PHILIP'S

STREET ATLAS
Liverpool
and Merseyside

www.philips-maps.co.uk

First published in 1997 by

Philip's, a division of
Octopus Publishing Group Ltd
www.octopusbooks.co.uk
2-4 Heron Quays, London E14 4JP
An Hachette Livre UK Company
www.hachettelivre.co.uk

Fourth edition 2007
Second impression 2008
MERDA

ISBN 978-0-540-09167-6 (spiral)

© Philip's 2007

Ordnance Survey®

This product includes mapping data licensed
from Ordnance Survey® with the permission of
the Controller of Her Majesty's Stationery Office.

© Crown copyright 2007. All rights reserved.
Licence number 100011710.

Data for the speed cameras provided by
PocketGPSWorld.com Ltd.

Ordnance Survey and the OS Symbol are
registered trademarks of Ordnance Survey, the
national mapping agency of Great Britain.

Printed and bound in China by Toppan

Contents

II **List of mobile speed cameras**

III **Key to map symbols**

IV **Key to map pages**

VI **Route planning**

VIII **Administrative and Postcode boundaries**

1 **Street maps** at 3½ inches to 1 mile

90 **Street map of Liverpool city centre**
at 7 inches to 1 mile

91 **Index** of towns, villages, streets, hospitals, industrial
estates, railway stations, schools, shopping centres,
universities and places of interest

Digital Data

The exceptionally high-quality mapping found in this atlas is available as digital data in TIFF format, which is
easily convertible to other bitmapped (raster) image formats.

The index is also available in digital form as a standard database table. It contains all the details found in the
printed index together with the National Grid reference for the map square in which each entry is named.

For further information and to discuss your requirements, please contact
victoria.dawbarn@philips-maps.co.uk

On-line route planner

For detailed driving directions and estimated driving times visit our free route planner at
www.philips-maps.co.uk

Mobile speed cameras

The vast majority of speed cameras used on Britain's roads are operated by safety camera partnerships. These comprise local authorities, the police, Her Majesty's Court Service (HMCS) and the Highways Agency.

This table lists the sites where each safety camera partnership may enforce speed limits through the use of mobile cameras or detectors. These are usually set up on the roadside or a bridge spanning the road and operated by a police or civilian enforcement officer. The speed limit at each site (if available) is shown in red type, followed by the approximate location in black type.

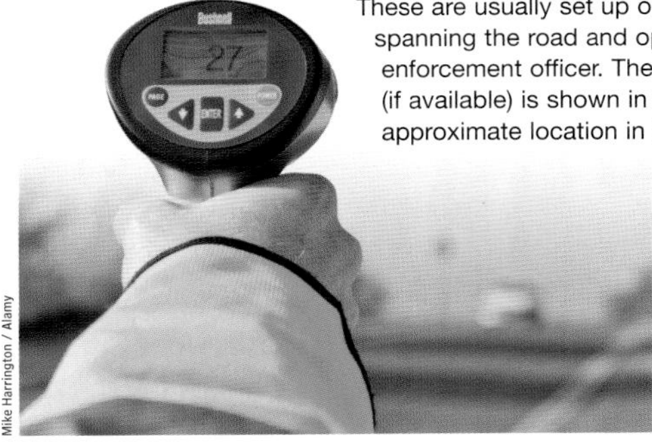

Mike Harrington / Alamy

A57
Liverpool, East
Prescot Rd

A58
St Helens, Prescot Rd

A506
Liverpool, Longmoor
Lane

A551
Wirral, Leasowe Rd

A553
Wirral, Laird Street

A561
Liverpool, Speke
Rd/Speke Boulevard

A562
Liverpool, Parliament
Street/Upper
Parliament Street

A572
St Helens, Common Rd

A580
Liverpool, Townsend
Avenue

St Helens, East
Lancashire Rd

A5038
Sefton, Southport Rd/
Liverpool Boundary to
Oxford Rd

Sefton, Southport
Rd/Oxford Rd to
Northfield Rd

A5080
Liverpool, Bowring
Park Rd/Roby Rd

A5098
Liverpool, Hornby Rd

B5136
Wirral, New Chester
Rd

UNCLASSIFIED
Liverpool, Great
Homer Street

Liverpool, Green Lane

Liverpool, Lower
House Lane/Dwerry
House Lane

Liverpool, Muirhead
Avenue

Liverpool, Netherfield
Rd North

Liverpool, Utting
Avenue East

Sefton, Park Lane

Motorway with junction number	
Primary route – dual/single carriageway	
A road – dual/single carriageway	
B road – dual/single carriageway	
Minor road – dual/single carriageway	
Other minor road – dual/single carriageway	
Road under construction	
Tunnel, covered road	
Speed cameras - single, multiple	
Rural track, private road or narrow road in urban area	
Gate or obstruction to traffic (restrictions may not apply at all times or to all vehicles)	
Path, bridleway, byway open to all traffic, road used as a public path	
Pedestrianised area	
Postcode boundaries	
County and unitary authority boundaries	
Railway, tunnel, railway under construction	
Tramway, tramway under construction	
Miniature railway	
Railway station	
Private railway station	
Metro station	
Tram stop, tram stop under construction	
Bus, coach station	

◆	**Ambulance station**
◆	**Coastguard station**
◆	**Fire station**
◆	**Police station**
✚	**Accident and Emergency entrance to hospital**
Ⓗ	**Hospital**
✛	**Place of worship**
𝒊	**Information Centre** (open all year)
🛒	**Shopping Centre**
P P&R	**Parking, Park and Ride**
PO	**Post Office**
⚕ ⛺	**Camping site, caravan site**
▶ ✕	**Golf course, picnic site**
Prim Sch	**Important buildings, schools, colleges, universities and hospitals**
	Built up area
	Woods
River Medway	**Water name**
	River, weir, stream
	Canal, lock, tunnel
	Water
	Tidal water
Church	**Non-Roman antiquity**
ROMAN FORT	**Roman antiquity**
87	**Adjoining page indicators and overlap bands** The colour of the arrow and the band indicates the scale of the adjoining or overlapping page (see scales below)
237	

Enlarged mapping only

	Railway or bus station building
	Place of interest
	Parkland

Acad	**Academy**	Inst	**Institute**	Recn Gd	**Recreation Ground**
Allot Gdns	**Allotments**	Ct	**Law Court**		
Cemy	**Cemetery**	L Ctr	**Leisure Centre**	Resr	**Reservoir**
C Ctr	**Civic Centre**	LC	**Level Crossing**	Ret Pk	**Retail Park**
CH	**Club House**	Liby	**Library**	Sch	**School**
Coll	**College**	Mkt	**Market**	Sh Ctr	**Shopping Centre**
Crem	**Crematorium**	Meml	**Memorial**	TH	**Town Hall/House**
Ent	**Enterprise**	Mon	**Monument**	Trad Est	**Trading Estate**
Ex H	**Exhibition Hall**	Mus	**Museum**	Univ	**University**
Ind Est	**Industrial Estate**	Obsy	**Observatory**	W Twr	**Water Tower**
IRB Sta	**Inshore Rescue Boat Station**	Pal	**Royal Palace**	Wks	**Works**
		PH	**Public House**	YH	**Youth Hostel**

■ The small numbers around the edges of the maps identify the 1 kilometre National Grid lines

■ The dark grey border on the inside edge of some pages indicates that the mapping does not continue onto the adjacent page

The scale of the maps on the pages numbered in blue is 5.52 cm to 1 km • 3½ inches to 1 mile • 1: 18103

0	¼	½	¾	1 mile
0	250 m	500 m	750 m	1 kilometre

The scale of the maps on pages numbered in red is 11.04 cm to 1 km • 7 inches to 1 mile • 1: 9051

0	220 yards	440 yards	660 yards	½ mile
0	125 m	250 m	375 m	½ kilometre

Walsall

South Shields

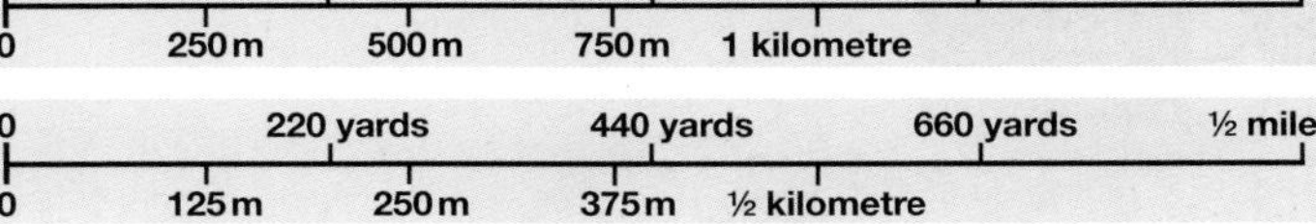

Key to map pages

45	Map pages at 3½ inches to 1 mile
90	Map pages at 7 inches to 1 mile

Scale

0 1 2 3 4 5 6 7 8 8 10 km

0 1 2 3 4 5 miles

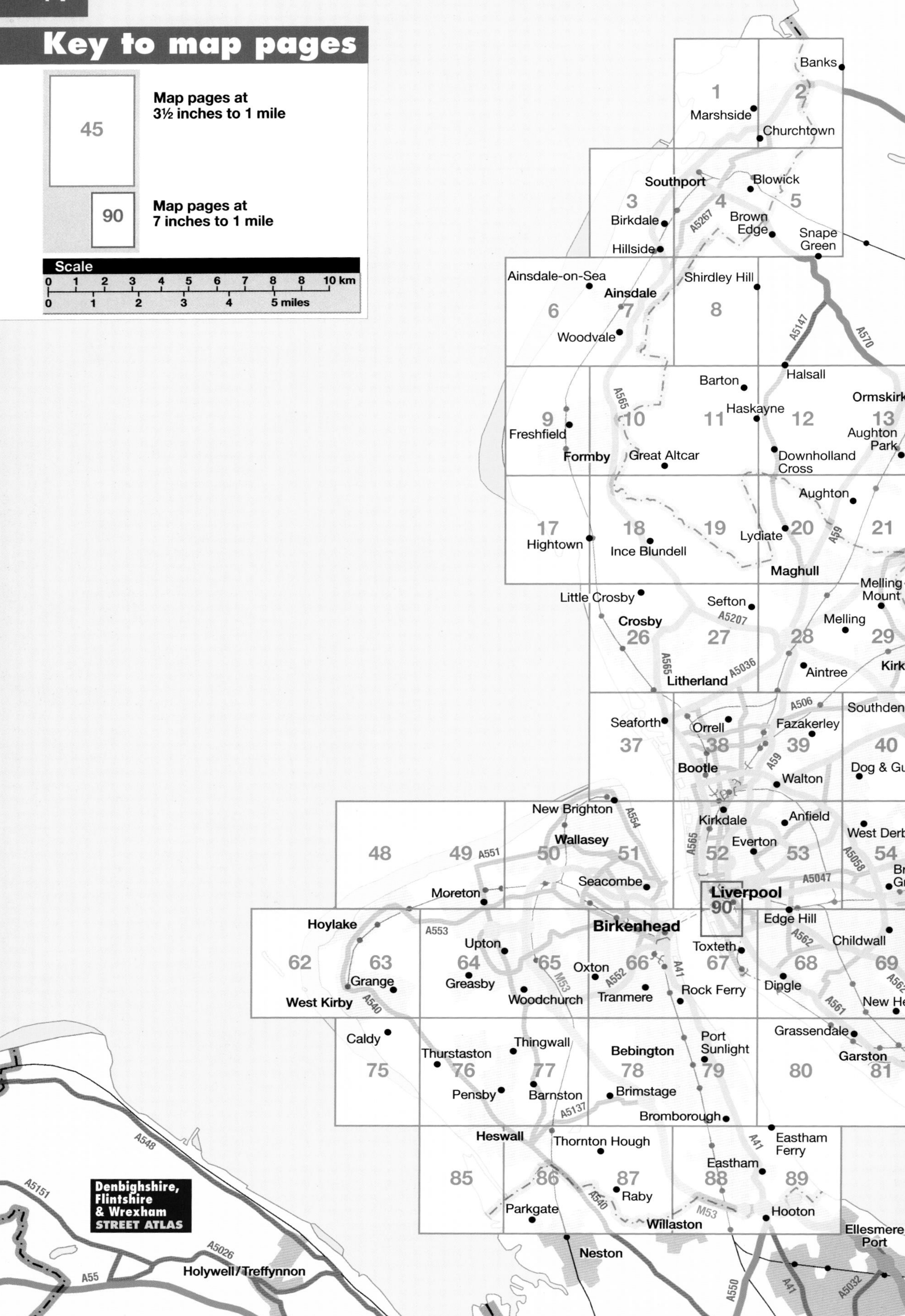

Banks

1 Marshside

2 Churchtown

Southport Blowick

3 Birkdale A5267 Brown 5 Snape
Hillside 4 Edge Green

Ainsdale-on-Sea Shirldey Hill

6 Ainsdale 7 8

Woodvale

Barton Halsall

Haskayne Ormskirk

9 10 11 12 13 Aughton
Freshfield Park

Formby Great Altcar Downholland
Cross

Aughton

17 18 19 20 21
Hightown Ince Blundell Lydiate

Maghull

Melling
Mount

Little Crosby Sefton

Crosby A5207 Melling

26 27 28 29
Kirkby

Litherland A565 A5036 Aintree

A506 Southdene

Seaforth Orrell Fazakerley 40

37 38 39 Dog & Gun

Bootle Walton

New Brighton A554 Kirkdale Anfield

Wallasey 52 Everton 53 West Derby 54
48 49 A551 50 51 Broad
Gree
Seacombe

Hoylake Liverpool
A553 Birkenhead 90 Edge Hill

62 63 64 Upton 65 Oxton 66 67 Toxteth 68 Childwall 69
Grange Greasby M53 A552 Rock Ferry Dingle New Heys
West Kirby A540 Woodchurch Tranmere A561
A41

Caldy Thingwall Grassendale

75 Thurstaston 76 77 Bebington Port 80 Garston 81
Pensby Barnston 78 Sunlight
A5137 Brimstage 79

Bromborough

Heswall Thornton Hough Eastham
Ferry

85 86 87 Raby 88 Eastham 89
Parkgate A540 M53 Hooton

Willaston Ellesmere
Port
Neston

Denbighshire,
Flintshire
& Wrexham
STREET ATLAS

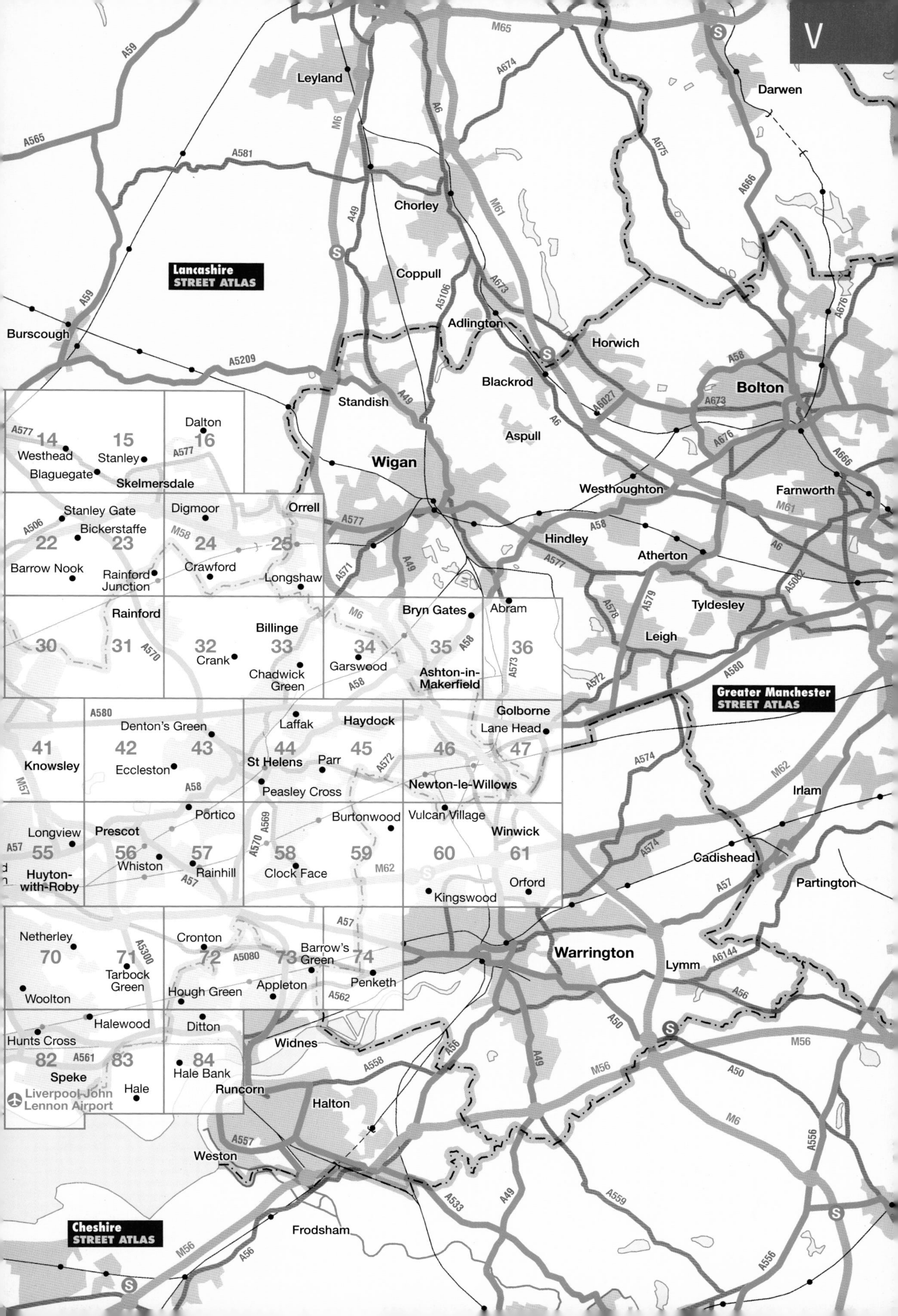
V
Lancashire STREET ATLAS
Greater Manchester STREET ATLAS
Cheshire STREET ATLAS
Leyland
Darwen
Chorley
Coppull
Adlington
Horwich
Blackrod
Bolton
Burscough
Standish
Wigan
Aspull
Westhoughton
Farnworth
Hindley
Atherton
Tyldesley
Leigh
Orrell
Abram
Golborne
Lane Head
Irlam
Cadishead
Partington
Warrington
Lymm
Widnes
Runcorn
Halton
Weston
Frodsham
Dalton
14 Westhead
15 Stanley
16
Blaguegate
Skelmersdale
Stanley Gate
Bickerstaffe
22 23
Barrow Nook
Rainford Junction
Digmoor
24 Crawford
25 Longshaw
Rainford
30 31
32 Crank
Billinge
33 Chadwick Green
34 Garswood
Bryn Gates
35 Ashton-in-Makerfield
36
41 Knowsley
Denton's Green
42 Eccleston
43
Laffak
44 St Helens
Haydock
45 Parr
Peasley Cross
46 47
Newton-le-Willows
Longview
55 Huyton-with-Roby
Prescot
56 Whiston
Portico
57 Rainhill
58 Clock Face
Burtonwood
59
Vulcan Village
60 Kingswood
Winwick
61 Orford
Netherley
70 Woolton
71 Tarbock Green
Cronton
72 Hough Green
73 Barrow's Green
74 Penketh
Appleton
Halewood
Ditton
Hunts Cross
82 Speke
83 Hale
84 Hale Bank
Liverpool John Lennon Airport
M65 A674 A6 M6 A675 A666 A581 A565 A59 A49 M61 A5106 A673 A676 A5209 A577 A6027 A673 A676 A666 M61 A58 A6 A5082 A506 M58 A571 A578 A579 A580 A570 A573 A572 M57 A574 M62 A57 A569 A5300 A5080 A562 A6144 A56 A50 M56 A561 A558 A557 A533 A559 A556

Route Planning

Scale
0 1 2 3 4 5 6 7 8 8 10 km
0 1 2 3 4 5 miles
Southport
ORMSKIRK
Formby
Maghull
LITHERLAND
Bootle
Wallasey
LIVERPOOL
HOYLAKE
West Kirby
Birkenhead
BEBINGTON
Heswall
Neston
Ellesmere Port
Liverpool Airport
Speke
Garston
Huyton
Prescot
Kirkby
Knowsley
Burscough
BELFAST 8:00
DOUGLAS 4:00 (Winter only)
DUBLIN 7:45
DOUGLAS 2:30
Crosby Channel
River Dee
Afon Dyfrdwy
Mersey
Merseyside

Farington
M65
Brindle
Belthorn
Waterside
Haslin
Midge Hall
Much Hoole
Clayton Green
Higher Wheelton
Abbey Village
Tockholes
DARWEN SERVICES
Blackburn
Sunnyhurst
Hoddlesden
LEYLAND
Broadfield
Clayton-le-Woods
Whittle-le-Woods
222
Withnell
Brinscall
Ryal Fold
DARWEN
with
Whitehall
Bent Gate
Helmshore
Wheelton
Whittlestone Head
Euxton
Ulnes Walton
Shaw Green
M6
B5249
Darwen
Cadshaw
Res.
Eden
White Coppice
Yarrow
Stubbins
Eccleston
CHORLEY
Cowling
Anglezarke Reservoir
Ramsbottom
Edgworth
Charnock Richard
Weld Bank
Mawdesley
Heskin Green
CHARNOCK RICHARD SERVICES
M61
Belmont
Chapeltown
Turton Bottoms
Woodhey
Egerton
Summerseat
Bispham Green
Wrightington Bar
Coppull
Rivington
WINTER HILL
456
Greenmount
Adlington
Grimeford Village
Toppings
Walmersley
Limefield
Hill Dale
Mossy Lea
Dangerous Corner
Parbold
Coppull Moor
Shevington Moor
Horwich
BOLTON WEST SERVICES
Astley Bridge
Bradshaw
Tottington
Bury
Walshaw
Standish
Blackrod
Bottom o' th' Moor
Halliwell
Harwood
Ainsworth
Bolton
Appley Bridge
Shevington Vale
Red Rock
Haigh
A6027
Breightmet
Dalton
Boars Head
Shevington
Beech Hill
Aspull
Lostock Junction
Darcy Lever
Redvales
Black Lane
Roby Mill
Marylebone
Deane
Skelmersdale
Gathurst
Wigan
WESTHOUGHTON
Wingates
Daubhill
Great Lever
Little Lever
Radcliffe
Orrell
Digmoor
Up Holland
Pemberton
Hart Common
Water's Nook
Highfield
FARNWORTH
Kearsley
Stand
M58
A577
Ince in Makerfield
Hindley
Daisy Hill
Over Hulton
M61
Higher End
Goose Green
Hindley Green
ATHERTON
Little Hulton
Walkden
Clifton
Green
PRESTWICH
Crawford
Longshaw
Platt Bridge
Bickershaw
Tyldesley
Swinton
Pendlebury
Rainford
Bryn Gates
Abram
Westleigh
Howe Bridge
Worsley
Bryn
Crank Wood
Billinge
Leigh
Charlestown
Crank
Garswood
Moss Bank
Chadwick Green
ASHTON-IN-MAKERFIELD
Plank Lane
Pennington
Astley Green
M60
M602
Eccles
SALFORD
Lowton Common
Lately Common
Golborne
Lowton
Denton's Green
Haydock
Twiss Green
Glazebury
BARTON
St Helens
Blackbrook
Broad Oak
Lane Head
Fowley Common
M62
Davyhulme
Trafford Park
Eccleston
Peasley Cross
Collins Green
Newton-le-Willows
New Lane End
Culcheth
Irlam
URMSTON
Sutton
Croft
Flixton
Thatto Heath
Burtonwood
Winwick
Glazebrook
Eccleston Park
Sutton Leach
Risley
Cadishead
Carrington
Rainhill
BURTONWOOD SERVICES
Houghton Green
Fearnhead
Birchwood
Hollins Green
Partington
Ashton upon Mersey
SALE
Sutton Manor
Clock Face
Dallam
Rainhill Stoops
Bold Heath
Orford
Woolston
Warburton
Brooklands
TOLL
Barrow's Green
Warrington
Great Sankey
Martinscroft
Manchester Ship Canal
Mossbrow
Broadheath
Dunham Town
Timperley
Cronton
Heatley
Warrington
Altrincham
Farnworth
Doe Green
Penketh
Thelwall
Oughtrington
Appleton
Latchford
Lymm
Hale
Ditton
Higher Walton
Grappenhall
Stockton Heath
Broomedge
Little Bollington
Bowdon
Halebarns
Widnes
Bowgreen
Hale Bank
Moore
LYMM SERVICES
Bollin
Appleton Thorn
M56
Runcorn
Keckwick
Sworton Heath
High Legh
Ashley
Thorns Green
Rostherne
Daresbury
Stretton
Halton
Hatton
Hoo Green
Bucklow Hill
New Mills
Morley Green
Lower Stretton
Mere
Norton
Arley
Preston Brook
Preston on the Hill
Higher Whitley
Over Tabley
Weston
Dutton
Bate Heath
Holehouses
Mobberley
Sutton Weaver
Lower Whitley
Knutsford
Newtown
Aston
Dones Green
Gib Hill
Great Budworth
Over Knutsford
Frodsham
Comberbach
KNUTSFORD SERVICES
Weaver
Pickmere
Ollerton
Overton
Fivecrosses
Higher Wincham
Little Leigh
Helsby
Barnton
Anderton
Marston
Plumley
Smithy Green
Newton
Acton Bridge
Wincham
Lostock Gralam
Over Peover
Kingsley
Hapsford

Major administrative and Postcode boundaries

Scale

0   5   10   15 km

0   5   10 miles

County and unitary authority boundaries

Postcode boundaries

Area covered by this atlas

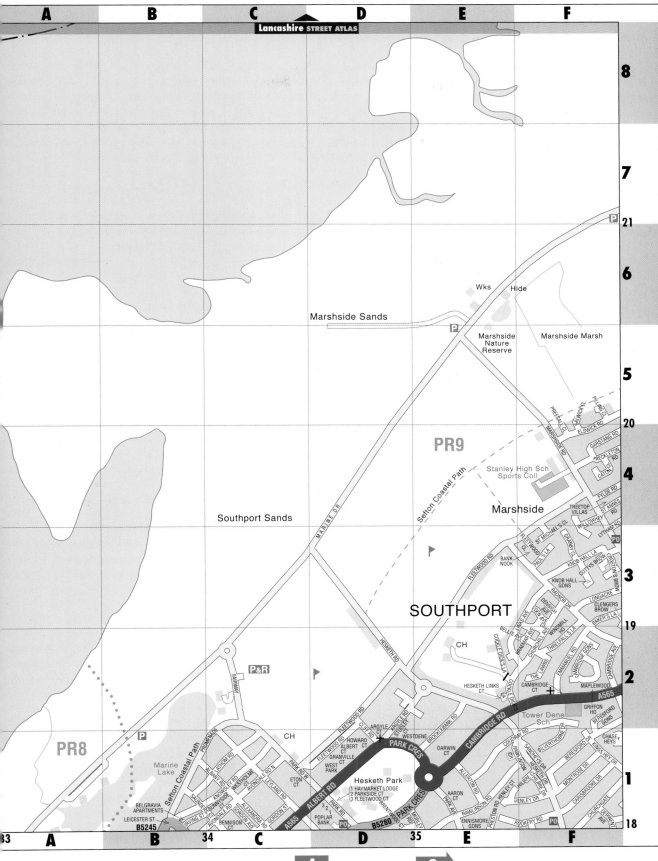

Lancashire STREET ATLAS

8

7

21

6

Wks   Hide

Marshside Sands

Marshside Marsh

P

Marshside
Nature
Reserve

5

PR9

20

Stanley High Sch
Sports Coll

4

Southport Sands

Sefton Coastal Path

Marshside

MARINE DR

FLEETWOOD RD

BANK
NOOK

3

SOUTHPORT

19

CH

2

HESKETH RD

HESKETH LINKS
CT

A565

FAIRWAY

P&R

Tower Dene
Sch

CAMBRIDGE RD

P

Marine
Lake

PR8

Sefton Coastal Path

PROMENADE

CH

FLEETWOOD RD

ARGYLE
CT

PARK CRES

DARWIN
CT

1

BELGRAVIA
APARTMENTS
LEICESTER ST
B5245

ALBERT RD

Hesketh Park
1 HAYMARKET LODGE
2 PARKSIDE CT
3 FLEETWOOD CT

PARK CRES

B5280

18

33   **A**   **B**   34   **C**   **D**   35   **E**   **F**

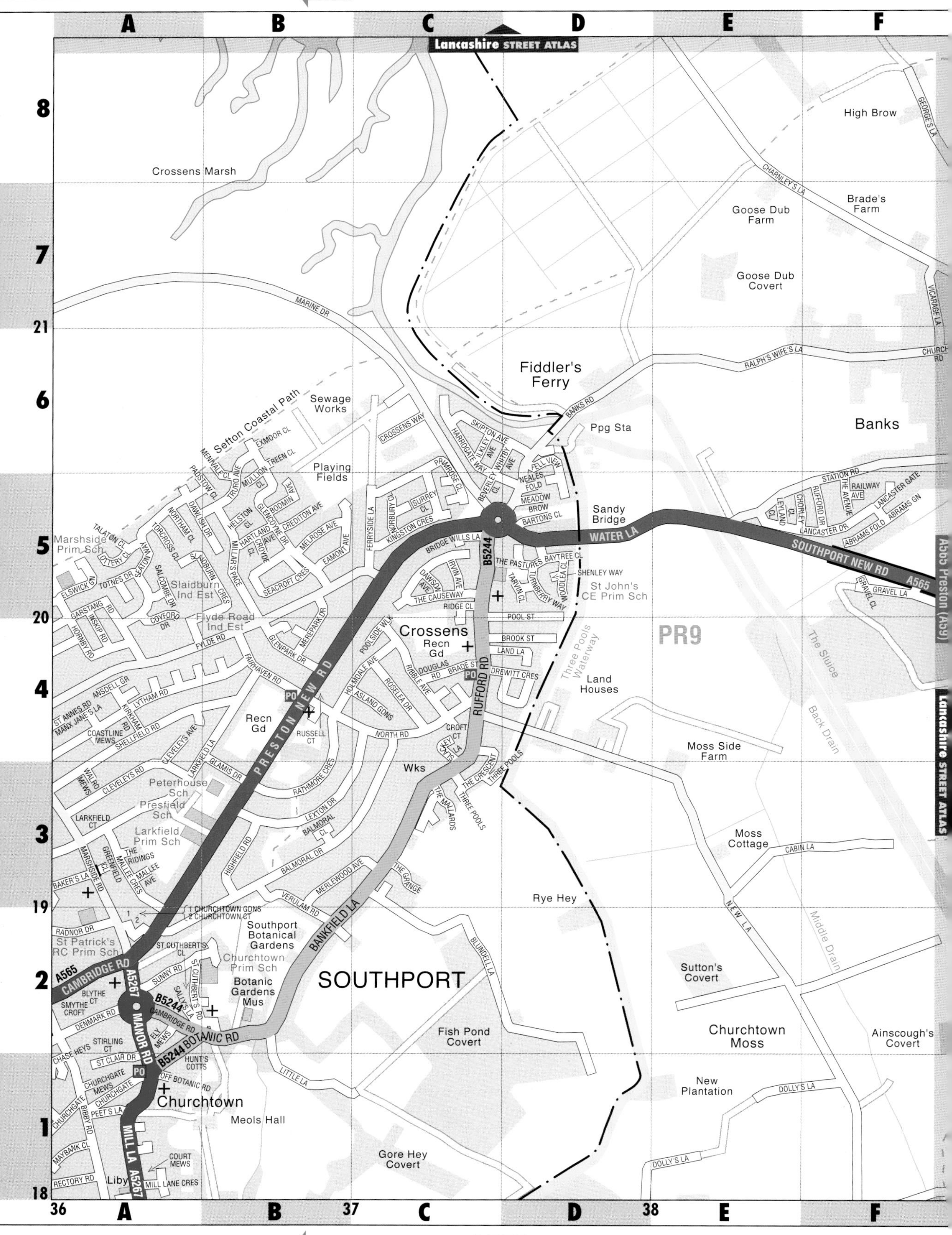
Lancashire STREET ATLAS
Crossens Marsh
Fiddler's Ferry
Sewage Works
Sefton Coastal Path
Playing Fields
Marshside Prim Sch
Slaidburn Ind Est
Flyde Road Ind Est
Crossens
Recn Gd
Sandy Bridge
WATER LA
SOUTHPORT NEW RD
PRESTON NEW RD
RUFFORD RD
St John's CE Prim Sch
PR9
Ppg Sta
Banks
High Brow
Goose Dub Farm
Brade's Farm
Goose Dub Covert
Land Houses
Moss Side Farm
Moss Cottage
Rye Hey
Wks
Peterhouse Sch
Presfield Sch
Larkfield Prim Sch
St Patrick's RC Prim Sch
Southport Botanical Gardens
Churchtown Prim Sch
Botanic Gardens Mus
SOUTHPORT
Fish Pond Covert
Churchtown
Meols Hall
Gore Hey Covert
Sutton's Covert
Churchtown Moss
New Plantation
Ainscough's Covert
The Sluice
Back Drain
Middle Drain
Three Pools Waterway
MARINE DR
CAMBRIDGE RD
BOTANIC RD
BANKFIELD LA
MANOR RD
MILL LA
Liby
A565
A5267
B5244
Preston (A59)
36
37
38
A
B
C
D
E
F
8
7
21
6
5
20
4
3
19
2
1
18

1
1
5

A B C D E F

8

Princes
Park

P&R P P 7
L Ctr 17

PRIORY MEWS 1
THE HOLLIES 2
THE OAKS 3
THE PINES 4
THE ELMS 5
THE WILLOWS 6
DONNINGTON LODGE 7
TUDOR MANS 8
SUNCOURT 9

Victoria
Park

Victoria Way

BEACH
PRIORY
GDNS 4 3
BEECHWD
4 3
ROTTEN ROW 2 1

Sunnymede
Sch

ST
WYBURN
CT
WESTCLIFFE
CT SHERWOOD
LODGE

TWISTFIELD 6

Queens Jubilee
Nature Trail

Birkdale Sands

KINGSWOOD PK
KINGSWOOD
HO
BLANDFORD
CL
WESTCLIFFE
RD
WARREN CT
LULWORTH
LODGE

PR8

CAMBERLEY CL
ASCOT
PALACE RD
HAYLEMERE
CT

WELD
RD
BRETWOOD

5

PRINCE CHARLES GDNS
SAXON RD SAXON
LODGE

SAXENHOLME

16

Dunes

WINDSOR CT
OXFORD
RD
LANCASTER
HO
SILVERDALE
CANDAISTIE
PRIORY
GDNS
CASP
CADBURY CL
YORK RD
CL 5 4

WESTBOURNE RD
THE HEYS
WESTBOURNE GDNS
LISMORE RD
REGENT RD
REGENCY
MEWS
BICKERTON ROW BICKERTON RD
Birkdale 4
P

LANCASTER
GDNS
LANCASTER CL
ROYAL PK

NELSON CT
TREESCE
CL
WALMER

ACRE
GR

SANDRINGHAM RD
Sch
GRANVILLE RD
GROSVENOR RD
GROSVENOR
CT
REGENCY
GDNS BROADLANDS
GROSVENOR
BELGRAVE PL
WORTHING
CL CROSBY RD
SELBY CL

BREEZE RD

SELWORTHY RD
GAINSBOROUGH
CHICHFIELD
CRICKET PATH
LLC
CRESCENT RD CAVENDISH

3

Trans Pennine Trail
Coastal Path
Sefton Coastal Path

SOUTHPORT

Royal Birkdale

TRAFALGAR RD
HARROD DR
GROSVENOR RD
CONYERS AVE
STANLEY AVE 15

Dunes

SHERRINGHAM RD
GREENBANK
DR
CROMLER RD
DOVERT RD
BLUNDELL
AVE
HARTLEY RD
HARTLEY
CRES

Birkdale 2

Greenbank
High Sch

BLUSDELL
CRES
BLUNDELL RD
DUNWIRK RD
KIRKSTALL RD
RICHMOND
RD
CLIVE LODGE
ST JOHN'S RD

HASTINGS RD
GRINSTEAD CL
KIRKLEES RD
CARDIGAN RD
CARNARVON
RD
Liby

CH Hillside CH
HILLSIDE RD
LYNTON DR
SANDON RD
Hillside 1

Birkdale
Hills LYNTON RD
PO LYNTON RD
DUNBAR RD
HAZELWOOD
LANGDALE
GDNS
NORFOLK
GR
THE BRIARS NORFOLK 14

ASH ON RD
LIVERPOOL RD
A565

A565

30 A B 31 C D 32 E F

F4
1 CARNEGHIE CT
2 WELD PAR
3 HOMECHASE HO
4 VICTORIA CT
5 WELDALE HO
6 OXFORD CT

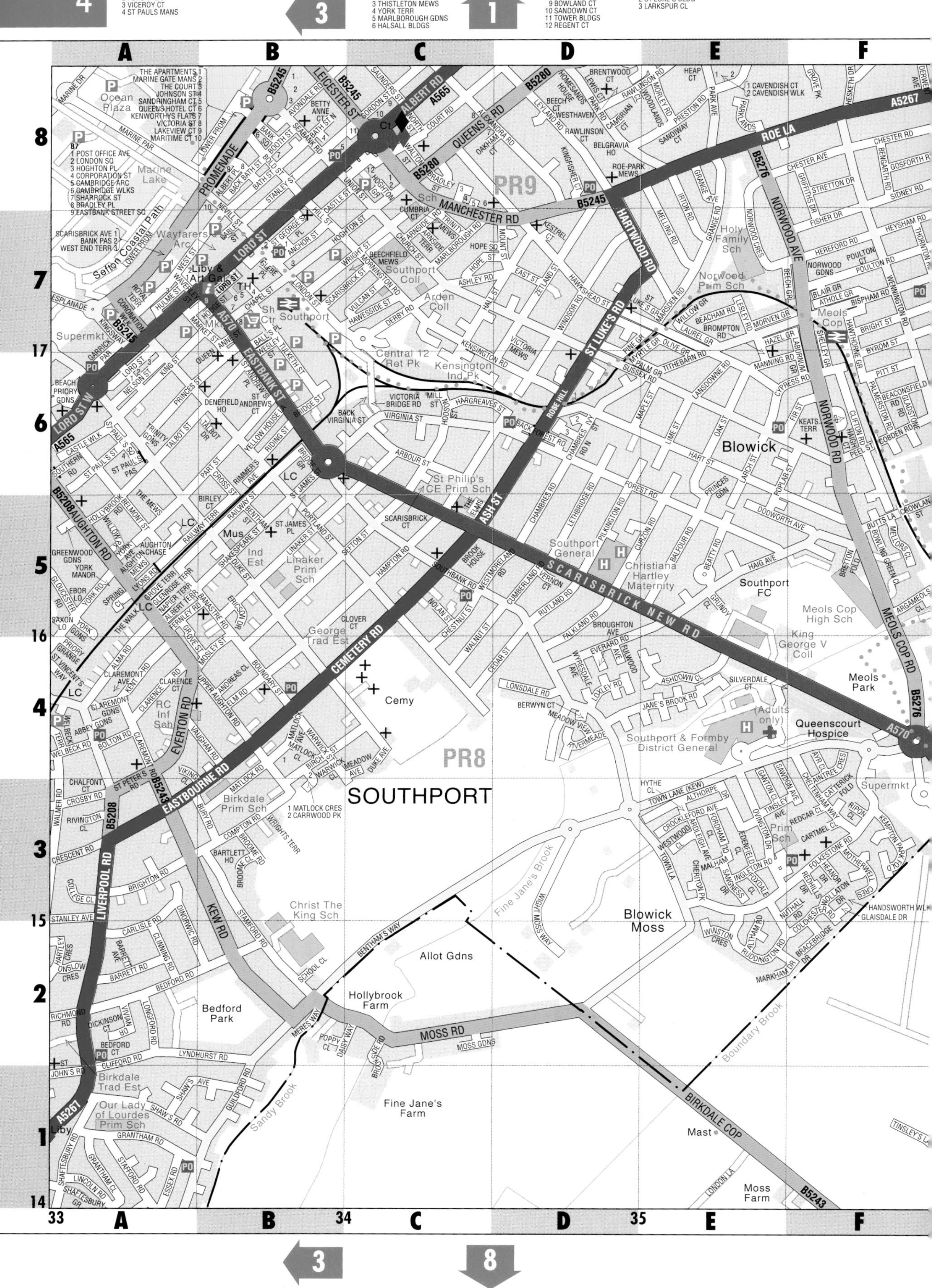

A **B** **C** **D** **E** **F**

8

BAMBER GDNS
ROE LA A5267
HIGH PARK PL
CHESTER RD
VERNON RD
SIDNEY RD
LEYSHAM RD
POULTON RD
BISPHAM RD
NEWTON ST
MILTON ST
RUSSELL AVE
High Park
WARREN CL
CHURCH CL
FARM LA
FINE JANE'S WAY
FOSTERS CL
TARLETON RD
DEVONSHIRE RD
BRADSHAW CT
LAWSON CT
SCOTT AVE
TEDDER AVE
WAVELL AVE
VICTORY AVE
BROOKE CL
WAVELL CT
RUSSELL AVE
MONTGOMERY AVE
CH
OLD LINKS CL
MOSS LA
PITTS HOUSE LA
Pool House Farm
Pitts House Covert

PR9

DOLLY'S LA
STRAIGHT UP LA
Peet's Farm
Wyke Hey Farm
Hooton's Cottages
LONG MEANYGATE
WYKE WOOD LA
MIDDLE DRAIN

17

Bishop David Sheppard CE Prim Sch
CHURCH MEWS
A.K.C.
CROWLAND ST
Southport A En Ctr Bsns Pk
Recn Gd
SALISBURY ST
COBDEN RD
CANNING RD
WENNINGTON
Wks
Blowick Ind Pk
Blowick Bsns Pk
Old Hall Farm Bsns Pk
Brook Farm Bridge
The Old Pool
Wyke House Farm

7

6

Wyke La
Big Wood
THE AVENUE
PERCH POOL LA

Hodge's Farm
FOUL LA
Twist's Covert
Wyke Thorn Farm
Heath Covert

5

16

Meols Cop Ret Pk
NEW FOUL LA
Kew Ret Pk
SCARISBRICK NEW RD
Sandy Brook
Sheepfold Farm
New House Farm
Pool Hey Crossing
LC
Shaw's Farm
Wyke Cop Crossing
LC
Scarisbrick Moss
Perch Pool Covert

4

40
MEOLS VIEW CL
Nursery
Pool Hey
POOL HEY LA
PR8
Drummersdale Drain
WOODMOSS LA
L40

3

15

High Brows Covert
COVERTSIDE RD
COVERT CL
Crem
KEN HOUSE DR
FIELDLANDS
ALDERLEE PK CVN SITE
BROWN EDGE CL
SOUTHPORT RD
Brown Edge
Black Brook
NEW HALL DR
PINEWOOD CL
GREENFIELD RD
WYKE COP RD
Wyke Road Farm
Sandy Brook

2

TURNING LA
TINSLEY'S LA
Boundary Farm
A570
HARES LA
Carr Cross
Sandy Brook Farm
Snape Green
RIMMER GN
SNAPE GN
CAT TAIL LA

1

14

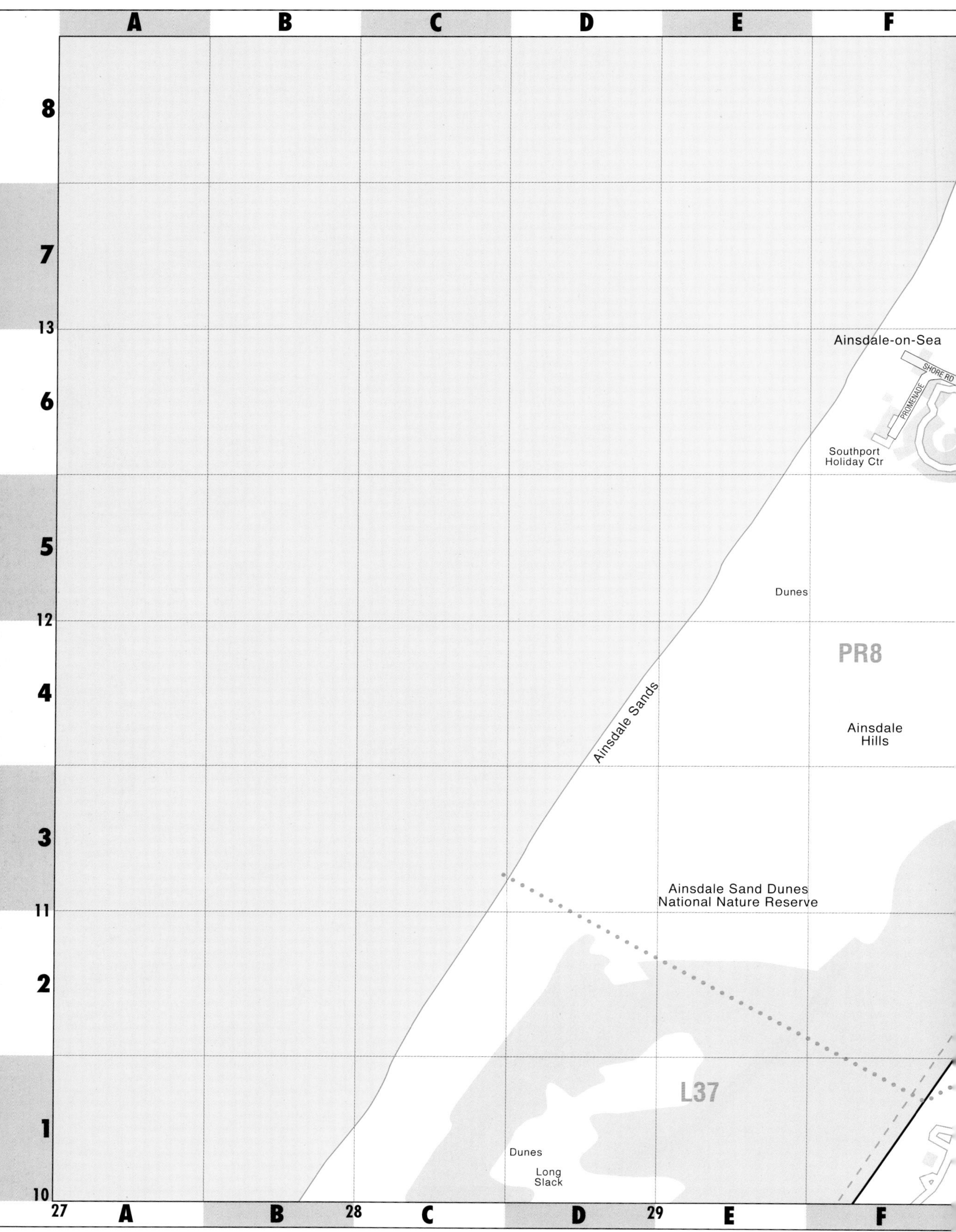

Ainsdale-on-Sea

SHORE RD

PROMENADE

Southport
Holiday Ctr

Dunes

PR8

Ainsdale
Hills

Ainsdale Sands

Ainsdale Sand Dunes
National Nature Reserve

L37

Dunes

Long
Slack

3
8

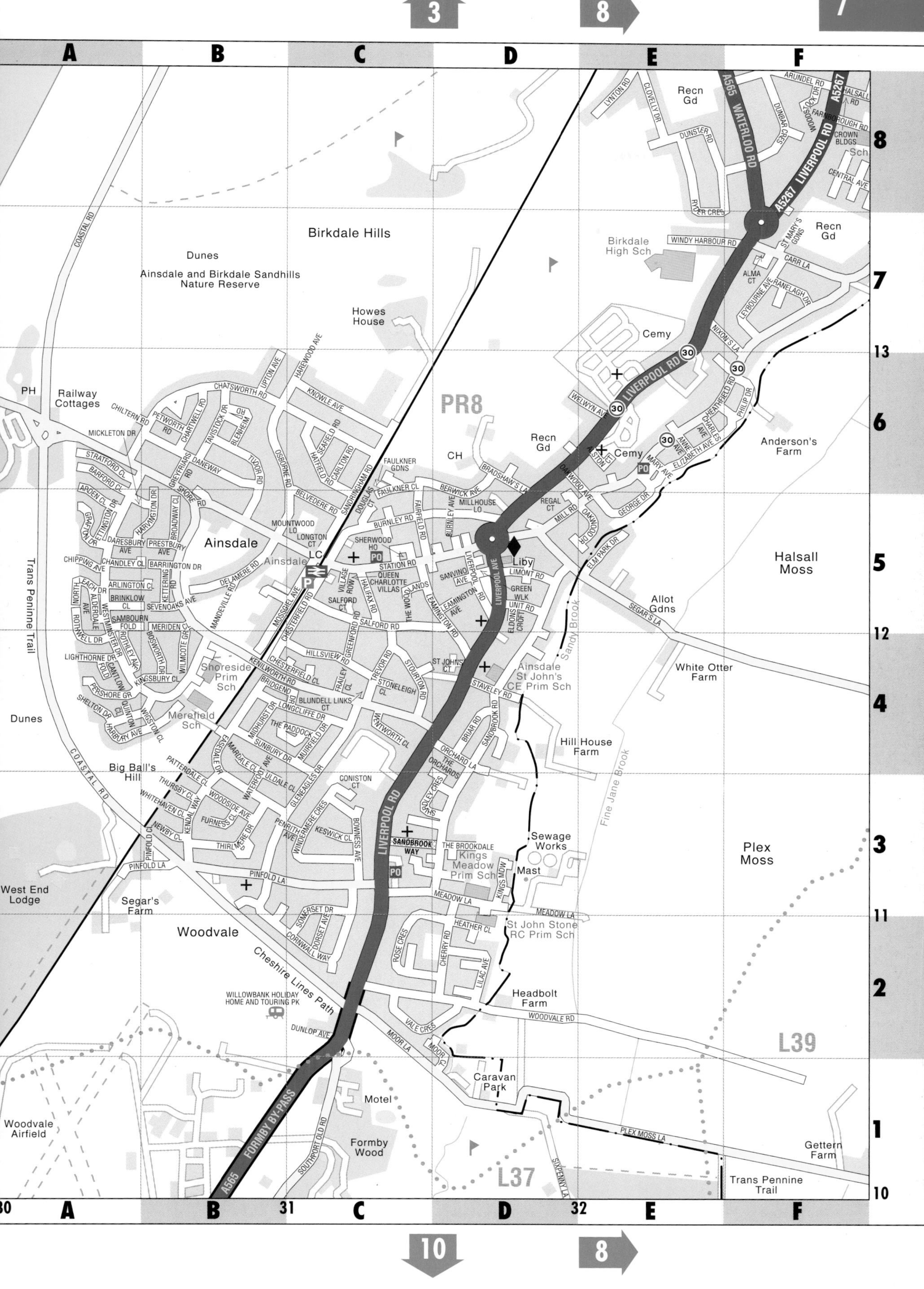
A
B
C
D
E
F
Birkdale Hills
Dunes
Ainsdale and Birkdale Sandhills
Nature Reserve
Howes
House
Recn
Gd
A565 WATERLOO RD
A5267 LIVERPOOL RD
A5267
Birkdale
High Sch
WINDY HARBOUR RD
CARR LA
Cemy
LIVERPOOL RD
PR8
PH
Railway
Cottages
CH
Anderson's
Farm
Ainsdale
Ainsdale
LC
Liby
Halsall
Moss
Allot
Gdns
SEGAR'S LA
Trans Pennine Trail
COASTAL RD
Shoreside
Prim
Sch
Merefield
Sch
Ainsdale
St John's
CE Prim Sch
White Otter
Farm
Dunes
Big Ball's
Hill
Hill House
Farm
Sandy Brook
Fine Jane Brook
LIVERPOOL RD
Sewage
Works
Kings
Meadow
Prim Sch
Mast
Plex
Moss
West End
Lodge
Segar's
Farm
Woodvale
St John Stone
RC Prim Sch
Cheshire Lines Path
Headbolt
Farm
WOODVALE RD
WILLOWBANK HOLIDAY
HOME AND TOURING PK
L39
MOOR LA
Caravan
Park
Motel
Woodvale
Airfield
A565 FORMBY BY-PASS
Formby
Wood
PLEX MOSS LA
Gettern
Farm
L37
Trans Pennine
Trail
8
7
13
6
5
12
4
3
11
2
1
10
30
31
32

10
8

A   B   C   D   E   F

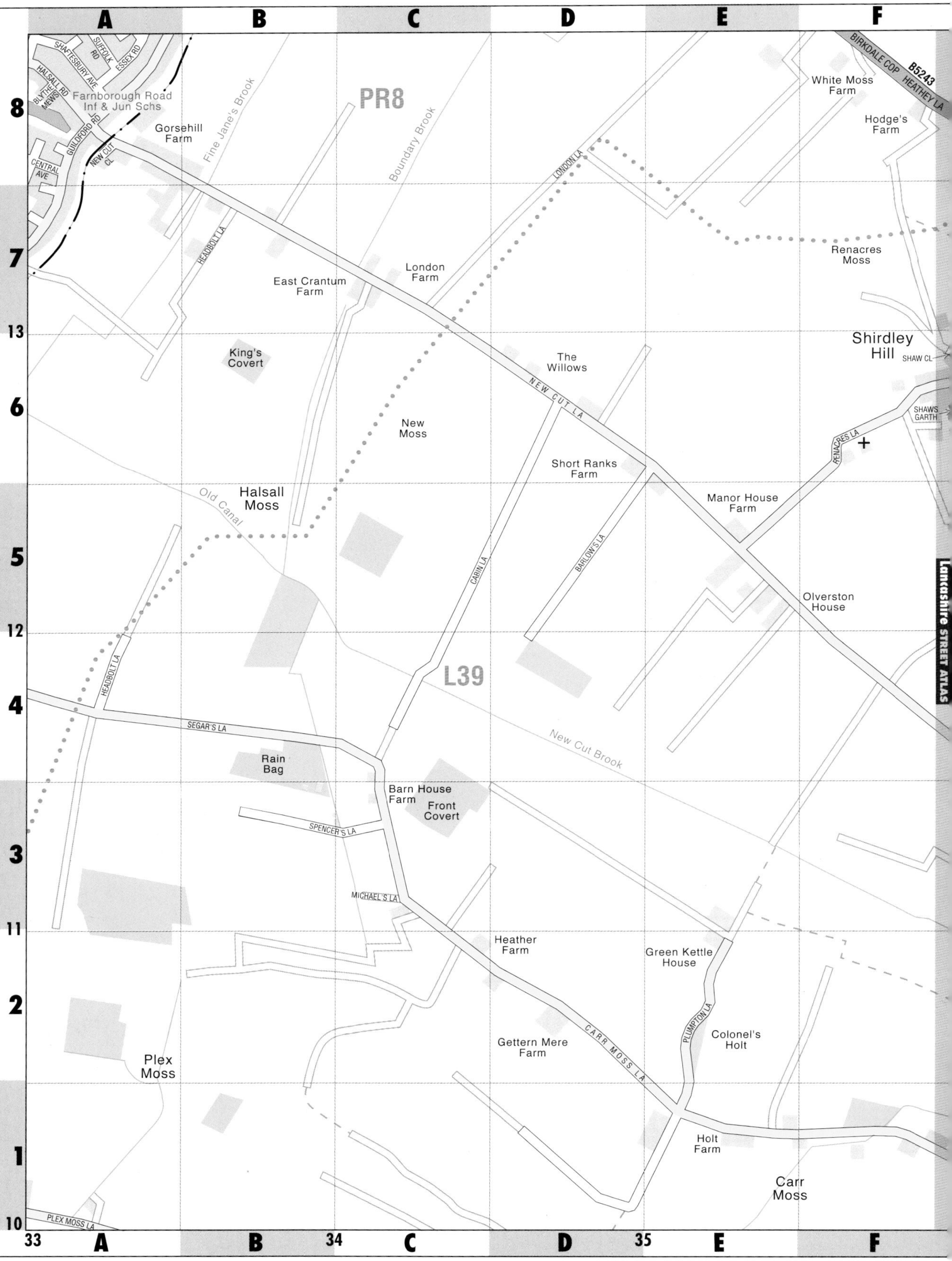

BIRKDALE COP HEATHEY LA

B5243

8

Farnborough Road
Inf & Jun Schs

SHAFTESBURY AVE
SUFFOLK RD
ESSEX RD
HALSALL RD
BLYTHE MEWS
CENTRAL AVE
GUILFORD RD
NEW CUT CL

PR8

Gorsehill
Farm

White Moss
Farm

Hodge's
Farm

Fine Jane's Brook

Boundary Brook

London LA

7

East Crantum
Farm

London
Farm

HEADBOLT LA

Renacres
Moss

13

King's
Covert

The
Willows

Shirdley
Hill

SHAW CL

6

New
Moss

NEW CUT LA

Short Ranks
Farm

RENACRES LA

SHAWS
GARTH

+

Old Canal

Halsall
Moss

CABIN LA

BARLOW'S LA

Manor House
Farm

5

Olverston
House

12

HEADBOLT LA

L39

4

SEGAR'S LA

New Cut Brook

Rain
Bag

SPENCER'S LA

Barn House
Farm

Front
Covert

3

MICHAEL'S LA

11

Heather
Farm

Green Kettle
House

2

Plex
Moss

Gettern Mere
Farm

CARR MOSS LA

PLUMPTON LA

Colonel's
Holt

1

Holt
Farm

Carr
Moss

PLEX MOSS LA

10

Lancashire STREET ATLAS

6
10
17
10
A
B
C
D
E
F
Cloven-le-Dale
Woodvale Airfield
Fisherman's Path
Formby Hills
FRESHFIELD CVN PK
Nature Reserve
Clarence High Sch
Freshfield
L37
Formby High Sch
FORMBY
Sandfield Farm
St Jerome's RC Prim Sch
Woodlands Prim Sch
Formby
Liby
Eccles Crossing
Shorrocks Hill
FORMBY POINT CVN PK
St Luke's CE Prim Sch
Sewage Works
VICTORIA RD
SHIREBURN RD
BLUNDELL AVE
LIFEBOAT RD
WICKS LA
KIRKLAKE RD
BUSHBY'S LA
QUEEN'S RD
COLLEGE AVE
ST GEORGE'S RD
DUKE ST
RAVEN MEOLS LA
CAMBRIDGE RD
BARTON HEYS RD
ALTCAR LA
Bill's La

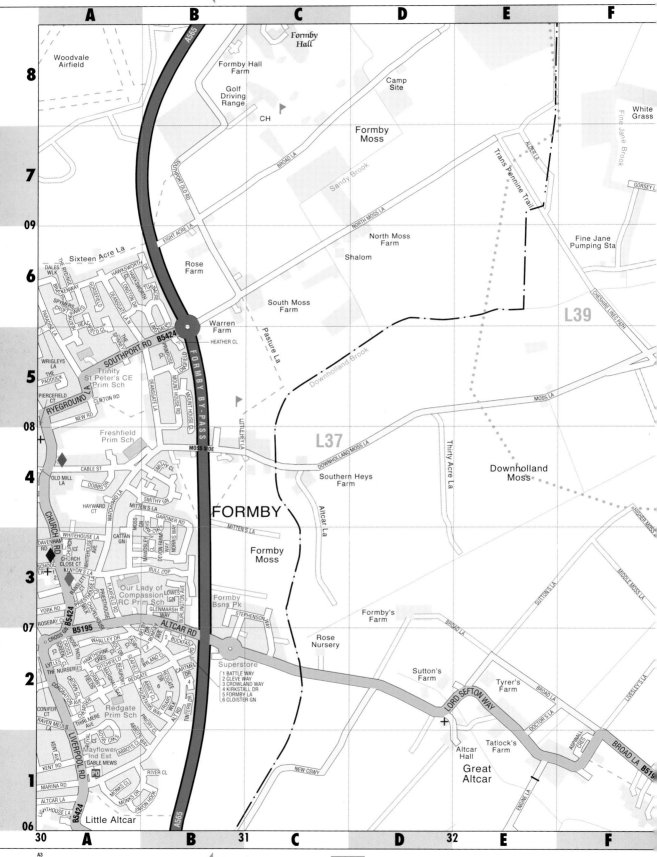

Woodvale
Airfield

Formby
Hall

Formby Hall
Farm

Golf
Driving
Range

CH

Camp
Site

Formby
Moss

White
Grass

Fine Jane Brook

GORSEY L

8

Broad La

Sandy Brook

North Moss La

Trans Pennine Trail

ALDER LA

7

09

North Moss
Farm

Shalom

Fine Jane
Pumping Sta

Sixteen Acre La

Rose
Farm

South Moss
Farm

CHESHIRE LINES PATH

L39

6

DALES WLK
THE PRINCES
BRACKENWAY
GORSEFIELD
GREENFIELD
HAWKSWORTH
HAWKSWORTH
LONGTON LA
TURNCROFT
SPYMERS
CROFT WAYS
HEATHEY CL
THE SPINNEY
DEANSGATE LA
LINDALE

Warren
Farm

HEATHER CL

Pasture La

Downholland Brook

MOSS LA

5

WRIGLEYS LA
THE PADDOCK
PIERCEFIELD CT
RYEGROUND LA

SOUTHPORT RD
B5424

Trinity
St Peter's CE
Prim Sch

PRIMROSE CL

DEANSGATE LA

MOUNT HOUSE LA

MOUNT HOUSE CL

FORMBY BY-PASS

CLIFTON RD
NEW RD

08

CHURCH RD

Freshfield
Prim Sch

MOSS SIDE

LITTLE HEY LA

L37

Downholland Moss La

Thirty Acre La

Downholland
Moss

4

OLD MILL LA

CABLE ST

DOBBS CR

HAYWARD CT

WATCHYARD LA

MOSS GN

SMITHY CL

SMITHY GN

Southern Heys
Farm

Altcar La

WHITEHOUSE LA
DAVENHAM RD
CHURCH CT
WHITEHOUSE AVE
CATTAN GN
MAWDSLEY CL
DEVON FARM CL
GARDNER RD
NORRIS WAY

FORMBY

MITTEN'S LA

3

SCHOOL LA
KENYON'S LA
CHURCH CLOSE CT
RANELETT
PRIESTHOUSE CL
PRIESTHOUSE
BULL COP
LOWES GN
BURLINGTON AVE

Our Lady of
Compassion
RC Prim Sch

Formby
Moss

07

YORK RD
ROSEBAY CL
B5424
B5195
CROSS GN
CROSS PATH
CROSS GREEN
ROSE PATH
EASBY
CHAPEL LA
FLAXFIELD RD
GLENMARSH WAY

ALTCAR RD

FORMBY LA

Formby
Bsns Pk

STEPHENSON WAY

Formby's
Farm

BROAD LA

2

WHALLEY DR
HAWTHORNE CRES
LYTLES
THE NURSERIES
FIELDS
FORMS
DITCHFIELD
EASBY
BYLAND CL
BEAUFORT
REDGATE
MARSHALSIDE
FOUNTAINS WAY
CARTMEL DR
BUCKFAST

Superstore
1 BATTLE WAY
2 CLEVE WAY
3 CROWLAND WAY
4 KIRKSTALL DR
5 FORMBY LA
6 CLOISTER GN

Rose
Nursery

Sutton's
Farm

Tyrer's
Farm

LIVESLEY'S LA

SUTTON'S LA

MIDDLE MOSS LA

LORD SEFTON WAY

DOCTOR'S LA

ASPINALL CRES

BROAD LA B515

CONIFER CT
CRAPLE
RAVEN MEOLS
CORONATION AVE
CROWN CL
THIRLMERE AVE
ROYAL CRES
ABBOTS WAY
PRIORY CL
FRIARS WALK
TINTERN DR

Redgate
Prim Sch

Mayflower
Ind Est
GABLE MEWS

RIVER CL

Altcar
Hall

Tatlock's
Farm

1

LIVERPOOL RD
KENT AVE
MARINA RD
ALTCAR LA
LIGHTHOUSE LA
B5424

MONKS CL
MONKS DR
MONKS HOOK

Little Altcar

NEW CSWY

ENGINE LA

Great
Altcar

A3
1 KENSINGTON CT
2 SPRINGFIELD HO

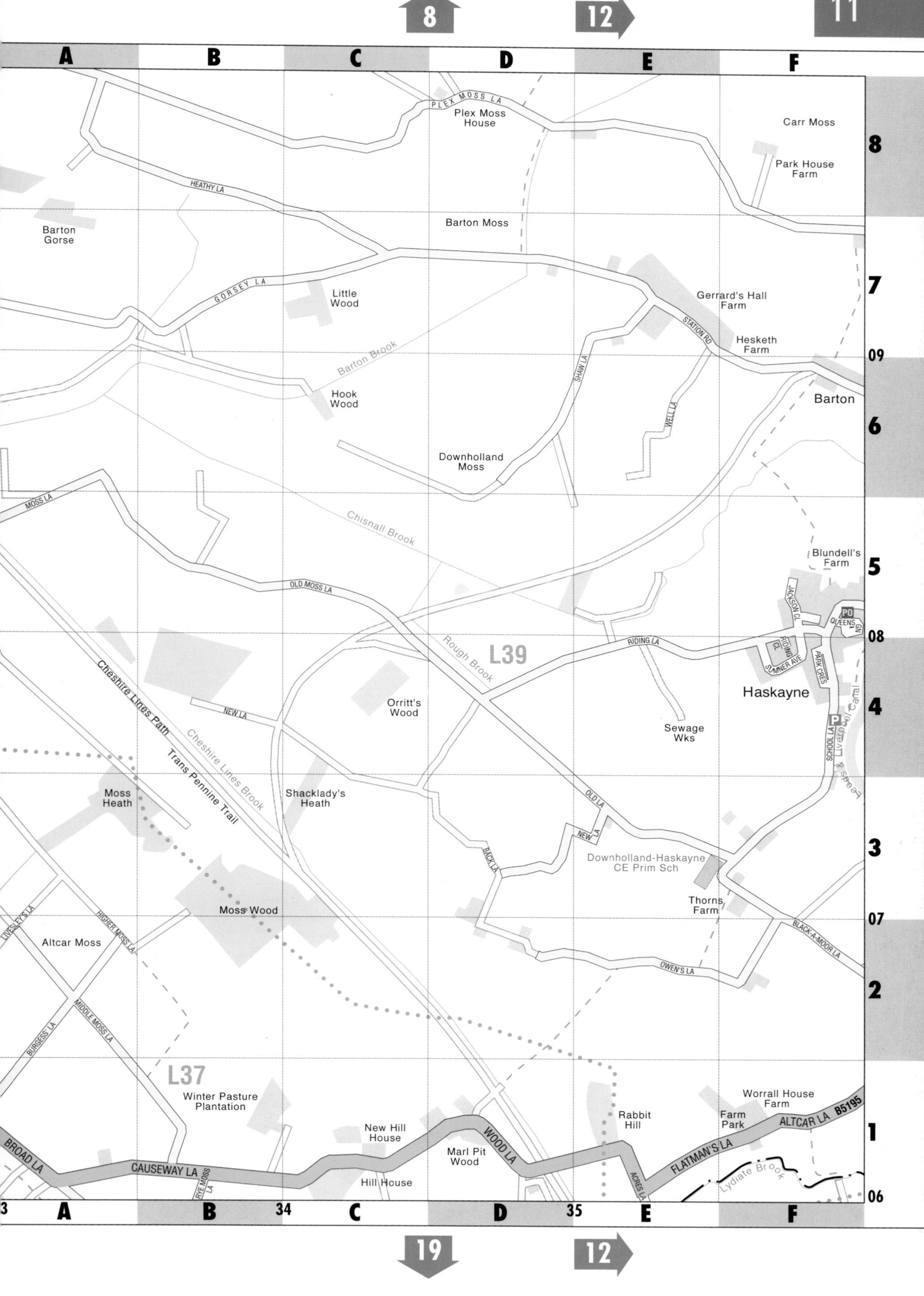
8
12
A
B
C
D
E
F
PLEX MOSS LA
Plex Moss House
Carr Moss
Park House Farm
HEATHY LA
Barton Gorse
Barton Moss
GORSEY LA
Little Wood
Gerrard's Hall Farm
STATION RD
Hesketh Farm
Barton Brook
Hook Wood
SHAW LA
Barton
WELL LA
Downholland Moss
MOSS LA
Chisnall Brook
Blundell's Farm
OLD MOSS LA
JACKSON CL
PO
QUEENS GN
RIDING LA
L39
Rough Brook
RIDING CL
SUMNER AVE
PARK CRES
Haskayne
Cheshire Lines Path
NEW LA
Orritt's Wood
Sewage Wks
P
SCHOOL LA
Leeds & Liverpool Canal
Trans Pennine Trail
Cheshire Lines Brook
Moss Heath
Shacklady's Heath
OLD LA
NEW LA
BACK LA
Downholland-Haskayne CE Prim Sch
Thorns Farm
Moss Wood
LIVESLEY'S LA
HIGHER MOSS LA
Altcar Moss
BLACK-A-MOOR LA
OWEN'S LA
MIDDLE MOSS LA
BURGESS LA
L37
Worrall House Farm
Winter Pasture Plantation
Rabbit Hill
New Hill House
WOOD LA
Farm Park
ALTCAR LA
B5195
BROAD LA
CAUSEWAY LA
Marl Pit Wood
FLATMAN'S LA
RYE MOSS LA
Hill House
ACRES LA
Lydiate Brook
8
7
09
6
5
08
4
3
07
2
1
06
3
A
B
34
C
D
35
E
F
19
12

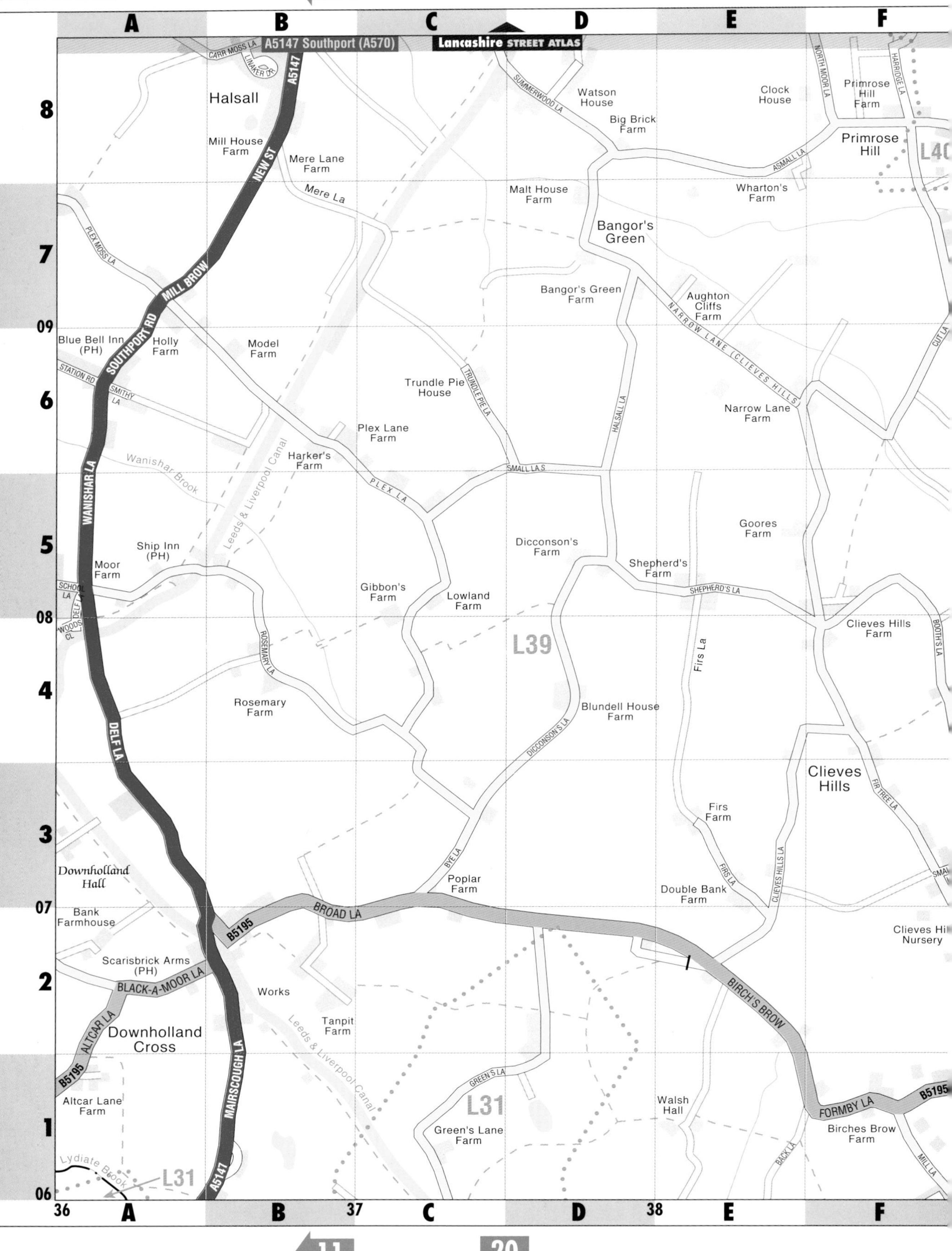

11

A B C D E F

Lancashire STREET ATLAS

8

Halsall

CARR MOSS LA
LINAKER DS
A5147 Southport (A570)
A5147
NEW ST
Mill House Farm
Mere Lane Farm
Mere La

Summerwood La
Watson House
Big Brick Farm
Malt House Farm

Clock House
ASMALL LA
Wharton's Farm

NORTH MOOR LA
HARROGE LA
Primrose Hill Farm
Primrose Hill

L40

Bangor's Green

7

MILL BROW

Bangor's Green Farm

Aughton Cliffs Farm

NARROW LANE (CLIEVES HILLS)

GILFA

09

Blue Bell Inn (PH)
SOUTHPORT RD
STATION RD
Holly Farm
SMITHY LA

Model Farm

Trundle Pie House

TRUNDLE PIE LA

HALSALL LA

Narrow Lane Farm

6

Wanishar Brook

Plex Lane Farm

Harker's Farm

PLEX LA

SMALL LA S

Leeds & Liverpool Canal

WANISHAR LA

Ship Inn (PH)

Dicconson's Farm

Shepherd's Farm

Goores Farm

5

Moor Farm

Gibbon's Farm

Lowland Farm

SHEPHERD'S LA

Clieves Hills Farm

BOOTHS LA

SCHOOL LA
DELF
WOODS CL

08

ROSEMARY LA

L39

Firs La

4

DELF LA

Rosemary Farm

Blundell House Farm

DICCONSON S LA

Clieves Hills

FIR TREE LA

3

Downholland Hall

BYE LA

Firs Farm

FIRS LA

CLIEVES HILLS LA

SMA

07

Bank Farmhouse

Poplar Farm

BROAD LA

Double Bank Farm

Clieves Hi Nursery

B5195

BIRCH'S BROW

2

Scarisbrick Arms (PH)

BLACK-A-MOOR LA

Works

Tanpit Farm

ALTCAR LA

Downholland Cross

MAIRSCOUGH LA

Leeds & Liverpool Canal

GREEN S LA

Walsh Hall

BACK LA

FORMBY LA

B5195

Birches Brow Farm

1

B5195

Altcar Lane Farm

Green's Lane Farm

L31

MILL LA

Lydiate Brook

L31

A5147

06

36 A B 37 C D 38 E F

14

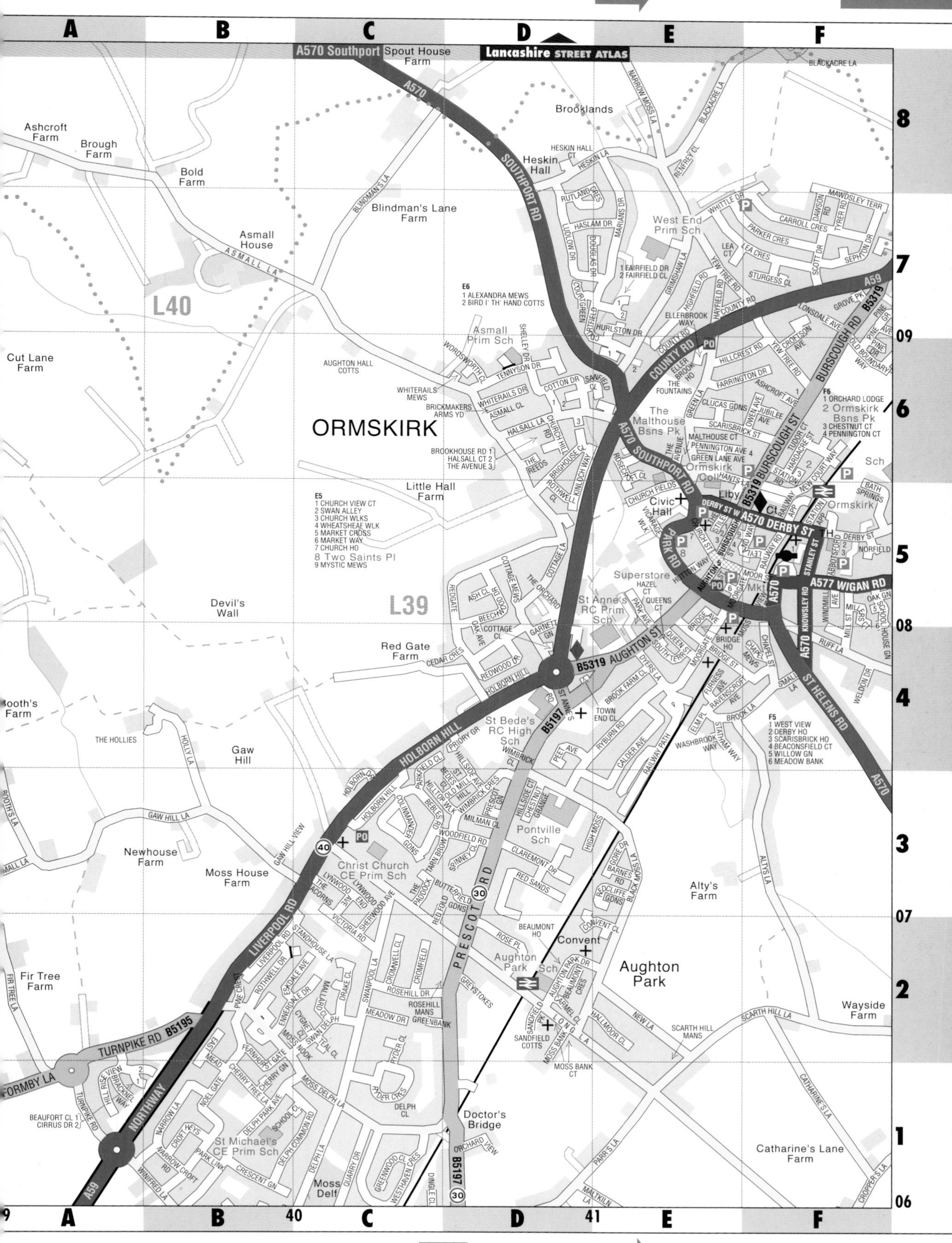
A570 Southport
Lancashire STREET ATLAS
Spout House Farm
Brooklands
Ashcroft Farm
Brough Farm
Bold Farm
Heskin Hall
Blindman's Lane Farm
West End Prim Sch
Asmall House
L40
Cut Lane Farm
Asmall Prim Sch
ORMSKIRK
The Malthouse Bsns Pk
Ormskirk Coll
Little Hall Farm
Civic Hall
Ormskirk
Superstore
Devil's Wall
L39
St Anne's RC Prim Sch
Red Gate Farm
St Bede's RC High Sch
Gaw Hill
Pontville Sch
Newhouse Farm
Moss House Farm
Christ Church CE Prim Sch
Alty's Farm
Fir Tree Farm
Convent
Aughton Park
Aughton Park Sch
Wayside Farm
Doctor's Bridge
St Michael's CE Prim Sch
Catharine's Lane Farm
Moss Delf
E6
1 ALEXANDRA MEWS
2 BIRD I' TH' HAND COTTS
E5
1 CHURCH VIEW CT
2 SWAN ALLEY
3 CHURCH WLKS
4 WHEATSHEAF WLK
5 MARKET CROSS
6 MARKET WAY
7 CHURCH HO
8 Two Saints Pl
9 MYSTIC MEWS
F6
1 ORCHARD LODGE
2 Ormskirk Bsns Pk
3 CHESTNUT CT
4 PENNINGTON CT
F5
1 WEST VIEW
2 DERBY HO
3 SCARISBRICK HO
4 BEACONSFIELD CT
5 WILLOW GN
6 MEADOW BANK

21

14

A59 Preston

Heyes Farm

Sycamore House Farm

HIGH LA

A59

Abbey Farm

Burscough Priory

ABBEY LA

ABBEY FARM CVN.PK

Jump's Farm

Bullen's Wood

MILL DAM LA

BLYTHE LA

LADY ALICE'S DR

Needless Inn Farm

Mains Wood

Grove Farm

Bath Lodge

Timbobbin Farm

SANDY LA

Robinsons Farm

CRANES LA

BROOK LANDS AVE

Ormskirk Ind Pk

A59

Bath Farm

Dark Lane Farm

DARK LA

LATHOM LA

Leas Farm

CH

New Park Brook

Nursery Ave

QUARRY MOUNT

Hettings House

Charlesbye Mews

LDY'S WLK

Leveldale

New Park Wood

Halsall's Lodge

WATERWORKS RD

PENDLE DR

CHARLESBYE CL

CHARLESBYE AVE

Ormskirk CE Prim Sch

ORME HO

ORME CL

THOMPSON AVE FIELD WLK

Ormskirk Sch

CASTLE LA

L40

Otterheads Farm

GREETBY HILL

DELPH TOP

DERBY HILL CRES

EDGLEY DR

TOWER HS

TAYLOR AVE

LATHAM AVE

Cross Hall Farm

DERBY HILL RD

TANFIELD DR

SUNNYFIELDS

A577

WIGAN RD

Seton Brook

Birchenholt

PO

HART BROW CL

Mawdsley's Farm

PH

OSMOND AVE

HALTON CL(HAL)

GREENACRE

MEADOW

MEADOWBRIDGE CL

DICK'S LA

CROSSHALL BROW

40

H

CROSS HALL CT

DICCONSON WAY

Ormskirk & District General

(Children only)

FORGE CL

FURLONGS CL

Dingle Heyes Farm

MILTON DR

NORMANHURST

BEECH MEADOW

Westhead

Westhead Lathom St James CE Prim Sch

B5240 PLOUGH LA

BLAIRGOWRIE GDNS

WOODLANDS CL

RUFF LA

Ruff Wood

Threlfalls Farm

Ruff Farm

Wellfield

HOLLY CL

DICKET'S BROOK

L39

Edge Hill Univ

VICARAGE CL

ST JAMES CL

VICARAGE LA

SCHOOL LA

A577 DICKET'S

DICKET'S BROW

A570

BEWCASTLE DR

VARLIAN CL

WELLFIELD LA

WN8

B5240

ST HELENS RD

Slack House Farm

SCARTH HILL LA

Turner's Farm

WHITELEYS LA

Westhead Farm

Goose Brook

SCARTH HILL LA

Wtr Twr

Delph Farm

Fosters Farm

LYELAKE LA

POPPY LA

Brookdale Farm

Scarth Hill

Scarth Hill Farm

Stuart's Farm

Grapel's Farm

CROPPER'S LA

ORMSKIRK RD

A570

White House Farm

Wiswall's Farm

B5240

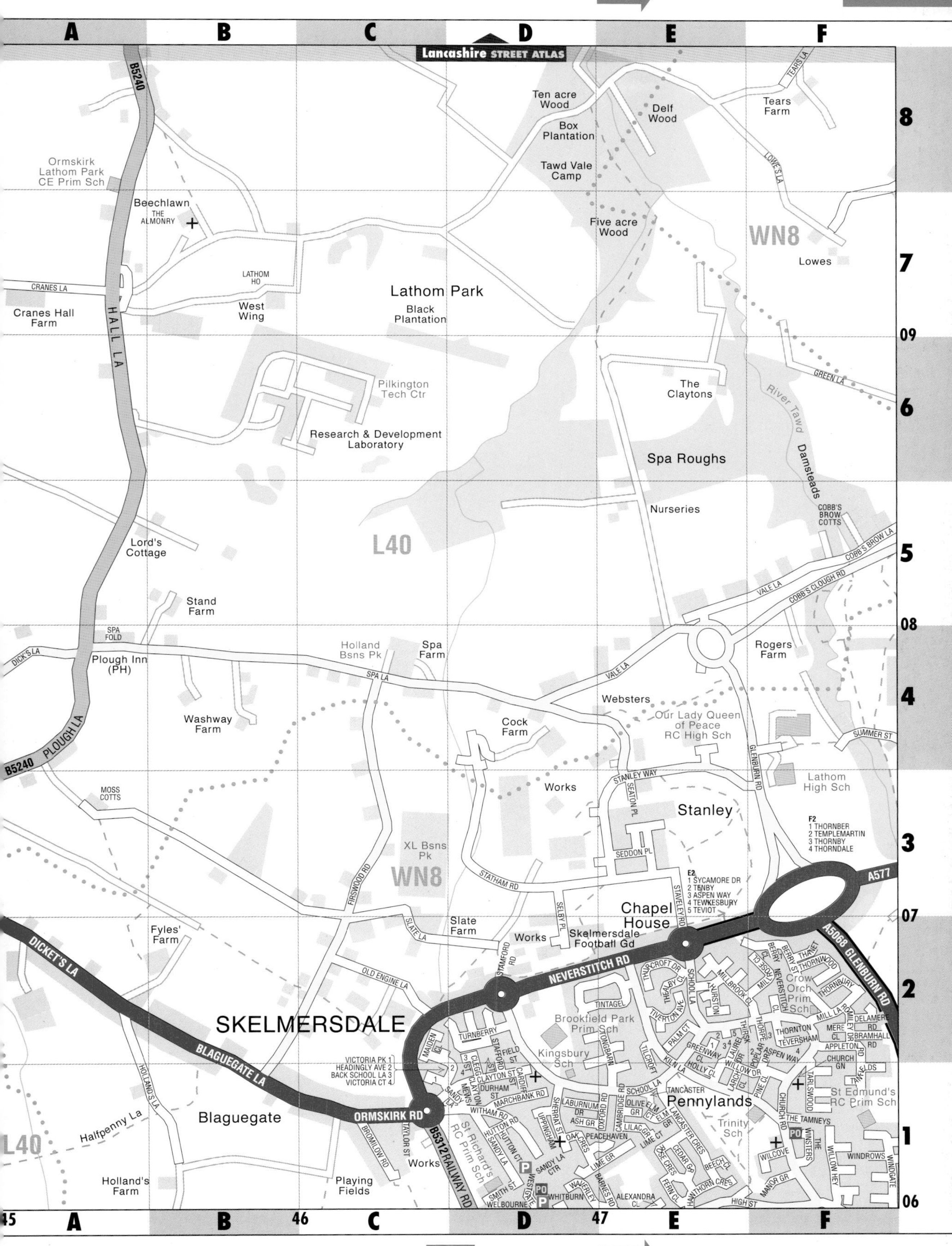

Lancashire STREET ATLAS

Ten acre Wood

Delf Wood

Tears Farm

Box Plantation

Tawd Vale Camp

Ormskirk Lathom Park CE Prim Sch

Beechlawn
THE ALMONRY

Five acre Wood

WN8

Lowes

LATHOM HO

Lathom Park

Black Plantation

West Wing

CRANES LA

Cranes Hall Farm

HALL LA

B5240

Pilkington Tech Ctr

Research & Development Laboratory

The Claytons

River Tawd

GREEN LA

Spa Roughs

Damsteads

COBB'S BROW COTTS

Lord's Cottage

L40

Nurseries

COBB'S BROW LA

COBB'S CLOUGH RD

Stand Farm

SPA FOLD

DICK'S LA

Plough Inn (PH)

Holland Bsns Pk

Spa Farm

VALE LA

Rogers Farm

PLOUGH LA

B5240

Washway Farm

SPA LA

MOSS COTTS

Cock Farm

Works

Our Lady Queen of Peace RC High Sch

GLENBURN RD

SUMMER ST

Lathom High Sch

STANLEY WAY

SEATON PL

Stanley

F2
1 THORNBER
2 TEMPLEMARTIN
3 THORNBY
4 THORNDALE

XL Bsns Pk

WN8

FIRSWOOD RD

SLATE LA

STATHAM RD

SEDDON PL

E2
1 SYCAMORE DR
2 TENBY
3 ASPEN WAY
4 TEWKESBURY
5 TEVIOT

A577

A5068 GLENBURN RD

Fyles' Farm

Slate Farm

Works

Chapel House

Skelmersdale Football Gd

STANLEY RD

Crow Orch Prim Sch

DICKET'S LA

OLD ENGINE LA

STATHFORD RD

SELBY PL

NEVERSTITCH RD

THE CROFT DR

SCHOOL LA

MILL BROOK CL

THORNBY

NEVERSTITCH CL

MERE CL

MILL LA

DELAMERE RD

BRAMHALL RD

SKELMERSDALE

BLAGUEGATE LA

MAIDEN

Turnberry

STAFFORD ST

Brookfield Park Prim Sch

STONEBARN

Kingsbury Sch

TINTAGEL

PALM CT

PALM CT

GREENWAY

LAUREL CL

THORP RD

ASPEN WAY

APPLETON RD

CHURCH GN

Pennylands

St Edmund's RC Prim Sch

THE TAMNEYS

VICTORIA PK 1
HEADINGLY AVE 2
BACK SCHOOL LA 3
VICTORIA CT 4

Blaguegate

ORMSKIRK RD

TAYLOR LA

CLEGGS CLAYTON ST

CARDIFF ST

MARCHBANK RD

DURHAM

SHERRAT ST

LABURNUM DR

SANDY LA

CAMBRIDGE RD

SCHOOL LA

OLIVE GR

LANCASTER RD

LARCHWOOD

PINE CL

WILLOW GR

KILN LA

HOLLY GR

VARLSWOOD

CHURCH RD

WILCOVE

Trinity Sch

PO

MANOR GR

THE WINSTERS

WILLOW HEY

WINDROWS

WINGATE

L40

Halfpenny La

Holland's Farm

B5312 RAILWAY RD

St Richard's RC Prim Sch

HUTTON CT

WESTGATE

Works

BROMILOW RD

SMITH ST

WELBOURNE

WHITBURN

PO P P

WITHAM RD

OAK GR

PEACEHAVEN

WHARFE ST

BARNES RD

ASH GR

LILAC

LIME CT

ALEXANDRA CL

LIME GR

CEDAR GR

HAWTHORN CRES

BEECH GR

FERN CL

HIGH ST

Playing Fields

A   B   46   C   D   47   E   F

45   06   07   08   09   5   6   7   8

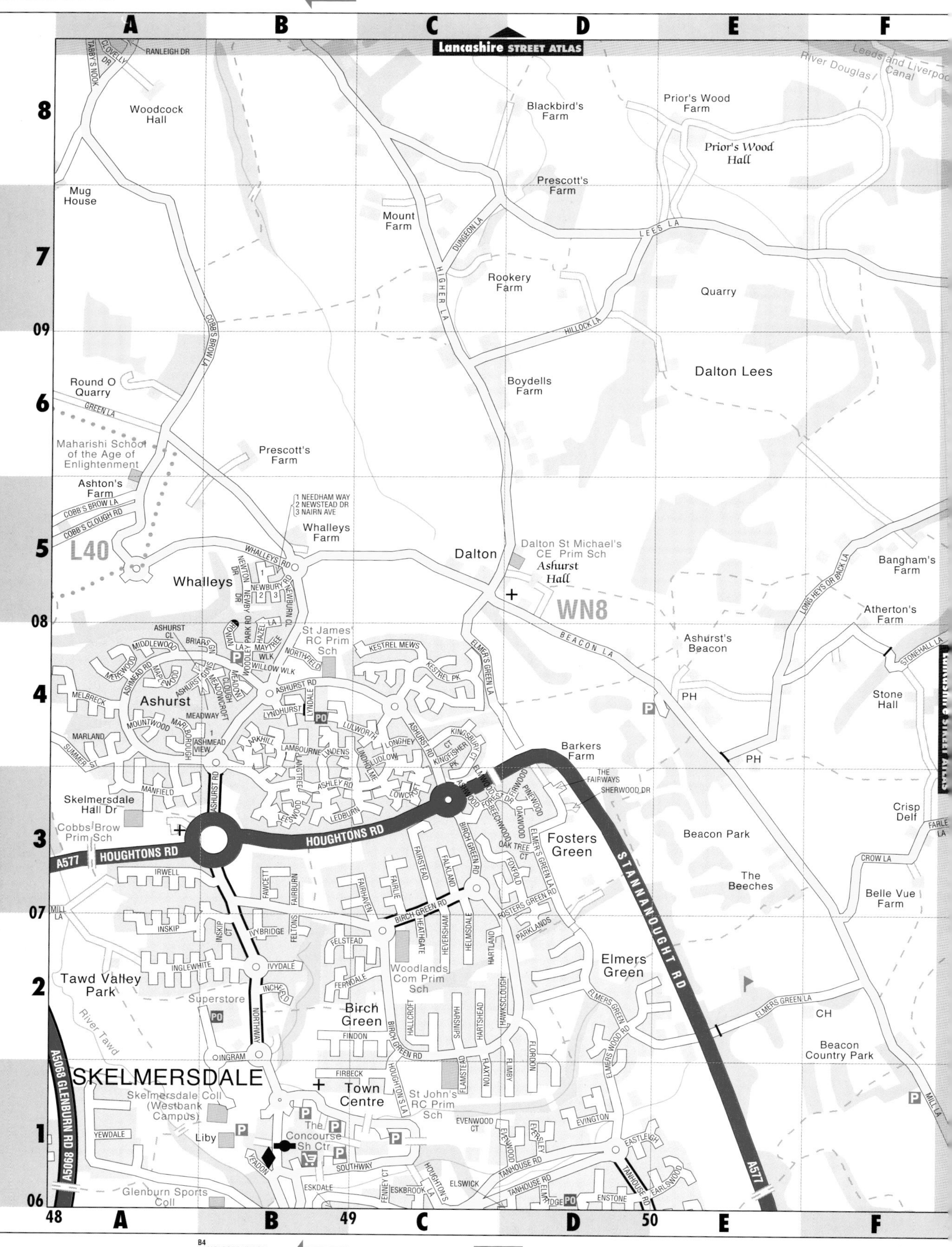

Lancashire STREET ATLAS

8

7

09

6

5

08

4

3

07

2

1

06

A   B   C   D   E   F

Woodcock Hall

Ranleigh Dr

Mug House

Round O Quarry

Maharishi School of the Age of Enlightenment

Ashton's Farm

Whalleys

Ashurst

Tawd Valley Park

Superstore

SKELMERSDALE

Skelmersdale Coll (Westbank Campus)

Glenburn Sports Coll

Prescott's Farm

Whalleys Farm

1 NEEDHAM WAY
2 NEWSTEAD DR
3 NAIRN AVE

Mount Farm

Blackbird's Farm

Prescott's Farm

Rookery Farm

Boydells Farm

Dalton

Dalton St Michael's CE Prim Sch

Ashurst Hall

WN8

Ashurst's Beacon

St James' RC Prim Sch

Kestrel Mews

Barkers Farm

THE FAIRWAYS

Fosters Green

Birch Green

Woodlands Com Prim Sch

Elmers Green

Town Centre

St John's RC Prim Sch

The Concourse Sh Ctr

Prior's Wood Farm

Prior's Wood Hall

Quarry

Dalton Lees

Bangham's Farm

Atherton's Farm

Stone Hall

Crisp Delf

Belle Vue Farm

Beacon Park

The Beeches

Beacon Country Park

CH

L40

48   A   B   49   C   D   50   E   F

A   B   C   D   E   F

Mount Pleasant

ELSWORTH CL

Marsh Farm

Sewage Works

ALEXANDRA RD

ALBERT RD

ST LUKE'S CHURCH RD

STAPLETON RD

Range High Sch

HOGG'S HILL LA

PARK CL

Works

8

L37

Raven Meols Hills

Sefton Coastal Path

7

Raven Meols Hills Nature Reserve

Cambrai Cottage

05

DANGER AREA

Grange Farm

Altcar Training Camp

LC

GRANGE RD

6

Battery Cottage

River Alt

DANGER AREA

FLOODGATES RD

DANGER AREA

Altcar Rifle Range

L38

ST GEORGE'S RD

5

04

MARK RD

ST STEPHEN'S RD

HESTER CL

ISLAKE WAY

4

LOWER ALT RD

ALT RD

PO

TUDOR GDNS

RATHBONE RD

DANGER AREA

NORTH DUNES

RIVERSIDE

WESTWAY

VILLAGE WAY

THE OUTLOOK

THE ROUNDEL

SANDILANDS GR

BLUNDELL AVE

WIGNALLS MDW

BANKSIDE

SANDHILLS

OLD ACRE

LARKHILL GR

BLUNDELL GR

Formby Bank

MOORHOUSES

BRIARY CROFT

HORNBECK AVE

WITHINS FIELD

3

03

Liverpool Bay

Hightown

ALTON CL

BRENTWOOD CL

WHITEFT

CLOD CL

LANGLEY RD

BLUNDELL RD

2

RICHMOND CL

OAKFIELD RD

MAYFAIR CL

1

02

17 10

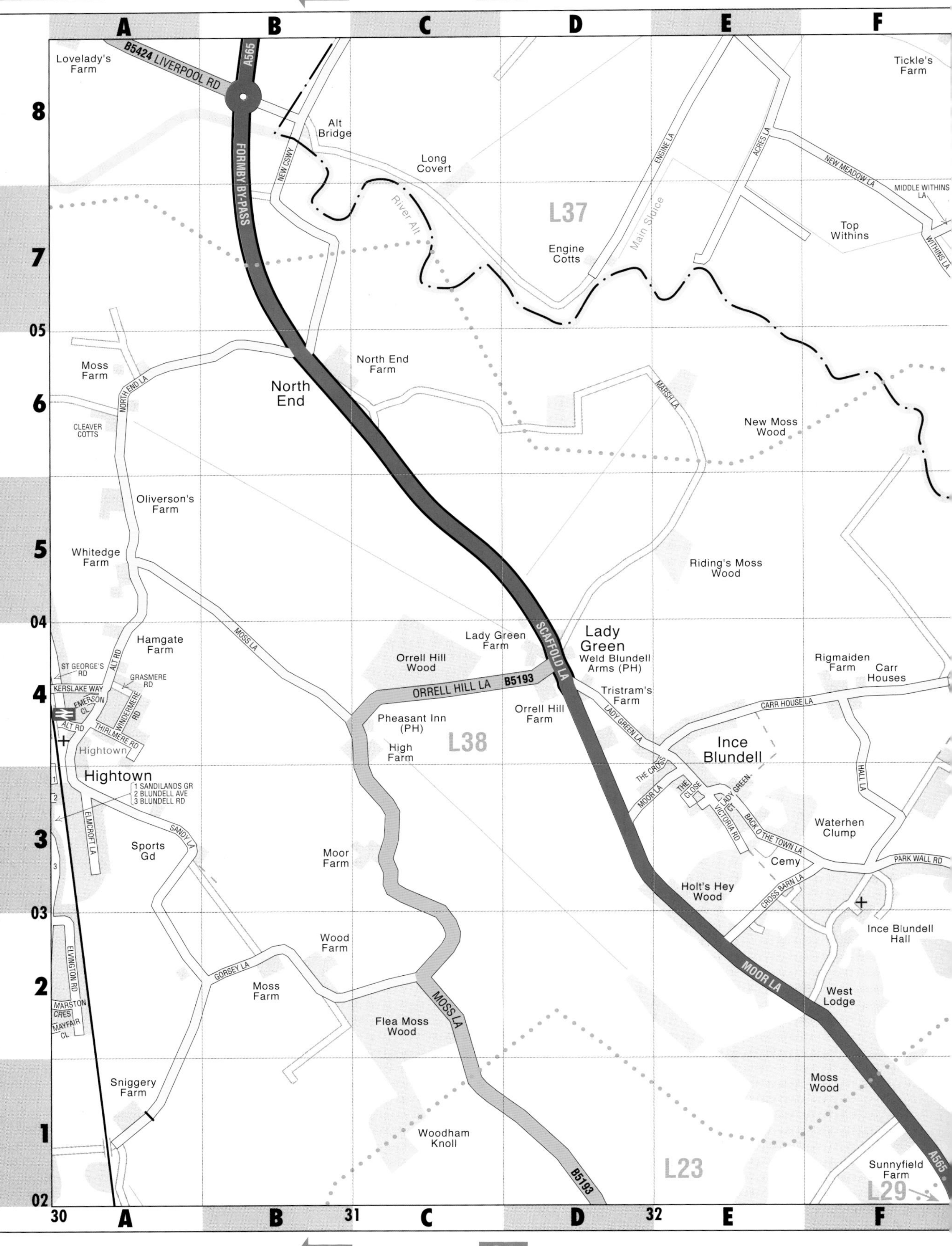
A B C D E F
8 7 05 6 5 04 4 3 03 2 1 02
30 31 32
Lovelady's Farm
B5424 LIVERPOOL RD
A565
FORMBY BY-PASS
NEW CSWY
Alt Bridge
Long Covert
River Alt
L37
ENGINE LA
Main Sluice
Engine Cotts
ACRES LA
NEW MEADOW LA
MIDDLE WITHINS LA
Tickle's Farm
Top Withins
WITHINS LA
Moss Farm
NORTH END LA
North End
North End Farm
CLEAVER COTTS
MARSH LA
New Moss Wood
Oliverson's Farm
Whitedge Farm
Riding's Moss Wood
MOSS LA
Hamgate Farm
ST GEORGE'S RD
ALT RD
GRASMERE RD
KERSLAKE WAY
EMERSON CL
WINDERMERE RD
THIRLMERE RD
Hightown
Lady Green Farm
Orrell Hill Wood
SCAFFOLD LA
Lady Green
Weld Blundell Arms (PH)
ORRELL HILL LA B5193
Pheasant Inn (PH)
High Farm
L38
Orrell Hill Farm
Tristram's Farm
LADY GREEN LA
Rigmaiden Farm
Carr Houses
CARR HOUSE LA
Ince Blundell
THE CROSS
MOOR LA
THE CLOSE
LADY GREEN CT
VICTORIA RD
BACK O' THE TOWN LA
HALL LA
Waterhen Clump
1 SANDILANDS GR
2 BLUNDELL AVE
3 BLUNDELL RD
ELMCROFT LA
SANDY LA
Sports Gd
Moor Farm
Holt's Hey Wood
Cemy
PARK WALL RD
CROSS BARN LA
Ince Blundell Hall
ELVINGTON RD
Wood Farm
GORSEY LA
Moss Farm
MARSTON CRES
MAYFAIR CL
Flea Moss Wood
MOSS LA
MOOR LA
West Lodge
Sniggery Farm
Moss Wood
Woodham Knoll
B5193
L23
Sunnyfield Farm
L29

17 26

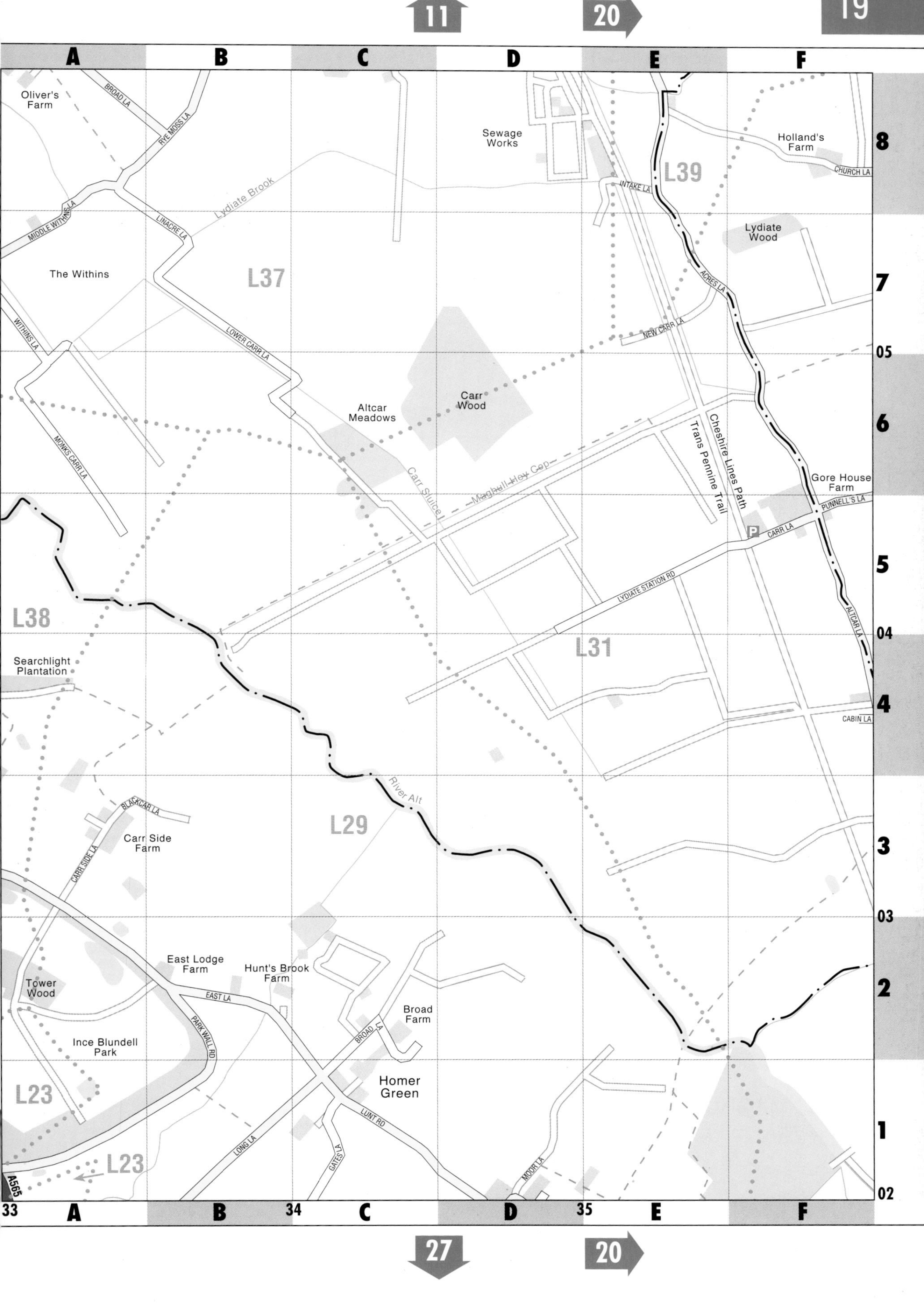
11
20
A
B
C
D
E
F
Oliver's Farm
BROAD LA
RYE MOSS LA
Sewage Works
Holland's Farm
L39
CHURCH LA
INTAKE LA
MIDDLE WITHINS LA
Lydiate Brook
LINACRE LA
Lydiate Wood
The Withins
L37
ACRES LA
WITHINS LA
LOWER CARR LA
NEW CARR LA
Altcar Meadows
Carr Wood
MONKS CARR LA
Carr Sluice
Maghull Hey Cop
Trans Pennine Trail
Cheshire Lines Path
Gore House Farm
PUNNELL'S LA
CARR LA
LYDIATE STATION RD
L38
ALTCAR LA
Searchlight Plantation
L31
CABIN LA
River Alt
BLACKCAR LA
L29
Carr Side Farm
CARR SIDE LA
East Lodge Farm
Hunt's Brook Farm
Tower Wood
EAST LA
Broad Farm
PARK WALL RD
BROAD LA
Ince Blundell Park
Homer Green
L23
LUNT RD
LONG LA
GATES LA
MOOR LA
L23
A565
8
7
05
6
5
04
4
3
03
2
1
02
33
34
35
27
20

19 12

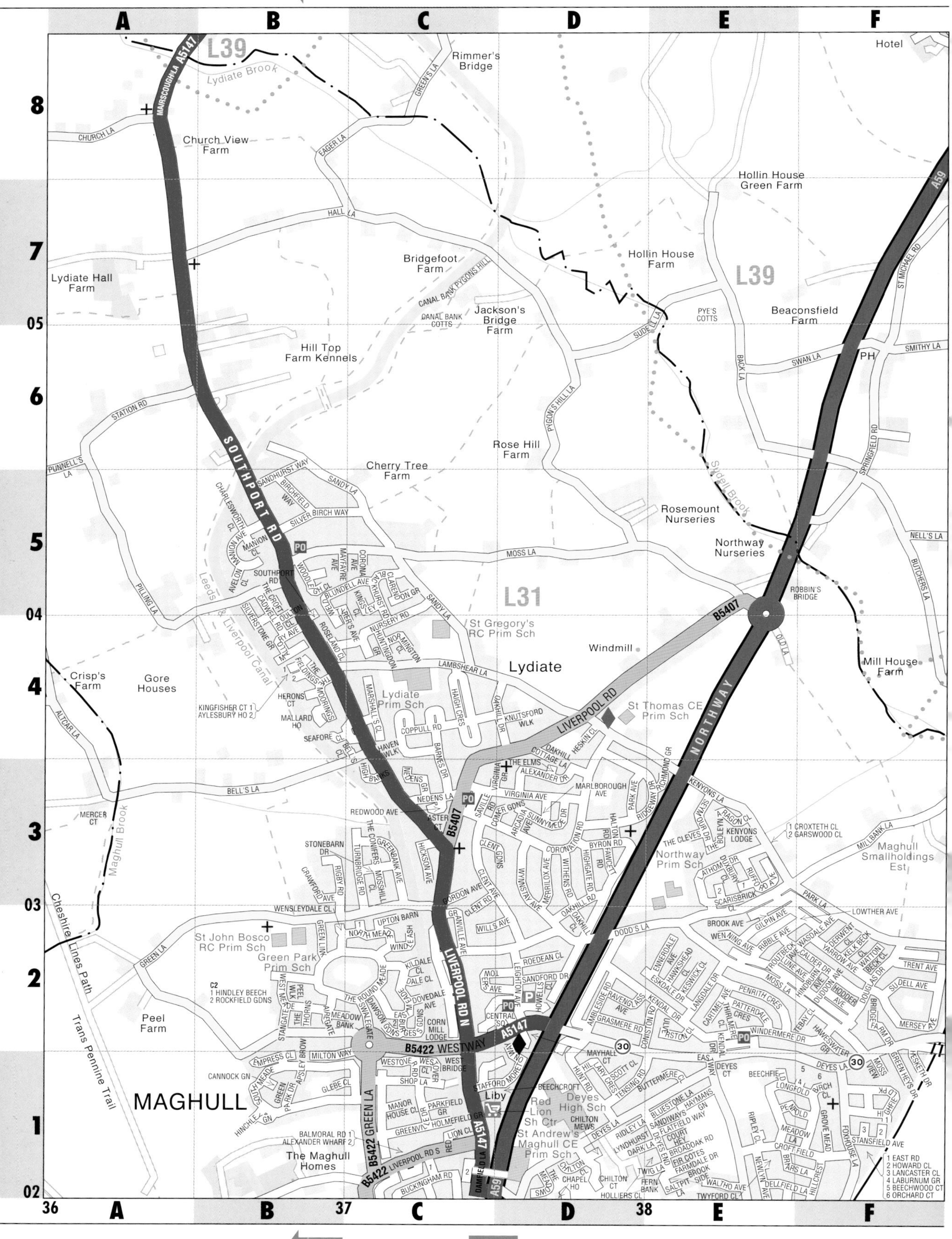

L39
L31
Lydiate
MAGHULL
SOUTHPORT RD
LIVERPOOL RD N
NORTHWAY
LIVERPOOL RD
B5422 WESTWAY
Rimmer's Bridge
Church View Farm
Lydiate Hall Farm
Bridgefoot Farm
Jackson's Bridge Farm
Hill Top Farm Kennels
Hollin House Green Farm
Hollin House Farm
Beaconsfield Farm
Rose Hill Farm
Cherry Tree Farm
Rosemount Nurseries
Northway Nurseries
St Gregory's RC Prim Sch
Windmill
Mill House Farm
Crisp's Farm
Gore Houses
Lydiate Prim Sch
St Thomas CE Prim Sch
Northway Prim Sch
Maghull Smallholdings Est
St John Bosco RC Prim Sch
Green Park Prim Sch
Peel Farm
Deyes High Sch
Red Lion Sh Ctr
St Andrew's Maghull CE Prim Sch
The Maghull Homes
Trans Pennine Trail
Cheshire Lines Path
Leeds & Liverpool Canal
Hotel

19 28

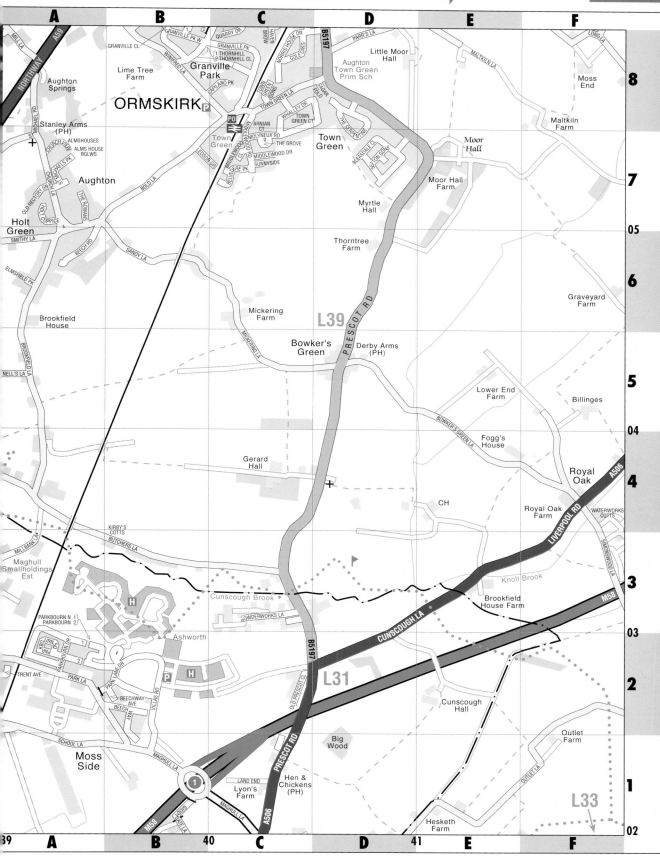
13
22

A B C D E F

Mill La
A59
Northway
Granville Cl
Granville Pk W
Quarry Dr
Haven Brow
Granville Pk
1 Thornhill
2 Thornhill Cl
Norris House Dr
Cole Cres
B5197
Parr's La
Little Moor Hall
Malt Kiln La
Long La
Lime Tree Farm
Winifred La
Granville Park
Capilano Pk
Aughton Town Green Prim Sch
Aughton Springs
Moss End
8
ORMSKIRK
Town Green Gdns
Town Green La
Sagar Fold
Michael Rd
Whalley Dr
Town Green Ct
PO
Maltkiln Farm
Stanley Arms (PH)
Arnian Ct
Middlewood Rd
The Serpentine
Almshouses
Church View
Alms House Bglws
Molyneux Rd
Town Green
The Grove
Town Green
Moor Hall
Bleasdale Cl
Sefton Gdns
Middlewood Dr
Ledson Gr
Haels Pk
Middlewood Cl
Sunnyside
St Michaels Cl
Belvedere Pk
Church La
Aughton
7
Moor Hall Farm
Bold La
Old Rectory Gn
The Rowans
Holt Coppice
Myrtle Hall
Holt Green
Smithy La
05
Thorntree Farm
Beech Rd
Sandy La
Elmsfield Pk
6
Graveyard Farm
Mickering Farm
Brookfield House
L39
Prescot Rd
Mickering La
Bowker's Green
Derby Arms (PH)
Brookfield La
Nell's La
5
Lower End Farm
Billinges
Bowker's Green La
04
Fogg's House
Gerard Hall
Royal Oak
A506
4
CH
Royal Oak Farm
Liverpool Rd
Waterworks Cotts
Kirby's Cotts
Butchers La
Millbank La
Maghull Smallholdings Est
Simonswood La
Knoll Brook
3
Cunscough Brook
Brookfield House Farm
M58
Parkbourn N 1
Parkbourn 2
Powderworks La
Cunscough La
03
Ashworth
Parkbourn Sq
Parkbourn Dr
B5197
Trent Ave
Park La
Park Lane Dr
L31
Old Prescot Cl
2
Beechway Ave
Beech Way
Villas Rd
Cunscough Hall
Outlet Farm
School La
Prescot Rd
Big Wood
Moss Side
Maghull La
Hen & Chickens (PH)
Land End
Lyon's Farm
Outlet La
1
L33
A506
Maghull La
Giddygate La
M58
Hesketh Farm
02

39 A B 40 C D 41 E F

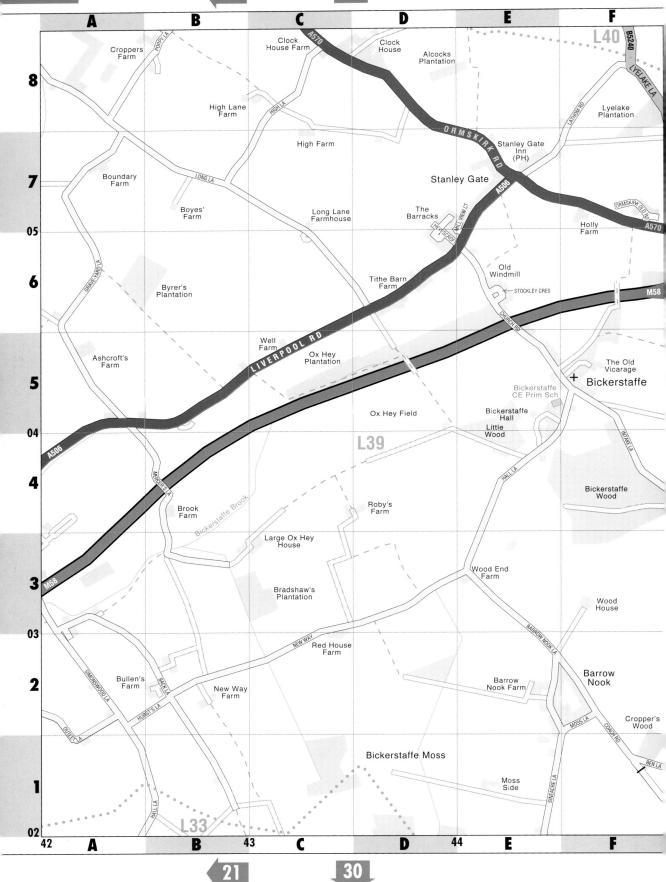

A   B   C   D   E   F

8

7

05

6

05

L40   B5240

LYELAKE LA

Croppers
Farm

POPPY LA

Clock
House Farm

Clock
House

Alcocks
Plantation

LATHOM RD

Lyelake
Plantation

High Lane
Farm

HIGH LA

High Farm

ORMSKIRK RD

Stanley Gate
Inn
(PH)

Boundary
Farm

LONG LA

Stanley Gate

A506

ORMSKIRK OLD RD

Boyes'
Farm

Long Lane
Farmhouse

The Barracks

HEYS CROFT

MILL VIEW CT

Holly
Farm

A570

GRAVE YARD LA

Byrer's
Plantation

Tithe Barn
Farm

Old
Windmill

STOCKLEY CRES

M58

6

04

5

04

Ashcroft's
Farm

LIVERPOOL RD

Well
Farm

Ox Hey
Plantation

CHURCH RD

The Old
Vicarage

Bickerstaffe
CE Prim Sch

Bickerstaffe

A506

Ox Hey Field

Bickerstaffe
Hall

Little
Wood

INTAKE LA

L39

MERCER'S LA

Brook
Farm

Bickerstaffe Brook

Roby's
Farm

HALL LA

Bickerstaffe
Wood

4

03

3

02

M58

Large Ox Hey
House

Bradshaw's
Plantation

NEW WAY

Red House
Farm

Wood End
Farm

BARROW NOOK LA

Wood
House

SIMONSWOOD LA

Bullen's
Farm

BACK LA

New Way
Farm

Barrow
Nook Farm

Barrow
Nook

MOSS LA

COACH RD

Cropper's
Wood

OURLEY LA

HURST'S LA

HALL LA

Bickerstaffe Moss

SINEACRE LA

Moss
Side

BEN LA

2

1

L33

42   A   B   43   C   D   44   E   F   02

15
24

A B C D E F

L40

Blaguegate Moss

Primrose Farm

PARKSIDE AVE 1
STANDSIDE PK 2
OLD TOWN CL 3
OLD TOWN WAY 4
VILLAGE WAY 5
WEST PARK CL 6

WELBOURNE

B5312

LIVERPOOL RD

KEGFOOT'S LA

DERBY RD

SWIFT S

Lyelake Farm

SKELMERSDALE RD

Four Lane Ends

B5240

B5312

Stanley Farm

LYELAKE LA

A570

3

RAINFORD RD

Colliery Plantation

WHITE MOSS RD

WHITE MOSS RD S

WAVERLEY

WESTGATE

WALDRON

VILLAGE CL

WHITE MOSS RD

ASHWALL

ST

WHEATACRE

JUBILEE DR

GARDNERS PL

GLADDEN PL

BIRCH

HIGH ST

ANN ST

WHITE ST

WHITEHEY

WHITE STOCK

WALLCROFT

WOODROW

WINSTANLEY RD

WOODCROFT

WOLVERTON

WIGAN RD

WINDSGATE

B5312

GLENBURN RD

A5063

RAILWAY RD

West Gillibrands Ind Est

West Gillibrands

GILLIBRANDS RD

GERRARD PL

GREENEY PL

Peel Farm

SKELMERSDALE

WN8

White Moss

4

M58

8

7

05

MAPLE VIEW

MOSS LANE VIEW

Whitemoss Bsns Pk

MOSS LA

Moss Lane Farm

6

Wash Farm

Rose Farm

Ivy House

RAINFORD RD

Bickerstaffe Moss

Higherend Farm

Hey's Crossing

5

04

L39

Long Plantation

Brookdale

COAL PIT LA

Barker's Brook

HOLLY LA

Holly Lane Farm

Big Ferny Knoll Farm

Ferny Knoll

HOLLY FOLD LA

FERNY KNOLL RD

4

WA11

3

03

Intake Farm

Ben Lane Farm

INTAKE LA

BEN LANE CL

BEN LA

Holly Fold Farm

Park Hill

ORMSKIRK RD

PH

BUSHEY LA

SPRING FIELD

KESWICK WAY 1
CONISTON WAY 2

WINDERMERE DR

BUTTERMERE CRES

KENDAL CL

KENDAL DR

NEWS LA

RAIL CL

Rainford Junction

Rainford

PO

PH

2

Bridge Farm

Moss House Farm

COACH RD

45

Lodge Farm

Kenyon's Wood

Rigby's Wood

LODGE LA

SIDING LA

SIDING LA

Red Delph Farm

RED DELPH LA

ORMSKIRK RD

A570

B5203

JUNCTION RD

1

02

A B C D E F

31
24

46 47

23
16

A B C D E F
8
7
05
6
5
04
4
3
03
2
1
02
48
49
50
SKELMERSDALE
Glenburn Sports Coll
Skelmersdale Coll (Westbank Campus)
Delph Side Com Prim Sch
Hillside Com Prim Sch
Beacon Sch
Tanhouse
East Gillibrands
Tawd Bridge
Skelmersdale Sports Ctr
Holland Moor Prim Sch
Holland Moor
Moorside Com Prim Sch
Little Digmoor Prim Sch
Bishop Martin CE Prim Sch
Digmoor
Playing Fields
GRIMSHAW RD
B5312
WINDMILL RD
A577
STANNANOUGHT RD
NEWGATE RD
M58
A5068
Moss Farm
Moss Side Farm
River Tawd
WN8
West Pimbo
West Pimbo Ind Est
East Pimbo
Hotel
Holland Moss
Moor Side Farm
Barton House
Upholland
Lower Balcony Farm
Nursery
Balcarres Farm
Crawford Village Prim Sch
Millets
WA11
Crawford
Maggots Nook Farm
Red House Farm
Billinge Bounty Farm
The Crawford (PH)
Strawberry Cottage
Black Brook
Scythe Stone Delph Farm
Hay's House
Maddocks
PIMBO RD
PEEL RD
POTTER PL
PRESCOTT RD
DUKE'S WOOD LA
CRAWFORD RD
LONG LA
PIMBO LA
LANGWOOD LA
MAGGOTS NOOK RD
FERNY KNOLL RD
HOLLAND MOSS
NIPE LA
WHITELEDGE RD
DIGMOOR RD
ORMSKIRK RD
GILLIBRANDS RD
MOSS LA

23
32

A7
1 DENHOLME
2 FIELDVIEW
3 MEADOWFIELD

E5
1 COSGATE CL
2 MIDDLECOT CL
3 THE ORCHARDS

F7
1 THIRLMERE AVE
2 LATIMER CL
3 BYRON CL
4 WINCHESTER CL

Lancashire STREET ATLAS

Greater Manchester STREET ATLAS

18

C4
1 HOMEDOVE HO
2 SANDHURST
3 FORTON LODGE

D5
1 CLAREMONT TERR
2 SPRINGFIELD COTTS
3 PINFOLD CT

E4
1 CHURCH RD
2 CENTRAL BLDGS
3 CROWN BLDGS
4 THE PRECINCTS

E5
1 ALLENGATE
2 GLENN BLDGS
3 TELEGRAPH HO
4 MOOR HO
5 RICHMOND CT

CROSBY

Little Crosby

Hill Farm

St Mary's RC Prim Sch

Bens Gorse

Crosby Hall

Sniggery Wood

Little Crosby Mus

Cottage Farm

The Lodge

Memorial Chapel

Playing Field

Crosby High Sch

Moor Park

Blundellsands

Blundellsands & Crosby

Great Crosby

Waterloo

Brighton le Sands

Sefton Coastal Path

L38 L29 L23 L22 L21

MOOR LA

LIVERPOOL RD

THE BY-PASS

CROSBY RD N

A565

Merchant Taylors' Boys' Sch

Sacred Heart RC Coll

Liby Civic Hall

Rimrose Valley Country Park

Waterloo EMI Day

Boating Lake

B3
1 LINDEN CT
2 WARRENHURST CT
3 GLENDOWER CT
4 BLUNDELLSANDS CT
5 THE KNOWLE
6 THE LAWNS
7 INVERCLYDE CT
8 NICHOLAS CT
9 SOMERFORD HO

C2
1 PURLEY RD
2 HOLDEN RD E
3 SANDPIPERS CT
4 BRIGHTON VALE
5 SUSSEX ST
6 WORTHING ST
7 HOLDEN GR
8 HOLDEN TERR
9 RIVER VIEW

C3
1 INGLESIDE CT
2 HOMEWOOD
3 ABBOTSFORD CT
4 WARREN CT
5 BACK BRIDGE RD
6 FORMBY LODGE

D1
1 BACK MOUNT ST
2 CANNING ST
3 WELBECK ST
4 GREENACRES
5 WELLINGTON GDNS
6 MOUNT PLEASANT FLATS
7 SANDON CT

D3
1 WINCHESTER AVE
2 COLLEGE GN
3 ALEXANDRA GN

E1
1 WINSTANLEY HO
2 BLUEBELL CL
3 CREMONA CNR
4 PARKHOLME
5 KENWOOD
6 LEESWOOD
7 KENMORE

E3
1 THE MEWS
2 ARGYLE CT

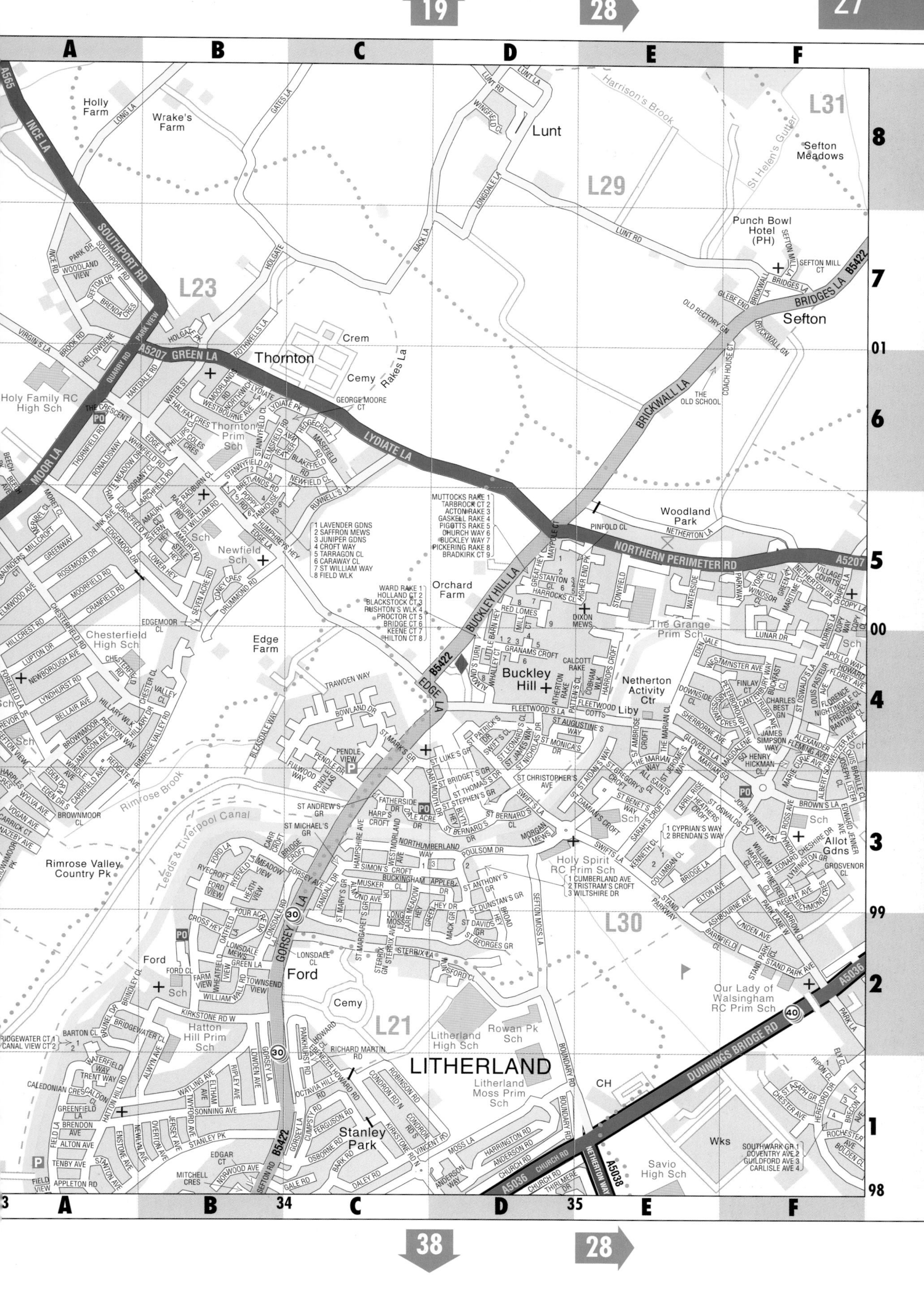
19
28
A
B
C
D
E
F
8
7
01
6
5
00
4
3
99
2
1
98
34
35
38
28
Holly Farm
Wrake's Farm
Lunt
Harrison's Brook
L31
Sefton Meadows
St Helen's Gutter
L29
Punch Bowl Hotel (PH)
Sefton
L23
Thornton
Crem
Cemy
Rakes La
Holy Family RC High Sch
Thornton Prim Sch
Newfield Sch
Woodland Park
NORTHERN PERIMETER RD
Orchard Farm
The Grange Prim Sch
Chesterfield High Sch
Edge Farm
Buckley Hill
Netherton Activity Ctr
Liby
Rimrose Brook
Leeds & Liverpool Canal
Rimrose Valley Country Pk
Holy Spirit RC Prim Sch
Allot Gdns
L30
Ford
Hatton Hill Prim Sch
Cemy
L21
Litherland High Sch
Rowan Pk Sch
LITHERLAND
Litherland Moss Prim Sch
Our Lady of Walsingham RC Prim Sch
CH
Wks
Savio High Sch
Stanley Park
SOUTHPORT RD
INCE LA
MOOR LA
GREEN LA
LYDIATE LA
BRICKWALL LA
BRIDGES LA
BUCKLEY HILL LA
EDGE LA
GORSEY LA
DUNNINGS BRIDGE RD
CHURCH RD
NETHERTON WAY
SEFTON MOSS LA
BOUNDARY RD
LUNT RD
BACK LA
A565
A5207
B5422
A5036
A5038
1 LAVENDER GDNS
2 SAFFRON MEWS
3 JUNIPER GDNS
4 CROFT WAY
5 TARRAGON CL
6 CARAWAY CL
7 ST WILLIAM WAY
8 FIELD WLK
MUTTOCKS RAKE 1
TARBROCK CT 2
ACTON RAKE 3
GASKELL RAKE 4
PIGOTTS RAKE 5
CHURCH WAY 6
BUCKLEY WAY 7
PICKERING RAKE 8
BRADKIRK CT 9
WARD RAKE 1
HOLLAND CT 2
BLACKSTOCK CT 3
RUSHTON'S WLK 4
PROCTOR CT 5
BRIDGE CT 6
KEENE CT 7
HILTON CT 8
1 CUMBERLAND AVE
2 TRISTRAM'S CROFT
3 WILTSHIRE DR
1 CYPRIAN'S WAY
2 BRENDAN'S WAY
SOUTHWARK GR 1
COVENTRY AVE 2
GUILDFORD AVE 3
CARLISLE AVE 4

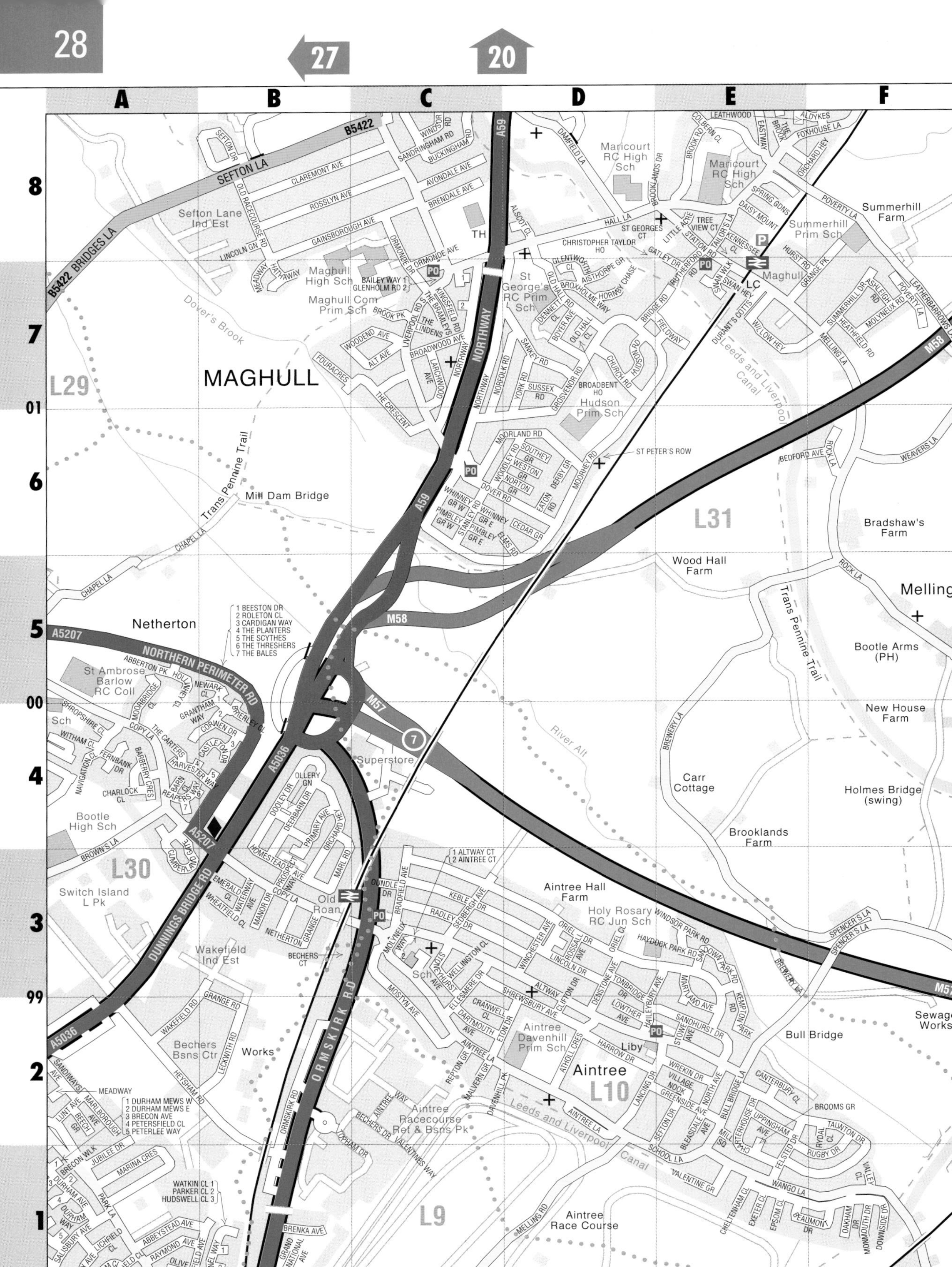

A B C D E F

8
7
01
6
5
00
4
3
99
2
1
98

L29

MAGHULL

B5422

SEFTON LA

B5422 BRIDGES LA

Sefton Lane Ind Est

Dover's Brook

Trans Pennine Trail

Mill Dam Bridge

Chapel La

Netherton

A5207

NORTHERN PERIMETER RD

St Ambrose Barlow RC Coll Sch

Bootle High Sch

L30

Switch Island L Pk

DUNNINGS BRIDGE RD

A5036

Wakefield Ind Est

Bechers Bsns Ctr

Works

MEADWAY

1 DURHAM MEWS W
2 DURHAM MEWS E
3 BRECON AVE
4 PETERSFIELD CL
5 PETERLEE WAY

A5036

A59

ORMSKIRK RD

Old Roan

Netherton Grange

L9

Aintree Racecourse Retl & Bsns Pk

Aintree Race Course

NORTHWAY

A59

Maghull High Sch

Maghull Com Prim Sch

TH

St George's RC Prim Sch

Christopher Taylor Ho

Hudson Prim Sch

St Peter's Row

M58

M57

7

Superstore

River Alt

1 ALTWAY CT
2 AINTREE CT

Aintree Hall Farm

Holy Rosary RC Jun Sch

Aintree Davenhill Prim Sch

Aintree

L10

Liby

Leeds and Liverpool Canal

Maricourt RC High Sch

Maricourt RC High Sch

St Georges

Summerhill Prim Sch

Summerhill Farm

Maghull

LC

L31

Wood Hall Farm

Bradshaw's Farm

Melling

Bootle Arms (PH)

New House Farm

Carr Cottage

Holmes Bridge (swing)

Brooklands Farm

Trans Pennine Trail

M57

Sewage Works

Bull Bridge

Leeds and Liverpool Canal

29
21
30
E5
1 ST PATRICK'S CL
2 WINDMILL CL
3 REDMOOR CRES
4 SANDRINGHAM CL
5 BALMORAL CL
6 APPLEBY RD
E5
7 FARNWORTH GR
8 ST ANDREW'S VIEW
9 FAIRLAWNE CL
E6
1 HORTON CL
2 KERR CL
3 FRANKLIN GR
4 LEWIS WLK
A B C D E F
8
7
01
6
5
00
4
3
99
2
1
98
Whinny Brook
M58
Mast
Moss Nook Farm
MOSS NOOK LA
Whitegates Farm
SPURRIER'S LA
OUTLET LA
A506
PRESCOT RD
Basford Farm
MOSS LA
Melling Mount
Ash Holt Farm
Pear Tree Inn (PH)
L33
Simonswood Hall
1 MULBERRY CL
2 COLMOOR CL
3 CARLILE WAY
4 LEDSON PK
5 WOODBERRY CL
6 KENYON CL
7 MEADOWSIDE DR
Moorfield House
GIDDYGATE LA
Simonswood Brook
Bank Hall Farm
GLENEAGLES CL 1
ANNANDALE CL 2
LEATHERBARROWS LA
Glovers Farm
Melling House Farm
L31
ANGERS LA
SANDY LA
OLD SCHOOL
SCHOOL LA
TITHEBARN LA
Barnes' Farm
Melling House
BANK LA
The Moorfield Ctr
SS Peter & Paul's RC Prim Sch
Tower Hill
Ravenscroft Com Prim Sch
Eastcroft Park Sch
WADDICAR LA
Wadacre Farm
Waddicar
THIRLMERE WLK 1
ULLSWATER CL 2
GRASMERE CL 3
Overdale Prim Sch
Leeds and Liverpool Canal
Ledsons Bridge
Kirkby Park
Kirkby
Millbrook Com Prim Sch
L32
Kirkby CE Prim Sch
Kirkby Brook
Ruffwood Sch
FELCROFT WAY 1
QUARRY DALE 2
DALESIDE WLK 3
Old Rough
CEDAR TWRS
OAK TWRS
Holy Angel's RC Prim Schs
HALL LA
A506
A5208
COUNTY RD
Westvale Prim Sch
Westvale
Mkt Sq
Liby
Knowsley Com Coll
Simonswood Prim Sch
Trans Pennine Trail
VALLEY RD
KIRKBY
BIRCHMUIR HEY 1
BURLEY CL 2
ASHMUIR HEY 3
LANGDALE CL 4
LEYLAKE GDNS 5
All Saints RC High Sch
River Alt
L10
M57
Kirkby Stadium
39 A B 40 C D 41 E F
A3
1 DAPPLE HEATH AVE
2 BIRCHTREE DR
3 IRIS PARK WLK
4 COLUMBINE CL
5 LARKSPUR CT
C1
1 TRENTHAM WLK
2 PATELEY CL
3 AMPLEFORTH CL
4 CORBET WLK
5 STRATTON WLK
5 HALSTEAD WLK
6 MARNWOOD WLK
7 OAKDALE CL
8 NEWICK PK
9 DOWNGREEN CL
C2
1 EMSTREY WLK
2 FRANTON WLK
3 BOLTON WLK
4 CORBET WLK
5 HARRON CL
6 HEYDON AVE
7 LEDSHAM WLK
C3
1 GLOVERS CT
2 PARK CT
3 KIRKBY ROW COTTS
4 BRAMLEY WAY
40
D5
1 APOSTLES WAY
2 EASEDALE WLK
3 CONWAY CL
4 ST PETERS CL
5 HOSTA CL
6 BELLIS GR
7 IRIS GR
8 SALVIA WAY
9 CLEMENTS WAY
10 GIBSON CL
11 BRETT CL
30
E1
1 BRACKNELL CL
2 PONDWATER CL
3 MEADOWBARN CL
E4
1 REDBROW WAY
2 HEATHER CL
3 DAVENPORT GR
4 DEVONSHIRE CL
5 BR AMPTON CL
6 MILLBECK CL
7 SOUTHCROFT
F2
1 KRAMAR WLK
2 BURNARD WLK
3 HARGATE WLK
4 TARVES WLK
5 RETFORD WLK
F4
1 SANDLEWOOD GR
2 LINSLADE CRES
3 KINGSWOOD CT
4 ROCKINGHAM CT
5 BUCKINGHAM CT
6 CRASK WLK
7 BEDALE WLK
8 RIVERSDALE CL

29 22

A B C D E F
8 7 01 6 5 00 4 3 99 2 1 98
42 43 44
Brookfield Farm
Voces Farm
Hesketh's Shroggs
Sewage Works
WALKDEN COTTS
Walkden House Farm
Grayson's Farm
HALL LA
Simonswood Brook
New Bridge Farm
Caravan Site
Barrow Nook Hall
SINEACRE LA
L39
High Barn Farm
Abram's Farm
Wood House Farm
STOPGATE LA
SIDING LA
Hall's Folly
Wild Goose Slack
SHEVINGTON'S LA
Gate House Bridge
Timber Yard
Simonswood Ind Pk
CALDER CL
1 GARDENERS VIEW
2 WINDFIELD CL
3 GREENSIDE CL
4 WHITELY GR
5 BLACKLEY GR
6 EPSOM GR
1 WINMOSS DR
2 SPRING CL
3 BROMPTON AVE
4 LOUGHLIN DR
5 SUNSET CL
6 KALE GR
7 DORCHESTER DR
8 CROFTERS LA
9 GLENDALE GR
10 BIRCHWOOD WAY
11CHERRY VIEW
PINGWOOD LA
ANDERS DR
FRECKLETON DR
ALVINA LA
HEADBOLT LA
Woodwards Plantation
Woods Farm
Bridge Farm
1 LAPFORD WLK
2 BYTON WLK
3 NORTHFIELD CL
4 WOODCOTE CL
5 WHITBURN RD
6 KENBURY CL
Southead
L33
NORTH PERIMETER RD
Spencer's House Farm
Eccleston House
Simonswood Moss
DALE LA
BRAMCOTE CL
BRAMCOTE RD
LAPFORD CRES
CARFAX RD
PENTLAND RD
SHACKLADY RD
TRECASTLE RD
WARRENHOUSE RD
ROUGHWOOD DR
OAKLEE GR
FOSCOTE RD
DEYCROFT AVE
DEYCROFT WLK
KENBURY RD
GILESCROFT AVE
WATTS CL
JARRETT RD
JARRETT WLK
CHANGFORD RD
Acorn Venture Urban Farm
Works
WA11
Ashcroft's Plantation
DEPOT RD
North Mersey Bsns Ctr
WOODWARD RD
MOSS END WAY
BROOK HEY DR
BIGDALE DR
QUERNMORE RD
1 JADE CL
2 WINGATE WLK
3 BROOK HEY WLK
4 QUERNMORE WLK
5 CHANGFORD GN
6 BIRBECK WLK
7 FAIRTHORN WLK
8 BURWELL CL
9 HARLESTON WLK
10 KENMAY WAY
MARL RD
HAMMOND RD
BRADMAN RD
Sch
Northwood
CLORAIN CL
CLORAIN RD
BIRBECK RD
DARMOND RD
SANDERLING RD
HARLESTON RD
MOSS LA
ASHCROFT RD
QUARRYSIDE DR
SIMONSWOOD LA
Courtyard Works
NEWSTET RD
Knowsley Ind Pk
BIRCHILL RD
STOCKPIT RD
DRAW WELL RD
ACORNFIELD RD
PERIMETER RD
Top House Farm
BOUNDARY LA
RETFORD RD
CYGNET CT
COLWALL RD
COLWALL CL
1 COLWALL WLK
2 SIMONSWOOD WLK
3 LIFTON RD
KIRKBY
Football Academy
ARBOUR CT
MINSTEAD AVE
WYLLIN RD
ORMONDE CRES
MINTOR RD
GLESSIDE RD
MADRYN AVE
BARN HEY RD
FARRIER RD
ARBOUR LA
Manor Complex
KIRKBY BANK RD
LEES RD
WEBBER RD
Orchard Works
CRANSTON RD
Capitol Trad Est
WESTHEAD AVE
4 WESTHEAD WLK
5 WESTHEAD CL
Acorn Bsns Ctr
Yardley Ctr
YARDLEY RD
Kirkby Moss
Charley Wood
A5208
COUNTY RD
GLADESWOOD RD
Venture Works
Sports Ctr
L32
RUSHDEN RD
DELFBY CRES
DULAS GN
DULAS RD
CROSLAND RD
LINKS RD
VALE GR
BROAD LA
MOSSLAWN RD
CHARLEY WOOD RD
CUSSON RD
Deltic Pl
Enterprise Workshops
DELTIC WAY
GORES RD

29 41

A B C D E F
Birchall's Wood
Moss Farm
Camholes Wood
L39
Coach Road Farm
Rainford Brook
Nursery Plantation
Dairy Farm
DAIRY FARM RD
COACH RD
WA11
Mast
Blackburn's Plantation
RAINFORD
A570
B5203
RAINFORD BY-PASS
ORMSKIRK RD
KNOWSLEY VIEW
JUNCTION RD
TUDOR CL
RANDLE BROOK CT
RANDLE AVE
EDEN AVE
HARRISON DR
STANLEY AVE
HELEN BANK DR
GRAYSONS RD
OLD LA
RUFFORD RD
SCARISBRICK RD
LATHOM DR
ASTLEY CL
PARKLANDS
LORDS FOLD
Works
Prim Sch
Sch
VICTORIA HO
Lower Shades
MOSS BROW
FERN BANK
PINE DALE
CENTRAL DR
CARTWRIGHT CT
BROOKSIDE AVE
BEECH GDNS
VICTORIA ST
ALFRED ST
ARNIAN RD
ARNIAN WAY
THE SPINNEY
CROXTETH AVE
CROSS PIT LA
B5205
CARTWRIGHT CL
Parson's Brow
PARSON'S BROW
ELM GDNS
WHALLEY AVE
ASH GR
LIME GR
THE AVENUE
LEYLAND RD
PILKINGTON ST
CHURCH RD
WEST VIEW
SCHOOL HOUSE CT
PO
MOSS NOOK LA
Inglenook Farm
Moss Nook
Mossnook Farm
Clare's Moss Plantation
Moor Game Farm
Clare's Wood
MOSSBOROUGH RD
Reed's Farm
REED'S LA
Brown Birch Farm
Aspinwall's Wood
Sharples Plantation
Simonswood Brook
Bunker Hill
Mossborough Hall
MOSSBOROUGH HALL LA
Moss Plantation
Brown Birches
Reed's Moss
NEW CUT LA
L33
Mossborough Moss
BLIND FOOT RD
Harrison's Wood
Blind Foot Farm
8 7 01 6 5 00 4 3 99 2 1 98
45 46 47

31
24

A
B
C
D
E
F
8
7
01
6
5
00
4
3
99
2
1
98
48
49
50
RAINFORD
WA11
WN8
Hyde's Brow Farm
Reeds Brow
Moss House
Pear Tree House
Rainford High Tech Coll
Rainford Brook Lodge Com Prim Sch
Holiday Moss
King's Moss Farm
King's Moss
Fir Tree Farm
Murray's Barn
Kings Moss
Collier's Arms (PH)
Pennsylvania
Holiday Moss Farm
King's Bridge Farm
Sch
King's Moss Plantation
Fire Clay Farm
Myer's Farm
Liby
Mill House Farm
Fairhurst's Plantation
Alderley Farm
Rookery Farm
Diamond Bsns Pk
Alder Lane Farm
Works
Red Cat Hotel
PH
Pasture Lane Bsns Ctr
Shawhurst
Mill Lane Farm
Crank
Rainford Ind Est
Heysome House
Crank Farm
Barrows House Farm
Millbrook Bsns Pk
Crank Hall Farm
Barrows Farm
Rainford Brook
Crank House
The Cottage
Hill Foot Farm
Fairfield
Hill Top Farmhouse
Rainford Hall
The Bottle & Glass (PH)
Lion House Wood
Hill Top House
Square Wood
Moss Plantation
Grey House Farm
Fenny Bank Farm
Inglewood Farm
Pottery Farm
Dagnals Bridge Farm
HENDERSON DR
NEWS LA
REEDS BROW
LANGWOOD LA
ROBIN'S LA
HYDE'S BROW
SPRING VALE
OLD LA
PIMBO RD
WITTON WAY
TYBURY CL
HIGHER LA
STANDISH DR
GARSWOOD AVE
SCARISBRICK RD
KING'S MOSS LA
FIR TREE CL
BROOK LA
CRANK RD
CROXTETH DR
OLD HALL GDNS
B5205
CROSS PIT LA
HEYES AVE
MUNCASTER DR
HEYES GR
NORWOOD GR
SANDON GR
KENWAY
LAKESIDE GDNS
LAKESIDE CT
MASSAM CL
PILKINGTON ST
SOUTHERN'S LA
EAGLE CRES
ROOKERY DR
FINCH AVE
RED CAT LA
GORES LA
HOLLY CRES
DERBY DR
BACK LA
ALL SAINTS CT
FESTIVAL RD
WALMESLEY DR
CARTER AVE
HERON GR
THICKWOOD MOSS LA
CHURCH RD
GREEN LA
ROOKERY LA
HIGHER LA
ROSE PL
STAR INN COTTS
ROSE DR
HOPWOOD CRES
MOSS LA
ALDER LA
WELLFIELD
HESKETH CT
B5201
HIGHFIELD DR
CRANK HILL
CHAPEL VIEW
A570
SANDWASH CL
THE MANOR
HEYSOME CL
PASTURE LA
MILL LA
RAINFORD BY-PASS
REED'S LA
FAIRFIELD GDNS
HILL TOP RD
ST HELENS RD
BERRINGTON'S LA
INGLEMOSS DR
LONGWOOD CL
INGLEWOOD RD
SANDY LA

31
43

25
34

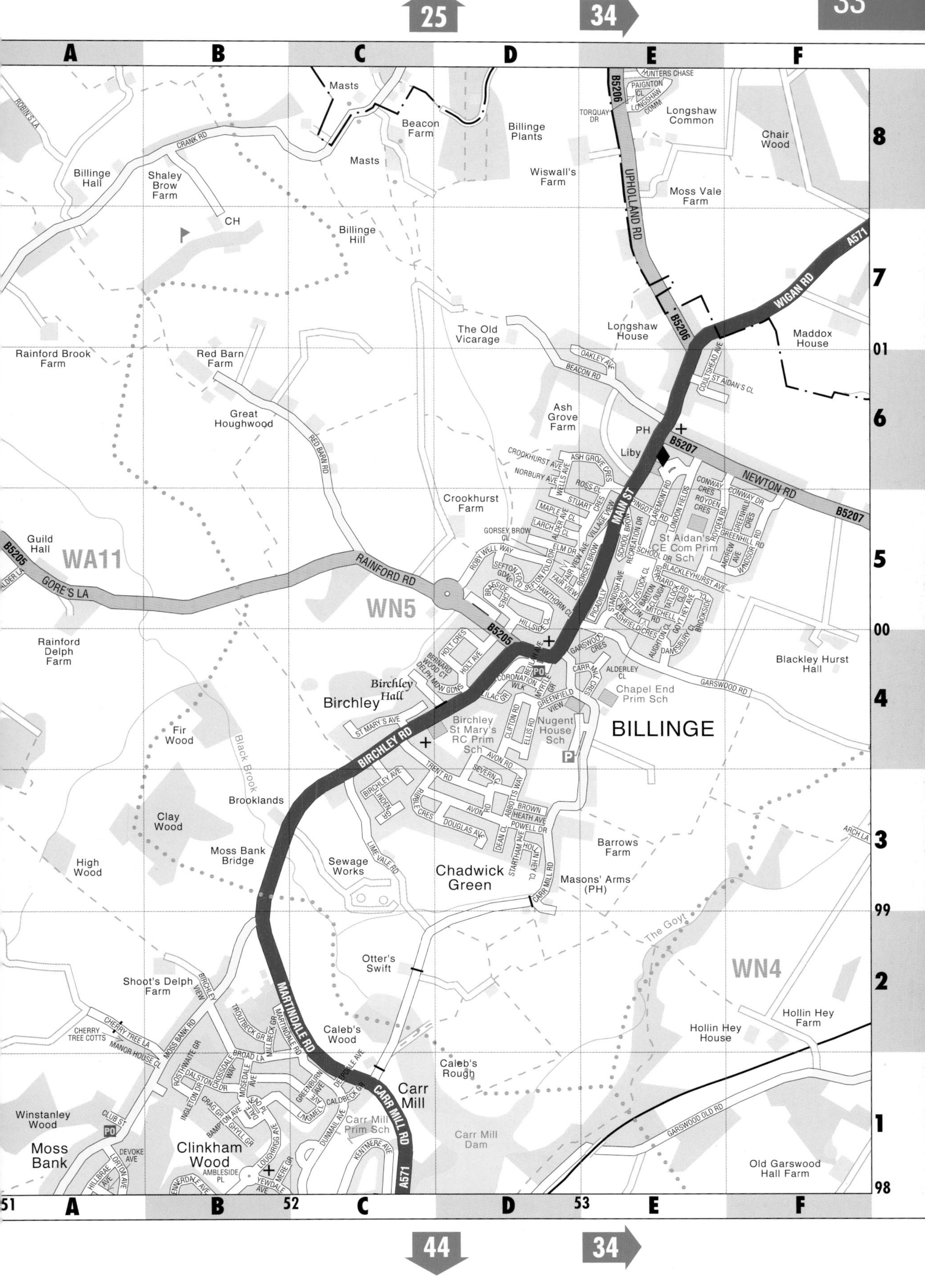
A
B
C
D
E
F
8
7
01
6
5
00
4
3
99
2
1
98
51
52
53
Masts
Beacon Farm
Billinge Plants
HUNTERS CHASE
PAIGNTON CL
LONGSHAW COMM
TORQUAY DR
B5206
Longshaw Common
Chair Wood
ROBIN'S LA
CRANK RD
Billinge Hall
Shaley Brow Farm
Masts
Wiswall's Farm
UPHOLLAND RD
Moss Vale Farm
CH
Billinge Hill
A571
WIGAN RD
Longshaw House
Maddox House
The Old Vicarage
Rainford Brook Farm
Red Barn Farm
OAKLEY AVE
BEACON RD
COULTSHEAD AVE
ST AIDAN'S CL
Great Houghwood
Ash Grove Farm
PH
Liby
B5207
NEWTON RD
RED BARN RD
CROOKHURST AVE
ASH GROVE CRES
NORBURY AVE
WELLS AVE
ROSS CL
CONWAY CRES
CONWAY DR
ROYDEN CRES
Crookhurst Farm
MAIN ST
STUART CRES
MAPLE AVE
LARCH CL
ALDER AVE
VILLAGE VIEW
CLAREMONT RD
LONDON FIELDS
ROYDEN RD
GREENHILL CRES
GREENHILL RD
GORSEY BROW CL
ELM DR
SCHOOL BROW
RECREATION DR
St Aidan's CE Com Prim Sch
SCHOOL DR
ANDREW AVE
WINDSOR RD
Guild Hall
WA11
B5205
GORE'S LA
RAINFORD RD
ROBY WELL WAY
SEFTON FOLD GDNS
SEFTON FOLD DR
FAIR VIEW AVE
GORSEY BROW
BLACKLEYHURST AVE
WN5
BRAESIDE CRES
HAWTHORN CL
PICADILLY
STANDISH AVE
LOSTOCK CL
BARTON CL
MITCHELL RD
MATLOCK RD
GOYT HEY AVE
BROOKSIDE
HILLSIDE CL
ASHFIELD CRES
AUGHTON CL
DANESBURY CL
Rainford Delph Farm
HOLT CRES
HOLT AVE
BEULAH AVE
GARSWOOD CRES
Blackley Hurst Hall
BERNARD WOOD CT
DELPH MOUNT GDNS
PO
CORONATION WLK
MYRTLE GR
CARR MILL CRES
ALDERLEY CL
GARSWOOD RD
Birchley Hall
LILAC GR
GREENFIELD VIEW
Chapel End Prim Sch
Birchley
ST MARY'S AVE
Birchley St Mary's RC Prim Sch
CLIFTON RD
ELLIS RD
Nugent House Sch
BILLINGE
Fir Wood
Black Brook
BIRCHLEY RD
AVON RD
P
TRENT RD
SEVERN CL
BIRCHLEY AVE
LINDEN GR
RIBBLE CRES
Brooklands
AVON RD
ABBOTTS WAY
BROWN HEATH AVE
POWELL DR
Clay Wood
DOUGLAS AVE
DEAN CL
HOLLY HEY CL
STARTHAM AVE
Barrows Farm
ARCH LA
High Wood
Moss Bank Bridge
Sewage Works
LIME VALE RD
Chadwick Green
CARR MILL RD
Masons' Arms (PH)
The Goyt
WN4
Otter's Swift
Shoot's Delph Farm
BIRCHLEY VIEW
MARTINDALE RD
Hollin Hey Farm
Hollin Hey House
CHERRY TREE LA
CHERRY TREE COTTS
MANOR HOUSE CL
MOSS BANK RD
TROUTBECK GR
MILLBECK GR
Caleb's Wood
BROAD LA
ROSTHWAITE GR
DALSTON DR
CROSSDALE WAY
MOSEDALE AVE
DERWENT AVE
Caleb's Rough
Carr Mill
INGLETON DR
CRAG GR
BAMPTON AVE
GHYLL GR
DALE END PL
GREENBURN AVE
LINGMELL AVE
CALDBECK GR
DUNMAIL AVE
Carr Mill Prim Sch
CARR MILL RD
Carr Mill Dam
GARSWOOD OLD RD
Winstanley Wood
CLUB ST
PO
Moss Bank
DEVOKE AVE
Clinkham Wood
LOUGHRIGG AVE
KENTMERE AVE
AMBLESIDE PL
MERE GR
YEWDALE AVE
HILLBRAE AVE
LORTON AVE
ENNERDALE AVE
Old Garswood Hall Farm

44
34

Greater Manchester STREET ATLAS

A | **B** | **C** | **D** | **E** | **F**

WINSTANLEY RD →

M6 Orrell

M6

A49 Wigan

Cranberry
Ley

WN3

Cranberry
Hotel

Haslemere Ind Est 1
Landgate Ind Est 2

Windy
Arbour

Sandy Forth
Farm

Windy Arbour
Farm

HILLSIDE AVE 3
PARKSIDE AVE 4
BROOKSIDE AVE 5
THE BUNGALOWS 6

30

Link 25
Bsns Pk

8

WIGAN RD

A571

A571

ASHTON RD

Sch

ELDER CL

LYON
ST

Low Brooks
Farm

DRUMMER'S LA

Drummersfield
Farm

Rose
Hill

7

Opencast
Workings

Ryecroft
Farm

25

A49

WINSTANLEY RD

BROCKSTEDES RD

P

01

WN5

Barton
Clough

Gladden Hey
Brow

Brocstedes
Farm

MALIKA PL

SOUGHER'S LA

CHIMES RD

DOWNALL GREEN RD

Our Lady
Immaculate
RC Prim Sch

B5207

Bryn

6

Tatlock's
Hillock

Down Brook

Leyland
Green

LEYLAND GREEN RD

CORONATION
ST

BROOKSTEDES AVE

MELROSE CL

P

North
Ashton

PASTURE CL

JENNET HEY

MEADOWCROFT

SEFTON RD

CHANTRY WLK

Rectory
CE
Prim Sch

BOOTH'S BROW RD

B5207

NEWTON RD

Leyland
Green

WN4

HAWTHORN AVE

PALM AVE

BIRCH GR

LILAC AVE

ELM AVE

POPLAR AVE

CEDAR
GR

THE
BRAMBLES

RECTORY RD

EVERTON RD

BOLTON RD

GASKELL'S BROW

OLD RD

DOWNALL GREEN RD

Mill
Farm

F5
1 ELMSBURY ST
2 COLUMBUS ST
3 BEVINGTON ST
4 RUFFORD ST
5 HADDON ST
6 CLARENCE ST
7 POULTON DR
8 WALKDEN HO

HALE GR

5

Billinge Lane
Farm

Simm's Lane
End

BILLINGE RD

Downall
Green

KELVIN CL 1
RANMORE AVE 2
CORN MILL CL 3
WHITBURN CL 4

FERN CL

STIRLING DR

THORNTON CL

00

Weathercock Hill
Farm

SMOCK LA

PEEBLES CL

THORNHILL RD

OBAN DR

FALKLAND DR

OBAN DR

ARGYLL CL

SELKIRK AVE

HAMILTON RD

VICTORIA DR

ELGIN AVE

ELSTEAD
GR

ABINGER RD

AVIEMORE

SPINDLE HILLOCK

GORDON AVE

AUSTIN AVE

LOW BANK RD

4

Weathercock
Hill

GARSWOOD RD

Senely Green
Farm

DARYL AVE

KINROSS AVE

LANGTON AVE

DUNBLANE AVE

GIRVAN CRES

COLLISTONE DR

THE CLOUGH

KENMORE
GR

HILLBECK CRES

CAMP RD

WOLFSON SQ 1
CAMPION GR 2
PETERHOUSE WLK 3

TENBURY DR

ORIEL DR

BALTON WAY

SALFORD

24

Charity
Farm

Montrey
Resr

Montrey
House

Arch Lane
Farm

ARCH LA

The Stag
(PH)

STATION RD

OLD COLLIERY YD

Prim
Sch

MELSTRANGE RD

MANDY CL

FORBES RD

NEWBRIDGE

LEDMORE GR

Long
Covert

Park
Ind Est

A58

M6

3

Garswood

Liby

P

SCHOOL LA

STATION MEWS

Garswood

GIBBON'S RD

99

GARSWOOD OLD RD

ARCH LA

Tithe Barn
Hillock

TITHEBARN RD

Tithe Barn
Farm

Ashton
Cross

LIVERPOOL RD

Garswood Park

CH

2

Carter's Fold
Farm

GARSWOOD OLD RD

LIVERPOOL RD

TV FAIRWAYS

MILLFIELD LA

Oil Depot

1

Old Garswood
Park

WA11

Millfield
Farm

Old Garswood
Hall Farm

A58

Pewfall

Haydock Lane
Ind Est

HAYDOCK LA

ANDOVER

WINCHESTER
RD

HALL WOOD AVE

98

54 | **A** | **B** | **55** | **C** | **D** | **56** | **E** | **F**

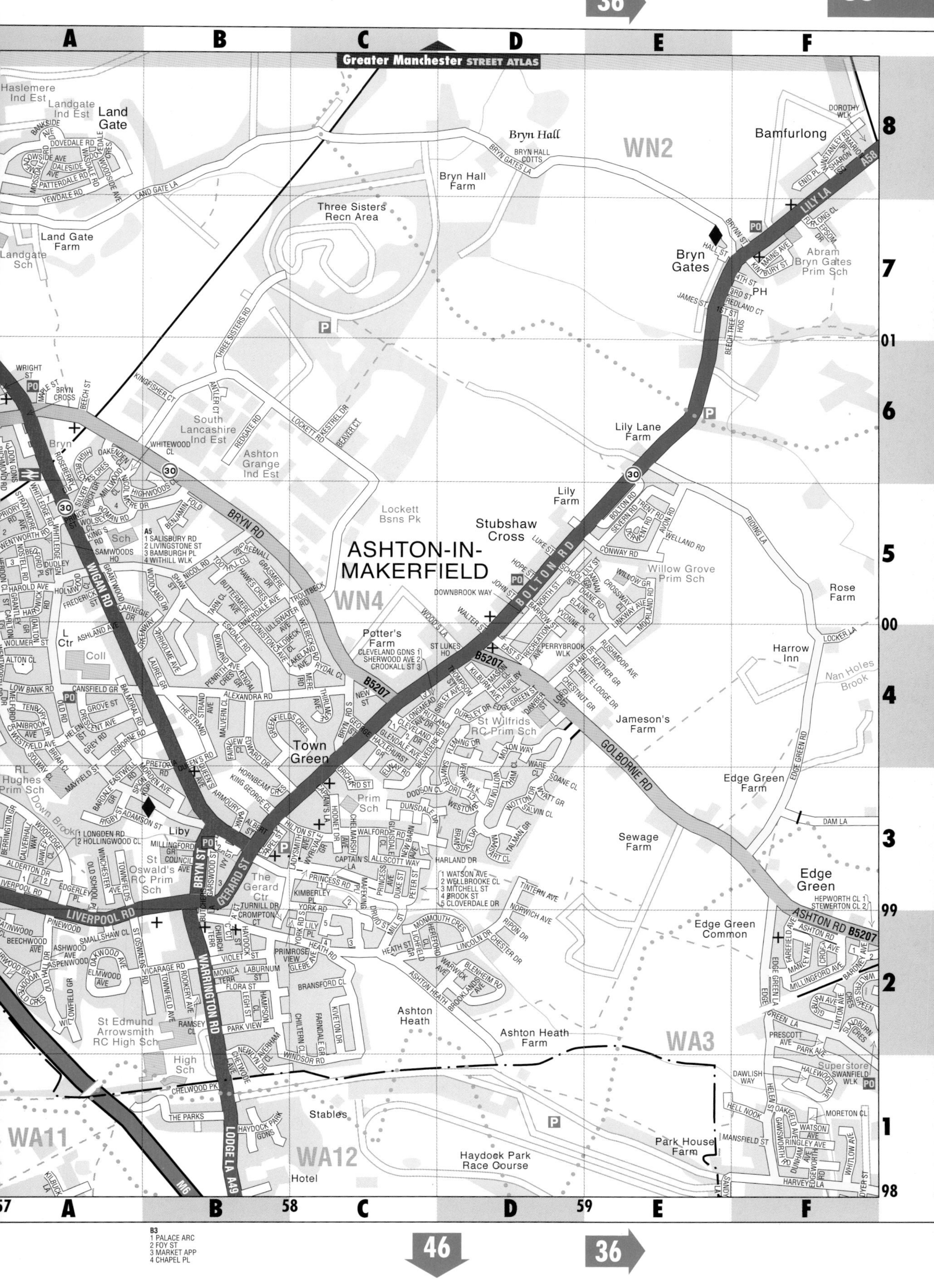
36
Greater Manchester STREET ATLAS
A
B
C
D
E
F
Haslemere Ind Est
Landgate Ind Est
Land Gate
Land Gate Farm
Landgate Sch
Bryn Hall
BRYN HALL COTTS
BRYN GATES LA
Bryn Hall Farm
WN2
Bamfurlong
DOROTHY WLK
Three Sisters Recn Area
Bryn Gates
Abram Bryn Gates Prim Sch
LILY LA
A58
THREE SISTERS RD
KINGFISHER CT
South Lancashire Ind Est
Ashton Grange Ind Est
LOCKETT RD
KESTREL DR
Bryn
WIGAN RD
BRYN RD
Lockett Bsns Pk
Lily Lane Farm
Lily Farm
Stubshaw Cross
ASHTON-IN-MAKERFIELD
WN4
BOLTON RD
Willow Grove Prim Sch
Rose Farm
Potter's Farm
B5207
Harrow Inn
Nan Holes Brook
L Ctr
Coll
Town Green
St Wilfrids RC Prim Sch
Jameson's Farm
GOLBORNE RD
Edge Green Farm
RL Hughes Prim Sch
Down Brook
Liby
Prim Sch
Sewage Farm
DAM LA
St Oswald's RC Prim Sch
The Gerard Ctr
Edge Green
LIVERPOOL RD
BRYN ST
GERARD ST
Edge Green Common
ASHTON RD B5207
WARRINGTON RD
St Edmund Arrowsmith RC High Sch
Ashton Heath
Ashton Heath Farm
WA3
High Sch
Superstore
Stables
WA11
WA12
Park House Farm
Haydock Park Race Course
Hotel
LODGE LA A49
M6
8
7
01
6
5
00
4
3
99
2
1
98
57
58
59
B3
1 PALACE ARC
2 FOY ST
3 MARKET APP
4 CHAPEL PL
46
36

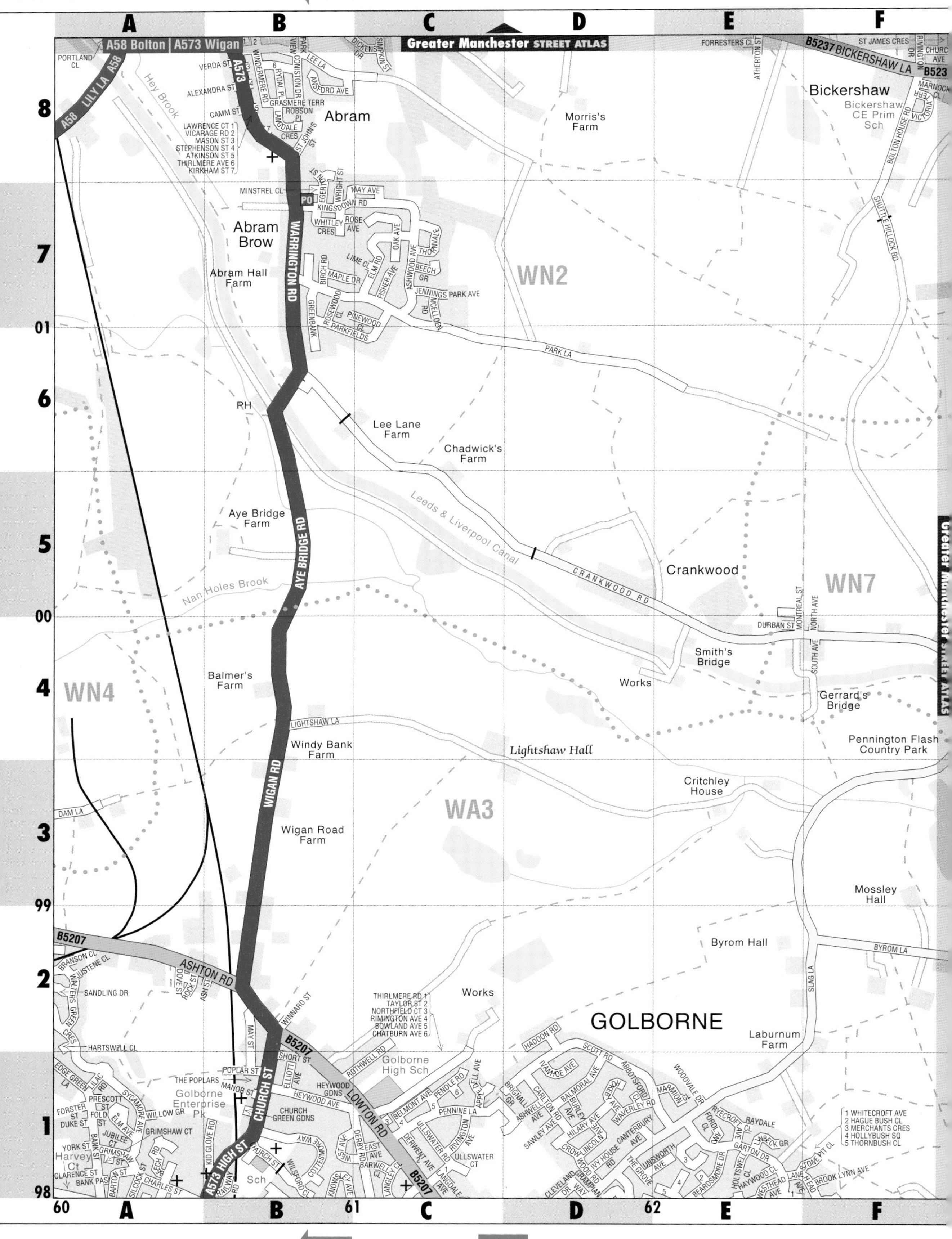

WN2

WN7

WN4

WA3

Abram

Abram Brow

Abram Hall Farm

Aye Bridge Farm

Balmer's Farm

Windy Bank Farm

Wigan Road Farm

Bickershaw

Bickershaw CE Prim Sch

Morris's Farm

Lee Lane Farm

Chadwick's Farm

Crankwood

Smith's Bridge

Works

Gerrard's Bridge

Pennington Flash Country Park

Lightshaw Hall

Critchley House

Mossley Hall

Byrom Hall

GOLBORNE

Golborne High Sch

Golborne Enterprise Pk

Laburnum Farm

Works

Leeds & Liverpool Canal

Greater Manchester Street Atlas

A B C D E F

Sefton Coastal Path

MARINE CRES
DUKE ST
SOUTH RD
DEAN'S RD
MARINE TERR
BATH RD
QUEEN'S RD
WESLEY ST
OLIVE ST
WALMER RD
ST SEFTON RD
CROSBY RD N
A565
BRAMHALL RD
PARK
ANGRA
BANK
GREENBANK
BROOKFIELD RD
BROOKSIDE AVE
BROOK VALE

ALBERT RD 1
DEACON CL 2
CHAPEL HO 3
DEAN HO 4

YORK RD
GREAT GEORGE'S RD
ST GEORGE'S RD
ST ANDREWS
B5421
SANDRINGHAM RD
NEW ARDS RD

Marine
Lake

L22

Lakeside
View

ALEXANDRA RD
CHATHAM CT
VICTORIA RD
MELROSE
RD
KINROSS RD
MARLBOROUGH RD

THE ESPLANADE
BRIDGE RD
BRUNSWICK PDE
PRINCETON MEWS
TULLIALLEN RD
CAMBRIDGE RD
HEREFORD RD
GRECIAN
WOODLAND RD
DORIC RD
CRESTED RD
ADELAIDE RD
CORINTHIAN

E8
1 WATER ST
2 SANDRINGHAM AVE
3 MELROSE PK
4 SOUTH VIEW CT

BOSSOM
CT SUNDENE
LO

Seaforth

Radar
Sta

Seaforth
Nature Reserve

Port of Liverpool
Euro Rail Terminal

F7
1 BEDFORD PL
2 GLADSTONE AVE
3 RIVERSDALE RD
4 BELGRAVE RD
5 SANDY HO
6 CHURCHILL HO
7 ALEXANDER HO
8 MONTGOMERY HO

LC

L21

Royal Seaforth
Container Terminal

F6
1 LATHOM CL
2 LATHOM AVE
3 CLARENDON RD
4 ELM GDNS

CROSBY RD S
PRITCHARD AVE
RAWSON RD
BOWER RD
CLAREMONT RD
BEACONSFIELD RD
GLADSTONE RD
HARROWBY RD
GORDON RD
CECIL RD

PRINCESS WAY
A5036
ELM DR
BARKELEY RD
ELM RD
POPLAR GR
HOLLY GR
CHURCH RD
BEECH GR
CARADOC RD
VERDI
TERR
CHURCH GR

40

97

6

Wind Turbines

Royal Seaforth Dock

Mast

LC
SHORE RD

5

96

Gladstone
Dock

4

L20

River Mersey

3

Alexandra
Dock

95

Rock
Lighthouse

Perch
Rock

2

1 MARINE PARK MANS
2 BECKENHAM RD
3 NELSON CT
4 RODNEY CT

CH45

Marine
Lake

UNION
TERR
MARINE PROM

1 TIVOLI VILLA'S
2 WATERS EDGE
APARTMENTS

A554
KING'S PAR

KING'S PAR

PORTLAND
ST
ATHERTON ST
PORTLAND
CT
REDCLIFFE
WELLINGTON ST
CAVENDISH ST
RIMROSE RD
DARLINGTON ST
A554
VIRGINIA RD
RICHMOND
RD
BELMONT
RD
VICTORIA PAR
ALBERT ST
BALMORAL
RD
TOLLEMACHE ST
TOWER
PROM

LB
Sta

WINDSOR RD

94

0 A B 31 C D 32 E F

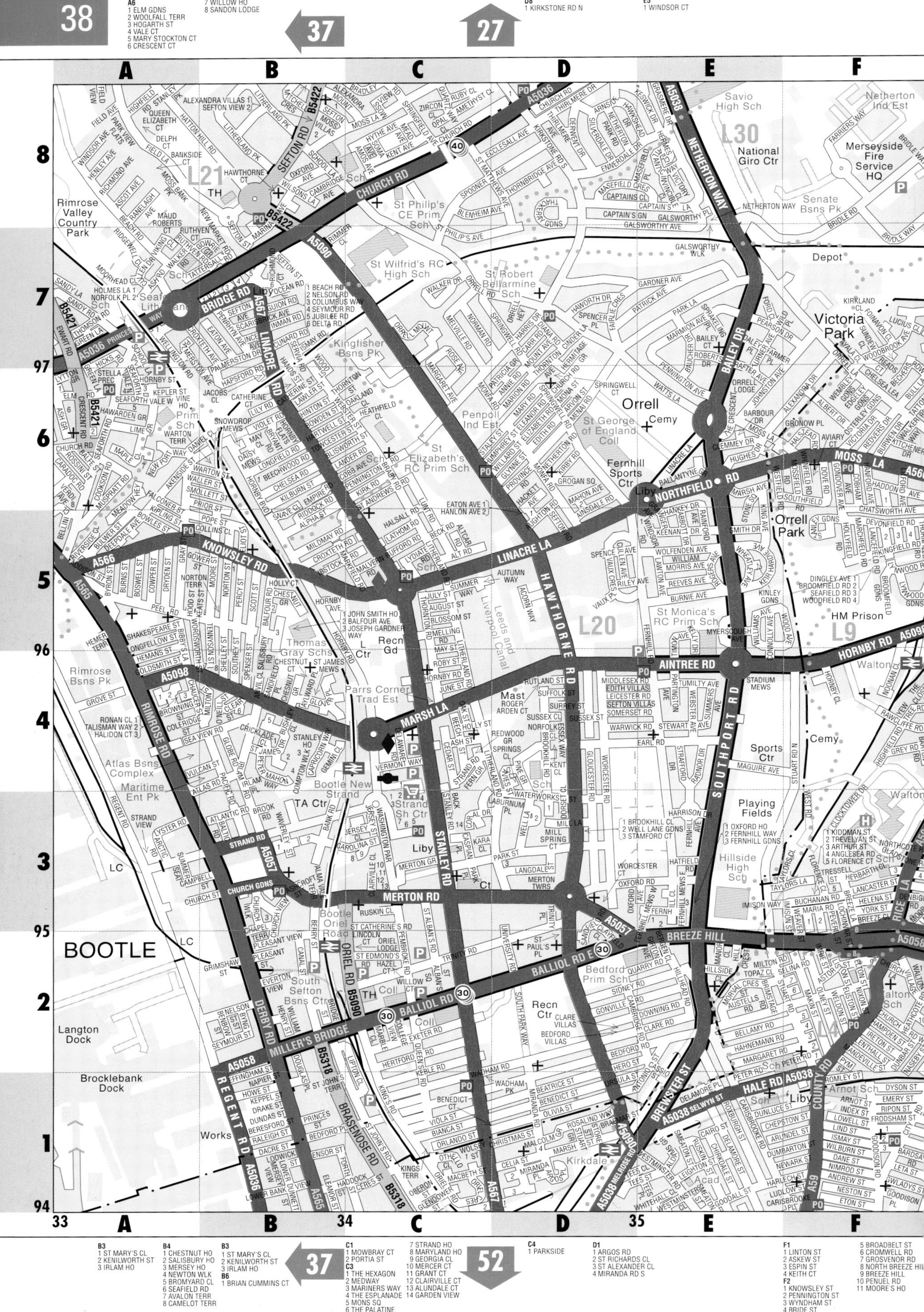

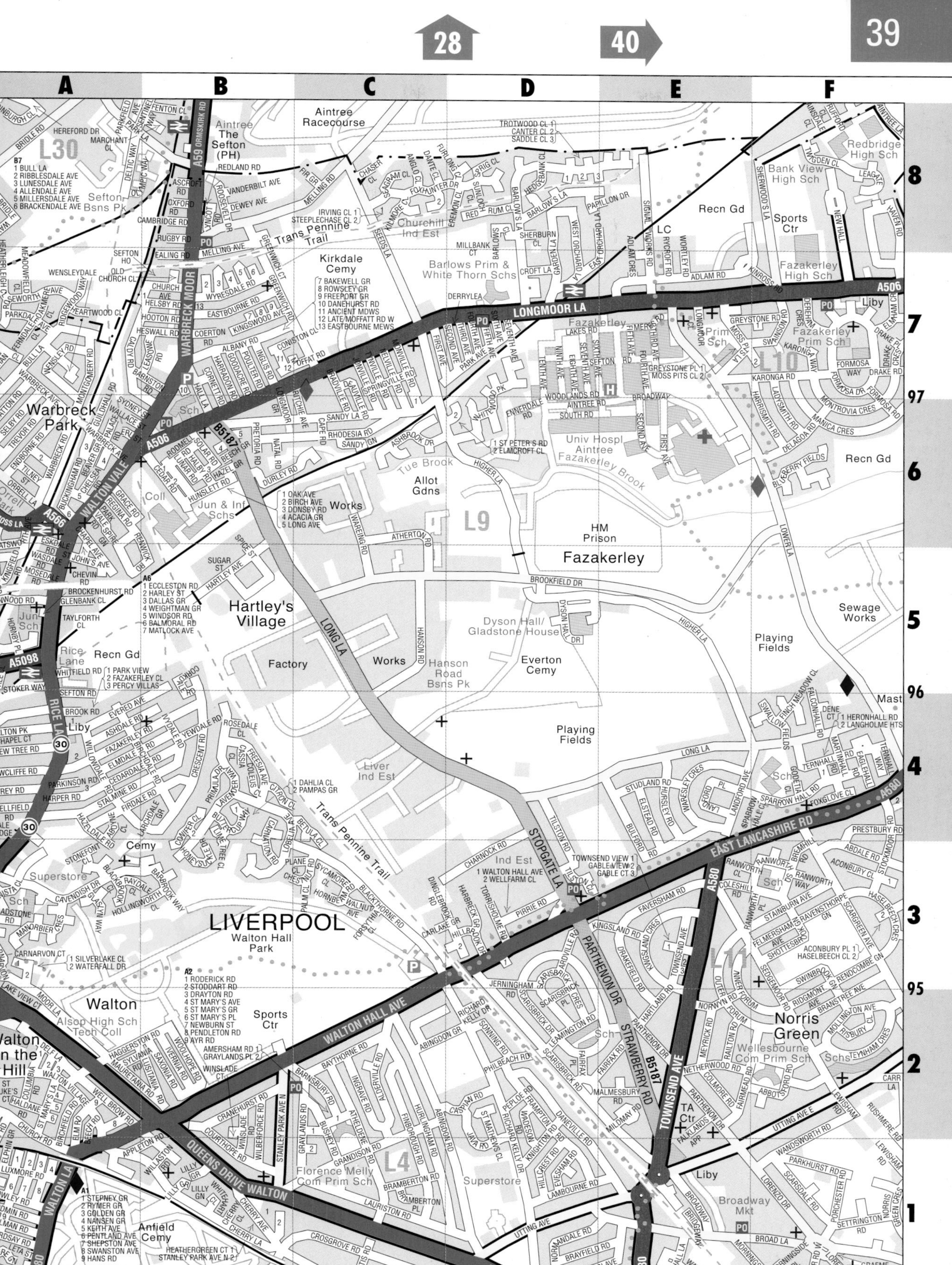
A
B
C
D
E
F
Aintree Racecourse
Aintree
The Sefton (PH)
L30
Sefton Bsns Pk
Trans Pennine Trail
Kirkdale Cemy
Churchill Ind Est
Barlows Prim & White Thorn Schs
LONGMOOR LA
Recn Gd
Bank View High Sch
Redbridge High Sch
Sports Ctr
Fazakerley High Sch
Fazakerley Prim Sch
L10
Warbreck Park
WARBRECK MOOR
WALTON VALE
A506
A565
Orrell Park
Coll
Jun & Inf Schs
Works
Allot Gdns
Tue Brook
L9
Univ Hospl Aintree
Fazakerley Brook
HM Prison
Fazakerley
Hartley's Village
LONG LA
Factory
Works
Hanson Road Bsns Pk
Dyson Hall/ Gladstone House
Everton Cemy
Sewage Works
Playing Fields
Rice Lane
Recn Gd
A5098
RICE LA
Liby
Liver Ind Est
Playing Fields
Mast
Cemy
Superstore
Sch
Trans Pennine Trail
STOPGATE LA
Ind Est
EAST LANCASHIRE RD
A580
LIVERPOOL
Walton Hall Park
WALTON HALL AVE
PARTHENON DR
L11
Norris Green
Walton
Alsop High Sch Tech Coll
Sports Ctr
Walton on the Hill
STRAWBERRY RD
B5187
TOWNSEND AVE
Wellesbourne Com Prim Sch
TA Ctr
QUEENS DRIVE WALTON
L4
Florence Melly Com Prim Sch
Superstore
Liby
Broadway Mkt
Anfield Cemy
Gwladys Street Prim Sch
WALTON LA
A5058
36
37
38
94
95
96
97
1
2
3
4
5
6
7
8

40
39
29
F8
1 THURSBY CRES
2 THURSBY CL
3 THURSBY WLK
4 GAYWOOD GN
5 GAYWOOD CL
6 LINDENWOOD
7 MIDDLEWOOD
8 MEREWOOD
9 MAPLEWOOD
10 GORLESTON MEWS
11 ROWLINGS WAY
12 MEDBOURNE CT
A
B
C
D
E
F
8
7
97
6
5
96
4
3
95
2
1
94
39
40
41
Southdene
Sports Ctr
CH
Burton's Farm
Burton's Bridge
Brookfield High Sch
L32
L10
Springfield Sch
Cherryfield Prim Sch
Gillmoss
Gillmoss Ind Est
Shrog's Farm
Knowsley Bridge
Knowsley Wood
Sewage Works
Works
L34
Randle's Bridge Farm
L9
Our Lady & St Swithin's RC Prim Sch
Croxteth Com Comp Sch
Liby
Croxteth
L11
Ret Pk
Craven Wood
Stand Lodge
Croxteth Com Prim Sch
Cemy
St John Bosco Arts Coll
Dam Wood
Emmaus CE & RC Prim Sch
Dog & Gun
De La Salle RC High Sch
L12
Mull Wood
Croxteth Country Park
Kennels
LIVERPOOL
Croxteth Hall
Monksdown Prim Sch
Home Farm House
Lodge
Old Kennels House
A506 LONGMOOR LA
VALLEY RD
EAST LANCASHIRE RD
A580
M57
A5207
MOORGATE RD
1 MOOR CT
2 COPPLE HOUSE CT
1 FIONA WLK
2 KATHERINE WLK
3 JOYCE WLK
1 BRADSTONE CL
2 PENTIRE CL
Knowsley Brook
Fazakerley Brook
Sugar Brook
Croxteth Brook
River Alt
C4
1 DRAGON WLK
2 THRONE WLK
3 ORB WLK
C3
1 SOVEREIGN HEY
2 DYMOKE WLK
3 HEBDEN PAR
4 SWORD CL
5 CARILLION CL
E3
1 ALDRIDGE CL
2 CHARMOUTH CL
3 ST CUTHBERT'S CL
1 TEWKESBURY CL
2 GOLDCREST CL
1 HOLLINGBOURNE PL
2 COTTESBROOK PL
3 COTTESBROOK CL
C2
1 HORWOOD CL
2 MORVAH CL
3 ELDERBERRY CL
F3
1 GREENFINCH CL
2 MISTLE THRUSH WAY
3 THORNBECK CL
B1
1 ROSEWOOD GDNS
2 MARCHAM WAY
3 ETAL CL
1 RHOSESMOR CL
2 RHOSESMOR RD
A1
1 BRANTHWAITE CL
2 HELMDON CL
3 GLASSONBY WAY
4 BRANTHWAITE GR
5 BLAISDON CL
6 NORRIS GREEN WAY
39
54

30
42
A
B
C
D
E
F
8
7
97
6
5
96
4
3
95
2
1
94
43
44
55
42
Park Brow Com Prim Sch
A5207
A5208
DIXON RD
BECKETT CL
GORES RD
SOUTH BOUNDARY RD
ADMIN RD
GALE RD
Bsns Resource Ctr
Acorn Field Plantation
PERIMETER RD
Sandy Brow
RED CUT LA
Sandy Brow Cottage
SANDY BROW LA
L33
Sandy Lane Farm
CUT LA
MOLLY'S LA
Cooper's Moss Farm
A8
1 GROSMONT RD
2 SHALDON GR
3 SHALDON CL
4 BIRKIN WLK
5 SHALDON WLK
6 GARTH WLK
7 BUXTED WLK
8 MOORGATE LA
9 SOUTHWOOD CL
Tokenspire Park
MOORGATE RD
L32
HORNHOUSE LA
ABERCROMBIE RD
OWEN RD
FARADAY RD
Knowsley Ind Pk
A7
1 WOODENE CL
2 CLEADON CL
3 KINSAIL RD
4 ALBURY RD
5 HARTWOOD CL
6 HARTWOOD RD
COOPER'S LA
Knowsley Brook
HEWITT'S LA
Moss Side
New Road Farm
A580
EAST LANCASHIRE RD
B5202
Knowsley Bsns Pk
PENRHYN RD
Quarry Farm
VILLIERS RD
VILLIERS CT
KITLING RD
AINSWORTH LA
NUNTHORPE RD
LOCKTON RD
Canrow Farm
Moss Plantation
CANROW LA
Scamper Plantation
PATTEN'S WLK
SCHOOL LA
GELLINGS RD
RANDLES RD
GELLINGS LA
KITLING LA
OVERBROOK LA
MILLBROOK CT
Maypole Farm
MAYPOLE CT
BEN'S CT
CADDICK RD
B5194
MILL LA
Delph Farm
Davis's Pits
Homer Wood
Keeper's house
OLD MDW
DUMBREEZE GR
ORMSKIRK RD
OLD MILL LA
Mill Plantation
TEYNHAM AVE
BLACKING DR
WHITEGATE CL
OLD MILL LANE COTTS
L34
CHURCH LA
Knowsley
KNOWSLEY LA
MAPLE CT 1
CEDAR CT 2
PH
MIDDLEHEY RD
GUILD HEY
QUAKERS MDW
LONGMEADOW RD
Knowsley Park
Howard's Pits
SHOP RD
STANLEY BGLWS
St John Fisher RC Prim Sch
TITHEBARN RD
CORNCROFT RD
Berry Hill
Meakins' Pits
PINFOLD LA
SYDERS GR
SINGLETON DR
HOMER RD
WILTONS DR
FREDERICK LUNT AVE
A3
1 DENHAM CL
2 HATFIELD CL
THE COPPICE
WOODVIEW
Thunderbolt Cottages
Maidens Bower Farm
Syders' Grove
PARKLANDS
SUGAR LA
ROSS CL
FOUNTAIN RD
BERRY HILL AVE
Berry Hill Strip
ALDER LA
LONGBOROUGH RD
Knowsley Village Sch
RIDING HILL WLK
RIDING HILL RD
Home Farm
JACK'S BROW
Whitehouse Lodge
WATTON CL
L12
ALBURY CL
The Roughs
WHITESTONE CL
HOME FARM RD
BROOK LA
FLUKER'S LA
Fluker's Brook Farm
SHANNONS LA
Knowsley Cottage
Ash Plantation
DARK ENTRY
Boat House Lodge
White Man's Dam
Nine Tree Prim Sch
Little Wood
Little Wood Lodge
M57
L28
CROXTETH LA
HOLLOW CROFT
BOODE CROFT
B5194
Orchard Lodge
Bridge Lodge

55
42

A B C D E F

8

New Cut
Farm

RED CUT LA
NEW CUT LA

Woodside
Farm

B5203
BLIND FOOT RD

Windle
Moss

WA11

L33

Crab Tree
Plantation

COACH RD

Emma
Wood

MOSS LA

7

CUT LA

Moss
Cottages

Coach
Road
Farm

Lodge

Grace's
Wood

Big
Longborough

B5203

Brandreth
House

Watery Lane
Farm

SADLER'S LA

Windle Brook

97

A580

EAST LANCASHIRE RD

A580

6

Longborough
Lodge

Little
Longborough

The
Gorse

The Royal Oak
(PH)

Catsdale Moss
Farm

B5203

Lower
Barrow Field
Farm

HOUGHTON'S LA

Catchdale
Moss

5

Potato Pie House
(Hunting Lodge)

Moss
Wood

Dead Man's
Corner

Longborough
Wood

Catchdale Moss
House

Orith
Farm

CATCHDALE MOSS LA

Hilton's
Farm

GREEN LA

PATTEN'S WLK

96

Patten's Bank

Park Side
Farm

Howard's
Farm

HOWARD'S LA

Mill Brook

VILLERS CR

RICHMOND

LAUREL

4

Pony
Coppice

Crab Tree Drive
Plantation

Blue Door
Lodge

Jim's
Wood

WA10

Brook House
Farm

GRIFFIN

3

Knowsley
Park

Chain Acre
Wood

Clay Lane
Farm

CLAY LA

Poplar
Farm

GILLAR'S LA

GILLARS GREEN
DR STANWOOD CL
ORITH AVE
HIGHAM AVE
SUMMERFIELD
AVE

KNOWSLEY HO DR

PO

SEDDON C

The
Nightcap

Parkside
Farm

Stanley Arms
(PH)

B5201

95

White Man's
Dam

L34

Shaw's
Plantation

Park
Farm

Trap
Wood

Burgesses
Farm

B5203

BURROW'S LA

2

Deer Park

Hag Brow

Knowsley
Safari Park

Singleton's
Hill

Gillar's
Green

Mere View
Farm

1

Hag
Delph

Burrow's Lane
Farm

Trap
Lodge

Ivy House
Farm

Roughly's Brow
Farm

B5201

Stand
Wood

No 4 Resr

94

32
44
A
B
C
D
E
F
8
7
97
6
5
96
4
3
95
2
1
94
Moss Farm
WA11
Potter's House Farm
Windle Park Wood
Windle Hall Farm
Windle Hall
Windle Hall Bridge
RAINFORD BY-PASS
RAINFORD RD
CRANK RD
MOSS LA
EAST LANCASHIRE RD
A580
A570
B5201
Windle Brook Bridge
Windle Farm
Windle Smithies
St Helens Crem
Cemy
St Thomas of Canterbury RC Prim Sch
Bleak Hill
BLEAK HILL RD
Cowley Language Coll
Windlehurst
Victoria Park
Cowley Hill
Recn Gd
Liby
Bleak Hill Prim Sch
Windle Brook
Rivington Prim Sch
ST HELENS
Denton's Green
WA10
MILLBROOK LA
GREENFIELD RD
DENTONS GREEN LA
LINGHOLME RD
Queens Park CE/URC Prim Sch
Queens Park Recn Ctr
De La Salle Sch
Mill Brook
Eccleston
CHAPEL LA
Mill Bridge
CHURCH LA
Newtown
Sports Gd
Mill Wood
Works
BURROW'S LA
Prim Sch
St. Helens RLFC
DUKE ST
KING ST
A571
KIRKLAND ST
LINKWAY W
A58
Superstore
TA Ctr
Green Bank
Hall Farm
Big Dam
Eccleston Mere
West Park
BOROUGH RD
PRESCOT RD
Works
Resr
Ravenhead
L34
Carmel Coll
Toll Bar
CH
WA9
1 HEREFORD CL
2 FLINTSHIRE GDNS
3 LANCASHIRE GDNS
4 WILTSHIRE GDNS
5 HAMPSHIRE GDNS
1 CHAPEL CT
2 OWEN CL
3 BATES CRES
4 DERRINGSTONE CL
5 MARGARET CT
6 ALEXANDRA ST
7 CHATTERISS CT
CONWAY ST 1
HOLLY MOUNT 2
OLIVE MOUNT 3
CROPPERS HILL CT 1
MAXWELL ST 2
BANK ST 3
8
49
50
57
44
F3
1 NEW CROSS ST
2 CHALON WAY W
3 BANNER WLK
F4
1 MORLEY WAY
2 OXFORD ST
3 VOLUNTEER ST
4 LEACH ST
5 RANDON GR
6 NEW CROSS ST
7 PALMER CL
8 BURNELL CL
9 PATRICIA CT

ST HELENS

WA11
WA10
WA9
WN4

Green Leach
Haresfinch
Laffak
Gerard's Bridge
Sand Lodge
Pocket Nook
Finger Post
Parr Stocks
Broad Oak
Moss Nook
Peasley Cross
Sutton Bridge
Parr

East Lancashire Rd — A580
Carr Mill Dam
Carr Mill Bridge
Glass House Close Wood
Stanley Bank Wood
Stanley Bank Farm
Sankey Valley Park
Stanley House Farm
Catherine Way
Ebenezer St
Blackbrook St Mary's RC Prim Sch
Ashurst Prim Sch
Visitor Ctr
St Augustine of Canterbury RC High Sch
Sewage Works
St Helens Canal (dis)
Merton Bank Prim Sch
Collins Ind Est
Parr Bridge
Works
Moorfoot Road Ind Est
Broad Oak Rd — A572
Chancery La
Parr Stocks Rd — A572
Lansbury Bridge Sch
Liby
Allanson Street Prim Sch
Parr Ind Est
St Cuthbert's RC Com Coll
Ravenhead Ret Pk
Grove's Dam
Bsns Pk
St Helens Pk
Superstore
Sutton Oak Dr
Sports Gd
Chalon Way Ind Est
St Helens Ret Pk
Westside Ind Est
Eastside Ind Est
Works
St Helens Linkway — A570
A58 Linkway
Superstore Mus
St Helens Central
St Helens Coll (Tech Campus)
Playing Field

Rainford Brook
Washway La
Green Leach La — A571
Haresfinch Rd
College St
Carr Mill Rd — A571
Blackbrook Rd
Stanley Bank Way
Park Rd
Parr St
Broad Oak Rd
A572
A571
A570
A569

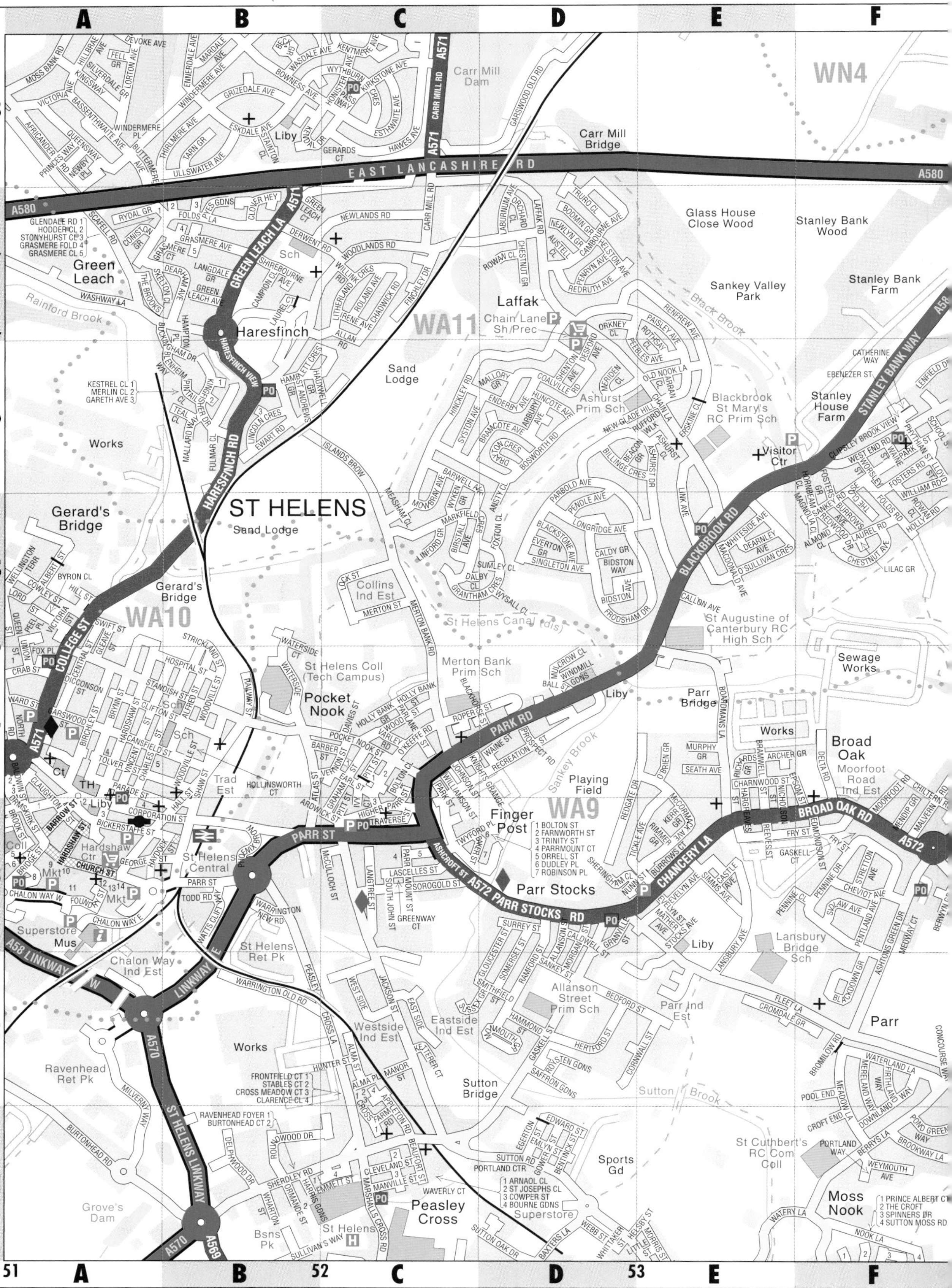

A3
1 COTHAM ST
2 VICTORIA SQ
3 LIBRARY ST
4 CATAPULT TOO
5 WATERLOO ST
6 CROSS ST
7 MILK ST
8 EXCHANGE ST
9 LAGRANGE ARC
10 PALATINE ARC
11 MARKET ST
12 CHURCH SQ
13 ST MARY'S ARC
14 BROWNLOW ARC

A4
1 NORMAN SALISBURY CT
2 WILLIAM ST
3 NORTH JOHN ST
4 TOLVER HO
5 PROVIDENCE CT

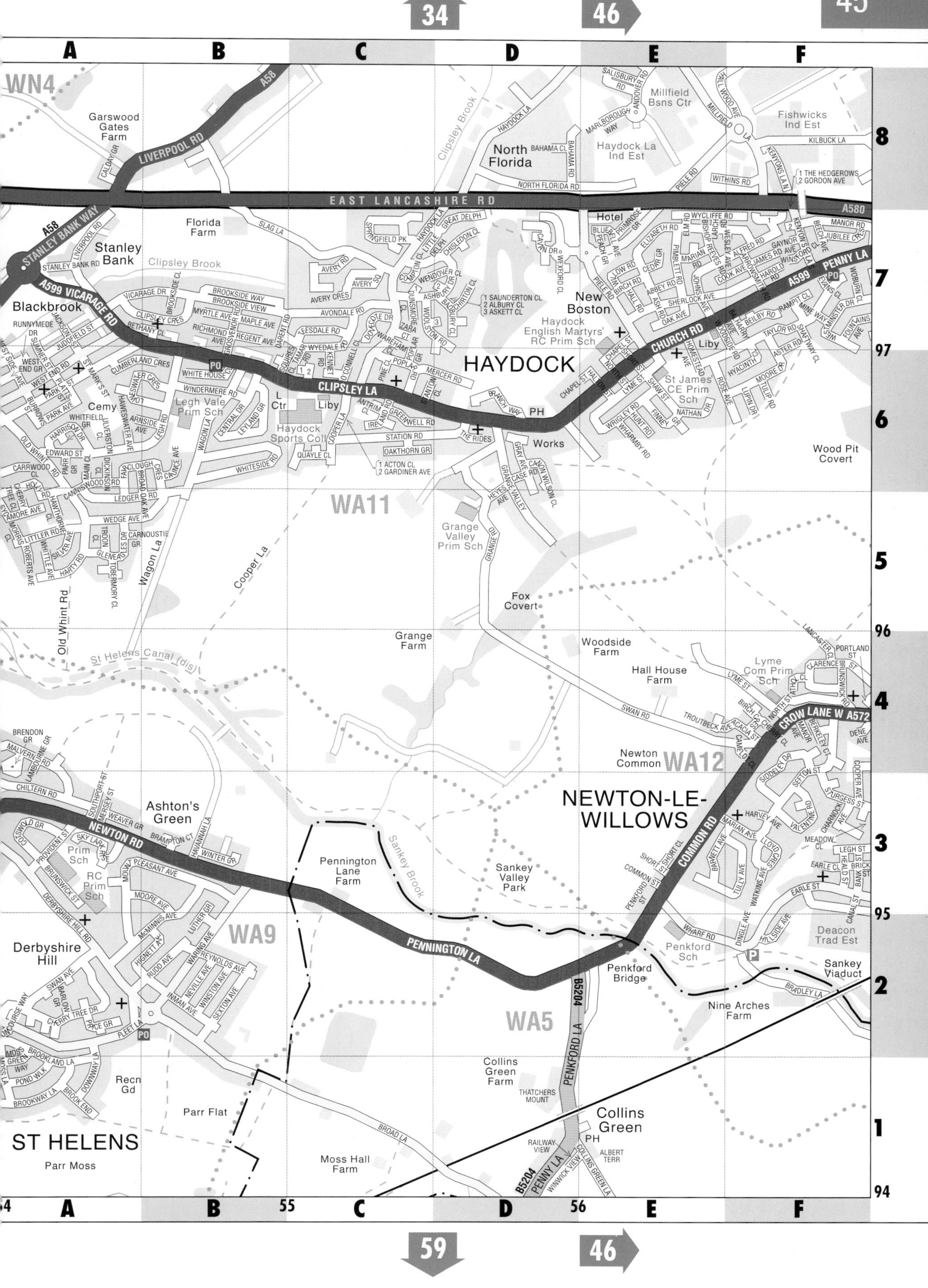
34
46
A
B
C
D
E
F
WN4
A58
Garswood Gates Farm
LIVERPOOL RD
Clipsley Brook
HAYDOCK LA
North Florida
Haydock La Ind Est
Millfield Bsns Ctr
Fishwicks Ind Est
KILBUCK LA
8
EAST LANCASHIRE RD
A580
STANLEY BANK WAY
Florida Farm
Stanley Bank
Clipsley Brook
Blackbrook
A599 VICARAGE RD
Hotel
1 SAUNDERTON CL
2 ALBURY CL
3 ASKETT CL
New Boston
Haydock English Martyrs' RC Prim Sch
7
CHURCH RD
A599 PENNY LA
Liby
97
HAYDOCK
CLIPSLEY LA
L Ctr
Liby
Legh Vale Prim Sch
Cemy
Haydock Sports Coll
St James' CE Prim Sch
PH
Works
6
Wood Pit Covert
WA11
Grange Valley Prim Sch
5
Cooper La
Wagon La
Old Whint Rd
Fox Covert
Grange Farm
96
St Helens Canal (dis)
Woodside Farm
Hall House Farm
Lyme Com Prim Sch
4
SWAN RD
CROW LANE W A572
Newton Common
WA12
NEWTON-LE-WILLOWS
Ashton's Green
NEWTON RD
COMMON RD
Prim Sch
RC Prim Sch
3
Pennington Lane Farm
Sankey Brook
Sankey Valley Park
95
Derbyshire Hill
WA9
PENNINGTON LA
Penkford Bridge
Penkford Sch
Deacon Trad Est
Sankey Viaduct
2
B5204
Nine Arches Farm
WA5
PENKFORD LA
Recn Gd
Collins Green Farm
Parr Flat
Collins Green
PH
1
ST HELENS
Parr Moss
Moss Hall Farm
BROAD LA
PENNY LA
94
55
56
59
46

45
35

A
B
C
D
E
F
HAYDOCK
Yew Tree Farm Trad Est
Old Boston Trad Est
Old Boston
Hotel
Haydock Park Racecourse
Haydock Park
White Door Covert
White Door Dam
Lady Hill Plantation
GOLBORNE
WA4
WA3
WA11
WA12
WA5
WA2
M6
A49
LODGE LA
A599
PENNY LA
A580
EAST LANCASHIRE RD
23
B5209
Haydock Park Farm
Fox Covert
Dean Dam
Dean Dam Farm
Ellam's Brook
Ellam's Rough
Newton-Haydock Bridge
WOODLANDS PK
Woodlands Ind Est
Lawson's Farm
Hollows Bridge
CH
L Ctr
VISTA RD
ASHTON RD
Newton-le-Willows Com High Sch
ROB LA
NEWTON LA
HIGH ST
A572
CROW LANE W
CROW LANE E
CHURCH ST
SOUTHWORTH RD
Newton Bank Sch
Newton Lake
Liby
St Helens Coll Newton Campus
The District CE Prim Sch
St Mary's RC Jun Sch
Inf Sch
St Aelred's RC Tech Coll
St Peter's CE Prim Sch
Newton-le-Willows Prim Sch
Newton-le-Willows
Mill Green Sch
Stones Crossing
MILL LA
MARKET ST
Earlestown
Wargrave
NEWTON-LE-WILLOWS
Deacon Trad Est
Mast
Sankey Valley Ind Est
Newton Community
Newton Park Farm
NEWTON PARK DR
WINWICK RD
Cemy
Newton Brook
Wargrave House Sch
Sch
Sankey Brook
Sankey Canal (dis)
Vulcan Ind Est
Works
Red Bank
New Hey Farm
HERMITAGE GREEN LA
BRADLEY LA
8
7
97
6
5
96
4
3
95
2
1
94
57
58
59

45
60

D8
1 SARSFIELD AVE
2 FOXGLOVE CL
3 GROSVENOR AVE
4 RIDGEWELL AVE

E8
1 TURRET HALL DR
2 ROYSTON CL
3 SANDFIELD CL
4 ARIEL WLK
5 BALLANTYNE WAY
6 BUNTING CL

7 REDSTART CL
8 WILD ARUM CL
9 HUDSON GR
10 STONECHAT CL
11 SPEEDWELL CL
12 LUNEHURST
13 CONINGSBY GDNS

F8
1 SCOTIA WLK
2 TYRER WLK
3 ROBSON WAY
4 HORNCASTLE CL
5 HOPWOOD CL
6 BIRCH TREE RD

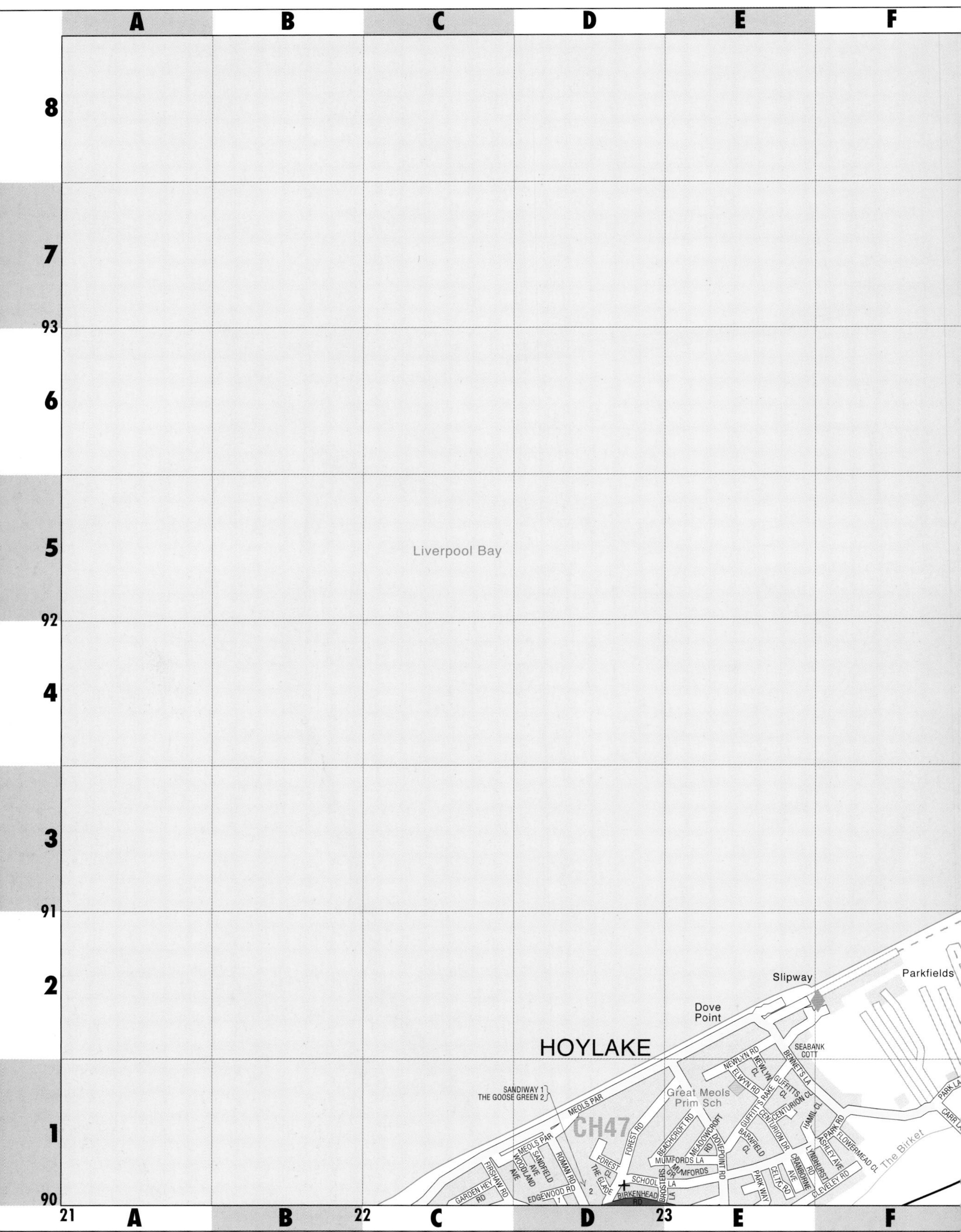

Liverpool Bay

Parkfields

Slipway

Dove
Point

SEABANK
COTT

HOYLAKE

SANDIWAY 1
THE GOOSE GREEN 2

Great Meols
Prim Sch

MEOLS PAR

CH47

NEWLYN RD

MEOLS PAR

FIRSWAY RD

SAMFIELD

WOODLAND
AVE

ROMAN RD

FOREST RD

FOREST
THE GLADE

EDGEWOOD RD

GARDEN HEY RD

BIRKENHEAD
RD

SCHOOL

MUMFORDS LA

MUMFORDS

MUMFORDS LA

LA LA1

BEACHCROFT RD

MEADONCROFT
RD

DOVEPOINT RD

BARNFIELD

BENNET'S LA

ELWYN RD

GUFFITTS RAKE

CENTURION DR

GUFFITTS CL

HAMIL CL

PARK WAY

DELTA CL

LYNHURST
AVE

CARBORNE

ASHLEY AVE

LOWERMEAD CL

CLEVELEY RD

PARK RD

THE Birket

CABRI LA

PARK LA

21   22   23

90 91 92 93

8 7 6 5 4 3 2 1

A B C D E F

8
7
93
6
5
92
4
3
91
2
1
90

Liverpool Bay

North Wirral Coastal Park

Caravan Pk

CH

Leasowe Castle Hotel

1 SHANNON HO
2 LAGAN HO
3 CAUSEWAY HO

COASTAL POINT

CASTLEFIELDS

A551

Wallasey Embankment

LEASOWE RD

Leasowe Common

Caravan Site

Lighthouse (dis)

LINGHAM LA

The Birket

Lingham Farm

Parkfield House

MEREHEATH GDNS

LEASOWE GDNS

OAKMERE CL

THE SANDHILLS

THE BEECHES

THE STAKES

HEATH CL

MARSHFIELD CT

CASTLEHEATH CL

DITTON LA

THE HEATHLANDS

THE LAURELS

CASTLEGRANGE CL

CASTLEFORD RISE

GARSWOOD CL

FARNWORTH AVE

CRONTON AVE

FINDLEY DR

NEWBURY WAY

EPSOM RD

CHELTENHAM CRES

DUNSTALL CL

GOODWOOD DR

AINTREE CL

Ditton Lane Nature Area

MURRAYFIELD DR

RAVENHILL CRES

WAKEFIELD DR

BLACKHEATH DR

WHITEHEATH WAY

GREENHEATH WAY

REEDS LA

TWICKENHAM DR

REEDS AVE E

REEDS AVE W

FARMSIDE

BIRKET AVE

BIRKET SQ

PO

WALLASEY

Leasowe Hotel (PH)

REEDVILLE GR

ROSSALL CT

Works

TARRAN WAY N

TARRAN WAY W

TARRAN WAY E

TARRAN RD

TARRAN DR

TARRAN WAY S

SUNNYSIDE

PASTURE RD

Moreton

STATION APP

CH46

CH47

PARK LA

Arrowe Brook

WASTDALE CT 1

WASTDALE MEWS 2

CURLEW CT

CURLEW WAY

LINGHAM CL

BERRYLANDS RD

BRAMBLE WAY

MEADFOOT RD

BRADMAN RD

GLASIER RD

LINGHAM LA

TERN WAY

WASTDALE DR

MALLARD WAY

ELEANOR RD

HEATHMOOR RD

FLAXHILL

HARVEST LA

BERRYLANDS CL

FURZE WAY

WESTWAY SQ

MAURICE JONES CT

WEST WAY

WITLEY AVE

WITLEY CL

IVY LA

PASTURE AVE

PASTURE CRES

SCHOOL CL

EAST WAY

OUNDLE RD

ROSSALL RD

YEW WAY

DANGER LA

YEW TREE RD

LOMBARD RD

KINGSMEAD RD

SUNFIELD RD

SAXON RD

DANESWELL DR

AVONDALE AVE

Eastway Prim Sch

BLUNDELLS DR

Sacred Heart RC Prim Sch

FAIRMEAD RD

HOYLAKE RD

A553

STUART AVE

BURNLEY RD

BURNLEY GR

ASHBY CL

MILLHOUSE LA

MILLHOUSE CL

DESFORD CL

GLENFIELD CL

ANSTEY CL

OAKHAM DR

CARNOUSTIE CL

BRADGATE CL

FOXTON CL

TURNBERRY CL

BELFRY CL

ST AUSTELL CL

TANWORTH GR

CARR LA

LC

ESKDALE AVE

BERMUDA RD

SMILIE AVE

TOWN MEADOW LA

HARDIE AVE

BURDEN RD

KESTREL RD

LINEAR PK

E1
1 GARDEN LA
2 OAKENHOLT RD

Lingham Prim Sch

EDGEHILL RD

DIGG LA

FELICITY GR

OVERGREEN GR

WILLASTON RD

HARVEST CT

MARYLAND LA

OLD MARYLAND LA

LITHERLAND AVE

BARNSTON LA

Liby

SILVERBURN AVE

LYONS RD

LYONS CL

KNUTSFORD RD

ORCHARD RD

KNUTSFORD GN

24 A B 25 C D 26 E F

64
50

Liverpool Bay

PENINSULA CL 1
CORMORANT CT 2
REDCAP CL 3
DUNLINS CT 4
ROSEATE CT 5

KING'S PAR

THE CLIFF

COMPASS CT 1
ENNERDALE CT 2

Slipway

COASTAL DR

SMUGGLERS WAY

THE CHANNEL

THE BANKS

BAYVIEW DR

PH

Harrison Park

WARREN PK

St George's
Prim Sch
(Annexe)

Wallasey
Grove Road

CH45

Greenleas
Prim Sch

Dunes

Wallasey
Village

St Mary's
RC Coll

St George's
Prim Sch

GREEN LA

LEASOWE RD

HEYES DR

WALLASEY VILLAGE

Liby

Liby

Our Lady of Lourdes
RC Sch

The
Mosslands
Sch

St Hilary Brow

A551

Leasowe

Castleway
Prim Sch

Liby

ROSS AVE

WALLASEY

Recn Gd

CH46

L Ctr

Wallasey
Sch

Leasowe
Prim Sch

The Birket

CH

A5139

A59

M53

A5139

Junction One
Ret Pk

CH44

Superstore

Bidston
Moss

Bidston
Ind Est

F4
1 BLETCHLEY AVE
2 BRYNMOSS AVE
3 CROMARTY RD
4 MILLTHWAITE CT

Factory

Bidston

CH43

Leasowe
P&R

Superstore

Sports
Ctr

CH41

Works

BALLANTYNE
WLK

Bsns
Pk
Works

Birkenhead
North

Clare Mount
Sch

Fender
Bridge

FENDER LA

Bidston Village
CE Prim Sch

Vyner
Prim Sch

Holy Cross
RC Prim Sch

A5050 WALLASEY

BRIDGE RD

A5088

Fender
Farm

A553

Bidston
Hall

Bidston

HOYLAKE RD

BOUNDARY RD

B5151

A553

Fender Hts

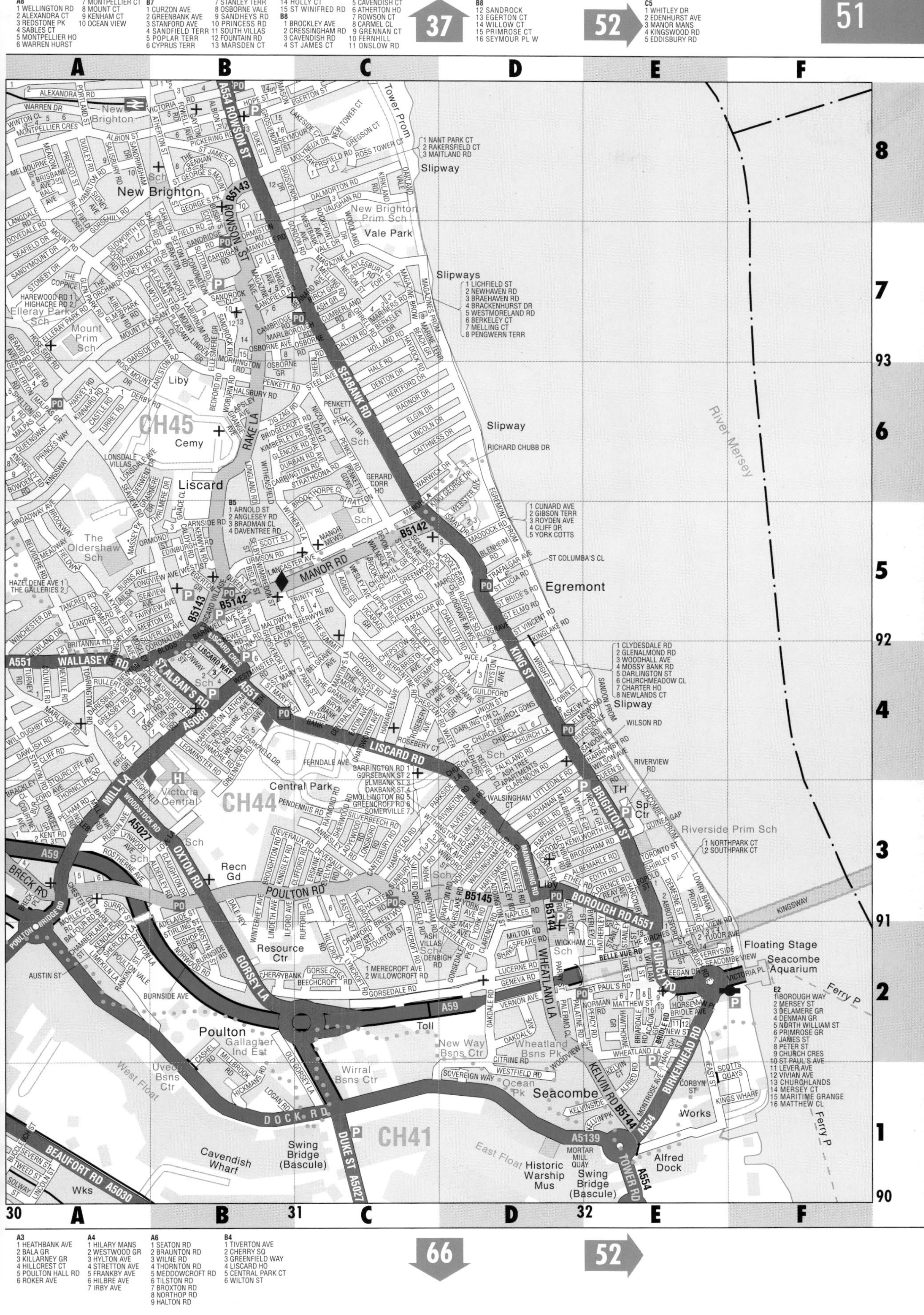

51
A8
1 WELLINGTON RD
2 ALEXANDRA CT
3 REDSTONE PK
4 SABLES CT
5 MONTPELLIER HO
6 WARREN HURST
7 MONTPELLIER CT
8 MOUNT CT
9 KENHAM CT
10 OCEAN VIEW
B7
1 CURZON AVE
2 GREENBANK AVE
3 STANFORD AVE
4 SANDFIELD TERR
5 POPLAR TERR
6 CYPRUS TERR
7 STANLEY TERR
8 OSBORNE VALE
9 SANDHEYS RD
10 PRINCESS RD
11 SOUTH VILLAS
12 FOUNTAIN RD
13 MARSDEN CT
14 HOLLY CT
15 ST WINIFRED RD
B8
1 BROCKLEY AVE
2 CRESSINGHAM RD
3 CAVENDISH RD
4 ST JAMES CT
5 CAVENDISH CT
6 ATHERTON HO
7 ROWSON CT
8 CARMEL CL
9 GRENNAN CT
10 FERNHILL
11 ONSLOW RD
37
B8
12 SANDROCK
13 EGERTON CT
14 WILLOW CT
15 PRIMROSE CT
16 SEYMOUR PL W
52
C5
1 WHITLEY DR
2 EDENHURST AVE
3 MANOR MANS
4 KINGSWOOD RD
5 EDDISBURY RD
A B C D E F
8 7 93 6 5 92 4 3 91 2 1 90
New Brighton
Slipway
1 NANT PARK CT
2 RAKERSFIELD CT
3 MAITLAND RD
New Brighton Prim Sch
Vale Park
Slipways
1 LICHFIELD ST
2 NEWHAVEN RD
3 BRAEHAVEN RD
4 BRACKENHURST DR
5 WESTMORELAND RD
6 BERKELEY CT
7 MELLING CT
8 PENGWERN TERR
Elleray Park Sch
Mount Prim Sch
Liby
CH45
Cemy
Liscard
Slipway
RICHARD CHUBB DR
River Mersey
1 CUNARD AVE
2 GIBSON TERR
3 ROYDEN AVE
4 CLIFF DR
5 YORK COTTS
B5
1 ARNOLD ST
2 ANGLESEY RD
3 BRADMAN CL
4 DAVENTREE RD
The Oldershaw Sch
HAZELDENE AVE 1
THE GALLERIES 2
ST COLUMBA'S CL
Egremont
MANOR RD
WALLASEY RD
A551
KING ST
SEABANK RD
ROWSON ST
RAKE LA
1 CLYDESDALE RD
2 GLENALMOND RD
3 WOODHALL AVE
4 MOSSY BANK RD
5 DARLINGTON ST
6 CHURCHMEADOW CL
7 CHARTER HO
8 NEWLANDS CT
Slipway
WILSON RD
LISCARD RD
RIVERVIEW RD
BARRINGTON RD 1
GORSEBANK ST 2
ELMBANK ST 3
OAKBANK ST 4
MOLLINGTON RD 5
GREENCROFT RD 6
SOMERVILLE 7
Central Park
CH44
Victoria Central
BRIGHTON ST
Riverside Prim Sch
1 NORTHPARK CT
2 SOUTHPARK CT
Recn Gd
POULTON RD
OXTON RD
BOROUGH RD
KINGSWAY
Floating Stage
Seacombe Aquarium
Resource Ctr
1 MERECROFT AVE
2 WILLOWCROFT RD
WHEATLAND LA
CHURCH RD
E2
1 BOROUGH WAY
2 MERSEY ST
3 DELAMERE GR
4 DENMAN GR
5 NORTH WILLIAM ST
6 PRIMROSE GR
7 JAMES ST
8 PETER ST
9 CHURCH CRES
10 ST PAUL'S AVE
11 LEVER AVE
12 VIVIAN AVE
13 CHURCHLANDS
14 MERSEY CT
15 MARITIME GRANGE
16 MATTHEW CL
Ferry P
Poulton
Gallagher Ind Est
Toll
New Way Bsns Ctr
Wheatland Bsns Pk
Uveco Bsns Ctr
West Float
Wirral Bsns Ctr
Ocean Pk
Seacombe
Works
DOCK RD
CH41
Swing Bridge (Bascule)
Cavendish Wharf
East Float
Historic Warship Mus
Swing Bridge (Bascule)
Alfred Dock
BEAUFORT RD A5030
Wks
DUKE ST A5027
TOWER RD
30 31 32
A3
1 HEATHBANK AVE
2 BALA GR
3 KILLARNEY GR
4 HILLCREST CT
5 POULTON HALL RD
6 ROKER AVE
A4
1 HILARY MANS
2 WESTWOOD GR
3 HYLTON AVE
4 STRETTON AVE
5 FRANKBY AVE
6 HILBRE AVE
7 IRBY AVE
A6
1 SEATON RD
2 BRAUNTON RD
3 WILNE RD
4 THORNTON RD
5 MEDDOWCROFT RD
6 TILSTON RD
7 BROXTON RD
8 NORTHOP RD
9 HALTON RD
B4
1 TIVERTON AVE
2 CHERRY SQ
3 GREENFIELD WAY
4 LISCARD HO
5 CENTRAL PARK CT
6 WILTON ST
66
52

52
D5
1 ST AUGUSTINE ST
2 McKEOWN CL
3 WESTMORELAND PL
4 WILBRAHAM PL
5 St Anthony's Sh Ctr
6 MILLERSMEDE
D7
1 JAMES HOPKINS WAY
2 WULSTAN ST
3 PINCROFT WAY
4 FOUNTAINS CT
5 EASBY RD
6 ELSTOW ST
51
D7
7 SWINDON CL
8 CHELMSFORD CL
9 SHARPEVILLE CL
10 BACK BLACKFIELD TERR
38
E8
1 DELAMORE ST
2 CHIRKDALE ST
3 BACK WESTMINSTER RD
4 BRUNSWICK CL
5 DRYBURGH WAY
6 WARDEN ST
7 BRADEWELL CL
8 ROCKLEY ST
9 ST HILDA ST
10 LONGRIDGE WLK
11 MILNTHORPE CL
F7
1 TEULON CL
2 LUTYENS CL
3 COCKERELL CL
4 HARTLEY CL
5 WYRE RD
6 GOSCHEN ST
7 ELM BANK
8 YORK VILLAS
9 PULFORD ST
10 BALFOUR ST
11 GORST ST
12 RANDOLPH ST
13 GURNALL ST
14 HAYFIELD ST
15 ATTWOOD ST
16 NORGATE ST
17 SAKER ST
18 LAMBRIGG RD
A
B
C
D
E
F
BOOTLE
Canada Dock
Huskisson Dock
Sandon Dock
Nelson Dock
Victoria Tower
River Mersey
Trafalgar Dock
Waterloo River Entrance
King Edward Ind Est
Princes Dock
Royal Liver Building
Liverpool Landing Stage
Sandhills
Vauxhall
Kirkdale
Everton
Everton Football Gd
Stanley Park
Leeds & Liverpool Canal
L20
L3
L4
L5
L6
L7
8
7
93
6
5
92
4
3
91
2
1
90
33
34
35
REGENT RD
WATERLOO RD
GREAT HOWARD ST
DERBY RD
BANKHALL ST
SANDHILLS LA
BOUNDARY ST
BLACKSTONE ST
COMMERCIAL RD
VAUXHALL RD
SCOTLAND RD
KIRKDALE RD
STANLEY RD
MELROSE RD
WALTON LA
WALTON BRECK RD
HEYWORTH ST
ST DOMINGO RD
LEEDS ST
TITHEBARN ST
OLD HALL ST
BYROM ST
ST ANNE ST
A580 NEW ISLINGTON
ISLINGTON A58
LONDON RD
LIME ST
HANOVER ST
STRAND ST
WATER ST
DALE ST
JAMES ST
Lime Street
Liverpool One
John Moores Univ
For full street detail of the highlighted area see page 90.
51
C3
1 GLADSTONE ST
2 STOCKDALE CL
3 WALDRON CL
4 MARLBOROUGH ST
5 MARLBOROUGH PL
6 PICKOP ST
D3
1 LIMEKILN LA
2 WELLINGTON ST
67
D3
3 NICHOLAS ST
4 ST STEPHENS PL
5 HOLY CROSS CL
6 BISPHAM HO
7 ADLINGTON ST
8 ADLINGTON HO
D4
1 BURROUGHS GDNS
2 BEVINGTON HILL
3 ENNERDALE ST
4 KINGSWAY CT
E3
1 BICKERSTAFFE ST
2 DRINKWATER GDNS
3 RODERICK ST
4 TRINITY WLK
E4
1 ST MARTIN'S MEWS
2 CLIFTON GR
3 SHERIFF CL
4 HIGHAM SQ
5 UPPER BUTE ST
6 WATMOUGH ST
7 BERESFORD ST
8 BACK BEAU ST
9 UPPER BEAU ST
10 ASHBURNHAM WAY
F3
1 CANTERBURY WAY
2 TICHBOURNE WAY
3 MELDA CL
4 TRAFALGAR WAY
5 Erskin Ind Est
6 THE COLLEGIATE
F4
1 NORTHCOTE CL
2 FISHGUARD CL
3 SPINDLE CL
4 EMBER CRES
5 RICHARD ALLEN WAY
6 ST AMBROSE WAY
7 MARSWORTH DR
8 WILSTONE CL

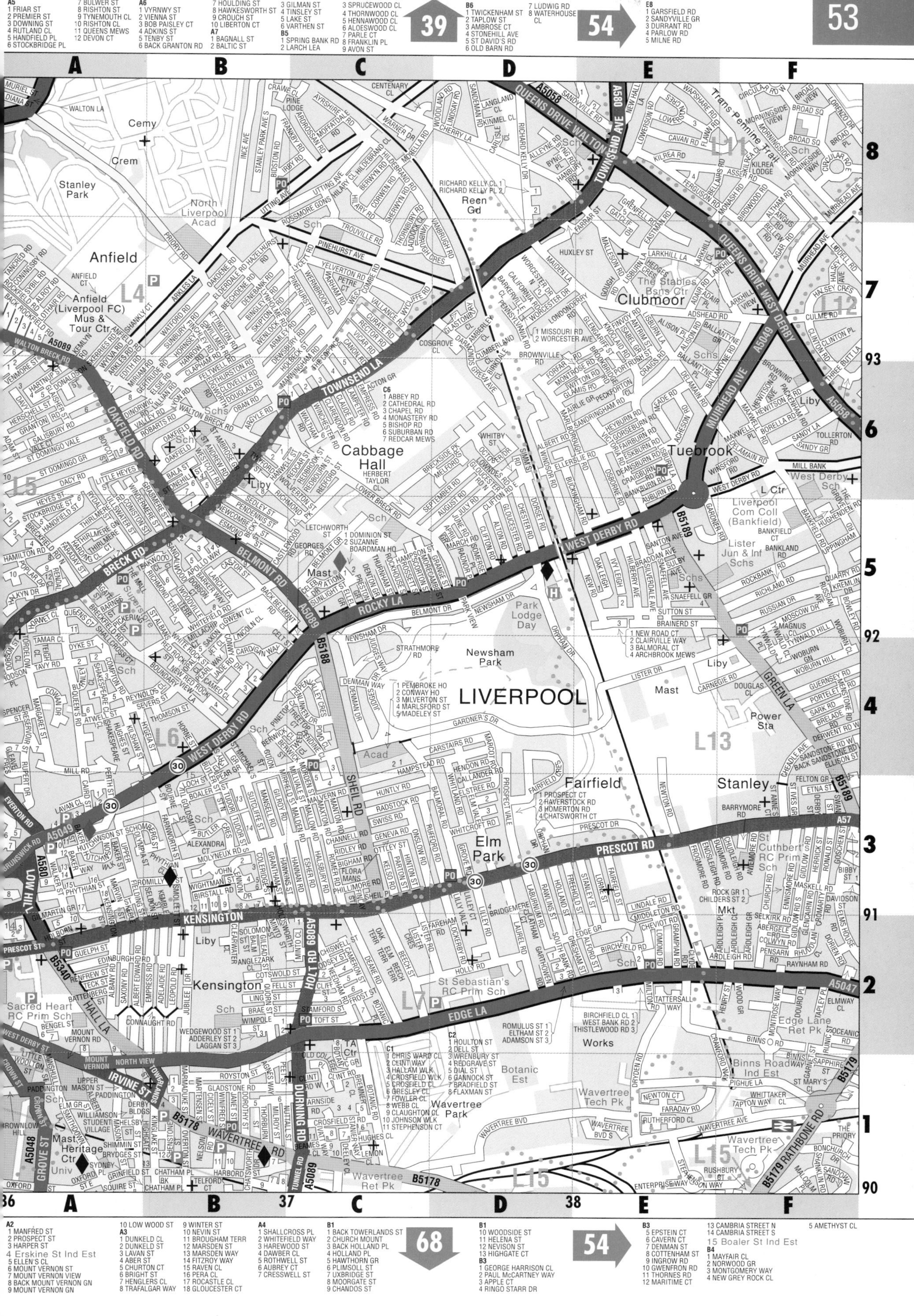
A5
1 FRIAR ST
2 PREMIER ST
3 DOWNING ST
4 RUTLAND CL
5 HANDFIELD PL
6 STOCKBRIDGE PL
7 BULWER ST
8 RISHTON ST
9 TYNEMOUTH CL
10 RISHTON CL
11 QUEENS MEWS
12 DEVON CT
A6
1 VYRNWY ST
2 VIENNA ST
3 BOB PAISLEY CT
4 ADKINS ST
5 TENBY ST
6 BACK GRANTON RD
7 HOULDING ST
8 HAWKESWORTH ST
9 CROUCH ST
10 LIBERTON CT
A7
1 BAGNALL ST
2 BALTIC ST
3 GILMAN ST
4 TINSLEY ST
5 LAKE ST
6 VARTHEN ST
B5
1 SPRING BANK RD
2 LARCH LEA
3 SPRUCEWOOD CL
4 THORNWOOD CL
5 HENNAWOOD CL
6 ALOESWOOD CL
7 PARLE CT
8 FRANKLIN PL
9 AVON ST
39
B6
1 TWICKENHAM ST
2 TAPLOW ST
3 AMBROSE CT
4 STONEHILL AVE
5 ST DAVID'S RD
6 OLD BARN RD
7 LUDWIG RD
8 WATERHOUSE CL
54
E8
1 GARSFIELD RD
2 SANDYVILLE GR
3 DURRANT RD
4 PARLOW RD
5 MILNE RD
A B C D E F
8 7 93 6 5 92 4 3 91 2 1 90
36 37 38
Anfield
Stanley Park
Cemy
Crem
North Liverpool Acad
Anfield (Liverpool FC) Mus & Tour Ctr
Cabbage Hall
Clubmoor
Tuebrook
LIVERPOOL
Newsham Park
Park Lodge Day
Fairfield
Stanley
Elm Park
Kensington
Botanic Est
Wavertree Park
Wavertree Tech Pk
Edge Lane Ret Pk
Binns Road Ind Est
Wavertree Ret Pk
Heritage Ctr
Sacred Heart RC Prim Sch
St Sebastian's RC Prim Sch
St Cuthbert's RC Prim Sch
Liverpool Com Coll (Bankfield)
Lister Jun & Inf Schs
Power Sta
Reen Gd
The Stables Bsns Ctr
Trans Pennine Trail
QUEENS DRIVE WALTON
QUEENS DRIVE WEST DERBY
TOWNSEND AVE
TOWNSEND LA
WEST DERBY RD
ROCKY LA
BRECK RD
BELMONT RD
OAKFIELD RD
PRESCOT RD
KENSINGTON
EDGE LA
WAVERTREE RD
DURNING RD
HOLT RD
SHEIL RD
GREEN LA
MUIRHEAD AVE
LOW HILL
IRVINE ST
WAVERTREE BVD
RATHBONE RD
A5058 A580 A5089 A5049 A5047 A57 B5189 B5188 B5178 B5179 B5340 A5048
L4 L5 L6 L7 L11 L12 L13 L15
A2
1 MANFRED ST
2 PROSPECT ST
3 HARPER ST
4 Erskine St Ind Est
5 ELLEN'S CL
6 MOUNT VERNON ST
7 MOUNT VERNON VIEW
8 BACK MOUNT VERNON GN
9 MOUNT VERNON GN
10 LOW WOOD ST
A3
1 DUNKELD CL
2 DUNKELD ST
3 LAVAN ST
4 ABER ST
5 CHURTON CT
6 BRIGHT ST
7 HENGLERS CL
8 TRAFALGAR WAY
9 WINTER ST
10 NEVIN ST
11 BROUGHAM TERR
12 MARSDEN ST
13 MARSDEN WAY
14 FITZROY WAY
15 RAVEN CL
16 PERA CL
17 ROCASTLE CL
18 GLOUCESTER CT
A4
1 SHALLCROSS PL
2 WHITEFIELD WAY
3 HAREWOOD ST
4 DAWBER CL
5 ROTHWELL ST
6 AUBREY CT
7 CRESSWELL ST
B1
1 BACK TOWERLANDS ST
2 CHURCH MOUNT
3 BACK HOLLAND PL
4 HOLLAND PL
5 HAWTHORN GR
6 PLIMSOLL ST
7 UXBRIDGE ST
8 MOORGATE ST
9 CHANDOS ST
68
B1
10 WOODSIDE ST
11 HELENA ST
12 NEVISON ST
13 HIGHGATE CT
B3
1 GEORGE HARRISON CL
2 PAUL McCARTNEY WAY
3 APPLE CT
4 RINGO STARR DR
54
B3
5 EPSTEIN CT
6 CAVERN CT
7 DENMAN ST
8 COTTENHAM ST
9 INGROW RD
10 GWENFRON RD
11 THORNES RD
12 MARITIME CT
13 CAMBRIA STREET N
14 CAMBRIA STREET S
15 Boaler St Ind Est
B4
1 MAYFAIR CL
2 NORWOOD GR
3 MONTGOMERY WAY
4 NEW GREY ROCK CL
5 AMETHYST CL

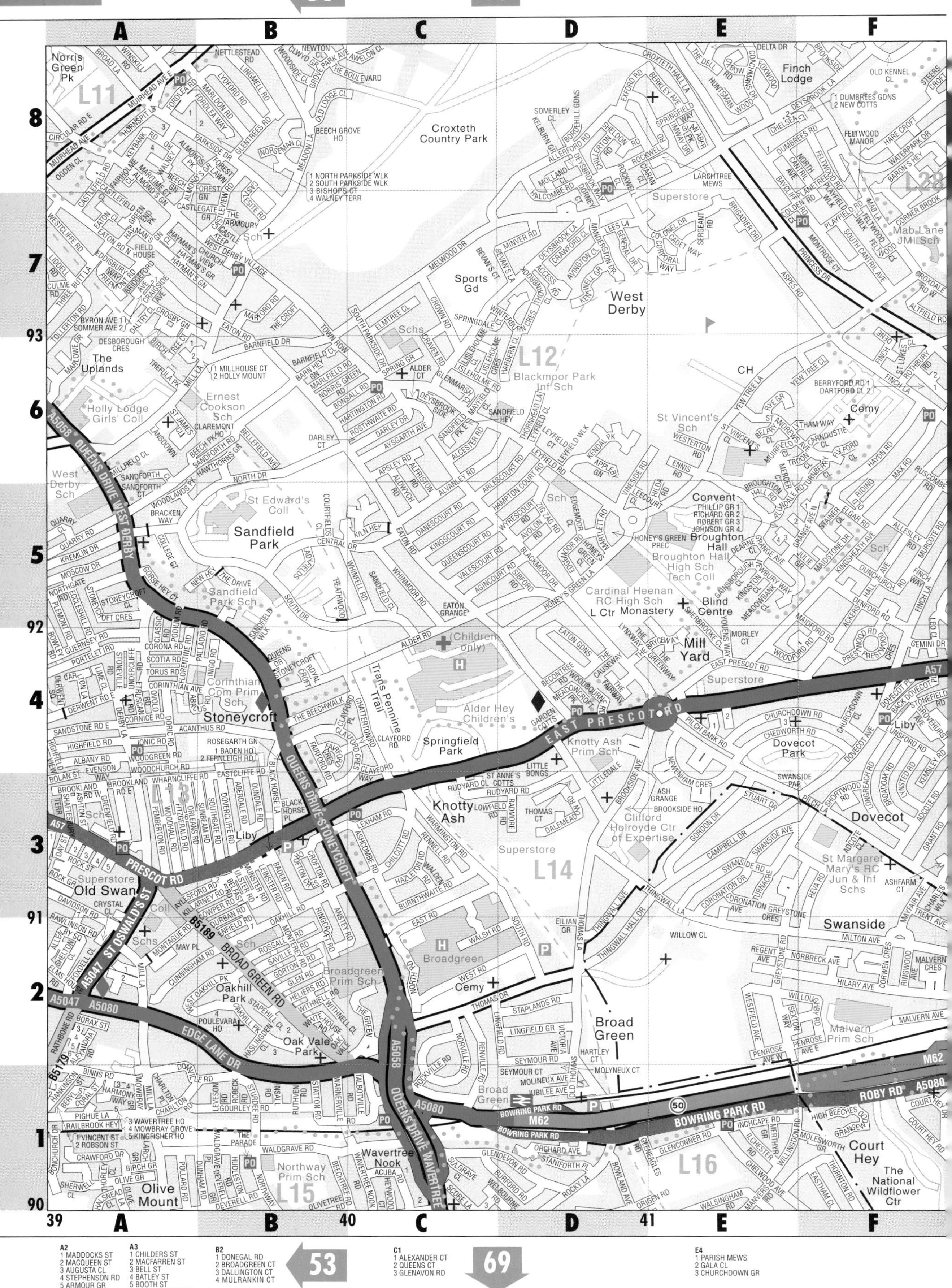

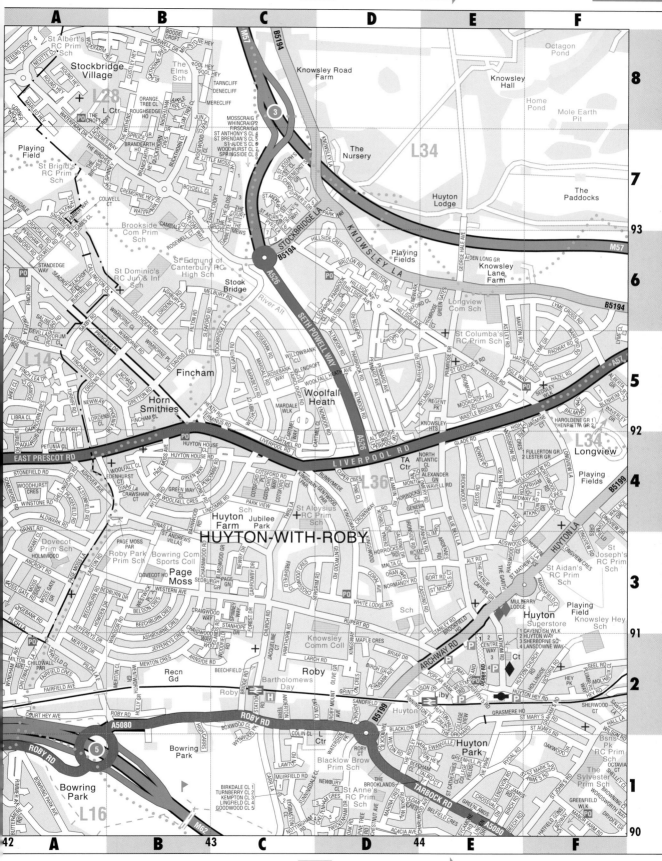

41
56

A B C D E F

Stockbridge Village
St Albert's RC Prim Sch
The Elms Sch
L28
Playing Field
St Brigid's RC Prim Sch
Brookside Com Prim Sch
St Edmund of Canterbury RC High Sch
St Dominic's RC Jun & Inf Sch
Stock Bridge
River Alt
Knowsley Road Farm
The Nursery
L34
Knowsley Hall
Octagon Pond
Home Pond
Mole Earth Pit
The Paddocks
Huyton Lodge
Playing Fields
Knowsley Lane Farm
Longview Com Sch
St Columba's RC Prim Sch
M57
B5194
A526
SETH POWELL WAY
KNOWSLEY LA
STOCKBRIDGE LA
MOSSCRAIG 1
WHINCRAIG 2
FIRSCRAIG 3
ST ANTHONY'S CL 4
ST BRENDAN'S CL 5
ST JUDE'S CL 6
WOODHURST CL 7
SPRINGSIDE CL 8
L14
Fincham
Horn Smithies
Woolfall Heath
EAST PRESCOT RD
LIVERPOOL RD
A57
L36
TA Ctr
Longview
Playing Fields
HAROLDENE GR 1
HENRIETTA GR 2
FULLERTON GR 1
2 LESTER GR
Huyton Farm
Jubilee Park
St Aloysius RC Prim Sch
HUYTON-WITH-ROBY
Dovecot Prim Sch
Roby Park Prim Sch
Bowring Com Sports Coll
Page Moss
St Aidan's RC Prim Sch
St Joseph's RC Prim Sch
Huyton
Superstore
Playing Field
Knowsley Hey Sch
1 CAVENDISH WLK
2 HUYTON WAY
3 SHERBORNE SQ
4 LANSDOWNE WAY
Knowsley Comm Coll
Recn Gd
Roby
Bartholomews Day
Liby
Ct
ARCHWAY RD
HUYTON LA
B5199
ROBY RD
A5080
Bowring Park
L16
M62
Blacklow Brow Prim Sch
St Anne's RC Prim Sch
Huyton Park
Bsns Pk RC Prim Sch
The Sylvester Prim Sch
TARBOCK RD
BIRKDALE CL 1
TURNBERRY CL 2
KEMPTON CL 3
LINGFIELD CL 4
GOODWOOD CL 5

8
7
93
6
5
92
4
3
91
2
1
90

42 A B 43 C D 44 E F

70
56

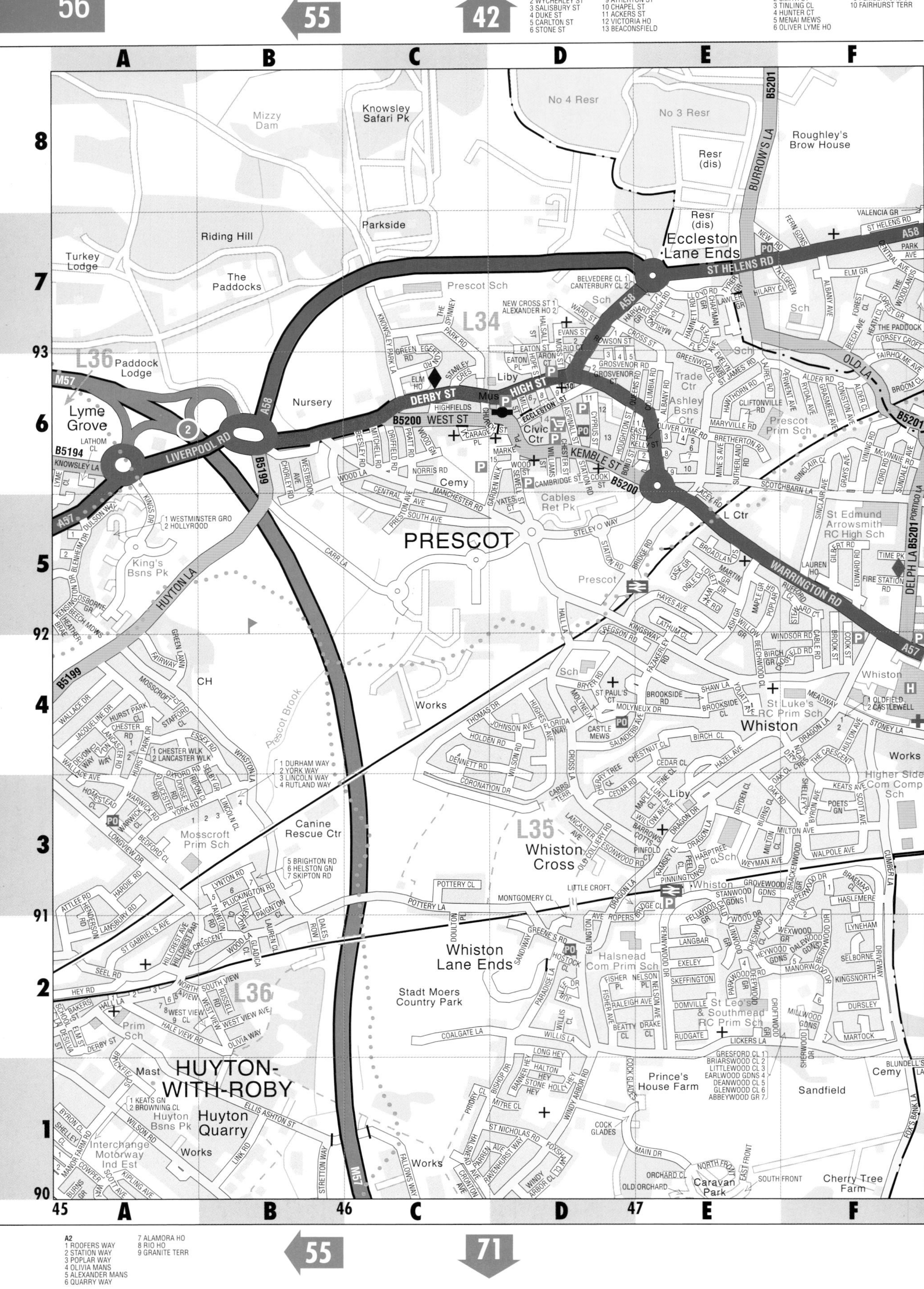
55
42
D6
1 SEDDONS CT
2 WYCHERLEY ST
3 SALISBURY ST
4 DUKE ST
5 CARLTON ST
6 STONE ST
7 HILL ST
8 LEYLAND ST
9 ATHERTON ST
10 CHAPEL ST
11 ACKERS ST
12 VICTORIA HO
13 BEACONSFIELD
14 Prescot Sh Ctr
15 GREENALL CT
E6
1 POTTERY FIELDS
2 SMITH ST
3 TINLING CL
4 HUNTER CT
5 MENAI MEWS
6 OLIVER LYME HO
7 LAVENDER CRES
8 DERBY SQ
9 PEMBERTONS CT
10 FAIRHURST TERR
A
B
C
D
E
F
8
7
93
6
5
92
4
3
91
2
1
90
No 4 Resr
No 3 Resr
Mizzy Dam
Knowsley Safari Pk
Roughley's Brow House
Resr (dis)
Riding Hill
Parkside
Turkey Lodge
The Paddocks
Eccleston Lane Ends
ST HELENS RD
BURROW'S LA
B5201
Prescot Sch
L34
L36
Paddock Lodge
M57
Lyme Grove
Nursery
DERBY ST
HIGH ST
WEST ST
B5200
Mus
Liby
Civic Ctr
Trade Ctr
Ashley Bsns Ctr
Prescot Prim Sch
LIVERPOOL RD
A58
B5199
B5194
A57
KEMBLE ST
Cemy
Cables Ret Pk
PRESCOT
L Ctr
St Edmund Arrowsmith RC High Sch
WARRINGTON RD
King's Bsns Pk
HUYTON LA
Prescot
CARR LA
STATION RD
OLD LA
DELPH LA
1 WESTMINSTER GRO
2 HOLLYROOD
CH
Works
Prescot Brook
Whiston
St Luke's RC Prim Sch
Higher Side Com Comp Sch
1 OLDFIELD
2 CASTLEWELL
1 CHESTER WLK
2 LANCASTER WLK
1 DURHAM WAY
2 YORK WAY
3 LINCOLN WAY
4 RUTLAND WAY
Canine Rescue Ctr
Mosscroft Prim Sch
L35
Whiston Cross
5 BRIGHTON RD
6 HELSTON GN
7 SKIPTON RD
POTTERY LA
Whiston Lane Ends
Halsnead Com Prim Sch
Stadt Moers Country Park
St Leo's & Southmead RC Prim Sch
HUYTON-WITH-ROBY
Prim Sch
Mast
1 KEATS GN
2 BROWNING CL
Huyton Bsns Pk
Huyton Quarry
Interchange Motorway Ind Est
Prince's House Farm
Sandfield
GRESFORD CL 1
BRIARSWOOD CL 2
LITTLEWOOD CL 3
EARLWOOD GDNS 4
DEANWOOD CL 5
GLENWOOD CL 6
ABBEYWOOD GR 7
Caravan Park
Cherry Tree Farm
Cemy
45
46
47
55
71
A2
1 ROOFERS WAY
2 STATION WAY
3 POPLAR WAY
4 OLIVIA MANS
5 ALEXANDER MANS
6 QUARRY WAY
7 ALAMORA HO
8 RIO HO
9 GRANITE TERR

A
B
C
D
E
F
ST HELENS
Thatto Heath
Thatto Heath Com Prim Sch
Grange Park
WA10
Portico
Valencia Farm
Eccleston Park
L34
Playing Fields
Hospice
St Austin's RC Prim Sch
Nutgrove Meth Prim Sch
Brown Edge
Sutton Heath
Depot
Eccleston Park
The Lodge
CH
Nutgrove
Scott Clinic
Two Butt La
Lea Green
Glasshouse Farm
Elton Head Hall Farm
Lowfield Ind Est
Longton Lane Com Prim Sch
Holt
Pendlebury Brook
Lea Green Ind Est
Lea Green Bsns Pk
L35
Stoney La Ind Est
Rainhill
Micklehead Farm
Micklehead Green Farm
Sports Ground
Sch
Liby
Brookhouse Bridge
Rainhill High Sch
Home Farm
Blundell's Hill
Loyola Hall
Chapel House Farm
Wood's House Farm
Oakdene Prim Sch
Willis Hall Farm
Rainhill Stoops
St Bartholomew's RC Prim Sch
Shirebrook
Rainhill Hall Farm
Tower Coll
PRESCOT RD
A58
ST HELENS RD
B5413
THATTO HEATH RD
NUTGROVE RD
RAINHILL RD
B5204
ELTON HEAD RD
ST HELENS LINKWAY
A570
WARRINGTON RD
A57
M62
BLUNDELL'S LA
CHAPEL LA
SCHOOL LA
MILL LA
HALL LA
CRONTON LA
1 CROWN ST
2 COMMON ST
3 GORSEFIELD
4 OAKFIELD CL
5 BILLINGHAM RD
1 SUDBURY GDNS
2 GOODWOOD CT
3 HOLKHAM GDNS
1 OULTON GDNS
2 SURLINGHAM GDNS
3 ROLLESBY GDNS
4 ORMESBY GDNS
5 HICKLING GDNS
6 SALHOUSE GDNS
7 RANWORTH GDNS
1 HOLLEY CT
2 BRAITHWAITE CL
3 Victoria Trad Est
4 STATION ST
5 STATION RD
6 HOUGHTON ST
1 WIDDALE AVE
2 KINGSDALE AVE
1 ALVA RD
2 ELGIN CT
TOFTWOOD GDNS 1
ANDERSON CL 2
OAK MEADOWS CT 1
NORBURY FOLD 2
8
7
93
6
5
92
4
3
91
2
1
90
48
49
50

57
44
F8
1 PRINCE ALBERT CT
2 THE CROFT
3 SPINNERS DR
4 COTTON TERR
A
B
C
D
E
F
8
7
93
6
5
92
4
3
91
2
1
90
51
52
53
ST HELENS
A570 ST HELENS LINKWAY
A569 SCORECROSS
MARSHALLS CROSS RD
THE CARAVAN PK
SHERDLEY RD
Sherdley Bsns Pk
SULLIVAN'S WAY
C8
1 WALNUT GR
2 BAY TREE GR
3 BRIDLE CT
4 DELLSIDE GR
5 MARSHALL AVE
St Helens
Robins Lane Com Prim Sch
Fishwicks Ind Est
D7
1 ST NICHOLAS GR
2 EAGLESFIELD CL
3 AMBERGATE CL
4 KERRYSDALE CL
5 SIMONSTONE GR
6 KIDSTONE CL
7 ORMSIDE GR
Works
Sutton
Sutton Oak CE Prim Sch
WATERY LA
WORSLEY BROW
ELLAMSBRIDGE RD
ELLEN GDN
JUNCTION LA
HOGHTON RD
ELIZABETH ST
CH
Sherdley Hall Farm
Sherdley Park
THE SCORE
St Helens Junction
MONASTERY LA
St Anne's RC Prim Sch
1 KERSWELL CL
2 HOLYWELL CL
3 FRESHFORD
Penlake Ind Est
B5204 BOLD RD
1 FRANCIS ST
2 ELIZA ST
3 HENLLAN GDNS
4 SUTTON CT
5 ORVILLE ST
The Dam
C6
1 HEWARD AVE
2 COTTERDALE CL
3 BRACEWELL CL
4 FREDA AVE
5 EVENWOOD
6 SHIREGREEN
Eaves Prim Sch
Sutton High Sports Coll
Sutton Hall Cottages
Sutton L Ctr
B5204
ELTON HEAD RD
P&R
Sherdley Prim Sch
REGINALD RD
Reginald Road Ind Pk
CLOVELLY AVE
Abbotsfield Road Ind Pk
Abbotsfield Road
MILL LA
B5204
Little Lea Green Farm
Peet's Bridge
Lea Green
PH
Sutton Mill Dam
Sutton Leach
Big Lea Green Farm
B5419
Marshall's Cross
C4
1 MORETON AVE
2 HAZELFIELD CT
3 THE WILLOWS
4 WOODCROFT WAY
5 CHURCHFIELDS
6 FALLOW CL
7 GREENWOOD CT
8 HAYFIELD WAY
9 COTTAGE PL
10 HARVEST WAY
11 LINDALE DR
12 BRACKEN CT
13 MILLERSDALE
14 BROCK HALL CL
15 WHINBURY CT
16 LITTLECOTE CL
Fog Cottages
WA9
Works
CHESTER LA
Willow Tree Prim Sch
1 WILLOW CT
2 MANOR CT
3 WHITFIELD LODGE
Tunstall's Farm
Sh Ctr
Liby
1 ELIZABETH ST
2 MARY ST
3 BARBARA ST
4 FRENCHFIELD ST
5 ST AIDANS CT
Lea Green Ind Est
Sch
Clock Face
CLOCK FACE RD
AUTUMN WAY 1
FERNHILL WLK 2
POLLITT ST 3
ROUGHDALE AVE 1
WALKER AVE 2
LAITHWAITE CL 3
Clock Face Colliery Country Park
Middle Field Farm
Sutton Manor Com Prim Sch
Sutton Manor
JUBITS LA
Sutton Road Farm
Yew Tree Farm
BUSHELL'S FARM
M62
BELL LA
PH
L35
Union Bridge Farm
FINGER HOUSE LA
Union Bridge
Crow's Nest Farm
Coney Green Wood
WA8
UNION BANK LA
Union Bank Farm
TIBBS CROSS LA
Kebb's Farm
A569
57
73

45
60

Sutton Moss
Burtonwood Moss
White House Farm
B5204
Higher Farm
Bold Moss
Burtonwood Brewery
Yew Tree Farm
LUMBER LA
BOLD LA
Bold Bsns Ctr
Derby Farm
Burtonwood Com Prim Sch
BACK LA
EPWORTH CL 1
ARNCLIFFE DR 2
ARUNDELL CL 3
DORCHESTER WAY 4
TRAVERS' ENTRY
1 PEONY GDNS
2 ARABIS GDNS
3 CAMELLIA GDNS
AZALEA GDNS 1
IBERIS GDNS 2
HYDRANGEA WAY 3
LAVENDER GDNS 4
SUNFLOWER CL 5
NEW BOLD CT
Phipps' Bridge
Burtonwood Ind Ctr
Bold
Travers' Farm
Wheatacre Farm
Haley Head Farm
Bold Ind Pk
Liby
Cemy
Rose Hill Farm
DOUGLAS AVE
ROSEHILL AVE
GORSEY LA
Burtonwood
Ashton's Farm
Northfield Riding Ctr
WA9
Moat House
Old Lodge Farm
Clay Lane Farm
CLAY LA
Abbotsfield Farm
Lodge Wood
Park Cottage
Maypole Farm
Moat House Farm
WA5
Nursery
Hollin Wood
Joy Lane Farm
Ivy Cottage
Highfield
HALL LA
JOY LA
Finger Post
BURTONWOOD RD
Home Farm
LIMEKILN LA
WRIGHT'S LA
Dog Kennel Plantation
Limekiln Farm
M62
WA8
Booth's Wood
Old Hall Farm
Duck Wood
ORION BVD
OMEGA BVD
A
B
C
D
E
F
8
7
93
6
5
92
4
3
91
2
1
90
54
55
56

74
60

A B C D E F

8

7

93

6

5

92

4

3

91

2

1

90

Bradlegh Old Hall
New Bradlegh Hall Farm
BRADLEY LA
HALL LA
THE BRAMBLES
LUMBER LA
MELROSE AVE
BAKEWELL RD
FIR TREE LA
PINEWOOD RD
CAMBOURNE RD
Boarded Barn Farm
The Old Vicarage
Stoneyard Cottage
Roxborough Cl
Primrose Hill Farm
KAREN CL
CHACE
FARMER'S LA
Tan House Farm
ALDER LA
Hall Lane Farm
Red House Farm
Clayton's House Farm
The Fiddle i'th Bag Inn
CH
Alder Root Farm
ALDER ROOT LA
Lower Alder Root Farm
Cop Holt Farm
Asps Wood

HEY WOOD CL
LONDON ROW
CHESTER ROW
SHEFFIELD ROW
LIVERPOOL ROW
MANCHESTER ROW
KIRKACRE AVE
HEY LOCK CL
CONROY WAY
WARGRAVE RD
DERBY RD

Vulcan Village
WA12
Newton Brook
Sankey Canal (dis)

WA2

HOLLINS LA
Hollins Park
H
BROWNING CL

NEWTON RD
A49
A49

WA5
Phipps' Brook
Brook Head Farm
TAN HOUSE LA
Forest Farm
Dial Post Farm

Sankey Brook
OLD ALDER LA
WATERY LA
Sankey Valley Park
Causeway Bridges Farm
Causey Bridge

DELPH LA
M62
CARPENTON CT
MILL LA
CRAVEN CL
CALVER RD

Burtonwood Service Area
M62
8
BURTONWOOD RD
CHARON WAY
BUTTS CT
BUTTS GN
ARDERS GREEN
FALCONERS GN
EAST PEEL CT
DELTA CRES
KINGSWOOD RD
Kingswood
KINGSWOOD
TOURNEY GN
HERALDS GN
CASTLE GN
CASTLE GN
WESTBROOK CRES
COPPICE GN
DOVEC
Westbrook Centre
WESTBROOK WAY
St Philip (Westbrook) CE Prim Sch
WESTBROOK CTR
Liby
Superstore
FIRMAN CL
P
WHITTLE AVE
MATLOCK CL
TENBURY CL
HARROGATE CL
BRISTOW CL
BLACKSHAW DR
BARROW
GARWOOD CL
GARWOOD CL
A574
A574 Warrington (A57)

Superstores
Superstore
EUROPA BVD
TAURUS PK
Gemini
WARRINGTON
Gemini Bsns Pk
A574
WILLOW CT
WEST DULY RD

CROMWELL AVE
PETERSWAY
HOLYHEAD
FAIRBOURNE CL
GOLDCLIFF CL
ST ASAPH DR
BALA
CHEPSTOW
RUTHIN LA
LAMPETER CL
Little Moss Wood
Callands Prim Sch
PD
NEWBRIDGE CL
STAINER CL
PENSARN GDNS
PEMARK
CRESSINGTON CL
WESTPOOL CL
BEECH CL
BRECON
GRANSTON
OLWEN CL
ST DAVID'S CL
ST JOHN'S CL
LYDSTEP CT
SUMMERFIELD AVE
RUTTER AVE
SAUNDERSFOOT
ROSSETT CL
PHOENIX AVE
LEWIS AVE
DAGNALL AVE
MARSHALL AVE
Dallam
Callands Rd
Callands
LANGLAND CL
TINTERN
BARMOUTH CL
Dallam Com Prim Sch
PD
HARRISON SQ
OLLENSHAW RD
Calland's Farmhouse
CARMARTHEN
GRANT CL
BURY CL
BEDFORD CL
Big Wood
NORTH PARK BROOK RD
BOVERTON CL
ABEY CL
CANDLESTON CL
ORNWEY
MARCROSS
WREXHAM CL
LADYWOOD
BEECROFT CL
HINDLE AVE
HIGHAM AVE
HAWLEY'S CL
HYSCASTLE CL
GALE AVE
CALDWELL AVE
BOULTING AVE
Gullivers World Theme Park

Cheshire STREET ATLAS

57 A 58 B C D 59 E F

A
B
C
D
E
F
8
7
93
6
5
92
4
3
91
2
1
90
HERMITAGE GREEN LA
The Hermit Inn (PH)
A573
GEROSA AVE
M6
WINWICK LA
A579
22
A49
ROSEMOUNT COTTS
Sand Pit
Island Plantation
Cockshot Farm
Southworth Hall
SMITHY BROW
Smithy Brow
Highfields
WATERWORKS LA
HIGHFIELD LA
GOLBORNE RD
Cockshot Bridge
Cockshot Brook
OLD SCHOOL HOUSE LA
GREEN LANE CL
GREEN LA
THE PRIORY
SPIRES GDNS
SOUTHWORTH LA
WA3
DAM LA
Cheshire STREET ATLAS
Mill House Brow
CHURCH WLK
HORNBY LA
PILGRIM CL
ILEX AVE
ST OSWALDS CL
MYDDLETON LA
Winwick
PO
Winwick CE Prim Sch
ASH RD
MAPLE RD
WINWICK LINK RD
Arbury
Myddleton Hall Farmhouse
HOLLINS LA
HOLLINS DR
BALLANTYNE PL
MARRYAT CL
L Ctr
PH
FLEMING DR
ALCOTT PL
CROMPTON DR
AUSTEN DR
BRONTE CL
RECTORY LA
RECTORY CL
ST ANTHONY PL
FARRINGDON RD
FALCONDALE RD
LINKSIDE AVE
ARBURY LA
M6 Stoke-on-Trent
DELPH LA
21a
BROWNING DR
WINWICK PARK AVE
CHESTERTON DR
SHERIDAN PL
BECKETT DR
MASEFIELD DR
Mainfield
Spa Well Cottage
NEWTON RD
M62 Manchester (M602)
Delph Farm
DELPH LA
TOWNSFIELD LA
Midhops Farm
10
M62
Delph Park
9
Houghton Green
PH
MILL LA
KINROSS CL
SOLWAY CL
DUNDEE CL
ENFIELD PARK RD
WA2
Peel Hall
ELM RD
WOBURN RD
BIRCH AVE
TOLL BAR PL
Hotel
POPLARS AVE
Radley Plantation
Recn Gd
RADLEY LA
SHETLAND CL
GAIRLOCH CL
KILSYTH CL
NEWHAVEN RD
HASTINGS AVE
HEYHILL AVE
BALLATER DR
CAMERON CT
COTSWOLD PL
ULVERSTON AVE
SEAFORD PL
LANCING AVE
Cinnamon Brow
WARRINGTON
MONTROSE CL
GRISEDALE AVE
CRAWLEY AVE
CHILTERN RD
KENTMERE PL
GRASMERE AVE
ENNERDALE AVE
COTSWOLD RD
PENNYFIELDS
MILL CL
COLDSTREAM CL
CINNAMON LA N
GABLES CL
ROSYTH CL
PERTH CL
WAYWELL CL
MILL LA
CALVER RD
ESKDALE AVE 1
BUTTERMERE CRES 2
TOLL BAR RD
WANSFELL PL
PENTLAND AVE
CLEVELAND RD
PETWORTH AVE
HORSESHOE CRES
MILL FARM CL
BRIERS CL
Sch
OXENHAM RD
WINDERMERE AVE
BRENDON AVE
CHEVIOT AVE
COLVILLE CT
St Andrew's CE Prim Sch
THIRLMERE AVE
ULLSWATER AVE
RAVENSDALE CL
OSPREY CL
DELAFIE LD CL
WASLEY CL
Winwick Quay
Hulme
BUTTERMERE AVE
MEREWOOD CL
LINNET CL
PARK VIEW
ACKERLEY CL
CHILTERN CL
MENDIP CL
CARTMEL AVE
SCAFELL AVE
QUAIL CL
GRASMERE CL
TEAL CL
ENFIELD PARK RD
GOTHAM CT
St Stephen's RC Prim Sch
POPLARS AVE
MALLARD CL
DUNLIN CL
MORVEN CL
FOXFIELD
ST STEPHEN'S AVE
BENTHAM AVE
AVOCET CL
DOVEDALE CL
DARLEY AVE
HUNTER AVE
SANDY LA W
L Ctr
BORROWDALE AVE
HOWSON RD
APPLEBY RD
CANBERRA AVE
BITTERN CL
SANDALWOOD CL
CROWE AVE
ST BRIDGET CL
CROMWELL AVE
A574
AJAX AVE
MARDALE AVE
PENRITH AVE
KESWICK AVE
KIRKSTONE AVE
HONISTER AVE
KENDAL AVE
CONCORDE PL
HALIFAX CL
METEOR CRES
GREENWOOD CRES
LANGDALE CL
MERRICK CL
CINNAMON LA
PARKFIELDS LA
WA5
MILLBROOK CL
ACHILLES AVE
POOLE AVE
SINCLAIR AVE
COOPER AVE
LOCKER AVE
POOLE CRES
KESWICK CRES
BONNESS AVE
PATTERDALE AVE
TROSSACH CL
BRANTFIELD CT
WELLINGTON CL 1
LANCASTER CL 2
VULCAN CL
APPLETREE GR
LYNDALE AVE
GAYHURST AVE
BYRON CT
STATHAM AVE
SMALL CRES
HUGHES PL
CATTERALL AVE
AVERY CL
ORANGE GR
BLACKBROOK AVE
VALIANT CL
Dallam Brook
GOUGH AVE
MARRON AVE
SANDY LA
THE COPPINS
SHAKESPEARE GR
KEATS GR
BURNS GR
MORGAN AVE
FESTIVAL AVE
FESTIVAL CRES
POPLARS PL
CAPESTHORNE RD
Blackbrook
HUDSON RD
VISCOUNT RD
HARRIS RD
INSALL RD
Liby
DEAN CRES
CURRANS RD
ARMOUR AVE
DENSHAM AVE
NORTHWAY
CLOUGH AVE
FISHER AVE
DRYDEN PL
TENNYSON DR
LEE CT
RUSKIN AVE
PRIMROSE CL
CALDBECK AVE
Liby
PO
Orford
LYSANDER CL
WESTLAND DR
FEARNHEAD CROSS
ANTRIM RD
Meadowside Com Prim Sch
COSLACK AVE
KIPLING AVE
FIELDVIEW DR
NEVILLE AVE
HANDLEY DR
MANNGAN CT
WADDINGTON CL
Padgate Com High Sch
Alban Ret Pk
Longford
CLIVE AVE
HARDING AVE
Brook Acre Com Prim Sch
HILDEN RD
BIGGIN CT
GOSPORT CL
HAWLEY'S LA
A50
LONG LA
MILVAIN DR
BEATTY AVE
MARINA DR
Sch
SCHOOL RD
COVEY RD
PARK RD
WARREN RD
BURTON RD
WOODCOT
BRUCE AVE
DEREK AVE
MARTIN AVE
BOYLE AVE
VALLEY CT
A574 Leigh
Hawley's Lane Trad Pk
Winstanley Ind Est
LONGFIELD RD
TE CL
BIRTLES RD
OSBORNE AVE
DARWEN GDNS
RUDLOE CT
A574 BIRCHWOOD WAY
EAGLE PARK DR
ATHLONE RD
Warrington Collegiate
William Beamont Com High Sch
Warrington Bsns Pk
ORFORD GN
A50
SYLVIA CRES
SEALAND CL
ANDOVER CL
CATFOSS CL
DUXFORD CT
FINNINGLEY CT
1 POCKLINGTON CT
2 UNSWORTH CT
WEST AVE
A49
St Mary's
ST MARGARET'S AVE 1
VALE OWEN RD 2
MALCOLM AVE
FERGUSON DR
WOODVALE
Padgate
Recn Gd
A49 Warrington
Cheshire STREET ATLAS
HALLOWS AVE
A50 M6 Junction 20
A574 Warrington (A57)
61
62

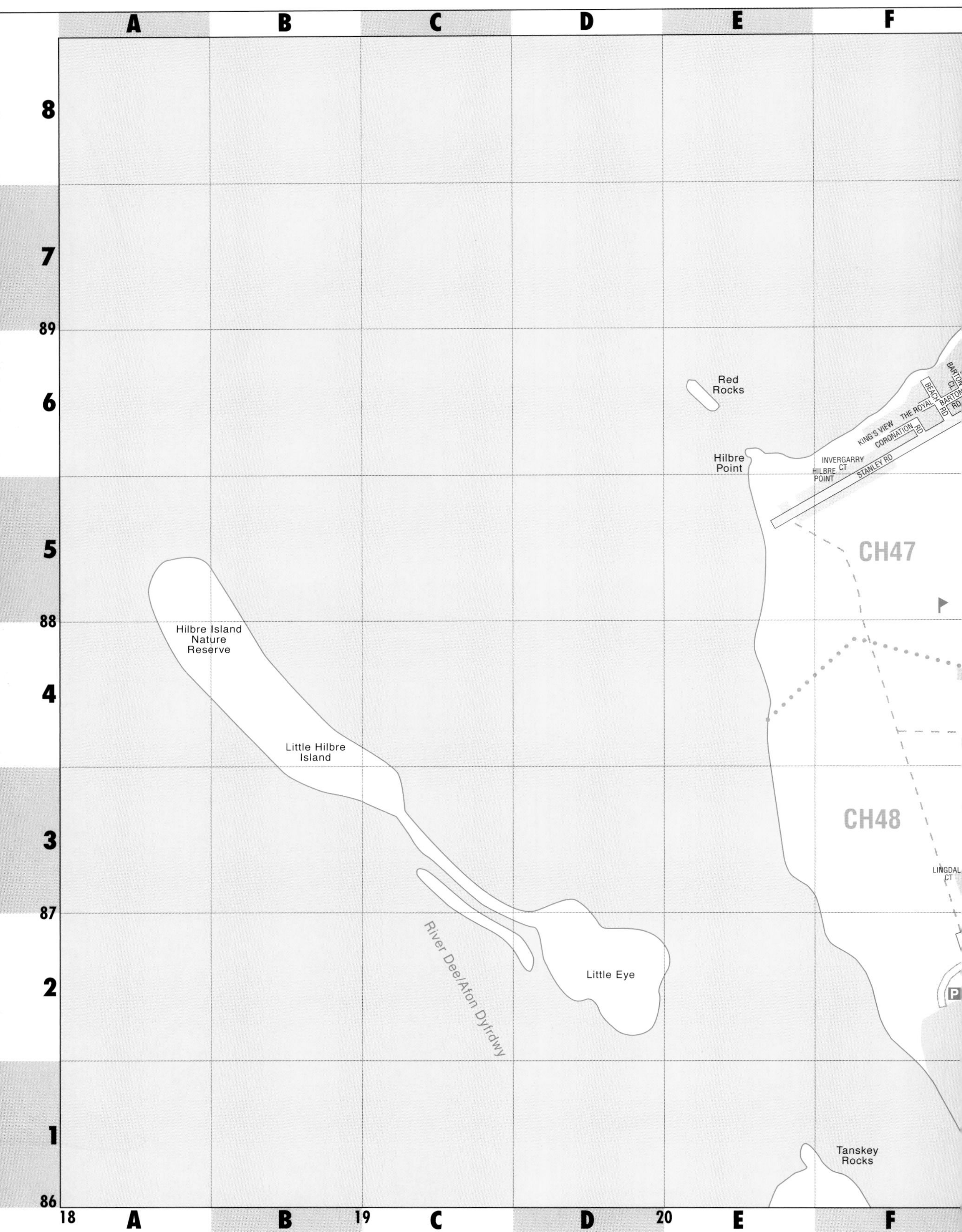

Red Rocks

Hilbre Point

CH47

CH48

Hilbre Island Nature Reserve

Little Hilbre Island

Little Eye

River Dee/Afon Dyfrdwy

Tanskey Rocks

KING'S VIEW
THE ROYAL
CORONATION
INVERGARRY
CT
HILBRE POINT
STANLEY RD
BARTON CL
BARTON RD
BEACH

LINGDAL CT

P

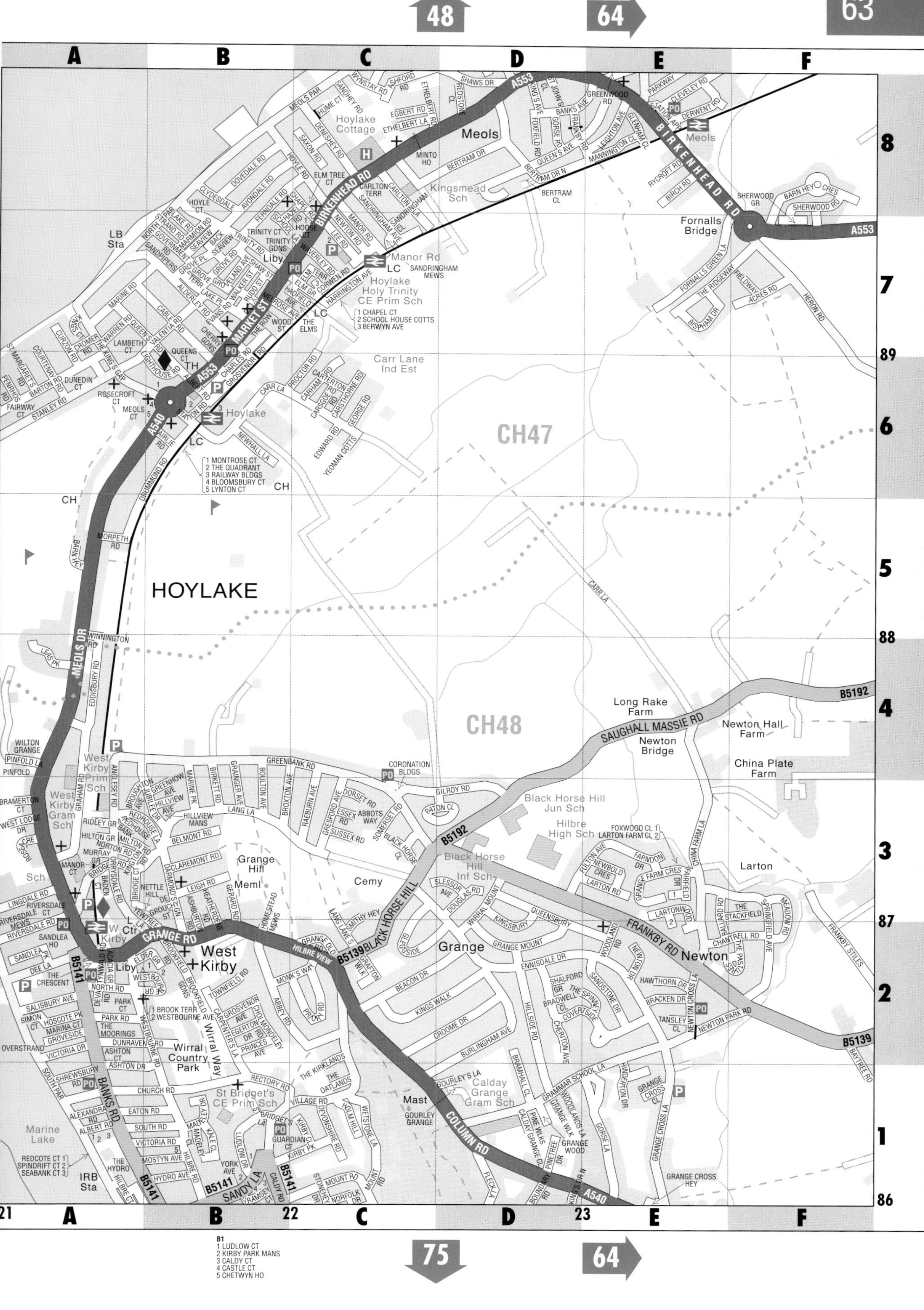

63 49

A B C D E F

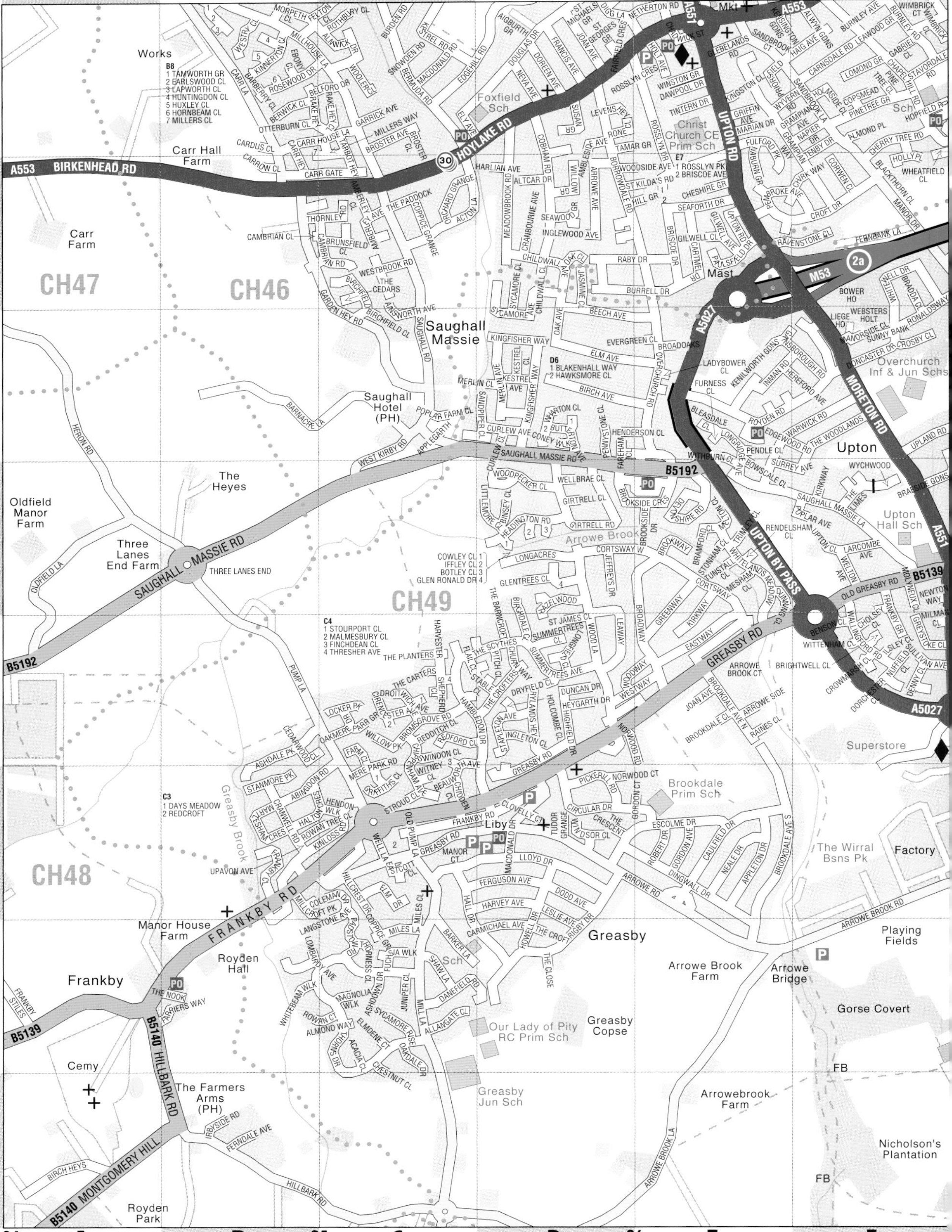

8

Works
B8
1 TAMWORTH GR
2 EARLSWOOD CL
3 LAPWORTH CL
4 HUNTINGDON CL
5 HUXLEY CL
6 HORNBEAM CL
7 MILLERS CL

Carr Hall
Farm

Foxfield
Sch

Christ
Church CE
Prim Sch

E7
1 ROSSLYN AVE
2 BRISCOE AVE

A553 BIRKENHEAD RD

POOL HOYLAKE RD 30

7

CH47

Carr
Farm

CH46

Saughall
Massie

Mast

89

The
Cedars

Saughall
Hotel
(PH)

M53 2a

Bower
HO
Websters
Holt
Sunny Bank

Overchurch
Inf & Jun Schs

6

Oldfield
Manor
Farm

The
Heyes

Poplar Farm CL

WEST KIRBY RD

SAUGHALL MASSIE ROW

D6
1 BLAKENHALL WAY
2 HAWKSMORE CL

Ladybower
CL

Upton

Upton
Hall Sch

B5192

5

Three
Lanes
End Farm

SAUGHALL MASSIE RD

THREE LANES END

Arrowe Brook

UPTON BY PASS

Upton
Hall Sch

B5139

B5192

88

CH49

C4
1 STOURPORT CL
2 MALMESBURY CL
3 FINCHDEAN CL
4 THRESHER AVE

The Planters

The Carters

The Scythes

GREASBY RD

BRIGHTWELL CL

OLD GREASBY RD

A5027

4

CH48

C3
1 DAYS MEADOW
2 REDCROFT

Greasby Brook

UPAVON AVE

FRANKBY RD

Liby

Brookdale
Prim Sch

The Wirral
Bsns Pk

Factory

Superstore

3

Manor House
Farm

Royden
Hall

Greasby

Arrowe Brook
Farm

Arrowe
Bridge

Playing
Fields

87

Frankby

PO

THE NOOK
SPIERS WAY

Sch

Greasby
Copse

Gorse Covert

2

B5139

B5140 HILLBARK RD

The Farmers
Arms
(PH)

Our Lady of Pity
RC Prim Sch

FB

Cemy

Greasby
Jun Sch

Arrowebrook
Farm

86

B5140 MONTGOMERY HILL

Royden
Park

BIRCH HEYS

HILLBARK RD

Nicholson's
Plantation

FB

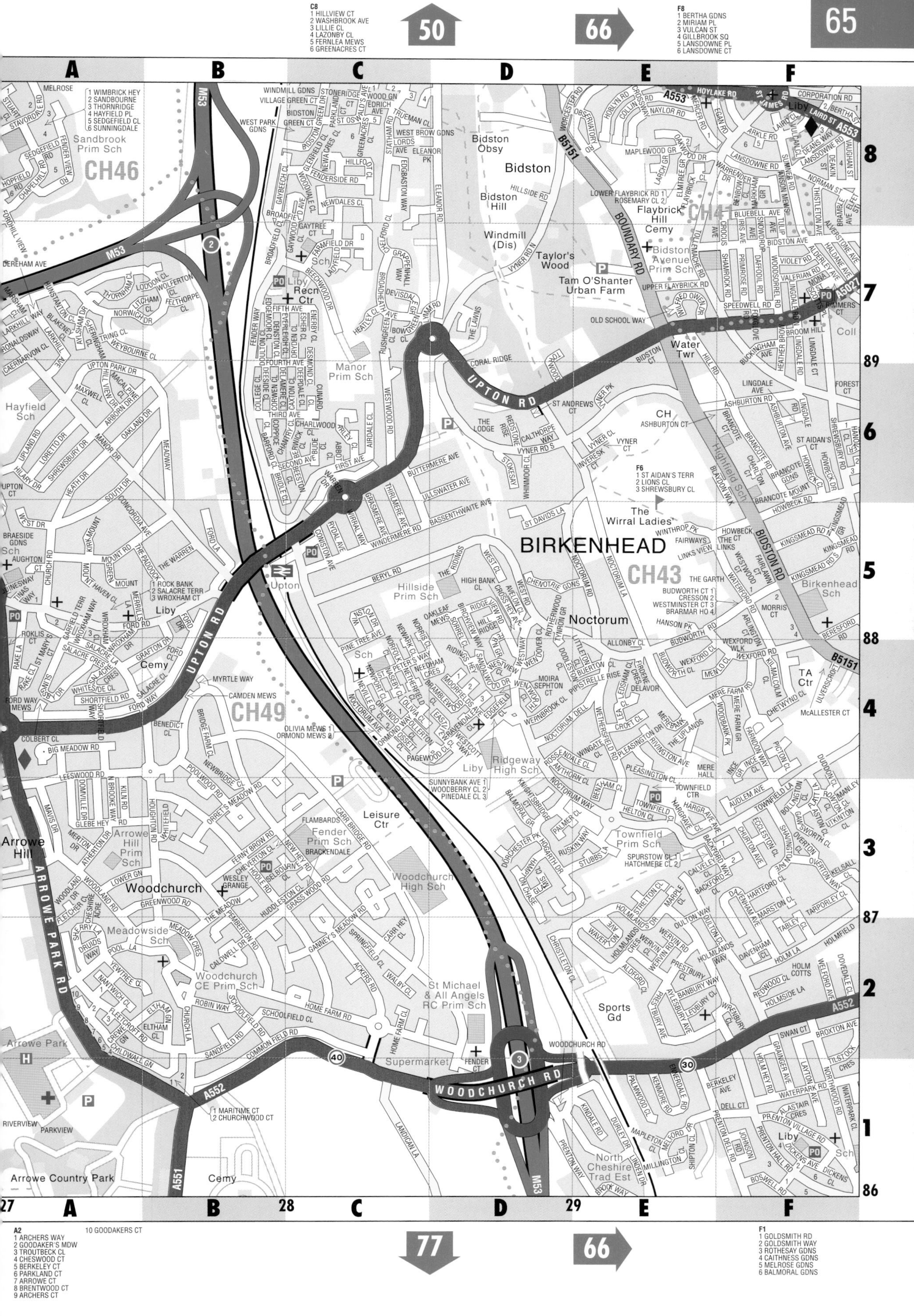

65
C8
1 HILLVIEW CT
2 WASHBROOK AVE
3 LILLIE CL
4 LAZONBY CL
5 FERNLEA MEWS
6 GREENACRES CT
50
66
F8
1 BERTHA GDNS
2 MIRIAM PL
3 VULCAN ST
4 GILLBROOK SQ
5 LANSDOWNE PL
6 LANSDOWNE CT
A
B
C
D
E
F
1 WIMBRICK HEY
2 SANDBOURNE
3 THORNRIDGE
4 HAYFIELD PL
5 SEDGEFIELD CL
6 SUNNINGDALE
Sandbrook Prim Sch
CH46
M53
DEREHAM AVE
Hayfield Sch
CH49
1 ROCK BANK
2 SALACRE TERR
3 WROXHAM CT
Liby
Cemy
UPTON RD
Upton
Manor Prim Sch
Recn Ctr
Bidston Obsy
Bidston
Bidston Hill
Windmill (Dis)
Taylor's Wood
Tam O'Shanter Urban Farm
Flaybrick Hill Cemy
Bidston Avenue Prim Sch
CH41
BOUNDARY RD
B5151
A553
A5027
Coll
Water Twr
UPTON RD
F6
1 ST AIDAN'S TERR
2 LIONS CL
3 SHREWSBURY CL
The Wirral Ladies'
BIRKENHEAD
CH43
Noctorum
Hillside Prim Sch
Birkenhead Sch
BIDSTON RD
Ridgeway High Sch
TA Ctr
OLIVIA MEWS 1
ORMOND MEWS 2
SUNNYBANK AVE 1
WOODBERRY CL 2
PINEDALE CL 3
Leisure Ctr
Fender Prim Sch
Arrowe Hill Prim Sch
Arrowe Hill
Woodchurch
Woodchurch High Sch
Townfield Prim Sch
Meadowside Sch
Woodchurch CE Prim Sch
St Michael & All Angels RC Prim Sch
Sports Gd
ARROWE PARK RD
Arrowe Park
Supermarket
WOODCHURCH RD
A552
A551
1 MARITIME CT
2 CHURCHWOOD CT
North Cheshire Trad Est
Arrowe Country Park
Cemy
8
89
7
6
5
88
4
3
87
2
1
86
27
28
29
A2
1 ARCHERS WAY
2 GOODAKER'S MDW
3 TROUTBECK CL
4 CHESWOOD CT
5 BERKELEY CT
6 PARKLAND CT
7 ARROWE CT
8 BRENTWOOD CT
9 ARCHERS CT
10 GOODAKERS CT
77
66
F1
1 GOLDSMITH RD
2 GOLDSMITH WAY
3 ROTHESAY GDNS
4 CAITHNESS GDNS
5 MELROSE GDNS
6 BALMORAL GDNS

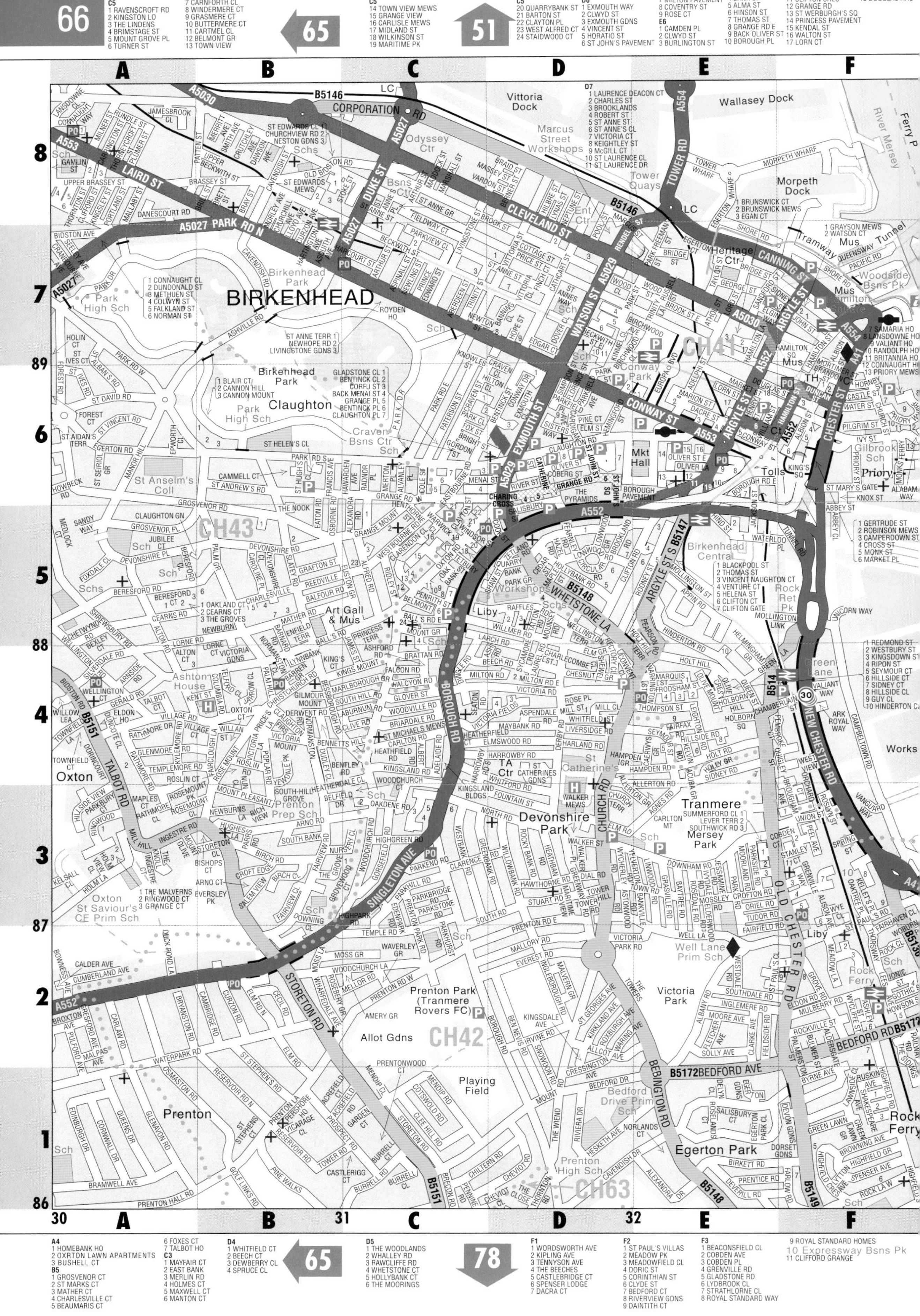

66
C5
1 RAVENSCROFT RD
2 KINGSTON LO
3 THE LINDENS
4 BRIMSTAGE ST
5 MOUNT GROVE PL
6 TURNER ST
7 CARNFORTH CL
8 WINDERMERE CT
9 GRASMERE CT
10 BUTTERMERE CT
11 CARTMEL CL
12 BELMONT GR
13 TOWN VIEW
65
C5
14 TOWN VIEW MEWS
15 GRANGE VIEW
16 CARLISLE MEWS
17 MIDLAND ST
18 WILKINSON ST
19 MARITIME PK
51
C5
20 QUARRYBANK ST
21 BARTON ST
22 CLAYTON PL
23 WEST ALFRED CT
24 STAIDWOOD CT
D6
1 EXMOUTH WAY
2 CLWYD ST
3 EXMOUTH GDNS
4 VINCENT ST
5 HORATIO ST
6 ST JOHN'S PAVEMENT
7 MILTON PAVEMENT
8 COVENTRY ST
9 ROSE CT
E6
1 CAMDEN PL
2 CLWYD ST
3 BURLINGTON ST
4 BANK ST
5 ALMA ST
6 HINSON ST
7 THOMAS ST
8 GRANGE RD E
9 BACK OLIVER ST
10 BOROUGH PL
11 CLIFTON CRES
12 GRANGE RD
13 ST WERBURGH'S SQ
14 PRINCESS PAVEMENT
15 KENDAL ST
16 WALTON ST
17 LORN CT
18 DOUGLAS ARC
A
B
C
D
E
F
8
7
89
6
5
88
4
3
87
2
1
86
30
31
32
BIRKENHEAD
Birkenhead Park
Claughton
Oxton
Prenton
Devonshire Park
Tranmere
Egerton Park
Rock Ferry
Vittoria Dock
Wallasey Dock
Morpeth Dock
River Mersey
Marcus Street Workshops
Tower Quays
CH41
CH42
CH43
CH63
CORPORATION RD
CLEVELAND ST
CONWAY ST
LAIRD ST
PARK RD N
BOROUGH RD
SINGLETON AVE
STORETON RD
CHURCH RD
BEBINGTON RD
OLD CHESTER RD
NEW CHESTER RD
CHESTER ST
ARGYLE ST
WHETSTONE LA
BEDFORD AVE
BEDFORD RD
TALBOT RD
Prenton Park (Tranmere Rovers FC)
Allot Gdns
Playing Field
Victoria Park
Mersey Park
St Anselm's Coll
Birkenhead Central
Art Gall & Mus
Well Lane Prim Sch
Bedford Drive Prim Sch
Prenton High Sch
Oxton St Saviour's CE Prim Sch
A4
1 HOMEBANK HO
2 OXRTON LAWN APARTMENTS
3 BUSHELL CT
B5
1 GROSVENOR CT
2 ST MARKS CT
3 MATHER CT
4 CHARLESVILLE CT
5 BEAUMARIS CT
6 FOXES CT
7 TALBOT HO
C3
1 MAYFAIR CT
2 EAST BANK
3 MERLIN RD
4 HOLMES CT
5 MAXWELL CT
6 MANTON CT
D4
1 WHITFIELD CT
2 BEECH CT
3 DEWBERRY CL
4 SPRUCE CL
65
D5
1 THE WOODLANDS
2 WHALLEY RD
3 RAWCLIFFE RD
4 WHETSTONE CT
5 HOLLYBANK CT
6 THE MOORINGS
78
F1
1 WORDSWORTH AVE
2 KIPLING AVE
3 TENNYSON AVE
4 THE BEECHES
5 CASTLEBRIDGE CT
6 SPENSER LODGE
7 DACRA CT
F2
1 ST PAUL'S VILLAS
2 MEADOW PK
3 MEADOWFIELD CL
4 DORIC ST
5 CORINTHIAN ST
6 CLYDE ST
7 BEDFORD CT
8 RIVERVIEW GDNS
9 DAINTITH CT
F3
1 BEACONSFIELD CL
2 COBDEN AVE
3 COBDEN PL
4 GRENVILLE RD
5 GLADSTONE RD
6 LYDBROOK CL
7 STRATHLORNE CL
8 ROYAL STANDARD WAY
9 ROYAL STANDARD HOMES
10 Expressway Bsns Pk
11 CLIFFORD GRANGE

F8
1 SOUTH HUNTER ST
2 BACK BEDFORD ST
3 SUGNALL ST
4 UPPER HOPE PL
5 PHILHARMONIC CT
6 BEDFORD CL

F8
7 BEDFORD WLK
8 HOPE WAY
9 BACK CATHARINE ST
10 ST BRIDE ST
11 BACK ST BRIDE ST
12 LITTLE ST BRIDE ST

13 SIR HOWARD ST
14 SIR HOWARD WAY
15 SANDON ST
16 CAMBRIDGE ST
17 AGNES JONES HO
18 BLACKBURNE TERR

E5
1 WOLFE ST
2 LAMPORT ST
3 SOUTHWELL PL
4 MILL VIEW
5 SADDLESTONE GR
6 DODDRIDGE RD

F5
1 WINKLE ST
2 TUPMAN ST
3 SEIONT HO
4 PECKSNIFF CL
5 MALTA WLK

F4
1 HAWKHURST CL
2 UPCHURCH CL
3 CHILHEM CT
4 LINDFIELD CL
5 SHELMORE DR
6 PAULTON CL
7 IRONBRIDGE VIEW
8 MONTPELIER DR
9 RIVERVIEW WLK
10 ALEXANDER WAY
11 STOPFORD ST
12 PARK HILL CT
13 KIRKBURN CL

LIVERPOOL

River Mersey

Toxteth

Rock Park

F6
1 UPPER HILL ST
2 MAKEPEACE WLK
3 RADLEY'S CT
4 KENYON CT
5 COMBERMERE CT
6 WINDSOR CT
7 THACKERAY CT
8 THACKERAY ST

F7
1 CATHEDRAL CT
2 BACK HUSKISSON ST
3 BIRLEY CT
4 MAHON CT
5 LITTLE CANNING ST
6 BACK LITTLE CANNING ST
7 BEDFORD CT
8 BACK EGERTON ST N
9 BACK EGERTON ST S

10 BERKLEY PL
11 RIALTO CL
12 SELBORNE ST
13 PRINCES AVE
14 ALEXANDRA TERR

1 NELSON HO
2 KINGS WLK
3 NELSON CT
4 ST PETER'S CT
5 PETERWOOD

1 MELVILLE
2 THORBURN CT
3 THORBURN LODGE
4 THE ESPLANADE

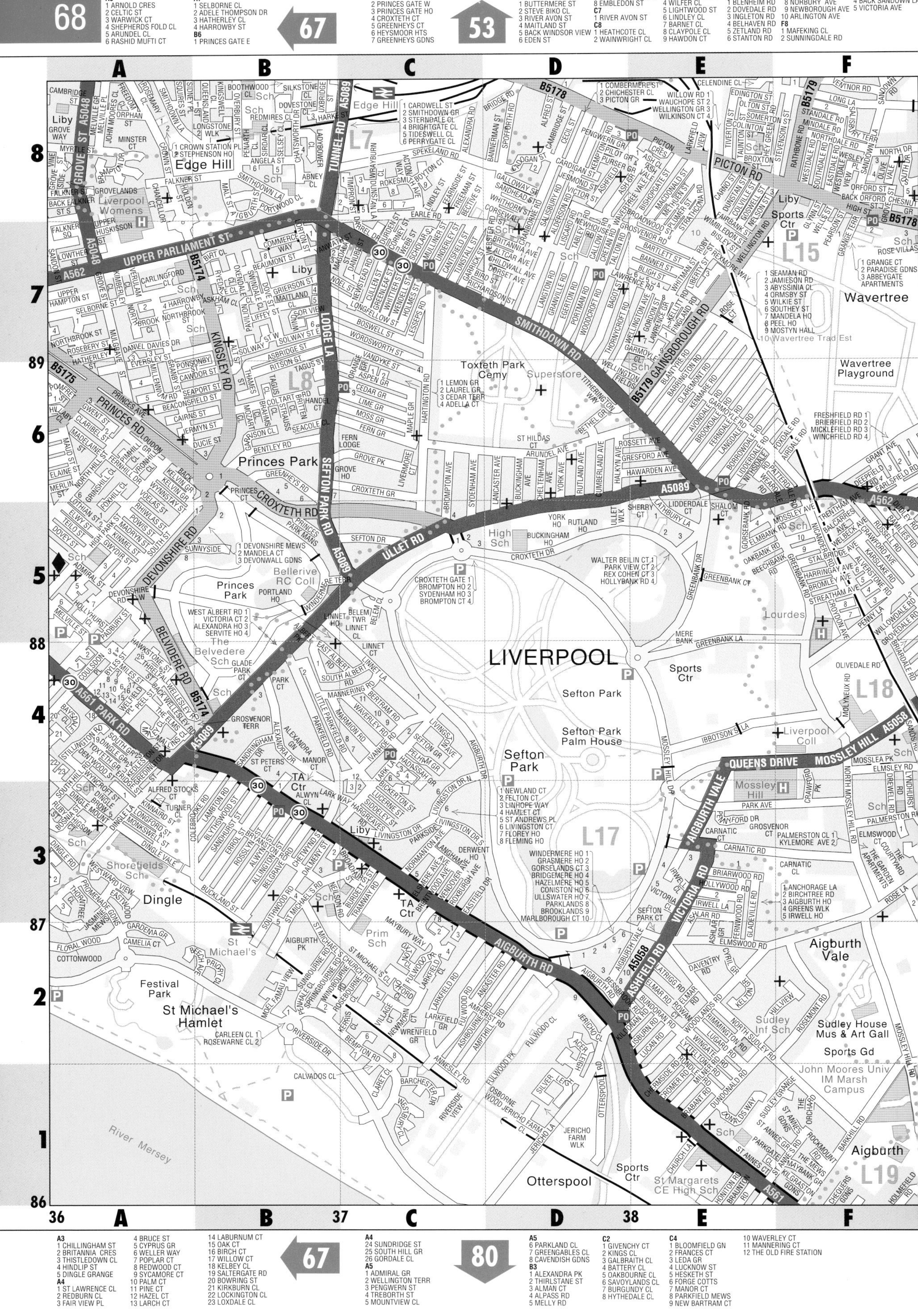

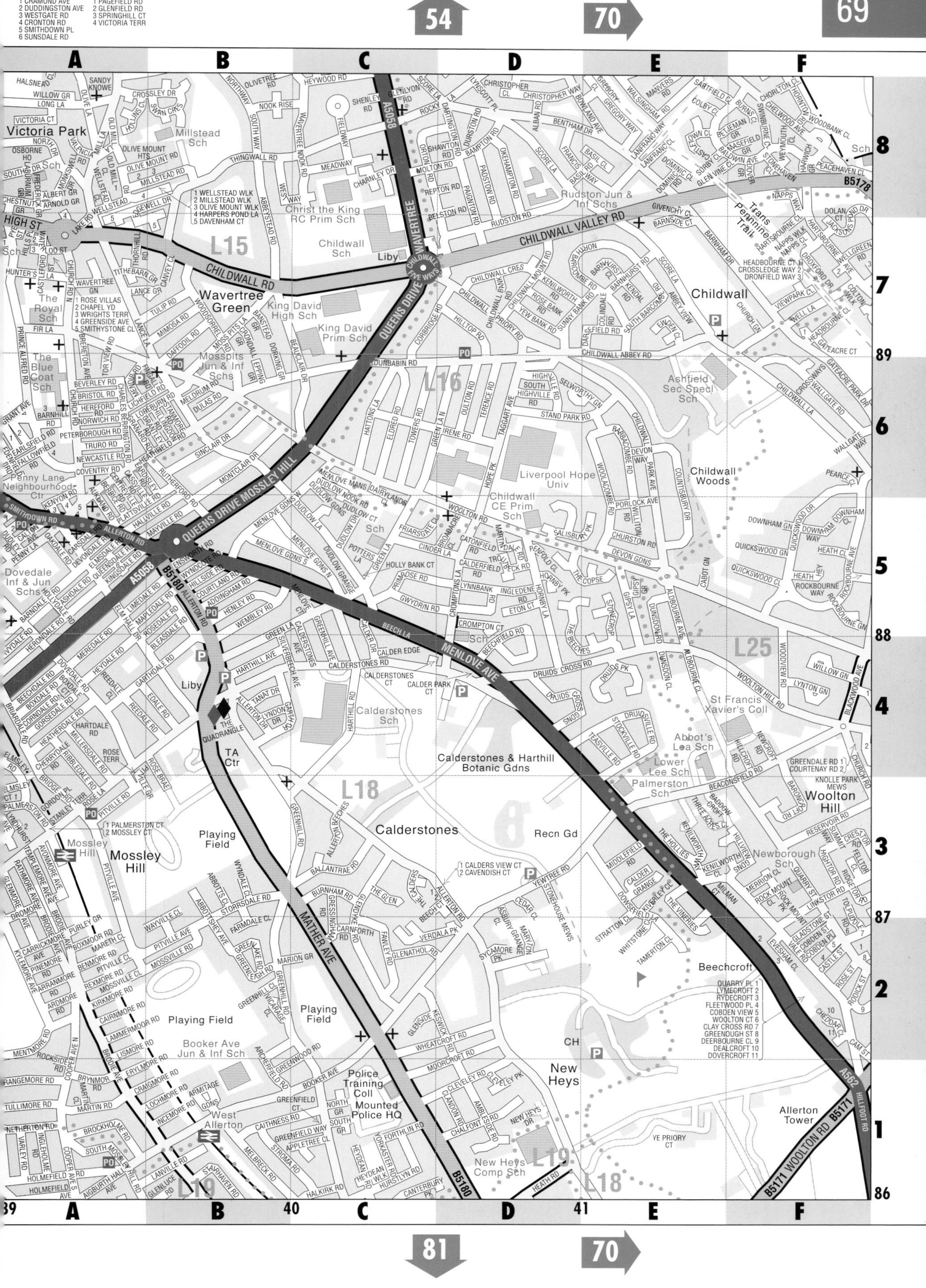
A5
1 CRAMOND AVE
2 DUDDINGSTON AVE
3 WESTGATE RD
4 CRONTON RD
5 SMITHDOWN PL
6 SUNSDALE RD
A6
1 PAGEFIELD RD
2 GLENFIELD RD
3 SPRINGHILL CT
4 VICTORIA TERR
54
70
A B C D E F
8 89 6 5 88 4 3 87 2 1 86
39 40 41
81
70
Victoria Park
Millstead Sch
Christ the King RC Prim Sch
Childwall Sch
Rudston Jun & Inf Schs
L15
CHILDWALL RD
CHILDWALL VALLEY RD
Wavertree Green
King David High Sch
King David Prim Sch
The Royal Sch
The Blue Coat Sch
Mosspits Jun & Inf Schs
L16
Childwall
Ashfield Sec Specl Sch
Liverpool Hope Univ
Childwall CE Prim Sch
Childwall Woods
Penny Lane Neighbourhood Ctr
QUEENS DRIVE MOSSLEY HILL
QUEENS DRIVE WAVERTREE
Dovedale Inf & Jun Schs
MENLOVE AVE
L25
Calderstones Sch
St Francis Xavier's Coll
Abbot's Lea Sch
Lower Lee Sch
Palmerston Sch
Calderstones & Harthill Botanic Gdns
L18
Woolton Hill
TA Ctr
Mossley Hill
Playing Field
Calderstones
Recn Gd
Newborough Sch
MATHER AVE
Beechcroft
QUARRY PL 1
LYMECROFT 2
RYDECROFT 3
FLEETWOOD PL 4
COBDEN VIEW 5
WOOLTON CT 6
CLAY CROSS RD 7
GREENOUGH ST 8
DEERBOURNE CL 9
DEALCROFT 10
DOVECROFT 11
Booker Ave Jun & Inf Sch
Police Training Coll
Mounted Police HQ
New Heys
New Heys Comp Sch
West Allerton
Allerton Tower
L19
B5171 WOOLTON RD
A562

69 55

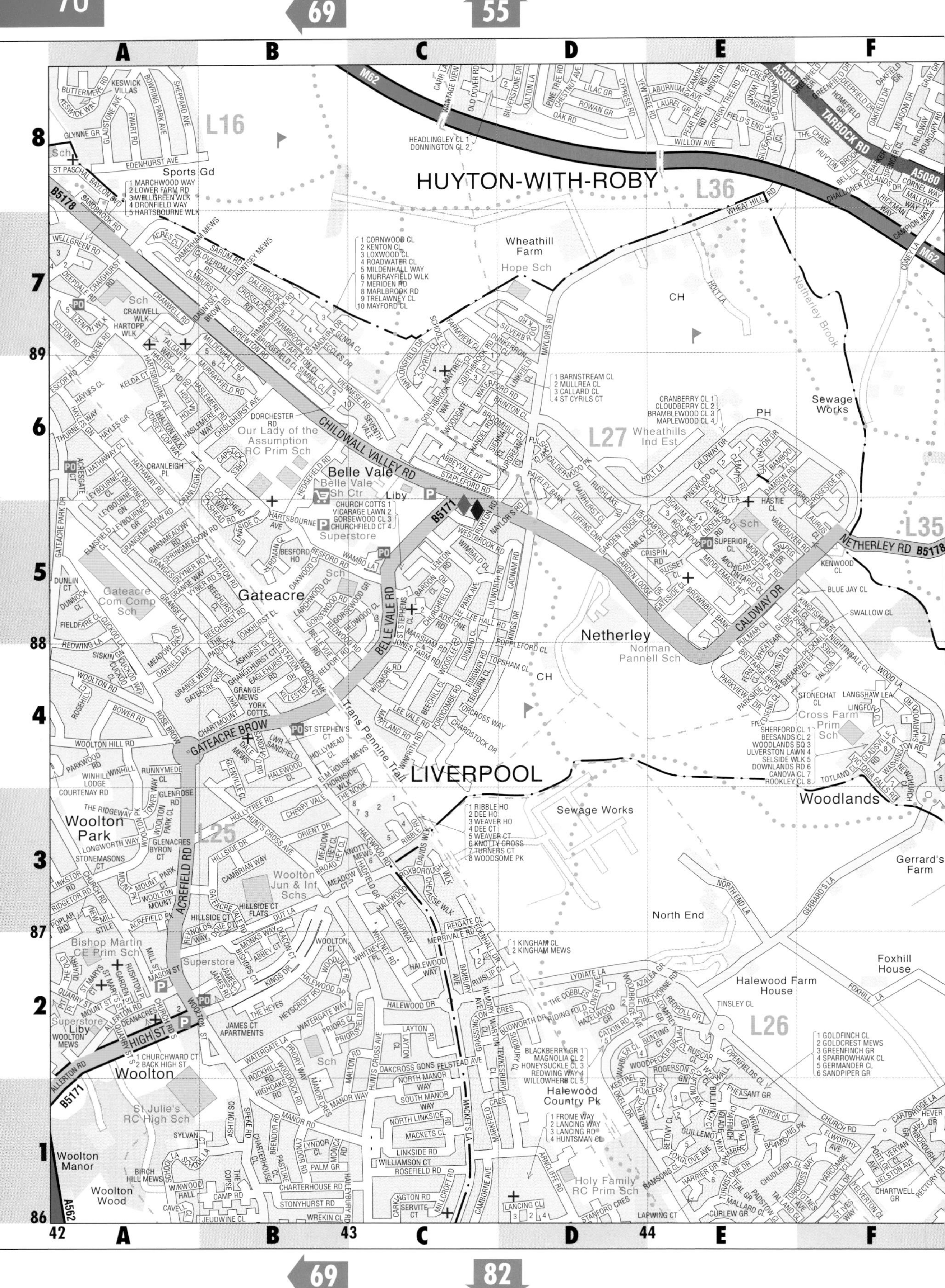
A B C D E F
8
7
89
6
5
88
4
3
87
2
1
86
42
43
44
HUYTON-WITH-ROBY
L16
L36
L27
L35
L25
L26
M62
A5080
B5178
B5171
A562
TARBOCK RD
Sports Gd
1 MARCHWOOD WAY
2 LOWER FARM RD
3 WELLGREEN WLK
4 DRONFIELD WAY
5 HARTSBOURNE WLK
HEADLINGLEY CL 1
DONNINGTON CL 2
1 CORNWOOD CL
2 KENTON CL
3 LOXWOOD CL
4 ROADWATER CL
5 MILDENHALL WAY
6 MURRAYFIELD WLK
7 MERIDEN RD
8 MARLBROOK RD
9 TRELAWNEY CL
10 MAYFORD CL
Wheathill Farm
Hope Sch
CH
Netherley Brook
Sewage Works
1 BARNSTREAM CL
2 MULLREA CL
3 CALLARD CL
4 ST CYRILS CT
CRANBERRY CL 1
CLOUDBERRY CL 2
BRAMBLEWOOD CL 3
MAPLEWOOD CL 4
PH
Wheathills Ind Est
Our Lady of the Assumption RC Prim Sch
CHILDWALL VALLEY RD
Belle Vale
Belle Vale Sh Ctr
Liby
CHURCH COTTS 1
VICARAGE LAWN 2
GORSEWOOD CL 3
CHURCHFIELD CT 4
Superstore
NETHERLEY RD
CALDWAY DR
Gateacre
Gateacre Com Comp Sch
BELLE VALE RD
Netherley
Norman Pannell Sch
BLUE JAY CL
SWALLOW CL
GATEACRE BROW
Trans Pennine Trail
LIVERPOOL
STONECHAT CL
LANGSHAW LEA
Cross Farm Prim Sch
SHERFORD CL 1
BEESANDS CL 2
WOODLANDS SQ 3
ULVERSTON LAWN 4
SELSIDE WLK 5
DOWNLANDS RD 6
CANOVA CL 7
ROOKLEY CL 8
Woodlands
1 RIBBLE HO
2 DEE HO
3 WEAVER HO
4 DEE CT
5 WEAVER CT
6 KNOTTY CROSS
7 TURNERS CT
8 WOODSOME PK
Sewage Works
Woolton Park
Woolton Jun & Inf Schs
Gerrard's Farm
North End
ACREFIELD RD
Bishop Martin CE Prim Sch
1 KINGHAM CL
2 KINGHAM MEWS
Foxhill House
Halewood Farm House
Superstore
Liby
HIGH ST
1 CHURCHWARD CT
2 BACK HIGH ST
Woolton
1 GOLDFINCH CL
2 GOLDCREST MEWS
3 GREENFINCH GR
4 SPARROWHAWK CL
5 GERMANDER CL
6 SANDPIPER GR
BLACKBERRY GR 1
MAGNOLIA CL 2
HONEYSUCKLE CL 3
REDWING WAY 4
WILLOWHERB CL 5
Halewood Country Pk
St Julie's RC High Sch
1 FROME WAY
2 LANCING WAY
3 LANCING RD
4 HUNTSMAN CL
Woolton Manor
Woolton Wood
Holy Family RC Prim Sch
MACKETS LA
HALEWOOD DR

69 82

56
72
A
B
C
D
E
F
Interchange Motorway Est
1 CONEY LA
2 BOUNDARY WLK
3 CARNABY CL
4 WARKWORTH CL
Warehouse
Windy Arbor
Hotel
Round Clump
Big Water
ORCHARD GDNS
WOODEND
LAKE VIEW
MAIN FRONT 1
OLD HALL 2
SOUTH FRONT 3
Caravan Park
Halsnead Park
L36
Works
Whitefield Lane End
PH
Huyton Bsns Pk
TARBOCK RD
CRONTON RD
A5080
M57
A5300
M62
Old Halsnead
SHAW ENTRY
FOX'S BANK LA
COPPICE LA
SEVENOAK GR
WILSON RD
STRETTON WAY
FALLOWS WAY
WINDY ARBOR RD
WINDY ARBOR BROW
SIMONS CL
WINDY ARBOR CL
EDINBURGH DR
ALDER AVE
COWPER WAY
SCOTT AVE
TENNYSON RD
KIPLING AVE
ELIZABETH RD
DARWICK DR
BOUNDARY RD
MANLEY RD
LOGWOOD RD
HASTINGS DR
NEWSHAM RD
BRIDGEWATER WAY
BRADLEY FOLD
BARDLEY CRES
HAWKE GN
OAKWORTH DR
RICHMOND WAY
MELLOR CL
RIBCHESTER WAY
ROSCOE CL
SMITHFORD WLK
CRONTON RD
DACRE'S BRIDGE LA
PENNY LA
Higher Park Farm
A5080
WHITEFIELD LA
OX LA
Ochre Brook
Yew Tree Farm
Yew Tree Farm
White House Farm
PRESCOT RD
Tarbock Hall
Mill Bridge
L35
Water Lane Farm
Four Oaks
Wayside Farm
WATER LA
Mill Brook
Mill Bridge Farm
1 EGREMONT LAWN
2 EGREMONT CL
3 KIRKBRIDE WLK
4 KIRKBRIDE LAWN
5 HEALY CL
6 WOODLANDS SQ
7 SELSIDE LAWN
8 APPLEBY WLK
9 APPLEBY LAWN
Water Lane Bridge
KNOWSLEY EXPRESSWAY
Dog Clog Brook
ALDER LA
Dog Clog Bridge
Brewery Farm
Marklands Farm
Dale Farm
STOCKSWELL RD
Stockswell Farm
10 HEYSHAM LAWN
11 MARDALE LAWN
12 MARDALE WLK
13 MARDALE CL
14 LAKESIDE LAWN
15 RIDSDALE LAWN
16 HONISTER WLK
17 SCAFELL LAWN
Brick Wall Inn (PH)
NETHERLEY RD
Tarbock Green
WA8
CROSS HILLOCKS LA
Georgeson's Farm
L27
Netherley Brook
Dye House Farm
Green's Bridge Farm
Barn Hey Farm
Foxhill Farm
L26
GREENSBRIDGE LA
Cross Hillocks Farm
B5178
Plumptons Farm
CARTBRIDGE LA
Bridgefield Forum (L Ctr)
Green's Bridge Plantation
APPLEWOOD CT
REDOAKS WAY
Ditton Brook
GARNETTS LA
Spring Farm
A1
1 ABINGDON GR
2 AMBASSADOR DR
3 HARESFINCH CL
4 WILLIAMSON CT
PH
Prim Sch
CHURCH RD
Springfield Farm
A5300
8
7
89
6
5
88
4
3
87
2
1
86
46
47
83
72

71
57

A B C D E F
8
7
89
6
5
88
4
3
87
2
1
86
48 49 50
L35
WA8
Mill Wood
M62
A57
WARRINGTON RD A57
WATKINSON WAY A557
Sandhill Farm
Higher Shaw Farm
Rough Head
Cronton Wood
Fox's Bank Brook
Pex Hill Visitor Ctr
Pex Hill
Town End
Penny Lane Farm
A5080
Nursery
Mast
Cronton Farm
Holy Family RC Prim Sch
Cronton CE Prim Sch
Nicolford Hall
Hotel
CRONTON LA
CRONTON RD
Cronton
Smaller Gorse Farm
Caxton Lodge
Upton Rocks
Rose Farm
Holly Farm
Upton
Stock's Well House
All Saints Upton CE Prim Sch
St Basil's RC Prim Sch
Hough Green
Rugby Football Ground
WIDNES
Ball o' Ditton
Saints Peter & Paul RC High Sch
The Bankfield Sch
Ditton CE Prim Sch
LIVERPOOL RD
Ditton Prim Sch
Ashley Sch
Chestnut Lodge Specl Sch
B5178 NETHERLEY RD
WARRINGTON RD 1
LOYOLA HEY 2
NORLAND'S LA 3
CRONTON FARM CT 1
STOCKWELL FARM CT 2
HOLLY FARM CT 3
ROSEWOOD FARM CT 4
BELLFLOWER CL 5
HAREBELL CL 6
DARLEY CL 1
BROXTON CL 2
FENTON CL 3
CAXTON CL 4
MADELINE McKENNA CT 5
BUCHANAN CL 1
FILLMORE GR 2
WASHINGTON CL 3
JEFFERSON GDNS 4
TRUMAN CL 5
1 ST THOMAS TERR
2 ST THOMAS CT
1 CHESTNUT CT
2 ELIZABETH TERR
3 VERONICA MEWS
NEW BANK PL 1
MANOR PL 2
KENDAL RD 1
LUNE WAY 2
DERWENT RD 3

71
84

8

7

89

6

5

88

4

87

2

1

86

A1
1 CLAYTON CRES
2 HENDERSON RD
3 SQUIRES AVE
4 BRUNNER RD
5 MOND RD

B1
1 ALBERT SQ
2 ALBERT RD
3 BROOK ST
4 SAXON TERR

B2
1 HAWTHORN AVE
2 WILLOW AVE
3 LIME AVE
4 PINE AVE
5 MAPLE AVE
6 PLUMPTON CROSS

C1
1 PARR ST
2 RUNNYMEDE CT
3 CLIFFE ST
4 HENRY ST
5 RUNNYMEDE GDNS

C2
1 BROOKLANDS PK
2 KNOWLES ST
3 RUNNYMEDE WLK

D1
1 ASHFORD WAY
2 MELVILLE CL
3 KINGHAM CL
4 WILSON CL
5 HARGREAVES HO

73
59

WARRINGTON
WA8
WA5
WA4
Lingley Green
Penketh
Cuerdley Cross
Lingley Mere
Lingley Mere Bsns Pk
Finch's Plantation
Eccles Plantation
South Park Plantation
Park Farm
Bargyloo
Dawson House
Hayfield Farm
The Trigger Pond (PH)
Greenside Farm
Laburnum Farm
Sandy Lane Farm
Camp (dis)
Four Top'd Oak
Brook Farm
Doe Green
Fowl Farm
Cross Lane Farm Cottages
Newspaper House
Marsh End Farm
Power Station
River Mersey
Ferry Inn (PH)
Swing Bridge
Riverside Trad Est
Fiddler's Ferry
Trans Pennine Trail
St Helens Canal (disused)
Great Sankey High Sch
Barrow Hall Com Prim Sch
Brow Farm
Park Road Com Prim Sch
Penketh Com Prim Sch
St Vincent's RC Prim Sch
Penketh South Com Prim Sch
Recn Gd
L Ctr
Liby
A57
WARRINGTON RD
LIVERPOOL RD
A5080
SOUTH LA
FARNWORTH RD
A562
WIDNES RD
MOWCROFT LA
SANDY LA
LABURNUM LA
MARSH LA
Cheshire STREET ATLAS

63
76

A
B
C
D
E
F
Marine Lake
Tell's Tower
Avalon Sch
Caldy Hill
Fleck La
Stapledon Wood
Caldy
CH48
Caldy Blacks
Wirral Country Park
Wirral Way
CH
CH61
Shore Cottage
Visitor Ctr
River Dee/Afon Dyfrdwy
B5141
B5140
A540
CALDY RD
COLUMN RD
TELEGRAPH RD
MONTGOMERY HILL
PIKES HEY RD
EAST FARM MEWS
GRANGE CROSS HEY
BOUNDARY RD
FLECK LA
1 STONEHEY DR
2 NORFOLK DR
SURREY DR
KIRBY MOUNT
WARWICK DR
RAMSEY CT
YORK AVE
HILBRE CT
BANKS RD
SOUTH PAR
SANDY LA
RIVERSIDE
HEADLAND CL
MACDONA DR
BEACH WLK
HEATH CL
WORDSWORTH WLK
SHELLEY WAY
CARISBROOKE CL
MELLONCROFT DR
MELLONCROFT DR W
THORSWAY
KING'S DR
CALDY MEWS
CALDY WOOD
THE GREEN
CALDY CHASE DR
LONG HEY RD
CROFT DR W
CROFT DR
CROFT DR E
SHORE RD
BEATTY CL
DAVENPORT CL
ASHMORE CL
CUNNINGHAM CL
JELLICOE CL
MILL HEY RD
RUBBING STONE
BARTON HEY DR
WESTWARD HO
BADGER'S SET
THE FINNEY
SIMONSBRIDGE
THE STEEPLE
THE FAIRWAYS
PARKDALE
MEREWORTH
HEATHERLEIGH
LINKS HEY RD
STATION RD
8
7
85
6
5
84
4
3
83
2
1
82
22
23

76

75
64

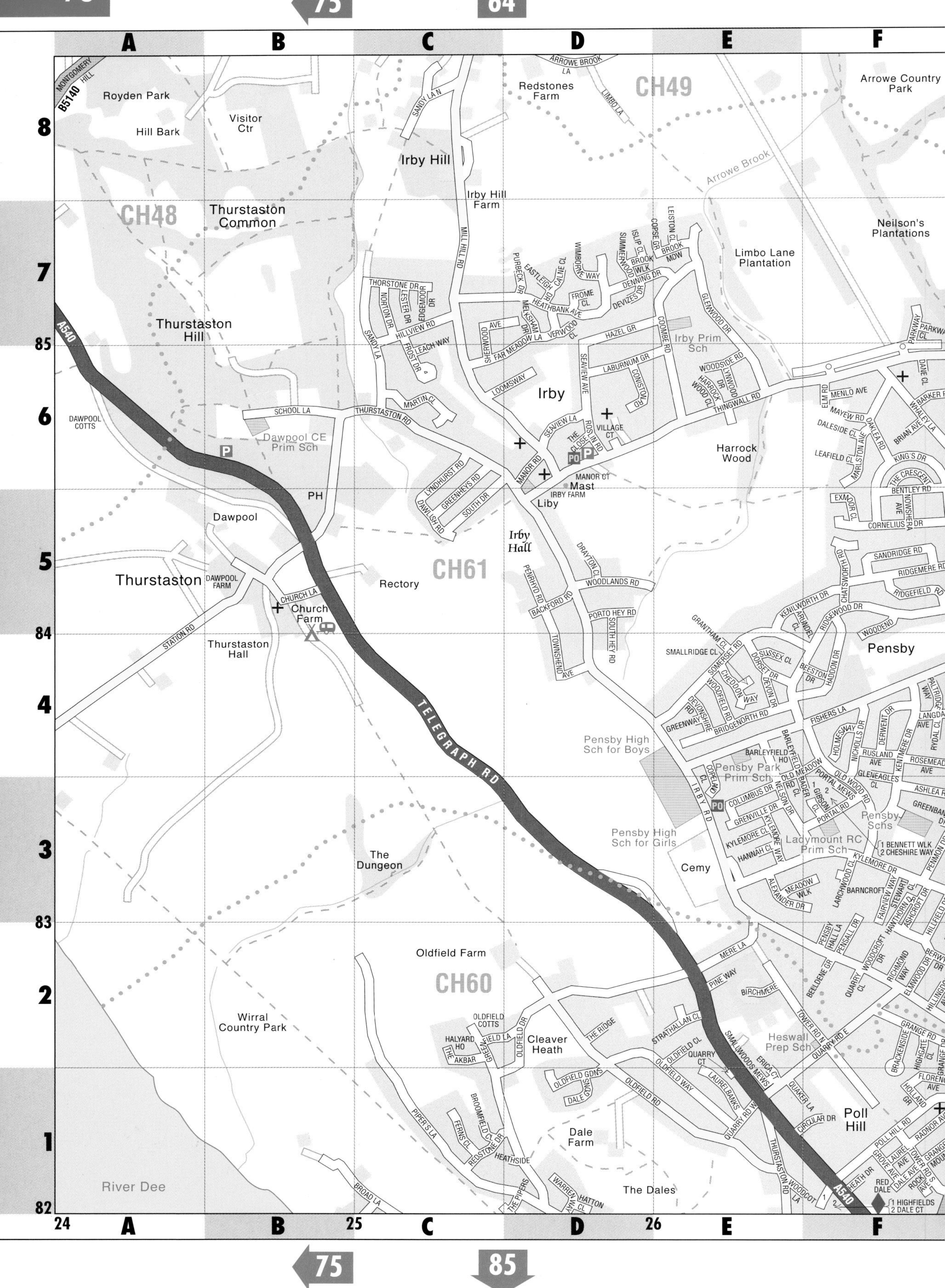
A
B
C
D
E
F
8
7
85
6
5
84
4
3
83
2
1
82
24
25
26
Royden Park
Hill Bark
Visitor Ctr
Redstones Farm
CH49
Arrowe Country Park
Irby Hill
Arrowe Brook
CH48
Thurstaston Common
Irby Hill Farm
Neilson's Plantations
Limbo Lane Plantation
Thurstaston Hill
A540
Irby
Irby Prim Sch
DAWPOOL COTTS
SCHOOL LA
THURSTASTON RD
Dawpool CE Prim Sch
VILLAGE CT
Harrock Wood
MANOR CT
Mast
IRBY FARM
Liby
PH
Dawpool
Irby Hall
CH61
Thurstaston
DAWPOOL FARM
Rectory
CHURCH LA
Church Farm
STATION RD
Thurstaston Hall
Pensby
TELEGRAPH RD
Pensby High Sch for Boys
Pensby Park Prim Sch
Pensby Schs
Pensby High Sch for Girls
Ladymount RC Prim Sch
The Dungeon
Cemy
Oldfield Farm
CH60
Wirral Country Park
OLDFIELD COTTS
HALYARD HO
Cleaver Heath
Heswall Prep Sch
Poll Hill
Dale Farm
River Dee
The Dales
1 HIGHFIELDS
2 DALE CT
1 BENNETT WLK
2 CHESHIRE WAY

75
85

A
B
C
D
E
F
8
7
85
6
5
84
4
3
83
2
1
82
27
28
29
Crem
Cemy
CH
PH
A551
ARROWE PARK RD
Home Farm
Landican
LANDICAN LA
CH49
Old Hall Farm
LANDICAN RD
North Cheshire Trad Est
M53
BROOK WAY
BADGER WAY
PARKVALE AVE
PRENTON WAY
DURLEY PARK CL
CH43
BYRON CL
GARRICK RD
PRENTON DELL RD
RICHMOND WAY
B5138
THINGWALL RD E
HAZELDENE WAY
The Farm
Caravan Park
Cow Hey Covert
Thingwall Prim Sch
Stanley Sch
MANOR PARK CL
HEYWOOD CL
HEYWOOD BLVD
THINGWALL DR
TORRINGTON DR
HAZELDENE AVE
TORRINGTON GDNS
THINGWALL GRANGE
GALLOPERS LA
BEVERLEY GDNS
BEAUMARIS DR
MILL RD
MILL YD
THE FOXES
HOWARDS RD
NURSE RD
CLEMERE DR
MILTON GN
SPARKS LA
TURMAR AVE
THE LEAS
PH
Stanley Wood
M53
CH63
PENRHYN AVE
AMBLESIDE CL
ANDERSON CL
HEATHFIELD RD
PO
Liby
QUARRY LA
REGENTS CL
BARNSDALE AVE
Murrayfield
Prenton Brook
AXHOLME RD
AXHOLME CL
SEVEN ACRES LA
WIMBOURNE AVE
LYNDHURST CL
CORNELIUS DR
PENSBY CL
ELMS PK
CESTRIAN DR
HESWALL MOUNT
GWENDOLINE CL
Thingwall
RYLAND PK
LOWER THINGWALL LA
HOLMWOOD AVE
Cross Hill
HOLMWOOD DR
CH61
Mast
STATION RD
PRIVATE DR
OVERDALE AVE
NORTHRIDGE RD
SOUTHRIDGE RD
RIDGEWOOD DR
SUNNINGDALE DR
DALE VIEW CL
THORNCROFT DR
LOW WOOD GR
WOODLANDS DR
DALE END RD
FISHERS LA
BEECH AVE
MARLFIELD LA
GILLS LA
New Hay Covert
LAURELHURST AVE
1 SHEARMAN CL
2 SHEARMAN RD
3 CHRISTOPHERS CL
PENSBY RD
FENDER WAY
MARKSWAY
Tree Tops
BARNSTON RD
STORETON LA
OAKS LA
Ley Farm
ROSEMEAD AVE
BELMONT DR
ASHLEA RD
Beech Farm
Bank Farm
Barnston
GREENBANK DR
KINGSLEY CL
HILLFIELD DR
LYNDHURST AVE
KYLEMORE DR
Manor Farm
Carnsdale Farm
NAPPS WAY
DOWNHAM RD N
Greenhayes Cottages
RAVENSWOOD RD
OAKLANDS TERR
OAKLANDS DR
CH63
1 MARANATHA BGLWS
2 ROSE BRAE CT
3 CONSTANTINE AVE
RABY CT
Heswall Prim Sch
WHITFIELD LA
HESWALL
CH60
BRUNSTATH CL
WHITEHOUSE LA
Whitehouse Farm
Fairfield
The Brooklet
A5137
BENT WAY
SANDY LA
HEATHER RD
SHREWSBURY RD
HESKETH DR
DOWNHAM RD S
GORSEHILL RD
MILTON CRES
FOREST RD
Whitfield Common
BRIARY CL
MILNER RD
BUFFS LA
PARK RD
PINE RD
MAPLE TREE GR
A551
PEAR TREE CL
ACRE LA
FIELDWAY
MEADOWCROFT
BROOKLET RD
BARCOMBE RD
NORTHWAY
Dunster House
BRIMSTAGE RD
MANOR RD
EPPING CT
B5138

77
66

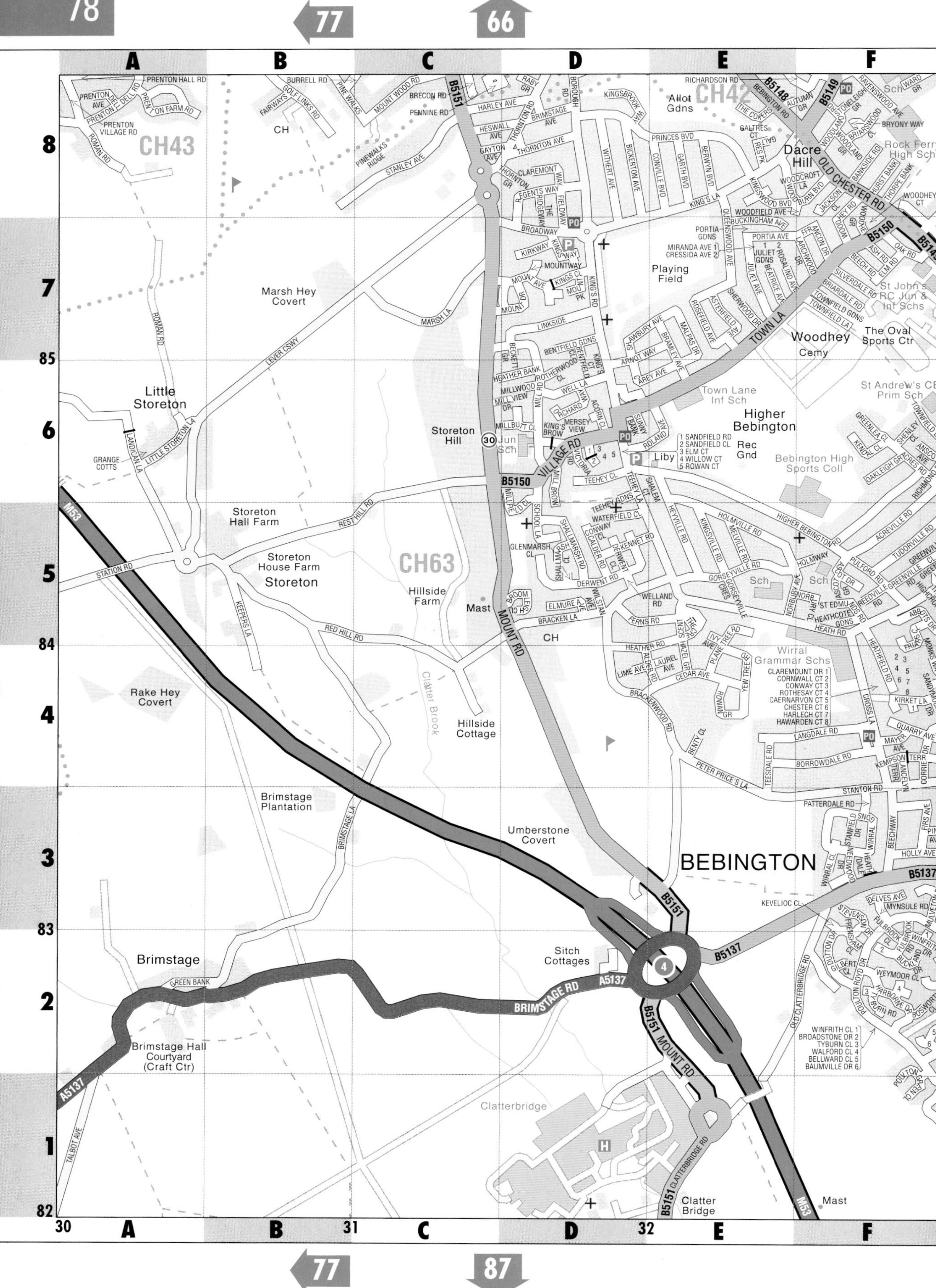
A
B
C
D
E
F
8
7
85
6
5
84
4
3
83
2
1
82
30
31
32
CH43
CH42
CH63
PRENTON HALL RD
PRENTON VILLAGE RD
ROMAN RD
BURRELL RD
GOLF LINKS RD
FAIRWAYS
PINE WALKS
MOUNT WOOD RD
BRECON RD
PENNINE RD
PINEWALKS RIDGE
STANLEY AVE
B5151
HARLEY AVE
HESWALL AVE
GAYTON AVE
THORNTON AVE
BRIMSTAGE AVE
CLAREMONT WAY
REGENTS WAY
BROADWAY
FIELDWAY
KIRKWAY
KINGS WAY
MOUNTWAY
KINGS CL
LINKSIDE
BENTFIELD GDNS
HEATHER BANK
ROTHERWOOD CL
MILLWOOD
MILL VIEW DR
WELL LA
RICHARD AVE
MERSEY VIEW
MILL RD
KING'S RD
KING'S BROW
VILLAGE RD
B5150
TEEHEY CL
TEEHEY GDNS
WATERFIELD CL
SCHOOL LA
GLENMARSH CL
SHALLMARSH RD
CALDER RD
DERWENT RD
KENNET RD
ELMURE AVE
WILSTAN AVE
BRACKEN LA
MOUNT RD
KINGSBROOK WAY
WITHERT AVE
BICKERTON AVE
CONVILLE BVD
GARTH BVD
BERWYN BVD
PRINCES BVD
KING'S LA
RICHARDSON RD
Allot Gdns
B5148
BEBINGTON RD
AUTUMN GR
B5149
Dacre Hill
OLD CHESTER RD
WOODCROFT LA
KINGSWOOD BVD
WOODFIELD AVE
BUCKINGHAM AVE
PORTIA GDNS
PORTIA AVE
MIRANDA AVE
CRESSIDA AVE
JULIET GDNS
JULIET AVE
QUEENSWOOD AVE
Playing Field
ROSEFIELD AVE
MALPAS DR
BRAMLEY AVE
AWBURY AVE
ARNOT WAY
AREY AVE
TOWN LA
Town Lane Inf Sch
Higher Bebington
SUNNY BANK
ROLAND AVE
1 SANDFIELD RD
2 SANDFIELD CL
3 ELM CT
4 WILLOW CT
5 ROWAN CT
Liby
Rec Gnd
Bebington High Sports Coll
Woodhey Cemy
The Oval Sports Ctr
St John's RC Jun & Inf Schs
St Andrew's CE Prim Sch
Rock Ferry High Sch
HEYVILLE RD
KINGSVILLE RD
MELVILLE RD
HOLMVILLE RD
GORSEVILLE RD
HIGHER BEBINGTON RD
HOLMWAY
Sch
ST EDMUNDS RD
HEATHCOTE GDNS
HEATH RD
WELLAND RD
FERNS RD
HEATHER RD
LIME AVE
LAUREL AVE
CEDAR AVE
BRACKENWOOD RD
Wirral Grammar Schs
CLAREMOUNT DR 1
CORNWALL CT 2
CONWAY CT 3
ROTHESAY CT 4
CAERNARVON CT 5
CHESTER CT 6
HARLECH CT 7
HAWARDEN CT 8
LANGDALE RD
BORROWDALE RD
PETER PRICE'S LA
STANTON RD
PATTERDALE RD
BENTY CL
KIRKET LA
QUARRY AVE
CROSS LA
HEATHFIELD RD
BEBINGTON
B5137
KEVELIOC CL
DELVES AVE
MYNSULE RD
WEYMOOR CL
WINFRITH CL 1
BROADSTONE DR 2
TYBURN CL 3
WALFORD CL 4
BELLWARD CL 5
BAUMVILLE DR 6
OLD CLATTERBRIDGE RD
POULTON ROYD DR
Little Storeton
LANDICAN LA
LITTLE STORETON LA
GRANGE COTTS
LEVER CSWY
Marsh Hey Covert
MARSH LA
Storeton Hill
Jun Sch
Storeton Hall Farm
REST HILL RD
STATION RD
Storeton House Farm
Storeton
KEEPERS LA
RED HILL RD
Hillside Farm
Mast
CH
Clatter Brook
Hillside Cottage
Rake Hey Covert
M53
Brimstage Plantation
BRIMSTAGE LA
Umberstone Covert
Brimstage
GREEN BANK
BRIMSTAGE RD
A5137
Sitch Cottages
Brimstage Hall Courtyard (Craft Ctr)
Clatterbridge
CLATTERBRIDGE RD
Clatter Bridge
TALBOT AVE

B6
1 ELMBANK RD
2 WILLOWBANK RD
3 ST MICHAEL'S PK
4 PHILIP LEVERHULME LODGE
5 MANOR LODGE
6 SUNLIGHT LODGE

A B C D E F

8

7

85

6

CH42

River Mersey

New Ferry

Bebington

1 BROWNLOW RD
2 WINSTANLEY HO
3 MAYFIELDS HO
4 SHOREFIELDS HO
5 UNDERLEY TERR

1 PORTBURY CL
2 PORTBURY WAY
3 PORTBURY WLK

Art Gall

DUKE OF YORK COTTS

Mus

Sch

Works

Bromborough Pool

Factory

1 APSLEY GR
2 WELLESLEY GR
3 WELLINGTON CL

THE CAUSEWAY

Lower Bebington

York St

Manor Pl

South View

The Green

5

Poets Cnr

Port Sunlight

Liby

TH

THE VILLAGE

Church Farm

Port Sunlight

84

Old Court House Rd

Dock Rd S

CH62

Collingwood Rd

Works

Works

4

CH63

Port Cswy

Northways

Fairway

Crossways

Greenway

Wirral International Bsns Pk

Georgia Ave

Ringways

3

Riverbank Rd

Thermal Rd

Coronation Rd

40

Magazine Rd

Magazine Wlk

South Wirral Ret Pk

Wirral L Pk

Commercial Rd

BRIMSTAGE RD

P&R

Spital

Spital Heyes

Spital

83

Works

Works

2

Poulton

1 BURDETT CL
2 HOCKENHULL CL
3 HARRIS CL
4 BURDETT AVE
5 LANGLEY CL

Woods-Lee Cotts

Woodslee Prim Sch

Croft Bsns Pk

Mosedale Rd

Caldbeck Rd

Lumina

Mast

Croft Bsns Pk

Plantation Bsns Pk

1

Bromborough

The Cross

The Precinct

Mast

Apex Ct

Brunel Rd

Old Hall Rd

82

33 A B 34 C D 35 E F

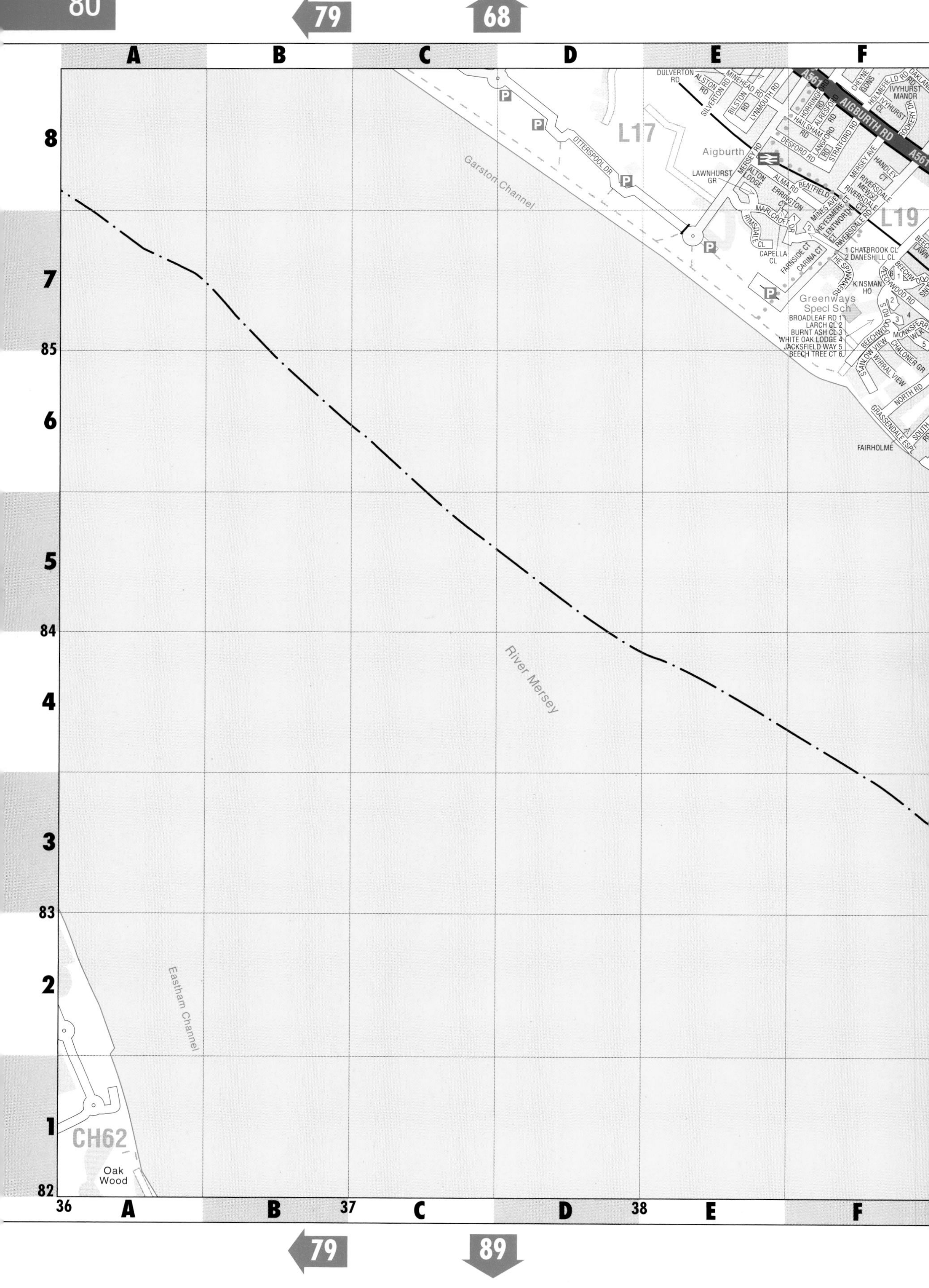

A B C D E F

8

L17

Garston Channel

Otterspool Dr

Aigburth

DULVERTON RD
ALSTON RD
SILVERTON RD
BILSTON RD
MINEHEAD RD
LYMOUTH RD
HALSHAM RD
LANFORD RD
STRATFORD RD
DESFORD RD
ALMA RD
BENTFIELD
MINNS AVE
ERRINGTON
LEWTMORE CL
LETTWORTH
IMMERDALE
RINSCALE CL
CAPELLA CL
CARINA CT
MARLCROFT RD
FARNSIDE CT
THE SPINNEY
MERSEY AVE
RIVERSDALE
HANDLEY CT
RIVERSDALE MEWS

AIGBURTH RD
A561
A561

CHEYNE GDNS
SPRING GR
HOLMEFIELD LD
HOLMEFIELD RD
OAKLAND
IVYHURST MANOR

L19

LAWNHURST
GR
LAWNHURST
LODGE

BEECH LAWN
BEECHWOOD RD
LINNET WOOD RD

Greenways
Specl Sch
BROADLEAF RD 1
LARCH CL 2
BURNT ASH CL 3
WHITE OAK LODGE 4
JACKSFIELD WAY 5
BEECH TREE CT 6
1 CHATBROOK CL
2 DANESHILL CL
KINSMAN HO

SANLOW VIEW
WIRRAL VIEW
MONKSFERRY
CHALONER GR

85

7

6

NORTH RD

GRASSENDALE ESP
SOUTH RD

FAIRHOLME

River Mersey

5

84

4

3

83

Eastham Channel

2

1

CH62

Oak
Wood

82

36 A B 37 C D 38 E F

A   B   C   D   E   F

DEE SIDE
TARGET RD
THE PIPERS
PIPER'S PK CL
PIPER'S CL
PIPER'S END
PIPER'S LA
PIPER'S LA
QUEENS DR
Sewage Works
Wirral Country Park
Heswall Dales
Dawstone CT
DALE CT
BROOMLANDS
Superstore
A540 TELEGRAPH RD
B5138
PENSBY RD
BROAD LA
BUSH WAY
QUEENS PK
FEATHER LA
FEATHER LA
CASTLE DR
PARKVIEW CT
BANKS RD
CROSSLEY DR
SANDFIELD DR
DALESWAY
PHILLIPS WAY DR
THURSTASTON RD
DIE VIEW RD
HIGH MOUNT
THE MOUNT AVE
P
MOSTYN AVE
CROFTSWAY
DELAVOR RD
DELAVOR CL
HAWTHORN COTTS
MOUNT MEWS
THE MOORINGS
TEALS WAY
HAWKS WAY
ROOKS WAY
HERBERTS RD
ROCKY LA
Sch
ROCKS WAY
FARR HALL RD
DAWSTONE RISE
DAWSTONE RD
P
WITTERING LA
BULLS WAY
LINNETS WAY
FARR HALL DR
HESWALL
FARR HALL DR
JANETS WAY
ST PETER'S CL
BROW LA
CHURCH FARM CT
THE RASCOT
DAVENPORT RD
RECTORY LA
MACKETS LA
RABY CL
TIVERTON CL
ROSCOTE CL
WALLRAKE
PARK W
BROMILEY CL
RECTORY CL
THE CLYDALE
HESSLE DR
MARINE DR
MANNERS LA
SCHOOL HILL
SCHOOL RD
STRANHEAT
SEAFIELD
HILL CL
HILLSIDE AVE
SEABANK RD
RONALDSWAY
STATION RD
GAYTON DR
LAPWING CL
CLOSEBURN AVE
WESTWAY
MEADOWAY
VICTORIA AVE
CH60
RIVERBANK CL
RIVERBANK RD
WOODBURN DR
HAVERTON DR
LONG MDW
P
LILLYFIELD
COTTAGE LA
COTTAGE DR W
COTTAGE DR E
Gayton Cott
Gayton Sands
River Dee/Afon Dyfrdwy
CH64

8
7
81
6
5
80
4
3
79
2
78

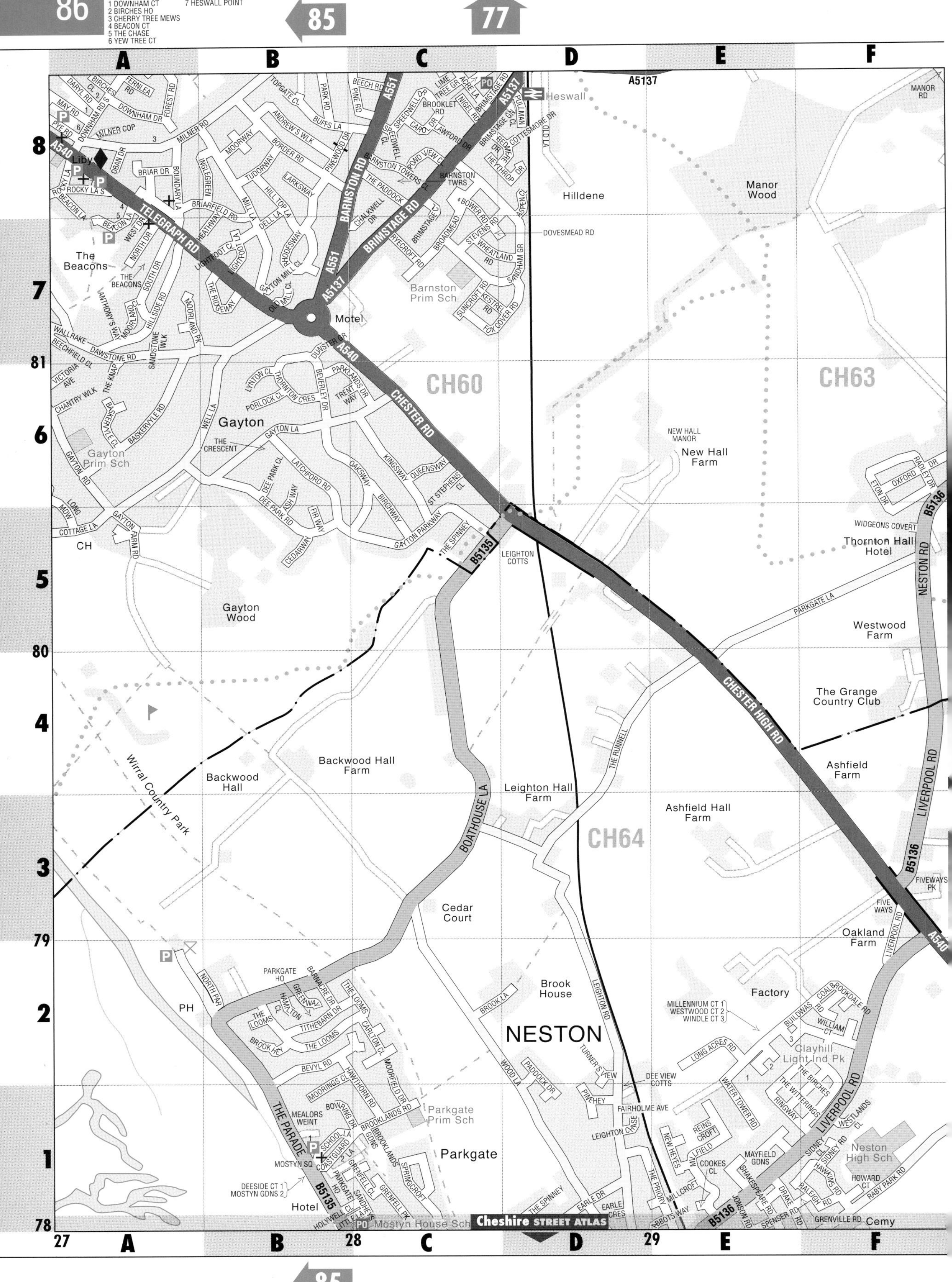

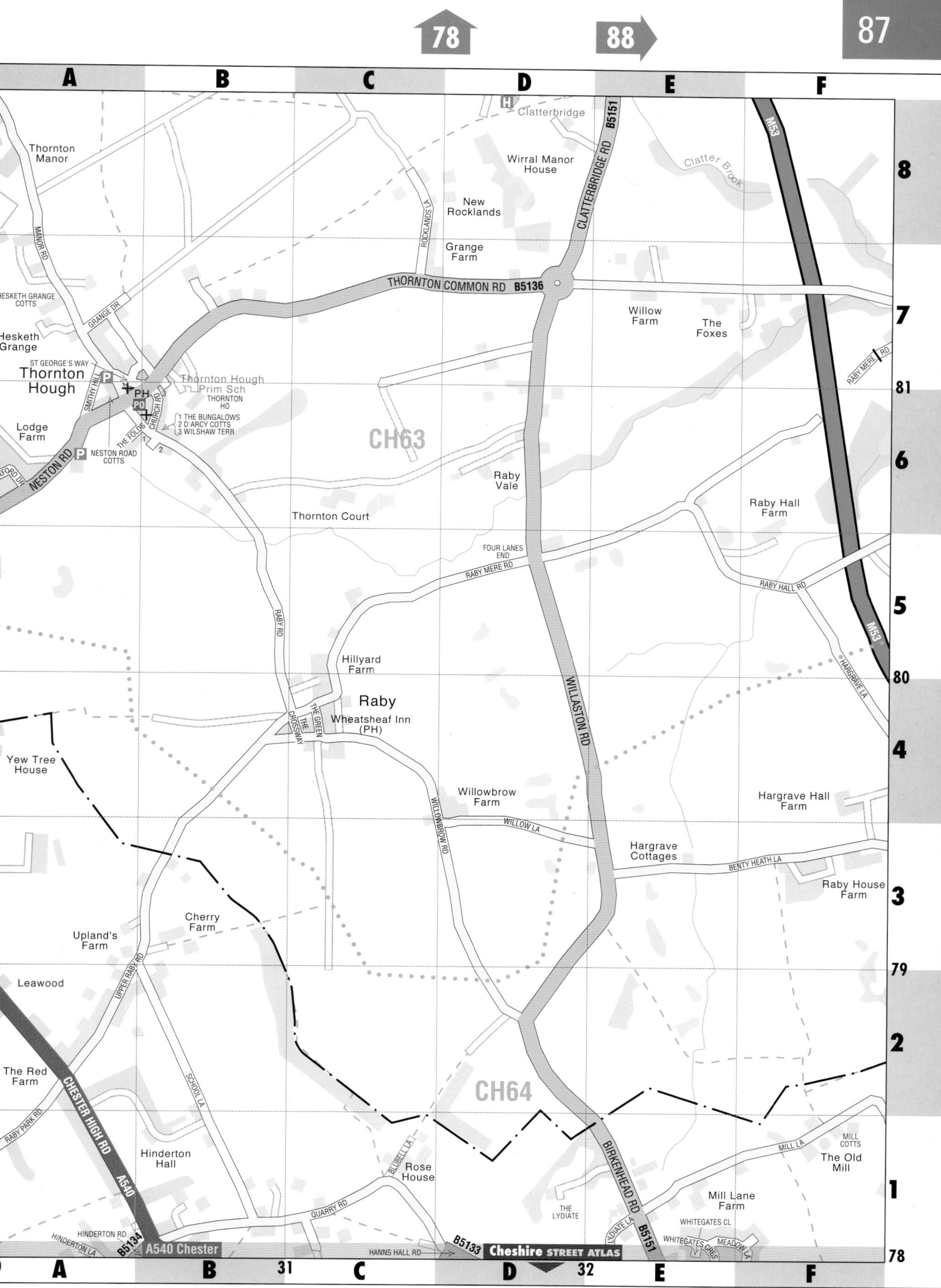

A   B   C   D   E   F

8

Thornton
Manor

Clatterbridge

Wirral Manor
House

Clatter Brook

M53

HESKETH GRANGE
COTTS

Hesketh
Grange

New
Rocklands

Grange
Farm

THORNTON COMMON RD   B5136

Willow
Farm

The
Foxes

RABY MERE RD

7

81

St George's Way
Thornton
Hough

P

PH
PO

Thornton Hough
Prim Sch
THORNTON
HO

CH63

1 THE BUNGALOWS
2 D'ARCY COTTS
3 WILSHAW TERR

Lodge
Farm

P

NESTON ROAD
COTTS

OXFORD RD

NESTON RD

Raby
Vale

Raby Hall
Farm

6

Thornton Court

FOUR LANES
END

RABY MERE RD

RABY HALL RD

HARGRAVE LA

80

RABY RD

Hillyard
Farm

5

Yew Tree
House

THE CROSSWAY

THE GREEN

Raby

Wheatsheaf Inn
(PH)

WILLASTON RD

Hargrave Hall
Farm

M53

4

Willowbrow
Farm

WILLOWBROW RD

WILLOW LA

Hargrave
Cottages

BENTY HEATH LA

Raby House
Farm

79

Upland's
Farm

Cherry
Farm

UPPER RABY RD

Leawood

3

The Red
Farm

RABY PARK RD

CHESTER HIGH RD

A540

SCHOOL LA

CH64

Hinderton
Hall

BIRKENHEAD RD

MILL LA

MILL
COTTS

The Old
Mill

2

Rose
House

BLUEBELL LA

B5151

Mill Lane
Farm

1

THE
LYDIATE

LYDIATE LA

WHITEGATES CRES

WHITEGATES CL

MEADOW LA

HINDERTON RD

B5134

QUARRY RD

A540 Chester

HANNS HALL RD

B5133

Cheshire STREET ATLAS

78

A B C D E F

8

7

81

6

5

80

4

3

79

2

1

78

Lancelyn Farm
The Vineyard Farm
Bromborough Rake
WOODLAND WLK 1
ECCLESTON AVE 2
HADLEY AVE 3
CHESTNUT GR
BROTHERTON CL
THE RAKE
PARK VIEW
THE OAKS
MANOR HO
BRADMOOR RD
Civic Hall Liby
PARKWOOD CL
HOWARD AVE
GRASSMOOR CL
Factory
HARDKNOTT RD
GARSDALE

Poulton Hall
POULTON HALL RD
POULTON RD
BEBINGTON
THORNTON COMMON RD
Clatter Brook
Raby Mere

MAPLE GR
BEECHWOOD DR
OAKFIELD RD
THE AVENUE
ASHFIELD RD
VALLEY RD
DALE RD
OTLEY AVE
MAINWARING RD
FOXWOOD RD
RONWOOD RD
HEYS AVE
ALLPORT LN
JUNE AVE
HARROW GR
CAMBRIDGE RD
NEVILLE RD
Mendell Prim Sch
A41
NEW CHESTER RD
WRYNOSE RD
TEBAY RD
Christ The King RC Prim Sch

KENYA CL
RUGABY CL
DIRMINGDALE RD
MEADOW RD
GREENACRE DR
GRENVILLE CRES
BLYTH RD
MARFORDS AVE
GREENFIELDS CRES
DAMFORD DR
GREENFIELDS AVE
CALDICOTT AVE
ACRE LA
MOSSLEY AVE
MEADOWSIDE RD
THE MEADOWS
GORDON AVE
ELYN AVE
AMBLESIDE CL
BRIDLE CL
OSBOURNE
WOODYEAR RD
Cemy

Raby Mere
Blakeley Dene
BLAKELEY CT
RABY PK
ORMESBY GR
BLAKELEY BROW
BLAKELEY DELL
CARYL CL
RABY AVE
LYNNS AVE
MERE AVE
RABY HALL RD
DIBBINS GN
MORE WAY
MAELOR CL
DELL
ALDFORD CL
Bromborough
MARTEN AVE
MARLINE AVE
P&R
BRUCE CRES
ANGUS RD
PLYMYARD CL
CROFT
THE WESTERINGS
LINEHURST
WOODCOTES
BROWNSBOROUGH
GREENWAYS CT
OAKLANDS
ANDERSON CT
MIDLAND AVE
Raeburn Prim Sch
WESTMINSTER RD
BRIQ
PK
PRINCES AVE
MANOR RD
KILBURN AVE
Pav
CH62
THE HEYS
PARK RD
RIBBLESDALE AVE

Raby Hall
CH63
CH
SOMERVILLE CL
BIRKDALE AVE
SUNNINGDALE DR
SANDIWAY
AINSDALE CL
BROOKHURST CL
COTTAGE CL
M CRES
Brookhurst Prim Sch
ALISTAIR DR
TAVENER CL
WESTHOUSE CL
DEARNFORD CL
SPRINGHILL
BRININGTON RD
BELTISFIELD AVE
DEARNFORD AVE
REDBROOK
WOODLEY
WHITE LODGE CL
EDGEWOOD DR
Heygarth Prim Sch
HEYGARTH RD
EDALE DR
RAEBURN AVE
ELGAR AVE
SWALEDALE AVE
WENSLEYDALE AVE
DOVEDALE AVE
DARLEYDALE DR
AVONDALE AVE
MALLOWDALE CL
CARLETT BVD
Eastham
WHARFEDALE AVE
MCLERGSAL
HANDFORD AVE
The Lyndale Sch
Liby
P
P

Brookhurst
BOWNESS AVE
KESWICK GDNS
CHINK AVE
CONISTON AVE
BROOKHURST AVE
KESWICK AVE
KINTORE
RHONE
TURRET DR
CULLEN CL
DUNCANSBY DR
NAIRN CL
TROON CL
FAIRHAVEN DR
WENTWORTH DR
THE CHASE
OAKWOOD PK
NORTREE AVE
OAKDENE CL
LANGFIELD
MILEY GR
WINGATE RD
HILLARY RD
HALEDENE CL
ATHOL CL
CHESTERFIELD RD
HARGATE
HARROGATE
GRAMPIAN WAY
SELGRA AVE
ANDREW CL
LYNDALE AVE
PAISLEY CL
GLENBURN AVE
BERWICK AVE
ADASTON CL
CRANFORD CL
Hargrave House Farm
Dibbinsdale Brook
KESWICK AVE
CHESTERFIELD RD
ARGYLL AVE
South Wirral High Sch
ROTHESAY DR
Millfields Prim Sch
ARCHERS
WILLINGTON AVE
DELAMERE CL
TARVIN RD
CRAIGLEIGH AVE
CROSTHWAITE
PICKMERE RD
DUNHAM CL
A41

M53
Hargrave House Farm
HARGRAVE LA
Eastham Rake
BOWELL CL
SCAFELL CL
AIRDRIE
EASTHAM RAKE
MARSH LN
PICTON CL
HATTON AVE
CLIFTON AVE
STRETTON
MILL PARK DR
HELSBY RD
P

Raby Nurseries
CH64
BENTY HEATH LA
PLINCE CL
STANLEY RD
KELSALL AVE
KELSALL AVE
KELGILL
THORNLEIGH
M53

Street Hey
STREET HEY LA
Nursery
Works
CH66
DALE HEY
Hooton Works
Railway Cotts
Hooton Bridge
Hooton Farm

Willaston
MILL LA
BRIARDALE RD
OVERDALE RD
STREET HEY LA
LAUREL DR
HAWTHORNE DR
FIELD HEY LA
BEECH HEY LA
KEELE HEY
CROSBY HEY
HEATH LA
Nursery
HOOTON RD
Hooton
Roften Ind Est
PH
OAK RD
WATERWORKS LA
P
B5133
SCHOOL LA

River Mersey

Eastham Country Park
Visitor Ctr

Eastham Ferry

Eastham Ferry Hotel

The Warrens Farm

Wirral Metropolitan Coll

WOOD HEATH WAY

PORT-DA
CHAPEL VIEW

CH

Custom House

Eastham Locks

Queen Elizabeth II Dock

MAYFIELD DR

SEAVIEW AVE

CH62

ST DAVID RD

ST JOHN'S RD

Tanks

Tanks

Oil Storage Depot

Tanks

Manchester Ship Canal

VICARAGE ROW

Tanks

Tanks

Tanks

B5132

EASTHAM VILLAGE RD

Eastham Mews

HALL FARM EASTHAM HO

CHURCH RD

B5132

10

David's Rough

Hooton Park

LC

Tanks

LC

ERIC FOUNTAIN RD

CH65

NORTH RD

Booston Wood

A41

5

NEW CHESTER RD

6

Kennel Wood

MERTON RD

DUDLEY CRES

RIVACRE RD

RIVACRE RD

79

REDVERS AVE

VERNON AVE

HOOTON WAY

HOOTON RD

B5133

CHRISTIE CL

GRANGE CRES

CRANSTON CL

DERWENT DR

Park Farm

HOOTON GN

NEW SCHOOL LA

HOOTON LA

Motor Vehicle Works

Hooton

CH66

WOODCLOSE

A550

CHESTER RD

WELSH ST RD

A41

Rivacre Wood

B5132

7

M53

B5132

M53 Chester (A56)

90
A4
1 EXCHANGE PAS W
2 EXCHANGE PAS E
3 PROGRESS PL
4 CHEAPSIDE ALLEY
5 HEWITTS PL
6 TEMPLE SQ
7 POWNALL SQ
8 WESTMORLAND DR
9 IRWELL CHAMBERS
10 FAZAKERLEY CT
11 HARLEY BLDGS
52
12 COLONIAL CHAMBERS
13 IMPERIAL CHAMBERS
14 NEW CENTURY BLDG
15 THE CABLE YARD
52
52
Scale: 7 inches to 1 mile
0 110 yards 220 yards
0 125 m 250 m
A
B
C
4
905
3
900
2
895
1
890
340
345
350
LIVERPOOL
L1
L2
L3
L8
River Mersey
A3
1 OLD CHURCH YD
2 ORIEL CL
3 GEORGES DOCKWAY
4 EXCHANGE ST W
5 QUEEN AVE
6 OLD ROPERY
7 CASTLE HILL
8 THE CORN EXCHANGE
1 BACK COMMUTATION ROW
2 COMMUTATION ROW
1 MITCHELL PL
2 RANELAGH PL
3 LIME CT
SEDDON ST 1
BECKWITH ST 2
DICKENSON ST 3
A
B
C
67
B3
1 OLD POST OFFICE PL
2 Clayton Sq
3 TYRER ST
4 HOUGHTON LA
5 ST JOHN'S WAY
6 CHARLOTTE WAY
7 HOUGHTON WAY
67
B3
8 MARKET WAY
9 MARKET SQ
10 ST JOHN'S SQ
11 ST GEORGE'S WAY
12 DAWSON WAY
13 WILLIAMSON SQ
14 RAINFORD GDNS
15 LYCEUM PL
16 GOSTINS BLDG
67
C2
1 BALTIMORE ST
2 LITTLE HARDMAN ST
3 ST LUKE'S PL
4 ROPEWALKS SQ
One-way streets
House numbers
HIGH ST

Index

Place name May be abbreviated on the map

Location number Present when a number indicates the place's position in a crowded area of mapping

Locality, town or village Shown when more than one place has the same name

Postcode district District for the indexed place

Page and grid square Page number and grid reference for the standard mapping

Church Rd [6] Beckenham BR2.........**53** C6

Cities, towns and villages are listed in CAPITAL LETTERS

Public and commercial buildings are highlighted in magenta **Places of interest** are highlighted in blue with a star★

Abbreviations used in the index

Acad	**Academy**	Comm	**Common**	Gd	**Ground**	L	**Leisure**	Prom	**Promenade**
App	**Approach**	Cott	**Cottage**	Gdn	**Garden**	La	**Lane**	Rd	**Road**
Arc	**Arcade**	Cres	**Crescent**	Gn	**Green**	Liby	**Library**	Recn	**Recreation**
Ave	**Avenue**	Cswy	**Causeway**	Gr	**Grove**	Mdw	**Meadow**	Ret	**Retail**
Bglw	**Bungalow**	Ct	**Court**	H	**Hall**	Meml	**Memorial**	Sh	**Shopping**
Bldg	**Building**	Ctr	**Centre**	Ho	**House**	Mkt	**Market**	Sq	**Square**
Bsns, Bus	**Business**	Ctry	**Country**	Hospl	**Hospital**	Mus	**Museum**	St	**Street**
Bvd	**Boulevard**	Cty	**County**	HQ	**Headquarters**	Orch	**Orchard**	Sta	**Station**
Cath	**Cathedral**	Dr	**Drive**	Hts	**Heights**	Pal	**Palace**	Terr	**Terrace**
Cir	**Circus**	Dro	**Drove**	Ind	**Industrial**	Par	**Parade**	TH	**Town Hall**
Cl	**Close**	Ed	**Education**	Inst	**Institute**	Pas	**Passage**	Univ	**University**
Cnr	**Corner**	Emb	**Embankment**	Int	**International**	Pk	**Park**	Wk, Wlk	**Walk**
Coll	**College**	Est	**Estate**	Intc	**Interchange**	Pl	**Place**	Wr	**Water**
Com	**Community**	Ex	**Exhibition**	Junc	**Junction**	Prec	**Precinct**	Yd	**Yard**

Index of towns, villages, streets, hospitals, industrial estates, railway stations, schools, shopping centres, universities and places of interest

1st St WN2 35 E7
3rd St WN2 35 E7
4th St WN2 35 F7

A

Aaron Ct PR9 1 E1
Abacus Rd L13 54 B4
Abberley Cl WA10 43 F3
Abberley Rd L25 82 D8
Abberton Pk L30 28 A5
Abbey Cl
  Birkenhead CH41 66 F5
  Formby L37 10 B2
  Kirkby L33 29 F2
  Up Holland WN8 25 C7
  Widnes WA8 84 C8
Abbey Ct L25 70 B2
Abbey Dr WN5 25 E6
Abbey Farm Cvn Pk L40 14 C8
Abbeyfield Dr L12 40 D3
Abbeyfield Ho WA10 43 E5
Abbeygate Apartments L15 68 F7
Abbey Gdns PR8 4 A4
Abbey La L40 14 C8
Abbey Rd
  Haydock WA11 45 E7
  [1] Liverpool L6 53 C6
  St Helens WA10 43 E7
  West Kirby CH48 63 B2
  Widnes WA8 84 C8
Abbey St CH41 66 F5
Abbeystead WN8 24 C7
Abbeystead Ave L30 28 A1
Abbeystead Rd L15 69 B7
Abbeyvale Dr L25 70 C6
Abbey View L16 69 E7
Abbeyway N WA11 46 A7
Abbeyway S WA11 46 A7
Abbeywood WN8 24 C6
Abbeywood Gr L35 56 F2
Abbot Cl CH43 65 C6
Abbotsbury Way L12 40 E3
Abbots Cl L37 10 A1
Abbots Dr CH63 78 F5
Abbotsfield Rd WA9 58 E5
Abbotsfield Rd Ind Pk WA9 58 E6
Abbotsford L39 13 F5
Abbotsford Cl WA3 36 D1
Abbotsford Ct [3] L23 26 C3
Abbotsford Gdns L23 26 C3
Abbotsford Rd
  Crosby L23 26 C3
  Liverpool L11 39 F2
Abbotsford St CH44 51 E2
Abbots Hall Ave WA9 58 D2
Abbot's Lea Sch L25 69 E4
Abbots Quay CH41 67 A6
Abbots Way
  Formby L37 10 B1
  Neston CH64 86 E1
  West Kirby CH48 63 C3
Abbott Dr L20 38 E5
Abbotts Cl L18 69 B3
Abbottshey Ave L18 69 B2
Abbotts Way WN5 33 D3
Abdale Rd L11 39 F3
Abercrombie Rd L33 41 C7
Abercromby Sq L7 52 F1
Aberdale Rd L13 54 B3
Aberdare Cl WA5 60 E1
Aberdeen St CH41 66 C7
Aberford Ave CH45 50 E5
Abergele Rd L13 53 F2
Aber St [4] L6 53 A3
Abingdon Gr
  [1] Halewood L26 71 A1
  Liverpool, Walton L4 39 C2
Abingdon Rd
  Birkenhead CH49 64 B3
  Liverpool L4 39 C2
Abinger Rd WN4 34 D4
Abney Cl L7 68 B8
Aboyne Cl L9 39 A4
ABRAM 36 B8
ABRAM BROW 36 B7
Abram Bryn Gates Prim Sch WN2 35 F7
Abrams Fold PR9 2 F5
Abrams Gn PR9 2 F5
Abram St L5 52 E5
Abratio St CH41 66 D6
Abyssinia Cl L15 68 E7
Acacia Ave
  Huyton-w-R L36 55 D1
  Widnes WA8 73 B3
Acacia Cl CH49 64 C2
Acacia Gr
  Liverpool L9 39 B6
  St Helens WA10 43 A4
  Wallasey CH44 51 E2
  West Kirby CH48 63 A2
Acacia St WA12 45 F4
Academy The [1] PR9 4 C8
Acad of St Francis of Assisi The L6 53 C4
Acanthus Rd L13 54 B4
Access Rd L12 54 D7
Acer Leigh L17 68 D2
Acheson Rd L13 53 E6
Achilles Ave WA2 61 B2
Ackerley Cl WA2 61 F3
Ackers Hall Ave L14 54 F5
Ackers La
  Crosby L23 26 C7
  St Helens WA10 43 C4
Ackers Rd CH49 65 C2
Ackers St [11] L34 56 D6
Acland Rd CH44 51 B4
Aconbury Cl L11 39 F3
Aconbury Pl L11 39 F3
Acorn Bsns Ctr L33 30 B1
Acorn Cl
  Bebington CH63 78 D6
  St Helens WA9 58 C4
Acorn Ct L8 67 F6
Acornfield Cl L33 41 C8
Acornfield Rd L33 30 D2
Acorn St WA12 46 D3
Acorns The L39 13 C3
Acorn Venture Urban Farm★ L33 30 D4
Acorn Way L20 38 D5
Acrefield Ct CH42 66 B1
Acrefield Pk L25 70 A3
Acrefield Rd
  Birkenhead CH42 66 C1
  Liverpool L25 70 A3
  Widnes WA8 72 B1
Acregate WN8 24 C7
Acre Gn L26 83 A6
Acre Gr PR8 3 F3
Acre La
  Bebington CH62 88 D8
  Heswall CH60 77 C1
Acres Cl L25 70 A7
Acresgate Ct L25 70 A6
Acres La
  Great Altcar L37 18 E8
  Maghull L31, L39 19 E7
Acres Rd
  Bebington CH63 78 F6
  Hoylake CH47 63 F7
Acreville Rd CH63 78 F5
'A' Ct WN4 35 B2
Acton Cl WA11 45 C6
Acton Gr L6 53 C6
Acton La CH46 64 C7
Acton Rake L30 27 D5
Acton Rd
  Birkenhead CH42 67 A1
  Burtonwood WA5 59 E6
  Kirkby L32 29 C2
Acton Way L7 68 C8
Acuba Gr CH42 66 E4
Acuba Rd L15 54 C1
Adair Pl L13 53 E7
Adair Rd L13 53 E7
Adam Cl L19 81 C5
Adams Cl WA12 46 D2
Adamson Ho WA7 84 E3
Adamson St
  Ashton-in-M WN4 35 A3
  Liverpool L7 53 D2
Adam St L5 52 F6
Adaston Ave CH62 88 F4
Adcote Cl L14 54 F3
Adcote Rd L14 54 F3
Addenbrooke Dr L24 82 C7
Adderley St L7 53 B2
Addingham Ave WA8 84 C7
Addingham Rd L18 69 B5
Addington St CH44 51 D3
Addison Cl L32 40 D8
Addison Sq WA8 73 A1
Addison St
  Bootle L20 38 A5
  Liverpool L3 52 D3
Addison Way L3 52 D3
Adelaide Ave WA9 57 E7
Adelaide Pl L5 52 E4
Adelaide Rd
  Birkenhead CH42 66 C4
  Liverpool L7 53 B2
  Seaforth L21 37 F7
Adelaide St CH44 51 B3
Adelaide Terr L22 26 C1
Adela Rd WA7 84 F2
Adele Thompson Dr [2] L8 68 A7
Adella Ct L17 68 C6
Adelphi St CH41 66 E6
Adkins St [4] L5 53 A6
Adlam Cres L9 39 E7
Adlam Rd L10, L9 39 E7
Adler Way L3 67 F3
Adlington Ho [8] L3 52 D3
Adlington St [7] L3 52 D3

Admin Rd L33 41 C8
Admiral Gr [1] L8 68 A5
Admirals Quay L23 26 A4
Admiral St L8 68 A5
Adrian's Way L32 29 E2
Adshead Rd L13 53 E7
Adstone Rd L25 70 C5
Adswood Rd L36 55 E3
Africander Rd WA11 44 A8
Afton WA8 72 A2
Agar Rd L11 53 F7
Agate St L5 53 A5
Agincourt Rd L12 54 C5
Agnes Gr CH44, CH45 51 C5
Agnes Jones Ho [17] L7, L8 67 F8
Agnes Rd
  Birkenhead CH42 66 E3
  Crosby L23 26 C3
Agnes St WA9 58 C3
Agnes Way L7 53 B1
Aiden Long Gr L34 55 E6
AIGBURTH 68 F1
Aigburth Dr L17 68 C4
Aigburth Gr CH46 64 D8
Aigburth Hall Ave L19, L18 81 A8
Aigburth Hall Rd L19 81 A8
Aigburth Ho L17 68 E3
Aigburth Pk L17 68 B2
Aigburth Rd L17, L8 68 D2
Aigburth St L7 68 B8
Aigburth Sta L17 80 E8
AIGBURTH VALE 68 F2
Aigburth Vale
  Liverpool L17 68 D2
  Liverpool L17, L18 68 E3
Ailsa Rd CH45 51 A5
Aindow Ct PR8 3 F3
AINSDALE 7 B5
Ainsdale & Birkdale Sandhills Nature Reserve★ PR8 7 B7
Ainsdale Cl
  Bebington CH63 88 C5
  Heswall CH61 77 A5
  Liverpool L10 39 F8
  Warrington WA5 74 F4
AINSDALE-ON-SEA 6 F6
Ainsdale Rd L20 38 D6

Ainsdale St John's CE Prim Sch PR8 . . . 7 D4
Ainsdale Sand Dunes Nature Reserve* PR8 . . . 6 E3
Ainsdale Sta PR8 . . . 7 C5
Ainsworth Ave CH46 . . . 64 C6
Ainsworth La L34 . . . 41 B6
Ainsworth Rd WA10 . . . 43 D5
Ainsworth St L3 . . . 90 C3
AINTREE . . . 28 D2
Aintree Cl CH46 . . . 49 F3
Aintree Cres PR8 . . . 4 F4
Aintree Ct L10 . . . 28 C3
Aintree Davenhill Prim Sch L10 . . . 28 D2
Aintree La
Aintree L10, L9 . . . 28 C2
Liverpool L10 . . . 40 A8
Aintree Race Course L9 . . . 28 D1
Aintree Racecourse Ret & Bsns Pk L9 . . . 28 C2
Aintree Rd
Bootle L20 . . . 38 E4
Liverpool L9 . . . 39 D6
Aintree Sta L30 . . . 39 B8
Aintree Way L9 . . . 28 C2
Airdale Cl CH43 . . . 65 C6
Airdale Rd L15 . . . 68 F6
Airdrie Cl CH62 . . . 88 D3
Aire WA8 . . . 72 B2
Airedale Cl WA5 . . . 74 F7
Airegate L31 . . . 20 B2
Airlie Gr L13 . . . 53 D6
Airlie Rd CH47 . . . 63 B6
Aisthorpe Gr L31 . . . 28 D7
Ajax Ave WA2 . . . 61 B2
Akbar The CH60 . . . 76 C2
A K Bsns Pk PR9 . . . 5 A6
Akenside St L20 . . . 38 A6
Alabama Way CH41 . . . 66 F6
Alamein Rd L36 . . . 55 D4
Alamora Ho [7] L36 . . . 56 A2
Alans Way L33 . . . 29 E4
Alastair Cres CH43 . . . 65 F1
Alban Rd L16 . . . 69 D8
Alban Ret Pk WA2 . . . 61 A1
Albany Ave L34 . . . 56 F7
Albany Rd
Birkenhead CH42 . . . 66 E2
Liverpool, Elm Park L7 . . . 53 A2
Liverpool L13 . . . 54 A4
Liverpool, Warbreck Pk L9 . . . 39 B7
Prescot L34 . . . 56 E6
Southport PR9 . . . 1 C1
Albemarle Rd CH44 . . . 51 E3
Alberta Gr L34 . . . 55 F5
Albert Ct PR9 . . . 1 D1
Albert Dock* L3 . . . 90 A2
Albert Dr
Liverpool L20, L9 . . . 38 F6
Warrington WA5 . . . 74 D6
Albert Edward Rd L7 . . . 53 A2
Albert Gr
Crosby L23 . . . 26 D4
Liverpool L15 . . . 69 A8
Albert Pk L8 . . . 68 B5
Albert Pl PR9 . . . 4 B8
Albert Rd
Birkenhead CH42 . . . 66 C4
Formby L37 . . . 17 B8
Hoylake CH47 . . . 63 B6
Liverpool L13 . . . 53 D6
Seaforth L22 . . . 37 D8
Southport PR9 . . . 1 D1
West Kirby CH48 . . . 63 A1
[2] Widnes WA8 . . . 73 B1
Albert Schweitzer Ave L30 . . . 27 F4
Albert Sq [1] WA8 . . . 73 B1
Albert St
Ashton-in-M WN4 . . . 35 B3
Liverpool L7 . . . 53 A1
St Helens WA10 . . . 44 A5
Wallasey CH45 . . . 37 C1
Albert Terr
Collins Green WA5 . . . 45 E1
Southport PR8 . . . 4 A5
Albion Pl CH45 . . . 51 B8
Albion St
Birkenhead CH41 . . . 66 F6
Birkenhead CH41 . . . 66 F7
Liverpool L5 . . . 52 F6
St Helens WA10 . . . 43 E4
Wallasey CH45 . . . 51 A8
Albourne Rd L32 . . . 41 A8
Albright Rd WA8 . . . 84 A6
Albury Cl
Haydock WA11 . . . 45 D7
Liverpool L12 . . . 41 A2
Albury Rd [4] L32 . . . 41 A7
Alcester Rd L12 . . . 54 C6
Alcott Pl WA2 . . . 61 A6
Aldams Gr L4 . . . 38 E1
Aldbourne Ave L25 . . . 69 E5
Aldbourne Cl L25 . . . 69 E4
Aldcliffe WA3 . . . 47 F8
Alder Ave
Ashton-in-M WN4 . . . 34 F5
Billinge WN5 . . . 33 D5
Huyton-w-R L36 . . . 71 A8
Widnes WA8 . . . 73 B3
Alderbank Rd WA5 . . . 74 F6
Alder Cl L34 . . . 56 F6
Alder Cres L32 . . . 29 D3
Alder Ct L12 . . . 54 C6
Alderdale Ave PR8 . . . 7 A5
Alderfield Dr L24 . . . 83 A3
Alder Gr L22 . . . 26 D2
Alder Hey Children's Hospl L14 . . . 54 C4
Alder Hey Rd WA10 . . . 43 C4
Alder La
Burtonwood WA2, WA5 . . . 60 C7
Crank WA11 . . . 32 F4
Cronton WA8, L35 . . . 72 A5
Formby L37, L39 . . . 10 E7
Knowsley L34 . . . 41 C2
Alderlee Pk Cvn Site PR8 . . . 5 A2
Alderley WN8 . . . 24 C6
Alderley Ave
Birkenhead CH41 . . . 65 F7
Golborne WA3 . . . 47 D7
Alderley Cl WN5 . . . 33 E5
Alderley Rd
Hoylake CH47 . . . 63 B7
Wallasey CH44 . . . 51 B3
Alderman Rd L24 . . . 82 C7
Alderney Rd L5 . . . 52 D5
Alder Rd
Bebington CH63 . . . 78 E4
Golborne WA3 . . . 47 F8
Liverpool L12 . . . 54 C4
Prescot L34 . . . 56 F6
Alder Root La WA2 . . . 60 D7
Aldersey St L3 . . . 52 D3
Aldersgate CH42 . . . 66 F2
Aldersgate Dr L26 . . . 83 A6
Alderson Cres L37 . . . 9 F4
Alderson Rd L15 . . . 68 D8
Alder St WA12 . . . 46 C3
Alderton Cl L26 . . . 83 A7
Alderton Dr WN4 . . . 35 A3
Alderville Rd L4 . . . 39 C2
Alder Wood Ave L24 . . . 82 F4
Alderwood Ct WA8 . . . 72 E4
Alderwood Lo L24 . . . 83 A3
Aldford Cl
Bebington CH63 . . . 88 B6
Birkenhead CH43 . . . 65 E2
Aldford Rd L32 . . . 40 E7
Aldridge Cl [1] L12 . . . 40 E3
Aldridge Dr WA5 . . . 59 F7
Aldrins La L30 . . . 27 F5
Aldwark Rd L14 . . . 55 A4
Aldwych Rd L12 . . . 54 C5
Aldykes L31 . . . 28 F8
Alexander Ct
[1] Liverpool L15 . . . 54 C1
St Helens WA9 . . . 57 D8
Alexander Dr
Heswall CH61 . . . 76 E3
Maghull L31 . . . 20 D3
Widnes WA8 . . . 84 D8
Alexander Fleming Ave L30 . . . 27 F4
Alexander Gn L36 . . . 55 E4
Alexander Ho
Prescot L34 . . . 56 D7
[7] Seaforth L21 . . . 37 F7
Alexander Mans [5] L36 . . . 56 A2
Alexander Way [10] L8 . . . 67 F4
Alexander Wharf L31 . . . 20 C1
Alexander Wlk L4 . . . 52 F8
Alexandra Cl WN8 . . . 15 E1
Alexandra Ct
[3] Crosby L23 . . . 26 D3
Liverpool L6 . . . 53 B3
[2] Wallasey CH45 . . . 51 A8
Alexandra Dr
Birkenhead CH42 . . . 66 E1
Bootle L20 . . . 38 F6
Liverpool L17 . . . 68 B4
St Helens WA10 . . . 43 D2
Alexandra Gn L17 . . . 68 B4
Alexandra Gr L26 . . . 82 F7
Alexandra Ho L17 . . . 68 B4
Alexandra Ind Est WA8 . . . 84 F7
Alexandra Mews
[1] Ormskirk L39 . . . 13 E6
[8] Southport PR9 . . . 4 C8
Alexandra Mount L21 . . . 38 B8
Alexandra Pk [1] L17 . . . 68 B3
Alexandra Rd
Ashton-in-M WN4 . . . 35 B4
Birkenhead CH43 . . . 66 C5
Crosby L23 . . . 26 D4
Formby L37 . . . 9 B1
Liverpool L7 . . . 68 C8
Liverpool, Stanley L13 . . . 54 A2
Seaforth L22 . . . 37 E8
Southport PR9 . . . 4 D8
Wallasey CH45 . . . 51 A8
West Kirby CH48 . . . 63 A1
Alexandra St
Abram WN2 . . . 36 B8
St Helens WA10 . . . 43 D1
Alexandra Terr [14] L8 . . . 67 F7
Alexandra Villas L21 . . . 38 B8
Alexandria Rd L19 . . . 81 C7
Alex Cl L8 . . . 67 F6
Alfonso Rd L4 . . . 52 D8
Alford Ave WA9 . . . 58 B4
Alford St L7 . . . 53 E2
Alfred Mews L1 . . . 90 C1
Alfred Rd
Birkenhead CH43 . . . 66 C5
Haydock WA11 . . . 45 F7
Wallasey CH44 . . . 51 E1
Alfred St
Liverpool L15 . . . 68 D8
Newton-le-W WA12 . . . 46 E3
Rainford WA11 . . . 31 F7
St Helens WA10 . . . 44 B4
Alfred Stocks Ct L8 . . . 68 A3
Alfriston Rd L12 . . . 54 C6
Algernon St WA7 . . . 84 F3
Alice St WA9 . . . 58 E8
Alicia Wlk L10 . . . 40 B7
Alison Ave CH42 . . . 66 F3
Alison Pl L13 . . . 53 E7
Alison Rd L13 . . . 53 E7
Alistair Dr CH63 . . . 88 C6
Allangate Cl CH49 . . . 64 C2
Allangate Rd L19 . . . 81 B8
Allan Rd WA11 . . . 44 C7
Allanson St WA9 . . . 44 D3
Allanson Street Prim Sch WA9 . . . 44 D2
Allcot Ave CH42 . . . 66 D2
Allenby Ave L22, L23 . . . 26 F2
Allenby Sq L13 . . . 54 A2
Allendale Ave
[4] Liverpool L9 . . . 39 B7
Rainhill L35 . . . 57 D3
Allengate [1] L23 . . . 26 E5
Allerby Way WA3 . . . 47 E8
Allerford Rd L12 . . . 54 D8
ALLERTON . . . 81 E8
Allerton Beeches L18 . . . 69 C3
Allerton Dr L18 . . . 69 B4
Allerton Gr CH42 . . . 66 E3
Allerton Rd
Birkenhead CH42 . . . 66 E3
Liverpool, Calderstones L18, L25 . . . 69 D3
Liverpool L18 . . . 69 B5
Liverpool, Wavertree L18 . . . 69 A5
Liverpool, Woolton L25 . . . 70 A2
Southport PR9 . . . 1 E1
Wallasey CH45 . . . 51 A6
Widnes WA8 . . . 73 B1
Allesley Rd L14 . . . 54 F5
Alleyne Rd L4 . . . 53 D8
All Hallows Dr L24 . . . 82 F4
Allington St L17 . . . 68 B3
Allonby Cl CH43 . . . 65 E4
Allport La CH62 . . . 88 D8
Allport Rd CH62, CH63 . . . 88 D7
Allports The CH62 . . . 88 D7
All Saints Cl L30 . . . 27 E3
All Saints Ct WA11 . . . 32 A5
All Saints RC High Sch L32 . . . 29 E1
All Saints RC Prim Sch
Golborne WA3 . . . 47 B8
Liverpool L4 . . . 53 B6
All Saints Rd L24 . . . 82 C4
All Saints Upton CE Prim Sch WA8 . . . 72 B3
Allscott Way WN4 . . . 35 C3
Alma Cl
Liverpool L10 . . . 40 B7
Up Holland WN8 . . . 25 C7
Almacs Cl L23 . . . 26 B3
Alma Ct
Southport PR8 . . . 7 F7
Up Holland WN8 . . . 25 C7
Alma Hill WN8 . . . 25 C7
Alma Hill Est WN8 . . . 25 C7
Alman Ct [3] L17 . . . 68 B3
Alma Par WN8 . . . 25 C7
Alma Pl WA9 . . . 44 C2
Alma Rd
Liverpool L17 . . . 80 E8
Southport PR8 . . . 4 A4
Up Holland WN8 . . . 25 C7
Alma St
[5] Birkenhead CH41 . . . 66 E6
Newton-le-W WA12 . . . 46 B3
St Helens WA9 . . . 44 C2
Alma Vale Terr L20 . . . 38 B3
Almeda Rd L24 . . . 83 A2
Almond Ave L30 . . . 27 C3
Almond Cl
Liverpool L26 . . . 82 E8
St Helens WA11 . . . 44 F5
Almond Ct L19 . . . 81 E5
Almond Dr WA5 . . . 59 F6
Almond Gr WA8 . . . 84 D8
Almond Pl CH46 . . . 64 F8
Almond's Gn L12 . . . 54 A8
Almond's Gr L12 . . . 54 A8
Almonds Pk L12 . . . 54 A8
Almonds The L26 . . . 82 E8
Almond's Turn L30 . . . 27 D4
Almond Tree Cl L24 . . . 83 E1
Almond Way CH49 . . . 64 C2
Almonry The L40 . . . 15 B7
Alms House Bglws L39 . . . 21 A7
Almshouses L39 . . . 21 A7
Alness Dr L35 . . . 57 D2
Alnwick Dr CH46 . . . 64 C8
Aloeswood Cl [6] L6 . . . 53 B5
Alpass Rd [4] L17 . . . 68 B3
Alpha Dr CH42 . . . 67 A1
Alpha St L20, L21 . . . 38 B5
Alpine Cl WA10 . . . 43 C4
Alpine St WA12 . . . 46 A3
Alresford Rd L19 . . . 80 F8
Alroy Rd L4 . . . 53 A7
Alscot Ave L10 . . . 40 B7
Alscot Cl L31 . . . 28 D8
Alsop High Sch Tech Coll L4 . . . 39 A2
Alston Cl CH62 . . . 79 C1
Alston Ct PR8 . . . 7 E6
Alstonfield Rd L14 . . . 55 A4
Alston Rd L17 . . . 80 E8
Alt WA8 . . . 72 B2
Alt Ave L31 . . . 28 C7
Altbridge Pk L11 . . . 40 B4
Alt Bridge Rd L36 . . . 55 D4
Altcar Ave L15 . . . 68 D7
Altcar Dr CH46 . . . 64 D7
Altcar La
Formby L37 . . . 9 F1
Haskayne L39 . . . 12 A2
Maghull L31 . . . 19 F5
Altcar Rd
Bootle L20 . . . 38 C5
Formby L37 . . . 10 B2
Altcross Rd L11 . . . 40 C4
Altcross Way L11 . . . 40 C4
Altfield Rd L14 . . . 54 F7
Altfinch Cl L14 . . . 55 A7
Altham Rd
Liverpool L11 . . . 53 F8
Southport PR8 . . . 4 E2
Althorpe Dr PR8 . . . 4 E3
Althorp St L8 . . . 67 F3
Altmoor Rd L36 . . . 55 D5
Alton Ave L21 . . . 27 A1
Alton Cl
Ashton-in-M WN4 . . . 35 A4
Hightown L38 . . . 17 F2
Alton Ct CH43 . . . 66 A4
Alton Lo L17 . . . 80 E8
Alton Rd
Birkenhead CH43 . . . 66 A5
Liverpool L6 . . . 53 D5
Alt Rd
Bootle L20 . . . 38 C5
Formby L37 . . . 10 B2
Hightown L38 . . . 18 A4
Huyton-w-R L36 . . . 55 E3
Alt Side Ct L10 . . . 40 B7
Alt St L8 . . . 68 B7
Altway L10 . . . 28 D3
Altway Ct L10 . . . 28 C3
Altys La L39 . . . 13 F3
Alundale Ct [13] L20 . . . 38 C3
Alundale Rd L12 . . . 54 E5
Alvanley Gn L32 . . . 29 C2
Alvanley Pl CH43 . . . 66 C6
Alvanley Rd
Kirkby L32 . . . 29 C2
Liverpool L12 . . . 54 C6
Alva Rd L35 . . . 57 D2
Alvega Cl CH62 . . . 79 C7
Alverstone Ave CH41 . . . 65 F7
Alverstone Cl WA5 . . . 74 C7
Alverstone Rd
Liverpool L18 . . . 68 F5
Wallasey CH44 . . . 51 D3
Alverton Cl WA8 . . . 84 D8
Alvina La
Kirkby L33 . . . 30 A5
Liverpool L4 . . . 52 E7
Alwain Gn L24 . . . 82 F3
Alwen St CH41 . . . 50 F1
Alwyn Ave L21 . . . 27 B1
Alwyn Cl L17 . . . 68 B3
Alwyn Gdns CH46 . . . 64 F8
Alwyn St L17 . . . 68 B3
Amanda Rd
Liverpool L10 . . . 40 B7
Rainhill L35 . . . 57 B5
Amanda Way L31 . . . 29 B4
Amaury Cl L23 . . . 27 B5
Amaury Rd L23 . . . 27 B5
Ambassador Dr [2] L26 . . . 71 A1
Ambergate WN8 . . . 24 B7
Ambergate Cl [3] WA9 . . . 58 D7
Ambergate Rd L19 . . . 81 B8
Amberley Ave CH46 . . . 64 C7
Amberley Cl
Birkenhead CH46 . . . 64 C7
Liverpool L6 . . . 53 D7
Amber Way L14 . . . 55 A7
Ambleside Ave CH46 . . . 64 D8
Ambleside Cl
Bebington CH62 . . . 88 E7
Heswall CH61 . . . 77 A6
Ambleside Cres WA2 . . . 61 C3
Ambleside Dr L33 . . . 29 D4
Ambleside Pl WA11 . . . 33 B1
Ambleside Rd
Liverpool L18 . . . 69 D1
Maghull L31 . . . 20 D2
Ambrose Ct [3] L4 . . . 53 B6
Amelia Cl
Liverpool L6 . . . 52 F3
Widnes WA8 . . . 73 B4
Amersham WN8 . . . 24 C7
Amersham Rd L4 . . . 39 C2
Amery Gr CH42 . . . 66 C2
Amethyst Cl
Litherland L21 . . . 38 C8
[5] Liverpool L6 . . . 53 B4
Amherst Rd L17 . . . 68 C2
Amis Gr WA3 . . . 47 E8
Amity St L8 . . . 67 F5
Amos Ave L21 . . . 38 C8
Ampleforth Cl [3] L32 . . . 29 C1
Ampthill Rd L17 . . . 68 D2
Ampulla Rd L11 . . . 40 C3
Amy Wlk L10 . . . 40 B7
Ancaster Rd L17 . . . 68 D2
Ancholme Cl L35 . . . 57 A6
Anchorage La L18 . . . 68 E3
Anchorage The L3 . . . 67 D6
Anchor St PR9 . . . 4 B7
Ancient Mdws L9 . . . 39 B7
Ancroft Rd L14 . . . 55 A3
Ancrum Rd L33 . . . 29 D6
Anders Dr L33 . . . 30 A5
Anderson Cl
Heswall CH61 . . . 77 A6
Rainhill L35 . . . 57 D1
Anderson Ct CH62 . . . 88 D6
Anderson Rd L21 . . . 27 D1
Anderson St L5 . . . 52 E6
Anderson Way L21 . . . 27 D1
Anderton Terr L36 . . . 55 C2
Andover Cl WA2 . . . 61 E1
Andover Rd WA11 . . . 45 E8
Andover Way L25 . . . 82 D9
Andreas Cl PR8 . . . 4 B4
Andrew Ave
Billinge WN5 . . . 33 F5
Kirkby L31 . . . 29 B3
Andrew Cl WA8 . . . 84 C8
Andrews Cl L37 . . . 9 E1
Andrews La L37 . . . 9 E1
Andrew St L4 . . . 38 F1
Andrew's Wlk CH60 . . . 86 B8
Andrews Yort L37 . . . 9 E1
Andromeda Way WA9 . . . 59 B7
Anemone Way WA9 . . . 59 A7
ANFIELD . . . 53 A7
Anfield Ct L4 . . . 53 A7
Anfield Inf Sch L4 . . . 53 B6
Anfield Jun Sch L4 . . . 53 B6
Anfield (Liverpool FC) Mus & Tour Ctr* L4 . . . 53 A7
Anfield Rd L4 . . . 53 A7
Angela St L7 . . . 68 B8
Angers La L31 . . . 29 B6
Anglesea Rd L9 . . . 38 F3
Anglesea Way L8 . . . 67 F4
Anglesey Rd
[2] Wallasey CH44 . . . 51 B5
West Kirby CH48 . . . 63 A3
Anglezark Cl L7 . . . 53 B2
Anglia Way L25 . . . 82 C9
Anglican Ct L8 . . . 90 C1
Anglo Cl L9 . . . 39 C8
Angra Bank L22 . . . 37 E8
Angus Rd
Bebington CH63 . . . 88 C6
Liverpool L11 . . . 53 F8
Annandale Cl L33 . . . 29 D6
Annandale Gdns WN8 . . . 25 A7
Annan Gr WN4 . . . 35 E5
Anne Ave PR8 . . . 7 E6
Anne Gr WA9 . . . 58 C7
Annesley Rd
Liverpool L17 . . . 68 C1
Wallasey CH44 . . . 51 C3
Anne St WA9 . . . 58 D3
Annette Ave WA12 . . . 46 A5
Annie Rd L20 . . . 38 D6
Ann St WN8 . . . 23 E8
Anscot Ave CH63 . . . 78 F6
Ansdell Dr WA10 . . . 43 B5
Ansdell Gr PR9 . . . 2 A4
Ansdell Rd WA8 . . . 73 C2
Ansdell Villas' Rd L35 . . . 57 C4
Ansford Ave WN2 . . . 36 B8
Anson Mews CH43 . . . 65 F8
Anson St L3 . . . 52 F2
Anstey Cl CH46 . . . 49 B1
Anstey Rd L13 . . . 54 B2
Ansty Cl WA11 . . . 44 D6
Anthony's Way CH60 . . . 86 A7
Anthorn Cl CH43 . . . 65 D4
Antler Ct WN4 . . . 35 B6
Antonio St L20 . . . 38 E1
Antons Cl L26 . . . 82 F7
Antons Ct L26 . . . 83 A6
Antons Rd
Heswall CH61 . . . 77 A5
Liverpool L26 . . . 82 F7
Antrim Cl WA11 . . . 45 C6
Antrim Rd WA2 . . . 61 A2
Antrim St L13 . . . 53 E7
Anvil Cl
Bootle L20 . . . 38 B4
Orrell WN5 . . . 25 D5
Anzacs The CH62 . . . 79 C6
Anzio Rd L36 . . . 55 D4
Apartments The PR9 . . . 4 B8
Apex Ct CH62 . . . 79 E1
Apollo Cres L33 . . . 29 E4
Apollo Ct L3 . . . 90 C4
Apollo Way
Litherland L30 . . . 27 F4
Liverpool L6 . . . 53 B5
Apostles Way [1] L33 . . . 29 D5
Appin Rd CH41 . . . 66 E5
Appleby Cl WA8 . . . 84 C8
Appleby Dr L30 . . . 27 D3
Appleby Gn L12 . . . 54 D6
Appleby Gr CH62 . . . 88 D6
Appleby Lawn L27 . . . 71 A4
Appleby Rd
[6] Kirkby L33 . . . 29 E5
Warrington WA2 . . . 61 C3
Appleby Wlk
Liverpool L27 . . . 71 A4
[5] Widnes WA8 . . . 84 C8
Applecorn Cl WA9 . . . 58 D5
Apple Ct [3] L6 . . . 53 B3
Apple Dell Ave WA3 . . . 36 C1
Appledore Ct L24 . . . 82 B5
Appledore Gr WA9 . . . 58 C5
Applegarth CH46 . . . 64 C6
APPLETON . . . 73 A2
Appleton Dr CH49 . . . 64 E3
Appleton Rd
Kirkby L32 . . . 29 E4

Appleton Rd *continued*
Litherland L21 27 A1
Liverpool L4 39 A1
Skelmersdale WN8 15 F2
St Helens WA9 44 C1
Widnes WA8 73 B1
Appleton Village WA8 73 B1
Appletree Cl L18 69 C1
Apple Tree Cl
Hale L24 83 E1
Huyton-w-R L28 55 B8
Appletree Gr WA2 61 F2
Applewood Ct L26 71 A1
Applewood Gr L26 71 A1
April Gr L6 53 D5
April Rise L30 27 E3
Apsley Ave CH45 51 B6
Apsley Brow L31 20 B1
Apsley Gr CH63 79 A6
Apsley Rd
Bebington CH62 79 B8
Liverpool L12 54 C6
Aquarius Cl L14 55 A4
Arabis Gdns WA9 59 B7
Aragon Cl L31 20 E3
Aran Cl L24 83 D1
Arborn Dr CH49 65 A6
Arbour Ct L33 30 B2
Arbour La L33 30 B2
Arbour St PR8 4 C6
Arbury Ave WA11 44 D6
Arbury La WA2 61 C6
Arcadia Ave L31 20 D3
Archbishop Beck RC Sports Coll L9 39 B6
Archbishop Blanch CE High Sch L7 53 A1
Archbishop Warlock Ct L3 52 C4
Archbrook Mews L13 53 E5
Archer Cl L4 52 E7
Archerfield Rd L18 69 B1
Archer Gr WA9 44 E4
Archers Croft CH62 79 D1
Archers Ct [9] CH49 65 A2
Archers Fold L31 29 B4
Archers Gn CH62 88 E3
Archers Green Rd WA5 60 B3
Archer St L4 52 E7
Archers Way [1] CH49 65 A2
Arch La WN4 34 B3
Arch View Cres L1 90 C2
Archway Rd L36 55 E2
Archway Wlk WA12 46 E3
Arctic Rd L20 38 A3
Arden WA8 72 A2
Arden Cl PR8 7 A5
Arden Coll PR9 4 C7
Ardennes Rd L36 55 E3
Arderne Cl CH63 79 B2
Ardleigh Ave PR8 4 E3
Ardleigh Cl L13 53 F2
Ardleigh Gr L13 53 F2
Ardleigh Pl L13 53 F2
Ardleigh Rd L13 53 F2
Ardmore Rd L18 69 A2
Ardrossan Rd L4 53 C8
Ardville Rd L11 39 D3
Ardwick Rd L24 82 F4
Ardwick St WA9 44 C3
Argameols Cl PR8 4 F5
Argarmeols Gr L37 9 E5
Argarmeols Rd L37 9 E6
Argo Rd L22 26 D1
Argos Pl L20 38 D1
Argos Rd [1] L20 38 D1
Argyle Ct
[2] Crosby L23 26 E3
Southport PR9 1 D1
Argyle Rd
Liverpool, Cabbage Hall L4 53 B6
Liverpool, Garston L19 81 C6
Southport PR9 1 D2
Argyle St S CH41 66 E5
Argyle St
Birkenhead CH41 66 E6
Liverpool L1 90 B2
St Helens WA10 43 F5
Argyle Street Hamilton Sq CH41 66 E7
Argyll Ave CH62 88 D4
Argyll Cl WN4 34 C4
Ariel Wlk [4] WA3 47 E8
Aries Cl L14 55 A5
Ariss Gr L35 57 A5
Arkenstone Cl WA8 72 C2
Arkle Rd CH43 65 F8
Arkles La L4 53 B7
Arkles Rd L4 53 A6
Arklow Dr L24 83 D2
Ark Royal Way CH41 66 F4
Arkwood Cl CH62 79 C3
Arkwright St L5 52 E5
Arlescourt Rd L12 54 D6
Arley Cl CH43 65 C6
Arley Dr WA8 72 B2
Arley St L3 52 C4
Arlington Ave [10] L18 68 F5
Arlington Cl PR8 7 A5
Arlington Ct CH43 65 F5
Arlington Dr WA5 74 E4
Arlington Rd CH45 50 E6
Armill Rd L11 40 C3
Armitage Gdns L18 69 B1
Armley Rd L4 53 B7
Armour Ave WA2 61 B2
Armour Gr [5] L13 54 A2
Armoury Bank WN4 35 B3
Armoury The L12 54 B7
Armscot Cl L25 82 B8
Armscot Pl L25 82 B8
Armstrong Quay L3 67 F3
Arncliffe Dr WA5 59 F6
Arncliffe Rd L25 82 D9
Arnhem Rd L36 55 E3
Arnian Ct L39 21 C7
Arnian Rd WA11 31 F7
Arnian Way WA11 31 F7
Arno Ct CH43 66 B3
Arnold Ave WA10 43 D5
Arnold Cl WA9 44 C1
Arnold Cres [1] L8 68 A6
Arnold Gr L15 69 A8
Arnold Pl WA8 84 C7
Arnold St [1] CH45 51 B5
Arno Rd CH42, CH43 66 B3
Arnot Cl WA10 43 F5
Arnot Com Prim Sch L4 38 F1
Arnot St L4 38 F1
Arnot Way CH63 78 D7
Arnside L21 38 D8
Arnside Ave
Haydock WA11 45 B6
Rainhill L35 57 A4
Arnside Rd
Birkenhead CH43 66 A4
Huyton-w-R L36 55 B2
Liverpool L7 53 C1
Southport PR9 4 C7
Wallasey CH45 51 B5
Arnside Terr PR9 4 C7
Aron Ct L34 56 D6
Arrad St L1, L7 67 F8
Arran Cl WA11 44 E6
Arranmore Rd L18 69 A2
Arrowe Ave CH46 64 D7
Arrowe Brook Ct CH49 64 E4
Arrowe Brook La CH49 64 E1
Arrowe Brook Rd CH49 64 F3
Arrowe Ct [7] CH49 65 A2
Arrowe Ctry Pk★ CH49 65 A1
ARROWE HILL 65 A3
Arrowe Hill Prim Sch CH49 65 A3
Arrowe Park Hospl CH49 65 A2
Arrowe Park Rd CH49 65 A2
Arrowe Rd CH49 64 E3
Arrowe Side CH49 64 E4
Arrowsmith Rd WA11 45 F7
Arthur St
Birkenhead CH41 66 C7
Birkenhead CH41 66 C8
Liverpool, Garston L19 81 D5
Liverpool, Walton L9 38 F3
[8] Runcorn WA7 84 F2
Arundel Ave
Liverpool L17 68 D6
Wallasey CH45 50 F6
Arundel Cl
Heswall CH61 76 E5
[5] Liverpool L8 68 A6
Arundell Cl WA5 59 F6
Arundel Rd PR8 7 F8
Arundel St L4 38 F1
Arvon St L20 38 D6
Asbridge St L8 68 B7
Asbury Cl L18 69 D3
Asbury Rd CH45 50 D6
Ascot Ave L21 38 A8
Ascot Cl PR8 3 E5
Ascot Dr
Bebington CH63 78 F5
Kirkby L33 29 E5
Ascot Gr CH63 78 F5
Ascot Pk L23 26 F4
Ascroft Rd L9 39 B8
Ash Ave WA12 46 C2
Ashbank Rd L11 40 B2
Ashbourne Ave
Crosby L23 26 C4
Litherland L30 27 E2
Ashbourne Cres L36 55 B3
Ashbourne Rd L17 68 C2
Ashbrook Dr L9 39 C6
Ashbrook Terr CH63 79 A6
Ashburn Ave L33 29 E4
Ashburnham Way [10] L5 52 E4
Ashburton Ave CH43 65 F6
Ashburton Ct CH43 65 E6
Ashburton Rd
Birkenhead CH43 65 F6
Wallasey CH44 51 B4
West Kirby CH48 63 B2
Ashbury Dr WA11 45 D7
Ashbury Gables L19 81 B7
Ashbury Rd L14 55 B6
Ashby Cl CH46 49 B1
Ash Cl
Liverpool L15 68 E8
Ormskirk L39 13 D5
Ashcombe Rd L14 54 C3
Ash Cres L36 70 E8
Ashcroft Ave L39 13 F6
Ashcroft Dr CH61 76 F3
Ashcroft Rd
Formby L37 9 F1
Kirkby L33 30 C3
Ashcroft St
Bootle L20 38 B3
St Helens WA9 44 C3
Ashdale L36 55 D2
Ashdale Cl L37 9 C2
Ashdale Pk CH49 64 B4
Ashdale Rd
Crosby L22 26 D2
Liverpool, Hartley's Village L9 39 A4
Liverpool, Mossley Hill L18 69 A5
Ashdown Cl PR8 4 E4
Ashdown Cres WA9 58 C4
Ashdown Dr CH49 64 C2
Ashdown Gr L26 71 A1
Ashfarm Ct L14 54 F3
Ashfield
Liverpool L15 68 D8
Rainhill L35 57 D3
Ashfield Cres
Bebington CH62 88 D8
Billinge WN5 33 E4
Ashfield Rd
Bebington CH62 88 C8
Liverpool L17 68 E2
Ashfield Sec Specl Sch L16 69 E6
Ashfield St L5 52 C5
Ashford Cl L26 82 E8
Ashford Rd
Birkenhead CH41, CH42 66 C4
Hoylake CH47 63 C8
Ashford Way [1] WA8 73 D1
Ash Gr
Formby L37 9 C1
Golborne WA3 47 B8
Liverpool L15 68 D8
Orrell WN5 25 F6
Prescot L35 56 E5
Rainford WA11 31 F6
Seaforth L21 38 A6
Skelmersdale WN8 15 D1
St Helens WA9 58 C4
Wallasey CH45 51 C7
Widnes WA8 84 D8
Ash Grange L14 54 E3
Ash Grove Cres WN5 33 E6
Ash La WA8 84 A8
Ashland Ave WN4 35 A4
Ashlar Gr L17 68 E2
Ashlar Rd
Crosby L22 26 E2
Liverpool L17 68 E3
Ashlea Rd CH61 77 A3
Ashleigh Rd L31 28 F7
Ashley Ave CH47 48 F1
Ashley Bsns Ctr L34 56 E6
Ashley Cl
Kirkby L33 29 E5
Rainhill L35 57 D2
Ashley Gn WA8 84 D8
Ashley Rd
Skelmersdale WN8 16 B3
Southport PR9 4 C7
Ashley Sch WA8 72 D1
Ashley St CH42 66 F2
Ashley Way W WA8 84 F7
Ashmead Rd WN8 16 A4
Ashmead View WN8 16 A4
Ashmore Cl CH48 75 C6
Ashmuir Hey L32 29 F1
Ashover Ave L14 55 A4
Ash Priors WA8 72 D3
Ash Rd
Bebington CH63 78 F7
Birkenhead CH42 66 D4
Haydock WA11 45 E7
Litherland L21 38 A7
Warrington WA5 74 F4
Winwick WA2 61 B6
Ashridge St WA7 84 F3
Ash St
Bootle L20 38 C4
Golborne WA3 36 B2
Southport PR8 4 C5
Ashton Ave L35 57 C2
Ashton Cl CH62 88 E3
ASHTON CROSS 34 D2
Ashton Ct CH48 63 A2
Ashton Dr
Liverpool L25 82 C8
West Kirby CH48 63 A1
Ashton Grange Ind Est WN4 35 B6
Ashton Heath WN4 35 C2
Ashton House Hospl CH43 66 B4
ASHTON-IN-MAKERFIELD 35 C5
Ashton Pk L25 82 D9
Ashton Rd
Golborne WA3 36 A2
Newton-le-W WA12 46 C5
Southport PR8 3 F1
Windy Arbour WN5 34 B8
ASHTON'S GREEN 45 B3
Ashtons Green Dr WA9 44 F3
Ashton Sq L25 70 B1
Ashton St
Liverpool L3 52 F1
Liverpool, Stanley L13 54 A3
Ash Tree Apartments CH44 51 D3
Ashtree Gr L12 40 F4
ASHURST 16 A4
Ashurst Cl
Liverpool L25 70 B4
Skelmersdale WN8 16 A4
St Helens WA11 44 E6
Ashurst Ct L37 9 E2
Ashurst Dr WA11 44 E6
Ashurst Gdns WN8 16 B4
Ashurst Prim Sch WA11 44 D6
Ashurst Rd WN8 16 B4
Ash Vale L15 68 E8
Ash Villas CH44 51 C2
Ashville Rd
Birkenhead CH41, CH43 66 B7
Wallasey CH44 51 D2
Ashwall St WN8 23 E8
Ashwater Rd L12 40 C2
Ash Way CH60 86 B6
Ashwell Ave WA3 36 D1
Ashwell St L8 90 C1
Ashwood WN8 16 C3
Ashwood Ave
Abram Brow WN2 36 C7
Ashton-in-M WN4 35 A2
Golborne WA3 47 D8
Ashwood Cl
Kirkby L33 29 E5
Liverpool L27 70 E5
Widnes WA8 84 A7
Ashwood Ct CH43 50 C1
Ashwood Dr L12 40 D3
Ashworth Hospl L31 21 B2
Askern Rd L32 40 F8
Askett Cl WA11 45 C7
Askew Cl CH44 51 D4
Askew St [2] L4 38 F1
Askham Cl L8 68 B7
Asland Gdns PR9 2 C4
Asmall Cl L39 13 D6
Asmall La
Haskayne L39, L40 12 E8
Ormskirk L39, L40 13 B7
Asmall Prim Sch L39 13 D6
Aspen Cl
Heswall CH60 86 D8
Kirkby L33 29 F6
Aspendale Rd CH42 66 D4
Aspen Gdns WA9 57 C6
Aspen Gr
Formby L37 9 C1
Liverpool L8 68 C6
Aspen Way [3] WN8 15 E2
Aspenwood WN4 35 A2
Aspes Rd L12 54 E7
Aspinall Cres L37 10 F1
Aspinall St
Birkenhead CH41 66 C7
Prescot L34 56 D6
Asquith Ave CH41 66 B7
Asser Rd L11 53 F8
Assheton Cl WA12 46 B4
Assheton Wlk L24 83 E2
Assissian Cres L30 27 E4
Aster Ct L31 20 C3
Aster Dr L33 29 D5
Asterfield Ave CH63 78 E7
Aster Rd WA11 45 F7
Astley Cl
Rainford WA11 31 F7
Widnes WA8 72 C3
Astley Rd L36 55 E5
Aston Cl CH43 65 F3
Aston St L19 81 D5
Astonwood Rd CH42 66 D3
Astor St L4 38 F2
Atheldene Rd L4 39 C2
Athelstan Cl CH62 79 D1
Atherton Cl L5 52 E5
Atherton Dr CH49 65 A3
Atherton Ho [6] CH45 51 B8
Atherton House Sch L23 26 D4
Atherton Rake L30 27 D4
Atherton Rd L9 39 C6
Atherton St
Bickershaw WN2 36 E8
[9] Prescot L34 56 D6
St Helens WA10 43 F4
Wallasey CH45 51 B8
Athlone Rd WA2 61 A1
Athol Cl
Bebington CH62 88 E5
Newton-le-W WA12 45 F4
Athol Dr CH62 88 E5
Athole Gr PR9 4 F7
Atholl Cres L10 28 D2
Athol St
Birkenhead CH41 66 E7
Liverpool L5 52 B5
Liverpool L5 52 C5
Liverpool L5 52 D5
Atkinson Gr L36 55 F4
Atkinson St WN2 36 B8
Atlanta Ct L33 29 D6
Atlantic Point L3 52 D3
Atlantic Rd L20 38 B3
Atlantic Way
Bootle L30 38 E8
Liverpool L3 67 D4
Atlas Bsns Complex L20 38 A4
Atlas Rd L20 38 B4
Atlas St WA9 44 B4
Atterbury Cl WA8 72 C2
Atterbury St L8 67 E5
Attlee Rd L36 56 A3
Attwood St [15] L4 52 F7
Atwell St L6 53 A4
Aubourn Cl WA8 72 C3
Aubrey Ct [6] L6 53 A4
Auburn Rd
Liverpool L13 53 E6
Wallasey CH45 51 A7
Aubynes The CH45 50 E7
Audlem Ave CH43 65 F3
Audley St L3 90 C4
Audre Cl WA5 74 D6
Audrey Wlk L10 40 B7
AUGHTON 21 A7
Aughton Chase PR8 4 A5
Aughton Christ Church CE Prim Sch L39 13 C3
Aughton Cl WN5 33 E4
Aughton Ct CH49 65 A5
Aughton Hall Cotts L39 13 C6
Aughton Mews PR8 4 A5
AUGHTON PARK 13 E2
Aughton Park Dr L39 13 D2
Aughton Park Sta L39 13 D2
Aughton Rd
Bootle L20 38 D5
Southport PR8 4 A5
Aughton St Michael's CE Prim Sch L39 13 B1
Aughton St L39 13 E4
Aughton Town Green Prim Sch L39 21 D8
Augusta Cl [3] L13 54 A2
August Rd L6 53 D5
August St L20 38 C5
Aukland Gr WA9 57 D6
Aukland Rd L15, L18 69 A5
Aurorean Cl L27 70 D6
Austell Cl WA11 44 D7
Austen Dr WA2 61 A6
Austin Ave
Garswood WN4 34 E4
St Helens WA10 57 C8
Austin Cl L32 29 D2
Austin Rawlinson Sports Ctr L24 82 E4
Austin St CH44 51 A2
Autumn Gr CH42 78 E8
Autumn Way
Bootle L20 38 C5
St Helens WA9 58 C3
Avalon Sch CH48 75 C8
Avalon Terr [7] L20 38 B4
Avebury Cl
Golborne WA3 47 E8
Widnes WA8 73 F3
Avelon Cl
Birkenhead CH43 65 D5
Maghull L31 20 B5
Avenue The
Banks PR9 2 F5
Bebington CH62 88 C8
Halewood L26 82 E8
Huyton-w-R L36 55 E3
Liverpool, Garston L19 81 E5
Newton-le-W WA12 46 D4
Ormskirk L39 13 D6
Ormskirk L39 13 E6
Orrell WN5 25 D3
Rainford WA11 31 F6
Southport PR8 5 F5
St Helens WA10 43 B3
Averham Cl WN4 35 B2
Avery Cl WA2 61 E2
Avery Cres WA11 45 C7
Avery Rd WA11 45 C7
Avery Sq WA11 45 C7
Aviary Ct L9 38 F6
Aviemore Cl WN4 34 D4
Aviemore Rd L13 53 F3
Avington Cl L12 54 D7
Avis Wlk L10 40 B7
Avocet Cl
Newton-le-W WA12 46 C4
Warrington WA2 61 D3
Avolon Rd L12 54 D5
Avon WA8 72 A2
Avon Ave WA5 74 F4
Avon Cl
Kirkby L33 29 F6
Liverpool L4 52 E8
Avon Ct L23 26 E5
Avondale Ave
Bebington CH62 88 F5
Maghull L31 28 C8
Wallasey CH46 49 F1
Avondale Dr WA8 72 B1
Avondale Rd
Haydock WA11 45 C7
Hoylake CH47 63 B8
Liverpool L15 68 E6
Southport PR9 4 B8
Avondale Rd N PR9 1 C1
Avonmore Ave L18 69 A3
Avon Rd
Ashton-in-M WN4 35 E5
Billinge WN5 33 D3
Avon St
[9] Liverpool L6 53 B5
Wallasey CH41 50 F1
Awelon Cl L12 54 C8
Axbridge Ave WA9 58 D5
Axholme Cl CH61 77 B5
Axholme Rd CH61 77 A5
Ayala Cl L9 38 F7
Aycliffe Rd WA9 57 D6
Aycliffe Wlk [6] WA8 84 C8
Aye Bridge Rd WA3 36 B5
Ayers Ct WA9 57 E7
Aylesbury Ave CH43 65 E2
Aylesbury Ho L31 20 B4
Aylesbury Rd CH45 51 C7

Aylesford Rd L13 54 B3
Aylsham Cl WA8 72 C4
Aylsham Dr CH49 65 A7
Aylton Rd L36 55 B4
Aylward Pl L20 38 B4
Aynsley Ct WA9 57 B6
Ayr Cl PR8 4 F4
Ayr Rd [9] L4 39 A2
Ayrshire Gdns WA10 43 E2
Ayrshire Rd L4 53 C8
Aysgarth Ave L12 54 C6
Aysgarth Rd CH45 50 F6
Azalea Gdns WA9 59 A7
Azalea Gr L26 70 D2

B

Babbacombe Rd
Liverpool L16 69 E6
Warrington WA5 74 E4
Back Barlow La L4 52 E8
Back Bath St PR9 4 B8
Back Beau St [8] L5 52 E4
Back Bedford St [2] L7, L69 67 F8
Back Belmont Rd L6 53 B5
Back Berry St L1 90 C2
Back Blackfield Terr [10] L4, L5 52 D7
Back Bold St L1 90 B3
Back Boundary St L5 52 D6
Back Bridge Rd [5] L23 26 C3
Back Bridge St WA12 46 B3
Back Bridport St L3 90 C3
Back Brow WN8 25 C7
Back Canning St L1, L8 67 F8
Back Catharine St [9] L8 67 F8
Back Chadwick Mount L5 52 E7
Back Chatham Pl L7 53 B1
Back Commutation Row L3 90 C4
Back Cross La WA12 46 B4
Back Dovecot Pl L14 54 F4
Back Egerton St N [8] L8 67 F7
Back Egerton St S [9] L8 67 F7
Back Falkner St S L8 68 A8
Backford Cl CH43 65 F3
Backford Rd CH61 76 D5
Backford Way CH43 65 F3
Back Forest Rd PR8 4 D6
Back Gillmoss La L11 40 C6
Back Granton Rd [6] L5 53 A6
Back Guilford St L6 52 F3
Back High St L25 70 A2
Back Holland Pl [3] L7 53 B1
Back Hope Pl L1 90 C2
Back Huskisson St [2] L8 67 F7
Back Kelvin Gr L8 68 A6
Back Knight St L1 90 C2
Back La
Burtonwood WA5 59 D7
Clieves Hills L39 12 E1
Crank WA11 32 F5
Crosby, Moor Park L23 26 F8
Crosby, Thornton L29 27 C7
Haskayne L39 11 D3
Maghull L39 20 E6
Royal Oak L39 22 B2
Skelmersdale, Digmoor WN8 24 D6
Skelmersdale, Holland Moor WN8 24 E7
Warrington WA5 74 A3
Back Langham St L4 52 F8
Back Leeds St L3 52 B2
Back Legh St WA12 46 A3
Back Lime St L1 90 B3
Back Little Canning St [6] L8 67 F7
Back Luton Gr L4 52 F8
Back Market St WA12 46 A3
Back Maryland St L1 90 C2
Back Menai St CH41 66 C6
Back Mersey View L22 26 C2
Back Mount St [1] L22 26 D1
Back Mount Vernon Gn [8] L7 53 A2
Back Mulberry St L7 67 F8
Back Oliver St [9] CH41 66 E6
Back Orford St L15 68 F8
Back O The Town La L38 18 E3
Back Percy St L8 67 F7
Back Renshaw St L1 90 C3
Back Rockfield Rd L4 53 A7
Back St Bride St [11] L7 67 F8
Back Sandon St L8 67 F7
Back Sandown La [4] L15 68 F8
Back Sandstone Rd L13 53 F4
Back School La
Skelmersdale WN8 15 D2
Up Holland WN8 25 C7
Back Seaview CH47 63 B7
Back Sea View CH47 63 B7
Back Seel St L1 90 B2
Back Sir Howard St L8 67 F8
Back South Rd L22 26 E1
Back Stanley Rd L20 38 C3
Back Towerlands St [1] L7 53 B1
Back Virginia St PR8 4 C6
Back Wellesley Rd L8 68 A4
Back Westminster Rd [3] L4 52 E8
Back Windsor View [5] L8 68 B7
Back Winstanley Rd L22 26 E2
Back York Terr L5 52 E6
Badbury Cl WA11 45 D7
Badby Wood L33 29 F4
Baddow Croft L25 69 E3
Baden Ct CH48 63 A3
Baden Ho L13 54 B3
Baden Rd L13 54 B3
Bader Cl CH61 76 E3
Badgers Rake L37 9 C5
Badger's Set CH48 75 D6
Badger Way CH43 77 E8
Badminton St L8 67 F3
Baffin Cl CH46 50 A4
Bagnall St [1] L4 53 A7
Bagot St L15 68 D7
Baguley Ave WA8 84 A5
Bahama Cl WA11 45 D8
Bahama Rd WA11 45 D8
Bailey Ct L20 38 E7
Bailey Dr L20 38 E7
Baileys Cl WA8 73 A5
Baileys La L26 83 A7
Bailey's La
Hale L24 83 A1
Liverpool L24 82 A4
Bailey St L1 90 C2
Bailey Way L31 28 C7
Bainbridge Ave WA3 47 F8
Bainbridge Cres WA5 74 E8
Bainton Cl L32 41 A7
Bainton Rd L32 41 A7
Bakers Green Rd L36 55 E4
Baker's La PR9 1 F3
Bakers St L36 56 A2
Baker St
Liverpool L6 53 A3
St Helens WA9 44 C3
Baker Way L6 53 A3
Bakewell Gr L9 39 B7
Bakewell Rd WA5 60 A7
Bala Cl WA5 60 E2
Bala Gr [2] CH44 51 A3
Bala St L4 53 B6
Balcarres Ave L18 68 F5
Baldwin Ave L16 69 F8
Baldwin St WA10 44 A4
Bales The L30 28 A4
Balfe St L21 38 A6
Balfour Ave L20 38 B5
Balfour Rd
Birkenhead CH43 66 B5
Bootle L20 38 B5
Southport PR8 4 E5
Wallasey CH41, CH44 51 A4
Balfour St
[10] Liverpool L4 52 F7
Runcorn WA7 84 F1
St Helens WA10 43 D3
Balham Cl WA8 73 A4
Balharry Ave WA11 45 E7
Balker Dr WA10 43 F5
Ballantrae Rd L18 69 C3
Ballantyne Dr CH43 50 C1
Ballantyne Gr
Bootle L20 38 E6
Liverpool L13 53 F7
Ballantyne Pl
Liverpool L13 53 E6
Winwick WA2 61 A6
Ballantyne Rd L13 53 F7
Ballantyne Way [5] WA3 47 E8
Ballantyne Wlk CH43 50 C1
Ballard Rd CH48 63 E3
Ballater Dr WA2 61 E4
Ball Ave CH45 51 A8
Balliol Cl CH43 50 C1
Balliol Gr L23 26 B2
Balliol Rd L20 38 C2
Balliol Rd E L20 38 D2
Balliol Way WN4 34 F4
BALL O' DITTON 72 E2
Ball Pathway WA8 72 E1
Ball's Pl PR8 4 B7
Ball's Rd CH41, CH43 66 B5
Ball's Rd E CH41 66 C5
Ball St WA9 44 D4
Balmer St WA9 57 D8
Balmoral Ave
Crosby L23 26 E3
Golborne WA3 36 D1
St Helens WA9 58 C7
Balmoral Cl
[5] Kirkby L33 29 E5
Southport PR9 2 B3
Balmoral Ct L13 53 E5
Balmoral Dr
Formby L37 9 E1
Southport PR9 2 B3
Balmoral Gdns [6] CH43 65 F1
Balmoral Gr CH43 65 D3
Balmoral Rd
Ashton-in-M WN4 35 A4
Liverpool, Elm Park L6 53 D3
[6] Liverpool L9 39 A6
Balmoral Rd *continued*
Maghull L31 20 C1
Wallasey CH45 37 C1
Widnes WA8 73 A4
Balmoral Way L34 55 F5
Balm St L7 53 B2
Balniel St WA9 58 E3
Balsham Cl L25 82 D8
Baltic Rd L20 38 B3
Baltic St [2] L4 53 A7
Baltimore St [1] L1 90 C2
Bamber Gdns PR9 5 A8
Bamboo Cl L27 70 E6
Bamburgh Pl [3] WN4 35 A5
BAMFURLONG 35 F8
Bampton Ave WA11 33 B1
Bampton Rd L16 69 D8
Banastre Dr WA12 46 F3
Banastre Rd PR8 4 B5
Banbury Ave L25 70 C2
Banbury Rd WN5 25 D2
Banbury Way CH43 65 E2
Bancroft Cl L25 82 C9
Bancroft Rd WA8 73 D2
Bandon Cl L24 83 D2
Banff Ave CH63 88 D5
Bangor Rd CH45 50 D6
BANGOR'S GREEN 12 D7
Bangor St L5 52 C5
Bank Ave WN5 25 D5
Bankburn Rd L13 53 E6
Bank Dene CH42 79 A8
Bankfield WN8 24 C7
Bankfield Ct L13 53 F5
Bankfield La PR9 2 B2
Bankfield Rd
Liverpool L13 53 F5
Widnes WA8 72 C1
Bankfield Sch The WA8 72 D1
Bankfields Dr CH62 89 B5
Bankfield St L20 52 B8
Bank Gdns WA5 74 E4
Bankhall La L20 52 C7
Bankhall St L20 52 C8
Bankhall Sta L20 52 C8
BANK HEATH 47 A8
Bank La L31, L33 29 D5
Bankland Rd L13 53 F5
Bank Nook PR9 1 F3
Bank Pas
Golborne WA3 36 A1
Southport PR8 4 A7
Bank Rd L20 38 B3
BANKS 2 F6
Banks Ave CH47 63 D8
Banksbarn WN8 24 C7
Bankside L38 17 F3
Bankside Ave WN4 35 A8
Bankside Ct L21 38 A8
Bankside Rd CH42 78 F8
Bank's La
Liverpool, Garston L19 81 D4
Speke L24 81 F2
Bank Sq PR9 4 B8
Banks Rd
Heswall CH60 85 D8
Southport PR9 2 D6
West Kirby CH48 63 A1
Bank's Rd L19 81 D4
Banks Road Prim Sch L19 81 D4
Bank St
[4] Birkenhead CH41 66 E6
Golborne WA3 36 A1
Newton-le-W WA12 45 F3
St Helens WA10 43 E3
Banks The CH45 50 E7
Bank's Way L19 81 D4
Bank View High Sch L10 39 F8
Bankville Rd CH42 66 E3
Banner Hey L35 56 D1
Bannerman St L7 68 D8
Banner St
Liverpool L15 68 E7
St Helens WA10 43 F3
Banner Wlk [3] WA10 43 F3
Banning Cl CH41 66 D7
Banstead Gr L15 69 B7
Barbara Ave L10 40 B7
Barbara St WA9 58 E3
Barberry Cl CH46 64 B8
Barberry Cres L30 28 A4
Barber St WA9 44 C4
Barbondale Cl WA5 74 F7
Barbour Dr L20 38 E6
Barbrook Way L9 39 B3
Barchester Dr L17 68 C1
Barclay St L8 67 F4
Barcombe Rd CH60 77 D1
Bardale Gr WN4 35 A3
Bardley Cres L36 71 A7
Bardney Ave WA3 35 F2
Bardon Cl L25 70 C5
Bardsay Rd L4 39 A1
Bardsley Ave WA5 60 F1
Bardsley Cl WN8 25 A7
Barford Cl
Birkenhead CH43 65 B6
Southport PR8 7 A6
Up Holland WN8 25 A7
Warrington WA5 60 B1
Barford Rd
Huyton-w-R L36 55 F5
Liverpool L25 82 B7
Bargate Water WA9 57 E6
Barkbeth Rd L36 55 C5
Barkeley Dr L21 37 F6
Barker Cl L36 70 F8
Barker La CH49 64 C2
Barker Rd CH61 76 F6
Barkerville Cl L13 53 D7
Barker Way L6 53 B5
Barkfield Ave L37 9 E4
Barkfield La
Formby L37 9 D4
Formby L37 9 E4
Barkhill Rd L17, L19 68 F1
Barkiss Cl L8 67 F5
Bark Rd L21 27 C1
Barleyfield CH61 76 E4
Barleyfield Ho CH61 76 E4
Barlow Ave CH63 79 A6
Barlow Gr WA9 45 A2
Barlow La L4 52 E8
Barlows Cl L9 39 D8
Barlow's La
Liverpool L9 39 D8
Shirdley Hill L39 8 D5
Barlows Prim Sch L9 39 D7
Barlow St L4 52 E8
Barmouth Cl WA5 60 E2
Barmouth Rd CH45 50 D6
Barmouth Way L5 52 C5
Barnacre Dr CH64 86 B2
Barnacre La CH46, CH48 64 B6
Barnard Rd CH43 66 B5
Barn Cl L30 28 A4
Barncroft CH61 76 F3
Barncroft Pl L23 26 E6
Barn Croft Rd L26 83 A7
Barncroft The CH49 64 D4
Barndale Rd L18 69 A5
Barnes Cl
Kirkby L33 29 E6
Widnes WA8 73 D2
Barnes Dr L31 20 C3
Barnes Gn CH63 79 A2
Barnes Rd
Ormskirk L39 13 E3
Skelmersdale WN8 15 E1
Widnes WA8 73 C2
Barnes St L6 53 A5
Barneston Rd WA8 73 E3
Barnet Cl [7] L7 68 C8
Barnett Ave WA12 45 E3
Barnfield Cl
Hoylake CH47 48 E1
Litherland L30 27 E2
Liverpool L12 54 B6
Barnfield Dr
Liverpool L12 54 B6
Skelmersdale WN8 24 E7
Barnham Cl
Golborne WA3 47 A8
Liverpool L24 82 B5
Barnham Dr L16 69 E7
Barn Hey CH47 63 A5
Barn Hey Cres CH47 63 F8
Barn Hey Gn L12 54 B6
Barn Hey Rd L33 30 A2
Barnhill Rd L15 69 A6
Barnhurst Cl L16 69 E7
Barnhurst Rd L16 69 E7
Barn La WA3 46 F8
Barnmeadow Rd L25 70 A5
Barnsbury Rd L4 39 C2
Barnsdale Ave CH61 77 B5
Barnside Ct L16 69 E7
Barnstaple Way WA5 74 E4
BARNSTON 77 C3
Barnston La CH46 49 E1
Barnston Prim Sch CH60 86 C7
Barnston Rd
Heswall CH60, CH61 77 B4
Liverpool L9 39 B7
Barnston Towers Cl CH60 86 C8
Barnston Twrs CH60 86 C8
Barnstream Cl L27 70 C6
Barnton Cl WA3 47 D7
Barn Way WA12 46 B3
Barnwell Ave CH44, CH45 51 B5
Barnwood Rd L36 55 B4
Baroncroft Rd L25 69 F3
Baron's Cl WA8 84 C8
Baron's Hey L28 54 F8
Barren Gr CH43 66 B4
Barrett Ave PR8 4 A2
Barrett Rd PR8 4 A2
Barrington Dr PR8 7 B5
Barrington Rd
Liverpool L15 68 E6
Wallasey CH44 51 C3
Barrow Ave WA2 61 E2
Barrow Cl L12 40 C1
Barrowdale Rd WA3 47 B8
Barrowfield Rd WA10 43 A5
Barrow Hall Com Prim Sch WA5 74 E7
Barrow Hall La WA5 74 E7
Barrow La WA2 47 C2
BARROW NOOK 22 F2
Barrow Nook La L39 22 E2
Barrows Cotts L35 56 E3
BARROW'S GREEN 73 E4
Barrow's Green La WA8 73 E3
Barrow's Row WA8 73 B4
Barrow St
Ashton-in-M WN4 35 D5
St Helens WA10 44 A3
Barry Dr L19 81 B6
Barrymore Rd L13 53 F3
Barrymore Way CH63 88 B6
Bartholomew Cl L35 57 E1
Bartholomews Day Hospl L36 55 C2
Bartlett Ho PR8 4 B3
Bartlett St L15 68 E7
BARTON 11 F6
Barton Cl
Hoylake CH47 62 F6
Litherland L21 27 A2
St Helens WA10 43 F4
Barton Clough WN5 33 E5
Barton Hey Dr CH48 75 D6
Barton Heys Rd L37 9 D1
Barton Rd
Hoylake CH47 63 A6
Liverpool L9 38 F4
Bartons Cl PR9 2 D5
Barton St
[21] Birkenhead CH41 66 C5
Golborne WA3 36 A1
Barwell Ave WA11 44 C6
Barwell Cl WA3 36 C1
Basil Cl L16 69 E8
Basildon Cl WA9 57 F7
Basil Rd L16 69 D8
Basing St L19 81 C7
Baskervyle Cl CH60 86 A6
Baskervyle Rd CH60 86 A6
Basnett St L1 90 B3
Bassendale Rd CH62 79 E2
Bassenthwaite Ave
Birkenhead CH43 65 D5
Kirkby L33 29 D4
St Helens WA11 44 A8
Bates Cres WA10 57 D8
Batey Ave L35 57 B4
Bathgate Way L33 29 D6
Bath St N PR9 4 B8
Bath Springs L39 13 F5
Bath St
Bebington CH62 79 B5
Liverpool L3 52 B2
Seaforth L22 37 D8
Southport PR9 4 B8
St Helens WA10 43 F3
Bathurst Rd L19 81 B7
Batley St [4] L13 54 A3
Battenberg St L7 53 A2
Battersea Ct WA8 72 F3
Battery Cl [4] L17 68 C2
Battle Way L37 10 B2
Baucher Dr L20 38 E7
Baumville Dr CH63 78 F2
Bawtry Ct WA2 61 E1
Baxters La WA9 58 D8
Baycliff Rd L12 54 E7
Bayfield Rd L19 81 A7
Bayhorse La L3 52 F2
Baysdale Cl L8 68 A4
Bayswater Ct CH45 50 D6
Bayswater Gdns CH45 50 D7
Bayswater Rd CH45 50 D6
Baythorne Rd L4 39 C2
Baytree Cl PR9 2 D5
Baytree Gr L31 29 A3
Bay Tree Gr [2] WA9 58 C8
Baytree Rd
Birkenhead CH42 66 E3
West Kirby CH48 63 F2
Bayview Dr CH45 50 D7
Beacham Rd PR8 4 E7
Beach Bank L22 26 C2
Beachcroft Rd CH47 48 E1
Beach Gr CH45 51 C7
Beach Lawn L22 26 C1
Beachmews PR8 3 F6
Beach Priory Gdns PR8 4 A6
Beach Rd
Bootle L21 38 B7
Hoylake CH47 62 F6
Litherland L21 38 A7
Southport PR8 3 F6
Beach Road Prim Sch L21 38 A7
Beach Wlk CH48 75 B8
Beacon CE Prim Sch The L5 52 F5
Beacon Ct [4] CH60 86 A8
Beacon Ctry Pk* WN8 16 F2
Beacon Dr CH48 63 C2
Beacon Gr WA11 44 D6
Beacon Ho L5 52 E4
Beacon Hts WN8 25 A8
Beacon La
Heswall CH60 86 A7
Liverpool L5 52 F6
Skelmersdale L40, WN8 16 D4
Beacon Rd WN5 33 E6
Beacon Sch WN8 24 E8
Beaconsfield [13] L34 56 D6
Beaconsfield Cl [1] CH42 66 F3
Beaconsfield Cres WA8 73 A4
Beaconsfield Ct [4] L39 13 F5
Beaconsfield Gr WA8 73 B4
Beaconsfield Rd
Bebington CH62 79 B7
Liverpool L25 69 F3
Runcorn WA7 84 E1
Seaforth L21 37 F7
Southport PR9 4 F6
St Helens WA10 43 C5
Widnes WA8 73 B4
Beaconsfield St L8 68 A6

Beaconsfield Terr L19 ... 81 B6
Beacons The CH60 .... 86 A7
Beacon View Dr WN8 .... 25 B7
Beadnell Dr WA5 .... 74 F3
Beames Cl L7 .... 53 C1
Beardsmore Dr WA3 ..... 36 E1
Bearncroft WN8 .... 24 D6
Beatles Story (Mus) The★
L3 .... 90 A2
Beatrice Ave CH63 .... 78 E7
Beatrice St L20 .... 38 D1
Beattock Cl L33 .... 29 D6
Beatty Ave WA2 .... 61 C1
Beatty Cl
Prescot L35 .... 56 D2
West Kirby CH48 .... 75 C6
Beatty Rd
7 Liverpool L13 .... 54 A3
Southport PR8 .... 4 E5
Beauclair Dr L15 .... 69 C6
Beaufort L37 .... 10 A2
Beaufort Cl
Ormskirk L39 .... 13 A1
Widnes WA8 .... 84 A8
Beaufort Dr CH44 .... 50 E4
Beaufort Park Prim Sch
L8 .... 67 F5
Beaufort Rd CH41 .... 51 A1
Beaufort St
Liverpool L8 .... 67 E5
St Helens WA9 .... 44 C1
Beaumaris Ct 5 CH43 .... 66 B5
Beaumaris Dr CH61 ...... 77 B6
Beaumaris Rd CH45 ...... 50 D6
Beaumaris St L20 .... 52 C8
Beaumont Ave WA10 ..... 43 D4
Beaumont Cres L39 ...... 13 D2
Beaumont Dr L10 .... 28 F1
Beaumont Ho L39 .... 13 D2
Beaumont St L8 .... 68 B7
Beau St L3 .... 52 E4
Beauworth Ave CH49 ..... 64 C3
Beaver Ct WN4 .... 35 C6
Beaver Gr L9 .... 39 A6
Beavers La WN8 .... 24 D6
BEBINGTON 78 E3
Bebington High Sports
Coll CH63 .... 78 F6
Bebington Rd
Bebington CH62 .... 79 A6
Birkenhead CH42 .... 66 E1
Bebington Sta CH63 ..... 79 A7
Bebles Rd L39 .... 13 C3
Bechers WA8 .... 72 B3
Bechers Bsns Ctr L30 .... 28 B2
Bechers Ct L9 .... 28 B3
Bechers Dr L9 .... 28 C2
Bechers Row L9 .... 38 F6
Beck Cl L10 .... 40 B7
Beckenham Ave 7 L18 .... 68 F5
Beckenham Cl WA8 ...... 73 D4
Beckenham Rd CH45 ..... 37 B1
Becket St L4 .... 52 D7
Beckett Cl L33 .... 41 C8
Beckett Dr WA2 .... 61 A5
Beckett Gr CH63 .... 78 D7
Beck Gr WA11 .... 44 B8
Beckinsale Cl L26 .... 71 A1
Beck Rd L20 .... 38 C5
Beckwith St E CH41 ..... 66 D7
Beckwith St
Birkenhead CH41 .... 66 C7
Liverpool L1 .... 90 B2
Becky St L6 .... 53 B5
Becontree Rd L12 .... 54 D4
Bective St L7 .... 68 C8
Bedale Wlk 7 L33 .... 29 F4
Bedburn Dr L36 .... 55 B3
Bede Cl L33 .... 29 E6
Bedford Ave
Birkenhead CH42 .... 66 E1
Maghull L31 .... 28 F6
Bedford Cl
Huyton-w-R L36 .... 56 A3
6 Liverpool L7 .... 67 F8
Bedford Ct
7 Birkenhead CH42 ...... 66 F2
7 Liverpool L8 .... 67 F7
Southport PR8 .... 4 A2
Bedford Dr CH42 .... 66 D1
Bedford Drive Prim Sch
CH42 .... 66 D1
Bedford Pl
Ashton-in-M WN4 .... 35 A5
Birkenhead CH42 .... 67 A2
Liverpool L20 .... 38 B1
1 Seaforth L21 .... 37 F7
Bedford Prim Sch L20 ... 38 D2
Bedford Rd
Birkenhead CH42 .... 66 F2
Bootle L20, L4 .... 38 D2
Southport PR8 .... 4 A2
Wallasey CH45 .... 51 B6
Bedford Rd E CH42 ...... 67 A2
Bedford St N L7 .... 52 F1
Bedford St S L7, L8, L69 ... 67 F8
Bedford St WA9 .... 44 D2
Bedford Villas L20 .... 38 D2
Bedford Wlk 7 L7 .... 67 F8
Beecham Cl L36 .... 55 D1
Beech Ave
Birkenhead CH49 .... 64 D6
Crosby L23 .... 27 A6
Golborne WA3 .... 47 F7
Haydock WA11 .... 45 F7
Heswall CH61 .... 77 A4
Kirkby L31 .... 29 B3
Liverpool L17 .... 68 B2
Beech Ave *continued*
Prescot L34 .... 56 F7
St Helens WA9 .... 58 C4
Warrington WA5 .... 74 C3
Beechbank Rd L18 .... 68 F5
Beechburn Cres L36 ..... 55 B3
Beechburn Rd L36 .... 55 A3
Beech Cl
Kirkby L32 .... 29 C3
Liverpool L12 .... 40 D3
Newton-le-W WA12 ...... 46 C2
Skelmersdale WN8 .... 15 E1
Beechcroft L31 .... 20 D1
Beechcroft Rd CH44 ..... 51 C2
Beech Ct
2 Birkenhead CH42 ...... 66 D4
Liverpool L18 .... 69 D3
Southport PR9 .... 4 D8
Widnes WA8 .... 72 B3
Beechdale Rd L18 .... 69 A4
Beechdene Rd L4 .... 53 B7
Beech Dr L37 .... 9 D4
Beechenhurst Sch L18 ... 69 D4
Beeches The
4 Birkenhead CH42 ...... 66 F1
Liverpool L18 .... 69 D4
St Helens WA9 .... 58 D5
Wallasey CH46 .... 49 E3
Widnes WA8 .... 73 D4
Beechfield
Huyton-w-R L36 .... 55 C2
Maghull L31 .... 20 E1
Beechfield Cl
Heswall CH60 .... 86 A7
Liverpool L26 .... 82 E7
Beechfield Gdns PR8 ...... 3 F6
Beechfield Mews PR9 ..... 4 C7
Beechfield Rd L18 .... 69 D4
Beech Gdns WA11 .... 31 E6
Beech Gn L12 .... 54 A8
Beech Gr
Abram Brow WN2 .... 36 C7
Litherland L30 .... 28 A2
Liverpool L9 .... 39 B6
Seaforth L21 .... 37 F6
Southport PR9 .... 4 F7
Beech Grove Ho L12 ..... 54 B8
Beech Hey La CH64 ...... 88 B1
Beechill Cl L25 .... 70 C4
Beech La L18 .... 69 C5
Beech Lawn L19 .... 80 F7
Beech Mdw L39 .... 14 A4
Beech Mdws L34 .... 56 A5
Beech Pk
Crosby L23 .... 27 A6
Liverpool L12 .... 54 A6
Beech Rd
Aughton L39 .... 21 A6
Bebington CH63 .... 78 F7
Birkenhead CH42 .... 66 D4
Golborne WA3 .... 36 A1
Heswall CH60 .... 86 C8
Huyton-w-R L36 .... 55 E1
Liverpool L4 .... 39 A2
Beech St
Ashton-in-M WN4 .... 35 A6
Bootle L20 .... 38 C4
Liverpool L7 .... 53 C2
St Helens WA10 .... 57 D8
Beech Terr L7 .... 53 C2
Beech Tree Ct L19 .... 80 F7
Beech Tree Hos WN2 .... 35 F7
Beechtree Rd L15 .... 54 B1
Beechtrees WN8 .... 24 D7
Beechurst Cl L25 .... 70 B5
Beechurst Rd L25 .... 70 B5
Beechwalk The L14 ...... 54 B4
Beechway
Bebington CH63 .... 78 F3
Maghull L31 .... 21 B2
Beechway Ave L31 .... 21 B2
Beechwood WN8 .... 16 C3
Beechwood Ave
Ashton-in-M WN4 .... 35 A2
Liverpool L26 .... 82 F8
Newton-le-W WA12 ...... 46 D4
Wallasey CH45 .... 50 E5
Warrington WA5 .... 74 F5
Beechwood Cl
Liverpool L19 .... 81 A7
Prescot L35 .... 56 E4
St Helens WA9 .... 58 C4
Beechwood Cres WN5 ... 25 E6
Beechwood Ct
Maghull L31 .... 20 F1
Skelmersdale WN8 .... 24 D6
Beechwood Dr
Birkenhead CH43 .... 65 C7
Formby L37 .... 9 C1
Ormskirk L39 .... 13 D5
Beechwood Gdns L19 .... 80 F7
Beechwood Gn L19 ...... 81 A7
Beechwood Rd
Bebington CH62 .... 88 C8
Bootle L21 .... 38 B6
Liverpool, Grassendale
L19 .... 80 F7
Beechwood Rd S L19 .... 80 F7
Beecroft Cl WA5 .... 60 D1
Beeford Dr WN5 .... 25 E5
Beesands Cl L27 .... 70 F4
Beesley Rd L34 .... 56 C6
Beeston Cl CH43 .... 65 C6
Beeston Dr
Heswall CH61 .... 76 F4
Litherland L30 .... 28 B5
Beeston Gr L19 .... 81 A7
Beeston St L4 .... 52 F8
Beetham Way L33 .... 29 F3
Begonia Gdns WA9 ...... 59 A7
Beilby Rd WA11 .... 45 E7
Belair Ind Est L23 .... 26 F3
Beldale Pk L32 .... 29 C4
Beldon Cres L36 .... 55 B3
Belem Cl L17 .... 68 C5
Belem Twr L17 .... 68 C5
Belfast Rd L13 .... 54 B3
Belfield WN8 .... 24 D6
Belfield Cres L36 .... 55 E1
Belfield Dr CH43 .... 66 B3
Belford Dr CH46 .... 64 C8
Belfort Rd L25 .... 70 B4
Belfry Cl
Liverpool L12 .... 54 E6
Wallasey CH46 .... 49 B1
Belgrave Ave CH44 ...... 51 C4
Belgrave Cl WA8 .... 73 E3
Belgrave Pl PR8 .... 3 F3
Belgrave Rd
Liverpool L17 .... 68 B3
4 Seaforth L21 .... 37 F7
Southport PR8 .... 3 F3
Belgrave St CH44 .... 51 C4
Belgravia Apartments
PR9 .... 1 B1
Belgravia Ct WA8 .... 72 F3
Belgravia Ho PR9 .... 4 D8
Belhaven Rd 4 L18 ...... 68 F5
Bellair Ave L23 .... 27 A4
Bellairs Rd L11 .... 53 E8
Bellamy Rd L4 .... 38 E2
Bella Vista Ct L23 .... 26 B3
Bell Cl L36 .... 70 F8
Belldene Gr CH61 .... 76 F2
Bellefield Ave L12 .... 54 B6
Bellerive RC Coll L8 ..... 68 B5
BELLE VALE 70 C6
Belle Vale Com Prim Sch
L25 .... 70 B5
Belle Vale Rd L25 .... 70 C5
Belle Vale Sh Ctr L25 .... 70 B6
Belle Vue Rd
Liverpool L25 .... 70 B4
Wallasey CH44 .... 51 E2
Bellew Rd L11 .... 53 F7
Bellfield Cres CH45 ..... 51 A8
Bellflower Cl WA8 .... 72 E4
Bellgreen Rd L11 .... 40 A2
Bell House Rd WA8 ..... 73 C1
Bellini Cl L21 .... 38 A6
Bellis Ave PR9 .... 1 F2
Bellis Gr 6 L33 .... 29 D5
Bell La L35, WA9 .... 58 A2
Bellmore St L19 .... 81 C7
Bell Rd CH44 .... 51 D3
Bell's Cl L31 .... 20 C4
Bell's La L31 .... 20 B3
Bell St 3 L13 .... 54 A3
Belltower Rd L20 .... 52 B7
Bellward Cl CH63 .... 78 F2
Belmont CH41 .... 66 C5
Belmont Ave
Bebington CH62 .... 79 C1
Golborne WA3 .... 36 C1
Orrell WN5 .... 25 D3
Belmont Cres WA5 ...... 74 F6
Belmont Dr
Heswall CH61 .... 77 A3
Liverpool L6 .... 53 D5
Belmont Gr
12 Birkenhead CH43 ..... 66 C5
Liverpool L6 .... 53 C5
Belmont Pl L19 .... 81 C6
Belmont Rd
Liverpool L6 .... 53 B5
Wallasey CH45 .... 37 B1
West Kirby CH48 .... 63 B3
Widnes WA8 .... 73 E2
Belmont St
Southport PR8 .... 4 A5
St Helens WA10 .... 43 D3
Beloe St L8 .... 67 F4
Belper St L19 .... 81 B7
Belsford Way L24 .... 82 B5
Belston Rd L16 .... 69 D8
Belton Cl WA3 .... 47 A7
Belton Rd L36 .... 55 D6
Belvedere Ave WA9 ..... 58 D6
Belvedere Cl L34 .... 56 E7
Belvedere Dr L37 .... 9 F1
Belvedere Pk L39 .... 21 C7
Belvedere Rd
Ashton-in-M WN4 .... 35 C4
Newton-le-W WA12 ...... 46 B5
Southport PR8 .... 7 C5
Belvedere Sch (Girls Jun)
L17 .... 68 B4
Belvedere Sch The L8 .... 68 A4
Belvidere Pk L23 .... 26 E3
Belvidere Rd
Crosby L23 .... 26 E3
Liverpool L8 .... 68 A4
Wallasey CH45 .... 51 A5
Belvoir Rd
Liverpool L18 .... 81 C8
Widnes WA8 .... 73 B1
Bembridge Cl
Warrington WA5 .... 74 C7
Widnes WA8 .... 72 F4
Bempton Rd L17 .... 68 C2
Benbow Cl CH43 .... 65 F8
Benbow St L20 .... 38 B2
Benedict Cl CH49 .... 65 B4
Benedict Ct L20 .... 38 C1
Benedict's Gr L36 .... 55 C7
Benedict St L20 .... 38 D1
Bengarth Rd PR9 .... 4 F8
Bengel St L7 .... 53 A2
Benjamin Fold WN4 ..... 35 B5
Ben La L39 .... 23 A1
Ben Lane Ct L39 .... 23 B2
Benledi St L5 .... 52 D5
Benmore Rd L18 .... 69 A2
Bennet's La CH47 .... 48 E1
Bennett Dr WN5 .... 25 D4
Bennetts Hill CH43 ...... 66 B4
Bennett's La WA8 .... 73 E1
Bennett St L19 .... 81 C6
Bennett Wlk CH61 .... 76 F3
Ben Nevis Rd CH42 ...... 66 D2
Bennison Ct PR9 .... 1 C1
Bennison Dr L19 .... 81 A7
Ben's Ct L34 .... 41 B5
Benson Cl CH49 .... 64 F4
Benson St L1 .... 90 C3
Bentfield L17 .... 80 F8
Bentfield Cl CH63 .... 78 D7
Bentfield Gdns CH63 .... 78 D7
Bentham Ave WA2 .... 61 C3
Bentham Cl CH43 .... 65 E3
Bentham Dr L16 .... 69 D8
Bentham St PR8 .... 4 B5
Bentham's Way PR8 ...... 4 C2
Bentinck Cl CH41 .... 66 D6
Bentinck Pl CH41, CH43 ... 66 C6
Bentinck St
Birkenhead CH41 .... 66 D6
Liverpool L5 .... 52 B5
Runcorn WA7 .... 84 F3
St Helens WA9 .... 44 D1
Bentley Rd
Birkenhead CH43 .... 66 B4
Heswall CH61 .... 76 F5
Liverpool L8 .... 68 B6
Bentley St WA9 .... 58 C3
Benton Cl L5 .... 52 D6
Bent Way CH60 .... 77 A1
Benty Cl CH63 .... 78 E4
Benty Farm Gr CH61 ..... 77 A5
Benty Heath La CH64,
CH66 .... 88 B3
Benwick Rd L32 .... 29 B2
Berbice Rd L15, L18 ..... 69 A5
Beresford Ave CH63 ..... 79 A7
Beresford Cl CH43 ...... 66 A5
Beresford Ct CH43 ...... 66 A5
Beresford Dr PR9 .... 1 F1
Beresford Gdns PR9 ...... 1 F2
Beresford Rd
Birkenhead CH43 .... 66 A5
Liverpool L8 .... 67 F4
Wallasey CH45 .... 50 F7
Beresford St
Bootle L20 .... 38 B1
7 Liverpool L5 .... 52 E4
St Helens WA9 .... 57 E7
Bergen Cl L20 .... 38 E2
Berkeley Ave CH43 ...... 65 E1
Berkeley Ct
5 Birkenhead CH49 ...... 65 A2
Newton-le-W WA12 ...... 45 F4
Wallasey CH45 .... 51 C7
Berkeley Dr CH45 .... 51 C7
Berkeley Rd L23 .... 26 C5
Berkeswell Rd L11 .... 40 A1
Berkley Ave L12 .... 54 E8
Berkley Pl 10 L8 .... 67 F7
Berkley St L8 .... 67 F7
Berkshire Gdns WA10 ... 43 F2
Bermondsey Gr WA8 .... 73 D4
Bermuda Rd CH46 .... 64 C8
Bernard Ave CH45 ...... 51 C7
Bernard Wood Ct WN5 ... 33 D4
Berner's Rd L19 .... 81 B7
Berner St CH41 .... 66 D8
Berrington Gr WN4 ..... 35 A3
Berrington's La WA11 ... 32 C1
Berry Cl WN8 .... 15 F2
Berryford Rd L14 .... 54 F6
Berry Hill Ave L34 ...... 41 D3
Berrylands Cl CH46 ..... 49 D1
Berrylands Rd CH46 ..... 49 D2
Berry Rd WA8 .... 72 D1
Berrys La WA9 .... 44 F1
Berry St
Bootle L20 .... 38 B2
Liverpool L1 .... 90 C2
Skelmersdale WN8 .... 15 F2
Berrywood Dr L35 .... 56 F2
Bertha Gdns 1 CH41 ..... 65 F8
Bertha St CH41 .... 65 F8
Bertram Cl CH47 .... 63 D8
Bertram Dr CH47 .... 63 D8
Bertram Dr N CH47 ...... 63 D8
Bertram Rd L17 .... 68 C4
Bertram St WA12 .... 46 A4
Berwick Ave
Bebington CH62 .... 88 E4
Southport PR8 .... 7 D5
Berwick Cl
Birkenhead, Bidston
CH43 .... 65 C6
Birkenhead, Moreton
CH46 .... 64 B8
Liverpool L6 .... 53 B4
Berwick Dr L23 .... 26 C5
Berwick St L6 .... 53 B4
Berwyn Ave
Heswall CH61 .... 77 A6
Hoylake CH47 .... 63 C7
Berwyn Bvd CH63 .... 78 E8
Berwyn Ct PR8 .... 4 D4
Berwyn Dr CH61 .... 77 A2
Berwyn Gr WA9 .... 44 F3
Berwyn Rd
Liverpool L4 .... 53 C8
Wallasey CH44 .... 51 C5
Beryl Rd CH43 .... 65 C5
Beryl St L13 .... 54 A1
Beryl Wlk L10 .... 40 B7
Besford Ho L25 .... 70 B5
Besford Rd L25 .... 70 B5
Bessborough Rd CH43 ... 66 B4
Bessbrook Rd L17 .... 68 E2
Bessemer St L8 .... 67 F4
Beta Cl CH62 .... 79 A7
Bethany Cl WA11 .... 45 B7
Bethany Cres CH63 ..... 79 A5
Bethel Gr L17 .... 68 D6
Betjeman Gr L16 .... 69 E8
Betony Cl L26 .... 70 E1
Bettisfield Ave CH62 .... 88 D6
Betty Anne Ct PR9 .... 4 B8
Betula Cl L9 .... 39 C4
Beulah Ave WN5 .... 33 D4
Bevan Cl WA9 .... 57 D6
Bevan's Ct L12 .... 54 C7
Bevan's La L12 .... 54 D7
Beverley Ave WN5 .... 25 E1
Beverley Cl PR9 .... 2 C5
Beverley Dr CH60 .... 86 B6
Beverley Gdns CH61 ..... 77 B6
Beverley Rd
Bebington CH62 .... 79 B8
Liverpool L15 .... 69 A6
Wallasey CH45 .... 50 F6
Beversbrook Rd L11 ..... 40 B2
Bevington Bush L3 .... 52 D3
Bevington Hill 2 L3 ..... 52 D4
Bevington St
3 Ashton-in-M WN4 ...... 34 F5
Liverpool L3 .... 52 D4
Bevyl Rd CH64 .... 86 B2
Bewcastle Dr L40 .... 14 C3
Bewey Cl L8 .... 67 E4
Bewley Dr L32 .... 40 E8
Bewsey St WA10 .... 43 D1
Bexhill Ave WA2 .... 61 B4
Bexhill Cl L24 .... 82 B5
Bexhill Gdns WA9 .... 57 C6
Bexley Ct CH43 .... 66 A5
Bianca St L20 .... 38 C1
Bibby Rd PR9 .... 2 A1
Bibby's La L20 .... 38 A5
Bibby St L13 .... 53 F3
BICKERSHAW 36 F8
Bickershaw CE Prim Sch
WN2 .... 36 F8
Bickershaw La WN2 ..... 36 F8
BICKERSTAFFE 22 F5
Bickerstaffe CE Prim Sch
L39 .... 22 E5
Bickerstaffe St
1 Liverpool L3 .... 52 E3
St Helens WA10 .... 44 A3
Bickerton Ave CH63 ..... 78 D8
Bickerton Rd PR8 .... 3 F4
Bickerton St L17 .... 68 C3
Bickley Cl WA2 .... 61 F3
Bidder St L3 .... 52 E3
Bideford Ave WA9 ...... 58 C5
Bideford Rd WA5 .... 74 E4
BIDSTON 50 D1
Bidston Ave
Birkenhead CH41 .... 65 F7
St Helens WA11 .... 44 D5
Wallasey CH45 .... 50 E6
Bidston Avenue Prim Sch
CH41 .... 65 E7
Bidston Ct CH43 .... 65 E7
Bidston Green Ct CH43 ... 65 C8
Bidston Green Dr
CH43 .... 65 C8
Bidston Ind Est CH44 .... 50 D3
Bidston Moss CH44 ..... 50 D3
Bidston Rd
Birkenhead CH43 .... 65 F5
Liverpool L4 .... 53 B8
Bidston Sta CH43 .... 50 C2
Bidston Station App
CH43 .... 50 C2
Bidston View CH43 ...... 50 C1
Bidston Village CE Prim
Sch CH43 .... 50 C1
Bidston Village Rd
CH43 .... 50 C1
Bidston Way WA11 ..... 44 D5
Bigdale Dr L33 .... 30 A3
Biggin Ct WA2 .... 61 E1
Bigham Rd L6 .... 53 C3
Biglands Dr L36 .... 70 F8
Big Meadow Rd CH49 ... 65 A4
BILLINGE 33 E4
Billinge Cres WA11 ..... 44 D6
Billinge Hospl WN5 ..... 25 D2
Billinge Rd WN4 .... 34 C5
Billingham Rd WA9 ..... 57 D7
Billings Cl L5 .... 52 D6
Billington Ave WA12 .... 46 C5
Billington Cl WA5 .... 74 E8
Billington Rd WA8 ...... 72 B3
Bilston Rd L17 .... 80 E8
Bilton Cl WA8 .... 73 E2
Bingley Rd L4 .... 53 B7
Binns Rd L13, L7 .... 53 F2
Binns Road Ind Est L13 .. 53 F1
Binns Way L13 .... 53 F1
Binsey Cl CH49 .... 64 D5
Birbeck Rd L33 .... 30 A3

Birbeck Wlk L33 30 A3
Birchall St L20 52 C7
Birch Ave
Birkenhead CH49 64 D6
Liverpool L9 39 B6
St Helens WA10 43 F6
Warrington WA2 61 A4
Birch Cl
Birkenhead CH43 66 B3
Maghull L31 20 F1
Prescot L35 56 E4
Birch Cres WA12 45 F4
Birch Ct 16 L8 68 A4
Birchdale Cl CH49 64 D4
Birchdale Rd
Crosby L22 26 D1
Liverpool L9 39 B4
Birchen Rd L26 83 A7
Birches Cl CH60 86 A8
Birches Ho 2 CH60 86 A8
Birches The
Formby L37 9 E5
Huyton-w-R L28 55 A7
Neston CH64 86 F2
Wallasey CH44 51 E2
Birchfield CH46 64 C7
Birchfield Ave WA8 73 A2
Birchfield Cl
Birkenhead CH46 64 C6
Liverpool L7 53 E2
Birchfield Rd
Liverpool, Fairfield L7 53 E2
Liverpool, Walton on the Hill L4 39 A2
Widnes, Appleton WA8 73 A1
Widnes, Farnworth WA8 73 A3
Birchfield St
Liverpool L3 52 E3
St Helens WA9 57 D7
Birchfield Way L31 20 B5
Birch Gdns WA10 43 F6
Birch Gn L37 9 D4
Birch Gr
Downall Green WN4 34 D5
Huyton-w-R L36 55 D2
Liverpool L15 54 A1
Prescot L35 56 E4
Wallasey CH45 51 C7
BIRCH GREEN 16 C2
Birch Green Rd WN8 16 C3
Birch Heys CH48 64 A1
Birch Hill Mews L25 70 A1
Birchill Rd L33 30 C2
BIRCHLEY 33 C4
Birchley Ave WN5 33 C3
Birchley Rd WN5 33 C4
Birchley St Mary's RC Prim Sch WN5 33 D4
Birchley St WA10 44 A4
Birchley View WA11 33 B2
Birchmere CH60 76 E2
Birchmuir Hey L32 29 F1
Birch Rd
Abram Brow WN2 36 B7
Bebington CH63 79 A4
Birkenhead CH43 66 B3
Haydock WA11 45 E7
Hoylake CH47 63 E8
Huyton-w-R L36 55 E1
Widnes WA8 73 B3
Birchridge Cl CH62 79 C2
Birch's Brow L39 12 E2
Birch St
Liverpool L5 52 B5
Skelmersdale WN8 23 E8
Southport PR8 4 B4
Birch Tree Ave WA11 43 F8
Birch Tree Ct L12 54 A6
Birchtree Dr 2 L31 29 A3
Birchtree Rd L17 68 E3
Birch Tree Rd 6 WA3 47 F8
Birchview Way CH43 65 D5
Birchway CH60 86 C5
Birchwood Ave CH41 66 D7
Birchwood Cl CH41 66 E7
Birchwood Way L33 30 A5
Bird i' th' Hand Cotts 2 L39 13 E6
Bird St L7 68 C7
Birdwood Rd L11 53 F8
BIRKDALE 3 F2
Birkdale Ave CH63 88 C6
Birkdale Cl
Huyton-w-R L36 55 C1
Liverpool L6 53 D6
Birkdale Cop PR8 4 E1
Birkdale High Sch PR8 7 E7
Birkdale Prim Sch PR8 4 B3
Birkdale Rd
Warrington WA5 74 F4
Widnes WA8 73 B5
Birkdale Sch for the Hearing Impaired PR8 3 D4
Birkdale Sta PR8 3 F4
Birkdale Trad Est PR8 4 A2
BIRKENHEAD 66 B7
Birkenhead Central Sta CH41 66 E5
Birkenhead High Sch for Girls CH43 66 A5
Birkenhead North Sta CH41 50 F1
Birkenhead Park Sta CH41 66 B7
Birkenhead Prep Sch CH43 66 A5
Birkenhead Priory* CH41 66 F6
Birkenhead Rd
Hoylake CH47 63 E8
Wallasey CH41, CH44 51 E2
Willaston CH64 87 E1
Birkenhead Sch CH43 65 F5
Birkenhead Sixth Form Coll CH43 65 F7
Birkenshaw Ave L23 26 B4
Birket Ave CH46 50 A3
Birket Cl CH46 50 A3
Birket Sq CH46 49 F3
Birkett Rd
Birkenhead CH42 66 E1
West Kirby CH48 63 B3
Birkett St L3 52 E3
Birkey La L37 9 F2
Birkin Cl L32 41 A8
Birkin Rd L32 41 A8
Birkin Wlk 4 L32 41 A8
Birkrig WN8 24 D6
Birley Ct
3 Liverpool L8 67 F7
Southport PR8 4 B5
Birley St WA12 46 D4
Birleywood WN8 24 D6
Birnam Dr L35 57 D2
Birnam Rd CH44 51 D3
Birstall Ave WA11 44 C5
Birstall Rd L6 53 B3
Birt Cl L8 68 B7
Birtles Rd WA2 61 D1
Birtley Ct WA8 72 B1
Bishopdale Cl WA5 74 F7
Bishopdale Dr L35 57 E2
Bishop David Sheppard CE Prim Sch PR9 5 B7
Bishop Dr L35 56 D1
Bishopgate St L15 68 E8
Bishop Martin CE Prim Sch
Liverpool L25 70 A2
Skelmersdale WN8 24 D6
Bishop Rd
5 Liverpool L6 53 C6
St Helens WA10 43 E5
Wallasey CH44 51 B2
Bishop Reeves Rd WA11 45 E7
Bishops Ct
Birkenhead CH43 66 B3
Liverpool, Croxteth L12 54 A8
Liverpool, Woolton L25 70 B2
Warrington WA2 61 A4
Bishop Sheppard Ct L3 52 C4
Bishops Way WA8 73 D3
Bisley St
Liverpool L15 68 E7
Wallasey CH45 51 B5
Bispham Ct WN5 25 D2
Bispham Dr
Ashton-in-M WN4 34 F5
Hoylake CH47 63 E7
Bispham Hall Bsns Pk WN5 25 C2
Bispham Ho 6 L3 52 D3
Bispham Rd PR9 4 F7
Bittern Cl WA2 61 D3
Bixteth St L2, L3 90 A4
Blackacre La L39, L40 13 E8
Black-A-Moor La L39 12 A2
Blackberry Gr L26 70 D2
BLACKBROOK
Haydock 45 A7
Warrington 61 E2
Blackbrook Ave WA2 61 F2
Blackbrook Cl
Liverpool L9 39 A3
Widnes WA8 72 C3
Blackbrook Rd WA11, WA9 44 E5
Blackbrook St Mary's RC Prim Sch WA11 44 E6
Blackburn Cl WA3 47 E8
Blackburne Ave WA8 84 B5
Blackburne Dr
Liverpool L25 82 D8
Newton-le-W WA12 46 A4
Blackburne Pl L1, L8 67 F8
Blackburne St L19 81 D3
Blackburne Terr 18 L8 67 F8
Blackcar La L29 19 B3
Black Denton's Pl WA8 73 C1
Blackdown Gr WA9 44 F2
Blackfield St L5 52 D6
Blackheath Dr CH46 49 F3
Black Horse Cl CH48 63 C3
Black Horse Hill CH48 63 C3
Black Horse Hill Inf Sch CH48 63 D3
Black Horse Hill Jun Sch CH48 63 D3
Black Horse La L13 54 B3
Black Horse Pl L13 54 B3
Blackhorse St WA9 44 D4
Blackhurst Rd L31 20 C5
Blackledge Cl WN5 25 E5
Blackley Gr L33 30 A6
Blackleyhurst Ave WN5 33 E5
Blacklock Hall Rd L24 82 C5
Blacklow Brow L36 55 D2
Blacklow Brow Prim Sch L36 55 D1
Blackmoor Dr L12 54 D5
Blackmoor Park Inf Sch L12 54 D6
Blackmoor Park Jun Sch L12 54 D5
Black Moss La L39 13 E3
Blackpool St CH41 66 E5
Blackrod Ave L24 82 C4
Blackshaw Dr WA5 60 B1
Blacksmith Pl L25 82 D9
Blackstock Ct L30 27 D4
Blackstock St L3 52 D3
Blackstone Ave WA11 44 D5
Blackstone St L5 52 B6
Blackthorn Cl CH46 64 F7
Blackthorne Cres L28 55 B8
Blackthorne Rd L4, L9 39 C3
Blackwater Rd L11 40 D4
Blackwood Ave L25 69 F4
BLAGUEGATE 15 B1
Blaguegate La WN8 15 B2
Blair Ct CH43 66 B6
Blair Dr WA8 72 C3
Blairgowrie Gdns L39 14 A4
Blair Gr PR9 4 F7
Blair Pk CH63 79 B3
Blair St L8 90 C1
Blair Wlk L26 82 F7
Blaisdon Cl 5 L11 40 A1
Blakeacre Cl L26 82 F7
Blakeacre Rd L26 83 A6
Blakefield Rd L23 27 C6
Blakehall WN8 24 D7
Blakeley Brow CH63 88 A6
Blakeley Ct CH63 88 A7
Blakeley Dell CH63 88 B6
Blakeley Dene CH63 88 B7
Blakeley Rd CH63 88 A6
Blakeney Cl CH49 65 A7
Blakenhall Way CH49 64 D6
Blaking Dr L34 41 D4
Blandford Cl PR8 3 F5
Blantyre Rd L15 68 E6
Blantyre St WA7 84 F3
Blay Cl L25 82 D9
Blaydon Cl L30 27 F1
Blaydon Gr WA9 57 D7
Blaydon Pk WN8 24 D7
Blaydon Wlk CH43 65 F6
BLEAK HILL 43 B6
Bleak Hill Cl WA10 43 C7
Bleak Hill Prim Sch WA10 43 B6
Bleak Hill Rd WA10 43 B6
Bleasdale Ave L10 28 E2
Bleasdale Cl
Birkenhead CH49 64 E6
Ormskirk L39 21 D7
Bleasdale Rd
Liverpool L18 69 B5
Newton-le-W WA12 46 C4
Bleasdale Way L21, L23 27 B4
Blenheim Ave L21 38 C8
Blenheim Cl WA2 61 F2
Blenheim Dr L34 56 A5
Blenheim Rd
Ashton-in-M WN4 35 D2
1 Liverpool L18 68 F5
Southport PR8 7 B6
Wallasey CH44 51 D5
Blenheim St L5 52 D5
Blenheim Way
Liverpool L24 82 B4
St Helens WA11 44 B6
Blessed Sacrament RC Inf Sch L9 39 B6
Blessed Sacrament RC Jun Sch L9 39 B6
Blessington Rd L4 52 F7
Bletchley Ave 1 CH44 50 F4
Bligh St L15 68 E7
Blind Foot Rd WA10, WA11 42 D8
Blindman's La L39 13 C7
Blisworth St L21 38 B6
Blomfield Rd L19 81 D8
Bloomfield Gn 1 L17 68 C4
Bloomsbury Ct CH47 63 A6
Bloomsbury Way WA8 72 D3
Blossom Gr L32 40 F7
Blossom St L20 38 C5
BLOWICK 4 E6
Blowick Bsns Pk PR9 5 A6
Blowick Ind Pk PR9 5 A6
BLOWICK MOSS 4 E3
Blubell La CH64 87 C1
Blucher St L22 26 C1
Bluebell Ave
Birkenhead CH41 65 F8
Haydock WA11 45 E7
Bluebell Cl
2 Crosby L22 26 E1
Kirkby L32 29 E4
Blue Bell La L36 55 E4
Blueberry Fields L10 39 F6
Blueberry Pk L14 54 F5
Bluecoat Arts Ctr* L1 90 B3
Blue Coat Sch The L15 69 A6
Bluefields St L8 67 F6
Blue Jay Cl L27 70 F5
Blue Ridge Cl WA5 74 E7
Bluestone La L31 20 E1
Bluewood Dr CH41 50 D1
Blundell Ave
Formby L37 9 B4
Hightown L38 17 F3
Southport PR8 3 F2
Blundell Cres PR8 3 F2
Blundell Dr PR8 3 F2
Blundell Gr L38 17 F3
Blundell La PR9 2 C2
Blundell Links Ct PR8 7 C4
Blundell Rd
Hightown L38 17 F3
Widnes WA8 84 D8
BLUNDELLSANDS 26 B4
Blundellsands L23 26 B3
Blundellsands & Crosby Sta L23 26 C4
Blundellsands Ct 4 L23 26 B3
Blundellsands Rd E L23 26 C4
Blundellsands Rd W L23 26 B3
Blundells Dr CH46 49 F1
BLUNDELL'S HILL 57 B2
Blundell's La L35 57 B2
Blundell St L1 90 B1
Blythe Ave WA8 73 B5
Blythe Ct PR9 2 A2
Blythe La L40 14 D8
Blythe Mews PR8 8 A8
Blythewood WN8 24 D7
Blyth Hey L30 27 D3
Blyth Rd CH63 88 C7
Blythswood St L17 68 B3
Boaler St Ind Est 15 L6 53 B3
Boaler St L6 53 B3
Boardmans La WA11, WA9 44 E4
Boathouse La CH64 86 C3
Bobbies La WA10 43 A3
Bob Paisley Ct 3 L5 53 A6
Bodden St WA9 58 D4
Bodley St L4 52 F7
Bodmin Ave PR9 2 B5
Bodmin Gr WA11 44 D7
Bodmin Rd L4 39 A1
Bodmin Way L26 82 F9
Bognor Cl L24 82 B5
Bolan St L13 54 A3
BOLD 59 B6
Bold Bsns Ctr WA9 59 B7
Bold Cross WA8 73 E7
Bolden Cl L30 27 F1
Bolde Way CH63 79 A1
BOLD HEATH 73 E7
Bold Ind Est WA8 73 C5
Bold Ind Park WA9 59 B6
Bold La
Ormskirk L39 21 B7
St Helens WA5, WA9 59 C7
Bold Pl L1 90 C2
Bold Rd WA9 58 F7
Bold St
Liverpool L1 90 C3
Southport PR9 4 B8
St Helens WA10 43 F3
Boleyn The L31 20 E3
Bollington Cl CH43 65 F3
Bolton Ave L32 29 C2
Bolton Cl
Formby L37 10 A2
St Helens WA9 44 C4
Bolton House Rd WN2 36 F8
Bolton Rd
Ashton-in-M WN2, WN4 35 D5
Bebington CH62 79 B5
Southport PR8 4 A4
Bolton Rd E CH62 79 C6
Bolton St
Downall Green WN4 34 D5
Liverpool L1, L3 90 C3
St Helens WA9 44 C4
Bolton Wlk 3 L32 29 C2
Bonchurch Dr L15 53 F1
Bond St
Liverpool L3 52 D4
Prescot L34 56 D6
Bonnington Ave L23 26 C5
Bonnington Cl WA10 43 C3
Bonsall Rd L12 54 C6
Boode Croft L28 41 B1
Booker Ave L18 69 C1
Booker Ave Jun & Inf Sch L18 69 B1
Booth's Brow Rd WN4 34 D6
Booth's La L39 12 F4
Booth St
5 Liverpool L13 54 A3
Southport PR9 4 B8
St Helens WA9 57 D7
Boothwood Cl L7 68 B8
BOOTLE 38 A2
Bootle High Sch L30 28 A4
Bootle New Strand Sta L20 38 C4
Bootle Oriel Road Sta L20 38 B2
Borax St L13 54 A2
Bordehill Gdns L12 54 D8
Border Rd CH60 86 B8
Border Way L5 52 E6
Borella Rd L13 53 F6
Borough Pavement CH41 66 D6
Borough Pl 10 CH41 66 E6
Borough Rd
Bebington CH42 78 D8
Birkenhead CH41, CH42 66 C4
Birkenhead CH42 66 D2
St Helens WA10 43 E2
Wallasey CH44 51 E3
Borough Rd E
Birkenhead CH41 66 E6
Wallasey CH44 51 E2
Borough Way 1 CH44 51 E2
Borron Ct WA12 46 B4
Borron Rd WA12 46 B5
Borron Road Ind Est WA12 46 C4
Borrowdale L37 9 F5
Borrowdale Ave WA2 61 C3
Borrowdale Rd
Bebington CH63 78 F4
Birkenhead CH46 64 D7
Liverpool L15 68 E6
St Helens WA10 57 C8
Widnes WA8 84 C8
Bosco Ct L11 40 B4
Boscow Cres WA9 58 D7
Bosnia St L8 68 A3
Bossom Ct L22 37 E7
Bostock St L5 52 E5
Boswell Rd CH43 65 F1
Boswell St
Bootle L20 38 A5
Liverpool L8 68 C7
Bosworth Cl CH63 78 F2
Bosworth Dr PR8 7 B4
Bosworth Rd WA11 44 D6
Botanic Est L7 53 D1
Botanic Gardens Mus* PR9 2 B2
Botanic Gr L7 53 C1
Botanic Pl L7 53 C2
Botanic Rd
Liverpool L7 53 C1
Southport PR9 2 B2
Botany Rd L24 82 C6
Botley Cl CH49 64 D5
Boulevard Ind Pk L24 82 E6
Boulevard The L12 54 B8
Boulting Ave WA5 60 F1
Boulton Ave
Bebington CH62 79 B8
West Kirby CH48 63 B3
Boundary Dr
Crosby L23 26 D5
Liverpool L25 82 D8
Boundary Farm Rd L26 82 E7
Boundary La
Heswall CH60 86 A8
Kirkby L33 30 F2
Liverpool L6 53 B4
Boundary Rd
Bebington CH62 79 B7
Birkenhead CH43 65 E7
Huyton-w-R L36 71 A8
Litherland L21 27 D1
St Helens WA10 43 E3
Wallasey CH43 50 D1
West Kirby CH48 75 D8
Boundary St E L5 52 E6
Boundary St
Liverpool L5 52 B6
Liverpool L5 52 C6
Southport PR8 4 B4
Boundary Wlk L36 71 A8
Bourne Ave WA3 47 D8
Bourne Gdns WA9 44 C1
Bourne St L6 53 B3
Bourton Rd L25 82 B8
Bousfield St L4 52 E7
Boverton Cl WA5 60 E1
Bowden Cl L12 40 E2
Bowden Rd
Liverpool L19 81 B6
Wallasey CH45 51 A6
Bowden St L21 38 B6
Bowdon Cl WA10 43 B2
Bowen Cl WA8 72 D4
Bower Gr L21 37 F7
Bower Ho CH46 64 F7
Bower Rd
Heswall CH60 86 C8
Huyton-w-R L36 55 E4
Liverpool L25 70 A4
Bower St WA8 73 C1
Bowfell Cl CH62 88 D3
Bowfield Rd L19 81 B7
Bowgreen Cl CH43 65 C7
BOWKER'S GREEN 21 D5
Bowker's Green La L39 21 E4
Bowland Ave
Ashton-in-M WN4 35 B4
Golborne WA3 36 C1
Liverpool L16 69 D8
St Helens WA9 58 B3
Bowland Cl CH62 79 D1
Bowland Ct 9 PR9 4 C8
Bowland Dr L21 27 C4
Bowles St L20 38 A5
Bowley Rd L13 53 F5
Bowling Green Cl PR8 4 F5
Bowness Ave
Bebington CH63 88 C5
Birkenhead CH43 66 A2
Southport PR8 7 C3
St Helens WA11 44 B8
Warrington WA2 61 C2
Bowood Ct WA2 61 A4
Bowood St L8 67 F3
Bowring Com Sports Coll L36 55 B3
Bowring Dr CH64 86 B1
BOWRING PARK 55 A1
Bowring Park Ave L16 55 A1
Bowring Park Rd L13, L14, L16 54 E1
Bowring St 20 L8 68 A4

Bowscale Cl CH49 64 E5
Bowscale Rd L11 40 A2
Boxdale Ct L18 69 A4
Boxdale Rd L18 69 A4
Boxgrove Cl WA8 73 B3
Boxmoor Rd L18 69 A2
Boxtree Cl L12 40 F4
Boxwood Cl L36 55 C2
Boycott St L5 53 A6
Boyd Cl CH46 50 B3
Boydell Cl L28 55 B7
Boyer Ave L31 28 D7
Boyes Brow L33 29 D4
Boyle Ave WA2 61 E1
Boyton Ct L7 68 C8
Brabant Rd L17 68 E1
Braby Rd L20, L21 38 C6
Bracebridge Dr PR8 4 F2
Bracewell Cl [3] WA9 58 C6
Bracken Ct [12] WA9 58 C4
Brackendale CH49 65 C3
Brackendale Ave [6] L9 39 B7
Bracken Dr CH48 63 E2
Brackenhurst Dr CH45 51 C7
Brackenhurst Gn L33 29 E2
Bracken La CH63 78 D5
Brackenside CH60 76 F2
Brackenway L37 10 A6
Bracken Way L12 54 A5
Bracken Wood L12 40 E4
Brackenwood Dr WA8 84 A8
Brackenwood Gr L35 56 F3
Brackenwood Inf Sch CH63 78 F5
Brackenwood Jun Sch CH63 78 E5
Brackenwood Rd CH63 78 E4
Brackley Cl CH44 51 A3
Brackley St WA7 84 F3
Bracknell Ave L32 40 E8
Bracknell Cl [1] L32 29 E1
Bracknel Way L39 13 A1
Bradbourne Cl L12 40 E3
Bradda Cl CH49 64 F7
Braddan Ave L13 53 E5
Bradden Cl CH63 79 B2
Brade St PR9 2 C4
Bradewell Cl [7] L4 52 E8
Bradfield Ave L10 28 C3
Bradfield St [7] L7 53 C2
Bradgate Cl CH46 49 B1
Bradkirk Ct L30 27 D5
Bradlegh Rd WA12 46 B1
Bradley Fold L35 71 A8
Bradley La WA5, WA12 46 A1
Bradley Pl [8] PR8 4 B7
Bradley Rd L21 38 C8
Bradley St PR9 4 C8
Bradley Way WA8 73 B1
Bradman Cl [3] CH45 51 B5
Bradman Rd
Kirkby L33 30 D3
Wallasey CH46 49 C1
Bradmoor Rd CH62 88 D8
Bradshaw Cl WA10 43 D4
Bradshaw Ct PR9 5 A7
Bradshaw's La PR8 7 D6
Bradshaw St WA8 73 A2
Bradstone Cl L10 40 B6
Bradville Rd L9 39 C7
Bradwell Cl CH48 63 D2
Bradwell Rd WA3 47 E7
Braehaven Rd CH45 51 C7
Braemar Ave PR9 1 E2
Braemar Cl L35 56 F3
Braemar Ho CH43 65 F5
Braemar St L20 38 D1
Braemore Rd CH44 50 F4
Braeside Cres WN5 33 D5
Braeside Gdns CH49 64 F5
Brae St L7 53 B2
Brahms Cl L8 68 B6
Braid St CH41 66 D8
Braidwood Ct [24] CH42 66 C5
Brainerd St L13 53 E5
Braithwaite Cl L35 57 C3
Braithwaite Rd WA3 47 D8
Bramberton Pl L4 39 C1
Bramberton Rd L4 39 C1
Bramble Ave CH41 65 F8
Bramble Cl WA5 74 E3
Brambles The
Burtonwood WA5 60 A7
Downall Green WN4 34 D5
Bramble Way CH46 49 D2
Bramblewood Cl L27 70 E5
Brambling Pk L26 70 E1
Brambling Way WA3 47 E7
Bramcote Ave WA11 44 D6
Bramcote Cl L33 30 A4
Bramcote Rd L33 30 A4
Bramcote Wlk L33 29 F4
Bramerton Ct CH48 63 A3
Bramford Cl CH49 64 E5
Bramhall Cl
Liverpool L24 82 E3
West Kirby CH48 63 D1
Bramhall Dr CH62 88 F4
Bramhall Rd
Seaforth L22 37 E8
Skelmersdale WN8 15 F2
Bramley Ave CH63 78 E7
Bramley Cl L27 70 E5
Bramleys The L31 28 C7
Bramley Way [4] L32 29 C3
Bramley Wlk L24 82 D3
Brampton Cl [5] L32 29 E4
Brampton Ct WA9 45 B3
Brampton Dr L8 68 A8
Bramwell Ave CH43 66 A1
Bramwell St WA9 44 E4
Branch Way WA11 45 D6
Brancker Ave L35 57 B4
Brancote Ct CH43 65 F6
Brancote Gdns
Bebington CH62 88 D7
Birkenhead CH43 65 F6
Brancote Mount CH43 65 F6
Brancote Rd CH43 65 F6
Brandearth Hey L28 55 B7
Brandearth Ho L28 55 B7
Brandon WA8 72 B2
Brandon Cl WN8 25 A7
Brandon St CH41 66 F6
Brandreth Cl L35 57 C3
Brandwood Ave WA2 61 B2
Branfield Cl L12 40 E3
Bransdale Cl WA5 74 F7
Bransdale Dr WN4 35 D3
Bransford Cl WN4 35 C2
Branson Cl WA3 36 A2
Branstree Ave L11 39 F2
Brantfield Ct WA2 61 E2
Branthwaite Cl [1] L11 40 A1
Branthwaite Cres L11 40 A1
Branthwaite Gr [4] L11 40 A1
Brasenose Rd L20 38 C1
Brassey St
Birkenhead CH41 66 B8
Liverpool L8 67 E6
Brathay Cl WA2 61 C3
Brattan Rd CH41 66 C4
Braunton Rd
Liverpool L17 68 E1
[2] Wallasey CH45 51 A6
Braybrooke Rd L11 40 A3
Braydon Cl L25 82 C7
Brayfield Rd L4 39 D1
Bray Rd L24 82 C5
Bray St CH41 66 B8
Brechin Rd L33 29 F2
Breckfield Pl L5 52 F5
Breckfield Prim Sch L5 52 F6
Breckfield Rd N L5 53 A5
Breckfield Rd S L6 53 A5
Breck Pl CH44 51 A3
Breck Rd
Liverpool L6 53 A5
Wallasey CH44 50 F4
Widnes WA8 73 B1
Breckside Ave CH44 50 E4
Breckside Pk L6 53 D6
Brecon Ave L30 27 F1
Brecon Ct WA5 60 E2
Brecon Rd
Bebington CH42 78 C8
Birkenhead CH42 66 C1
Brecon Wlk L30 28 A1
Bredon Ct L37 9 E4
Breeze Cl L9 38 F3
Breeze Hill
Bootle L20, L4 38 E2
[9] Liverpool L4 38 F2
Breeze La L9 38 F3
Breeze Rd PR8 3 E2
Brelade Rd L13 53 F4
Bremhill Rd L11 39 F3
Bremner Cl L7 53 C1
Brenda Cres L23 27 A7
Brendale Ave L31 28 C8
Brendan's Way L30 27 E3
Brendon Ave
Litherland L21 27 A1
Warrington WA2 61 A3
Brendon Gr WA9 45 A4
Brendor Rd L25 70 B1
Brenig St CH41 50 F1
Brenka Ave L9 28 B1
Brentfield WA8 72 D2
Brent Way L26 82 F7
Brentwood Ave
Crosby L23 26 F5
Liverpool L17 68 C3
Brentwood Cl
Hightown L38 17 F2
St Helens WA10 43 B3
Brentwood Ct
[8] Birkenhead CH49 65 A2
Southport PR9 1 D1
Brentwood Gr L33 29 E6
Brentwood St CH44 51 C3
Brereton Ave
Bebington CH63 79 A6
Liverpool L15 69 A7
Bretherton Pl L35 57 C4
Bretherton Rd L34 56 E6
Bretlands Rd L23 27 B6
Brett Cl [11] L33 29 D5
Bretton Fold PR8 4 F5
Brett St CH41 66 B8
Brewery La
Aintree L31 28 E4
Formby L37 9 F6
Brewster St L20, L4 38 E1
Breydon Gdns WA9 57 E6
Brian Ave CH61 76 F6
Brian Cummings Ct [1] L21 38 B6
Briar Cl WN4 35 A4
Briardale Rd
Bebington CH63 78 F7
Birkenhead CH42 66 C4
Liverpool L18 69 A4
Wallasey CH44 51 E2
Willaston CH64 88 A1
Briar Dr
Heswall CH60 86 A8
Huyton-w-R L36 55 D2
Briarfield Ave WA8 72 A1
Briarfield Rd CH60 86 B8
Briar Rd
Golborne WA3 47 B8
Southport PR8 7 D4
Briars Cl L35 57 D1
Briars Gn
Skelmersdale WN8 16 B4
St Helens WA10 43 F5
Briars La L31 20 E1
Briar St L4, L5 52 D7
Briars The PR8 3 F1
Briarswood Cl
Bebington CH42 78 F8
Prescot L35 56 F3
Briar Wlk WA3 47 B8
Briarwood L23 26 B6
Briarwood Rd L17 68 E3
Briary Cl CH60 77 B1
Briary Croft L38 17 F3
Brickfields L36 56 A1
Brickmakers Arms Yd L39 13 D6
Brick St
Liverpool L1 90 B1
Newton-le-W WA12 45 F3
Brickwall Gn L29 27 F7
Brickwall La L29, L30 27 E6
Bride St [4] L4 38 F2
Bridewell Ct WA8 73 B3
Bridge Ave L39 13 E5
Bridge Bank Cl WA3 47 B7
Bridge Croft L21, L30 27 C3
Bridgecroft Rd CH45 51 B6
Bridge Ct
Litherland L30 27 D4
West Kirby CH48 63 A3
Bridge Farm Cl CH49 65 B4
Bridge Farm Dr L31 20 F2
Bridgefield Cl L25 70 B7
Bridgefield Forum (L Ctr) L26 71 A2
Bridgeford Ave L12 54 A7
Bridge Gdns L12 40 F1
Bridge Gr PR8 4 B6
Bridgehall Dr WN8 25 B7
Bridge Ho L39 13 E4
Bridge Ind Est L24 82 B6
Bridge La L30 27 E3
Bridgeman St WA10 43 D3
Bridgemere Cl L7 53 D3
Bridgemere Ho L17 68 D2
Bridgend Cl WA8 72 D3
Bridgend Dr PR8 7 B4
Bridgenorth Rd CH61 76 E4
Bridge Rd
Bootle L21 38 B7
Crosby L23 26 C3
Huyton-w-R L36 55 C2
Liverpool L7 68 D8
Liverpool, Mossley Hill L18 69 A3
Maghull L31 28 D7
Prescot L34, L35 56 E5
St Helens WA9 58 D2
West Kirby CH48 63 A3
Bridges La
Maghull L29, L31 28 A8
Sefton L29 27 F7
Bridge St
Bebington CH62 79 B5
Birkenhead CH41 66 E7
Bootle L20 38 B2
Golborne WA3 47 A7
Newton-le-W WA12 46 B3
Ormskirk L39 13 E4
Southport PR8 4 B6
St Helens WA10 44 A3
Bridgeview Dr L33 29 F4
Bridgewater Cl L21 27 A2
Bridgewater Ct L21 27 A2
Bridgewater St L1 90 B1
Bridgewater Way L36 71 A8
Bridgeway L11 39 E1
Bridge Wills La PR9 2 C5
Bridle Ave CH44 51 E2
Bridle Cl
Bebington CH62 88 E7
Birkenhead CH43 65 B6
Bridle Ct [3] WA9 58 C8
Bridle Pk CH62 88 E7
Bridle Rd
Bebington CH62 88 E6
Bootle L30 38 F8
Litherland L30 28 A1
Wallasey CH44 51 E2
Bridle Way
Bootle L30 38 F7
Kirkby L33 29 D6
Bridport St L3 90 C4
Brierfield WN8 24 D6
Brierfield Rd L15 68 F6
Brierley Cl L30 28 B4
Briers Cl WA2 61 F3
Briery Hey Ave L33 29 F2
Brigadier Dr L12 54 E7
Brighouse Cl L39 13 D6
Brightgate Cl L7 68 B8
BRIGHTON LE SANDS 26 B3
Brighton Rd
Crosby L22 26 D1
Huyton-w-R L36 56 B3
Southport PR8 4 A3
Brighton St CH44 51 E3
Brighton Vale [4] L22 26 C2
Bright St
Birkenhead CH41 66 C6
[6] Liverpool L6 53 A3
Southport PR9 4 F7
Brightwell Cl
Birkenhead CH49 64 F4
Warrington WA5 74 E5
Brignall Gr WA3 36 D1
Brill St CH41 66 B8
Brimelow Cres WA5 74 E3
BRIMSTAGE 78 A2
Brimstage Ave CH63 78 D8
Brimstage Cl CH60 86 C8
Brimstage Gn CH60 86 D8
Brimstage Hall Courtyard (Craft Ctr)* CH63 78 A2
Brimstage La CH63 78 B3
Brimstage Rd
Bebington CH63 78 D2
Heswall CH60 86 C7
Liverpool L4 38 E2
Brimstage St [4] CH41 66 C5
Brindley Cl L21 27 A2
Brindley Rd
Kirkby L32 29 C2
St Helens WA9 58 F6
Brindley St
Liverpool L8 67 D6
Runcorn WA7 84 F3
Brinklow Cl PR8 7 A5
Brinley Cl CH62 88 D5
Brinton Cl
Liverpool L27 70 D6
Widnes WA8 84 E8
Brisbane Ave CH45 51 A8
Brisbane St WA9 57 D8
Briscoe Ave [2] CH46 64 E7
Briscoe Dr CH46 64 E7
Bristol Ave CH44 51 C4
Bristol Rd L15 69 A6
Bristow Cl WA5 60 B1
Britannia Ave L15 68 D7
Britannia Cres [2] L8 68 A3
Britannia Ho CH41 66 F6
Britannia Rd CH45 51 A4
British Lawnmower Mus* PR8 4 B5
Britonside Ave L32 41 A8
Brittarge Brow L27 70 E4
Britten Cl L8 68 B6
Broadacre WN8 25 A6
Broadacre Cl L18 69 D5
Broadbelt St [5] L4 38 F2
Broadbent Ho L31 28 D7
Broadfield Ave CH43 65 C8
Broadfield Cl CH43 65 B8
Broadgate Ave WA9 58 C8
BROAD GREEN 54 D2
Broadgreen Ct [2] L13 54 B2
Broadgreen High Sch Tech Coll L13 54 C2
Broadgreen Hospl L14 54 C2
Broadgreen Prim Sch L13 54 B2
Broad Green Rd L13 54 B2
Broad Green Sta L14 54 D1
Broadheath Ave CH43 65 C7
Broadheath Terr WA8 72 D1
Broad Hey L30 27 D3
Broad Hey Cl L25 70 B3
Broadhurst St L17 68 C3
Broad La
Billinge WA11 33 B1
Burtonwood WA5 59 E8
Formby L37 10 E2
Great Altcar L37, L38 19 A8
Haskayne L39 12 B2
Haydock WA5, WA9 45 C1
Heswall CH60 85 C8
Kirkby L32 40 F8
Liverpool L11, L4 39 F1
Maghull, Homer Green L29 19 C2
Broadlands
Prescot L35 56 E5
Southport PR8 3 E3
Broadleaf Rd L19 80 F7
Broadley Ave WA3 47 C7
Broadmead
Heswall CH60 86 C7
Liverpool L19 81 E7
BROAD OAK 44 F4
Broad Oak Ave
Haydock WA11 45 A6
Warrington WA5 74 E4
Broad Oak Com Prim Sch WA9 45 A3
Broadoak Rd
Liverpool L14 54 F3
Maghull L31 20 E1
Broad Oak Rd WA9 44 F3
Broadoaks CH49 64 E6
Broad Pl L11 53 F8
Broad Sq L11 53 F8
Broad Square Com Prim Sch L11 53 F8
Broads The WA9 57 E6
Broadstone Dr CH63 78 F2
Broad View L11 53 F8
Broadway
Bebington CH63 78 D7
Birkenhead CH49 64 E4
Liverpool, Fazakerley L9 39 E7
Liverpool, Norris Green L11 39 E1
St Helens, Grange Park WA10 57 C8
Broadway *continued*
St Helens, Windlehurst WA10 43 B5
Wallasey CH45 50 F5
Widnes WA8 72 A1
Broadway Ave CH45 50 F5
Broadway Cl PR8 7 B5
Broadway Mkt L11 39 E1
Broadwood Ave L31 28 C7
Broadwood St L15 68 E7
Brockenhurst Rd L9 39 A5
Brock Gdns L24 83 E2
Brockhall Cl L35 57 A6
Brock Hall Cl [14] WA9 58 C4
Brockholme Rd L18, L19 69 A1
Brocklebank La L19 81 D8
Brocklebank Rd PR9 1 E2
Brockley Ave [1] CH45 51 B8
Brock St L4 52 E8
Brockstedes Ave WN4 34 E6
Brocstedes Rd WN4 34 D7
Brodie Ave L18, L19 69 A1
BROMBOROUGH 79 D1
BROMBOROUGH POOL 79 D5
Bromborough Rake Sta CH62 88 C8
Bromborough Rd CH62, CH63 79 B4
Bromborough Sta CH63 88 C7
Bromborough Village Rd CH62 79 E1
Brome Way CH63 79 B2
Bromilow Rd
Skelmersdale WN8 15 C1
St Helens WA9 44 F2
Bromley Ave
Golborne WA3 47 D7
Liverpool L18 68 F5
Bromley Cl
Heswall CH60 85 E7
Liverpool L26 71 A1
Warrington WA2 61 F3
Bromley Rd CH45 51 A7
Brompton Ave
Crosby L23 26 C3
Kirkby L33 30 A5
Liverpool L17 68 C6
Wallasey CH44 51 C4
Brompton Ct L17 68 C5
Brompton Ho L17 68 C5
Brompton Rd PR8 4 E7
Bromsgrove Rd CH49 64 C4
Bromyard Cl [5] L20 38 B4
Bronington Ave CH62 88 D6
Bronshill Ct L23 26 A4
Bronte Cl
Crosby L23 26 B4
Winwick WA2 61 A6
Bronte St
Liverpool L3 90 C4
St Helens WA10 43 D4
Brook Acre Com Prim Sch WA2 61 E1
Brook Ave L31 20 E2
Brookbank Ct L10 40 B7
Brookbridge Rd L13 53 E6
Brook Cl
Cronton WA8 72 C6
Wallasey CH44, CH45 51 C5
Brookdale WA8 72 A3
Brookdale Ave N CH49 64 E4
Brookdale Ave S CH49 64 E3
Brookdale Cl CH49 64 E4
Brookdale Prim Sch CH49 64 E3
Brookdale Rd L15 68 E6
Brookdale The PR8 7 D3
Brooke Cl PR9 5 B7
Brook End WA9 45 A1
Brooke Rd E L22, L23 26 D2
Brooke Rd W L22 26 C2
Brook Farm Cl L39 13 E4
Brookfield Ave
Crosby L23 26 D3
Rainhill L35 57 C5
Seaforth L22 37 F8
Brookfield Dr L9 39 D5
Brookfield Gdns CH48 63 B2
Brookfield High Sch L32 40 D8
Brookfield Ho L36 55 E3
Brookfield La L39 21 A5
Brookfield Park Prim Sch WN8 15 D2
Brookfield Rd
Up Holland WN8 25 B7
West Kirby CH48 63 B2
Brookfields Sch WA8 73 D2
Brookfield St WA12 46 B3
Brook Hey CH64 86 B2
Brook Hey Dr L33 30 A3
Brook Hey Wlk L33 30 A3
Brookhill Cl L20 38 D3
Brookhill Rd L20 38 D4
Brook Ho PR8 4 C5
Brook House Gr WA10 43 A3
Brookhouse Rd L39 13 D6
BROOKHURST 88 C5
Brookhurst Ave CH63 88 C5
Brookhurst Cl CH63 88 C5
Brookhurst Prim Sch CH63 88 C6

Brookhurst Rd CH63 88 C5
Brook La
Crank WA11 32 F7
Neston CH64 86 C2
Ormskirk L39 13 E4
Brookland La WA9 45 A1
Brookland Rd CH41 66 D5
Brookland Rd E L13 54 A3
Brookland Rd W L13 54 A3
Brooklands
3 Birkenhead CH41 66 D7
Liverpool L17 68 D2
Ormskirk L39 14 A6
Brooklands Ave
Ashton-in-M WN4 35 D2
Seaforth L22 37 E8
Brooklands Dr
Maghull L31 28 D8
Orrell WN5 25 D5
Brooklands Gdns CH64 86 C1
Brooklands Pk 1 WA8 73 C2
Brooklands Rd
Neston CH64 86 C1
St Helens WA10 43 A4
Up Holland WN8 25 C7
Brooklands The L36 55 E1
Brooklet Rd CH60 77 C1
Brook Lynn Ave WA3 36 F1
Brook Mdw CH61 76 E7
Brook Pk L31 28 C7
Brook Rd
Bootle L20 38 B3
Crosby L23 27 A7
Liverpool L9 39 A4
Maghull L31 28 E8
Brook St E CH41 66 E7
Brooks Alley L1 90 B3
Brookside L12 54 F8
Brook Side L31 20 E1
Brookside Ave
Ashton-in-M WN4 34 F8
Liverpool L14 54 D3
Rainford WA11 31 E7
Seaforth L22 37 F8
St Helens WA10 43 C5
Brookside Cl
Billinge WN5 33 E5
Haydock WA11 45 B7
Prescot L35 56 E4
Brookside Com Prim Sch L28 55 B7
Brookside Cres CH49 64 E5
Brookside Ct L23 26 E4
Brookside Dr CH49 64 E5
Brookside Ho L14 54 D3
Brookside Rd
Prescot L35 56 E4
Southport PR8 4 C2
Brookside View WA11 45 B7
Brookside Way WA11 45 B7
Brooks Rd L37 9 D2
Brook St
Ashton-in-M WN4 35 C2
Bebington CH62 79 A6
Birkenhead CH41 66 D8
Golborne, Bank Heath WA3 47 A8
Liverpool L3 52 B2
Prescot L35 56 F4
Southport PR9 2 D4
St Helens WA10 44 A3
3 Widnes WA8 73 B1
Brooks The WA11 44 A7
Brooks Way L37 9 D2
Brook Terr CH48 63 B2
Brook The L31 28 E8
Brookthorpe Cl CH45 51 C6
Brook Vale L22 37 F8
Brookvale Cl WA5 59 F6
Brookway
Birkenhead, Upton CH49 64 E5
Wallasey CH45 51 A5
Brook Way CH43 77 E8
Brookway La WA9 45 A1
Brook Wlk CH61 76 D7
Brookwood Rd L36 55 E4
Broom Cl L34 56 F6
Broome Cl PR8 4 B3
Broome Rd PR8 4 B3
Broomfield Cl CH60 76 C1
Broomfield Gdns L9 38 F5
Broomfield Rd L9 38 F5
Broom Hill CH43 65 F7
Broomhill Cl L27 70 D6
Broomlands CH60 85 E8
Broomleigh Cl CH63 78 D5
Broom Rd WA10 57 B8
Brooms Gr L10 28 E2
Broom Way L26 82 E8
Broseley Ave CH62 79 C1
Broster Ave CH46 64 C8
Broster Cl CH46 64 C8
Brosters La CH47 48 D1
Brotherhood Dr WA9 58 D7
Brotherton Cl CH62 88 C8
Brotherton Way WA12 46 B4
Brougham Ave CH41 66 F3
Brougham Rd CH44 51 E3
Brougham Terr 11 L6 53 A3
Broughton Ave
Golborne WA3 47 D7
Southport PR8 4 D4
West Kirby CH48 63 A3
Broughton Dr L19 81 A7
Broughton Hall High Sch Tech Coll L12 54 E5
Broughton Hall Rd L12 54 E5
Broughton Rd CH44 51 B3
Broughton Way WA8 84 B5
Brow La CH60 85 F7
Brownbill Bank L27 70 E5
BROWN EDGE
Southport 5 A2
St Helens 57 D7
Brown Edge Cl PR8 5 A2
Brown Heath Ave WN5 33 D3
Browning Ave
Birkenhead CH42 66 F1
Widnes WA8 84 F8
Browning Cl L36 56 A1
Browning Dr WA2 61 A6
Browning Rd
Crosby L22 26 D2
Liverpool L13 53 F6
Wallasey CH45 50 D5
Browning St L20 38 A4
BROWNLOW 25 C1
Brownlow Arc 14 WA10 44 A3
Brownlow Hill L1, L3, L7 52 F1
Brownlow La WN5 25 C1
Brownlow Rd CH62 79 B7
Brownlow St L3 52 F1
Brownmoor Cl L23 27 A3
Brownmoor La L23 26 F3
Brownmoor Pk L23 26 F3
Brown's La L30 28 A3
Brownville Rd L13 53 E6
Brow Rd CH43 50 D1
Brows Cl L37 9 E3
Brow Side L5, L6 52 F4
Brows La L37 9 E3
Broxholme Way L31 28 D7
Broxton Ave
Birkenhead CH43 65 F2
Orrell WN5 25 F7
West Kirby CH48 63 B3
Broxton Cl WA8 72 C3
Broxton Rd 7 CH45 51 A6
Broxton St L15 68 E8
Bruce Ave WA2 61 D1
Bruce Cres CH63 88 C6
Bruce St
4 Liverpool L8 68 A4
St Helens WA10 43 E3
Brunel Dr L21 27 A2
Brunel Rd CH62 79 E1
Brunner Rd 4 WA8 73 A1
Brunsborough Cl CH62 88 C6
Brunsfield Cl CH46 64 C7
Brunstath Cl CH60 77 C1
Brunswick Bsns Pk L3 67 D4
Brunswick Cl 4 L4 52 E8
Brunswick Ct CH41 66 F7
Brunswick Ent Ctr L3 67 D5
Brunswick Mews
Birkenhead CH41 66 E7
Seaforth L22 37 E7
Brunswick Par L22 37 E8
Brunswick Pl L20 52 B8
Brunswick Rd
Liverpool L6 52 F3
Newton-le-W WA12 45 F4
Brunswick St
Liverpool, Garston L19 81 C3
Liverpool L2, L3 90 A3
St Helens WA9 45 A3
Brunswick Sta L8 67 E4
Brunswick Way L3 67 D5
Brunt La L19, L24 81 E7
Brushford Cl L12 40 B2
Bruton Rd L36 55 D6
Bryanston Rd
Birkenhead CH42 66 A2
Liverpool L17 68 B3
Bryant Rd L21 38 B6
Bryceway The L12 54 E4
Brydges St L7 53 A1
Bryer Rd L35 56 D4
BRYN 34 F6
Bryn Bank CH44 51 C4
Bryn Cross WN4 35 A6
BRYN GATES 35 E7
Bryn Gates La WN2 35 D8
Bryn Hall Cotts WN2 35 D8
Brynmor Rd L18 69 A1
Brynmoss Ave 2 CH44 50 F4
Brynn St
Ashton-in-M WN2 35 F7
St Helens WA10 44 A4
Bryn Rd WN4 35 B5
Bryn Rd S WN4 35 C4
Bryn St Peter's CE Prim Sch WN4 34 F6
Bryn St WN4 35 B3
Bryn Sta WN4 35 A6
Bryony Cl WN5 25 D5
Bryony Way CH42 78 F8
Brythen St L1 90 B3
Bsns Resource Ctr L33 41 C8
Buccleuch St CH41 50 F1
Buchanan Cl WA8 72 F3
Buchanan Rd
Liverpool L9 38 F3
Wallasey CH44 51 D3
Buckfast Ave WA11 46 A7
Buckfast Cl
Litherland L30 27 F4
Warrington WA5 74 E3
Buckfast Dr L37 10 B2
Buckingham Ave
Bebington CH63 78 E7
Birkenhead CH43 65 F7
Liverpool L17 68 D6
Widnes WA8 73 A4
Buckingham Cl
Litherland L30 27 C3
St Helens WA10 43 F2
Buckingham Ct 5 L33 29 F4
Buckingham Dr WA11 44 B6
Buckingham Gr L37 9 E1
Buckingham Ho L17 68 D5
Buckingham Rd
Liverpool, Tuebrook L13 53 E5
Liverpool, Warbreck Park L9 39 A6
Maghull L31 28 C8
Wallasey CH44 50 F4
Buckingham St L5 52 E5
Buckland Cl WA8 84 D7
Buckland Dr CH63 78 F2
Buckland St L17 68 B3
BUCKLEY HILL 27 D4
Buckley Hill La L23, L29, L30 27 D5
Buckley Way L30 27 D5
Buckley Wlk L24 82 D3
Buckthorn Cl L28 55 B7
Buckthorn Gdns WA9 57 C6
Bude Cl CH43 65 C6
Bude Rd WA8 72 E2
Budworth Ave
St Helens WA9 58 B4
Widnes WA8 72 D2
Budworth Cl CH43 65 E4
Budworth Ct CH43 65 F5
Budworth Dr L25 70 D2
Budworth Rd CH43 65 E5
Buerton Cl CH43 65 E4
Buffs La CH60 86 B8
Buildwas Rd CH64 86 F2
Bulford Rd L9 39 E3
Bulkeley Rd CH44 51 D3
Bull Bridge La L10 28 E2
Bull Cop L37 10 B3
Bullens Rd
Kirkby L32 29 F1
Liverpool L4 52 F8
Bullfinch Ct L26 70 E1
Bull La 1 L9 39 B7
Bullrush Dr CH46 50 A2
Bulrushes The L17 67 F3
Bulwer St
Birkenhead CH42 66 F2
Bootle L20 38 A5
7 Liverpool L5 53 A5
Bundoran Rd L17 68 E2
Bungalow Rd WA12 46 E1
Bungalows The
Ashton-in-M WN4 34 F7
Thornton Hough CH63 87 B6
Bungalow The L23 26 B4
Bunter Rd L32 40 F7
Bunting Cl 6 WA3 47 E8
Bunting Ct L26 70 D2
Burbo Bank Rd L23 26 B3
Burbo Bank Rd N L23 26 A5
Burbo Bank Rd S L23 26 B3
Burbo Cres L23 26 B3
Burbo Mans L23 26 B3
Burbo Way CH45 50 E8
Burden Rd
Birkenhead CH46 64 C8
Wallasey CH46 49 C1
Burdett Ave CH63 79 A2
Burdett Cl CH63 79 A2
Burdett Rd
Crosby L22 26 D2
Wallasey CH45 50 D5
Burdett St L17 68 C3
Burford Ave CH44 51 A3
Burford Rd L16 54 D1
Burgess Gdns L31 20 C2
Burgess' La L37 11 A2
Burgess St L3 90 C4
Burghill Rd L12 40 F4
Burgundy Cl 7 L17 68 C2
Burkhardt Dr WA12 46 E3
Burland Cl WA7 84 F1
Burland Rd L26 83 A6
Burleigh Mews L5 52 F6
Burleigh Rd N L4, L5 52 F7
Burleigh Rd S L4, L5 52 F6
Burley Ave WA3 36 D1
Burley Cl L32 29 F1
Burlingham Ave CH48 63 D2
Burlington Ave L37 10 B3
Burlington Rd
Southport PR8 3 F3
Wallasey CH45 37 B1
Burlington St
3 Birkenhead CH41 66 E6
Liverpool L3, L5 52 C4
Burman Cres L19 81 C7
Burman Rd L19 81 D7
Burnage Ave WA9 58 C4
Burnage Cl L24 82 F3
Burnand St L4 52 F7
Burnard Cl L33 29 F2
Burnard Cres L33 29 F2
Burnard Wlk 2 L33 29 F2
Burnell Cl 8 WA10 43 F4
Burnfell WA3 47 E7
Burnham Cl
Warrington WA5 74 F5
Widnes WA8 72 C3
Burnham Rd L18 69 C3
Burnie Ave L20 38 E5
Burnley Ave
Birkenhead CH46 64 F8
Southport PR8 7 D5
Burnley Cl L6 53 A4
Burnley Gr CH46 49 F1
Burnley Rd
Birkenhead CH46 64 F8
Southport PR8 7 C5
Burnsall Ave WA3 47 F8
Burnsall Dr WA8 72 C3
Burnsall St L19 81 E5
Burns Ave CH45 51 A5
Burns Cl
Ashton-in-M WN4 34 F6
Liverpool L16 69 F8
Longshaw WN5 25 D1
Prescot L35 56 E3
Burns Cres WA8 84 F8
Burns Gr
Huyton-w-R L36 56 A1
Warrington WA2 61 C2
Burnside Ave CH44 51 B2
Burnside Rd CH44 51 B2
Burns Rd WA9 58 A3
Burns St L20 38 A5
Burnt Ash Cl L19 80 F7
Burnthwaite Rd L14 54 C3
Burnt Mill La WA8 83 D5
Burrell Cl CH42 66 C1
Burrell Ct CH42 66 C1
Burrell Dr CH46 64 E7
Burrell Rd
Bebington CH42 78 B8
Birkenhead CH42 66 C1
Burrell St L4 52 F8
Burroughs Gdns 1 L3 52 D4
Burrows Ave WA11 44 F5
Burrows Ct
Liverpool L3, L5 52 C4
St Helens WA9 44 E3
Burrow's La L34, WA10 42 E2
Burrows St WA11 45 A6
Bursar Cl WA12 46 D4
Burscough Rd L39 13 F7
Burscough St L39 13 F6
Burton Ave
Rainhill L35 57 A4
Wallasey CH45 50 E5
Burton Cl
Liverpool L1 90 B2
Rainhill L35 57 A4
Widnes WA8 72 F3
Burtonhead Ct WA9 44 B1
Burtonhead Rd WA9, WA10 44 A1
Burton Rd WA2 61 D1
Burton St L5 52 C6
Burtons Way L10, L32 40 C8
BURTONWOOD 59 E6
Burtonwood Com Prim Sch WA5 59 E7
Burtonwood Ind Ctr WA5 59 E7
Burtonwood Rd WA5 60 A2
Burtree Rd L14 55 A6
Burwell Ave L37 9 D1
Burwell Cl L33 30 A3
Burwen Dr L9 38 F6
Bury Rd PR8 4 B3
Busby's Cotts CH45 51 B8
Bushby's La L37 9 C2
Bushby's Pk L37 9 D2
Bushell Ct 3 CH43 66 A4
Bushell's Farm WA8 58 E2
Bushel's Dr WA9 58 E3
Bushey La WA11 23 E2
Bushey Rd L4 39 C1
Bushley Cl L20 38 B4
Bush Rd WA8 84 F5
Bush Way CH60 85 D8
Butchers La
Ashton-in-M WN4 35 B3
Maghull L39 21 B3
Bute St
Liverpool L3 52 E3
Liverpool L5 52 E4
Butleigh Rd L36 55 E5
Butler Cres L6 53 B3
Butler St L6 53 B3
Buttercup Cl
Crosby L22 26 F1
Wallasey CH46 50 A2
Buttercup Way L9 39 B4
Butterfield Gdns L39 13 D3
Butterfield St L4 52 F7
Buttermere Ave
Ashton-in-M WN4 35 B5
Birkenhead CH43 65 C6
St Helens WA11 44 A8
Warrington WA2 61 C3
Buttermere Cl
Formby L37 9 D3
Kirkby L33 29 D4
Maghull L31 20 E1
Buttermere Cres
Rainford WA11 23 F2
Warrington WA2 61 C3
Buttermere Ct 10 CH41 66 C5
Buttermere Gdns L23 26 F2
Buttermere Rd L16 70 A8
Buttermere St 1 L8 68 B7
Butterton Ave CH49 64 D6
Butterwick Dr L12 40 E3
Button St L2 90 B3
Butts Gn WA5 60 A3
Butts La PR8 4 F5
Buxted Rd L32 41 A8
Buxted Wlk 7 L32 41 A8
Buxton La CH44 50 E5
Buxton Rd CH42 67 A2
Bye La L39 12 C3
Byerley St CH44 51 E3
Byland Cl
Formby L37 10 B2
Widnes WA8 73 C5
Byles St L8 68 A4
Byng Pl L4 53 D8
Byng Rd L4 53 D8
Byng St L20 38 B2
By-Pass The L23 26 E5
Byrchall High Sch The WN4 35 B1
Byrne Ave CH42 66 F1
Byrom La WA3 36 F2
Byrom St
Liverpool L1, L3 90 B4
Southport PR9 4 F7
Byron Ave
Liverpool L12 54 A7
Prescot L35 56 F3
Byron Cl
Birkenhead CH43 77 F8
Formby L37 9 F4
Huyton-w-R L36 56 A1
3 Orrell WN5 25 F7
St Helens WA10 44 A5
Byron Ct
Liverpool L25 70 A3
Warrington WA2 61 C2
Byron Rd
Crosby L23 26 C4
Maghull L31 20 D3
Byron St
Bootle L20 38 A5
Liverpool L19 81 C5
Byton Wlk L33 30 A4
Byway The L23 26 E5

C

CABBAGE HALL 53 C6
Cabes Cl L14 55 A6
Cabin La
Halsall Moss L39 8 C5
Maghull L31 19 F4
Southport, Churchtown Moss PR9 2 F3
Cable Rd
Hoylake CH47 63 B7
Prescot L35 56 F4
Cables Ret Pk L34 56 D5
Cable St
Formby L37 10 A4
Southport PR8 4 B7
Cable Yard The 15 L3 90 A4
Cabot Cl WA5 60 C1
Cabot Gn L25 69 E5
Cadbury Cl L12 40 B2
Caddick Rd L34 41 B5
Cadet Way L12 54 E7
Cadnam Rd L25 70 D5
Cadogan St L15, L7 68 D8
Cadwell Rd L31 20 B5
Caernarvon Cl CH49 65 A6
Caernarvon Ct CH63 78 F4
Caerwys Gr CH42 66 E4
Cain's Brewery* L8 67 E6
Caird St L6 53 A3
Cairn Brae WA12 46 C4
Cairn Ct WA9 57 D8
Cairnmore Rd L18 69 A2
Cairns St L8 68 A6
Cairo St
Liverpool L4 38 E1
St Helens WA10 43 D1
Caister Cl WN8 24 E8
Caithness Dr
Crosby L23 26 F3
Wallasey CH45 51 C6
Caithness Gdns 4 CH43 65 F1
Caithness Rd L18 69 B1
Calcott Rake L30 27 E4
Calday Gr WA11 45 A8
Calday Grange Cl CH48 63 D1
Calday Grange Gram Sch CH48 63 D1
Caldbeck Ave WA2 61 D2
Caldbeck Cl WN4 35 B4
Caldbeck Gr WA11 33 C1
Caldbeck Rd CH62 79 E2
Calder Ave
Birkenhead CH43 66 A2
Ormskirk L39 13 E4
Calder Cl
Kirkby L33 30 A6
Widnes WA8 73 F3
Calder Dr
Liverpool L18 69 C4
Maghull L31 20 F2
Rainhill L35 57 C3
Calder Edge L18 69 C4
Calderfield Rd L18 69 D5
Calder Grange L18 69 E3
Calderhurst Dr WA10 43 B6
Calder Park Ct L18 69 D4
Calder Rd
Bebington CH63 78 D5
Liverpool L5 52 F6
Calders The L18 69 C3
CALDERSTONES 69 C3
Calderstones Ave L18 69 C4
Calderstones Ct L18 69 C4

- Calderstones & Harthill Botanic Gdns★ L18 69 D4
- Calderstones Rd L18 69 C4
- Calderstones Sch L18 69 C4
- Calders View Ct L18 69 C3
- Calderwood Pk L27 70 D6
- Caldicott Ave CH62 88 D7
- Caldon Cl L21 27 A1
- Caldway Dr L27 70 E6
- Caldwell Ave WA5 60 F2
- Caldwell Cl L33 29 F5
- Caldwell Dr CH49 65 B2
- Caldwell Rd L19 81 D7
- Caldwell St WA9 44 D3
- CALDY 75 D7
- Caldy Chase Dr CH48 75 D7
- Caldy Ct 3 CH48 63 B1
- Caldy Gr WA11 44 D5
- Caldy Mews CH48 75 D7
- Caldy Rd
  - Liverpool L9 39 A7
  - Wallasey CH45 51 B5
  - West Kirby CH48 75 D7
- Caldy Wood CH48 75 D7
- Caldywood Dr L35 56 E3
- Caledonian Cres L21 27 A1
- Caledonia St L7, L8 67 F8
- Calgarth Rd L36 55 C5
- California Rd L13 53 D7
- Callaghan Cl L5 52 D5
- Callander Rd L6 53 D3
- Callands Prim Sch WA5 60 E2
- Callands Rd WA5 60 D2
- Callard Cl L27 70 C6
- Callestock Cl L11 40 D6
- Callington Cl L14 55 A6
- Callon Ave WA11 44 E5
- Callow Rd L15 68 D7
- Calmet Cl L5 52 E6
- Calne Cl CH61 76 D7
- Calstock Cl WA5 74 E3
- Calthorpe St L19 81 B7
- Calthorpe Way CH43 65 D6
- Calton Ave L15, L18 69 A5
- Calvados Cl L17 68 C1
- Calveley Ave CH62 88 F4
- Calveley Cl CH43 65 E3
- Calveley Rd L26 83 A6
- Calverhall Way WN4 35 A3
- Calver Rd WA2 61 A3
- Camberley Cl PR8 3 E5
- Camberley Dr L25 82 D9
- Camberwell Park Rd WA8 73 D4
- Camborne Ave L25 70 C1
- Cambourne Ave WA11 44 D7
- Cambourne Rd WA5 59 F6
- Cambrian Cl CH46 64 B7
- Cambrian Ct PR9 4 D8
- Cambrian Rd CH46 64 C7
- Cambrian Way L25 70 B3
- Cambria Street N 13 L6 53 B3
- Cambria Street S 14 L6 53 B3
- Cambridge Arc 5 PR8 4 B7
- Cambridge Ave
  - Crosby L23 26 D5
  - Litherland L21 38 B8
  - Southport PR9 1 F2
- Cambridge Ct
  - Liverpool L7 67 F8
  - Southport PR9 1 F2
- Cambridge Dr
  - Crosby L23 26 C5
  - Liverpool L26 82 F9
- Cambridge Gdns PR9 1 F2
- Cambridge Rd
  - Bebington CH62 88 E8
  - Birkenhead CH42 66 B2
  - Bootle L20 38 D2
  - Crosby L23 26 C5
  - Formby L37 9 D1
  - Liverpool L9 39 B8
  - Orrell WN5 25 F8
  - Seaforth L21, L22 37 E8
  - Skelmersdale WN8 15 E1
  - Southport PR9 1 E2
  - St Helens WA10 43 E4
  - Wallasey CH45 51 B7
- Cambridge St
  - 16 Liverpool, Edge Hill L7, L69 67 F8
  - Liverpool, Wavertree L15 68 D8
  - Prescot L34 56 D6
- Cambridge Wlks 6 PR8 4 B7
- Camdale Cl L28 55 B7
- Camden Mews CH49 65 B4
- Camden Pl 1 CH41 66 E6
- Camden St L3 90 C4
- Camelford Rd L11 40 C5
- Camelia Ct L17 68 A2
- Camellia Gdns WA9 59 B7
- Camelot Cl WA12 45 F4
- Camelot Terr 8 L20 38 B4
- Cameo Cl L6 53 B4
- Cameron Ct WA2 61 A4
- Cameron Rd CH46 50 B3
- Cameron St L7 53 C2
- Cammell Ct CH43 66 B6
- Camm St WN2 36 B8
- Campania St L19 81 C4
- Campbell Cres
  - Kirkby L33 29 D6
  - Warrington WA5 74 F6
- Campbell Dr L14 54 E3
- Campbell Sq L1 90 B2
- Campbell St
  - Bootle L20 38 B3
  - Liverpool L1 90 B2
  - St Helens WA10 43 E4
- Campbeltown Rd CH41 66 F4
- Camperdown St CH41 66 F6
- Camphill Rd L25 82 A9
- Campion Cl WA11 44 B7
- Campion Gr WN4 34 F4
- Campion Way L36 70 F7
- Camp Rd
  - Garswood WN4 34 E4
  - Liverpool L25 70 B1
- Campsey Ash WA8 72 F4
- Cam St L25 69 F2
- Canada Bvd L3 52 B1
- Canal Bank Cotts L31 20 C7
- Canal Bank Pygons Hill L31 20 C7
- Canalside Gr L5 52 C5
- Canal St
  - Bootle L20 38 B2
  - Newton-le-W WA12 45 F3
  - St Helens WA10 43 F2
- Canal View L31 29 A3
- Canal View Ct L21 27 A2
- Canberra Ave
  - St Helens WA9 57 E8
  - Warrington WA2 61 D3
- Canberra La L11 40 C5
- Canberra Sq WA2 61 D2
- Candia Twr L5 52 E6
- Candleston Cl WA5 60 E1
- Canning Pl L1 90 A2
- Canning Rd PR9 5 A6
- Canning St
  - Birkenhead CH41 66 F7
  - 2 Crosby L22 26 D1
  - Liverpool L8 67 F7
- Canniswood Rd WA11 45 A6
- Cannock Gn L31 20 B1
- Cannon Hill CH43 66 B6
- Cannon Mount CH43 66 B6
- Cannon St WA9 58 C3
- Canon Rd L6 53 C7
- Canon St WA7 84 F3
- Canon Wilson Cl WA11 45 D6
- Canova Cl L27 70 F4
- Canrow La L34 41 E5
- Cansfield Gr WN4 35 A4
- Cansfield High Specialist Language Coll WN4 35 A4
- Cansfield St WA10 44 A4
- Canterbury Ave
  - Crosby L22 26 D3
  - Golborne WA3 36 D1
- Canterbury Cl
  - Aintree L10 28 E2
  - Formby L37 9 F5
  - Prescot L34 56 E7
  - Southport PR8 3 F4
- Canterbury Pk L18 81 C8
- Canterbury Rd
  - Birkenhead CH42 67 A1
  - Wallasey CH44 51 C3
  - Widnes WA8 84 C8
- Canterbury St
  - Liverpool, Garston L19 81 D4
  - Liverpool L3 52 E3
  - St Helens WA10 43 E5
- Canterbury Way
  - Litherland L30 27 F4
  - 1 Liverpool L3 52 F3
- Canter Cl L9 39 D8
- Cantlow Fold PR8 7 A4
- Cantsfield St L7 68 C7
- Canvey Cl L15 69 B7
- Capella Cl L17 80 E7
- Cape Rd L9 39 C6
- Capesthorne Cl WA8 84 E8
- Capesthorne Rd WA2 61 D2
- Capilano Pk L39 21 C8
- Capitol Trad Est L33 30 C2
- Caplin Cl L33 29 E6
- Capper Gr L36 55 E3
- Capricorn Cres L14 55 A5
- Capricorn Way L20 38 B4
- Capstick Cres L25 70 B6
- Captains Cl L30 38 D8
- Captains Gn L30 38 D8
- Captain's La
  - Ashton-in-M WN4 35 C3
  - Bootle L30 38 E8
- Caradoc Rd L21 38 A6
- Caravan Pk The WA9 58 A8
- Caraway Cl L23 27 B5
- Caraway Gr WA10 43 D4
- Carbis Cl L10 40 B6
- Carden Cl L4 52 E8
- Cardiff St WN8 15 D1
- Cardiff Way L19 81 B6
- Cardigan Ave CH41 66 D6
- Cardigan Cl
  - St Helens WA10 43 F2
  - Warrington WA5 60 D2
- Cardigan Rd
  - Southport PR8 3 F1
  - Wallasey CH45 51 B7
- Cardigan St L15 68 D8
- Cardigan Way
  - Litherland L30 28 B4
  - Liverpool L6 53 B4
- Cardinal Heenan RC High Sch L12 54 D5
- Cardus Cl CH46 64 B8
- Cardwell Rd L19 81 D6
- Cardwell St L7 68 B8
- Carey Ave CH63 78 D6
- Carey St WA8 73 B1
- Carfax Rd L33 30 A4
- Carfield WN8 24 E6
- Cargill Gr CH42 79 B8
- Carham Rd CH47 63 C6
- Carillion Cl L11 40 C3
- Carina Ct L17 80 F7
- Carisbrooke Cl CH48 75 C8
- Carisbrooke Dr PR9 1 F1
- Carisbrooke Pl L4 38 F1
- Carisbrooke Rd L20, L4 38 E1
- Carkington Rd L25 70 C1
- Carlake Gr L9 39 D3
- Carland Cl L10 40 B6
- Carlaw Rd CH42 66 A2
- Carleen Cl L17 68 B2
- Carleton House Prep Sch L18 68 F3
- Carlett Bvd CH62 88 F5
- Carley Wlk L24 82 E3
- Carlile Way L33 29 F6
- Carlingford Cl L8 68 A7
- Carlisle Ave L30 27 F1
- Carlisle Cl L4 53 D8
- Carlisle Mews 16 CH43 66 C5
- Carlisle Rd PR8 4 A2
- Carlis Rd L32 40 F8
- Carlow Cl L24 83 D2
- Carlow St WA10 43 D1
- Carl's Way L33 30 A6
- Carlton Ave WN8 25 A7
- Carlton Cl
  - Ashton-in-M WN4 35 A5
  - Neston CH64 86 C2
- Carlton La
  - Hoylake CH47 63 C8
  - Liverpool L13 54 A4
- Carlton Mt CH42 66 E3
- Carlton Rd
  - Bebington CH63 79 B4
  - Birkenhead CH42 66 C4
  - Golborne WA3 36 D1
  - Southport PR8 7 C6
  - Wallasey CH45 51 B7
- Carlton St
  - Liverpool L3 52 B4
  - 5 Prescot L34 56 D6
  - St Helens WA10 43 E3
- Carlton Terr CH47 63 C8
- Carlyon Way L26 82 E9
- Carmarthen Cl WA5 60 D2
- Carmarthen Cres L8 67 D6
- Carmel Cl
  - Ormskirk L39 13 D2
  - 8 Wallasey CH45 51 B8
- Carmel Coll WA10 43 B1
- Carmel Ct WA8 73 B4
- Carmelite Cres WA10 43 A5
- Carmichael Ave CH49 64 D2
- Carnaby Cl L36 71 A8
- Carnarvon Ct L9 39 A3
- Carnarvon Rd
  - Liverpool L9 39 A3
  - Southport PR8 3 F1
- Carnarvon St WA9 57 D8
- Carnatic Cl L18 68 F3
- Carnatic Ct L18 68 E3
- Carnatic Rd L17, L18 68 E3
- Carnation Rd L9 39 B3
- Carneghie Ct 1 PR8 3 F4
- Carnegie Ave L23 26 D3
- Carnegie Cres WA9 58 E8
- Carnegie Dr WN4 35 A5
- Carnegie Rd L13 53 E4
- Carnforth Ave L32 29 F1
- Carnforth Cl
  - 7 Birkenhead CH41 66 C5
  - Liverpool L12 40 C1
- Carnforth Rd L18 69 C2
- Carno St L15 68 E8
- Carnoustie Cl
  - Liverpool L12 54 F6
  - Southport PR8 3 F4
  - Wallasey CH46 49 B1
- Carnoustie Gr WA11 45 A5
- Carnsdale Rd CH46 64 F8
- Carol Dr CH60 86 C8
- Carole Cl WA9 58 E6
- Carolina St L20 38 C3
- Caroline Pl CH43 66 B5
- Caronia St L19 81 C4
- Carpathia St L19 81 C4
- Carpenter's La CH48 63 B2
- Carpenters Row L1 90 B2
- Carraway Rd L11 40 C6
- Carr Bridge Rd CH49 65 C3
- Carr Cl L11 40 B2
- Carr Croft L21 27 B3
- CARR CROSS 5 D1
- Carrfield Ave L23 27 A3
- Carr Gate CH46 64 C7
- Carr Hey CH46 64 B7
- Carr Hey Cl CH49 65 C2
- Carr House La
  - Birkenhead CH46 64 B8
  - Ince Blundell L38 18 E4
- Carriage Cl L24 83 D1
- Carrick Ct L23 27 A3
- Carrickmore Ave L18 69 A2
- Carrington Rd CH45 51 C6
- Carrington St CH41 66 A8
- Carr La
  - Hale L24, WA8 83 E4
  - Hoylake CH47 63 B6
  - Huyton-w-R L36 55 C1
  - Liverpool L11 40 A2
  - Maghull L31 19 F5
- Carr La *continued*
  - Prescot L34 56 B5
  - Southport PR8 7 F7
  - Wallasey CH46, CH47 49 A1
  - West Kirby CH48 63 E5
- Carr La E L11 40 B3
- Carr La Ind Est CH47 63 C6
- Carr Meadow Hey L30 27 C3
- CARR MILL 33 C1
- Carr Mill Cres WN5 33 E4
- Carr Mill Prim Sch WA11 33 C1
- Carr Mill Rd
  - Billinge WA11, WN5 33 D3
  - St Helens WA11 44 C8
- Carr Moss La
  - Haskayne L39 12 B8
  - Southport L39 8 D2
- Carrock Rd CH62 79 E2
- Carroll Cres L39 13 F7
- Carrow Cl CH46 64 B7
- Carr Rd L20 38 D7
- Carr's Cres L37 9 E1
- Carr's Cres W L37 9 D1
- Carr Side La L29 19 A3
- Carr St WA10 43 D5
- Carrs Terr L35 56 D3
- Carruthers St L3 52 C3
- Carrville Way L12 41 A3
- Carrwood Cl WA11 45 A6
- Carrwood Pk PR8 4 B4
- Carsdale Rd L18 69 A5
- Carsgoe Rd CH47 63 C6
- Carsington Rd L11 40 A2
- Carstairs Rd L6 53 D4
- Carsthorne Rd CH47 63 C6
- Cartbridge La L26, L35 71 A2
- Carter Ave WA11 32 A5
- Carter St L8 67 F6
- Carters The
  - Birkenhead CH49 64 C4
  - Litherland L30 28 A4
- Carterton Rd CH47 63 C6
- Cartier Cl WA5 60 C1
- Cartmel Ave
  - Maghull L31 20 E2
  - Warrington WA2 61 C3
- Cartmel Cl
  - 11 Birkenhead CH41 66 C5
  - Huyton-w-R L36 55 D4
  - Southport PR8 4 F3
  - Warrington WA5 60 E2
- Cartmel Dr
  - Birkenhead CH46 64 E7
  - Formby L37 10 B2
  - Liverpool L12 40 C1
  - Rainhill L35 57 A4
- Cartmell Ave WA10 43 E7
- Cartmel Rd L36 55 C4
- Cartmel Terr L11 40 C3
- Cartmel Way L36 55 C4
- Cartwright Cl WA11 31 F6
- Cartwright Ct WA11 31 F7
- Cartwrights Farm Rd L24 82 A5
- Carver St L3 52 F3
- Caryl Gr L8 67 E4
- Caryl St
  - Liverpool L8 67 D6
  - Liverpool L8 67 E4
  - Liverpool, Toxteth L8 67 D5
- Cascade Rd L24 82 C7
- Case Gr L35 56 E5
- Case Rd WA11 45 D6
- Cases St L1 90 B3
- Cashel Rd CH44 51 B2
- Caspian Pl L20 38 C3
- Caspian Rd L4 39 D2
- Cassia Cl L9 39 B4
- Cassino Rd L36 55 E3
- Cassio St L20 38 E2
- Cassley Rd L24 83 A3
- Cassville Rd L15, L18 69 A6
- Castell Gr WA10 43 F3
- Castle Ave WA9 44 E3
- Castlebridge Ct 5 CH42 66 F1
- Castle Cl CH46 50 A3
- Castle Ct 4 CH48 63 B1
- Castle Dr
  - Formby L37 9 F1
  - Heswall CH60 85 F8
- Castlefield Cl L12 54 A7
- Castlefield Rd L12 54 A8
- Castlefields CH46 49 F4
- Castleford Rise CH46 49 E3
- Castleford St L15 69 A7
- Castlegate Gr L12 54 B7
- Castle Gn WA5 60 B2
- Castlegrange Cl CH46 49 E4
- Castleheath Cl CH46 49 E3
- Castlehey WN8 24 E6
- Castle Hill
  - 7 Liverpool L2 90 A3
  - Newton-le-W WA12 46 E4
- Castle Keep L12 54 B7
- Castle La L40 14 E5
- Castle Mews L35 56 D4
- Castle Rd CH45 51 A6
- Castlerigg Ct CH42 66 C1
- Castlesite Rd L12 54 B7
- Castle St
  - Birkenhead CH41 66 F6
  - Liverpool L2 90 A3
  - Liverpool, Woolton Hill L25 69 F2
  - Southport PR9 4 B8
  - Widnes WA8 73 D1
- Castleton Dr L30 28 B4
- Castletown Cl L16 69 E8
- Castleview Rd L12 54 B7
- Castleway N CH46 50 A4
- Castleway Prim Sch CH46 50 A4
- Castleway S CH46 50 A3
- Castlewell L35 56 F4
- Castle Wlk PR8 4 A6
- Castlewood Rd L6 53 B5
- Castor St L6 53 B5
- Catapult Too 4 WA10 44 A3
- Catchdale Moss La WA10 42 E5
- Catford Cl WA8 72 C2
- Catford Gn L24 82 F4
- Catfoss Cl WA2 61 E1
- Catharine's La L39 13 F1
- Catharine St L8 67 F8
- Cathcart St CH41 66 D7
- Cathcart Street Prim Sch CH41 66 D7
- Cath CE (Cathedral Church of Christ)★ L1 90 C1
- Cathedral Cl L1 90 C1
- Cathedral Ct 1 L8 67 F7
- Cathedral Gate L1 90 C2
- Cathedral Rd 2 L6 53 C6
- Cathedral Wlk L3 52 F1
- Catherine Ct L21 38 B6
- Catherine St
  - Birkenhead CH41 66 D6
  - Bootle L21 38 B6
- Catherine Way
  - Newton-le-W WA12 46 B2
  - St Helens WA11 44 F6
- Catkin Rd L26 70 D2
- Caton Cl PR9 1 F4
- Catonfield Rd L18 69 D5
- Cat Tail La PR8 5 E1
- Cattan Gn L37 10 B3
- Catterall Ave
  - St Helens WA9 58 D6
  - Warrington WA2 61 D2
- Catterick Cl L26 82 F9
- Catterick Fold PR8 4 F3
- Caulfield Dr CH49 64 E3
- Caunce Ave
  - Golborne WA3 47 A7
  - Haydock WA11 45 B6
  - Newton-le-W WA12 46 C1
- Causeway Cl CH62 79 B6
- Causeway Ho CH46 49 E4
- Causeway La L37 11 B1
- Causeway The
  - Bebington CH62 79 B5
  - Liverpool L12 54 D4
  - Southport PR9 2 C5
- Cavalier Dr L19 81 E5
- Cavan Dr WA11 45 D7
- Cavan Rd L11 53 E8
- Cavell Cl L25 70 A1
- Cavendish Ct
  - Liverpool L18 69 D3
  - Southport PR9 4 E8
  - 5 Wallasey CH45 51 B8
  - Widnes WA8 72 F1
- Cavendish Dr
  - Birkenhead CH42 66 D1
  - Liverpool L9 39 A3
- Cavendish Gdns 8 L8 68 A5
- Cavendish Rd
  - Birkenhead CH41 66 B7
  - Crosby L23 26 C3
  - Southport PR8 3 F3
  - 3 Wallasey CH45 51 B8
- Cavendish St
  - Birkenhead CH41 66 B8
  - 7 Runcorn WA7 84 F2
- Cavendish Wlk
  - Huyton-w-R L36 55 E2
  - Southport PR9 4 E8
- Cavern Ct 6 L6 53 B3
- Cavern Wlks L2 90 A3
- Cawdor St
  - Liverpool L8 68 A6
  - Runcorn WA7 84 F3
- Cawfield Ave WA8 72 D1
- Cawthorne Ave L32 40 E8
- Cawthorne Cl L32 40 E8
- Cawthorne Wlk L32 40 E8
- Caxton Cl
  - Birkenhead CH43 65 C6
  - Widnes WA8 72 C3
- Caxton Rd L35 57 E1
- Cazneau St L3 52 D3
- 'C' Ct WN4 35 B2
- Cearns Ct CH43 66 A5
- Cearns Rd CH43 66 A5
- Cecil Dr WA10 43 A4
- Cecil Rd
  - Bebington CH62 79 B8
  - Birkenhead CH42 66 B2
  - Seaforth L21 37 F6
  - Wallasey CH44 51 B4
- Cecil St
  - Liverpool L15 68 D8
  - St Helens WA9 58 F7
- Cedar Ave
  - Bebington CH63 78 E4
  - Golborne WA3 47 F7
  - Widnes WA8 73 B2
- Cedar Cl
  - Liverpool L18 69 D3

Cedar Cl continued
Prescot L35 . . . . **56** E4
Cedar Cres
Huyton-w-R L36 . . . . **55** D1
Newton-le-W WA12 . . . . . **46** D2
Ormskirk L39 . . . . **13** D4
Cedar Ct L34 . . . . **41** C4
Cedardale Pk WA8 . . . . **73** E4
Cedardale Rd L9 . . . . **39** A4
Cedar Dr L37 . . . . **9** C1
Cedar Gr
Crosby L23 . . . . **26** D2
Downall Green WN4 . . . . . **34** D5
Haydock WA11 . . . . **45** E7
Liverpool L18 . . . . **68** C6
Maghull L31 . . . . **28** D6
Orrell WN5 . . . . **25** F6
Skelmersdale WN8 . . . . . . **15** E1
Cedar Rd
Liverpool L9 . . . . **39** B6
Prescot L35 . . . . **56** D3
Warrington WA5 . . . . **74** F6
Cedar St
Birkenhead CH41 . . . . **66** D5
Bootle L20 . . . . **38** C4
Newton-le-W WA12 . . . . . **46** C2
Southport PR8 . . . . **4** D4
St Helens WA10 . . . . **43** D2
Cedars The
Birkenhead CH46 . . . . **64** C7
Liverpool L12 . . . . **40** F3
Cedar Terr L8 . . . . **68** C6
Cedar Twrs L33 . . . . **29** F3
Cedarway CH60 . . . . **86** B5
Cedarwood Cl CH49 . . . . . . **64** B4
Cedarwood Ct L36 . . . . **70** E8
Celandine Way WA9 . . . . . . **59** B7
Celebration Dr L6 . . . . **53** C5
Celendine Cl L15 . . . . **68** E8
Celia St L20 . . . . **38** D1
Celtic Rd CH47 . . . . **48** E1
Celtic St 2 L8 . . . . **68** A6
Celt St L6 . . . . **53** C4
Cemeas St L3 . . . . **52** C5
Cemetery Rd PR8 . . . . **4** C4
Centenary Cl L4 . . . . **53** C8
Central Ave
Bebington CH62 . . . . **79** C1
Eccleston Park L34 . . . . . . **57** A7
Liverpool L24 . . . . **82** D4
Prescot L34 . . . . **56** C5
Southport PR8 . . . . **7** F8
Central Bldgs 2 L23 . . . . . **26** E4
Central Dr
Haydock WA11 . . . . **45** B6
Liverpool L12 . . . . **54** B5
Rainford WA11 . . . . **31** F7
Central Liverpool Coll of F
Ed L1 . . . . **90** C2
Central Par L24 . . . . **82** E4
Central Park Ave CH44 . . . **51** C4
Central Park Ct 5
CH44 . . . . **51** B4
Central Rd
Bebington, New Ferry
CH62 . . . . **79** B6
Bebington, Port Sunlight
CH62 . . . . **79** C4
Central Sh Ctr L1 . . . . **90** B3
Central Sq L31 . . . . **20** D2
Central St WA10 . . . . **44** A4
Central Sta L1 . . . . **90** B3
Central Way
Liverpool L24 . . . . **82** F3
Newton-le-W WA12 . . . . . **46** E2
Centreville Rd L15, L18 . . . **69** A6
Centre Way L36 . . . . **55** C2
Centurion Cl CH47 . . . . **48** E1
Centurion Dr CH47 . . . . **48** E1
Century Bldgs L3 . . . . **67** D5
Century Rd L23 . . . . **26** D4
Ceres St L20 . . . . **38** C1
Cestrian Dr CH61 . . . . **77** A5
Chadlow Rd L32 . . . . **40** F7
Chadwell Rd L33 . . . . **29** F4
CHADWICK GREEN **33** D3
Chadwick Rd WA11 . . . . . . **44** C7
Chadwick St
Birkenhead CH46 . . . . **64** E8
Liverpool L3 . . . . **52** B3
Chadwick Way L33 . . . . **29** E6
Chaffinch Cl L12 . . . . **40** F1
Chaffinch Glade L26 . . . . . **70** E1
Chainhurst Cl L27 . . . . **70** D5
Chain La WA11 . . . . **44** E6
Chain Lane Sh Prec
WA11 . . . . **44** D7
Chalfont Ct PR8 . . . . **4** A3
Chalfont Rd L18 . . . . **69** D1
Chalfont Way L28 . . . . **55** B7
Chalgrave Cl WA8 . . . . **73** F3
Chalkwell Dr CH60 . . . . **86** C7
Challis St CH41 . . . . **50** E1
Challoner Cl L36 . . . . **70** F8
Chaloner Gr L19 . . . . **80** F6
Chaloner St L1 . . . . **90** B1
Chalon Way E WA10 . . . . . . **44** A3
Chalon Way Ind Est
WA10 . . . . **44** A2
Chalon Way W WA10 . . . . . **44** A3
Chamberlain Dr L33 . . . . . . **29** F5
Chamberlain St
Birkenhead CH41 . . . . **66** F4
St Helens WA10 . . . . **43** D3

Chamberlain St continued
Wallasey CH44 . . . . **51** A2
Chambres Rd PR8 . . . . **4** D5
Chambres Rd N PR8 . . . . **4** D6
Chancellor Ct L8 . . . . **68** A8
Chancel St L4 . . . . **52** F7
Chancery La WA9 . . . . **44** E3
Chandlers Ct WA7 . . . . **84** E1
Chandlers Way WA9 . . . . . . **58** B3
Chandler Way WA3 . . . . **47** E8
Chandley Cl PR8 . . . . **7** A5
Chandos St 9 L7 . . . . **53** B1
Changford Gn L33 . . . . **30** A3
Changford Rd L33 . . . . **30** A3
Channell Rd L6 . . . . **53** C3
Channel Rd L23 . . . . **26** B3
Channel Reach L23 . . . . **26** B3
Channel The CH45 . . . . **50** E8
Chantrell Rd CH48 . . . . **63** F2
Chantry Cl CH43 . . . . **65** C6
Chantry The WA10 . . . . **43** D6
Chantry Wlk
Ashton-in-M WN4 . . . . **34** F5
Heswall CH60 . . . . **86** A6
Chapel Alley L37 . . . . **9** F3
Chapel Ave L9 . . . . **39** A5
Chapel Ct
Hoylake CH47 . . . . **63** C7
Liverpool L9 . . . . **39** A4
St Helens WA10 . . . . **43** D1
Chapel End Prim Sch
WN5 . . . . **33** E4
Chapel Gdns L5 . . . . **52** D5
Chapelhill Rd CH46 . . . . . . **64** F8
Chapel Ho
Maghull L31 . . . . **20** D1
Seaforth L22 . . . . **37** D8
CHAPEL HOUSE **15** E2
Chapelhouse Wlk L37 . . . . . **10** A3
Chapel La
Burtonwood WA5 . . . . **59** F6
Formby L37 . . . . **9** F3
Kirkby L31 . . . . **29** A4
Litherland L30 . . . . **27** F5
Litherland, Netherton
L30 . . . . **28** A5
Rainhill L35, WA9 . . . . **57** E2
St Helens, Eccleston
WA10 . . . . **43** B4
Widnes WA8 . . . . **72** C4
Chapel Mews L39 . . . . **13** F4
Chapel Pl
4 Ashton-in-M WN4 . . . . **35** B3
Liverpool L19 . . . . **81** C6
Chapel Rd
Hoylake CH47 . . . . **63** C8
3 Liverpool, Cabbage Hall
L6 . . . . **53** C6
Liverpool, Garston L19 . . . . **81** C6
Warrington WA5 . . . . **74** E3
Chapel St
Ashton-in-M WN4 . . . . **35** B3
Haydock WA11 . . . . **45** E6
Liverpool L3 . . . . **90** A4
Newton-le-W WA12 . . . . . **46** B3
Ormskirk L39 . . . . **13** F4
10 Prescot L34 . . . . **56** D6
Southport PR8 . . . . **4** B7
St Helens WA10 . . . . **43** F5
Chapel Terr L20 . . . . **38** B3
Chapel View
Bebington CH62 . . . . **89** A6
Crank WA11 . . . . **32** F4
Chapel Yd L15 . . . . **69** A7
Chapman Cl
Liverpool L8 . . . . **67** E5
Widnes WA8 . . . . **72** C4
Chapman Gr L34 . . . . **56** E7
Chardstock Dr L25 . . . . **70** C4
Charlecombe St CH42 . . . . . **66** D4
Charlecote St L8 . . . . **67** F3
Charles Ave
Southport PR8 . . . . **7** E6
Warrington WA5 . . . . **74** F6
Charles Berrington Rd
L15 . . . . **69** A6
Charles Best Gn L30 . . . . . . **27** F4
Charlesbye Ave L39 . . . . . . **14** B6
Charlesbye Cl L39 . . . . **14** B6
Charles Rd CH47 . . . . **63** B6
Charles St
2 Birkenhead CH41 . . . . **66** D7
Golborne WA3 . . . . **36** A1
St Helens WA10 . . . . **44** A4
Charleston Rd L8 . . . . **67** F4
Charlesville CH43 . . . . **66** B5
Charlesville Ct 4
CH43 . . . . **66** B5
Charlesworth Cl L31 . . . . . . **20** B5
Charley Wood Rd L33 . . . . . **30** C1
Charlock Cl L30 . . . . **28** A4
Charlotte Rd CH44 . . . . **51** D5
Charlotte's Mdw CH63 . . . . **79** A4
Charlotte Way 6 L1 . . . . . . **90** B3
Charlton Ct
Birkenhead CH43 . . . . **65** F6
Liverpool L25 . . . . **82** D8
Charlton Pl L13 . . . . **54** A1
Charlton Rd L13 . . . . **54** A1
Charlwood Ave L36 . . . . **55** E1
Charlwood Cl CH43 . . . . **65** C6
Charmalue Ave L23 . . . . . . **26** F4
Charmouth Cl
2 Liverpool L12 . . . . **40** E3
Newton-le-W WA12 . . . . . **46** B4
Charnley Dr L15 . . . . **69** C8
Charnley's La PR9 . . . . **2** E7

Charnock Ave WA12 . . . . . . **45** F3
Charnock Cotts L11 . . . . . . **40** A3
Charnock Rd L9 . . . . **39** D3
Charnwood Cl L12 . . . . **40** D3
Charnwood Rd L36 . . . . **55** B3
Charnwood St WA9 . . . . . . **44** E4
Charon Way WA5 . . . . **60** B3
Charter Ho CH44 . . . . **51** D4
Charterhouse Cl L25 . . . . . . **70** B1
Charterhouse Dr L10 . . . . . . **28** E2
Charterhouse Rd L25 . . . . . . **70** B1
Chartmount Way L25 . . . . . **70** B4
Chartwell Gr L26 . . . . **70** F1
Chartwell Rd PR8 . . . . **7** B6
Chase Cl PR8 . . . . **3** F4
Chase Heys PR9 . . . . **2** A1
Chaser Cl L9 . . . . **39** C8
Chase The
Bebington CH63 . . . . **88** C5
5 Heswall CH60 . . . . **86** A8
Huyton-w-R L36 . . . . **70** E8
Chase Way L5 . . . . **52** E4
Chatbrook Cl L17 . . . . **80** F7
Chatburn Ave WA3 . . . . **36** C1
Chater Cl L35 . . . . **57** A5
Chatham Cl L21 . . . . **37** F7
Chatham Ct L22 . . . . **37** E8
Chatham Pl L7 . . . . **53** B1
Chatham Rd CH42 . . . . **67** A2
Chatham St L7, L69 . . . . **67** F8
Chatsworth Ave
Liverpool L9 . . . . **38** F5
Wallasey CH44 . . . . **51** C4
Chatsworth Cl WN4 . . . . . . **34** F4
Chatsworth Ct L7 . . . . **53** D3
Chatsworth Dr
Liverpool L7 . . . . **68** B8
Widnes WA8 . . . . **72** C3
Chatsworth Rd
Birkenhead CH42 . . . . **67** A2
Heswall CH61 . . . . **76** F5
Rainhill L35 . . . . **57** B4
Southport PR8 . . . . **7** B6
Chatteriss St WA10 . . . . . . **43** D1
Chatterton Rd L14 . . . . **54** C4
Chaucer Dr L12 . . . . **40** F2
Chaucer Rd WA10 . . . . **43** D6
Chaucer St
Bootle L20 . . . . **38** A4
Liverpool L3 . . . . **52** D3
Cheadle Ave L13 . . . . **53** F4
Cheapside
Formby L37 . . . . **10** A2
Liverpool L2 . . . . **90** A4
Cheapside Alley 4 L2 . . . . . **90** A4
Cheddar Cl L25 . . . . **69** F2
Cheddar Gr
Burtonwood WA5 . . . . **59** F7
Kirkby L32 . . . . **40** E7
Cheddon Way CH61 . . . . . . **76** E4
Chedworth Dr WA8 . . . . **72** C4
Chedworth Rd L14 . . . . **54** C4
Cheldon Rd L12 . . . . **40** C2
Chelford Ave WA3 . . . . **47** D8
Chelford Cl CH43 . . . . **65** C7
Chellowdene L23 . . . . **27** A6
Chelmarsh Ave WN4 . . . . . . **35** C3
Chelmsford Cl 8 L4 . . . . . . **52** D7
Chelsea Cl L12 . . . . **54** E8
Chelsea Lea L9 . . . . **38** F6
Chelsea Rd
Bootle L21 . . . . **38** B6
Liverpool L9 . . . . **39** A6
Cheltenham Ave L17 . . . . . . **68** D6
Cheltenham Cl L10 . . . . **28** E1
Cheltenham Cres
Huyton-w-R L36 . . . . **55** D1
Wallasey CH46 . . . . **49** E3
Cheltenham Dr
Longshaw WN5 . . . . **25** D2
Newton-le-W WA12 . . . . . **46** C5
Cheltenham Rd CH45 . . . . . **50** E6
Cheltenham Way PR8 . . . . . . **4** F3
Chelwood Ave L14, L16 . . . **54** E1
Chelwood Pk L35 . . . . **35** B1
Chemical St WA12 . . . . **46** B3
Chemistry Rd L24 . . . . **82** C6
Chenotrie Gdns CH43 . . . . . **65** D5
Chepstow Ave CH44 . . . . . . **51** C4
Chepstow Cl WA5 . . . . **60** E3
Chepstow St L4 . . . . **38** F1
Chequer Cl WN8 . . . . **24** F5
Chequer La WN8 . . . . **24** F6
Chequers Gdns L19 . . . . . . **68** F1
Cheriton Ave CH48 . . . . **63** D2
Cheriton Cl L26 . . . . **82** E9
Cheriton Pk PR8 . . . . **4** E3
Chermside Rd L17 . . . . **68** E1
Cherry Ave L4 . . . . **39** B1
Cherrybank CH44 . . . . **51** B2
Cherry Cl
Liverpool L4 . . . . **39** B1
Newton-le-W WA12 . . . . . **45** F4
Cherrycroft WN8 . . . . **24** E6
Cherrydale Rd L18 . . . . **69** A4
Cherryfield Cres L32 . . . . . . **29** E2
Cherryfield Dr L32 . . . . **29** E2
Cherryfield Prim Sch
L32 . . . . **40** E7
Cherry Gdns
Hoylake CH47 . . . . **63** B7
Kirkby L32 . . . . **40** F7
Cherry Gn L39 . . . . **13** B1
Cherry La L4 . . . . **53** D8
Cherry Rd PR8 . . . . **7** D2
Cherry Sq 2 CH44 . . . . **51** B4
Cherrysutton WA8 . . . . **72** B3

Cherrysutton Mews
WA8 . . . . **72** B4
Cherry Tree Ave WA5 . . . . **74** F4
Cherry Tree Cl
Hale L24 . . . . **83** E1
Haydock WA11 . . . . **45** A5
Prescot L35 . . . . **56** D3
Cherry Tree Cotts
WA11 . . . . **33** A2
Cherry Tree Dr WA9 . . . . . . **45** A2
Cherry Tree La
Billinge WA11 . . . . **33** A2
Ormskirk WA9 . . . . **13** B1
Cherry Tree Mews 3
CH60 . . . . **86** A8
Cherry Tree Rd
Birkenhead CH46 . . . . **64** F8
Golborne WA3 . . . . **47** F8
Huyton-w-R L36 . . . . **70** E8
Cherry Vale L25 . . . . **70** B3
Cherry View L33 . . . . **30** A5
Cherrywood Ave L26 . . . . . **71** B1
Cherwell Cl WA2 . . . . **61** D2
Cheryl Dr WA8 . . . . **73** D1
Cheshire Acre CH49 . . . . . . **65** A2
Cheshire Ave L10 . . . . **40** B7
Cheshire Cl WA12 . . . . **46** E3
Cheshire Gdns WA10 . . . . . **43** E2
Cheshire Gr CH46 . . . . **64** E7
Cheshire Lines Path
L39 . . . . **10** E6
Cheshire Way CH61 . . . . . . **76** F3
Chesnell Gr L33 . . . . **29** F5
Chesney Cl L8 . . . . **67** E6
Chesnut Gr
Birkenhead CH42 . . . . **66** D4
Bootle L20 . . . . **38** B4
Chesnut Rd L21 . . . . **37** F8
Chester Ave
Golborne WA3 . . . . **47** D8
Litherland L30 . . . . **27** F1
Southport PR9 . . . . **4** E8
Chester Cl L23 . . . . **27** B4
Chester Ct CH63 . . . . **78** F4
Chester Dr WN4 . . . . **35** D2
Chesterfield Cl PR8 . . . . **7** C4
Chesterfield Dr L33 . . . . . . **29** E5
Chesterfield High Sch
L23 . . . . **27** A4
Chesterfield Rd
Bebington CH62 . . . . **88** D4
Crosby L23 . . . . **27** A4
Southport PR8 . . . . **7** C5
Chesterfield St L8 . . . . **90** C1
Chester High Rd CH64 . . . . **86** E4
Chester La WA9 . . . . **58** B4
Chester Rd
Heswall CH60, CH64 . . . . **86** C6
Hooton CH66 . . . . **89** A1
Huyton-w-R L36 . . . . **56** A4
Liverpool L6 . . . . **53** D5
Southport PR9 . . . . **4** E8
Chester Row WA12 . . . . **60** D8
Chester St
Birkenhead CH41 . . . . **66** F6
Liverpool L8 . . . . **90** C1
Prescot L34 . . . . **56** D6
Wallasey CH44 . . . . **51** A3
Widnes WA8 . . . . **73** B1
Chester Wlk L36 . . . . **56** A4
Chesterton Dr WA2 . . . . **61** A5
Chesterton St L19 . . . . **81** C4
Chester Wlk L36 . . . . **56** A4
Chestnut Ave
Crosby L23 . . . . **26** F6
Huyton-w-R L36 . . . . **70** D8
St Helens WA11 . . . . **44** F5
Warrington WA5 . . . . **74** F6
Widnes WA8 . . . . **73** B2
Chestnut Cl
Birkenhead CH49 . . . . **64** C2
Prescot L35 . . . . **56** E4
Chestnut Ct
Bootle L20 . . . . **38** B4
3 Ormskirk L39 . . . . **13** F6
Widnes WA8 . . . . **72** D1
Chestnut Gr
Ashton-in-M WN4 . . . . **35** D4
Bebington CH62 . . . . **88** C8
Bootle L20 . . . . **38** B5
Golborne WA3 . . . . **47** F8
Liverpool L15 . . . . **69** A8
St Helens WA11 . . . . **44** D7
Chestnut Grange CH49
L39 . . . . **13** D3
Chestnut Ho 1 L20 . . . . **38** B4
Chestnut Lodge Specl Sch
WA8 . . . . **72** E1
Chestnut Rd L9 . . . . **39** C3
Chestnut St
Liverpool L7 . . . . **52** F1
Southport PR8 . . . . **4** C5
Chestnut Tree Sch L23 . . . . **26** E4
Chestnut Way L37 . . . . **9** C1
Chestnut Wlk L31 . . . . **29** A4
Cheswood Cl L35 . . . . **56** E2
Cheswood Ct 4 CH49 . . . . . **65** A2
Chetham Ct WA2 . . . . **61** A3
Chetwode Ave WN4 . . . . . . **35** B1
Chetwood Ave L23 . . . . **26** F5
Chetwood Cl WA12 . . . . **46** B5
Chetwood Dr WA8 . . . . **72** B4
Chetwynd Cl CH43 . . . . **65** F4
Chetwynd Rd CH43 . . . . **66** A5
Chetwynd St L17 . . . . **68** B3
Chetwyn Ho 5 CH48 . . . . . . **63** B1
Chevasse Wlk L25 . . . . **70** C3
Cheverton Cl CH49 . . . . **65** B3
Chevin Cl L9 . . . . **39** A5

Cheviot Ave
St Helens WA9 . . . . **44** F3
Warrington WA2 . . . . **61** A3
Cheviot Cl CH42 . . . . **66** D1
Cheviot Rd
Birkenhead CH42 . . . . **66** D1
Liverpool L7 . . . . **53** C2
Cheviot Way L33 . . . . **29** F6
Cheyne Cl L23 . . . . **26** A3
Cheyne Gdns L19 . . . . **80** F8
Cheyne Wlk WA9 . . . . **57** F6
Chichester Cl L15 . . . . **68** D8
Chidden Cl CH49 . . . . **64** C3
Chigwell Cl L12 . . . . **40** E3
Chilcott Rd L14 . . . . **54** C3
Childers St 1 L13 . . . . **54** A3
CHILDWALL **69** E7
Childwall Abbey Rd
L16 . . . . **69** E7
Childwall Ave
Birkenhead CH46,
. . . . **64** D7
Liverpool L15 . . . . **68** D7
Childwall Bank Rd L16 . . . . **69** D7
Childwall CE Prim Sch
L16 . . . . **69** D5
Childwall Cl CH46 . . . . **64** D7
Childwall Cres L16 . . . . **69** D7
Childwall Five Ways
L15 . . . . **69** C7
Childwall Gn CH49 . . . . **65** A2
Childwall La
Huyton-w-R L36 . . . . **55** A2
Liverpool L16, L25 . . . . . . **69** F6
Childwall Mount Rd
L16 . . . . **69** D7
Childwall Par L14 . . . . **55** A2
Childwall Park Ave
L16 . . . . **69** E6
Childwall Priory Rd
L16 . . . . **69** D7
Childwall Rd L15 . . . . **69** B7
Childwall Sch L15 . . . . **69** C7
Childwall Valley Prim Sch
L25 . . . . **70** A7
Childwall Valley Rd L16, L25,
L27 . . . . **70** C6
Chilhem Cl 3 L8 . . . . **67** F4
Chilington Ave WA8 . . . . . . **74** F3
Chillerton Rd L12 . . . . **54** D8
Chillingham St 1 L8 . . . . . . **68** A3
Chiltern Cl
Ashton-in-M WN4 . . . . **35** C2
Kirkby L32 . . . . **29** C4
Liverpool L12 . . . . **40** F2
Chiltern Cres WA2 . . . . **61** A3
Chiltern Dr L32 . . . . **29** C4
Chiltern Pl WA2 . . . . **61** A3
Chiltern Rd
Birkenhead CH42 . . . . **66** C1
Southport PR8 . . . . **7** B6
St Helens WA9 . . . . **45** A3
Warrington WA2 . . . . **61** A3
Chilton Cl L31 . . . . **20** D1
Chilton Ct L31 . . . . **20** D1
Chilton Mews L31 . . . . **20** D1
Chilwell Cl WA8 . . . . **72** C4
Chimes Rd WN4 . . . . **34** F6
China Farm La CH48 . . . . . . **63** E3
Chindit Cl L37 . . . . **9** D2
Chippenham Ave CH49 . . . . **64** C3
Chipping Ave PR8 . . . . **7** A5
Chirkdale St L4 . . . . **38** E1
Chirk Way CH46 . . . . **64** F7
Chirton Cl WA11 . . . . **45** D7
Chisenhale St L3 . . . . **52** C4
Chisledon Cl WA11 . . . . **45** D7
Chisleburst Ave L25 . . . . . . **70** B6
Chislet Ct WA8 . . . . **72** E4
Chisnall Ave WA10 . . . . **43** C4
Chiswell St L7 . . . . **53** C2
Cholmley Dr WA12 . . . . **46** E2
Cholmondeley Rd
CH48 . . . . **63** B2
Cholsey Cl CH49 . . . . **64** F4
Chorley Cl PR9 . . . . **2** F5
Chorley Rd L34 . . . . **56** B6
Chorley's La WA8 . . . . **73** E3
Chorley St WA10 . . . . **43** F4
Chorley Way CH63 . . . . **79** A1
Chorlton Cl L16 . . . . **69** F8
Chorlton Gr CH45 . . . . **50** D5
Christ Church CE Prim
Sch
Birkenhead CH41 . . . . **66** C5
Birkenhead, Moreton
CH46 . . . . **64** E8
Bootle L20 . . . . **38** D4
Christchurch Rd CH43 . . . . **66** B4
Christiana Hartley
Maternity Hospl PR8 . . . . **4** D5
Christian Fellowship Sch
L7 . . . . **68** B8
Christian St L3 . . . . **52** E3
Christie Cl CH66 . . . . **89** A2
Christie St WA8 . . . . **73** D1
Christleton Cl CH43 . . . . . . **65** D2
Christmas St L20 . . . . **38** D1
Christopher Cl
Liverpool L16 . . . . **69** D8
Rainhill L35 . . . . **57** B2
Christopher Dr CH62 . . . . . . **89** A5
Christophers Cl CH61 . . . . . **77** A4
Christopher St L4 . . . . **52** F8
Christopher Taylor Ho
L31 . . . . **28** D8
Christopher Way L16 . . . . . . **69** D8
Christowe Wlk L11 . . . . **40** C5

Christ The King RC High Sch & Sixth Form Ctr PR8 4 B2
Christ The King RC Prim Sch
Bebington CH62 88 E7
Liverpool L15 69 C8
Chris Ward Cl 1 L7 53 C1
Chromolyte Ind Est PR8 4 B5
Chudleigh Cl L26 70 E1
Chudleigh Rd L13 53 F3
Chung Hok Ho L1 90 C1
Church Alley L1 90 B3
Church Ave
Bickershaw WN2 36 F8
Liverpool L9 39 B7
Church Cl
Formby L37 10 A3
Southport PR9 5 A8
Wallasey CH44 51 D4
Church Close Ct L37 10 A3
Church Cotts L25 70 C5
Church Cres 9 CH44 51 E2
Churchdown Cl L14 54 F4
Churchdown Gr 3 L14 54 E4
Churchdown Rd L14 54 E4
Church Dr
Bebington CH62 79 B6
Newton-le-W WA12 46 C1
Orrell WN5 25 D5
Church Drive Prim Sch CH62 79 B6
Church End L24 83 D1
Church End Mews L24 83 D1
Church Farm CH63 79 A5
Church Farm* CH61 76 B5
Church Farm Ct CH60 85 F7
Churchfield Ct L25 70 C4
Churchfield Rd L25 70 C5
Churchfields
Southport PR8 3 F3
5 St Helens WA9 58 C4
Widnes WA8 73 B5
Church Fields L39 13 E5
Churchgate PR9 1 F1
Churchgate Mews PR9 2 A1
Church Gdns
Bootle L20 38 B3
Wallasey CH44 51 D4
Church Gn
Formby L37 9 C2
Kirkby L32 29 E3
Liverpool L16 69 F7
Skelmersdale WN8 15 F1
Church Gr L21 37 F6
Church Green Gdns WA3 36 B1
Church Hill CH44, CH45 50 F5
Church Hill Rd L39 13 D6
Church Ho 7 L39 13 E5
Churchill Ave
Birkenhead CH41 66 B7
Southport PR9 1 F2
Churchill Gdns WA9 57 C6
Churchill Gr CH44 51 C5
Churchill Ho 6 L21 37 F7
Churchill Ind Est L9 39 C8
Churchill Way (Elevated Rd) L1, L2, L3 90 B4
Church La
Aughton L39 21 A7
Bebington, Bromborough CH62 79 D1
Bebington CH62 89 A4
Birkenhead CH49 65 B2
Golborne WA3 47 D7
Kirkby L34 41 C4
Liverpool L17 68 E1
Liverpool, Walton on the Hill L4 38 F2
Maghull L31 20 A8
St Helens WA10 43 A4
Thurstaston CH61 76 B5
Wallasey CH44 51 D4
Churchlands 13 CH44 51 E2
Churchmeadow Cl CH44 51 D4
Church Meadow La CH60 85 F7
Church Meadow Wlk WA8 84 B5
Church Mews
Birkenhead CH42 67 A1
Liverpool L24 82 B4
Southport PR9 5 A7
Church Mount 2 L7 53 B1
Church Rd
Banks PR9 2 F6
Bebington CH63 79 A4
Bickerstaffe L39 22 E6
Birkenhead, Devonshire Park CH42 66 D3
Birkenhead, Upton CH49 65 A5
Bootle L20 38 D6
1 Crosby L23 26 E4
Formby L37 10 A4
Hale L24 83 E1
Halewood L26 70 F1
Haydock WA11 45 E7
Huyton-w-R L36 55 C3
Litherland L21 38 C8
Litherland, Stanley Park L21 27 D1
Liverpool, Garston L19 81 C5
Liverpool, Stanley L13 53 F3
Liverpool, Walton on the Hill L4 39 A2
Church Rd *continued*
Liverpool, Wavertree Green L15, L18 69 A6
Liverpool, Woolton Park L25 70 A3
Maghull L31 28 D7
Rainford WA11 32 A5
Seaforth L22 37 E8
Skelmersdale WN8 15 F1
Thornton Hough CH63 87 B6
Wallasey CH44 51 E2
West Kirby CH48 63 B1
Church Rd N L15 69 A7
Church Rd S L25 70 A2
Church Rd W L4 38 F2
Church Sq 12 WA10 44 A3
Church St
Birkenhead CH41 66 F6
Bootle L20 38 A3
Golborne WA3 36 B1
Liverpool L1 90 B3
Newton-le-W WA12 46 E4
Ormskirk L39 13 E5
Orrell WN5 25 E5
Prescot L34 56 D6
Southport PR9 4 C7
St Helens WA10 44 A3
Up Holland WN8 25 C7
Wallasey CH44 51 D4
Church Terr
Ashton-in-M WN4 35 B2
Birkenhead CH42 66 D3
CHURCHTOWN 2 A1
Churchtown Ct PR9 2 A2
Churchtown Gdns PR9 2 A2
CHURCHTOWN MOSS 2 E2
Churchtown Prim Sch PR9 2 B2
Church View
Aughton L39 21 A7
Bootle L20 38 B3
Liverpool L12 54 B7
Church View Ct 1 L39 13 E5
Churchview Rd CH41 66 B8
Churchward Ct L25 70 A2
Church Way
Formby L37 9 C2
Kirkby L32 29 E3
Litherland L30 27 D5
Churchway Rd L24 83 A2
Church Wlk
Bootle L20 38 B3
St Helens WA10 43 A4
Winwick WA2 61 A6
Church Wlks 3 L39 13 E5
Churchwood Cl CH62 79 D1
Churchwood Ct CH49 65 B1
Churnet St L4 52 E8
Churn Way CH49 64 D4
Churston Rd L16 69 E5
Churton Ave CH43 65 F3
Churton Ct 5 L6 53 A3
Ciaran Cl L12 54 E8
Cicely St L7 53 B1
Cinder La
Bootle L20 38 D7
Liverpool L18 69 C5
CINNAMON BROW 61 F4
Cinnamon Brow WN8 25 C6
Cinnamon Brow CE Prim Sch WA2 61 F3
Cinnamon La WA2 61 F2
Cinnamon La N WA2 61 F3
Circular Dr
Bebington CH62 79 B7
Birkenhead CH49 64 D3
Heswall CH60 76 F1
Circular Rd CH41 66 D5
Circular Rd E L11 53 F8
Circular Rd W L11 53 F8
Cirencester Ave CH49 64 C4
Cirrus Dr L39 13 A1
Citrine Rd CH44 51 D2
Citron Cl L9 39 B4
City Gdns WA10 43 F6
City Rd
Liverpool L4 38 F1
St Helens WA10 43 F6
Civic Way
Bebington CH63 79 A5
Huyton-w-R L36 55 E2
Clairville PR8 3 F5
Clairville Cl L20 38 C3
Clairville Ct 12 L20 38 C3
Clairville Way L13 53 E5
Clamley Ct L24 83 A3
Clamley Gdns L24 83 E2
Clandon Rd L18 69 D1
Clanfield Ave WA8 72 C3
Clanfield Rd L11 40 B1
Clap Gate Cres WA8 84 B5
Clapham Rd L4 53 B6
Clare Cl WA9 57 E7
Clare Cres CH44 50 F4
Claremont Ave
Maghull L31 28 B8
Southport PR8 4 A4
Widnes WA8 73 C4
Claremont Cl L21 37 F7
Claremont Dr
Ormskirk L39 13 D3
Widnes WA8 73 B4
Claremont Gdns PR8 4 A4
Claremont Ho L12 54 B6
Claremont Rd
Billinge WN5 33 E5
Crosby L23 26 E4
Liverpool L15 68 E6
Claremont Rd *continued*
Seaforth L21 37 F7
Southport PR8 4 A4
West Kirby CH48 63 B3
Claremont Terr 1 L23 26 D5
Claremont Way CH63 78 D8
Claremount Ct CH45 50 F5
Claremount Dr CH63 78 F4
Claremount Rd CH44, CH45 50 F6
Clare Mount Sch CH46 50 A1
Clarence Ave
Warrington WA5 74 D6
Widnes WA8 73 A4
Clarence Cl WA9 44 C2
Clarence Ct
Newton-le-W WA12 46 A4
Southport PR8 4 A4
Clarence High Sch L37 9 F6
Clarence Rd
Birkenhead CH42 66 C3
Southport PR8 4 A4
Wallasey CH44 51 D3
Clarence St
6 Ashton-in-M WN4 34 F5
Golborne WA3 36 A1
Liverpool L3 90 C3
Newton-le-W WA12 45 F4
Runcorn WA7 84 F3
Clarendon Cl CH43 66 C5
Clarendon Ct WA2 60 F4
Clarendon Gr L31 20 C5
Clarendon Rd
Liverpool, Cabbage Hall L6 53 C6
Liverpool, Garston L19 81 C6
3 Seaforth L21 37 F6
Wallasey CH44 51 D4
Clare Rd L20 38 E2
Claret Cl L17 68 C1
Clare Villas L20 38 D2
Clare Way CH45 50 F5
Clare Wlk L10 40 B7
Claribel St L8 68 A6
Clarke Ave CH42 66 E2
Clarke's Cres WA10 43 B4
Classic Rd L13 54 A4
Clatterbridge Hospl CH63 78 D1
Clatterbridge Rd
Bebington CH63 78 E1
Thornton Hough CH63 87 D8
Claude Rd L6 53 C6
CLAUGHTON 66 B6
Claughton Cl 9 L7 53 C1
Claughton Dr CH44 51 B3
Claughton Firs CH43 66 B4
Claughton Gn CH43 66 B5
Claughton Pl CH41 66 C6
Claughton Rd CH41 66 D6
Claughton St WA10 44 A3
Clavell Rd L19 81 D8
Clay Brow Rd WN8 24 E6
Clay Cross Rd L25 69 F2
Claydon Ct L26 71 A1
Clayfield Cl L20 38 D3
Clayford Cres L14 54 C4
Clayford Pl L14 54 B4
Clayford Rd L14 54 C4
Clayford Way L14 54 C4
Clayhill Light Ind Pk CH64 86 F2
Clay La
Burtonwood WA5 59 E5
St Helens WA10 42 E3
Claypole Cl 8 L7 68 C8
Clay St L3 52 B4
Clayton Ave WA3 47 E8
Clayton Cl WA10 43 E3
Clayton Cres
Runcorn WA7 84 F1
Widnes WA8 72 F1
Clayton La CH44 51 A2
Clayton Mews WN8 15 D1
Clayton Pl 22 CH41 66 C5
Clayton Sq 2 L1 90 B3
Clayton St
Birkenhead CH41 66 C5
Skelmersdale WN8 15 D1
Cleadon Cl 2 L32 41 A7
Cleadon Rd L32 41 A7
Cleadon Way WA8 72 E4
Clearwater Cl L7 53 B2
Cleary St L20 38 B4
Cleaver Cotts L38 18 A6
Clee Hill Rd CH42 66 C1
Clegg St
Liverpool L5 52 E4
Skelmersdale WN8 15 D1
Clematis Rd L27 70 E6
Clement Gdns L3 52 C4
Clementina Rd L23 26 B4
Clements Way 9 L33 29 D5
Clemmey Dr L20 38 E6
Clengers Brow PR9 2 A3
Clent Ave L31 20 C3
Clent Gdns L31 20 C3
Clent Rd L31 20 C3
Cleopas St L8 67 F4
Cleveland Cl L32 29 D4
Cleveland Dr
Ashton-in-M WN4 35 C4
Golborne WA3 36 D1
Cleveland Gdns WN4 35 C4
Cleveland Rd WA2 61 B3
Cleveland Sq L1 90 B2
Cleveland St
Birkenhead CH41 66 D8
Cleveland St *continued*
St Helens WA9 44 C1
Cleveley Pk L18 69 D1
Cleveley Rd
Hoylake CH47 63 E8
Liverpool L18 69 D1
Cleveleys Ave
Southport PR9 2 A4
Widnes WA8 73 D2
Cleveleys Rd PR9 2 A3
Cleves The L31 20 E3
Cleve Way L37 10 B2
CLIEVES HILLS 12 F3
Clieves Hills La L39 12 E3
Clieves Rd L32 29 F1
Clifden Ct L37 9 F3
Cliff Dr CH44 51 D5
Cliffe St 3 WA8 73 C1
Clifford Gr 11 CH42 66 F3
Clifford Holroyde Ctr of Expertise L14 54 D3
Clifford Rd
Southport PR8 4 A2
Wallasey CH44 51 C3
Clifford St
Birkenhead CH41 66 A8
Liverpool L3 90 C4
Cliff Rd
Southport PR9 1 D1
Wallasey CH44 51 A4
Cliff St L7 53 C2
Cliff The CH45 50 F8
Clifton Ave
Bebington CH62 88 E3
Liverpool L26 70 E1
Clifton Cres 11 CH41 66 E6
Clifton Ct
Birkenhead CH41 66 E5
Liverpool L19 81 C8
Clifton Dr L10 28 D2
Clifton Gr
2 Liverpool L5 52 E4
Wallasey CH44 51 D4
Cliftonmill Mdws WA3 46 F8
Clifton Rd
Ashton-in-M WN4 34 F6
Billinge WN5 33 D4
Birkenhead CH41 66 D5
Formby L37 10 A5
Liverpool L6 53 D5
Southport PR8 4 F6
Clifton Rd E L6 53 D6
Clifton St
Liverpool L19 81 C6
St Helens WA10 44 A4
Cliftonville Rd L34 56 E6
Clincton Cl WA8 84 A8
Clincton View WA8 84 A8
CLINKHAM WOOD 33 B1
Clinning Rd PR8 4 A2
Clinton Pl L12 53 F7
Clinton Rd L12 53 F7
Clint Rd L7 53 C1
Clint Rd W L7 53 C1
Clint Way 2 L7 53 C1
Clipper View CH62 79 B8
Clipsley Brook View WA11 44 F6
Clipsley Cres WA11 45 B7
Clipsley La WA11 45 C6
Clive Ave WA2 61 C1
Clive Lo PR8 3 F2
Clive Rd
Birkenhead CH43 66 C4
Southport PR8 3 F2
CLOCK FACE 58 D3
Clock Face Colliery Ctry Pk* WA9 58 F3
Clock Face Rd
Bold Heath WA8 73 E8
St Helens WA8, WA9 58 D3
Clocktower Dr L9 38 F3
Clocktower St WA10 43 F3
Cloister Gn L37 10 B2
Cloisters The
Crosby L23 26 D3
Formby L37 9 F3
2 Southport PR9 4 C8
St Helens WA10 43 B4
Clorain Cl L33 30 A3
Clorain Rd L33 30 A3
Closeburn Ave CH60 85 E6
Close St WA9 57 E7
Close The
Birkenhead, Egerton Park CH63 66 D1
Birkenhead, Greasby CH49 64 D2
Crosby L23 26 D3
Huyton-w-R L28 55 C7
Ince Blundell L38 18 E3
Irby CH61 76 D6
Liverpool L9 38 F4
Newton-le-W WA12 46 E1
St Helens, Blackbrook WA11 44 F5
St Helens, Eccleston WA10 43 A5
Cloudberry Cl L27 70 E6
Clough Ave WA2 61 B2
Clough Gr WN4 34 F5
Clough Rd
Liverpool L26 71 A1
Speke L24 82 E5
Clough The WN4 34 D4
Clovelly Ave
St Helens WA9 58 E6
Warrington WA5 74 E7
Clovelly Ct CH49 64 D3
Clovelly Dr
Skelmersdale WN8 16 A8
Southport PR8 7 E8
Clovelly Rd L4 53 B6
Clover Ave L26 70 D2
Clover Ct PR8 4 C5
Cloverdale Dr WN4 35 C2
Cloverdale Rd L25 70 B7
Clover Dr CH41 50 E1
Clover Hey WA11 44 B7
CLUBMOOR 53 E7
Club St WA11 33 A1
Clucas Gdns L39 13 E6
Clwyd Gr L12 54 B8
Clwyd St
2 Birkenhead CH41 66 D6
2 Birkenhead CH41 66 E6
Wallasey CH45 51 B7
Clyde Rd L7 53 E2
Clydesdale Rd
Hoylake CH47 63 B8
Wallasey CH44 51 D4
Clyde St
6 Birkenhead CH42 66 F2
Liverpool L20 52 C8
Coach House Ct L29 27 F7
Coachmans Dr L12 40 E1
Coach Rd
Bickerstaffe L39 22 F2
Rainford L33, L39, WA11 31 B5
Coalbrookdale Rd CH64 86 F2
Coalgate La L35 56 C2
Coal Pit La L39 23 D4
Coalport Wlk WA9 57 C6
Coal St L1, L3 90 C4
Coalville Rd WA11 44 D6
Coastal Dr CH45 50 E8
Coastal Point CH46 49 E4
Coastal Rd
Southport, Birkdale PR8 3 C3
Southport, Woodvale PR8 7 A4
Coastguard La CH64 86 B1
Coastline Mews PR9 2 A4
Cobb Ave L21 38 B6
Cobbles The L26 70 D2
Cobblestone Cnr L19 81 A7
Cobb's Brow Cotts L40 15 F5
Cobb's Brow La L40, WN8 16 B6
Cobbs Brow Prim Sch WN8 16 A3
Cobb's Clough Rd L40 15 F5
Cobden Ave 2 CH42 66 F3
Cobden Ct CH42 66 F3
Cobden Pl
3 Birkenhead CH42 66 F3
Liverpool L25 69 F2
Cobden Rd PR9 5 A6
Cobden St
Liverpool L6 52 F3
Liverpool, Woolton Hill L25 69 F2
Newton-le-W WA12 46 D4
Cobden View L25 69 F2
Coberg St CH41 66 D6
Cobham Ave L9 38 F6
Cobham Rd CH46 64 D7
Cobham Wlk L30 27 E4
Cob Moor Ave WN5 25 D1
Cob Moor Rd WN5 25 D1
Coburg Dock (Marina)* L3 67 D6
Coburg Wharf L3 67 C6
Cochrane St L5 52 F5
Cockburn St L8 67 F3
Cockerell Cl 3 L4 52 F7
Cockerham Way L11 40 C5
Cock Glades L35 56 D1
Cocklade La L24 83 D1
Cock Lane Ends WA8 84 B4
Cockle Dick's La PR9 1 E2
Cockshead Rd L25 70 B5
Cockshead Way L25 70 B6
Cockspur St W L3 90 A4
Cockspur St L3 90 A4
Coerton Rd L9 39 B7
Cokers The CH42 78 E8
Colbern Cl L31 28 E8
Colbert Cl CH49 65 A4
Colby Cl L16 69 E8
Colchester Rd PR8 4 F3
Colden Cl L12 54 E7
Coldstone Dr WN4 34 D4
Coldstream Cl WA2 61 E3
Cole Ave WA12 46 C4
Colebrooke Rd L17 68 A3
Cole Cres L39 21 C8
Coleman Dr CH49 64 C3
Colemere Dr CH61 77 B6
Coleridge Ave WA10 43 D4
Coleridge Ct L32 40 D8
Coleridge Dr CH62 79 A7
Coleridge Gr WA8 72 E1
Coleridge Rd WN5 25 D1
Coleridge St
Bootle L20 38 A4
Liverpool L6 53 B3
Colesborne Rd L11 40 B2
Coles Cres L23 27 B6
Coleshill Rd L11 39 E3
Cole St CH43 66 C6
Cole Street Prim Sch CH43 66 C6

Colette Rd L10 40 B7
Coleus Cl L9 39 B4
Colin Cl L36 55 C2
Colindale Rd L16 69 E7
Colin Dr L3 52 C5
Colinmander Gdns L39 13 C3
Colinton WN8 24 E7
Colinton St L15 68 E8
College Ave
Crosby L23 26 D2
Formby L37 9 E4
College Cl
Birkenhead CH43 65 B6
Formby L37 9 D4
Southport PR8 4 A3
Wallasey CH45 50 E6
College Ct L12 54 A5
College Dr CH63 79 A7
College Fields
Huyton-w-R L36 55 E1
Widnes WA8 72 F5
College Gn 2 L23 26 D3
College La L1 90 B3
College Path L37 9 D5
College Rd
Crosby L23 26 D3
Up Holland WN8 25 B8
College Rd N L23 26 C5
College St N L6 52 F3
College St S L6 52 F3
College St WA10 44 A5
College View
Bootle L20 38 C2
Huyton-w-R L36 55 E2
Collegiate The 6 L6 52 F3
Collier St WA7 84 F3
Collingwood Cl L4 52 D8
Collingwood Rd
Bebington CH63 79 B4
Newton-le-W WA12 46 B3
Collin Rd CH43 65 E8
Collins Cl L20 38 A5
COLLINS GREEN 45 E1
Collins Green La WA5 45 E1
Collins Ind Est WA9 44 C5
Collisdene Rd WN5 25 E6
Colmoor Cl L33 29 F6
Colmore Ave CH63 79 A1
Colmore Rd L11 39 E2
Colne Dr WA9 58 D7
Colne Rd WA5 59 F6
Colonel Dr L12 54 E7
Colonial Chambers 12 L3 90 A4
Colquitt St L1 90 C2
Coltart Rd L8 68 B6
Colton Rd L25 70 A7
Colton Wlk L25 69 F7
Columban Cl L30 27 E3
Columbia Rd
Birkenhead CH43 66 B4
Liverpool L4 39 A2
Prescot L34 56 E6
Columbine Cl
4 Kirkby L31 29 A3
Widnes WA8 72 B4
Columbine Way WA9 59 B7
Columbus Dr CH61 76 E3
Columbus Quay L3 67 E3
Columbus St 2 WN4 34 F5
Columbus Way L21 38 B7
Column Rd CH48 63 D1
Colville Ct WA2 61 A3
Colville Rd CH44 51 A4
Colville St L15 68 E8
Colwall Cl L33 30 A2
Colwall Rd L33 30 A2
Colwall Wlk L33 30 A2
Colwell Cl L14 55 A6
Colwell Ct L14 55 A7
Colwell Rd L14 55 A6
Colworth Rd L24 82 B5
Colwyn Cl WA5 60 E2
Colwyn Rd L13 53 F2
Colwyn St CH41 66 A8
Colyton Ave WA9 58 D5
Combermere St
Liverpool L15 68 D8
5 Liverpool, Toxteth L8 67 F6
Comely Ave CH44 51 D4
Comely Bank Rd CH44 51 D4
Comer Gdns L31 20 C3
Comfrey Gr L26 70 E2
Commerce Way L8 68 B7
Commercial Rd
Bebington CH62 79 E3
Liverpool L20 52 C7
Common Field Rd CH49 65 B2
Common Rd WA12, WA5 45 E3
Common St
Newton-le-W WA12 45 E3
St Helens WA9 57 D7
Commutation Row L3 90 C4
Compass Ct CH45 50 F8
Compton Cl WA11 45 C7
Compton Rd
Liverpool L6 53 A4
Southport PR8 4 B3
Wallasey CH41 50 D1
Compton Way L26 82 F7
Compton Wlk L20 38 B4
Comus St L3 52 D3
Concert St L1 90 B3
Concorde Pl WA2 61 D2
Concordia Ave CH49 65 A5
Concourse Sh Ctr The WN8 16 B1
Concourse Way WA9 45 A2
Condor Cl L19 81 D6
Condron Rd N L21 27 C1
Condron Rd S L21 27 C1
Coney Cres L23 27 B5
Coney La
Huyton-w-R L36 71 A8
Liverpool L36 70 F7
Coney Wlk CH49 64 D6
Congress Gdns WA9 57 D7
Conifer Cl
Kirkby L33 29 E5
Liverpool L9 39 B4
Conifer Ct L37 10 A2
Conifer Gr WA5 74 F7
Conifers The L31 20 C3
Coningsby Dr CH45 51 A4
Coningsby Gdns 13 WA3 47 E8
Coningsby Rd L4 53 A7
Coniston Ave
Ashton-in-M WN4 35 B4
Bebington CH63 88 C4
Birkenhead CH43 65 C5
Orrell WN5 25 F7
Prescot L34 56 F6
Wallasey CH45 50 E7
Warrington WA5 74 D4
Coniston Cl
Hooton CH66 89 B2
Kirkby L33 29 D4
Liverpool L9 39 B7
Coniston Ct PR8 7 C3
Coniston Dr WN2 36 B8
Coniston Gr WA11 44 A7
Coniston Ho L17 68 D2
Coniston Rd
Formby L37 9 D2
Irby CH61 76 D6
Maghull L31 20 E2
Coniston St L5 53 A5
Coniston Way WA11 23 F2
Conleach Rd L24 82 E4
Connaught Cl CH41 66 A8
Connaught Dr WA12 46 C2
Connaught Ho CH41 66 F6
Connaught Rd L7 53 B2
Connaught Way CH41 66 A8
Connolly Ave L20 38 E5
Conroy Way WA12 60 C8
Conservation Ctr (Mus)* L1 90 B4
Consett Rd WA9 57 D6
Constance St
Liverpool L3 52 F2
St Helens WA10 43 D2
Constantine Ave CH60 77 A1
Convent Cl
Birkenhead CH42 66 D4
Liverpool L19 81 A7
Ormskirk L39 13 E2
Conville Bvd CH63 78 E8
Conway Ave WA5 60 F2
Conway Cl
Bebington CH63 78 D5
3 Kirkby L33 29 D5
Warrington WA5 74 F6
Conway Cres WN5 33 E6
Conway Ct CH63 78 F4
Conway Dr
Billinge WN5 33 F5
Birkenhead CH41 66 D6
Newton-le-W WA12 46 E3
Conway Ho L6 53 C4
Conway Park Stn CH41 66 E7
Conway Rd WN4 35 E5
Conway St
Birkenhead CH41 66 E6
Liverpool L5 52 E5
St Helens WA10 43 D2
Wallasey CH44 51 B4
Conwy Dr L6 53 B4
Conyers Ave PR8 3 F3
Coogee Ave WA5 74 E7
Cook Ave WA11 45 F7
Cookes Cl CH64 86 E1
Cooke St WN4 34 F6
Cook Rd CH46 50 B4
Cook's Ct L23 26 D5
Cookson Rd L21 38 A6
Cookson St L1 90 C1
Cooks Rd L23 26 D5
Cook St
Birkenhead CH41 66 D5
Liverpool L2 90 A3
Prescot, Eccleston Lane Ends L34 56 D6
Prescot, Whiston L35 56 F4
Coombe Rd CH61 76 E7
Cooperage Cl L8 67 E4
Cooper Ave
Newton-le-W WA12 45 F3
Warrington WA2 61 B2
Cooper Ave N L18 69 A2
Cooper Ave S L19 69 A1
Cooper Cl L19 81 A8
Cooper La WA11 45 C6
Cooper's La L33 41 D7
Coopers Row L22 37 E8
Cooper St
St Helens WA10 43 F4
Widnes WA8 73 B1
Copeland Cl CH61 76 E3
Copperas Hill L1, L3 90 C3
Copperas St WA10 43 F3
Copperfield Cl L8 67 F5
Copperwood Dr L35 56 F3
Coppice Cl CH43 65 B6
Coppice Cres L36 55 F4
Coppice Dr WN5 25 D2
Coppice Gn WA5 60 A1
Coppice Gr CH49 64 C2
Coppice Grange CH46 64 C7
Coppice La L35 71 C7
Coppice Leys L37 9 E3
Coppice The
Knowsley L34 41 D3
Liverpool L6 53 C6
Wallasey CH45 51 A7
Coppins The WA2 61 C2
Copple House Ct L10 40 A7
Copple House La L10 40 A7
Coppull Rd L31 20 C4
Copse Gr CH61 76 E7
Copse The
Liverpool, Childwall L18 69 D5
Liverpool, Woolton L25 70 B1
Newton-le-W WA12 46 B4
Copsmead CH46 64 F8
Copthorne Rd L32 29 B2
Copthorne Wlk L32 29 B2
Copy Cl L30 27 F5
Copy La L30, L9 28 B3
Copy Way L30 27 F5
Coral Ave
Huyton-w-R L36 55 D3
St Helens WA9 57 F7
Coral Cl L32 29 C2
Coral Dr L20 38 C3
Coralin Way WN4 34 F7
Coral Ridge CH43 65 D6
Coral St L13 54 A1
Corbet Cl L32 29 C2
Corbet Wlk 4 L32 29 C2
Corbridge Rd L16 69 C7
Corbyn St CH44 51 E1
Corfu St CH43 66 C6
Corinthian Ave L13 54 A4
Corinthian Com Prim Sch L13 54 B4
Corinthian St
5 Birkenhead CH42 66 F2
Seaforth L21 37 F7
Corinth Twr L5 52 E6
Corinto St L8 67 F6
Corkdale Rd L9 39 B5
Cormorant Ct CH45 50 E8
Cormorant Dr WA7 84 E2
Cornbrook WN8 24 E7
Corncroft Rd L34 41 D3
Corndale Rd L18 69 A4
Cornelian Gr WN4 34 F5
Cornelius Dr CH61 76 F5
Cornel Way L36 70 F8
Corner Brook L28 54 F7
Cornerhouse La WA8 72 D3
Cornett Rd L9 39 B7
Corn Exchange The 8 L2 90 A3
Corney St L7 68 C7
Cornfields Cl L19 81 B6
Cornflower Way CH46 50 A2
Cornforth Way WA8 72 F3
Cornhill L1 90 B2
Cornice Rd L13 54 A4
Corniche Rd CH62 79 B6
Corn Mill Cl WN4 34 D4
Corn Mill Lo L31 20 C2
Corn St L8 67 E5
Cornwall Cl CH62 79 B7
Cornwall Ct CH63 78 F4
Cornwall Dr CH43 66 A1
Cornwallis St
Liverpool L1 90 B1
Liverpool L1 90 C2
Cornwall Rd WA8 73 B3
Cornwall St WA9 44 E2
Cornwall Way PR8 7 C2
Cornwood Cl L25 70 B7
Corona Ave L31 20 C5
Corona Rd
Bebington CH62 79 C6
Crosby L22 26 D1
Liverpool L13 54 A4
Coronation Ave
Formby L37 10 A2
Huyton-w-R L14 54 E3
Wallasey CH45 51 B7
Coronation Bldgs
Wallasey CH44 51 B4
West Kirby CH48 63 C4
Coronation Dr
Bebington CH62 79 D3
Crosby L23 26 D3
Haydock WA11 46 A7
Huyton-w-R L14 54 E3
Newton-le-W WA12 46 E1
Prescot L35 56 C3
Warrington WA5 74 F4
Widnes WA8 84 C8
Coronation Rd
Crosby L23 26 D4
Hoylake CH47 62 F6
Maghull L31 20 D3
St Helens WA10 43 C5
Coronation St WN4 34 D6
Coronation Wlk
Billinge WN5 33 D4
Southport PR8 4 A7
Coroner's La WA8 73 A4
Coronet Rd L11 40 C3
Coronet Way WA8 84 B8
Corporal Way L12 54 E7
Corporation Rd CH41 66 C8
Corporation St
4 Southport PR8 4 B7
St Helens WA9, WA10 44 A3
Corpus Christi RC Prim Sch WA11 31 F7
Corrie Dr CH63 78 F4
Corsewall St L7 68 D8
Corsican Gdns L35 57 C7
Cortsway CH49 64 E5
Cortsway W CH49 64 D5
Corwen Cl
Birkenhead, Moreton CH46 64 F7
Birkenhead, Upton CH43 65 B6
Warrington WA5 60 E1
Corwen Cres L14 54 F2
Corwen Dr L30 28 B4
Corwen Rd
Hoylake CH47 63 C7
Liverpool L4 53 C8
Cosgate Cl 1 WN5 25 E5
Cosgrove Cl L6 53 D7
Cossack Ave WA2 61 C1
Costain St L20 52 C7
Cotham St 1 WA10 44 A3
Coton Way L32 29 C3
Cotsford Cl L36 55 C4
Cotsford Pl L36 55 C4
Cotsford Rd L36 55 C4
Cotsford Way L36 55 C4
Cotswold Ave WA3 47 D6
Cotswold Cres L26 82 E8
Cotswold Gr WA9 45 A3
Cotswold Pl WA2 61 B4
Cotswold Rd
Birkenhead CH42 66 C1
Warrington WA2 61 B3
Cotswold St L7 53 B2
Cottage Cl
Bebington CH63 88 C5
Kirkby L32 40 E7
Ormskirk L39 13 D4
Cottage Dr E CH60 85 F5
Cottage Dr W CH60 85 F5
Cottage La
Heswall CH60 85 F5
Ormskirk L39 13 D5
Cottage Mews L39 13 D5
Cottage Pl 9 WA9 58 C4
Cottage St CH41 66 D7
Cottenham St 8 L7 53 B3
Cotterdale Cl
2 St Helens WA9 58 C6
Warrington WA5 74 F7
Cottesbrook Cl L11 40 A3
Cottesbrook Pl L11 40 A3
Cottesbrook Rd L11 40 A3
Cottesmore Dr CH60 86 D8
Cottesmore Way WA3 36 B1
Cotton Dr L39 13 D6
Cotton Exchange L3 90 A4
Cotton St L3 52 B4
Cotton Terr 4 WA9 58 F8
Cottonwood L17 68 A2
Cottrell Cl L19 81 C4
Cottys Brow PR9 1 F3
Coudray Rd PR9 1 E1
Coulport Cl L14 55 A4
Coulsdon Pl L8 68 A4
Coulthard Rd CH42 79 A8
Coulton Rd WA8 73 F3
Coultshead Ave WN5 33 E6
Council Ave WN4 35 B3
Council St L35 57 A5
Countess Pk L11 40 C2
Countisbury Dr L16 69 E6
County Dr WA10 43 E2
County Rd
Kirkby L32 29 E2
Kirkby L32 29 E4
Liverpool L4 38 F1
Ormskirk L39 13 E6
Court Ave L26 71 A1
Courtenay Ave L22 26 C2
Courtenay Rd
Crosby L22 26 C2
Hoylake CH47 63 A6
Liverpool L25 70 A4
Courtfield L39 13 D7
Courtfields Cl L12 54 B5
Courtgreen L39 13 D7
COURT HEY 54 F1
Court Hey L31 20 E1
Court Hey Ave L14, L36 55 A2
Court Hey Dr L16 54 F1
Court Hey Rd L16 54 F1
Courthope Rd L4 39 B1
Courtland Rd L18 69 B5
Court Mews PR9 2 A1
Courtney Ave CH44 51 A3
Courtney Rd CH42 79 A8
Court Rd PR9 4 C8
Court The
Bebington CH63 79 A4
Huyton-w-R L28 55 C7
Southport PR9 4 B8
Courtyard The
Liverpool L18 68 F3
Newton-le-W WA12 46 E4
Courtyard Works L33 30 C2
Covent Gdn L2 90 A3
Coventry Ave L30 27 F1
Coventry Rd L15 69 A6
Coventry St 8 CH41 66 D6
Coverdale Ave L35 57 D3
Coverdale Cl WA5 74 F7
Covert Cl PR8 5 A2
Covertside CH48 63 D2
Covertside Rd PR8 5 A2
Cowan Dr L6 53 A4
Cowanway WA8 72 F5
Cowdrey Ave CH43 50 C1
Cowley Cl CH49 64 D5
COWLEY HILL 43 F5
Cowley Hill La WA10 43 E4
Cowley Language Coll WA10 43 E6
Cowley Rd L4 39 A1
Cowley St WA10 44 A5
Cowper Rd L13 54 B3
Cowper St
Bootle L20 38 A5
St Helens WA9 44 C1
Cowper Way L36 56 A1
Coyford Dr PR9 2 A4
Coylton Ave L35 57 D2
Crab St WA10 43 F4
Crabtree Cl
Liverpool L27 70 E5
Newton-le-W WA12 46 E3
Crab Tree Cl L24 83 E2
Cradley WA8 72 C2
Crag Gr WA11 33 B1
Craigburn Rd L13 53 E6
Craighurst Rd L25 70 A7
Craigleigh Gr CH62 88 F4
Craigmore Rd L18 69 A1
Craigside Ave L12 54 A7
Craigs Rd L13 53 E6
Craigwood Way L36 55 B3
Craine Cl L4 53 B8
Cramond Ave 1 L15, L18 69 A5
Cranberry Cl
Liverpool L27 70 E6
St Helens WA10 43 F5
Cranborne Ave CH47 48 E1
Cranborne Rd L15 68 D7
Cranbourne Ave
Birkenhead CH41 66 A7
Birkenhead, Saughall Massie CH46 64 D7
Cranbrook Ave WN4 35 A4
Crane Ave WA9 58 D6
Cranehurst Rd L4 39 B2
Cranes La L40 14 E7
Cranfield Rd L23 27 A5
Cranford Cl CH62 88 F4
Cranford Rd L19 81 B8
Cranford St CH44 51 C2
Cranham Ave WA3 47 E7
CRANK 32 F4
Crank Hill WA11 32 E4
Crank Rd
Billinge WA11, WN5 33 B8
Crank, Kings Moss WA11 32 F7
Crank WA11 32 E2
St Helens WA11 43 C7
CRANKWOOD 36 E5
Crankwood Rd WN2, WN7 36 D5
Cranleigh Gdns L23 26 D4
Cranleigh Pl L25 70 A6
Cranleigh Rd L25 70 A6
Cranmer St
Liverpool L5 52 C5
Liverpool L5 52 D6
Cranmore Ave L23 26 F2
Cranshaw Ave WA9 58 D3
Cranshaw La WA8 73 B6
Cranston Cl WA10 43 C5
Cranston Rd L33 30 C2
Crantock Cl
Halewood L26 82 F9
Liverpool, Croxteth L11 40 C4
Crantock Gr WA10 43 C7
Cranwell Cl L10 28 C2
Cranwell Rd
Birkenhead CH49 64 B3
Liverpool L25 70 A7
Cranwell Wlk L25 70 A7
Crask Wlk 6 L33 29 F4
Craven Ave WA3 47 E7
Craven Bsns Ctr CH41 66 C6
Craven Cl CH41 66 D6
Craven Ct WA2 60 F4
Craven Lea L12 40 E4
Craven Rd
Liverpool L12 54 C6
Rainhill L35 57 C3
Craven St
Birkenhead CH41 66 C6
Liverpool L3 90 C4
Cravenwood Rd L26 82 F8
CRAWFORD 24 E2
Crawford Ave
Liverpool L18 68 F5
Maghull L31 20 B3
Widnes WA8 72 B1
Crawford Cl
Liverpool L12 54 D7
St Helens WA9 58 D4
Crawford Dr L15 54 A1
Crawford Pk L18 68 F3
Crawford Rd WN8 24 D2
Crawford St WA9 58 E3
Crawford Village Prim Sch WN8 24 E3
Crawford Way L7 53 F1
Crawley Ave WA2 61 A3
Crawshaw Ct L36 55 B4
Crediton Ave PR9 2 B5
Crediton Cl L11 40 C5

Creek The CH45 50 E8
Cremona Cnr 3 L22 26 E1
Cremorne Hey L28 55 B7
Crescent Ave
Ashton-in-M WN4 35 A4
Formby L37 9 E1
Crescent Ct 6 L21 38 A6
Crescent Gn L39 13 B1
Crescent Rd
Crosby L23 26 B5
Liverpool L9 39 B4
Seaforth L21 38 A6
Southport PR8 3 F3
Wallasey CH44 51 C4
Crescents The L35 57 A4
Crescent The
Bebington CH63 78 E5
Birkenhead CH49 64 D3
Bootle L20 38 E6
Crosby, Thornton L23 27 A6
Crosby, Waterloo L22 26 E1
Heswall, Gayton CH60 86 B6
Heswall, Pensby CH61 76 F6
Huyton-w-R L36 56 B2
Liverpool L24 82 C5
Maghull L31 28 C6
Prescot L35 56 F4
Southport PR9 2 C3
West Kirby CH48 63 A2
Cressida Ave CH63 78 E7
Cressingham Rd 2
CH45 51 B8
Cressington Ave CH42 66 D1
Cressington Espl L19 81 A6
CRESSINGTON PARK 81 B6
Cressington Sta L19 81 A7
Cresson CH43 65 F5
Cresswell Cl
Liverpool L26 71 A1
Warrington WA5 60 D2
Cresswell St 7 L6 53 A4
Crestor Rd L25 69 F3
Creswell St WA10 43 E3
Cretan Rd L15 68 D7
Crete Twr L5 52 E6
Crewe Gn CH49 65 A2
Cricket Cl L19 81 D4
Cricket Path
Formby L37 9 F5
Southport PR8 3 F3
Cricklade Cl L20 38 B4
Cringles Dr L35 71 A7
Crispin Rd L27 70 E5
Crispin St WA10 43 E3
Critchley Rd L24 83 A3
Critchley Way L33 29 F5
Crockett's Wlk WA10 43 B5
Crockleford Ave PR8 4 E3
Crocus Ave CH41 65 F7
Crocus Gdns WA9 59 A7
Crocus St L5 52 D7
Croft Ave
Bebington CH62 79 D1
Golborne WA3 35 F2
Orrell WN5 25 D5
Croft Ave E CH62 79 D2
Croft Bsns Pk CH62 79 E2
Croft Cl CH43 65 E4
Croft Ct PR9 2 C4
Croft Dr
Birkenhead CH46 64 F7
West Kirby CH48 75 C7
Croft Dr E CH48 75 E6
Croft Dr W CH48 75 C7
Croft Edge CH43 66 B3
Croft End WA9 44 F1
Crofters La L33 30 A5
Crofters The CH49 64 D4
Croft Field L31 20 E1
Croft Gn CH62 79 D3
Croft Heys L39 13 B1
Croft La
Bebington CH62 79 D1
Liverpool L9 39 D7
Croftlands WN5 25 D4
Crofton Cres L13 54 B3
Crofton Rd
Birkenhead CH42 66 E3
Liverpool L13 54 B3
Runcorn WA7 84 E1
Croftson Ave L39 13 F7
Croft St WA3 47 A8
Croftsway CH60 85 D8
Croft The
Birkenhead CH49 64 D2
Huyton-w-R L28 55 A8
Kirkby L32 40 F7
Liverpool L12 54 B7
Maghull L31 20 B5
Orrell WN5 25 D3
St Helens WA9 44 F1
Croft Way L23 27 B5
Croftwood Gr L35 56 E2
Cromarty Rd
Liverpool L13 53 F3
3 Wallasey CH44 50 F4
Cromdale Gr WA9 44 E2
Cromdale Way WA5 74 E6
Cromer Dr CH45 51 A5
Cromer Rd
Hoylake CH47 63 A7
Liverpool L17 68 E1
Southport PR8 3 E2
Cromer Way L26 82 F7
Cromfield L39 13 C2
Cromford Rd L36 55 E5
Crompton Ct
Ashton-in-M WN4 35 B2

Crompton Ct *continued*
Liverpool L18 69 D5
Crompton Dr
Liverpool L12 40 E3
Winwick WA2 61 A6
Cromptons La L16, L18 69 D5
Crompton St L5 52 D5
Cromwell Cl
Newton-le-W WA12 46 A4
Ormskirk L39 13 C2
Cromwell Rd 6 L4 38 F2
Crondall Gr L15 69 B7
CRONTON 72 D5
Cronton Ave
Prescot L35 56 C1
Wallasey CH46 49 F3
Cronton CE Prim Sch
WA8 72 C6
Cronton Farm Ct WA8 72 E4
Cronton La
Rainhill L35, WA8 57 B1
Widnes WA8 72 F5
Cronton Park Ave WA8 72 C6
Cronton Park Cl WA8 72 C6
Cronton Rd
Cronton L35, WA8 72 C5
Huyton-w-R L35, L36 71 B7
4 Liverpool L15 69 A5
Cronulla Dr WA5 74 E7
Crookall St WN4 35 C4
Crookhurst Ave WN5 33 D6
Croome Dr CH48 63 D2
Croppers Hill WA10 43 E3
Croppers Hill Ct WA10 43 E3
Cropper's La L39 14 A1
Croppers Rd WA2 61 F3
Cropper St L1 90 C3
Cropton Rd L37 9 F3
CROSBY 26 D6
Crosby Cl CH49 64 F6
Crosby Gn L12 54 A7
Crosby Gr
St Helens WA10 43 D1
Willaston CH64 88 B1
Crosby High Sch L23 26 E6
Crosby Rd PR8 4 A3
Crosby Rd N L22 26 E1
Crosby Rd S L21 37 F7
Crosender Rd L23 26 C3
Crosfield Cl 5 L7 53 C1
Crosfield Rd
Liverpool L7 53 C1
Prescot L35 56 F4
Wallasey CH44 51 C3
Crosfield Wlk 4 L7 53 C1
Crosgrove Rd L4 39 C1
Crosland Rd L32 30 A1
Crossacre Rd L25 70 B7
Cross Barn La L38 18 E3
Crossdale Rd
Bebington CH62 88 D5
Crosby L23 26 C3
Crossdale Way WA11 33 B1
CROSSENS 2 C4
Crossens Way PR9 2 C6
Cross Farm Prim Sch
L27 70 F4
Cross Farm Rd WA9 44 C1
Crossfield Rd WN8 24 C8
Crossford Rd L14 55 A5
Crossgates WA8 73 F3
Cross Gn L37 10 A2
Cross Green Cl L37 10 A2
Crosshall Brow L40 14 C4
Cross Hall Ct L39 14 A4
Crosshall St L1, L2 90 B4
Cross Hey L21 27 B2
Cross Hey Ave CH43 65 D5
Cross Hillocks La L35,
WA8 71 E3
Crossings The WA12 46 C3
Cross La
Bebington CH63 78 F4
Newton-le-W WA12 46 B4
Orrell WN5 25 D3
Prescot L35 56 D4
Wallasey CH45 50 D4
Crossledge Way L16 69 F7
Crossley Dr
Heswall CH60 85 D8
Liverpool L15 69 B8
Crossley Rd WA10 43 D1
Cross Meadow Ct WA9 44 C2
Cross Pit La WA11 31 F6
Cross St
Bebington CH62 79 B5
Birkenhead CH41 66 F6
Crosby L22 26 D1
Golborne WA3 47 A7
Prescot L34 56 E7
Southport PR8 4 B6
6 St Helens WA10 44 A3
Widnes WA8 73 C1
Cross The
Bebington CH62 79 D1
Ince Blundell L38 18 E4
Crossvale Rd L36 55 E1
Crossway
Birkenhead CH43 65 E8
Widnes WA8 84 D8
Crossway Cl WN4 35 E5
Crossways
Bebington CH62 79 D3
Liverpool L25 69 F6
Crossway The CH63 87 C4
Crosswood Cres L36 55 C3
Crosthwaite Ave CH62 88 F4
Croston Ave L35 57 B5

Croston Cl WA8 72 C3
Croston's Brow PR9 1 F3
Crouch St
9 Liverpool L5 53 A6
St Helens WA9 58 D8
Crowe Ave WA2 61 B2
Crow La WN8 16 F3
Crowland Cl PR9 5 A6
Crowland St PR9 5 A6
Crowland Way L37 10 B2
Crow Lane E WA12 46 C4
Crow Lane W WA12 46 A4
Crowmarsh Cl CH49 64 F4
Crown Acres Rd L25 82 C9
Crown Ave WA8 84 B8
Crown Bldgs
3 Crosby L23 26 E4
Southport PR8 7 F8
Crown Cl L37 10 A2
Crown Fields Cl WA12 46 B5
Crown Gdns WA12 46 B4
Crown Park Dr WA12 46 B5
Crown Rd L12 54 C7
Crown St
Liverpool, Edge Hill L7,
L8 68 A8
Liverpool L7 53 A1
Newton-le-W WA12 46 A3
St Helens WA9 57 D7
Crown Station Pl L8 68 A8
Crownway L36 55 D4
Crow Orchard Prim Sch
WN8 15 F2
Crow St L8 67 D6
Crowther St WA10 43 E3
CROW WOOD 73 D3
Crow Wood La WA8 73 D2
Crow Wood Pl WA8 73 D3
Crow Wood Rd WA3 36 D1
Croxdale Rd L14 55 A6
Croxdale Rd W
Huyton-w-R L14 55 A7
Liverpool L14 54 F7
CROXTETH 40 C4
Croxteth Ave
Bootle L21 38 B7
Rainford WA11 31 F7
Wallasey CH44 51 B4
Croxteth Cl L31 20 E3
Croxteth Com Comp Sch
L11 40 C5
Croxteth Com Prim Sch
L11 40 D4
Croxteth Ct 4 L8 68 B6
Croxteth Ctry Pk* L12 40 D2
Croxteth Dr L17 68 D5
Croxteth Gate L17 68 C5
Croxteth Gr L8 68 C6
Croxteth Hall* L12 40 D1
Croxteth Hall La L11,
L12 40 C2
Croxteth La L28, L34 41 C1
Croxteth Rd
Bootle L20 38 B5
Liverpool L8 68 B5
Croxteth View L32 40 F6
Croyde Cl PR9 2 B5
Croyde Pl WA9 58 C4
Croyde Rd L24 83 A3
Croydon Ave L18 68 F5
Croylands St L4 52 E8
Crucian Way L12 40 D3
Crump St L1 90 C1
Crutchley Ave CH41 66 B8
Crystal Cl L13 54 A2
Cubbin Cres L5 52 D6
Cubert Rd L11 40 D4
Cuckoo Cl L25 70 A4
Cuckoo La L25 70 A5
Cuckoo Way L25 70 A4
Cuerden St L3 90 B4
CUERDLEY CROSS 74 A2
Cuerdley Gn WA5 74 A2
Cuerdley Rd WA5 74 C3
Cullen Ave L20 38 D5
Cullen Cl CH63 88 C4
Cullen Dr L21 38 A7
Cullen St L8 68 C7
Culme Rd L12 53 F7
Culzean Cl L12 40 E3
Cumber La L35 56 F3
Cumberland Ave
Birkenhead CH43 66 A2
Litherland L30 27 C3
Liverpool L17 68 D6
St Helens WA10 57 B8
Cumberland Cl L6 53 D7
Cumberland Cres
WA11 45 A6
Cumberland Gate L30 28 A3
Cumberland Rd
Southport PR8 4 D5
Wallasey CH45 51 C7
Cumberland St L1 90 A4
Cumbria Ct PR9 4 C7
Cumbria Way L12 40 C2
Cummings St L1 90 C2
Cummins Ave L37 9 E5
Cumpsty Rd L21 27 C1
Cunard Ave CH44 51 D5
Cunard Cl CH43 65 C6
Cunard Rd L21 38 B7
Cunliffe Ave WA12 46 B5
Cunliffe St L2 90 A4
Cunningham Cl
Warrington WA5 74 F5
West Kirby CH48 75 C6

Cunningham Dr
Bebington CH63 88 C7
Runcorn WA7 84 E1
Cunningham Rd
Liverpool L13 54 A2
Widnes WA8 84 D8
Cunscough La L31, L39 21 D3
Cuper Cres L36 55 D4
Curate Rd L6 53 C7
Curlender Cl CH41 50 E1
Curlender Way L24 83 E2
Curlew Ave CH49 64 D6
Curlew Cl
Birkenhead CH49 64 D6
Golborne WA3 47 D8
Curlew Ct CH46 49 C1
Curlew Gr L26 70 E1
Curlew Way CH46 49 C1
Currans Rd WA2 61 B2
Curran Way L33 29 D5
Curtana Cres L11 40 C3
Curtis Rd L4 39 C1
Curwell Cl CH63 79 B3
Curzon Ave
Birkenhead CH41 66 B7
1 Wallasey CH45 51 B7
Curzon Rd
Birkenhead CH42 66 B2
Crosby L22 26 E1
Hoylake CH47 63 A7
Southport PR8 4 E5
Curzon St 5 WA7 84 F1
Cusson Rd L33 30 B1
Custley Hey L28 55 B8
Cut La
Haskayne L39, L40 12 F6
Kirkby L33 41 F7
Cygnet Cl L39 13 C2
Cygnet Ct L33 30 A2
Cynthia Rd WA7 84 F1
Cypress Ave WA8 73 B2
Cypress Cl L31 29 A3
Cypress Croft CH63 79 B3
Cypress Gdns L35 57 C7
Cypress Rd
Huyton-w-R L36 70 D8
Southport PR8 4 F6
Cyprian's Way L30 27 E3
Cyprus Gr 5 L8 68 A4
Cyprus St L34 56 D6
Cyprus Terr 6 CH45 51 B7
Cyril Gr L17 68 E2

D

Dacre Ct 7 CH42 66 F1
DACRE HILL 78 F8
Dacre's Bridge La L35 71 D6
Dacre St
Birkenhead CH41 66 E6
Liverpool L20 38 B1
Dacy Rd L5 53 A6
Daffodil Cl WA8 73 E4
Daffodil Gdns WA9 59 A7
Daffodil Rd
Birkenhead CH41 65 F7
Liverpool L15 69 B7
Dagnall Ave WA5 60 F2
Dagnall Rd L32 29 D1
Dahlia Cl
Liverpool L9 39 B4
St Helens WA9 59 A7
Dailton Rd WN8 25 A7
Daintith Ct 9 CH42 66 F2
Dairy Farm Rd WA11 31 C7
Dairylands Cl L16 69 C6
Daisy Ave WA12 46 C2
Daisy Bank Rd WA5 74 F4
Daisy Mews L21 38 B6
Daisy Mount L31 28 E8
Daisy St L5 52 D7
Daisy Way PR8 4 C2
Dakin Wlk L33 29 F2
Dakota Dr L19 81 E3
Dalby Cl WA11 44 C5
Dale Acre Dr L21, L30 27 C3
Dale Ave
Bebington CH62 88 D8
Heswall CH60 76 F1
Dalebrook Cl L25 70 B7
Dale Cl
Maghull L31 20 C2
Widnes WA8 84 A8
Dale Cres WA9 58 D6
Dalecrest WN5 25 D1
Dale Ct
Heswall CH60 76 F1
Heswall CH60 85 F8
Dale End Rd CH61 77 C4
Dalegarth Ave L12 40 F1
Dale Gdns CH60 76 D1
Dalehead Pl WA11 33 B1
Dale Hey
Hooton CH66 88 E2
Wallasey CH44 51 B3
Dalehurst Cl CH44 51 D4
Dale La L33 30 B4
Dalemeadow Rd L14 54 D3
Dale Mews L25 70 B4
Dale Rd
Bebington CH62 88 D6
Golborne WA3 47 A7
Dale St (Queensway) L1,
L2 90 A4
Daleside Ave WN4 35 A8
Daleside Cl CH61 76 F6
Daleside Rd L33 29 F3

Daleside Wlk L33 29 F3
Dales Row L36 56 B2
Dale St L19 81 C5
Dalesway CH60 85 E8
Dales Wlk L37 10 A6
Dale The WA5 74 F5
Dale View WA12 46 E4
Dale View Cl CH61 77 A5
Dalewood L12 40 E3
Dalewood Gdns L35 56 F2
Daley Pl L20 38 E7
Daley Rd L21 27 C1
Dallam Com Prim Sch
WA5 60 F1
Dallas Gr 3 L9 39 A6
Dallington Ct 3 L13 54 B2
Dalmeny St L17 68 B3
Dalmorton Rd CH45 51 C8
Dalry Cres L32 40 F7
Dalrymple St L5 52 D5
Dalry Wlk L32 40 F7
Dalston Dr WA11 33 B1
DALTON 16 C5
Dalton Cl L12 40 C2
Dalton Gr WN4 35 A4
Dalton Rd CH45 51 C7
Dalton St Michael's CE
Prim Sch WN8 16 D5
Daltry Cl L12 54 A7
Damerham Mews L25 70 A7
Damfield La L31 28 D8
Damian Dr WA12 46 A5
Dam La
Ashton-in-M WN4 35 F3
Winwick WA3 61 F7
Damson Rd L27 70 E6
Damwood Rd L24 82 E3
Danbers WN8 24 F6
Danby Cl L5 52 F5
Danby Fold L35 57 B3
Dane Cl CH61 76 F6
Dane Ct L35 57 C3
Danefield Pl L19 81 D8
Danefield Rd
Birkenhead CH49 64 C2
Liverpool L19 81 D8
Danefield Terr L19 81 D7
Danehurst Rd
Liverpool L9 39 B7
Wallasey CH45 50 F7
Danesbury Cl WN5 33 E4
Danescourt Rd
Birkenhead CH41 66 A8
Liverpool L12 54 C5
Danescroft WA8 72 B3
Daneshill Cl L17 80 F7
Dane St L4 38 F1
Daneswell Dr CH46 49 F1
Daneswell Rd L24 83 A2
Daneville Rd L4 39 D2
Daneway PR8 7 B6
Danger La CH46 49 F1
Daniel Cl L20 38 A6
Daniel Davies Dr L8 68 A7
Daniels La WN8 24 C7
Dannette Hey L28 55 C7
Dansie St L3 52 F1
Dan's Rd WA8 73 E2
Dante Cl L9 39 C8
Danube St L7, L8 68 C7
Dapple Heath Ave 1
L31 29 A3
Darby Gr L19 81 B6
Darby Rd L19 81 A8
D'Arcy Cotts CH63 87 B6
Darent Rd WA11 45 B7
Daresbury Ave PR8 7 A5
Daresbury Cl L32 29 C2
Daresbury Ct WA8 73 E3
Daresbury Expressway 5
WA7 84 F2
Daresbury Rd
St Helens WA10 43 B5
Wallasey CH44 51 A4
Darfield WN8 24 F7
Dark Entry L34 41 E1
Dark La
Maghull L31 20 E1
Ormskirk L40 14 C6
Darley Ave WA2 61 E3
Darley Cl WA8 72 B3
Darley Ct L12 54 C6
Darleydale Dr CH62 88 F5
Darley Dr L12 54 C6
Darlington Cl CH44 51 D4
Darlington St CH44 51 D4
Darmond Rd L33 30 A3
Darmond's Gn CH48 63 B3
Darmonds Green Ave
L6 53 D7
Darnley St L8 67 E5
Darrel Dr L7 68 C7
Darsefield Rd L16 69 E7
Dartford Cl L14 54 F6
Dartington Rd L16 69 D8
Dartmouth Ave L10 28 C2
Dartmouth Dr
Litherland L30 27 C3
St Helens WA10 43 C6
Darvel Ave WN4 34 C4
Darwall Rd L19 81 D8
Darwen Gdns WA2 61 E1
Darwen St L5 52 B5
Darwick Dr L36 71 A8
Darwin Gr WA9 57 E7

Daryl Rd CH60 86 A8
Daulby St L3 52 F2
Dauntsey Brow L25 70 B7
Dauntsey Mews L25 70 B7
Davenham Ave CH43 65 F3
Davenham Cl CH43 65 F2
Davenham Ct L15 69 B7
Davenham Rd L37 9 F3
Davenhill Pk L10 28 C2
Davenport Cl CH48 75 C6
Davenport Gr 3 L33 29 E4
Davenport Rd CH60 85 E7
Daventree Rd 4 CH45 51 B5
Daventry Rd L17 68 E2
Davidson Rd L13 54 A3
David St L8 67 F4
Davids Wlk L25 70 C3
Davies Ave WA12 46 C4
Davies St
Bootle L20 38 D4
Liverpool L1, L2 90 A4
St Helens WA9 44 C4
Davis Rd CH46 50 B3
Davy Cl WA10 43 B5
Davy St L5 53 A6
Dawber Cl 4 L6 53 A4
Dawber St WN4 35 D4
Dawley Cl WN4 35 A3
Dawlish Cl L25 82 C9
Dawlish Dr PR9 2 A5
Dawlish Rd
Irby CH61 76 C5
Wallasey CH44 51 A4
Dawlish Way WA3 35 F1
Dawn Cl WA9 57 E7
Dawn Wlk L10 40 B6
Dawpool CE Prim Sch CH61 76 B6
Dawpool Cotts CH48 76 A6
Dawpool Dr
Bebington CH62 88 C7
Birkenhead CH46 64 E8
Dawpool Farm CH61 76 B5
Dawson Ave
Birkenhead CH41 66 B8
Southport PR9 2 C5
St Helens WA9 58 D7
Dawson Gdns L31 20 C2
Dawson Rd L39 13 F7
Dawson St L1 90 B3
Dawson Way 12 L1 90 B3
Dawstone Ct CH60 85 F8
Dawstone Rd CH60 86 A7
Dawstone Rise CH60 85 F7
Daybrook WN8 24 F7
Dayfield WN8 25 B7
Days Mdw 1 CH49 64 C3
Day St L13 54 A3
Deacon Cl L22 37 D8
Deacon Ct
Liverpool L25 70 B2
Seaforth L22 37 D8
Deacon Rd WA8 73 B1
Deacon Trad Est WA12 46 A2
Deakin St CH41 65 F8
Dealcroft L25 69 F2
Deanacres L25 70 A2
Dean Ave CH45 50 E6
Dean Cl
Billinge WN5 33 D3
Up Holland WN8 25 C7
Dean Cres WA2 61 B2
Dean Ct WA3 47 A7
Dean Dillistone Ct L1 90 C1
Deane Rd L7 53 C2
Dean Ho L22 37 D8
Dean Mdw WA12 46 C4
Dean Patey Ct L1 90 C1
Dean Rd WA3 47 A7
Deansburn Rd L13 53 E6
Deanscales Rd L11 40 A2
Deans Ct L37 9 F5
Deansgate La L37 10 B5
Deansgate La N L37 10 A6
Dean St L22 37 D8
Deansway WA8 84 C8
Deans Way CH41 65 F8
Dean Way WA9 58 B2
Dean Wood Ave WN5 25 E8
Deanwood Cl L35 56 F2
Dearden Way WN8 25 A7
Dearham Ave WA11 44 B7
Dearne Cl L12 54 E5
Dearnford Ave CH62 88 D6
Dearnford Cl CH62 88 D6
Dearnley Ave WA11 44 E5
Deauville Rd L9 39 C7
Debra Cl L31 29 B4
Dee Cl L33 29 F6
Dee Ct L25 70 C3
Dee Ho L25 70 C3
Dee La CH48 63 A2
Deeley Cl L7 53 C1
Dee Park Cl CH60 86 B6
Dee Park Rd CH60 86 B5
Deepdale WA8 72 C3
Deep Dale WA5 74 F6
Deepdale Ave
Billinge WA11 33 C1
Bootle L20 38 A5
Deepdale Cl CH43 65 C6
Deepdale Dr L35 57 D3
Deepdale Rd L25 70 A7
Deepfield Dr L36 70 F8
Deepfield Rd L15 68 F6
Deepwood Gr L35 56 E2
Deerbarn Dr L30 28 B4
Deerbolt Cl L32 29 C3
Deerbolt Cres L32 29 C3
Deerbolt Way L32 29 C3
Deerbourne Cl L25 69 F2
Dee Rd L35 57 B3
Dee Side CH60 85 C8
Deeside Cl CH43 65 B6
Deeside Ct CH64 86 B1
Dee View Cotts CH64 86 D1
Dee View Rd CH60 85 F8
De Grouchy St CH48 63 B3
De-Haviland Way WN8 24 E8
De Havilland Dr L24 81 E3
Deighton Cl WN5 25 E6
Deirdre Ave WA8 73 A1
Dekker Rd L33 29 E6
Delabole Rd L11 40 D5
Delafield Cl WA2 61 F3
Delagoa Rd L10 39 F6
Delamain Rd L13 53 E6
Delamare Pl 1 WA7 84 F1
Delamere Ave
Bebington CH62 88 E4
Golborne WA3 47 E6
St Helens WA9 58 A3
Widnes WA8 72 C1
Delamere Cl
Bebington CH62 88 E4
Birkenhead CH43 65 B6
Liverpool L12 40 D3
Delamere Ct CH62 88 E4
Delamere Gr 3 CH44 51 E2
Delamere Rd
Skelmersdale WN8 15 F2
Southport PR8 7 B5
Delamere Way WN8 25 A7
Delamore Pl L4 38 E1
Delamore St L4 38 E1
De La Salle RC High Sch L11 40 B2
De La Salle Sch WA10 43 B4
Delavor CH43 65 E4
Delavor Cl CH60 85 E8
Delavor Rd CH60 85 E8
Delaware Cres L32 29 C3
Delaware Rd L20 38 C4
Delfby Cres L32 30 A1
Delf La
Haskayne L39 12 A4
Liverpool, Hunt's Cross L24 82 B6
Liverpool, Walton on the Hill L4 39 A2
Dell Cl CH63 88 B6
Dell Ct CH43 65 F1
Dellfield La L31 20 E1
Dell Gr CH42 79 B8
Dell La CH60 86 B7
Dellside Cl WN4 34 D5
Dellside Gr 4 WA9 58 C8
Dell St 2 L7 53 C2
Dell The
Birkenhead CH42 67 B1
Liverpool L12 54 E8
Up Holland WN8 25 B7
Delph Cl L39 13 C1
Delph Common Rd L39 13 C1
Delph Ct L21 38 A8
Delph Hollow Way WA9 58 B8
Delph La
Formby L37 9 C3
Ormskirk L39 13 C1
Prescot L35 56 F5
Warrington, Houghton Green WA2 61 E6
Winwick WA2 61 A5
Delph Mdw Gdns WN5 33 D4
Delph Park Ave L39 13 B1
Delph Rd L23 26 D8
Delphside Cl WN5 25 D5
Delph Side Com Prim Sch WN8 24 C8
Delphside Rd WN5 25 D5
Delph Top L39 14 A6
Delphwood Dr WA9 44 B1
Delta Cres WA5 60 C2
Delta Dr L12 54 E8
Delta Rd
Bootle L21 38 B7
St Helens WA9 44 F4
Delta Rd E CH42 67 B1
Delta Rd W CH42 67 B1
Deltic Pl L33 30 B1
Deltic Way
Kirkby L33 30 B1
Liverpool L30 39 A8
Delves Ave CH63 78 F3
Delyn Cl CH42 66 E1
Demesne St CH44 51 E3
Denbigh Ave
Southport PR9 1 F3
St Helens WA9 58 C7
Denbigh Rd
Liverpool L9 38 F3
Wallasey CH44 51 D3
Denbigh St L5 52 B5
Dencourt Rd L11 40 B1
Dene Ave WA12 45 F4
Denebank Rd L4 53 B7
Denecliff L28 55 B8
Dene Ct L9 39 F4
Denefield Ho PR8 4 B6
Denehurst Cl WA5 74 F4
Deneshey Rd CH47 63 C8
Denes Way L28 55 A7
Denford Rd L14 54 F5
Denham Cl 1 L12 41 A3
Denholme
Skelmersdale WN8 24 F7
1 Up Holland WN8 25 A7
Denise Ave WA5 74 E5
Denise Rd L10 40 B7
Denison Gr WA9 57 E7
Denison St L3 52 B3
Denman Dr L6 53 C4
Denman Gr 4 CH44 51 E2
Denman St 7 L7 53 B3
Denman Way L6 53 C4
Denmark Rd PR9 2 A2
Denmark St L22 26 D1
Dennett Cl L31 28 D7
Dennett Rd L35 56 C4
Denning Dr CH61 76 D7
Dennis Ave WA10 57 C7
Denny Cl CH49 64 F4
Densham Ave WA2 61 B2
Denshaw WN8 24 F7
Denston Cl CH43 65 B7
Denstone Ave L10 28 D3
Denstone Cl L25 82 B9
Dentdale Dr L5 52 E4
Denton Dr CH45 51 C6
Denton Gr L6 53 C5
DENTON'S GREEN 43 D5
Dentons Green La WA10 43 E5
Denton St
Liverpool L8 67 F4
Widnes WA8 73 C1
Dentwood St L8 68 A4
Denver Rd L32 29 C1
Depot Rd L33 30 D4
Derby Bldgs L7 53 B1
Derby Cl WA12 46 B3
Derby Ct L37 9 E5
Derby Dr WA11 32 A5
Derby Gr L31 28 D6
Derby Hill Cres L39 14 A5
Derby Hill Rd L39 14 A5
Derby Ho 2 L39 13 F5
Derby La L13 54 A4
Derby Rd
Birkenhead CH41, CH42 66 D4
Bootle L20 38 B2
Formby L37 9 E5
Golborne WA3 47 C8
Huyton-w-R L36 55 E2
Liverpool L20 52 C7
Skelmersdale WN8 23 C8
Southport PR9 4 C7
Wallasey CH45 51 A6
Widnes, Barrow's Green WA8 73 D4
Widnes, Lunts Heath WA8 73 B4
Derby Row WA12 60 D8
Derby St W L39 13 E5
DERBYSHIRE HILL 45 A2
Derbyshire Hill Rd WA9 45 A2
Derby Sq
Liverpool L1 90 A3
8 Prescot L34 56 E6
Derby St
Huyton-w-R L36 56 A2
Liverpool, Garston L19 81 C4
Liverpool, Stanley L13 53 F3
Newton-le-W WA12 46 B3
Ormskirk L39 13 F5
Prescot L34 56 C6
Dereham Ave CH49 65 A7
Dereham Cres L10 39 F7
Derek Ave WA2 61 E1
Derna Rd L36 55 D3
Derringstone Cl WA10 43 D1
Derrylea L9 39 D7
Derwent Ave
Formby L37 9 D2
Golborne WA3 36 C1
Prescot L34 56 F6
Southport PR9 1 F1
Derwent Cl
Bebington CH63 78 D5
Kirkby L33 29 D4
Maghull L31 20 F2
Rainhill L35 57 B3
Derwent Dr
Bootle L21 38 D8
Heswall CH61 76 F4
Hooton CH66 89 B2
Wallasey CH45 51 A6
Derwent Ho L17 68 C3
Derwent Rd
Ashton-in-M WN4 35 E5
Bebington CH63 78 D5
Birkenhead CH43 66 B4
Crosby L23 26 F2
Hoylake CH47 63 E8
Orrell WN5 25 F8
St Helens WA11 44 B7
Widnes WA8 72 C1
Derwent Rd E L13 54 A4
Derwent Rd W L13 53 F4
Derwent Sq L13 54 A4
Desborough Cres L12 54 A7
Desford Ave WA11 44 D6
Desford Cl CH46 49 B1
Desford Rd L19 80 F8
Desilva St L36 56 A2
Desmond Cl CH43 65 C6
Desmond Gr L23 26 F3
Desoto Rd WA8 84 E5
Desoto Rd E WA8 84 F6
Desoto Rd W WA8 84 F6
Deva Cl L33 29 E7
Deva Rd CH48 63 A2
Deveraux Dr CH44 51 C3
Deveraux Rd CH44 51 C3
Deverell Gr L15 54 B1
Deverell Rd L15 54 B1
Deverill Rd CH42 66 E1
Devilla Cl L14 55 A5
De Villiers Ave L23 26 E5
Devisdale Gr CH43 65 C7
Devizes Dr CH61 76 D7
Devoke Ave WA11 33 A1
Devon Ave
Up Holland WN8 25 B6
Wallasey CH44, CH45 51 C5
Devon Cl L23 26 A3
Devon Ct 12 L6 53 A5
Devondale Rd L18 69 A5
Devon Dr CH61 76 E4
Devon Farm Way L37 10 B3
Devonfield Rd L9 38 F5
Devon Gdns
Birkenhead CH42 66 F1
Liverpool L16 69 E5
Devon Pl WA8 73 B3
Devonport St L8 67 F5
Devonshire Cl
Birkenhead CH43 66 B5
4 Kirkby L33 29 E4
Devonshire Gdns WA12 46 C2
Devonshire Mews L8 68 B5
DEVONSHIRE PARK 66 D3
Devonshire Park Prim Sch CH42 66 C2
Devonshire Pl
Birkenhead CH43 66 A5
Liverpool L5 52 E6
Devonshire Rd
Birkenhead CH43 66 B5
Birkenhead, Upton CH49 64 E5
Crosby L22, L23 26 C3
Heswall CH61 76 E4
Liverpool L8 68 A5
Southport PR9 5 A8
St Helens WA10 43 D5
Wallasey CH44 51 B4
West Kirby CH48 63 C1
Devonshire Rd W L8 68 A5
Devon St
Liverpool L3, L6 52 F2
St Helens WA10 43 D4
Devonwall Gdns L8 68 B5
Devon Way
Huyton-w-R L36 56 A4
Liverpool L16 69 E6
Dewberry Cl 3 CH42 66 D4
Dewberry Fields WN8 25 B7
Dewey Ave L9 39 B8
Dewlands Rd L21 37 F8
Dewsbury Rd L4 53 C7
Dexter St L8 67 E6
Dexter Way WN8 25 B6
Deycroft Ave L33 30 A4
Deycroft Wlk L33 30 A4
Deyes Ct L31 20 E1
Deyes End L31 20 E1
Deyes High Sch L31 20 D1
Deyes La
Maghull L31 20 D1
Maghull, Moss Side L31 20 F1
Deysbrook La L12, L28 54 F8
Deysbrook Side L12 54 C6
Deysbrook Way L12 54 D8
Dial Rd CH42 66 D3
Dial St 5 L7 53 C2
Diamond Bsns Pk WA11 32 B4
Diamond St L3, L5 52 D4
Diana Rd L20 38 D7
Diana St L4 53 A8
Diane Rd WN4 35 E5
Dibbinsdale Rd CH63 88 B7
Dibbins Gn CH63 88 B7
Dibbins Hey CH63 79 B2
Dibbinview Gr CH63 79 B2
Dibb La L23 26 C7
Dicconson's La L39 12 D4
Dicconson St WA10 44 A4
Dicconson Way L39 14 A5
Dickens Ave CH43 65 F1
Dickens Cl
Birkenhead CH43 65 F1
Liverpool L32 40 D8
Dickens Dr WN2 36 C8
Dickenson St L1 90 B2
Dickens Rd WA10 57 C8
Dickens St L8 67 F6
Dicket's Brow L40 14 F3
Dicket's La L40, WN8 15 A2
Dickinson Cl
Formby L37 9 F2
Haydock WA11 45 A6
Dickinson Ct PR8 4 A2
Dickinson Rd L37 9 F2
Dick's La L40 14 F4
Dickson St L3 52 B4
Didcot Cl L25 82 D9
Didsbury Cl L33 29 F2
Digg La CH46 49 D1
DIGMOOR 24 D6
Digmoor Dr WN8 24 C7
Digmoor Rd
Kirkby L32 40 F7
Skelmersdale WN8 24 D6
Dignum Mead L27 70 E5
Dilloway St WA10 43 E4
Dinaro Cl L25 70 C4
Dinas La L36 55 B4
Dinesen Rd L19 81 C7
DINGLE 68 A3
Dingle Ave
Newton-le-W WA12 45 F2
Up Holland WN8 25 C8
Dinglebrook Rd L9 39 D3
Dingle Brow L8 68 A3
Dingle Cl L39 13 C1
Dingle Gr L8 68 A4
Dingle Grange 5 L8 68 A3
Dingle La L17, L8 68 A3
Dingle Mount L8 68 A3
Dingle Rd
Birkenhead CH42 66 C4
Liverpool L8 68 A3
Up Holland WN8 25 B7
Dingle Vale L17, L8 68 A3
Dingley Ave L9 38 F6
Dingwall Dr CH49 64 E4
Dinmore Rd CH44 51 B4
Dinnington Ct WA8 72 E3
Dinorwic Rd
Liverpool L4 53 A6
Southport PR8 4 A2
Dinsdale Rd CH62 79 E2
Discovery Rd L19 81 D4
District CE Prim Sch The WA12 46 A4
Ditchfield L37 10 A2
Ditchfield Pl WA8 84 B8
Ditchfield Rd
Warrington WA5 74 E3
Widnes WA8 84 B8
DITTON 84 C8
Ditton CE Prim Sch WA8 72 A1
Ditton La CH46 49 E3
Ditton Prim Sch WA8 72 E1
Ditton Rd
Widnes WA8 84 D6
Widnes WA8 84 F6
Dixon Ave WA12 46 C5
Dixon Cl WA11 46 A8
Dixon Mews L30 27 E5
Dixon Rd L33 41 B8
Dobbs Dr L37 10 A4
Dobson Ct L6 53 B5
Dobson St L6 53 A4
Dock Rd
Liverpool L19 81 B5
Wallasey CH41, CH44 51 C1
Widnes WA8 84 F5
Dock Rd N CH62 79 C6
Dock Rd S CH62 79 D4
Doctor's La L37 10 E2
Dodd Ave
Birkenhead CH49 64 D3
St Helens WA10 43 C4
Doddridge Rd 6 L8 67 E5
Dodd's La L31 20 D2
Dodleston Cl CH43 65 D4
Dodman Rd L11 40 D5
Dodson Cl WN4 35 C3
Dodworth Ave PR8 4 E5
Doe Park Ctyd L25 82 B9
Doe's Meadow Rd CH63 88 B7
DOG & GUN 40 B2
Dolan Ct L25 69 F8
Dolly's La PR9 5 D8
Dolomite Ave L24 81 F6
Domar Cl L32 29 F1
Dombey St L8 67 F6
Domingo Dr L33 29 D5
Dominic Cl L16 69 E8
Dominic Rd L16 69 E8
Dominion St L6 53 C5
Domville L35 56 E2
Domville Dr CH49 65 A3
Domville Rd L13 54 A1
Donaldson St L5 53 A6
Donalds Way L17 68 E1
Doncaster Dr CH49 64 F6
Donegal Rd 1 L13 54 B2
Donne Ave CH63 79 A3
Donne Cl CH63 79 A3
Donnington Cl L36 70 D8
Donnington Lo PR8 3 F6
Donsby Rd L9 39 B6
Dooley Dr L30 28 B4
Doon Cl L4 52 E8
Dorbett Dr L23 26 F2
Dorchester Cl CH49 64 F4
Dorchester Dr L33 30 A5
Dorchester Pk CH43 65 D3
Dorchester Rd
Liverpool L25 70 B6
Up Holland WN8 25 A7
Dorchester Way WA5 59 F6
Doreen Ave CH46 64 D8
Dorgan Cl L35 57 C4
Doric Gn WN5 25 D3
Doric Rd L13 54 A4
Doric St
4 Birkenhead CH42 66 F2
Seaforth L21 37 F7
Dorien Rd L13 53 F2
Dorincourt CH43 66 A4
Dorking Gr L15 69 B6
Dorney Ct L12 54 D7
Dorothy St
Liverpool L7 53 B1
St Helens WA9 57 E8
Dorothy Wlk WN2 35 F8

Dorrit St L8 67 F6
Dorset Ave
Liverpool L15 68 D7
Southport PR8 7 C2
Dorset Cl L20 38 D3
Dorset Dr CH61 76 E4
Dorset Gdns CH42 66 F1
Dorset Rd
Huyton-w-R L36 56 A3
Liverpool L6 53 D5
St Helens WA10 43 D1
Wallasey CH45 51 A7
West Kirby CH48 63 C3
Douglas Arc 13 CH41 66 E6
Douglas Ave
Billinge WN5 33 D3
St Helens WA9 59 B6
Up Holland WN8 25 B7
Douglas Cl
Liverpool L13 53 F4
Widnes WA8 73 F3
Douglas Ct PR8 7 C5
Douglas Dr
Birkenhead CH46 64 D8
Maghull L31 20 F2
Ormskirk L39 13 D7
Orrell WN5 25 F7
Douglas Pl L20 38 B1
Douglas Rd
Liverpool L4 53 B6
Southport PR9 2 C4
West Kirby CH48 63 D3
Douglas St
Birkenhead CH41 66 E6
St Helens WA10 43 D3
Douglas Way L33 29 F6
Doulton Cl CH43 65 B7
Doulton Pl L35 56 C2
Doulton St WA10 43 D3
Douro Pl L13 53 F2
Douro St L3, L5 52 E4
DOVECOT 54 F3
Dovecot Ave L14 54 F4
Dovecote Dr WA11 45 C7
Dovecote Gn WA5 60 A1
Dovecot Ho L36 55 B3
Dovecot Pl L14 54 F4
Dovecot Prim Sch L14 55 A3
Dove Ct L25 70 B3
Dovedale Ave
Bebington CH62 88 E5
Maghull L31 20 C2
Dovedale Cl
Birkenhead CH43 65 F2
Warrington WA2 61 E3
Dovedale Cres WN4 35 A8
Dovedale Ct WA8 72 B3
Dovedale Inf & Jun Schs
L18 69 A5
Dovedale Rd
Ashton-in-M WN4 35 A8
Hoylake CH47 63 B8
2 Liverpool L18 68 F5
Liverpool L18 69 A4
Wallasey CH45 51 A7
Dovepoint Rd CH47 48 E1
Dover Cl CH41 66 D7
Dovercliffe Rd L13 54 B3
Dovercroft L25 69 F2
Dove Rd L9 38 F6
Dover Gr L16 69 F8
Dover Rd
Maghull L31 28 C6
Southport PR8 3 F2
Dover St L3 52 F1
Dovesmead Rd CH60 86 C7
Dove St
Golborne WA3 36 A2
Liverpool L8 68 B7
Dovestone Cl L7 68 B8
Dovey St L8 68 A5
Doward St WA8 73 C2
Dowhills Dr L23 26 B5
Dowhills Pk L23 26 B6
Dowhills Rd L23 26 B5
DOWNALL GREEN 34 C5
Downall Green Rd
WN4 34 E6
Downbrook Way WN4 35 D5
Downes Gn CH63 79 A1
Downgreen Cl 9 L32 29 C1
Downham Cl L25 69 F5
Downham Ct 1 CH60 86 A8
Downham Dr CH60 86 A8
Downham Gn L25 69 F5
Downham Rd CH42 66 E3
Downham Rd N CH61 77 A2
Downham Rd S CH60 77 A1
Downham Road S
CH60 86 A8
Downham Way L25 69 F5
Downham Wlk WN5 25 D1
DOWNHOLLAND CROSS
12 A2
Downholland-Haskayne
CE Prim Sch L39 11 E3
Downholland Moss La
L37 10 C4
Downing Cl CH43 66 B3
Downing Rd L20 38 E2
Downing St 3 L5 53 A5
Downlands Rd L27 70 F4
Download Way WA9 44 F2
Downside WA8 72 B3
Downside Cl L30 27 E4
Downside Dr L10 28 F1
Downs Rd WA10 43 D2
Downs The L23 26 B3
Downway La WA9 45 A1
Dowsefield La L18, L25 69 E3
Dragon Cl
Liverpool L11 40 C4
Skelmersdale WN8 24 E8
Dragon Cres L35 56 F4
Dragon Dr L35 56 E3
Dragon La L35 56 E3
Dragon Wlk 1 L11 40 C4
Dragon Yd WA8 73 B4
Drake Cl
Liverpool L10 40 A7
Ormskirk L39 13 C2
Prescot L35 56 E2
Warrington WA5 60 D1
Drake Cres L10 40 A7
Drakefield Rd L11 39 E3
Drake Gdns WA9 57 E6
Drake Pl L10 39 F7
Drake Rd
Liverpool L10 40 A7
Neston CH64 86 E1
Wallasey CH46 50 B4
Drake St
Bootle L20 38 B1
St Helens WA10 43 D4
Drake Way L10 40 A7
Draw Well Rd L33 30 D2
Draycott St L8 67 F3
Drayton Cl
Irby CH61 76 D5
Runcorn WA7 84 F1
Drayton Cres WA11 44 D6
Drayton Rd
3 Liverpool L4 39 A2
Wallasey CH44 51 D3
Drennan Rd L19 81 E8
Drewell Rd L18 68 F3
Drewitt Cres PR9 2 D4
Driffield Rd L34 56 C6
Drinkwater Gdns 2 L3 52 E3
Drive The L12 54 B5
Driveway L35 56 F2
Droitwich Ave CH49 64 C4
Dromore Ave L18 69 A3
Dronfield Way L25 69 F7
Droxford Dr L25 69 F7
Druids' Cross Gdns
L18 69 D4
Druids' Cross Rd L18 69 D4
Druids Pk L18 69 E4
Druid St WN4 35 C2
Druidsville Rd L18 69 E4
Druids Way CH49 65 A2
Drum Cl L14 55 A5
Drummer's La WN4 34 E7
Drummond Ct WA8 73 D2
Drummond Rd
Crosby L23 27 B5
Hoylake CH47 63 B6
Liverpool L4 39 C1
Drummoyne Ct L23 26 A5
Druridge Dr WA5 74 F4
Drury La L2 90 A3
Dryburgh Way 5 L4 52 E8
Dryden Ave WN4 34 F6
Dryden Cl
Birkenhead CH43 65 C7
Prescot L35 56 E3
Dryden Gr L36 55 F1
Dryden Pl WA2 61 C2
Dryden Rd L15, L7 53 E1
Dryden St
Bootle L20 38 A5
Liverpool L5 52 D4
Dryebeck Gr WA9 58 D6
Dryfield Cl CH49 64 D4
Dublin St L3 52 B4
Ducie St L8 68 B6
Duckinfield St L3 52 F1
Duck Pond La CH42 66 A2
Duddingston Ave
Crosby L23 26 E2
2 Liverpool L15, L18 69 A5
Duddon Ave L31 20 F2
Duddon Cl CH43 65 F3
Dudley Cl CH43 66 B4
Dudley Cres CH65 89 B3
Dudley Gr L23 26 E2
Dudley Pl WA9 44 D3
Dudley Rd
Liverpool L18 68 F5
Wallasey CH45 51 A8
Dudley St WN4 35 A5
Dudlow Ct L18 69 C5
Dudlow Dr L18 69 C5
Dudlow Gdns L18 69 C6
Dudlow Grange L18 69 C5
Dudlow La L18 69 C5
Dudlow Nook Rd L18 69 C6
Dugdale Cl L19 81 A7
Duke Ave PR8 4 C4
Duke Cl WA7 84 F2
Duke Of York Cotts
CH62 79 A6
DUKESFIELD 84 E3
Dukes Rd L5 52 E6
Duke St
Ashton-in-M WN4 35 C3
Birkenhead CH41 66 C8
Formby L37 9 F2
Golborne WA3 36 A1
Liverpool, Garston L19 81 C6
Liverpool L1 90 B2
Newton-le-W WA12 46 B3
4 Prescot L34 56 D6
Seaforth L22 37 D8
Southport PR8 4 B5
Duke St *continued*
St Helens WA10 43 F4
Wallasey CH45 51 B8
Dukes Terr L1 90 C2
Duke Street La L1 90 B2
Dukes Way L37 9 F2
Duke's Wood La WN8 24 D3
Dulas Gn L32 30 A1
Dulas Rd
Kirkby L32 30 A1
Liverpool L15 69 B6
Dulson Way L34 56 A5
Dulverton Rd L17 80 E8
Dumbarton St L4 38 F1
Dumbrees Gdns L12 54 E8
Dumbrees Rd L12 54 F8
Dumbreeze Gr L34 41 D4
Dumfries Way L33 29 D6
Dunacre Way L26 82 F8
Dunbabin Rd L15, L16 69 C6
Dunbar Cres PR8 7 F8
Dunbar Rd PR8 3 F1
Dunbar St L4 38 F2
Dunbeath Ave L35 57 D2
Dunbeath Cl L35 57 D1
Dunblane Cl WN4 34 C4
Duncan Ave WA12 46 C5
Duncan Cl WA10 43 F2
Duncan Dr CH49 64 D4
Duncansby Cres WA5 74 E6
Duncansby Dr CH63 88 C4
Duncan St
Birkenhead CH41 66 F6
Liverpool L1 90 C1
St Helens WA10 43 E3
Dunchurch Rd L14 54 F5
Duncombe Rd N L19 81 B7
Duncombe Rd S L19 81 B7
Duncote Cl
Birkenhead CH43 66 A4
Rainhill L35 57 A5
Dundale Rd L13 54 B3
Dundalk Rd WA8 84 E8
Dundas St L20 38 B1
Dundee Cl WA2 61 F4
Dundee Gr CH44 51 A3
Dundonald Rd L17 68 E1
Dundonald St CH41 66 A8
Dunedin Ct CH47 63 A6
Dunedin St WA9 57 E8
Dunes Dr L37 9 C4
Dunes Way L5 52 C6
Dunfold Cl L32 29 F1
Dungeon La
Liverpool L24 82 F2
Skelmersdale WN8 16 C7
Dunham Ave WA3 35 F1
Dunham Cl CH62 88 F3
Dunham Rd L15 54 B1
Dunkeld Cl 1 L6 53 A3
Dunkeld St 2 L6 53 A3
Dunkerron Cl L27 70 D7
Dunkirk Rd PR8 3 F2
Dunlin Ave WA12 46 C4
Dunlin Cl
Liverpool L27 70 E4
Warrington WA2 61 E3
Dunlin Ct L25 70 A5
Dunlins Ct CH45 50 E8
Dunlop Ave PR8 7 C2
Dunlop Dr L31 29 B4
Dunlop Rd L24 82 C3
Dunluce St L4 38 E1
Dunmail Ave WA11 33 C1
Dunmore Rd L13 53 F3
Dunmow Way L25 82 C9
Dunnerdale Rd L11 40 A2
Dunnett St L20 38 B1
Dunning Cl CH49 64 E5
Dunnings Bridge Rd L30,
L31 28 A3
Dunnock Cl
Liverpool L25 70 A5
Warrington WA2 61 E3
Dunraven Rd CH48 63 A2
Dunriding La WA10 43 D3
Dunscroft WA9 58 D7
Dunsdale Dr WN4 35 C3
Dunsdon Cl L18, L25 69 E4
Dunsdon Rd L25 69 E5
Dunsford WA8 72 B3
Dunsmore Cl WA11 45 C7
Dunsop Ave WA9 58 D4
Dunstall Cl CH46 49 E3
Dunstan La L7 68 C8
Dunstan St L15 68 E8
Dunster Gr
Heswall CH60 86 B7
St Helens WA9 58 D4
Dunster Rd PR8 7 E8
Durant's Cotts L31 28 E7
Durban Ave L23 26 E5
Durban Rd
Liverpool L13 54 B3
Wallasey CH45 51 C6
Durban St WN2, WN7 36 E4
Durden St L7 68 C7
Durham Ave L30 28 A1
Durham Mews E L30 28 A1
Durham Mews W L30 28 A1
Durham Rd
Seaforth L21 37 F7
Widnes WA8 73 B3
Durham St
Liverpool L19 81 D4
Skelmersdale WN8 15 D2
Durham Way
Huyton-w-R L36 56 A3
Durham Way *continued*
Litherland L30 28 A1
Durley Dr CH43 65 E1
Durley Park Cl CH43 77 E8
Durley Rd L9 39 B6
Durliston Cl WA8 72 C2
Durning Rd L7 53 C1
Durrant Rd 3 L11 53 E8
Durrell Way WA3 47 E8
Dursley L35 56 F2
Dursley Dr WN4 35 D4
Durston Rd L16 69 D8
Dutton Dr CH63 78 F2
Duxbury Cl
Maghull L31 20 E3
Rainford WA11 32 A7
Duxford Ct WA2 61 E1
Dwerryhouse La L11,
L12 40 B2
Dwerryhouse St L8 67 D6
Dyers La L39 13 E4
Dyer St WA3 35 F1
Dyke St L6 53 A4
Dykin Cl WA8 73 E3
Dykin Rd WA8 73 E3
Dylan Cl L4 52 F7
Dymchurch Rd L24 82 B5
Dymoke Rd 2 L11 40 C3
Dymoke Wlk L11 40 C3
Dyson Hall Dr L9 39 D5
Dyson Hall/Gladstone Ho
L9 39 D5
Dyson St L4 38 F1

E

Eager La L31 20 B8
Eagle Cres WA11 32 A6
Eagle Dene L10 40 A6
Eaglehall Rd L9 39 F4
Eaglehurst Rd L25 70 B4
Eagle Park Dr WA2 61 A1
Eagles Ct L32 29 E2
Eaglesfield Cl 2 WA9 58 D7
Ealing Rd L9 39 B7
Eamont Ave PR9 2 B5
Eardisley Rd L15, L18 69 B6
Earhart Cl WN8 24 E8
Earle Cl WA12 45 F3
Earle Cres CH64 86 D1
Earle Dr CH64 86 D1
Earle Rd L7 68 C8
Earle St
Liverpool L3 52 B2
Newton-le-W WA12 46 A3
EARLESTOWN 46 B2
Earlestown Sta WA12 46 B3
Earl Rd L20 38 E4
Earl's Cl L23 26 D3
Earlsfield Rd L15 68 F6
Earl St
Bebington CH62 79 B8
St Helens WA9 44 C4
Earlston Rd CH45 51 B6
Earlswood WN8 16 E1
Earlswood Cl 2 CH46 64 B8
Earlwood Gdns L35 56 E2
Earp St L19 81 C6
Easby Cl L37 10 A2
Easby Rd 5 L4 52 D7
Easby Wlk L4 52 D7
Easedale Dr PR8 7 B4
Easedale Wlk 2 L33 29 D5
Easenhall Cl WA8 73 C5
Easington Rd WA9 57 D6
East Albert Rd L17 68 B4
East Ave WA3 36 C1
East Bank 2 CH42 66 C3
Eastbank St PR8 4 B6
Eastbank Street Sq 9
PR8 4 B7
Eastbourne Mews L9 39 B7
Eastbourne Rd
Birkenhead CH41 66 C6
Crosby L22 26 B2
Liverpool L9 39 B7
Southport PR8 4 A3
Eastbury Cl WA8 73 C5
East Cl L34 57 A7
Eastcliffe Rd L13 54 B3
Eastcote Rd L19 81 C8
Eastcott Cl CH49 64 C3
Eastcroft Park Sch L33 29 F5
Eastcroft Rd CH44 51 C2
Eastdale Rd L15 68 F8
East Dam Wood Rd
L24 83 A2
Easter Ct WA5 60 B2
Eastern Ave
Bebington CH62 79 D3
Liverpool L24 82 F4
Eastern Dr L19 81 A7
East Farm Mews CH48 75 F8
Eastfield Dr L17 68 C3
Eastfield Wlk L32 29 C1
East Front L35 56 E1
EAST GILLIBRANDS 24 A8
EASTHAM 88 F5
Eastham Cl L16 54 F1
Eastham Cres WA9 58 C4
Eastham Ctry Pk*
CH62 89 A8
EASTHAM FERRY 89 B8
Eastham Gn L24 82 E5
Eastham Ho CH62 89 A4
Eastham Mews CH62 89 A4
Eastham Rake CH62,
CH64 88 D3
Eastham Rake Sta
CH63 88 D3
Eastham Village Rd
CH62 89 A5
East La L29 19 B2
Eastlake Ave L5 52 F5
East Lancashire Rd
Haydock WA11, WA12,
WA3 46 C7
Knowsley L34 41 C6
Liverpool L11 40 C5
St Helens WA10, WA11 43 C7
East Leigh WN8 16 D1
Eastleigh Dr CH61 76 D7
East Mains L24 83 A3
Eastman Rd L13 53 E7
East Mead L39 13 B2
East Meade L31 20 C2
East Millwood Rd L24 83 A4
East Mount WN5 25 F6
East O Hills Cl CH60 77 A1
Easton Rd
Bebington CH62 79 B8
Huyton-w-R L36 55 A3
East Orchard La L9 39 E7
EAST PIMBO 24 E5
East Prescot Rd L13,
L14 54 D4
East Rd
Halewood L24, L26 83 A5
Liverpool, Broad Green
L14 54 C2
Maghull L31 20 F1
East Side WA9 44 C2
Eastside Ind Est WA9 44 C2
East St
Ashton-in-M WN4 35 D4
Crosby L22 26 D1
Liverpool L3 90 A4
Prescot L34 56 E6
Southport PR9 4 D7
Wallasey CH41, CH44 51 E1
Widnes WA8 73 D1
Eastview Cl CH43 65 D4
Eastway
Birkenhead CH49 64 E4
Maghull L31 20 E1
Widnes WA8 72 D1
East Way CH46 49 F1
Eastway Prim Sch
CH46 49 F1
Eastwell Rd WN4 35 A3
Eastwood L17 68 A3
Eastwood Ave WA12 46 F3
Eastwood Rd WA5 59 F7
Eaton Ave
Bootle L21 38 B7
Bootle, Orrell Park L20 38 D5
Wallasey CH44 51 C4
Eaton Cl
Huyton-w-R L36 55 D2
Liverpool L12 54 A7
Eaton Gdns L12 54 D4
Eaton Grange L12 54 C5
Eaton Pl L34 56 D6
Eaton Rd
Birkenhead CH43 66 B5
Liverpool, Cressington Park
L19 81 A6
Liverpool, Sandfield Park
L12 54 C5
Maghull L31 28 D6
St Helens WA10 43 D6
West Kirby CH48 63 B1
Eaton Rd N L12 54 A7
Eaton St
Liverpool L3 52 C3
Prescot L34 56 D7
Wallasey CH44 51 B5
Eavesdale WN8 24 E8
Eaves La WA9 58 C6
Eaves Prim Sch WA9 58 C6
Ebenezer Howard Rd
L21 27 C1
Ebenezer St
Birkenhead CH42 67 A2
St Helens WA11 44 F6
Eberle St L2 90 A4
Ebony Cl CH46 64 B8
Ebony Way L33 29 E5
Ebor La L5 52 E4
Ebor Lo PR8 4 A5
Ebrington St L19 81 C7
Ecclesall Ave L21 38 D8
Eccles Dr L25 70 B7
Ecclesfield Rd WA10 43 A6
Eccles Gr WA9 58 E3
Eccleshall Rd CH62 79 C6
Eccleshill Rd L13 54 A5
Eccles Rd L37 9 D1
ECCLESTON 43 A4
Eccleston Ave CH62 79 C1
Eccleston Cl CH43 65 F3
Eccleston Gdns
St Helens, Portico
WA10 57 A8
St Helens WA10 43 B1
Eccleston Hall WA10 43 B3
ECCLESTON LANE ENDS
56 E7
Eccleston Lane Ends Prim
Sch L34 56 F7

Eccleston Mere Prim Sch
WA10 . . . . **43** A3
ECCLESTON PARK **57** A8
Eccleston Pk L35 . . . . . . **57** A6
Eccleston Rd **1** L9 . . . . **39** A6
Eccleston St
Prescot L34 . . . . **56** D6
St Helens WA10 . . . . **43** E3
Edale Cl CH62 . . . . **88** E5
Edale Rd L18 . . . . **69** B4
Edburton Ct WA3 . . . . . . **47** A8
Eddisbury Rd
5 Wallasey CH44 . . . . . **51** C5
West Kirby CH48 . . . . **63** A4
Eddisbury Way L12 . . . . . **54** A7
Eddleston St WN4 . . . . . . **34** F6
Eden Ave
Rainford WA11 . . . . **31** E7
Southport PR9 . . . . **1** F2
Eden Cl
Kirkby L33 . . . . **29** F6
Rainhill L35 . . . . **57** B2
Edendale WA8 . . . . **72** B2
Eden Dr N L23 . . . . **27** A3
Eden Dr S L23 . . . . **27** A3
Edenfield Cl PR8 . . . .**4** E3
Edenfield Cres L36 . . . . . . **55** F4
Edenfield Rd L15 . . . . **69** A6
Edenhall Dr L25 . . . . **70** C2
Edenhurst WN8 . . . . **24** E8
Edenhurst Ave
Huyton-w-R L16 . . . . **70** A8
2 Wallasey CH44 . . . . . **51** C5
Edenhurst Cl L37 . . . . **9** C2
Edenhurst Ct L36 . . . . **55** B4
Edenhurst Dr L37 . . . . **9** C2
Edenpark Rd CH42 . . . . . **66** C3
Eden St L30 . . . . **27** E4
Eden Vale L30 . . . . **27** E4
Edgar Ct
Birkenhead CH41 . . . . **66** D7
Litherland L21 . . . . **27** B1
Edgar St L3 . . . . **52** D3
Edgbaston Cl L36 . . . . **55** C1
Edgbaston Way CH43 . . . **65** C8
Edgefield Cl CH43 . . . . . . **65** D4
Edgefold Rd L32 . . . . **29** F1
Edge Gr L7 . . . . **53** E2
EDGE GREEN **35** F3
Edge Green La WA3 . . . . . **35** F2
Edge Green Rd WN4 . . . . . **35** F4
Edge Green St WA3 . . . . . **35** D4
Edge Hall Rd WN5 . . . . . . **25** E5
EDGE HILL **68** B8
Edgehill Rd CH46 . . . . **64** D8
Edge Hill Sta L7 . . . . **68** C8
Edge Hill Univ L39 . . . . . . **14** A3
Edge La
Crosby L23 . . . . **27** A5
Liverpool L13, L7 . . . . **53** D2
Edge Lane Dr L13 . . . . **54** B2
Edge Lane Ret Pk L13 . . . . **53** F2
Edgeley Gdns L9 . . . . **38** F6
Edgemoor Cl
Birkenhead CH43 . . . . **65** B7
Crosby L23 . . . . **27** A5
Liverpool L12 . . . . **54** D5
Edgemoor Dr
Crosby L23 . . . . **27** A5
Irby CH61 . . . . **76** C7
Liverpool L10 . . . . **40** A7
Edgemoor Rd L12 . . . . **54** D5
Edgerley Pl WN4 . . . . **35** A3
Edgerton Rd WA3 . . . . . . **47** F8
Edge St WA9 . . . . **57** C6
Edgewell Dr L15 . . . . **69** B8
Edgewood Dr CH62 . . . . . **88** D5
Edgewood Rd
Birkenhead CH49 . . . . **64** F6
Hoylake CH47 . . . . **48** D1
Edgeworth Cl WA3 . . . . . . **58** A8
Edgeworth Rd WA3 . . . . . **35** F1
Edgeworth St WA9 . . . . . . **58** E7
Edgley Dr L39 . . . . **14** A5
Edgworth Rd L4 . . . . **53** B6
Edinburgh Cl L30 . . . . . . **39** A8
Edinburgh Dr
Birkenhead CH43 . . . . **66** A1
Huyton-w-R L36 . . . . **71** B3
Edinburgh Rd
Formby L37 . . . . **9** E1
Liverpool L7 . . . . **53** A2
Wallasey CH45 . . . . **51** B5
Widnes WA8 . . . . **84** A8
Edington St L15 . . . . **68** E2
Edith Rd
Bootle L20 . . . . **38** D6
Liverpool L4 . . . . **53** A6
Wallasey CH44 . . . . **51** D4
Edith St
Runcorn WA7 . . . . **84** F3
St Helens WA9 . . . . **58** F7
Edith Villas L20 . . . . **38** E4
Edmondson St WA9 . . . . . **44** F3
Edmonton Cl L5 . . . . **52** D6
Edmund St L3 . . . . **90** A4
Edna Ave L10 . . . . **40** A7
Edrich Ave CH43 . . . . **65** C8
Edward Dr WN4 . . . . **35** B4
Edward Jenner Ave
L30. . . . . **27** F3
Edward Rd
Hoylake CH47 . . . . **63** C6
Prescot L35 . . . . **56** F5
Warrington WA5 . . . . **74** D6

Edward's La L24 . . . . **82** B7
Edwards Lane Ind Est
L24. . . . . **82** B7
Edward St
Haydock WA11 . . . . **45** A6
Liverpool L3 . . . . **90** C3
St Helens WA9 . . . . **44** D1
Widnes WA8 . . . . **73** D1
Edwards Way WA8 . . . . . . **84** C8
Edwin St WA8 . . . . **73** C1
Effingham St L20 . . . . **38** B1
Egan Ct CH41 . . . . **66** E7
Egan Rd CH43 . . . . **65** F8
Egbert Rd CH47 . . . . **63** C8
Egdon Cl WA8 . . . . **73** E2
Egerton Cl
Birkenhead CH41 . . . . **66** E7
13 Wallasey CH45 . . . . **51** B8
Egerton Dr CH48 . . . . **63** B2
Egerton Gdns CH42 . . . . . **66** E1
Egerton Gr CH45 . . . . **51** B5
EGERTON PARK **66** E1
Egerton Park Cl CH42 . . . **66** E1
Egerton Rd
Bebington CH62 . . . . **79** B7
Birkenhead CH43 . . . . **66** A6
Liverpool L15 . . . . **68** D7
Prescot L34 . . . . **56** C6
Egerton St
Abram Brow WN2 . . . . **36** B7
Liverpool L8 . . . . **67** F7
Runcorn WA7 . . . . **84** F3
St Helens WA9 . . . . **44** D1
Wallasey CH45 . . . . **51** C8
Egerton Wharf CH41 . . . . **66** E8
Eglington Ave L35 . . . . . . **56** D2
EGREMONT **51** D4
Egremont Cl L27 . . . . **71** A4
Egremont Lawn L27 . . . . . **71** A4
Egremont Prim Sch
CH44. . . . . **51** D4
Egremont Prom CH44,
CH45 . . . . **51** D5
Egypt St WA8 . . . . **84** F7
Eight Acre La L37 . . . . **10** B6
Eighth Ave L9 . . . . **39** D7
Eilian Gr L14 . . . . **54** D2
Elaine Cl
Ashton-in-M WN4 . . . . **35** D5
Widnes WA8 . . . . **73** C1
Elaine Price Ct **3** WA7 . . **84** F1
Elaine St L8 . . . . **67** F6
Elbow La L37 . . . .**9** F3
Elcombe Ave WA3 . . . . . . **47** E7
Elderberry Cl **3** L11 . . . . **40** C2
Elderdale Rd L4 . . . . **53** B7
Elderflower Rd WA10 . . . . **43** E5
Elder Gdns L19 . . . . **81** B8
Elder Gr CH48 . . . . **63** B2
Eldersfield Rd L11 . . . . . . **40** B2
Elderswood Rd L35 . . . . . **57** C4
Elderwood Rd CH42 . . . . . **66** E3
Eldon Cl WA10 . . . . **43** E2
Eldon Gdns WN4 . . . . **35** A6
Eldon Gr L3 . . . . **52** D4
Eldon Ho CH43 . . . . **66** A4
Eldonian Way L3, L5 . . . . . **52** C4
Eldon Pl L3 . . . . **52** D4
Eldon Rd
Birkenhead CH42 . . . . **66** F2
Wallasey CH44 . . . . **51** B4
Eldons Croft PR8 . . . . **7** D5
Eldon St
Liverpool L3 . . . . **52** C4
St Helens WA10 . . . . **43** E2
Eldred Rd L16 . . . . **69** C6
Eleanor Pk CH43 . . . . **65** C8
Eleanor Rd
Birkenhead CH43 . . . . **65** D8
Bootle L20 . . . . **38** D6
Wallasey CH46 . . . . **49** D1
Eleanor St L20 . . . . **38** B1
Elephant La WA9 . . . . **57** E2
Elfet St CH41 . . . . **65** F8
Elgar Ave CH62 . . . . **88** E5
Elgar Rd L14 . . . . **54** F5
Elgin Ave WN4 . . . . **34** D4
Elgin Ct L35 . . . . **57** D2
Elgin Dr CH45 . . . . **51** C6
Elgin Way CH41 . . . . **66** E7
Eliot Cl CH62 . . . . **79** A7
Eliot St L20 . . . . **38** B5
Elizabeth Ave PR8 . . . . . . **7** E6
Elizabeth Rd
Bootle L20 . . . . **38** D6
Haydock WA11 . . . . **45** E7
Huyton-w-R L36 . . . . **71** A8
Liverpool L10 . . . . **40** B6
Elizabeth St
Liverpool L3, L7 . . . . **52** F2
St Helens, Clock Face
WA9 . . . . **58** E3
St Helens, Sutton WA9 . . . **58** E8
Elizabeth Terr WA8 . . . . . **72** D1
Eliza St WA9 . . . . **58** F7
Elkan Cl WA8 . . . . **73** E2
Elkan Rd WA8 . . . . **73** E2
Elkstone Rd L11 . . . . **40** B1
Ellaby Rd L35 . . . . **57** C4
Ellamsbridge Rd WA9 . . . **58** E8
Ellel Gr L6 . . . . **53** C5
Ellen Gdn WN4 . . . . **58** E7
Ellen's Cl **5** L6 . . . . **53** A2
Ellen's La CH62, CH63 . . . **79** B5
Ellen St WN4 . . . . **58** E7
Elleray Dr L8 . . . . **67** F4
Elleray Park Rd CH45 . . . . **51** A7

Elleray Park Sch CH45 . . . **51** A7
Eller Brook Ho L39 . . . . . . **13** E6
Ellerbrook Way L39 . . . . . **13** E6
Ellergreen Rd L11 . . . . . . **40** A2
Ellerman Rd L3 . . . . **67** F3
Ellerslie Ave L35 . . . . **57** C5
Ellerslie Rd L13 . . . . **53** E6
Ellerton Cl WA8 . . . . **72** D3
Ellerton Way L12 . . . . **40** E3
Ellesmere Dr L10 . . . . **28** C3
Ellesmere Gr CH45 . . . . . **51** B7
Ellesmere Rd WN4 . . . . . . **34** F4
Elliot St
Liverpool L1 . . . . **90** B3
St Helens WA10 . . . . **43** D4
Elliott Ave WA3 . . . . **36** B1
Ellis Ashton St L36 . . . . . . **56** B1
Ellison Dr WA10 . . . . **43** C4
Ellison Gr L36 . . . . **55** E2
Ellison St L13 . . . . **53** F4
Ellis Pl L8 . . . . **67** F5
Ellis Rd WN5 . . . . **33** D4
Ellis St WA8 . . . . **84** F7
Ellon Ave L35 . . . . **57** D2
Elloway Rd L24 . . . . **83** A3
Ellwood Cl L24 . . . . **83** A3
Elmar Rd L17 . . . . **68** E2
Elm Ave
Birkenhead CH49 . . . . **64** D6
Crosby L23 . . . . **26** F6
Downall Green WN4 . . . . . **34** D5
Golborne WA3 . . . . **36** A1
Newton-le-W WA12 . . . . . **46** C2
Widnes WA8 . . . . **73** B2
Elm Bank **7** L5 . . . . **52** F7
Elmbank Rd
1 Bebington CH62 . . . . **79** B6
Liverpool L18 . . . . **68** E5
Elmbank St CH44 . . . . **51** C3
Elm Cl
Heswall CH61 . . . . **77** A4
Liverpool L12 . . . . **40** F3
Elmcroft L19 . . . . **39** D6
Elmcroft La L38 . . . . **18** A3
Elm Ct
Bebington CH63 . . . . **78** D6
Crosby L23 . . . . **26** C4
Skelmersdale WN8 . . . . . . **15** E1
Elmdale Cl L37 . . . . **9** D2
Elmdale Rd L9 . . . . **39** A4
Elmdene Ct CH49 . . . . **64** C2
Elm Dr
Billinge WN5 . . . . **33** D5
Birkenhead CH49 . . . . **64** C3
Formby L37 . . . .**9** D1
Seaforth L21 . . . . **37** F6
Elmers Gn WN8 . . . . **16** D2
ELMERS GREEN **16** D2
Elmer's Green La WN8 . . . **16** C4
Elmers Wood Rd WN8 . . . **16** D2
Elmfield Cl WA9 . . . . **57** E8
Elmfield Rd L9 . . . . **39** A5
Elm Gdns
Rainford WA11 . . . . **31** F6
1 Seaforth L21 . . . . **38** A6
Elm Gr
Birkenhead CH42 . . . . **66** D4
Hoylake CH47 . . . . **63** C7
Liverpool L7 . . . . **53** A1
Prescot L34 . . . . **56** F7
Skelmersdale WN8 . . . . . . **15** E1
Widnes WA8 . . . . **73** B1
Elm Hall Dr L18 . . . . **69** A5
Elmham Cres L10 . . . . **39** F7
Elm Ho
Crosby L22 . . . . **26** D1
Prescot L34 . . . . **56** C6
Elm House Mews L25 . . . . **70** B4
Elmhurst Rd L25 . . . . **70** B7
Elmore Cl L5 . . . . **52** F5
ELM PARK **53** D3
Elm Park Dr PR8 . . . .**7** E5
Elm Park Rd CH45 . . . . . . **51** A7
Elm Pl L39 . . . . **13** E4
Elm Rd
Abram Brow WN2 . . . . **36** C7
Bebington CH63 . . . . **78** F7
Birkenhead, Devonshire Park
CH42. . . . . **66** D3
Birkenhead, Prenton
CH42. . . . . **66** B2
Haydock WA11 . . . . **45** E7
Heswall CH61 . . . . **76** D5
Kirkby L32 . . . . **29** D3
Liverpool L4 . . . . **39** A2
Seaforth L21 . . . . **37** F6
Southport PR8 . . . .**4** B4
St Helens WA10, WA9 . . . . **57** E8
Warrington WA5 . . . . **74** F4
Warrington, Winwick Quay
WA2 . . . . **61** B4
Elm Rd N CH42 . . . . **66** B2
Elmridge WN8 . . . . **24** D8
Elmridge Ct WA3 . . . . **47** F8
Elmsbury St **1** WN4 . . . . **34** F5
Elmsdale Rd L18 . . . . **69** A5
Elmsett Cl WA5 . . . . **74** E5
Elmsfield Cl L25 . . . . **70** A5
Elmsfield Pk L39 . . . . **21** A6
Elmsfield Rd L25 . . . . **27** B6
Elms House Rd L13 . . . . . **53** F2
Elmsley Ct L18 . . . . **69** A3
Elmsley Rd L18 . . . . **68** F4
Elms Pk CH61 . . . . **77** A5
Elms Rd L31 . . . . **28** D6
Elms Sch The L28 . . . . . . **55** B8

Elm St
Birkenhead CH41. . . . . **66** D6
Huyton-w-R L36 . . . . **56** A2
Elmstead WN8 . . . . **24** D8
Elms The
Golborne WA3 . . . . **47** F7
Hoylake CH47 . . . . **63** C7
Liverpool L68 . . . . **68** A4
Maghull L31 . . . . **20** D3
Runcorn WA7 . . . . **84** F1
Southport, Birkdale PR8 . . . .**3** F6
Southport, Blowick PR8 . . . . .**4** C5
Elmswood Ave L35 . . . . . . **57** D1
Elmswood Ct L18 . . . . **68** F3
Elmswood Gr L36 . . . . **55** C3
Elmswood Rd
Birkenhead CH42 . . . . **66** D4
Liverpool L17, L18 . . . . . . **68** E2
Wallasey CH44 . . . . **51** D4
Elm Terr
Hoylake CH47 . . . . **63** C7
Liverpool L7 . . . . **53** C2
Elmtree Cl L12 . . . . **54** C7
Elm Tree Cl CH47 . . . . **63** C8
Elmtree Gr CH43 . . . . **65** E8
Elm Tree Rd WA3 . . . . **47** F8
Elmure Ave CH63 . . . . **78** D5
Elm Vale L6 . . . . **53** D3
Elmway Cl L13 . . . . **53** F2
Elmwood WN8 . . . . **16** C3
Elmwood Ave
Ashton-in-M WN4 . . . . **35** A2
Crosby L23 . . . . **27** A5
Elmwood Dr CH61 . . . . . . **76** F2
Elphin Gr L4 . . . . **39** A1
Elric Wlk L33 . . . . **29** F3
Elsbeck Gr WA9 . . . . **58** D6
Elsie Rd L4 . . . . **53** B6
Elsinore Ct L23 . . . . **26** C3
Elsmere Ave L17 . . . . **68** C3
Elson Rd L37 . . . .**9** D1
Elstead Gr WN4 . . . . **34** D4
Elstead Rd
Kirkby L32 . . . . **29** C1
Liverpool L9 . . . . **39** E2
Elstow St **6** L5 . . . . **52** D7
Elstree Ct WA8 . . . . **73** D4
Elstree Rd L6 . . . . **53** D3
Elswick WN8 . . . . **24** C8
Elswick Gn PR9 . . . .**2** A5
Elswick Gn PR9 . . . .**1** F4
Elswick St L8 . . . . **67** F3
Elsworth Cl L37 . . . . **17** C8
Eltham Ave L21 . . . . **27** B1
Eltham Cl
Ashton-in-M WN4 . . . . **35** D3
Birkenhead CH49 . . . . **65** B2
Widnes WA8 . . . . **73** E3
Eltham Gn CH49 . . . . **65** B2
Eltham St L7 . . . . **53** D2
Eltham Wlk WA8 . . . . **73** E3
Elton Ave
Crosby L23 . . . . **26** C4
Litherland L30 . . . . **27** E3
Elton Cl
Bebington CH62 . . . . **88** E3
Golborne WA3 . . . . **47** E7
Elton Dr CH63 . . . . **79** A3
Elton Head Rd
Nutgrove L35, WA9 . . . . . . **57** D6
St Helens, Marshall's Cross
WA9 . . . . **58** B5
Elton St L4 . . . . **38** F2
Elvington Rd L38 . . . . **18** A2
Elway Rd WN4 . . . . **35** C4
Elwick Dr L11 . . . . **40** C2
Elwood Cl L33 . . . . **29** E6
Elworth Ave WA8 . . . . **73** A5
Elworthy Ave L25 . . . . **70** F1
Elwyn Dr L26 . . . . **83** A3
Elwy Rd CH47 . . . . **48** E1
Elwy St L8 . . . . **68** A5
Ely Ave CH46 . . . . **64** C8
Ely Cl L30 . . . . **27** F1
Ely Mews PR9 . . . .**2** A2
Ember Cres **4** L6 . . . . . . **52** F4
Embledon St **8** L8 . . . . . **68** B7
Emerald Cl L30 . . . . **28** B3
Emerald St L8 . . . . **67** F3
Emerson Cl L38 . . . . **18** A4
Emerson St L8 . . . . **67** F7
Emery St L4 . . . . **38** F1
Emily St WA9 . . . . **44** D1
Emlyn St WN4 . . . . **34** E3
Emmanuel Rd PR9 . . . .**1** F2
Emmaus CE & RC Prim
Sch L12 . . . . **40** F3
Emmett St WA9 . . . . **44** C1
Empire Rd L21 . . . . **38** B6
Empress Cl L31 . . . . **20** B1
Empress Rd
Liverpool, Cabbage Hall
L6 . . . . **53** C6
Liverpool L7 . . . . **53** B2
Wallasey CH44 **1** **51** C4
Emstrey Wlk **1** L32 . . . . . **29** C2
Endborne Rd L9 . . . . **39** A6
Endbutt La L23 . . . . **26** E3
Enderby Ave WA11 . . . . . . **44** D6
Endfield Pk L19 . . . . **81** B8
Endmoor Rd L36 . . . . **55** D5
Endsleigh Rd
Crosby L22 . . . . **26** B2
Liverpool L13 . . . . **53** E3
Enerby Cl CH43 . . . . **65** C7
Enfield Ave L23 . . . . **26** E4
Enfield Park Rd WA2 . . . . . **61** F4

Enfield Rd L13 . . . . **54** B2
Enfield St WA10 . . . . **43** E2
Enfield Terr CH43 . . . . **66** B5
Enford Dr WA9 . . . . **58** D7
Engine La L37 . . . . **18** E8
English Martyr's RC Prim
Sch L21 . . . . **38** C8
Enid Pl WN2 . . . . **35** F8
Enid St L8 . . . . **67** F8
Enmore WN8 . . . . **24** D8
Ennerdale Ave
Ashton-in-M WN4 . . . . **35** B5
Bebington CH62 . . . . **88** F4
Billinge WA11 . . . . **33** B1
Maghull L31 . . . . **20** E2
Warrington WA2 . . . . **61** B3
Ennerdale Cl
Formby L37 . . . .**9** D3
Kirkby L33 . . . . **29** C5
Ennerdale Ct CH45 . . . . . . **50** F8
Ennerdale Dr
Bootle L21 . . . . **38** D8
Ormskirk L39 . . . . **13** B2
Ennerdale Rd
Birkenhead CH43 . . . . **65** E1
Formby L37 . . . .**9** E3
Liverpool L9 . . . . **39** D6
Wallasey CH45 . . . . **50** F8
Ennerdale St **3** L3 . . . . . **52** D4
Ennis Cl L24 . . . . **83** D2
Ennis Ct L11 . . . . **40** B3
Ennisdale Dr CH48 . . . . . . **63** D2
Ennismore Gdns PR9 . . . . . .**1** C3
Ennismore Rd
Crosby L23 . . . . **26** C5
Liverpool L13 . . . . **53** F3
Ennis Rd L12 . . . . **54** E6
Ensor St L20 . . . . **38** B1
Enstone WN8 . . . . **16** C1
Enstone Ave L21 . . . . **27** A1
Enstone Rd L25 . . . . **82** B7
Ensworth Rd L18 . . . . **69** B5
Enterprise Way L15 . . . . . **53** E1
Enterprise Workshops
L33 . . . . **30** B1
Epping Cl L35 . . . . **57** D2
Epping Ct CH60 . . . . **77** A1
Epping Gr L15 . . . . **69** B6
Epsom Cl L10 . . . . **28** E1
Epsom Dr WN2 . . . . **35** F7
Epsom Gr L33 . . . . **30** A6
Epsom Rd CH46 . . . . **49** F3
Epsom St WA9 . . . . **44** F4
Epsom Way L5 . . . . **52** D5
Epstein Ct **5** L6 . . . . **53** B3
Epworth Cl
Birkenhead CH43 . . . . **66** A6
Burtonwood WA5 . . . . **59** F7
Epworth St L6, L7 . . . . **52** F2
Eremon Cl L9 . . . . **39** D8
Erfurt Ave CH63 . . . . **79** A4
Erica Ct CH60 . . . . **76** E1
Eric Fountain Rd CH65 . . . **89** D3
Eric Gr CH44 . . . . **51** A4
Eric Rd CH44 . . . . **51** A4
Ericson Dr PR8 . . . .**5** A3
Eridge St L8 . . . . **68** A3
Erin Cl L8 . . . . **67** E6
Erl St L9 . . . . **39** A6
Ermine Cres L5 . . . . **52** F7
Ernest Cookson Sch
L13 . . . . **54** A6
Errington Ct L17 . . . . **80** F8
Errington St L5 . . . . **52** C6
Errol St L17 . . . . **68** B3
Erskine Cl WA11 . . . . **44** E6
Erskine Ind Est **5** L6 . . . . **52** F3
Erskine Rd CH44 . . . . **51** C3
Erskine St Ind Est 4
L7. . . . . **53** A2
Erskine St L6 . . . . **52** F2
Erylmore Rd L18 . . . . **69** A1
Escolme Dr CH49 . . . . **64** E3
Escor Rd L25 . . . . **70** A6
Escort Cl L25 . . . . **82** C9
Eshelby Cl L22 . . . . **26** F1
Esher Cl
Bebington CH62 . . . . **79** B8
Birkenhead CH43 . . . . **65** C7
Eshe Rd L23 . . . . **26** C4
Eshe Rd N L23 . . . . **26** C4
Esher Rd
Bebington CH62 . . . . **79** B8
Liverpool L6 . . . . **53** C3
Eskbank WN8 . . . . **24** C8
Eskbrook WN8 . . . . **16** C1
Eskburn Rd L13 . . . . **53** E6
Eskdale WN8 . . . . **24** B8
Eskdale Ave
Bebington CH62 . . . . **88** E5
Ormskirk L39 . . . . **13** C2
St Helens WA11 . . . . **44** B8
Wallasey CH46 . . . . **49** C1
Warrington WA2 . . . . **61** C3
Eskdale Dr
Formby L37 . . . .**9** D2
Maghull L31 . . . . **20** E2
Eskdale Rd
Ashton-in-M WN4 . . . . **35** B4
Liverpool L9 . . . . **39** A6
Esk St L20 . . . . **52** B8
Eslington St L19 . . . . **81** A7
Esmond St L6 . . . . **53** B5
Esonwood Rd L35 . . . . **56** D3
Espin St **3** L4 . . . . **38** F1

Esplanade
Birkenhead CH42 67 B2
Southport PR8 3 F7
Esplanade The
Birkenhead CH42 67 B1
4 Bootle L20 38 C3
Seaforth L22 37 D8
Esplen Ave L23 26 F5
Essex Rd
Huyton-w-R L36 56 B4
Southport PR8 8 A8
West Kirby CH48 63 C3
Essex St L8 67 F5
Essex Way L20 38 D4
Esthwaite Ave WA11 44 C8
Estuary Banks L24 81 F4
Estuary Bvd L24 81 F4
Estuary Commerce Pk L24 81 F4
Etal Cl 3 L11 40 B1
Ethelbert Rd CH47 63 C8
Ethel Rd CH44 51 D3
Etna St L13 53 F3
Eton Ct
Liverpool L18 69 D5
Southport PR9 1 C1
Eton Dr
Aintree L10 28 D2
Heswall CH63 86 F6
Eton Hall Dr WA9 58 C7
Eton St L4 38 F1
Eton Way WN5 25 F8
Etruria St L19 81 C4
Etruscan Rd L13 54 A4
Ettington Dr PR8 7 A5
Ettington Rd L4 53 B7
Ettrick Cl L33 29 D6
Eurolink WA9 57 F4
Europa Bvd
Birkenhead CH41 66 E6
Warrington WA5 60 D3
Euston Gr CH43 66 C5
Euston St L4 38 F2
Evans Cl WA11 45 F7
Evans Rd
Hoylake CH47 63 B7
Liverpool L24 82 C6
Evans St L34 56 D7
Evellynne Cl L32 29 D2
Evelyn Ave
Prescot L34 56 E6
St Helens WA9 44 E3
Evelyn Com Prim Sch L34 56 E7
Evelyn Rd CH44 51 C3
Evelyn St
Liverpool L5 52 D6
St Helens WA9 44 E3
Evenson Way L13 54 A4
Evenwood
Skelmersdale WN8 16 D1
5 St Helens WA9 58 C6
Evenwood Ct WN8 16 C1
Everard Rd PR8 4 D4
Everdon Wood L33 29 F3
Evered Ave L9 39 A4
Everest Rd
Birkenhead CH42 66 D2
Crosby L23 26 E4
Evergreen Cl
Birkenhead CH49 64 E6
Liverpool L27 70 E6
Evergreens The L37 9 D4
Evergreen Way WA9 59 A7
Everite Rd WA8 84 B7
Everite Road Ind Est WA8 84 B7
Everleigh Cl CH43 65 B7
Eversleigh Dr CH63 79 A4
Eversley
Skelmersdale WN8 16 D1
Widnes WA8 72 B2
Eversley Pk CH43 66 B3
Eversley St L8 68 A7
EVERTON 52 F5
Everton Brow L3, L5 52 E4
Everton Gr WA11 44 D5
Everton Rd
Liverpool L6 52 F4
Southport PR8 4 A4
Everton St WN4 34 D5
Everton Valley L4, L5 52 E7
Everton View L20 38 B2
Every St L6 53 B4
Evesham Cl L25 69 F2
Evesham Rd
Liverpool L4 39 D1
Wallasey CH45 50 F6
Evington WN8 16 D1
Ewanville L36 55 E1
Ewart Rd
Huyton-w-R L16 70 A8
Seaforth L21 38 A7
St Helens WA11 44 B6
Ewden Cl L16 69 E7
Exchange Pas E 2 L2 90 A4
Exchange Pas W 1 L2 90 A4
Exchange Pl L35 57 C3
Exchange St E L2 90 A4
Exchange St W 4 L2 90 A3
Exchange St 8 WA10 44 A3
Exeley L35 56 E2
Exeter Cl L10 28 E1
Exeter Rd
Bootle L20 38 C2
Wallasey CH44 51 C5
Exeter St WA10 43 D3
Exford Rd L12 54 D8
Exmoor Cl
Heswall CH61 76 F5
Southport PR9 2 B6
Exmouth Cl CH41 66 D6
Exmouth Gdns 3 CH41 66 D6
Exmouth St CH41 66 D6
Exmouth Way
1 Birkenhead CH41 66 D6
Burtonwood WA5 59 F6
Express Ind Est WA8 84 A7
Expressway Bsns Pk 10 CH42 66 F3
Extension View WA9 58 D8

F

FACT (Mus) L1 90 C2
Factory La WA8 73 B3
Factory Row WA10 43 E1
Fairacre Rd L19 81 A8
Fairacres Rd CH63 79 A4
Fairbairn Rd L22 26 E1
Fairbank St L15 68 E7
Fairbeech Ct CH43 65 C7
Fairbeech Mews CH43 65 C7
Fairbourne Cl WA5 60 E3
Fairbrook Dr CH41 50 E1
Fairbrother Cres WA2 61 D2
Fairburn WN8 16 B3
Fairburn Cl WA8 73 E3
Fairburn Rd L13 53 E6
Fairclough Cl L35 57 B3
Fairclough Cres WA11 45 A6
Fairclough La CH43 66 B4
Fairclough Rd
Huyton-w-R L36 55 C5
Rainhill L35 57 B3
St Helens WA10 43 C4
Fairclough St
Burtonwood WA5 59 E6
Liverpool L1 90 B3
Newton-le-W WA12 46 B3
Fairfax Pl L11 39 D2
Fairfax Rd
Birkenhead CH41 66 E4
Liverpool L11 39 E2
FAIRFIELD 53 E3
Fairfield L23 26 E4
Fairfield Ave L14, L36 55 A2
Fairfield Cl
Huyton-w-R L36 55 A2
Ormskirk L39 13 E7
Fairfield Cres
Birkenhead CH46 64 D8
Huyton-w-R L36 55 A2
Liverpool L6 53 D4
Fairfield Dr
Ormskirk L39 13 E7
West Kirby CH48 63 E3
Fairfield Gdns WA11 32 E2
Fairfield High Sch WA8 73 B3
Fairfield Hospl WA11 32 E2
Fairfield Inf Sch WA8 73 B2
Fairfield Jun Sch WA8 73 B2
Fairfield Rd
Birkenhead CH42 66 E2
Southport PR8 7 C5
St Helens WA10 43 D5
Widnes WA8 73 B2
Fairfield St L7 53 E3
Fairford Cres L14 54 B4
Fairford Rd L14 54 B4
Fairhaven
Kirkby L33 29 E5
Skelmersdale WN8 16 C3
Fairhaven Cl CH42 66 F2
Fairhaven Dr CH63 88 C5
Fairhaven Rd
Southport PR9 2 B4
Widnes WA8 73 C2
Fairholme L19 80 F6
Fairholme Ave
Ashton-in-M WN4 35 B4
Eccleston Park L34 57 A6
Neston CH64 86 D1
Fairholme Cl L12 54 A8
Fairholme Mews L23 26 E4
Fairholme Rd L23 26 E4
Fairhurst Terr 10 L34 56 E6
Fairlawn Cl CH63 88 A6
Fairlawn Ct CH43 65 F5
Fairlawne Cl 9 L33 29 E5
Fairlie WN8 16 C3
Fairlie Cres L20 38 D7
Fairlie Dr L35 57 D2
Fairmead Rd
Liverpool L11 39 E2
Wallasey CH46 49 F1
Fairoak Cl CH43 65 C7
Fairoak Mews CH43 65 C7
Fairstead WN8 16 C3
Fairthorn Wlk L33 30 A3
Fair View WN5 33 D5
Fairview Ave CH45 51 B5
Fair View Ave WN5 33 D5
Fairview Cl
Ashton-in-M WN4 35 B4
Birkenhead CH43 66 B3
Fair View Pl 3 L8 68 A4
Fairview Rd CH43 66 B3
Fairview Way CH61 76 F3
Fairway
Huyton-w-R L36 56 A4
Southport PR9 1 C2
St Helens WA10 43 C5
Fairway Cres CH62 79 D4
Fairway Ct CH47 63 A6
Fairway N CH62 79 D3
Fairways
Bebington CH42 78 B8
Birkenhead CH43 65 E5
Crosby L23 26 D5
Fairway S CH62 79 D3
Fairways Cl L25 82 B9
Fairways Ct L37 9 C5
Fairways The
Garswood WN4 34 D2
Liverpool L25 82 D9
Skelmersdale WN8 16 D3
West Kirby CH48 75 D6
Fairway The L12 54 D4
Fairway Trad Est WA8 84 E6
Faith Prim Sch L5 52 E4
Falcon Cres L27 70 F4
Falcondale Rd WA2 61 B6
Falconers Gn WA5 60 B2
Falconer St L20 38 A6
Falconhall Rd L9 39 F4
Falcon Hey L10 40 A6
Falcon Rd CH41, CH43 66 C4
Falkirk Ave WA8 72 F3
Falkland WN8 16 C3
Falkland Dr WN4 34 C4
Falkland Rd
Southport PR8 4 D5
Wallasey CH44 51 D4
Falklands App L11 39 E2
Falkland St
Birkenhead CH41 66 A8
Liverpool L3 52 F2
Falkner Sq L8 68 A7
Falkner St L1, L7, L8 67 F8
Fallbrook Dr L12 40 B1
Fallow Cl 6 WA9 58 C4
Fallowfield L33 29 E4
Fallowfield Rd L15 69 A6
Fallows Way L35 71 C8
Falmouth Dr WA5 74 E3
Falmouth Rd L11 40 D5
Falstaff St L20 52 C8
Faraday Rd
Knowsley L33 41 B7
Liverpool L13 53 E1
Faraday St L5 53 A5
Farefield Ave WA3 35 F2
Fareham Cl CH49 64 D6
Fareham Rd L7 53 D2
Faringdon Cl L25 82 B7
Farley Ave CH62 79 C1
Farley La WN8 16 F3
Farlow Rd CH42 66 F1
Farmbrook Rd L25 70 B7
Farm Cl
Birkenhead CH49 64 C4
Southport PR9 5 A8
St Helens WA9 58 D3
Farmdale Cl L18 69 B2
Farmdale Dr L31 20 E1
Far Meadow La CH61 76 D7
Farmer Pl L20 38 E7
Farmer's La WA5 60 A6
Farmfield Dr CH43 65 C7
Farm Meadow Rd WN5 25 E5
FAR MOOR 25 D4
Far Moss Rd L23 26 B6
Farm Pk★ L39 11 F1
Farm Rd WA9 58 D3
Farmside CH46 49 F3
Farm View L21 27 B2
Farmview Cl L27 70 C7
Farm Way WA12 46 E1
Farnborough Gr L26 70 F1
Farnborough Rd PR8 7 F8
Farnborough Road Inf & Jun Schs PR8 8 A8
Farndale WA8 73 A5
Farndale Cl WA5 74 F7
Farndale Gr WN4 35 C2
Farndon Ave
St Helens WA9 58 B4
Wallasey CH45 50 E6
Farndon Dr CH48 63 E3
Farndon Way CH43 65 F4
Farnham Cl L32 29 F1
Farnside Ct L17 80 F7
FARNWORTH 73 A3
Farnworth Ave CH46 49 F4
Farnworth CE Prim Sch WA8 73 A4
Farnworth Cl WA8 73 B4
Farnworth Ct WA8 73 B3
Farnworth Gr 7 L33 29 E5
Farnworth Rd WA5 74 C4
Farnworth St
Liverpool L6 53 B3
St Helens WA9 44 C4
Widnes WA8 73 B4
Farrar St L13 53 E7
Farrell Cl L31 29 B4
Farr Hall Dr CH60 85 E7
Farr Hall Rd CH60 85 F8
Farrier Rd L33 30 A2
Farriers Way
Birkenhead CH48 64 B2
Bootle L30 38 F8
Farrier Wlk WA9 58 C4
Farringdon Cl WA9 57 F6
Farringdon Rd WA2 61 B6
Farrington Dr L39 13 E6
Farthing Cl L25 82 B8
Farthingstone Cl L35 57 A6
Fatherside Dr L30 27 C3
Faulkner Cl PR8 7 C6
Faulkner Gdns PR8 7 C6
Faversham Rd L11 39 E3
Fawcett WN8 16 B3
Fawcett Rd L31 20 D3
Fawley Rd
Liverpool L18 69 C2
Rainhill L35 57 E1
FAZAKERLEY 39 D5
Fazakerley Cl L9 39 A4
Fazakerley High Sch L10 39 F7
Fazakerley Prim Sch L10 39 F7
Fazakerley Rd
Liverpool L9 39 A4
Prescot L35 56 E4
Fazakerley St L3 52 B2
Fazakerley Sta L9 39 D7
Fearnhead Cross WA2 61 F2
Fearnley Rd CH41 66 D5
Fearnley Way WA12 46 C1
Fearnside St L7 68 C8
Feather La CH60 85 F8
Feathers The WA10 43 D3
Feeny St WA9 58 B2
Feilden Rd CH63 79 A4
Felcroft Way L33 29 F3
Felicity Gr CH46 49 D1
Fell Gr WA11 44 A8
Fell St
Liverpool L7 53 B2
Wallasey CH44 51 E2
Felltor Cl L25 69 F3
Fell View PR9 2 D6
Fellwood Gr L35 56 E3
Felmersham Ave L11 39 F3
Felspar Rd L32 40 F7
Felstead WN8 16 B2
Felstead Ave L25 70 C2
Felsted Dr L10 28 E1
Felthorpe Cl CH49 65 B7
Felton Cl CH46 64 C8
Felton Ct L17 68 C3
Felton Gr L13 53 F3
Feltons WN8 16 B2
Feltwell Rd L4 53 B6
Feltwood Cl L12 54 F7
Feltwood Manor L12 54 F7
Feltwood Rd L12 54 F8
Feltwood Wlk L12 54 F7
Fendale Ave CH46 50 A1
Fender Ct CH49 65 D1
Fender Hts CH46 50 A1
Fender La CH43, CH46 50 B1
Fender Prim Sch CH49 65 C3
Fenderside Rd CH43 65 C8
Fender View Rd CH46 65 A8
Fender Way
Birkenhead CH43 65 B7
Heswall CH61 77 A4
Fenham Dr WA5 74 F4
Fenney Ct WN8 16 C1
Fenton Cl
Liverpool, Warbreck Pk L30 39 B8
Speke L24 82 D4
St Helens WA10 43 F4
Widnes WA8 72 C3
Fenton Gn L24 82 D3
Fenwick St L2 90 A3
Ferguson Ave CH49 64 D3
Ferguson Dr WA2 61 D1
Ferguson Rd
Litherland L21 27 C1
Liverpool L11 53 E8
Fern Ave WA12 46 D2
Fern Bank
Maghull L31 20 E1
Rainford WA11 31 E7
Fernbank Ave L36 55 D2
Fernbank Dr L30 28 A4
Fernbank La CH49 64 F7
Fern Cl
Kirkby L33 29 F4
Liverpool L27 70 E4
Skelmersdale WN8 15 E1
Ferndale WN8 16 C2
Ferndale Ave
Birkenhead CH48 64 B1
Wallasey CH44 51 C4
Ferndale Cl
Bold Heath WA8 73 E7
Liverpool L9 39 A7
Ferndale Rd
Crosby L22 26 E2
Hoylake CH47 63 B8
Liverpool L15 68 E6
Fern Gdns L34 56 F7
Fern Gr
Birkenhead CH43 65 D4
Bootle L20 38 C4
Liverpool L8 68 C6
Fern Hey L23 27 B5
Fernhill 10 CH45 51 B8
Fernhill Ave L20 38 E3
Fernhill Cl L20 38 E3
Fernhill Dr L8 68 A6
Fernhill Gdns L20 38 E3
Fernhill Mews E L20 38 E3
Fernhill Mews W L20 38 E3
Fernhill Rd L20 38 E4
Fernhill Sports Ctr L20 38 D6
Fernhill Way L20 38 E3
Fernhill Wlk WA9 58 C3
Fernhurst Gate L39 13 B1
Fernhurst Rd L32 29 C1
Fernie Cres L8 67 F5
Fernlea Ave WA9 57 D7
Fernlea Gr WN4 34 D5
Fernlea Mews 5 CH43 65 C8
Fernlea Rd CH60 86 A8
Fernleigh Rd L13 54 B3
Fernley Rd PR8 4 A5
Fern Lo L8 68 C6
Ferns Cl CH60 76 C1
Ferns Rd CH63 78 D5
Fernwood Dr L26 82 E9
Fernwood Rd L17 68 E3
Ferny Brow Rd CH49 65 B3
Ferny Knoll Rd WA11 23 F4
Ferrer St WN4 34 F6
Ferrey Rd L10 40 A7
Ferries Cl CH62 79 B8
Ferry Rd CH62 89 A6
Ferryside CH44 51 E2
Ferryside La PR9 2 C5
Ferry View Rd CH44 51 E2
Festival Ave WA2 61 D2
Festival Cres WA2 61 D2
Festival Ct L11 40 B3
Festival Rd WA11 32 A5
Ffrancon Dr CH63 78 F7
FIDDLER'S FERRY 2 D6
Fiddler's Ferry Rd WA8 73 D1
Fidler St WA10 43 D1
Field Ave L21 38 A8
Field Cl
Bebington CH62 79 C8
St Helens WA9 58 D3
Fieldfare Cl
Golborne WA3 47 D8
Liverpool L25 70 A5
Fieldgate WA8 84 B6
Field Hey La CH64 88 B1
Field Ho L12 54 A7
Fielding St L6 53 A3
Fieldings The L31 20 B4
Field La
Litherland L21 38 A8
Liverpool L10 40 B7
Fieldlands PR8 5 A2
Field Rd
St Helens WA9 58 D3
Wallasey CH45 51 B7
Field's End L36 70 E8
Fieldsend Cl L27 70 E4
Fieldside Rd CH42 66 E2
Field St
Liverpool L3 52 E3
Skelmersdale WN8 15 D2
Fieldton Rd L11 40 B3
Fieldview 2 WN8 25 A7
Field View L21 27 A1
Fieldview Dr WA2 61 C1
Fieldway
Bebington CH63 78 D8
Heswall CH60 77 C1
Hoylake CH47 63 F7
Huyton-w-R L36 70 F8
Liverpool L15 69 C8
Maghull L31 28 E7
Wallasey CH45 51 A5
Widnes WA8 73 E2
Field Way L35 57 C5
Fieldway Ct CH41 66 C8
Field Wlk
Crosby L23 27 B5
Ormskirk L39 14 B5
Fifth Ave
Aintree L9 39 D7
Birkenhead CH43 65 B7
Liverpool, Fazakerley L9 39 E7
Filbert Cl L33 29 F6
Filby Gdns WA9 57 E6
Fillmore Gr WA8 72 F3
Filton Rd L14 55 B6
Finborough Rd L4 39 C1
FINCHAM 55 B5
Fincham Cl L14 55 B5
Fincham Gn L14 55 B5
Fincham Rd L14 55 A5
Fincham Sq L14 55 A5
Finch Ave WA11 32 A5
Finch Cl WA9 58 D3
Finch Ct CH41 66 D7
Finchdean Cl 3 CH49 64 C4
Finch Dene L14 54 F6
Finch La
Halewood L26 83 B7
Huyton-w-R L14 55 A6
Liverpool, Mill Yard L14 54 F5
Finch Lea Dr L14 55 A5
Finchley Dr WA11 44 C7
Finchley Rd L4 53 B7
Finch Meadow Cl L9 39 F4
Finch Pl L3 52 F2
Finch Rd L14 55 A6
Finch Way L14 54 F5
Findlay Cl WA12 46 C2
Findley Dr CH46 49 F3
Findon WN8 16 C2
Findon Rd L32 40 F8
Fine Jane's Way PR9 5 B8
Fingall Rd L15 69 B6
Finger House La WA8 58 D1
FINGER POST 44 D3
Fingland Rd L15 68 E7
Finlan Rd WA8 84 F7
Finlay Ave WA5 74 E3
Finlay Ct L30 27 F4
Finlay St L6 53 C3

Finney Gr WA11 . . . . 45 E6
Finney The CH48 . . . . 75 D6
Finningley Ct WA2 . . . . 61 E1
Finsbury Pk WA8 . . . . 73 C5
Finstall Rd CH63 . . . . 79 A2
Finvoy Rd L13 . . . . 53 E7
Fiona Wlk L10 . . . . 40 B7
Fir Ave L26 . . . . 83 A8
Firbeck WN8 . . . . 16 C1
Firbrook Ct CH43 . . . . 50 C1
Fir Cl L26 . . . . 83 A8
Fir Cotes L31 . . . . 20 E1
Firdale Rd L9 . . . . 39 A4
Firdene Cres CH43 . . . . 65 E4
Fire Station Rd L35 . . . . 56 F5
Firethorne Rd L26 . . . . 70 D2
Fir Gr L9 . . . . 39 C8
Fir La L15 . . . . 69 A7
Firman Cl WA5 . . . . 60 B1
Fir Rd L22 . . . . 26 E2
Firs Ave CH63 . . . . 78 F3
Firs Cl L37 . . . . 9 D5
Firscraig L28 . . . . 55 C7
Firs Cres L37 . . . . 9 D5
Firshaw Rd CH47 . . . . 48 C1
Firs La L39 . . . . 12 E3
Firs Link L37 . . . . 9 D4
Fir St
 Southport PR8 . . . . .4 F6
 St Helens WA10 . . . . 57 D8
 Widnes WA8 . . . . 73 C2
First Ave
 Aintree L9 . . . . 39 C7
 Birkenhead CH43 . . . . 65 C6
 Crosby L23 . . . . 26 D4
 Liverpool, Fazakerley L9 . . 39 E6
 Rainhill L35 . . . . 57 B4
Firstone Gr L32 . . . . 40 E8
Firswood Rd L40, WN8 . . . . 15 C3
Firthland Way WA9 . . . . 44 F2
Fir Tree Ave WA3 . . . . 47 F8
Fir Tree Cl
 Crank WA11 . . . . 32 F7
 Skelmersdale WN8 . . . . . . 24 D7
Fir Tree Dr N L12 . . . . 40 E4
Fir Tree Dr S L12 . . . . 40 E3
Fir Tree La
 Burtonwood WA5 . . . . 60 A7
 Haskayne L39 . . . . 12 F3
 Ormskirk L39 . . . . 13 A2
Fir Tree Wlk WA3 . . . . 47 F8
Fir Way CH60 . . . . 86 B5
Firwood WN8 . . . . 16 D3
Firwood Gr WN4 . . . . 35 A2
Fisher Ave
 Abram Brow WN2 . . . . 36 C7
 Prescot L35 . . . . 56 D2
 Warrington WA2 . . . . 61 B2
Fisher Dr
 Orrell WN5 . . . . 25 E7
 Southport PR9 . . . . .4 F7
Fishermans Cl L37 . . . . .9 E6
Fisher Pl L37 . . . . 56 D2
Fishers La CH61 . . . . 76 F4
Fisher St
 Liverpool L8 . . . . 67 D6
 St Helens WA9 . . . . 58 E8
Fishguard Cl **2** L6 . . . . . . 52 F4
Fishwicks Ind Est
 Haydock WA11 . . . . 45 F8
 St Helens WA9 . . . . 58 D8
Fistral Cl L10 . . . . 40 B6
Fistral Dr WA10 . . . . 43 B6
Fitzclarence Way L6 . . . . . . 52 F7
Fitzgerald Rd L13 . . . . 54 A3
Fitzpatrick Ct L3 . . . . 52 C4
Fitzroy Way **14** L6 . . . . . . 53 A3
Fiveways L35 . . . . 43 A4
Five Ways CH64 . . . . 86 F3
Fiveways Pk CH64 . . . . 86 F3
Flail Cl CH49 . . . . 64 C4
Flambards CH49 . . . . 65 B3
Flamstead WN8 . . . . 16 C1
Flander Cl WA8 . . . . 72 C2
Flatfield Way L31 . . . . 20 E1
Flatman's La L39 . . . . 11 E1
Flatt La CH43 . . . . 65 F3
Flawn Rd L11 . . . . 53 E8
Flaxfield Rd L37 . . . . 10 A3
Flaxhill CH46 . . . . 49 D1
Flaxman St **8** L7 . . . . 53 C2
Flaxton WN8 . . . . 16 C1
Flaybrick Cl CH43 . . . . 65 E8
Fleck La CH48 . . . . 63 D1
Fleetcroft Rd CH49 . . . . 65 A2
Fleet La WA9 . . . . 44 E2
Fleet St L1 . . . . 90 B3
Fleetwood Cl PR9 . . . . .1 F3
Fleetwood Cotts L30 . . . . . . 27 E4
Fleetwood Ct PR9 . . . . .1 D1
Fleetwood Dr WA12 . . . . . . 46 B4
Fleetwood Gdns L33 . . . . . . 29 F5
Fleetwood Pl L25 . . . . 69 F2
Fleetwood Rd PR9 . . . . .1 E3
Fleetwood's La L30 . . . . 27 D4
Fleming Ct L3 . . . . 52 C4
Fleming Dr
 Ashton-in-M WN4 . . . . 35 D4
 Winwick WA2 . . . . 61 A6
Fleming Ho L17 . . . . 68 C3
Fleming Rd L24 . . . . 82 C7
Flemington Ave L4 . . . . 39 D1
Fleming Way CH46 . . . . 50 A2
Fletcher Ave
 Birkenhead CH42 . . . . 66 E2

Fletcher Ave continued
 Prescot L34 . . . . 56 E7
Fletcher Cl CH49 . . . . 65 A3
Fletcher Dr L19 . . . . 81 A7
Flimby WN8 . . . . 16 D1
Flint Dr L12 . . . . 40 D1
Flintshire Gdns WA10 . . . . . 43 F2
Flint St L1 . . . . 90 B1
Floodgates Rd L38 . . . . 17 F5
Floral Wood L17 . . . . 68 A2
Flora Mans L6 . . . . 53 C3
Flora St WN4 . . . . 35 B2
Flordon WN8 . . . . 16 D2
Florence Ave CH60 . . . . 76 F1
Florence Cl L9 . . . . 38 F3
Florence Ct L9 . . . . 38 F3
Florence Melly Com Prim
 Sch L4 . . . . 39 C1
Florence Nightingale Cl
 L30 . . . . 27 F4
Florence Rd CH44 . . . . 51 E3
Florence St
 Birkenhead CH41 . . . . 66 D6
 Liverpool L4 . . . . 52 F8
 St Helens L35 . . . . 57 C7
Florentine Rd L13 . . . . 54 A4
Florey Ho L17 . . . . 68 C3
Florida Ct L19 . . . . 81 B8
Florida Way L35 . . . . 56 D4
Flowermead Cl CH47 . . . . . . 48 F1
Fluker's Brook La L34 . . . . . 41 B2
Flyde Road Ind Est PR9 . . . . .2 B4
Foinavon Cl L9 . . . . 38 F7
Folds La WA11 . . . . 44 B7
Folds Rd WA11 . . . . 44 F5
Fold St WA3 . . . . 36 A1
Folds The CH63 . . . . 87 A6
Foley Cl L4 . . . . 52 E7
Foley St L4 . . . . 52 E7
Folkestone Rd PR8 . . . . .4 F3
Folly La CH44 . . . . 50 E5
Fontenoy St L3 . . . . 90 B4
Fonthill Cl L4 . . . . 52 D7
Fonthill Rd L4 . . . . 52 D8
FORD 27 C2
Ford Ave L33 . . . . 29 E6
Ford Cl
 Birkenhead CH49 . . . . 65 B4
 Bootle L20 . . . . 38 E7
 Litherland L21 . . . . 27 B2
Fordcombe Rd L25 . . . . 70 C4
Ford Dr CH49 . . . . 65 B5
Fordham Cl PR8 . . . . .4 E3
Fordham St L4 . . . . 52 E8
Fordhill View CH46 . . . . 65 A8
Ford La
 Birkenhead CH49 . . . . 65 B5
 Litherland L21 . . . . 27 B3
Fordland Cl L12 . . . . 54 A8
Fordlea Rd L12 . . . . 54 A8
Fordlea Way L12 . . . . 54 B8
Ford Rd
 Birkenhead CH49 . . . . 65 A5
 Prescot L35 . . . . 56 F6
Ford St L3 . . . . 52 C3
Ford View L21 . . . . 27 B3
Ford Way CH49 . . . . 65 B4
Ford Way Mews CH49 . . . . . 65 B4
Forefield Inf Sch L23 . . . . . . 27 A4
Forefield Jun Sch L23 . . . . . 27 A4
Forefield La L23 . . . . 27 A4
Foreland Cl WA5 . . . . 74 C7
Forest Cl
 Hoylake CH47 . . . . 48 D1
 Prescot L34 . . . . 56 F7
Forest Ct CH43 . . . . 65 F6
Forest Dr
 Huyton-w-R L36 . . . . 55 C3
 Skelmersdale WN8 . . . . . . 16 C3
Forest Gn L12 . . . . 54 B8
Forest Gr L34 . . . . 56 F7
Forest Lawn L12 . . . . 54 B8
Forest Mead WA10 . . . . 43 A3
Forest Rd
 Birkenhead CH43 . . . . 66 A6
 Heswall CH60 . . . . 86 A8
 Hoylake CH47 . . . . 48 D1
 Southport PR8 . . . . .4 D6
 St Helens WA9 . . . . 58 A2
Forfar Rd L13 . . . . 53 D6
Forge Cl
 Cronton WA8 . . . . 72 C5
 Westhead L40 . . . . 14 E4
Forge Cotts **6** L17 . . . . . . 68 C4
Forge Rd WA5 . . . . 74 F5
Forge St L20 . . . . 52 C8
Formby
 Formby L37 . . . . 10 B2
 Haskayne L39 . . . . 12 F1
Formby Lo **6** L23 . . . . 26 C3
Formby Point Cvn Pk
 L37 . . . . .9 B1
Formby Rd WA10 . . . . 43 D1
Formby St L37 . . . . .9 E2
Formby Sta L37 . . . . .9 E2
Formosa Dr L10 . . . . 39 F7
Formosa Rd L10 . . . . 39 F6
Formosa Way L10 . . . . 39 F7

Fornalls Green La
 CH47 . . . . 63 E7
Forres Gr WN4 . . . . 34 D4
Forrester Ave L35 . . . . 57 C7
Forresters Cl WN2 . . . . 36 E8
Forrest St L1 . . . . 90 B2
Forshaw Ave WA10 . . . . 57 C8
Forshaw's La WA5 . . . . 59 E8
Forster St WA3 . . . . 36 A1
Forsythia Cl L9 . . . . 39 C3
Forthlin Rd L18 . . . . 69 C1
Forth St L20 . . . . 52 C8
Forton Lo **3** L23 . . . . 26 C4
Fort St CH45 . . . . 51 C7
Forwood Rd CH62 . . . . 88 D8
Foscote Rd L33 . . . . 30 A4
Foster Cl L35 . . . . 57 A5
Foster Rd L37 . . . . .9 D2
Fosters Cl PR9 . . . . .5 B8
Fosters Gr WA11 . . . . 44 F5
FOSTERS GREEN 16 D3
Fosters Green Rd WN8 . . . . 16 D3
Fosters Rd WA11 . . . . 44 F6
Foster St
 Liverpool L20 . . . . 52 C7
 Widnes WA8 . . . . 73 B1
Foul La PR8, PR9 . . . . .5 A5
Foundry La WA8 . . . . 84 C5
Foundry St
 Newton-le-W WA12 . . . . . . 46 B3
 St Helens WA9 . . . . 44 A3
Fountain Ct L23 . . . . 26 A5
Fountain Rd
 Knowsley L34 . . . . 41 D3
 12 Wallasey CH45 . . . . . 51 B7
Fountains Ave WA11 . . . . . . 45 F7
Fountains Cl L4 . . . . 52 F7
Fountains Ct **4** L4 . . . . . . 52 D7
Fountains Rd L4 . . . . 52 D7
Fountain St
 Birkenhead CH42 . . . . 66 D3
 St Helens WA9 . . . . 57 C6
Fountains The L39 . . . . 13 E6
Fountains Way L37 . . . . 10 B2
Four Acre Dr L21 . . . . 27 B2
Four Acre La L35 . . . . 58 C4
Four Acre Lane Sh Ctr
 WA9 . . . . 58 B4
Fouracres L31 . . . . 28 B7
Four Lane Ends WA9 . . . . . . 57 F7
Four Lanes End CH63 . . . . . 87 D5
Fourth Ave
 Aintree L9 . . . . 39 D7
 Birkenhead CH43 . . . . 65 B6
 Liverpool, Fazakerley L9 . . 39 E7
Fowell Rd CH45 . . . . 51 B8
Fowler Cl **7** L7 . . . . 53 C1
Fox Bank Cl WA8 . . . . 74 F1
Foxcote WA8 . . . . 72 B2
Fox Cover Rd CH60 . . . . 86 D7
Foxcovers Rd CH63 . . . . . . 79 A3
Foxdale Cl
 Birkenhead CH43 . . . . 66 A5
 Southport PR8 . . . . .4 E3
Foxdale Rd L15 . . . . 68 F6
Foxdell Cl L13 . . . . 54 A2
Foxes Ct **6** CH43 . . . . 66 B5
Foxes The CH61 . . . . 77 A6
Foxfield Cl WA2 . . . . 61 E3
Foxfield Rd CH47 . . . . 63 D8
Foxfield Sch CH46 . . . . 64 D8
Foxfold WN8 . . . . 16 D3
Foxglove Ave L26 . . . . 70 E1
Foxglove Cl
 2 Golborne WA3 . . . . . . 47 D8
 Liverpool L9 . . . . 39 A4
Foxglove Rd CH41 . . . . 65 F7
Fox Hey Rd CH44 . . . . 50 F4
Foxhill Cl
 Formby L37 . . . . .9 C3
 Liverpool L8 . . . . 68 A6
Foxhill La L26 . . . . 70 E2
Foxhouse La L31 . . . . 20 F1
Foxhunter Dr L9 . . . . 39 C8
Foxleigh L26 . . . . 70 E1
Foxley Heath WA8 . . . . 84 E8
Fox Pl WA10 . . . . 44 A4
Fox's Bank La L35 . . . . 71 F7
Foxshaw Cl L35 . . . . 56 D1
Fox St
 Birkenhead CH41 . . . . 66 C6
 Liverpool L3, L5 . . . . 52 C4
Foxton Cl
 St Helens WA11 . . . . 44 D5
 Wallasey CH46 . . . . 49 B1
Foxwood
 Liverpool L12 . . . . 54 E8
 St Helens L35 . . . . 57 C7
Foxwood Cl
 Orrell WN5 . . . . 25 E5
 West Kirby CH48 . . . . 63 E3
Foy St **2** WN4 . . . . 35 B3
Frailey Cl PR8 . . . . .7 C4
Frampton Rd L4 . . . . 39 D2
Frances Ct **2** L17 . . . . 68 C4
Francine Cl L3 . . . . 52 C5
Francis Ave
 Birkenhead CH43 . . . . 66 B6
 Birkenhead, Moreton
 CH46 . . . . 64 D8
Francis Cl
 Rainhill L35 . . . . 57 C4
 Widnes WA8 . . . . 84 C8
Francis St WA9 . . . . 58 F7
Francis Way L16 . . . . 69 D8
FRANKBY 64 A2
Frankby Ave **5** CH44 . . . . 51 A4
Frankby Cl CH49 . . . . 64 B3

Frankby Gr CH49 . . . . 64 F5
Frankby Rd
 Birkenhead CH48,
 CH49 . . . . 64 B3
 Hoylake CH47 . . . . 63 D8
 Liverpool L4 . . . . 53 C8
 West Kirby CH48 . . . . 63 E2
Frankby Stiles CH48 . . . . . . 63 F2
Franklin Gr **3** L33 . . . . . . 29 E6
Franklin Pl **8** L6 . . . . 53 B5
Franklin Rd CH46 . . . . 50 A4
Frank St WA8 . . . . 73 C1
Franton Wlk **2** L32 . . . . . 29 C2
Fraser Rd WA5 . . . . 74 D6
Fraser St L3 . . . . 90 C4
Frawley Ave WA12 . . . . 46 C5
Freckleton Dr L33 . . . . 30 A5
Freckleton Rd
 Southport PR9 . . . . .1 F4
 St Helens WA11 . . . . 43 C1
Freda Ave **4** WA9 . . . . . . 58 C6
Frederick Banting Cl
 L30 . . . . 27 F4
Frederick Gr L15 . . . . 69 A8
Frederick Lunt Ave
 L34 . . . . 41 D3
Frederick St
 Ashton-in-M WN4 . . . . 35 A5
 St Helens WA9 . . . . 58 F8
 Widnes WA8 . . . . 73 B1
Frederick Terr WA8 . . . . 84 A4
Freedom Cl L7 . . . . 68 A4
Freehold St L7 . . . . 53 E3
Freeland St L4 . . . . 52 E7
Freeman St
 Birkenhead CH41 . . . . 66 E7
 Liverpool L7 . . . . 68 C8
Freemantle Ave WA9 . . . . . 57 F7
Freemasons' Row L3 . . . . . . 52 D3
Freemont Rd L12 . . . . 54 A7
Freeport Gr L9 . . . . 39 B7
Freesia Ave L9 . . . . 39 B4
Freme Cl L11 . . . . 40 B3
Frenchfield St WA9 . . . . 58 D3
French St
 St Helens WA10 . . . . 43 D1
 Widnes WA8 . . . . 73 D1
Frensham Cl CH63 . . . . 78 F2
FRESHFIELD 9 E5
Freshfield Cl L36 . . . . 55 C3
Freshfield Ct L37 . . . . .9 E4
Freshfield Cvn Pk L37 . . . . . .9 B6
Freshfield Gdns L37 . . . . . . .9 E4
Freshfield Prim Sch
 L37 . . . . 10 A4
Freshfield Rd
 Formby L37 . . . . .9 E4
 Liverpool L15 . . . . 68 F6
Freshfield Sta L37 . . . . .9 E5
Freshford L L11 . . . . 40 A1
Freshwater Cl WA5 . . . . 74 D7
Friars Ave WA5 . . . . 74 E5
Friars Cl CH63 . . . . 78 F5
Friarsgate Cl L18 . . . . 69 C5
Friar St
 1 Liverpool L5 . . . . 53 A5
 St Helens WA9 . . . . 43 E7
Friars Wlk L37 . . . . 10 B2
Friends La WA5 . . . . 74 D6
Frinsted Rd L11 . . . . 40 A1
Frobisher Rd CH46 . . . . 50 A4
Frodsham Dr WA11 . . . . 44 D5
Frodsham St
 Birkenhead CH41 . . . . 66 E4
 Liverpool L4 . . . . 38 F1
Frogmore Rd L13 . . . . 53 E3
Frome Cl CH61 . . . . 76 D7
Frome Rd L25 . . . . 70 D5
Frome Way L25 . . . . 70 D5
Frontfield Ct WA9 . . . . 44 C2
Frost Dr CH61 . . . . 76 C6
Frost St L7 . . . . 53 C2
Fry St WA9 . . . . 44 F3
Fuchsia Wlk CH49 . . . . 64 C2
Fulbeck WN8 . . . . 16 C2
Fulbrook Cl CH63 . . . . 78 F2
Fulbrook Rd CH63 . . . . 78 F2
Fulford Cl L12 . . . . 54 F6
Fulford Pk CH46 . . . . 64 C6
Fullerton Gr L36 . . . . 55 E4
Fulmar Cl
 Liverpool L27 . . . . 70 E5
 St Helens WA11 . . . . 44 B6
Fulshaw Cl L27 . . . . 70 D6
Fulton Ave CH48 . . . . 63 E3
Fulton St L5 . . . . 52 B6
Fulwood Ave PR8 . . . . .4 D4
Fulwood Cl L17 . . . . 68 D2
Fulwood Dr L17 . . . . 68 C2
Fulwood Pk L17 . . . . 68 D1
Fulwood Rd
 Golborne WA3 . . . . 47 F2
 Liverpool L17 . . . . 68 C2
Fulwood Way L21 . . . . 27 C4
Funchal Ave L37 . . . . .9 D1
Furlong Cl
 Ashton-in-M WN2 . . . . 35 F7
 Liverpool L9 . . . . 39 D8
Furness Ave
 Formby L37 . . . . .9 F3
 Liverpool L12 . . . . 40 C1
 Ormskirk L39 . . . . 13 C4
 St Helens WA10 . . . . 43 E7
Furness Cl
 Birkenhead CH49 . . . . 64 E6
 Southport PR8 . . . . .7 B3
Furness St L4 . . . . 52 E7
Furze Way CH46 . . . . 49 C1

Fylde Rd PR9 . . . . .2 B4

G

Gable Ct L11 . . . . 39 E3
Gable Mews L37 . . . . 10 A1
Gables Cl WA2 . . . . 61 F3
Gable St WA12 . . . . 46 B3
Gables The L23 . . . . 26 B3
Gable View L11 . . . . 39 E3
Gabriel Cl CH46 . . . . 64 F8
Gainford Cl WA8 . . . . 72 C3
Gainford Rd L14 . . . . 55 A6
Gainsborough Ave L31 . . . . 28 B8
Gainsborough Cl L12 . . . . . 54 E5
Gainsborough Ct WA8 . . . . . 72 B1
Gainsborough Rd
 Birkenhead CH49 . . . . 64 F6
 Liverpool L15 . . . . 68 C6
 Southport PR8 . . . . .3 E3
 Wallasey CH45 . . . . 50 E5
Gairloch Cl WA2 . . . . 61 F4
Gaisgill Ct WA8 . . . . 72 C1
Gala Cl **2** L14 . . . . 54 E4
Galbraith Cl **3** L17 . . . . . . 68 C2
Gale Ave WA5 . . . . 60 F1
Galemuele L11 . . . . 40 B3
Gale Rd
 Kirkby L33 . . . . 41 C8
 Litherland L21 . . . . 27 C1
Galion Way WA8 . . . . 72 F3
Gallagher Ind Est CH44 . . . . 51 B2
Galleries The CH45 . . . . 51 A3
Gallery The L37 . . . . .9 F3
Gallopers La CH61 . . . . 77 C6
Galloway Dr WN6 . . . . 25 B6
Galloway Rd L22 . . . . 26 C2
Galloway St L7 . . . . 68 D8
Galston Ave L35 . . . . 57 D2
Galston Cl L33 . . . . 29 E3
Galsworthy Ave L30 . . . . . . 38 E7
Galsworthy Pl L30 . . . . 38 E8
Galsworthy Wlk L30 . . . . . . 38 E7
Galton St L3 . . . . 52 B3
Galtres Ct CH63 . . . . 78 E8
Galtres Pk CH63 . . . . 78 E8
Galway Ave WA8 . . . . 72 E3
Gambier Terr L1 . . . . 67 F7
Gamble Ave WA10 . . . . 43 E6
Gamlin St CH41 . . . . 66 A8
Gamston Wood L32 . . . . . . 29 C1
Ganney's Meadow Rd
 CH49 . . . . 65 C2
Gannock St **6** L7 . . . . 53 C2
Gantley Ave WN5 . . . . 25 D3
Gantley Cres WN5 . . . . 25 D3
Gantley Rd WN5 . . . . 25 D3
Ganton Cl
 Southport PR8 . . . . .4 E3
 Widnes WA8 . . . . 73 B4
Ganworth Cl L24 . . . . 82 E3
Ganworth Rd L24 . . . . 82 E3
Garden Apartments The
 L18 . . . . 68 F3
Garden Cotts L12 . . . . 54 D4
Garden Ct CH42 . . . . 66 C1
Gardeners View L33 . . . . . . 30 A4
Gardeners Way L35 . . . . . . 57 C5
Garden Hey Rd
 Birkenhead CH46 . . . . 64 C6
 Hoylake CH47 . . . . 48 C1
Gardenia Gr L17 . . . . 68 A2
Garden La
 Liverpool, Everton L5 . . . . . 52 F4
 Liverpool L9 . . . . 39 D7
 1 Wallasey CH45 . . . . . 49 E1
Garden Lodge Gr L27 . . . . . 70 D5
Gardenside CH46 . . . . 50 B4
Gardenside St L6 . . . . 52 F3
Gardens Rd CH63 . . . . 79 B5
Garden St L25 . . . . 70 A2
Garden View **14** L20 . . . . 38 C3
Garden Wlk L34 . . . . 56 D6
Gardiner Ave WA11 . . . . . . 45 C6
Gardiners Pl WN8 . . . . 23 E8
Gardner Ave L20 . . . . 38 C7
Gardner Rd
 Formby L37 . . . . 10 B4
 Liverpool L13 . . . . 53 E5
Gardner's Dr L6 . . . . 53 D4
Gardner's Row L3 . . . . 52 D3
Gareth Ave WA11 . . . . 44 B6
Garfield Terr CH49 . . . . 65 A5
Garfourth Cl L19 . . . . 81 D7
Garfourth Rd L19 . . . . 81 D7
Garmoyle Cl L15 . . . . 68 E6
Garmoyle Rd L15 . . . . 68 E6
Garnet St
 Liverpool L13 . . . . 53 F1
 St Helens WA9 . . . . 58 E8
Garnett Ave L4 . . . . 52 E8
Garnett Gn L39 . . . . 13 C4
Garnett Pl WN8 . . . . 24 A7
Garnetts La
 Tarbock Green L35 . . . . . . 71 D1
 Widnes WA8 . . . . 84 A3
Garrick Ave CH46 . . . . 64 C8
Garrick Par PR8 . . . . .4 A6
Garrick Rd CH43 . . . . 77 F8
Garrick St L7 . . . . 68 C7
Garrigill Cl L8 . . . . 68 B6
Garrison Cl L8 . . . . 68 B6
Garrowby Dr L36 . . . . 55 C3
Garsdale Ave L35 . . . . 57 D2
Garsdale Cl WA5 . . . . 74 F7
Garsfield Rd **1** L4 . . . . . . 53 E8
Garside Ave WA3 . . . . 47 D4

Garstang Rd PR9 . . . . 2 A5
GARSTON 81 C5
Garston CE Prim Sch
L19 . . . . 81 D6
Garston Ind Est L19. . . . . . 81 C4
Garston Old Rd L19 . . . . . . 81 C7
Garston Way L19 . . . . 81 C6
GARSWOOD 34 C3
Garswood Ave WA11 . . . . . 32 A7
Garswood Cl
Maghull L31. . . . . 20 E3
Wallasey CH46 . . . . 49 E4
Garswood Cres WN5 . . . . . 33 E4
Garswood Old Rd WA11,
WN4. . . . . 33 E1
Garswood Prim Sch
WN4 . . . . 34 C4
Garswood Rd
Billinge WN5 . . . . 33 F4
Garswood WA11, WN4 . . . . 34 C3
Garswood St
Ashton-in-M WN4 . . . . 35 B3
Liverpool L8. . . . . 67 F3
St Helens WA10. . . . . 44 A4
Garswood Sta WN4 . . . . . . 34 D3
Garter Cl L11 . . . . 40 C3
Garth Bvd CH63. . . . . 78 E8
Garth Ct L22. . . . . 26 E1
Garthdale Rd L18 . . . . 69 B4
Garth Dr L18 . . . . 69 C4
Garthowen Rd L7. . . . . 53 D2
Garth Rd L32 . . . . 41 A8
Garth The
Birkenhead CH43. . . . . 65 F5
Huyton-w-R L36. . . . . 55 E3
Garth Wlk 6 L32 . . . . 41 A8
Garton Dr WA3 . . . . 36 E1
Gartons La WA9 . . . . 58 C3
Garway L25 . . . . 70 C3
Garwood Cl WA5 . . . . 60 C1
Gascoyne St L3. . . . . 52 C3
Gaskell Ct WA9. . . . . 44 F3
Gaskell Rake L30 . . . . 27 D5
Gaskell's Brow WN4 . . . . . 34 E5
Gaskell St WA9 . . . . 44 D2
Gaskill Rd L24 . . . . 82 D5
Gatclif Rd L13 . . . . 53 E7
GATEACRE 70 B5
Gateacre Brow L25 . . . . . . 70 B4
Gateacre Com Comp Sch
L25 . . . . 70 A5
Gateacre Ct L25 . . . . 69 F7
Gateacre Park Dr L25 . . . . 69 F6
Gateacre Rise L25 . . . . 70 B4
Gateacre Vale Rd L25 . . . . 70 B3
Gategill Gr WN5 . . . . 25 D3
Gateside Cl L27 . . . . 70 E5
Gates La L29 . . . . 19 C1
Gateway Complex L19 . . . 81 C5
Gathurst Ct WA8. . . . . 84 D8
Gathurst Rd WN5 . . . . 25 E8
Gatley Dr L31. . . . . 28 E7
Gatley Wlk L24 . . . . 82 F5
Gautby Rd CH41 . . . . 50 E1
Gavin Rd WA8 . . . . 84 B7
Gaw Hill La L39. . . . . 13 B3
Gaw Hill View L39 . . . . . . 13 B3
Gawsworth Cl
Birkenhead CH43. . . . . 65 F3
St Helens WA10. . . . . 43 B3
Gawsworth Rd WA3. . . . . . 35 F1
Gaybeech Cl CH43 . . . . 65 B8
Gayhurst Ave WA2 . . . . 61 F2
Gayhurst Cres L11 . . . . 40 A2
Gaynor Ave WA11. . . . . 45 F7
GAYTON 86 B6
Gayton Ave
Bebington CH63. . . . . 78 C8
Wallasey CH45 . . . . 51 B8
Gayton Farm Rd CH60. . . . 86 A5
Gayton La CH60. . . . . 86 B6
Gayton Mill Cl CH60. . . . . 86 B7
Gayton Parkway CH60. . . . 86 C5
Gayton Prim Sch CH60 . . . 86 A6
Gayton Rd CH60 . . . . 86 A6
Gaytree Ct CH43 . . . . 65 C7
Gaywood Ave L32. . . . . 40 F8
Gaywood Cl
Birkenhead CH43. . . . . 65 C7
5 Kirkby L32 . . . . 40 F8
Gaywood Ct L23 . . . . 26 B3
Gaywood Gn 4 L32 . . . . . . 40 F8
Gellings La L34. . . . . 41 A5
Gellings Rd L34. . . . . 41 A5
Gelling St L8 . . . . 67 F5
GEMINI 60 D3
Gemini Bsns Pk WA5. . . . . 60 E3
Gemini Cl L20 . . . . 38 B4
Gemini Dr L14. . . . . 54 F4
Gem St L5. . . . . 52 C5
General Dr L12 . . . . 54 D7
Geneva Cl L36 . . . . 55 D4
Geneva Rd
Liverpool L6. . . . . 53 C3
Wallasey CH44 . . . . 51 D2
Genista Cl L9. . . . . 39 A3
Genoa Cl L25 . . . . 70 B7
Gentwood Par L36. . . . . . . 55 D4
Gentwood Rd L36. . . . . 55 D3
George Dr PR8 . . . . 7 E5
George Hale Ave L34. . . . . 55 E6
George Harrison Cl 1
L6. 53 B3
George Moore Ct L23 . . . . 27 C6
George Rd CH47 . . . . 63 C6
George's Dock Gates L2,
L3. 52 B1
Georges Dockway L3 . . . . 52 B1
George's La PR9 . . . . 2 F8
Georges Par L3. . . . . 52 B1
Georges Pierhead L3 . . . . 52 B1
George's Prec WA5 . . . . . . 74 D6
Georges Rd L6 . . . . 53 C5
George St
Ashton-in-M WN4 . . . . 35 C4
Birkenhead CH41. . . . . 66 E7
Liverpool L2. . . . . 90 A4
Newton-le-W WA12. . . . . . . 46 A4
St Helens WA10. . . . . 44 A3
George Terr WN5. . . . . 25 D5
George Trad Est PR8 . . . . . . 4 B4
Georgia Ave
Bebington CH62. . . . . 79 E3
Kirkby L33 . . . . 29 D6
Georgia Cl 9 L20. . . . . 38 C3
Georgian Cl
Eccleston Park L35 . . . . 57 A6
Liverpool L26. . . . . 82 F7
Georgian Pl L37 . . . . 9 E1
Geraint St L8. . . . . 67 F6
Gerald Rd CH43. . . . . 66 A4
Gerard Ave CH45 . . . . 51 A7
Gerard Corr Ho CH45 . . . . 51 C6
Gerard Ctr The WN4 . . . . . 35 B3
Gerard Rd
Wallasey CH45 . . . . 50 F6
West Kirby CH48. . . . . 63 B3
GERARD'S BRIDGE 44 A5
Gerards Ct WA11 . . . . 44 C8
Gerards La WA9 . . . . 58 D7
Gerard St
Ashton-in-M WN4 . . . . 35 B3
Liverpool L3. . . . . 90 C4
Germander Cl L26 . . . . 70 E1
Gerneth Cl L24 . . . . 82 C5
Gerneth Rd L24. . . . . 82 B5
Gerosa Ave WA2. . . . . 61 B8
Gerrard Pl WN8. . . . . 23 F7
Gerrard Rd WN5 . . . . 33 E5
Gerrard's La L26. . . . . 70 F3
Gertrude Rd L4. . . . . 53 B6
Gertrude St
Birkenhead CH41. . . . . 66 F6
St Helens WA9. . . . . 57 D7
Geves Gdns L22 . . . . 26 E1
Ghyll Gr WA11. . . . . 33 B1
Gibbons Ave WA10. . . . . . . 43 C3
Gibbon's Rd WN4 . . . . 34 D3
Gibraltar Row L3 . . . . 52 B2
Gibson Cl
Heswall CH61 . . . . 76 F3
10 Kirkby L33 . . . . 29 D5
Gibson Rd L8. . . . . 67 F6
Gibson Terr CH44. . . . . 51 D5
Giddygate La L31 . . . . 29 B7
Gidlow Rd L13. . . . . 53 F3
Gidlow Rd S L13. . . . . 53 F2
Gilbert Cl CH63 . . . . 78 F2
Gilbert Ho WA7. . . . . 84 E3
Gilbert Rd L35. . . . . 56 F5
Gilbert St L1 . . . . 90 B2
Gilbrook Sch CH41. . . . . . . 66 F6
Gildarts Gdns L3. . . . . 52 C4
Gildart St L3 . . . . 52 F2
Gilead St L7. . . . . 53 B2
Gilescroft Ave L33 . . . . 30 A4
GILLAR'S GREEN 42 E2
Gillars Green Dr WA10 . . . 43 A3
Gillar's La WA10 . . . . 42 E3
Gillbrook Sq 4 CH41. . . . . 65 F8
Gilleney Gr L35. . . . . 57 A5
Gillibrands Rd WN8. . . . . . 24 A7
GILLMOSS 40 C6
Gillmoss Cl L11. . . . . 40 C4
Gillmoss Ind Est L10,
L11 . . . . 40 B6
Gillmoss La L11. . . . . 40 C5
Gills La CH61 . . . . 77 B4
Gill St L3. . . . . 52 F2
Gilman St 3 L4. . . . . 53 A7
Gilmartin Gr L6. . . . . 53 A3
Gilmour Jun Sch L19 . . . . 81 B7
Gilmour Mount CH43. . . . . 66 B4
Gilmour (Southbank) Inf
Sch L19. . . . . 81 B7
Gilpin Ave L31. . . . . 20 E2
Gilroy Rd
Liverpool L6. . . . . 53 B3
West Kirby CH48. . . . . 63 D3
Giltbrook Cl WA8 . . . . 72 F3
Gilwell Ave CH46, CH49 . . . 64 E7
Gilwell Cl CH46 . . . . 64 E7
Ginnel The CH62. . . . . 79 B5
Gipsy Gr L18. . . . . 69 E5
Gipsy La L16, L18. . . . . 69 E5
Girton Ave
Ashton-in-M WN4 . . . . 34 F4
Bootle L20. . . . . 38 E2
Girtrell Cl CH49. . . . . 64 D5
Girtrell Rd CH49 . . . . 64 D5
Girvan Cres WN4 . . . . 34 D4
Gisburn Ave WA3 . . . . 35 F2
Givenchy Cl L16 . . . . 69 E8
Givenchy Ct 1 L17. . . . . . . 68 C2
Gladden Pl WN8. . . . . 23 E8
Glade Park Ct L8 . . . . 68 B4
Glade Rd L36. . . . . 55 E4
Gladeswood Rd L33. . . . . . 30 B1
Glade The CH47 . . . . 48 D1
Gladeville Rd L17 . . . . 68 E3
Gladica Cl L36. . . . . 56 B2
Gladstone Ave
Huyton-w-R L16. . . . . 70 A8
2 Seaforth L21 . . . . 37 F7
Gladstone Cl CH41 . . . . 66 C6
Gladstone Hall Rd
CH62 . . . . 79 B4
Gladstone Rd
5 Birkenhead CH42. . . . . . . 66 F3
Liverpool, Edge Hill L7. . . . . 53 B1
Liverpool, Garston L19 . . . . 81 C6
Liverpool, Walton L9 . . . . . . 39 A3
Seaforth L21 . . . . 37 F7
Southport PR9. . . . . 4 F6
Wallasey CH44 . . . . 51 D3
Gladstone St
1 Liverpool, Vauxhall
L3 . . . . 52 C3
Liverpool, Woolton Hill
L25 . . . . 69 F2
St Helens WA10. . . . . 43 D3
Gladstone Way WA12 . . . . 46 B4
Gladsville Rd L27 . . . . 70 F4
Glaisdale Cl WN4 . . . . 35 C3
Glaisdale Dr PR8. . . . . 4 F3
Glaisher St L5. . . . . 53 A6
Glamis Cl CH43 . . . . 65 D3
Glamis Dr PR9. . . . . 2 B3
Glamis Gr WA9 . . . . 58 C7
Glamis Rd L13. . . . . 53 E6
Glamorgan Cl WA10. . . . . . 43 F2
Glan Aber Pk L12 . . . . 54 E8
Glasier Rd CH46 . . . . 49 C1
Glaslyn Way L9. . . . . 39 A3
Glasshouse Farm WA9 . . . 57 F5
Glassonby Cres L11. . . . . . 40 A1
Glassonby Way 3 L11. . . . 40 A1
Glastonbury Cl L6 . . . . 53 D7
Glasven Rd L33. . . . . 29 F3
Gleadmere WA8 . . . . 72 C2
Gleaner Cl WA7. . . . . 84 F3
Gleaston Cl CH62 . . . . 79 D1
Gleave Cres L6 . . . . 53 A4
Gleave Rd WA5 . . . . 59 F6
Gleave St WA10. . . . . 44 A5
Glebe Ave WN4. . . . . 35 C2
Glebe Cl L31. . . . . 20 B1
Glebe End L29. . . . . 27 F7
Glebe Hey L27. . . . . 70 E5
Glebe Hey Rd CH49 . . . . . . 65 A3
Glebe La WA8 . . . . 73 B5
Glebelands Rd CH46 . . . . . 64 E8
Glebe Pl PR8 . . . . 4 B7
Glebe Rd
Skelmersdale WN8 . . . . 24 A8
Wallasey CH45 . . . . 51 A6
Gleggside CH48. . . . . 63 C2
Glegg St L3 . . . . 52 B4
Glegside Rd L33 . . . . 30 A2
Glenacres L25. . . . . 70 A3
Glenalmond Rd CH44 . . . . 51 D4
Glenathol Rd L18 . . . . 69 C2
Glenavon Rd
Birkenhead CH43. . . . . 66 A1
3 Liverpool L16 . . . . 54 C1
Glenbank L22 . . . . 26 C2
Glenbank Cl L9 . . . . 39 A5
Glenburn Ave CH62 . . . . . . 88 E4
Glenburn Rd
Skelmersdale WN8 . . . . 15 F2
Skelmersdale WN8 . . . . 16 A1
Wallasey CH44 . . . . 51 D3
Glenburn Sports Coll
WN8. . . . . 24 B8
Glenby Ave L23. . . . . 26 F2
Glencairn Rd L13 . . . . 53 F3
Glencoe Rd CH45 . . . . 51 C6
Glenconner Rd L16 . . . . . . 54 E1
Glencourse Rd WA8. . . . . . 73 A5
Glencoyne Dr PR9 . . . . 2 B5
Glencroft Cl L36 . . . . 55 C5
Glendale Ave WN4. . . . . . . 35 C4
Glendale Cl L8. . . . . 67 F3
Glendale Gr
Bebington CH63. . . . . 79 B2
Kirkby L33 . . . . 30 A5
Glendale Rd WA11 . . . . 44 A7
Glendale Way L37 . . . . 9 F2
Glendevon Rd
Huyton-w-R L36. . . . . 55 E1
Liverpool L16. . . . . 54 D1
Glendower Ct 3 L23 . . . . . 26 B3
Glendower Rd L22 . . . . 26 E1
Glendower St L20. . . . . 38 C1
Glendyke Rd L18. . . . . 69 C3
Gleneagles Cl
Golborne WA3 . . . . 47 F7
Heswall CH61 . . . . 76 F3
Kirkby L33 . . . . 29 D6
Gleneagles Dr
Haydock WA11. . . . . 45 A5
Southport PR8. . . . . 7 C3
Widnes WA8 . . . . 73 B5
Gleneagles Rd L14, L16 . . . 54 D1
Glenfield Cl
Birkenhead CH43. . . . . 65 C8
Wallasey CH46 . . . . 49 B1
Glenfield Rd 2 L15 . . . . . . 69 A6
Glengariff St L13 . . . . 53 E7
Glenham Cl CH47 . . . . 63 E8
Glenhead Rd L19 . . . . 81 B8
Glenholm Rd L31 . . . . 28 C7
Glenluce Rd L19. . . . . 69 B1
Glenlyon Rd L15, L16 . . . . . 69 C8
Glenmarsh Cl
Bebington CH63. . . . . 78 D5
Liverpool L12. . . . . 54 C6
Glenmarsh Way L37. . . . . . 10 B3
Glenmaye Cl L12. . . . . 40 E2
Glenmore Ave L18 . . . . 69 A3
Glenmore Rd CH43. . . . . . . 66 A4
Glenn Bldgs 2 L23 . . . . . . 26 E5
Glenn Pl WA8 . . . . 72 E1
Glenpark Dr PR9. . . . . 2 B4
Glen Park Rd CH45. . . . . . . 51 A7
Glen Rd L13 . . . . 54 B2
Glen Ronald Dr CH49. . . . . 64 D5
Glenrose Rd L25. . . . . 70 A3
Glenrose Terr PR8 . . . . 4 A5
Glenside L18 . . . . 69 C2
Glen The
Bebington CH63. . . . . 79 C3
Liverpool L18. . . . . 69 C3
Glentrees Cl CH49 . . . . 64 D5
Glentrees Rd L12 . . . . 54 B8
Glentworth Cl L31 . . . . 28 D7
Glenville Cl L25. . . . . 70 B4
Glen Vine Cl L16. . . . . 69 F8
Glenway L33 . . . . 29 F6
Glenway Cl L12. . . . . 40 F4
Glenwood Cl L35 . . . . 56 F2
Glenwood Dr CH61. . . . . . . 76 E7
Glenwyllin Rd L22 . . . . 26 F1
Globe Rd L20. . . . . 38 B4
Globe St L4 . . . . 52 E7
Gloucester Ave WA3 . . . . . 47 B8
Gloucester Ct 18 L6. . . . . . 53 A3
Gloucester Rd
Bootle L20 . . . . 38 D4
Huyton-w-R L36. . . . . 56 A3
Liverpool L6. . . . . 53 D5
Southport PR8 . . . . 3 F5
Wallasey CH45 . . . . 50 E6
Widnes WA8 . . . . 73 B3
Gloucester Rd N L6. . . . . . 53 D6
Gloucester St WA9. . . . . . . 44 D2
Glover Pl L20. . . . . 38 B4
Glover's Brow L32 . . . . 29 C4
Glovers Ct 1 L32 . . . . 29 C3
Glover's La L30. . . . . 27 E4
Glover St
Birkenhead CH42. . . . . 66 C4
Newton-le-W WA12. . . . . . . 46 C3
St Helens WA10. . . . . 43 F3
Glyn Ave CH62 . . . . 88 E7
Glynne Gr L16 . . . . 70 A8
Glynne St L20 . . . . 38 D6
Glynn St L15. . . . . 68 F8
Glyn Rd CH44. . . . . 51 B5
Godetia Cl L9. . . . . 39 F4
Godshill Cl WA5 . . . . 74 D7
GOLBORNE 47 B7
Golborne Dale Rd WA3,
WA12. . . . . 47 A5
Golborne Enterprise Pk
WA3 . . . . 36 A1
Golborne Jun & Inf Sch
WA3 . . . . 47 A8
Golborne Rd
Ashton-in-M WN4 . . . . 35 E4
Golborne WA3 . . . . 47 C8
Winwick WA12, WA2 . . . . . . 61 A7
Golborne St WA12 . . . . 46 E4
Golbourne High Sch
WA3 . . . . 36 C1
Goldcliff Cl WA5 . . . . 60 D3
Goldcrest Cl L12. . . . . 40 F4
Goldcrest Mews L26 . . . . . 70 E1
Golden Gr 3 L4 . . . . 39 A1
Goldfinch Cl L26. . . . . 70 E1
Goldfinch Farm Rd
L24. . . . . 82 C4
Goldie St L4. . . . . 52 F7
Goldsmith Rd 1 CH43. . . . 65 F1
Goldsmith St
Bootle L20 . . . . 38 A4
Liverpool L6. . . . . 53 B3
Goldsmith Way 2
CH43 . . . . 65 F1
Goldsworth Fold L35. . . . . 57 B3
Gold Triangle Complex
WA8 . . . . 84 C5
Golf Links Rd CH42 . . . . . . 78 B8
Golf Rd L37 . . . . 9 E5
Gondover Ave L9 . . . . 38 F6
Gonville Rd L20. . . . . 38 D2
Gooch Dr WA12. . . . . 46 D2
Goodacre Rd L9 . . . . 39 B7
Goodakers Ct 10 CH49. . . . 65 A2
Goodaker's Mdw 2
CH49 . . . . 65 A2
Goodall Pl L4. . . . . 52 E8
Goodall St L4. . . . . 38 E1
Goodban St WA9 . . . . 58 E8
Goodison Ave L4 . . . . 52 F8
Goodison Park (Everton
FC)★ L4 . . . . 52 F8
Goodison Pl L4. . . . . 38 F1
Goodison Rd L4 . . . . 38 F1
Goodlass Rd L24. . . . . 82 A7
Goodleigh Pl WA9 . . . . 58 C5
Good Shepherd Cl L11 . . . 40 B2
Goodwood Cl L36. . . . . 55 D1
Goodwood Ct WA9. . . . . . . 57 D6
Goodwood Dr CH46 . . . . . . 49 F3
Goodwood St L5. . . . . 52 D5
Goose Green The
CH47 . . . . 48 D1
Goostrey Cl CH63 . . . . 79 B1
Gordale Cl
26 Liverpool L8. . . . . 68 A4
Warrington WA5 . . . . 74 F7
Gordon Ave
Bebington CH62. . . . . 88 E7
Birkenhead CH49. . . . . 64 E3
Crosby L22. . . . . 26 C2
Garswood WN4 . . . . 34 E4
Haydock WA11. . . . . 45 F7
Maghull L31. . . . . 20 C3
Southport PR9. . . . . 1 C1
Gordon Ct CH49 . . . . 64 E3
Gordon Dr
Huyton-w-R L14. . . . . 54 E3
Liverpool L19. . . . . 81 A7
Gordon Pl L18. . . . . 69 A3
Gordon Rd
Seaforth L21 . . . . 37 F6
Wallasey CH45 . . . . 51 C7
Gordon St
Birkenhead CH41. . . . . 66 C6
Liverpool L15. . . . . 68 E7
Southport PR9. . . . . 4 C8
Gordonstoun Cres
WN5. . . . . 25 F7
Gore Dr L39 . . . . 13 E3
Gores La
Crank WA11. . . . . 32 F6
Formby L37 . . . . 9 F5
Gore's La WA11. . . . . 33 A5
Gores Rd L33. . . . . 30 C1
Gore St L8 . . . . 67 E6
Gorleston Mews 10
L32. . . . . 40 F8
Gorleston Way L32. . . . . . . 29 F1
Gorse Ave L12. . . . . 40 B1
Gorsebank Rd L18 . . . . 68 E5
Gorsebank St CH44 . . . . . . 51 C3
Gorseburn Rd L13 . . . . 53 E6
Gorse Cres CH44. . . . . 51 C2
Gorsedale Pk CH44 . . . . . . 51 D2
Gorsedale Rd
Liverpool L18. . . . . 69 A4
Wallasey CH44 . . . . 51 C2
Gorsefield
Formby L37 . . . . 10 A6
St Helens WA9. . . . . 57 D7
Gorsefield Ave
Bebington CH62. . . . . 88 D5
Crosby L23. . . . . 27 A5
Gorsefield Cl CH62. . . . . . . 88 D5
Gorsefield Rd CH42 . . . . . . 66 C3
Gorse Hey Ct L12, L13 . . . . 54 A5
Gorsehill Rd
Heswall CH60 . . . . 77 A1
Wallasey CH45 . . . . 51 A8
Gorse La CH48. . . . . 63 E1
Gorselands Ct L17 . . . . 68 D2
Gorse Rd CH47 . . . . 63 D8
Gorse Way L37 . . . . 9 C4
Gorsewood Cl L25 . . . . 70 C5
Gorsewood Gr L25. . . . . . . 70 C5
Gorsewood Rd L25. . . . . . . 70 B5
Gorsey Ave L30. . . . . 27 C3
Gorsey Brow WN5 . . . . 33 E5
Gorsey Brow Cl WN5. . . . . 33 D5
Gorsey Cop Way L25 . . . . . 70 A6
Gorsey Croft L34. . . . . 56 F7
Gorsey La
Haskayne L39 . . . . 11 B7
Hightown L38. . . . . 18 B2
Litherland L21 . . . . 27 C2
St Helens WA5, WA9. . . . . . 59 C5
Wallasey CH41, CH44 . . . . . 51 B2
Widnes WA8 . . . . 73 E1
Gorsey Pl WN8 . . . . 24 B7
Gorseyville Cres CH63. . . . 78 E5
Gorseyville Rd CH63 . . . . . 78 E5
Gorst St 11 L4 . . . . 52 F7
Gorton Rd L13. . . . . 54 B2
Gort Rd L36 . . . . 55 E3
Goschen St
6 Liverpool, Everton
L5 . . . . 52 F7
Liverpool, Stanley L13. . . . . 53 F3
Gosford St L8 . . . . 67 F4
Gosforth Rd PR9. . . . . 4 F8
Gosport Cl WA2 . . . . 61 F1
Gostins Bldg 16 L1. . . . . . . 90 B3
Goswell St L15 . . . . 68 E8
Gotham Rd CH63. . . . . 79 B3
Gothic St CH42 . . . . 66 F2
Gough Ave WA2 . . . . 61 B2
Gough Rd L13 . . . . 53 E7
Gourley Rd L13 . . . . 54 B1
Gourley's La CH48 . . . . 63 D1
Government Rd CH47 . . . . 63 B7
Govett Rd WA9 . . . . 57 D7
Gower St
Bootle L20. . . . . 38 B5
Liverpool L1, L3. . . . . 90 A2
St Helens WA9. . . . . 44 D1
Gowrie Gr L21. . . . . 38 B7
Goyt Hey Ave WN5. . . . . . . 33 E5
Graburn Rd L37. . . . . 9 F4
Grace Ave L10. . . . . 40 A7
Grace Cl CH45 . . . . 51 B5
Grace Rd L9. . . . . 39 A6
Grace St
Liverpool L8. . . . . 67 F4
St Helens WA9. . . . . 58 C8
Gradwell St L1 . . . . 90 B3
Graeme Bryson Ct L11 . . . 39 F1
Grafton Cres L8 . . . . 67 E6
Grafton Dr
Birkenhead CH49. . . . . 65 B4
Southport PR8. . . . . 7 A5
Grafton Gr L8 . . . . 67 E4
Grafton Rd CH45. . . . . 51 B7
Grafton St
Birkenhead CH43. . . . . 66 B5
Liverpool, Dingle L8. . . . . . . 67 F3
Liverpool L8. . . . . 67 E4
Liverpool L8. . . . . 67 E6
Liverpool, Toxteth L8 . . . . . . 67 E5
Newton-le-W WA12. . . . . . . 46 B3
St Helens WA10. . . . . 43 D3

Grafton Wlk CH48 63 C2
Graham Cl WA8 72 C1
Graham Dr L26 83 A8
Graham Rd
West Kirby CH48 63 A3
Widnes WA8 84 C8
Graham's Rd L36 55 F2
Graham St WA9 44 C4
Grainger Ave
Birkenhead CH43 65 F1
Bootle L20 38 E5
West Kirby CH48 63 B3
Grain Ind Est L8 67 E4
Graley Cl L26 82 F7
Grammar School La CH48 63 D1
Grampian Ave CH46 64 E8
Grampian Rd L7 53 E2
Grampian Way
Bebington CH62 88 E4
Birkenhead CH46 64 E8
Golborne WA3 36 D1
Granams Croft L30 27 D4
Granard Rd L15 69 A6
Granary Way L3 67 D6
Granborne Chase L32 29 B3
Granby Cl PR9 1 F3
Granby Cres CH63 79 A2
Granby St L8 68 A6
Grandison Rd L4 39 C1
Grand National Ave L9 28 B1
GRANGE 63 D2
Grange Ave
Halewood L25 82 D8
Liverpool, Mill Yard L12 54 E5
Southport PR9 4 E8
Wallasey CH45 51 B6
Grange Ave N L12 54 F5
Grange Cl WA3 47 C6
Grange Cotts CH63 78 A6
Grange Cres CH66 89 A1
Grange Cross Cl CH48 63 E1
Grange Cross Hey CH48 63 E1
Grange Cross La CH48 63 E1
Grange Ct
Birkenhead CH43 66 A3
Liverpool L15 68 F7
Grange Dr
Heswall CH60 76 F2
St Helens WA10 57 B8
Thornton Hough CH63 87 A7
Widnes WA8 72 D1
Grange Farm Cres CH48 63 E3
Grangehurst Ct L25 70 B4
Grange La
Formby L37 9 E5
Liverpool L25 70 A5
Grangemeadow Rd L25 70 A5
Grange Mews L25 70 B4
Grange Mount
Birkenhead CH43 66 C5
Heswall CH60 76 F1
West Kirby CH48 63 D2
Grange Old Rd CH48 63 C2
GRANGE PARK 57 C8
Grange Park Rd WA10 57 C8
Grange Pk L31 28 F7
Grange Pl CH41 66 C6
Grange Prim Sch The L30 27 E5
Grange Rd
Ashton-in-M WN4 34 F6
Birkenhead CH41 66 D6
12 Birkenhead CH41 66 E6
Haydock WA11, WA12 45 D5
Heswall CH60 76 F2
Hightown L38 17 E6
Litherland L30 28 B2
Southport PR9 4 E7
West Kirby CH48 63 B2
Grange Rd E 8 CH41 66 E6
Grange Rd W CH41, CH43 66 C6
Grangeside L25 70 A5
Grange St L6 53 D5
Grange Terr L15 68 F7
Grange The
Southport PR9 2 C3
Wallasey CH44 51 C4
Grange Vale CH42 67 A1
Grange Valley WA11 45 D6
Grange Valley Prim Sch WA11 45 D5
Grange View 15 CH43 66 C5
Grange Way L25 70 A5
Grange Weint L25 70 B4
Grange Wlk CH48 63 D1
Grangewood L16 54 F1
Granite Terr 9 L36 56 A2
Granston Cl WA5 60 E2
Grant Ave L15 68 F6
Grant Cl
Huyton-w-R L14 55 A3
St Helens WA10 43 E4
Warrington WA5 60 D1
Grant Ct 11 L20 38 C3
Grantham Cl
Heswall CH61 76 E4
Southport PR8 4 A1
Grantham Cres WA11 44 D5
Grantham Rd
Kirkby L33 29 E5
Grantham Rd *continued*
Southport PR8 4 A1
Grantham St L6 53 B3
Grantham Way L30 28 B4
Grantley Rd L15 69 B6
Grantley St WN4 35 A5
Granton Cl L37 9 E3
Granton Rd L5 53 A6
Grant Rd
Huyton-w-R L14 55 A4
Wallasey CH46 50 C4
Grantwood WN4 35 A5
Granville Ave L31 20 C2
Granville Cl
Ormskirk L39 21 B8
Wallasey CH45 50 E6
Granville Ct
Southport PR9 1 D1
3 Wallasey CH45 50 E6
GRANVILLE PARK 21 C8
Granville Pk L39 21 C8
Granville Pk W L39 21 B8
Granville Rd
Liverpool, Garston L19 81 C6
Liverpool L15 68 D7
Southport PR8 3 D4
Granville St WA9 44 D3
Grappenhall Way CH43 65 C7
Grasmere Ave
Birkenhead CH43 65 C5
Orrell WN5 25 F8
Prescot L34 56 F6
St Helens WA11 44 B7
Up Holland WN8 25 B7
Warrington WA2 61 E3
Grasmere Cl
Kirkby L33 29 D4
St Helens WA11 44 B7
Grasmere Ct
9 Birkenhead CH41 66 C5
St Helens WA11 44 B7
Grasmere Dr
Ashton-in-M WN4 35 B5
Bootle L21 38 E8
Wallasey CH45 51 A6
Grasmere Fold WA11 44 B7
Grasmere Gdns L23 26 F3
Grasmere Ho
Huyton-w-R L36 55 E2
Liverpool L17 68 D2
Grasmere Rd
Formby L37 9 D3
Hightown L38 18 A4
Maghull L31 20 D2
Grasmere St L5 53 B5
Grasmere Terr WN2 36 B8
GRASSENDALE 81 A8
Grassendale Ct L19 81 A7
Grassendale Espl L19 80 F6
Grassendale La L19 81 A7
Grassendale Rd L19 81 A7
Grassington Cres L25 70 C2
Grassmoor Cl CH62 88 E8
Grasswood Rd CH49 65 C3
Grass Wood Rd CH49 65 C3
Grasville Rd CH42 66 E3
Gratrix Rd CH62 88 D8
Gratton Pl WN8 24 A8
Gravel Cl PR9 2 F5
Gravel La PR9 2 F5
Grave-Yard La L39 22 A6
Gray Ave WA11 45 B6
Gray Gr L36 70 F8
Graylands Pl L4 39 C1
Graylands Rd
Bebington CH62 79 C6
Liverpool L4 39 C2
Grayling Dr L12 40 D3
Grays Ave L35 56 F6
Grayson Mews CH41 66 F7
Graysons Rd WA11 31 F8
Grayson St L1 90 B2
Gray St L20 38 A5
Grayston Ave WA9 58 D6
GREASBY 64 D2
Greasby Inf Sch CH49 64 C2
Greasby Jun Sch CH49 64 C1
Greasby Rd
Birkenhead CH49 64 E4
Wallasey CH44 51 A4
GREAT ALTCAR 10 E1
Great Ashfield WA8 72 D3
Great Charlotte St
Liverpool L1 90 B3
Liverpool L1 90 B4
GREAT CROSBY 26 D4
Great Crosby RC Prim Sch L23 26 E4
Great Crosshall St L3 90 B4
Great Delph WA11 45 D7
Great George Pl L1 90 C1
Great George Sq L1 90 C1
Great George's Rd L22 37 E8
Great George St L1 90 C1
Great Hey L30 27 D5
Great Homer St L5 52 E5
Great Howard St L3, L5 52 B4
Great Meols Prim Sch CH47 48 E1
Great Mersey St L5 52 D6
Great Nelson St L3, L5 52 D4
Great Newton St L3 52 F1
Great Orford St L3 52 F1
Great Richmond St L3 52 E3
Great Sankey High Sch WA5 74 E7
Greaves St L8 67 F5
Grebe Ave WA10 57 B7
Grecian St L21 37 F8
Grecian Terr L5 52 F6
Gredington St L8 68 A4
Greek St
Liverpool L3 90 C4
Runcorn WA7 84 F3
Greenacre L40 14 E4
Greenacre Cl L25 82 C9
Greenacre Dr CH63 88 C7
Greenacre Rd L25 82 C9
Greenacres 4 L22 26 D1
Greenacres Cl CH43 65 C8
Greenacres Ct 6 CH43 65 C8
Greenall Ave WA5 74 D4
Greenall Ct 15 L34 56 D6
Greenall St
Ashton-in-M WN4 35 B5
St Helens WA10 43 E4
Greenbank
Abram Brow WN2 36 B7
Ormskirk L39 13 C2
Seaforth L22 37 E8
GREEN BANK 43 F2
Green Bank CH63 78 A2
Greenbank Ave
Maghull L31 20 C3
Orrell WN5 25 D3
2 Wallasey CH45 51 B7
Greenbank Cres WA10 43 F3
Greenbank Ct L17 68 E5
Greenbank Dr
Heswall CH61 77 A3
Liverpool, Gillmoss L10 40 B7
Liverpool L15, L17 68 E5
Southport PR8 3 E2
Greenbank High Sch PR8 3 E1
Greenbank La L17, L18 68 E5
Greenbank Prim Sch L18 68 F5
Greenbank Rd
Birkenhead CH42 66 C3
Liverpool L18 68 F5
West Kirby CH48 63 C4
Greenburn Ave WA11 33 C1
Greencroft Rd CH44 51 C3
Greendale Rd
Bebington CH62 79 B5
Liverpool L25 69 F4
Green End La WA9 58 C8
Green End Pk L12 54 A7
Greene's Rd L35 56 D2
Greenfield Cl PR9 2 A3
Greenfield Ct L18 69 C1
Greenfield Dr L36 70 F8
Greenfield Gr L36 70 F8
Greenfield La
Heswall CH60 76 C2
Litherland L21 27 A1
Greenfield Rd
Liverpool L13 54 A3
Southport PR8 5 C1
St Helens WA10 43 E5
Greenfields Ave CH62 88 C7
Greenfields Cl WA12 46 C4
Greenfields Cres
Ashton-in-M WN4 35 B4
Bebington CH62 88 C7
Greenfield View WN5 33 D4
Greenfield Way
Liverpool L18 69 C1
3 Wallasey CH44 51 B4
Greenfield Wlk L36 55 F1
Greenfinch Cl 1 L12 40 F3
Greenfinch Gr L26 70 E1
Greenford Cl WN5 25 D6
Greenford Rd PR8 7 C4
Greengables Cl 7 L8 68 A5
Green Gates L36 55 E6
Greengates Com Prim Sch L26 82 F8
Greenham Ave L33 29 F6
Greenhaven WN8 25 B7
Greenhaven Cl L10 40 A7
Greenheath Way CH46 49 F3
Green Hey Dr L30 27 D3
Greenhey Pl WN8 23 F8
Greenheys Ct 5 L8 68 B6
Green Heys Dr L31 20 F1
Greenheys Gdns 7 L8 68 B6
Greenheys Rd
Irby CH61 76 C5
Liverpool L8 68 B6
Wallasey CH44 51 B4
Greenhill Ave L18 69 C4
Greenhill Cl L18 69 B2
Greenhill Cres WN5 33 F5
Greenhill Pl L36 55 E1
Greenhill Rd
Billinge WN5 33 F5
Liverpool, Grassendale L19 81 C8
Liverpool, Mossley Hill L18 69 B2
Greenholme Cl L11 40 A3
Greenhow Ave CH48 63 B3
Green Jones Brow WA5 59 F6
Green La
Bebington CH63 79 A5
Birkenhead CH41 66 E4
Burtonwood WA5 59 E7
Crosby, Thornton L23 27 B6
Crosby, Waterloo L22 26 C2
Formby L37 9 F5
Litherland L21 27 B2
Liverpool, Calderstones L18 69 B5
Green La *continued*
Liverpool, Childwall L16, L18 69 C5
Liverpool L3 90 C3
Liverpool, Stanley L13 53 F4
Maghull L31 20 A2
Maghull L31 20 C1
Ormskirk L39 13 E6
Orrell WN5 25 D3
Rainford WA11 32 A5
Seaforth L21 38 A7
Skelmersdale L40 16 A6
Skelmersdale L40, WN8 15 F6
St Helens WA10 42 F5
Wallasey CH45 50 D6
Wallasey CH45, CH46 50 C5
Widnes WA8 72 E1
Winwick WA2 61 A7
Greenlake Rd L18 69 B2
Green La N L16 69 D6
Greenlands L36 55 E1
Greenland St L1 90 B1
Green Lane Ave L39 13 E6
Green Lane Cl WA2 61 A7
Green Lane Sta CH41 66 F4
Green Lawn
Birkenhead CH42 66 F1
Huyton-w-R L36 56 A4
Green Lawn Gr CH42 66 F1
GREEN LEACH 44 A7
Green Leach Ave WA11 44 B7
Green Leach Ct WA11 44 B7
Green Leach La WA11 44 B7
Greenlea Cl
Bebington CH63 78 F6
Orrell WN5 25 D5
Greenleaf St L8 68 C7
Greenleas Cl CH45 50 D5
Greenleas Prim Sch CH45 50 D6
Greenleas Rd CH45 50 D5
Greenleigh Rd L18 69 B2
Green Link L31 20 B2
Greenloon's Dr L37 9 C3
Greenloon's Wlk L37 9 C2
Green Mdws WA3 47 E5
Green Mount CH49 65 A5
Green Oaks Way WA8 73 C1
Greenock Mews WA8 72 E3
Greenock St L3 52 B3
Greenodd Ave L12 40 C1
Greenore Dr L24 83 D2
Greenough Ave L35 57 C5
Greenough St L25 69 F2
Green Park Dr L31 20 B1
Green Park Prim Sch L31 20 B2
Green Pk L30 27 F5
Green Rd L34 56 C7
Greensbridge La
Halewood L26 83 A8
Liverpool L26, L35 71 B2
Greenshank Cl WA12 46 C4
Greenside L6 52 F3
Greenside Ave
Aintree L10 28 E2
Liverpool L15 69 A7
Greenside Cl L33 30 A6
Green's La L31 12 C1
Greenslate Ct WN5 25 E3
Greenslate Rd WN5 25 E3
Green St L3, L5 52 C4
Greens Wlk L17 68 E3
Green The
Bebington CH62 79 D5
Crosby L23 26 D5
Hale L24 83 D1
Liverpool L13 54 C2
Prescot L34 56 F7
Thornton Hough CH63 87 C4
West Kirby CH48 75 D7
Greenville Cl CH63 78 F5
Greenville Dr L31 20 C1
Greenville Rd CH63 78 F5
Greenway
Ashton-in-M WN4 35 A4
Bebington CH62 79 D3
Birkenhead CH49 64 E5
Crosby L23 27 A5
Heswall CH61 76 E4
Neston CH64 86 B2
Warrington WA5 74 E7
Green Way L36 55 B4
Greenway Ave WN8 24 B8
Greenway Cl WN8 15 E2
Green Way Cl L36 55 B4
Greenway Ct WA9 44 C3
Greenway Rd
Birkenhead CH42 66 D3
Runcorn WA7 84 F1
Speke L24 83 A3
Widnes WA8 73 B1
Greenways WN5 25 D3
Greenways Ct CH62 88 C6
Greenways Specl Sch L19 80 F7
Greenway The L12 54 E4
Greenwell Rd WA11 45 C6
Greenwich Ave WA8 73 D4
Greenwich Ct L9 39 B8
Greenwich Rd L9 39 B7
Green Wlk PR8 7 D5
Greenwood Cl
Ormskirk L39 13 C1
Prescot L34 56 E6
Greenwood Cres WA2 61 E2
Greenwood Ct 7 WA9 58 C4
Greenwood Dr WA12 46 D2
Greenwood Gdns PR8 4 A5
Greenwood La CH44 51 C5
Greenwood Rd
Birkenhead CH49 65 B3
Hoylake CH47 63 E8
Liverpool L18 69 B1
Greetby Hill L39, L40 14 A6
Greetby Pl WN8 24 A8
Greetham St L1 90 B2
Gregory Cl L16 69 E8
Gregory Way L16 69 E8
Gregson Ct CH45 51 C8
Gregson Rd
Prescot L35 56 D5
Widnes WA8 73 C1
Gregson's Ave L37 9 E5
Gregson St L6 52 F3
Grenfell Cl CH64 86 C1
Grenfell Pk CH64 86 C1
Grenfell Rd L13 53 E8
Grennan Ct 9 CH45 51 B8
Grennan The CH45 51 B8
Grenville Cres CH63 88 C7
Grenville Dr CH61 76 E3
Grenville Rd
4 Birkenhead CH42 66 F3
Neston CH64 86 F1
Grenville St S L1 90 C2
Grenville Way CH42 66 F3
Gresford Ave
Birkenhead CH43 66 A2
Liverpool L17 68 E6
West Kirby CH48 63 C3
Gresford Cl
Prescot L35 56 F3
Warrington WA5 60 E1
Gresham St L7 53 E2
Gresley Cl 6 L7 53 C1
Gressingham Rd L18 69 C2
Gretton Rd L14 55 B5
Greyfriars WN4 34 F4
Greyfriars Rd PR8 7 B6
Greyhound Farm Rd L24 82 C5
Grey Rd
Ashton-in-M WN4 35 A4
Liverpool L9 39 A4
Grey St L8 67 F6
Greystoke Cl CH49 64 F4
Greystokes L39 13 D2
Greystone Cres L14 54 E3
Greystone Pl L10 39 F7
Greystone Rd
Huyton-w-R L14 54 E2
Liverpool L10 39 F7
Warrington WA5 74 F4
Gribble Rd L10 40 A7
Grierson St L8 68 B7
Grieve Rd L10 40 A7
Griffin Ave CH46 64 E8
Griffin Cl
Liverpool L11 40 C4
St Helens WA10 42 F4
Griffin Mews WA8 73 B3
Griffin St WA9 58 E7
Griffiths Cl CH49 64 C3
Griffiths Dr PR9 4 F8
Griffith's Rd L36 55 E2
Griffiths St L1 90 C2
Griffon Ho PR9 1 F2
Grimrod Pl WN8 24 A7
Grimshaw Ct WA3 36 A1
Grimshaw La L39 13 E7
Grimshaw Rd WN8 24 D8
Grimshaw St
Bootle L20 38 B2
Golborne WA3 36 A1
St Helens WA9 58 C6
Grinfield St L7 53 A1
Grinshill Cl L8 68 A6
Grinstead Cl PR8 3 F1
Grinton Cres L36 55 D2
Grisedale Ave WA2 61 B3
Grisedale Cl L37 9 E3
Grisedale Rd CH62 88 F8
Grizedale WA8 72 B2
Grizedale Ave WA11 44 B8
Groarke Dr WA5 74 D5
Groes Rd L19 81 B7
Grogan Sq L20 38 D6
Gronow Pl L20 38 E6
Grosmont Rd L32 40 F8
Grosomont Rd 1 L32 41 A8
Grosvenor Ave
Crosby L23 26 E2
3 Golborne WA3 47 D8
West Kirby CH48 63 B2
Grosvenor Cl
Litherland L30 27 F3
Southport PR8 3 E3
Grosvenor Ct
1 Birkenhead CH43 66 B5
Liverpool L18 68 E3
Prescot L34 56 D6
Southport PR8 3 E3
Grosvenor Dr CH45 51 B8
Grosvenor Gdns
Newton-le-W WA12 46 C2
Southport PR8 3 F3
Grosvenor Pl
Birkenhead CH43 66 A5
Southport PR8 3 F3
Grosvenor Rd
Birkenhead CH43 66 B5
Haydock WA11 45 B7
Hoylake CH47 63 B6

Grosvenor Rd *continued*
Liverpool, Cressington Park L19 81 A6
Liverpool L15 68 E7
7 Liverpool, Walton on the Hill L4 38 F2
Maghull L31 28 D7
Prescot L34 56 D6
Southport PR8 3 E4
St Helens WA10 43 D2
Wallasey CH45 51 B8
Widnes WA8 73 B5
Grosvenor St
Liverpool L3 52 D3
Wallasey CH44 51 B4
Grosvenor Terr L8 68 B4
Grove Ave CH60 76 F1
Grovedale Dr CH46 50 A1
Grovedale Rd L18 68 F5
Grove Ho L8 68 C6
Grovehurst Ave L14 54 F4
Groveland Ave
Hoylake CH47 63 B7
Wallasey CH45 50 D6
Groveland Rd CH45 50 D6
Grovelands L7 68 A8
Grove Mans 5 CH45 50 E6
Grove Mead L31 20 F1
Grove Park Ave L12 54 B8
Grove Pk
Liverpool L8 68 C6
Ormskirk L39 13 F7
Southport PR9 4 F8
Grove Pl
Hoylake CH47 63 B7
Liverpool L4 52 E7
Grove Rd
Birkenhead CH42 66 F2
Hoylake CH47 63 B7
Liverpool L6 53 D3
Up Holland WN8 25 C8
Wallasey CH45 50 F7
Groveside CH48 63 A2
Grove Side L7 68 A8
Grove Sq CH62 79 A7
Grove St
Ashton-in-M WN4 35 A4
Bebington CH62 79 B7
Bootle L20 38 A4
Liverpool, Edge Hill L7, L8 68 A8
Liverpool, Wavertree L15 68 F8
Runcorn WA7 84 F3
Southport PR8 4 A4
Groves The
Birkenhead CH43 66 A5
Kirkby L32 40 E7
Grove Street Prim Sch CH62 79 B7
Grove Terr
Hoylake CH47 63 B7
Southport PR8 4 A5
Grove The
Bebington CH63 79 A5
Birkenhead CH43 66 B3
Golborne WA3 36 D1
Huyton-w-R L28 55 C7
Liverpool L13 53 F5
Ormskirk L39 21 C7
St Helens WA10 43 C5
Wallasey CH44 51 C3
Warrington WA5 74 F4
Grove Way L7 68 A8
Grovewood PR8 3 E5
Grovewood Ct CH43 66 B3
Grovewood Gdns L35 56 E3
Grundy Cl
Southport PR8 4 E5
Widnes WA8 72 F3
Grundy St
Golborne WA3 47 A7
Liverpool L5 52 C6
Guardian Ct CH48 63 B1
Guelph St L7 53 A2
Guernsey Rd
Liverpool L13 54 A4
Widnes WA8 73 E3
Guffitts Cl CH47 48 E1
Guffitt's Rake CH47 48 E1
Guildford Ave L30 27 F1
Guildford Rd PR8 8 A8
Guildford St CH44 51 D4
Guildhall Rd L9 39 A6
Guild Hey L34 41 D4
Guillemot Way L26 70 E1
Guilsted Rd L11 40 A2
Guinea Gap CH44 51 E3
Guion Rd L21 38 B7
Guion St L6 53 B4
Gullivers World Theme Pk* WA5 60 E1
Gulls Way CH60 85 E7
Gunning Ave WA10 43 B5
Gunning Cl WA10 43 B5
Gurnall St 13 L4 52 F7
Gutticar Rd WA8 72 B1
Guy Cl CH41 66 E4
Gwendoline Cl CH61 77 A5
Gwendoline St L8 67 F6
Gwenfron Rd 10 L6 53 B3
Gwent Cl L6 53 B5
Gwent St L8 68 A6
Gwladys St L4 38 F1
Gwladys Street Prim Sch L4 39 A1
Gwydir St L8 68 A5
Gwydrin Rd L18 69 C5

H

Hackett Ave L20 38 D6
Hackins Hey L2 90 A4
Hackthorpe St L5 52 E7
Hadassah Gr L17 68 C4
Hadden Cl L35 57 A4
Haddock St L20 38 B1
Haddon Ave L9 38 F6
Haddon Dr
Heswall CH61 76 F4
Widnes WA8 72 C3
Haddon Rd
Birkenhead CH42 67 A2
Golborne WA3 36 D2
Haddon St 5 WN4 34 F5
Haddon Wlk L12 40 E3
Hadfield Ave CH47 63 B7
Hadfield Cl WA8 73 E2
Hadfield Gr L25 70 C3
Hadleigh Cl WA5 74 E5
Hadleigh Rd L32 29 F1
Hadley Ave CH62 79 C1
Hadstock Ave L37 9 D1
Hadwens Bldgs L3 90 A4
Haggerston Rd L4 39 A2
Hague Bush Cl WA3 36 E1
Hahnemann Rd L4 38 E2
Haig Ave
Birkenhead CH46 64 F8
Southport PR8 4 E5
Haigh Cres L31 20 C4
Haigh Ct PR8 4 F6
Haigh Rd L22 26 E1
Haigh St L3, L6 52 F3
Haig Rd WA8 73 A1
Haileybury Ave L10 28 D2
Haileybury Rd L25 82 B9
Hailsham Rd L19 80 F8
Halby Rd L9 39 B6
Halcombe Rd L12 54 D7
Halcyon Rd CH41 66 C4
Haldane Ave CH41 65 F7
Haldane Rd L4 39 A2
HALE 83 D1
HALE BANK 84 A4
Hale Bank CE Prim Sch WA8 84 A5
Halebank Rd WA8 84 A5
Hale Bank Terr WA8 84 A4
Hale CE Prim Sch L24 83 E1
Hale Ct WA8 84 A4
Hale Dr L24 82 E3
Halefield St WA10 43 F4
Hale Gate Rd
Hale WA8 83 F3
Widnes WA8 84 A3
Hale Gr WN4 34 F5
HALE HEATH 83 A1
Hale Rd
Hale L24 83 B2
Liverpool, Kirkdale L4 38 E1
Speke L24 82 C4
Speke L24 82 E3
Wallasey CH45 51 C6
Widnes WA8 84 C7
Hale Road Ind Est WA8 84 B4
Hale St L2 90 A4
Hale View Rd L36 56 A2
HALEWOOD 82 F9
Halewood Ave WA3 35 F1
Halewood CE Prim Sch L26 71 A1
Halewood Cl L25 70 B4
Halewood Coll L26 82 E8
Halewood Dr
Liverpool L25 70 B2
Liverpool L25 70 C2
Halewood Lane Ends L26 83 A8
Halewood Pl L25 70 C3
Halewood Rd L25 70 C3
Halewood Sta L26 82 F9
Halewood 'Triangle' Ctry Pk L26 82 E9
HALEWOOD VILLAGE 83 A8
Halewood Way L25 70 C2
Haley Rd N WA5 59 E6
Haley Rd S WA5 59 E5
Half Crown St L5 52 C6
Halfpenny Cl L19 81 B7
Halftide Wharf L3 90 A1
Halidon Ct L20 38 A4
Halifax Cl WA2 61 D2
Halifax Cres L23 27 B6
Halifax Rd PR8 7 C5
Halkirk Rd L18 69 C1
Halkyn Ave L17 68 D6
Halkyn Dr L5 53 A5
Hallam Wlk 3 L7 53 C1
Hall Ave WA8 72 A1
Hallbridge Gdns WN8 25 B8
Hall Brow Cl L39 14 B4
Hallcroft WN8 16 C2
Hall Dr
Birkenhead CH49 64 C2
Kirkby L32 29 E3
Hall Farm CH62 89 A4
Hallfields Rd WA2 61 D1
Hall Gn WN8 25 B7
HALL GREEN 25 A7
Hall Green Cl WN8 25 B7
Hall La
Bickerstaffe L39 22 E4
Cronton L35 72 C7
Huyton-w-R L36 56 A2
Ince Blundell L38 18 F3
Hall La *continued*
Kirkby L32 29 E2
Kirkby L33 30 A8
Liverpool, Kensington L7 53 A2
Liverpool, Walton L9 39 B6
Maghull L31 28 D8
Maghull, Lydiate L31 20 B7
Newton-le-W WA5 60 B8
Orrell WN5 25 F4
Prescot L34, L35 56 D5
Skelmersdale L40 15 A6
St Helens WA9 59 A4
Hallmoor Cl L39 13 E2
Hall Nook WA5 74 F3
Hallows Ave WA2 61 D1
Hall Rd WA11 45 E7
Hall Rd E L23 26 B6
Hall Rd W L23 26 A6
Hall Road Sta L23 26 A6
Hallsands Rd L32 40 E8
Hall's Cotts WA10 43 D6
Hallside Cl L19 81 A8
Hall St
Ashton-in-M WN2 35 E7
Southport PR9 4 C7
St Helens, Pocket Nook WA10 44 B4
St Helens WA9 58 E3
Hall Terr WA5 74 E7
Halltine Cl L23 26 A6
Hallville Rd L18 69 B5
Hall Wood Ave WA11 34 F1
HALSALL 12 B8
Halsall Bldgs 6 PR9 4 C8
Halsall Cl L23 26 E5
Halsall Ct L39 13 D6
Halsall Gn CH63 79 B1
Halsall La
Formby L37 9 F3
Haskayne L39 12 D6
Ormskirk L39 13 D6
Halsall Rd
Bootle L20 38 C5
Southport PR8 8 A8
Halsall's Cotts WA8 83 E5
Halsall St L34 56 D7
Halsbury Rd
Liverpool L6 53 C3
Wallasey CH45 51 B6
Halsey Ave L12 53 F7
Halsey Cres L12 53 F7
Halsnead Ave L35 56 C1
Halsnead Cl L13 54 A1
Halsnead Com Prim Sch L35 56 D2
Halstead Rd
Liverpool L9 38 F6
Wallasey CH44 51 C3
Halstead Wlk 5 L32 29 C1
Halton Chase L40 14 E4
Halton Cres CH49 64 B3
Halton Hey L35 56 D1
Halton Rd
Maghull L31 20 D3
9 Wallasey CH45 51 A6
Warrington WA5 74 F6
Halton St WA11 45 E6
HALTON VIEW 73 C1
Halton View Rd WA8 73 C1
Halton Wlk L25 70 C6
Halton Wood L32 29 B3
Halville Rd CH44 51 C3
Halyard Ho CH60 76 C2
Hambledon Dr CH49 64 D4
Hamble Dr WA5 74 F3
Hambleton Cl
Liverpool L11 40 B4
Widnes WA8 72 C3
Hamblett Cres WA11 44 B6
Hamer Ho CH45 50 E5
Hamer St WA10 43 F4
Hamil Cl CH47 48 E1
Hamilton Cl CH64 86 B2
Hamilton Ct L23 26 B4
Hamilton La CH41 66 E7
Hamilton Rd
Garswood WN4 34 D4
Liverpool L5 52 F5
St Helens WA10 43 C6
Wallasey CH45 51 A8
Hamilton Sq CH41 66 F7
Hamilton Square Sta CH41 66 F7
Hamilton St CH41 66 F6
Hamlet Ct L17 68 C3
Hamlet Rd CH45 50 F6
Hamlin Rd L19 81 D6
Hammersley Ave WA9 58 C3
Hammersley St WA9 58 C3
Hammersmith Way WA8 73 D4
Hammill Ave WA10 43 E6
Hammill St WA10 43 D5
Hammond Rd L33 30 C3
Hammond St WA9 44 D2
Hamnett Rd L34 56 E7
Hampden Gr CH42 66 E4
Hampden Rd CH42 66 E4
Hampden St L4 38 F2
Hampshire Ave L30 27 C3
Hampshire Gdns WA10 43 F2
Hampson Cl WN4 35 B2
Hampson St L6 53 C5
Hampstead Rd
Liverpool L6 53 C4
Wallasey CH44 51 C3
Hampton Chase CH43 65 D3
Hampton Cl WA8 73 E3
Hampton Court Rd L12 54 D5
Hampton Court Way WA8 73 D4
Hampton Dr WA8 72 C5
Hampton Pl WA11 44 B6
Hampton Rd
Formby L37 9 E1
Southport PR8 4 C5
Hampton St L8 67 F7
Hanbury Rd L4 53 D8
Handel Ct L8 68 B6
Handel Rd L27 70 C6
Handfield Pl 5 L5 53 A5
Handfield Rd L22 26 E1
Handfield St L5 53 A5
Handford Ave CH62 88 F5
Handley Ct L19 80 F8
Handley Dr WA2 61 E1
Handley St WA7 84 F3
Hands St L21 38 B6
Handsworth Wlk PR8 4 F3
Hanford Ave L9 38 F6
Hankey Dr L20 38 E5
Hankey St 2 WA7 84 F2
Hankinson St L13 54 A1
Hankin St L5 52 D5
Hanley Cl WA8 72 C1
Hanley Rd WA8 72 C1
Hanlon Ave L20 38 D6
Hanmer Rd L32 29 B2
Hannah Cl CH61 76 E3
Hannan Rd L6 53 C3
Hanns Hall Rd CH64 87 D1
Hanover Cl CH43 65 F6
Hanover St L1 90 B3
Hansard Ct WA9 57 D7
Hansby Cl WN8 24 E8
Hansby Dr L24, L25 82 C6
Hanson Pk CH43 65 E5
Hanson Rd L9 39 C5
Hanson Road Bsns Pk L9 39 C5
Hans Rd 9 L4 39 A1
Hanstock Cl WN5 25 E5
Hants La L39 13 E6
Hanwell St L6 53 B6
Hanworth Cl L12 40 E3
Hapsford Rd L21 38 B6
Hapton St L5 52 E6
Harbern Cl L12 54 D6
Harbord Rd L22 26 C1
Harbord St L7 53 B1
Harbord Terr L22 26 C1
Harborne Dr CH63 78 F2
Harbreck Gr L9 39 D3
Harbury Ave PR8 7 A4
Harcourt Ave CH44 51 E3
Harcourt St
Birkenhead CH41 66 C7
Liverpool L4 52 D7
Hardacre St L39 13 F6
Hardie Ave CH46 49 C1
Hardie Cl WA9 58 A3
Hardie Rd L36 56 A3
Harding Ave
Bebington CH63 79 A4
Warrington WA2 61 E1
Harding Cl L5 53 A5
Hardinge Rd L19 81 D8
Hardknott Rd CH62 88 E8
Hard La WA10 43 E6
Hardman St L1 90 C2
Hardshaw Ctr WA10 44 A3
Hardshaw St
St Helens WA10 44 A3
St Helens WA10 44 A4
Hardwick Rd WN4 35 A5
Hardy St
Liverpool, Garston L19 81 D4
Liverpool L1 90 B1
Liverpool L1 90 C2
Harebell Cl
Formby L37 9 F1
Widnes WA8 72 E4
Harebell St L5 52 D7
Hare Croft L28 54 F8
Harefield Gn L24 82 D4
Harefield Rd L24 82 D4
HARESFINCH 44 B7
Haresfinch Cl 3 L26 71 A1
Haresfinch Rd WA10, WA11 44 B6
Haresfinch View WA11 44 B6
Hares La PR8 5 D1
Harewell Rd L11 40 A1
Harewood Ave PR8 7 C6
Harewood Cl L36 55 E3
Harewood Rd CH45 51 A7
Harewood St 3 L6 53 A4
Harford Cl WA5 74 F4
Hargate Rd L33 29 F2
Hargate Wlk 3 L33 29 F2
Hargrave Ave CH43 65 E3
Hargrave Cl CH43 65 E3
Hargrave La
Bebington CH64 88 A4
Thornton Hough CH63, CH64 87 F5
Hargreaves Ct WA8 73 D1
Hargreaves Ho 5 WA8 73 D1
Hargreaves Rd L17 68 C3
Hargreaves St
Southport PR8 4 C6
St Helens WA9 44 E3
Harington Cl L37 9 D3
Harington Gn L37 9 D3
Harington Rd L37 9 D4
Harker St L3 52 E3
Harke St L7 68 B8
Harland Dr WN4 35 C3
Harland Gn
Liverpool L24 82 F4
Speke L24 83 A3
Harland Rd CH42 66 D4
Harlech Cl WA5 60 E2
Harlech Ct CH63 78 F4
Harlech Rd L23 26 C3
Harlech St
Ashton-in-M WN4 34 F5
Liverpool L4 38 F1
Wallasey CH44 51 E2
Harleston Rd L33 30 A3
Harleston Wlk L33 30 A3
Harley Ave CH63 78 C8
Harley Bldgs 11 L3 90 A4
Harley St 2 L9 39 A6
Harlian Ave CH46 64 D7
Harlow Cl WA9 57 F7
Harlow St L8 67 F4
Harlyn Cl L26 82 E7
Harlyn Gdns WA5 74 D3
Harmony Way L13 54 A1
Harold Ave WN4 35 A5
Haroldene Gr L34 55 F5
Harold Rd WA11 45 F7
Harper Rd L9 39 A4
Harpers Pond La L15 69 A8
Harper St 3 L6, L7 53 A2
Harp's Croft L30 27 C3
Harptree Cl L35 56 E3
Harradon Rd L9 39 B7
Harridge La L39 12 F8
Harrier Dr
Liverpool L26 70 E1
Skelmersdale WN8 24 E8
Harrier Rd WA2 61 F2
Harringay Ave L18 68 F5
Harrington Ave CH47 63 C7
Harrington Chambers L2 90 A3
Harrington Rd
Crosby L23 26 D4
Litherland L21 27 D1
Liverpool L3 67 E4
Harrington St L2 90 A3
Harris Cl CH63 79 A2
Harris Dr L20, L30 38 D7
Harris Gdns WA9 44 B1
Harris Grange WA10 43 C1
Harrismith Rd L10 39 F6
Harrison Dr
Bootle L20 38 E3
Haydock WA11 45 A6
Rainford WA11 31 F8
Wallasey CH45 50 E7
Harrison Hey L36 55 E1
Harrison Sq WA5 60 F1
Harrison St WA8 84 B6
Harrison Way
Liverpool L3 67 E4
Newton-le-W WA12 46 C4
Harris St
St Helens WA10 43 E4
Widnes WA8 73 C1
Harrocks Cl L30 27 D5
Harrock Wood Cl CH61 76 E6
Harrod Dr PR8 3 E3
Harrogate Cl
Bebington CH62 88 D4
Warrington WA5 60 A1
Harrogate Dr L5 52 F5
Harrogate Rd
Bebington CH62 88 D4
Bebington, Dacre Hill CH42 79 A8
Harrogate Way PR9 2 C6
Harrogate Wlk CH42 79 A8
Harron Cl 5 L32 29 C2
Harrops Croft L30 27 E4
Harrowby Cl L8 68 A7
Harrowby Rd
Birkenhead CH42 66 D4
Seaforth L21 37 F7
Wallasey CH44 51 E4
Harrowby Rd S CH42 66 C4
Harrowby St 4 L8 68 A7
Harrow Cl
Litherland L30 27 F2
Orrell WN5 25 F8
Wallasey CH44 50 F5
Harrow Dr L10 28 D2
Harrow Gr CH62 88 E8
Harrow Rd
Liverpool L4 53 B6
Wallasey CH44 50 F5
Harsnips WN8 16 C2
Harswell Cl WN5 25 E5
Hartdale Rd
Crosby L23 27 B6
Liverpool L18 69 A4
Hartford Cl CH43 65 F3
Harthill Ave L18 69 B4
Harthill Mews CH43 50 C1
Harthill Rd L18 69 C4
Hartington Ave CH41 66 B7
Hartington Rd
Liverpool, Garston L19 81 D6
Liverpool L8 68 C6
Liverpool, Sandfield Park L12 54 C6
St Helens WA10 43 D5

Hartington Rd *continued*
Wallasey CH44 .... 51 B4
Hartington Terr L19........ 81 B6
Hartismere Rd CH44 ..... 51 D3
Hartland WN8 .... 16 C2
Hartland Ave PR9.......... 2 B5
Hartland Cl WA8......... 73 A5
Hartland Gdns WA9...... 57 D6
Hartland Rd L11 .... 39 E2
Hartley Ave L9........... 39 B5
Hartley Cl [4] L4 .... 52 F7
Hartley Cres PR8 .... 3 F2
Hartley Ct L14 .... 54 D2
Hartley Gr
Kirkby L33 .... 29 F5
St Helens WA10.......... 57 C8
Hartley Quay L3 .... 90 A2
Hartley Rd PR8 .... 3 F2
HARTLEY'S VILLAGE 39 B5
Hartnup St
Liverpool, Anfield L5 ...... 53 A6
Liverpool, Everton L5...... 52 F6
Harton Cl WA8........... 72 E3
Hartopp Rd L25.......... 70 A6
Hartopp Wlk L25......... 70 A7
Hartsbourne Ave L25 .... 70 A6
Hartsbourne Cl L25 ...... 69 F7
Hartsbourne Wlk L25 .... 70 A7
Hartshead WN8.......... 16 C2
Hart's La WN8 .... 24 F8
Hart St
Liverpool L3............ 90 C4
Southport PR8 .... 4 E6
Hartswell Cl WA3 .... 36 A2
Hartwell St L21.......... 38 B6
Hartwood Cl [5] L32 .... 41 A7
Hartwood Rd
Kirkby L32 .... 40 F7
Southport PR9 .... 4 D7
Hartwood Sq L32 .... 40 F7
Harty Rd WA11 .... 45 A5
Harvard Ct WA2 .... 61 A3
Harvard Gr L34.......... 56 E7
Harvest Ct CH46 .... 49 D1
Harvester Way
Birkenhead CH49......... 64 C4
Litherland L30 .... 28 A4
Harvest La CH46 .... 49 D1
Harvest Way [10] WA9 ..... 58 C4
Harvey Ave
Birkenhead CH49......... 64 D3
Newton-le-W WA12....... 45 F3
Harvey Ct WA3 .... 36 A1
Harvey Ct WA2 .... 61 B3
Harvey La WA3 .... 35 F1
Harvey Rd
Wallasey CH46 .... 50 A2
Wallasey, Liscard CH45..... 51 A6
Harvington Dr PR8......... 7 B5
Harwich Gr L16.......... 69 F8
Harwood Rd L19.......... 81 D6
Haselbeech Cl L11....... 39 F3
Haselbeech Cres L11...... 39 F3
Haseldine St WN4 .... 34 F6
Hasfield Rd L11.......... 40 B2
HASKAYNE 11 F4
Haslam Dr L39........... 13 D7
Haslemere L35 .... 56 F3
Haslemere Dr WA5 ...... 74 D4
Haslemere Ind Est
WN4..................... 35 A8
Haslemere Rd L25 .... 70 B6
Haslemere Way L25...... 70 B6
Haslingden Cl L13 .... 54 B2
Haslington Gr L26 .... 83 A6
Hassal Rd CH42.......... 79 A8
Hastie Cl L27............ 70 E5
Hastings Ave WA2 .... 61 B4
Hastings Dr L36 .... 71 A8
Hastings Rd
Crosby L22............... 26 B2
Southport PR8............. 3 E1
Haswell Dr L28 .... 55 B8
Hatchmere Cl CH43 ...... 65 F3
Hatfield Cl
[2] Liverpool L12 .... 41 A3
St Helens WA9........... 57 F7
Hatfield Gdns L36........ 55 F1
Hatfield Rd
Bootle L20 .... 38 E3
Southport PR8............ 7 C6
Hathaway L31 .... 28 B7
Hathaway Cl L25......... 70 A6
Hathaway Rd L25 .... 70 A6
Hatherley Ave L22, L23 ... 26 E2
Hatherley Cl [3] L8 .... 68 A7
Hatherley St
Liverpool L8............. 68 A7
Wallasey CH44 .... 51 E2
Hathersage Rd L36 ...... 55 F5
Hatherton Gr L26 .... 83 A6
Hatton Ave CH62......... 88 E3
Hatton Cl CH60 .... 76 D1
Hatton Garden Ind Est
L3 .... 90 B4
Hatton Gdn L1, L2, L3 ..... 90 B4
Hatton Hill Prim Sch
L21 .... 27 B2
Hatton Hill Rd L21 .... 27 A1
Hattons La L16 .... 69 C6
Hauxwell Gr WA11 .... 44 B6
Havannah La WA9 .... 45 B3
Havelock Cl WA10 .... 43 F3
Haven Brow L39.......... 21 C8
Haven Rd L10........... 39 F8
Haven Wlk L31 .... 20 C4
Havergal St [4] WA7...... 84 F1
Haverstock Rd L6........ 53 D3
Haverton Wlk L12......... 40 E3
Haverty Prec WA12 ...... 46 B1
Hawarde Cl WA12........ 46 A4
Hawarden Ave
Birkenhead CH43......... 66 C6
Liverpool L17............ 68 E6
Wallasey CH44 .... 51 C4
Hawarden Ct CH63....... 78 F4
Hawarden Gr L21 .... 38 A6
Hawdon Ct [9] L7 .... 68 C8
Hawes Ave WA11 .... 44 C8
Hawes Cres WN4 .... 35 B5
Hawesside St PR9 .... 4 C7
Haweswater Ave WA11... 45 A6
Haweswater Cl L33 ...... 29 D5
Haweswater Gr L31 ...... 20 F2
Hawgreen Rd L32........ 29 B1
Hawick Cl L33 .... 29 D6
Hawke Gn L36 .... 71 A7
Hawker Dr WN8 .... 24 E8
Hawke St L3............. 90 C3
Hawkesworth St [8] L4 ... 53 A6
Hawkhurst Cl [1] L8 ...... 67 F4
Hawkins Rd CH64........ 86 F1
Hawkins St L6 .... 53 C3
Hawksclough WN8....... 16 D2
Hawkshead Ave L12...... 40 C1
Hawkshead Cl L31 .... 20 E2
Hawkshead Dr L21 .... 38 D8
Hawkshead Rd
Bebington CH62.......... 79 E1
Burtonwood WA5......... 59 E6
Hawkshead St PR8, PR9.... 4 D7
Hawksmoor Cl L10....... 40 A7
Hawksmoor Rd L10 ...... 40 A7
Hawksmore Cl CH49 ..... 64 D6
Hawkstone St L8 .... 68 A5
Hawks Way CH60 .... 85 E8
Hawksworth Cl L37 ...... 10 A6
Hawksworth Dr L37...... 10 A6
Hawleyís Lane Trad Pk
WA2 .... 61 A1
Hawley's Cl WA5......... 60 F1
Hawley's La WA2, WA5.... 61 A1
Haworth Dr L20.......... 38 D7
Hawthorn Ave
Downall Green WN4 ...... 34 D5
Newton-le-W WA12....... 46 D3
Orrell WN5.............. 25 F6
[1] Widnes WA8.......... 73 B2
Hawthorn Cl WN5........ 33 D5
Hawthorn Cotts CH60 .... 85 F8
Hawthorn Cres WN8 ..... 15 E1
Hawthorn Dr
Heswall CH61 .... 76 F2
St Helens WA10.......... 43 B4
West Kirby CH48......... 63 E2
Hawthorne Ave
Liverpool L26............ 82 F7
Warrington WA5 .... 74 F6
Hawthorne Cl WA11...... 45 A5
Hawthorne Cres L37 ..... 10 A2
Hawthorne Ct L21 .... 38 B8
Hawthorne Dr CH64...... 88 B1
Hawthorne Gr
Southport PR9............ 4 F7
Wallasey CH44 .... 51 E2
Hawthorne Rd
Birkenhead CH42......... 66 D3
Bootle L20, L21, L70 ...... 38 D5
St Helens WA9........... 58 D6
Hawthorn Gr [5] L7........ 53 B1
Hawthorn La CH62 .... 88 D8
Hawthorn Rd
Huyton-w-R L36.......... 55 C2
Neston CH64 .... 86 C1
Prescot L34 .... 56 E6
Hawthorns Gr L12 .... 54 B6
Haxted Gdns L19 .... 81 D6
Haydn Rd L14 .... 54 F6
HAYDOCK 45 D6
Haydock English Martyrs'
RC Prim Sch WA11 ..... 45 E7
Haydock La WA11........ 45 C7
Haydock La Ind Est
WA11 .... 45 E8
Haydock Park Gdns
WA12.................... 35 B1
Haydock Park Race
Course WA12........... 35 D1
Haydock Park Rd L10 .... 28 E3
Haydock Rd CH45........ 51 C7
Haydock Sports Coll
WA11 .... 45 C6
Haydock St
Ashton-in-M WN4 .... 35 B2
Newton-le-W WA12....... 46 A3
St Helens WA10.......... 44 A3
Hayes Ave L35........... 56 E5
Hayes Dr L31 .... 29 B3
Hayes St WA10 .... 57 C8
Hayfield Cl L26 .... 71 A1
Hayfield Pl CH46......... 65 A8
Hayfield Rd L39.......... 13 E7
Hayfield Sch CH49 .... 65 A6
Hayfield St [14] L4 .... 52 F7
Hayfield Way [8] WA9 .... 58 C4
Haylemere Ct PR8 .... 3 E5
Hayles Cl L25........... 70 A6
Hayles Gn L25 .... 70 A6
Hayles Gr L25 .... 70 A6
Haylock Cl L8 .... 67 F4
Hayman's Cl L12......... 54 A7
Haymans Gn L31......... 20 E1
Hayman's Gn L12 .... 54 A7
Hayman's Gr L12 .... 54 A7
Haymarket Lo PR9 .... 1 D1
Hayscastle Cl WA5....... 60 E1
Hayward Ct L37.......... 10 A4
Haywood Cl WA3 .... 36 E1
Haywood Gdns WA10 .... 43 D2
Hazel Ave
Kirkby L32 .... 29 C3
Prescot L35 .... 56 E4
Hazelbank Gdns L37 ...... 9 E5
Hazel Ct
Bootle L20 .... 38 C2
[12] Liverpool L8.......... 68 A4
Ormskirk L39............. 13 E5
Hazeldale Rd L9 .... 39 A4
Hazeldene Ave
Heswall CH61 .... 77 B6
Wallasey CH45 .... 51 A5
Hazeldene Way CH61 .... 77 B7
Hazelfield Ct [2] WA9..... 58 C4
Hazel Gr
Bebington CH63.......... 78 E4
Crosby L23.............. 26 F3
Golborne WA3 .... 47 B8
Irby CH61 .... 76 D7
Liverpool L9............. 39 B6
Southport PR8 .... 4 E7
St Helens WA10.......... 43 C3
Hazelhurst Rd L4 .... 53 B7
Hazel La WN8 .... 16 B4
Hazelmere Ho L17 .... 68 D2
Hazel Mews L31 .... 29 B3
Hazel Rd
Birkenhead CH41......... 66 D5
Hoylake CH47 .... 63 B7
Huyton-w-R L36.......... 55 F5
Hazelslack Rd L11 .... 40 A2
Hazelwood
Birkenhead CH49......... 64 D5
Southport PR8............. 3 F1
Hazelwood Cl
St Helens WA9........... 58 B3
Widnes WA8 .... 84 A8
Hazelwood Gr L26 .... 70 D2
Hazlehurst Cl L37......... 9 C2
Hazlehurst Gr WN4 ...... 35 C4
Hazleton Rd L14 .... 54 C3
Headbolt La
Kirkby L33 .... 29 F4
Southport L39 .... 8 A4
Southport PR8............ 8 B7
Headbourne Cl L25 ...... 69 F7
Headbourne Ct L25 ...... 69 F7
Headingley Cl
Huyton-w-R L36.......... 70 C8
St Helens WA9........... 58 C6
Headingly Ave WN8...... 15 D1
Headington Rd CH49..... 64 D5
Headland Cl
Golborne WA3 .... 47 E6
West Kirby CH48......... 75 B8
Headley Cl WA10 .... 43 F3
Head St L8 .... 67 E6
Heald St
Liverpool L19............ 81 C6
Newton-le-W WA12....... 45 F3
Healy Cl L27............. 71 A4
Heanor Dr PR8 .... 4 F3
Heap Ct PR9.............. 4 E8
Hearne Rd WA10......... 43 D4
Heartwood Cl L9 .... 39 A7
Heathbank Ave
Irby CH61 .... 76 D7
[1] Wallasey CH44........ 51 A3
Heathbank Rd CH42...... 66 D3
Heath Cl
Liverpool L25............ 69 F5
Prescot L34 .... 56 F7
West Kirby CH48......... 75 B8
Heathcote Cl [1] L7....... 68 C8
Heathcote Gdns CH63.... 78 F5
Heathcote Rd L4......... 38 F2
Heath Dale CH63......... 78 F3
Heath Dr
Birkenhead CH49......... 65 A6
Heswall CH60 .... 76 F1
Heather Bank CH63 ...... 78 D6
Heather Brae
Huyton-w-R L34.......... 56 A5
Newton-le-W WA12....... 46 A4
Heather Brow CH43....... 65 F7
Heather Cl
Formby L37 .... 10 B5
[2] Kirkby L33 .... 29 E4
Liverpool L4............. 52 F8
Southport PR8............ 7 D2
Heather Ct L4 .... 52 F8
Heatherdale Cl CH42..... 66 C4
Heatherdale Rd L18...... 69 A4
Heather Dene CH62...... 79 D2
Heatherdene Rd CH48.... 63 B3
Heatherfield Ct CH42 .... 66 C4
Heather Gr WN4......... 35 E4
Heathergreen Ct L4....... 39 B1
Heatherlea Cl WN8 ...... 25 C7
Heatherleigh
St Helens WA9........... 57 D6
West Kirby CH48......... 75 D6
Heatherleigh Cl L9....... 39 A7
Heather Rd
Bebington CH63.......... 78 D4
Heswall CH60 .... 77 A1
Heathers Croft L30 ...... 27 E3
Heather Way L23 .... 27 C6
Heatherways L37 .... 10 A6
Heathey La PR8........... 8 F8
Heathfield CH62 .... 79 D2
Heathfield Ave WA9...... 57 E8
Heathfield Cl
Bootle L21.............. 38 C6
Formby L37 .... 10 A6
Heathfield Dr L33........ 29 E4
Heathfield Ho CH61 ...... 77 A6
Heathfield Pk WA8....... 72 D3
Heathfield Rd
Bebington CH63.......... 78 F4
Birkenhead CH43......... 66 C4
Crosby L22.............. 26 C2
Liverpool L15, L18 .... 69 B6
Maghull L31............. 28 F7
Southport PR8 .... 7 F6
Heathfield St L1 .... 90 C3
Heathgate WN8.......... 16 C2
Heathgate Ave L24....... 83 A2
Heath Hey L25........... 69 F5
Heath La
Golborne, Kenyon WA3 .... 47 F2
Golborne WA3 .... 47 D6
Willaston CH64 .... 88 C1
Heathland WN8.......... 25 B7
Heathland Rd WA9....... 58 C4
Heathlands The CH46 .... 49 E3
Heathmoor Ave WA3..... 47 D6
Heathmoor Rd CH46 ..... 49 D1
Heath Rd
Ashton-in-M WN4 .... 35 C2
Bebington CH63.......... 78 F5
Huyton-w-R L36.......... 55 B5
Liverpool L19, L18 .... 81 D8
Warrington WA5 .... 74 F5
Widnes WA8 .... 72 D2
Heathside CH60.......... 76 D1
Heath St
Ashton-in-M WN4 .... 35 C2
Golborne WA3 .... 47 A8
St Helens WA9........... 57 D7
Heath View L21.......... 27 B3
Heathview Cl WA8 ...... 84 A5
Heathview Rd WA8 ...... 84 A5
Heathwaite Cres L11..... 40 A1
Heathway CH60.......... 86 B7
Heathwood L12.......... 54 B5
Heathy La L39 .... 11 B8
Heatley Cl CH43 .... 65 C7
Heaton Cl
Liverpool L24............ 82 F4
Up Holland WN8 .... 25 A7
Hebburn Way L12........ 41 A3
Hebden Par [3] L11....... 40 C3
Hebden Rd L11 .... 40 B3
Hebdon Cl WN4.......... 35 A5
Hedgebank Cl L9 .... 39 D8
Hedgecote L32 .... 40 E7
Hedgecroft L23.......... 27 C6
Hedgefield Rd L25....... 70 B6
Hedgerows The WA11.... 45 F7
Hedges Cres L13......... 53 E7
Hedingham Cl L26....... 71 A1
Hedworth Gdns WA9..... 57 D6
Heigham Gdns WA9..... 57 E6
Helena Rd WA9.......... 58 F7
Helena St
Birkenhead CH41......... 66 E5
Liverpool, Walton L9 ...... 38 F3
[11] Liverpool, Wavertree
L7....................... 53 B1
Helen Bank Dr WA11..... 31 F7
Helen St
Ashton-in-M WN4 .... 35 A4
Golborne WA3 .... 35 F1
Helford Cl L35........... 57 A6
Helford Rd L11 .... 40 D5
Heliers Rd L13.......... 54 B2
Hell Nook WA3 .... 35 F1
Helmdon Cl [2] L11....... 40 A1
Helmingham Gr CH41 .... 66 E4
Helmsdale WN8 .... 16 C2
Helmsley Rd L26......... 82 F8
Helsby Ave CH62......... 88 F3
Helsby Rd L9 .... 39 B7
Helsby St
Liverpool L7............. 53 A1
St Helens WA9........... 44 E1
Helston Ave
Liverpool L26............ 70 F1
St Helens WA11.......... 44 D7
Helston Cl
Southport PR9............ 2 B5
Warrington WA5 .... 74 E5
Helston Gn L36 .... 56 B3
Helston Rd L11 .... 40 D5
Helton Cl CH43 .... 65 E3
Hemans St L20 .... 38 A4
Hemer Terr L20.......... 38 A5
Hemingford St CH41 ..... 66 D6
Hemlock Cl L12.......... 40 D3
Hemmingsway L35....... 57 A3
Hempstead Cl WA9 ...... 57 F7
Henderson Cl
Birkenhead CH49......... 64 E6
Warrington WA5 .... 74 D6
Henderson Dr WA11 ..... 32 A8
Henderson Rd
Huyton-w-R L36.......... 56 A3
Widnes, Lower House
WA8 .... 84 F8
[2] Widnes WA8.......... 73 A1
Hendon Rd L6 .... 53 D4
Hendon Wlk CH49 .... 64 C3
Hengest Cl L33 .... 29 E6
Henglers Cl [7] L6........ 53 A3
Henley Ave L21 .... 38 A8
Henley Cl CH63 .... 79 A2
Henley Ct
Southport PR9............ 1 E1
St Helens WA10.......... 43 D1
Henley Dr PR9............. 1 F1
Henley Rd L18........... 69 B5
Henllan Gdns WA9....... 58 F7
Henlow Ave L32 .... 40 F8
Hennawood Cl [5] L6..... 53 B5
Henrietta Gr L34......... 55 F5
Henry Edward St L3...... 52 D3
Henry Hickman Cl L30 ... 27 F4
Henry St
Birkenhead CH41......... 66 E6
Liverpool L1............. 90 B2
Liverpool, Stanley L13 ..... 53 F2
St Helens WA10.......... 43 F4
[4] Widnes WA8.......... 73 C1
Henthorne Rd CH62...... 79 B8
Henthorne St CH43 ...... 66 C5
Hepworth Cl WN3........ 35 F2
Herald Ave L24 .... 81 F6
Herald Cl L11............ 40 C3
Heralds Cl WA8.......... 84 C8
Heralds Gn WA5 .... 60 A2
Herbarth Cl L9 .... 38 F3
Herberts La CH60 .... 85 F8
Herbert St
Burtonwood WA5......... 59 E6
St Helens WA9........... 58 F7
Herbert Taylor Cl L6 ..... 53 C5
Herculaneum Ct L8 ...... 67 F3
Herculaneum Rd L8...... 67 E4
Herdman Cl L25 .... 70 B5
Hereford Ave
Birkenhead CH49......... 64 E6
Golborne WA3 .... 47 B8
Hereford Cl
Ashton-in-M WN4 .... 35 C2
St Helens WA10.......... 43 F2
Hereford Dr L30 .... 27 F1
Hereford Gr WN8 .... 25 B6
Hereford Rd
Liverpool L15............ 69 A6
Seaforth L21 .... 37 F7
Southport PR9............. 4 F7
Heriot St L5 .... 52 D6
Hermes Cl L30........... 38 E8
Hermes Rd L11 .... 40 C6
Hermitage Gr L20........ 38 D6
Hermitage Green La WA2,
WA12.................... 61 A8
Hermitage The CH60 ..... 85 F7
Herm Rd L5 .... 52 C5
Heron Ct L26 .... 70 E1
Herondale Rd L18 .... 69 A5
Heron Gr WA11 .... 32 B5
Heronhall Rd L9 .... 39 F4
Heronpark Way CH63 .... 79 B2
Heron Rd CH47, CH48 ..... 64 A6
Herons Ct L31 .... 20 B4
Hero St L20 .... 38 D2
Herrick St L13 .... 53 F3
Herschell St L5.......... 53 A6
Hertford Cl L26.......... 82 F8
Hertford Dr CH45 .... 51 C6
Hertford Rd L20 .... 38 C2
Hertford St WA9......... 44 D2
Hesketh Ave CH42 .... 66 D1
Hesketh Cl WA5 .... 74 F4
Hesketh Ct WA11 .... 32 A4
Hesketh Dr
Heswall CH60 .... 77 A1
Maghull L31............. 20 F1
Southport PR9............. 1 F1
Hesketh Grange Cotts
CH63 .... 87 A7
Hesketh Links Ct PR9 ...... 1 E2
Hesketh Lo L37............ 9 E3
Hesketh Meadow La
WA3..................... 47 F8
Hesketh Rd
Hale L24 .... 83 E2
Southport PR9............ 1 D2
Hesketh St [5] L17........ 68 C4
Heskin Cl
Kirkby L32 .... 40 E7
Maghull L31............. 20 D4
Rainhill L35 .... 57 B3
Heskin Hall Ct L39 ...... 13 D8
Heskin La L39 .... 13 D8
Heskin Rd L32 .... 40 E7
Heskin Wlk L32.......... 40 E7
Hessle Dr CH60 .... 85 F7
Hester Cl L38............ 17 F4
HESWALL 77 B1
Heswall Ave
Bebington CH63.......... 78 C8
St Helens WA9........... 58 B4
Heswall Mount CH61..... 77 A5
Heswall Point [7] CH60 .... 86 A8
Heswall Prep Sch
CH60.................... 76 F2
Heswall Prim Sch
CH60..................... 77 A1
Heswall Rd L9 .... 39 B7
Heswall St Peter's CE Prim
Sch CH60 .... 85 F8
Heswall Sta CH60........ 86 D8
Hever Dr L26 .... 71 A1
Heversham WN8......... 16 C2
Heward Ave [1] WA9...... 58 C6
Hewitson Ave L13........ 53 F6
Hewitson Rd L13 .... 53 F6
Hewitt Ave WA10 .... 43 D4
Hewitt Bsns Pk WN5 ..... 25 E4
Hewitt's La L33, L34 ...... 41 E7
Hewitts Pl [5] L2 .... 90 A4
Hexagon The [1] L20 ..... 38 C3
Hexham Cl
Litherland L30 .... 28 A1
St Helens WA9........... 57 D6

Heyburn Rd L13 53 E6
Heydale Rd L18 69 A4
Heydean Rd L18 69 C1
Heydean Wlk L18 69 C1
Heydon Ave 6 L32 29 C2
Heydon Cl
Formby L37 9 D1
Halewood L26 83 A7
Heyes Ave
Haydock WA11 45 D5
Rainford WA11 32 A6
Heyescroft L39 22 D6
Heyes Dr CH45 50 C4
Heyes Gr WA11 32 A6
Heyesmere Ct L17 80 F7
Heyes Mount L35 57 C2
Heyes Rd
Orrell WN5 25 E6
Widnes WA8 84 C8
Heyes St L5 53 A5
Heyes The L25 70 B2
Heygarth Dr CH49 64 D4
Heygarth Prim Sch CH62 88 E5
Heygarth Rd CH62 88 E5
Heygreen Com Prim Sch L15 68 E8
Hey Green Rd L15 68 E8
Hey Lock Cl WA12 60 C8
Hey Pk L36 55 F2
Hey Rd L36 55 F2
Heys Ave CH62 88 D8
Heyscroft Rd L25 70 B2
Heysham Lawn L27 71 A4
Heysham Rd
Litherland L30, L9 28 A2
Southport PR9 4 F7
Heysmoor Hts 6 L8 68 B6
Heysome Cl WA11 32 E4
Heys The
Bebington CH62 88 F5
Southport PR8 3 D4
Heythrop Dr CH60 86 D8
Heyville Rd CH63 78 E5
Heywood Ave WA3 36 B1
Heywood Bvd CH61 77 A6
Heywood Cl
Formby L37 9 E3
Heswall CH61 77 A6
Hey Wood Cl WA12 60 C8
Heywood Ct L15 54 C1
Heywood Gdns
Golborne WA3 36 B1
Prescot L35 56 E2
Heywood Rd L15 69 C8
Heyworth St L5 52 F5
Hickling Gdns WA9 57 E6
Hickmans Rd CH41, CH44 51 B1
Hickory Gr L31 29 A2
Hickson Ave L31 20 C3
Hicks Rd
Crosby L22 26 E1
Seaforth L21 38 A7
Highacre Rd CH45 51 A7
Higham Ave
St Helens WA10 42 F3
Warrington WA5 60 F1
Higham Sq 4 L5 52 E4
High Bank Cl CH43 65 D5
Highbank Dr L19 81 E6
Highbanks L31 20 C3
High Beeches L16 54 F1
High Beeches Cres WN4 35 A6
High Carrs L36 55 B2
Highclere Cres L36 55 E5
Highcroft Ave CH63 79 A5
Highcroft Gn CH63 79 A5
Highcroft The CH63 78 F5
Higher Ashton WA8 72 F3
HIGHER BEBINGTON 78 E6
Higher Bebington Jun Sch CH63 78 D6
Higher Bebington Rd CH63 78 E5
HIGHER END 25 D3
Higher End Pk L30 27 E5
Higher La
Liverpool L9 39 D6
Rainford WA11 32 C5
Skelmersdale WN8 16 C7
Up Holland WN8 25 C7
Higher Moss La L37 11 A2
Higher Parr St WA9 44 C3
Higher Rd
Halewood L26, WA8 83 C5
Speke L25, L26 82 E8
Higher Side Com Comp Sch L35 56 F3
Higher View WN8 25 C6
Highfield L33 29 F5
Highfield Ave WA3 46 F8
Highfield Cl CH44 51 A4
Highfield Cres
Birkenhead CH42 66 F1
Widnes WA8 73 A2
Highfield Ct CH42 66 F1
Highfield Dr
Birkenhead CH49 64 D4
Crank WA11 32 E4
Highfield Gr
Birkenhead CH42 66 F1
Crosby L23 26 F5
Highfield La
Golborne WA3 47 C5
Winwick WA2 61 C7
Highfield Pk L31 20 F1
Highfield Rd
Birkenhead CH42 66 F1
Litherland L21 38 A8
Liverpool L13 54 A4
Liverpool, Walton L9 38 F4
Ormskirk L39 13 E7
Southport PR9 2 B3
Widnes WA8 73 A2
Highfields
Heswall CH60 76 F1
Prescot L34 56 C6
Highfield S CH42 79 A8
Highfield Sch
Birkenhead CH43 65 F6
Halewood L26 83 A7
Highfield St
Liverpool L2, L3 90 A4
St Helens WA9 58 D8
Highfield View L13 54 A4
Highgate Cl CH60 76 F2
Highgate Ct 13 L7 53 B1
Highgate Rd
Maghull L31 20 D3
Up Holland WN8 25 B7
Highgate St L7 53 A1
Highgreen Rd CH42 66 C3
Highgrove Pk L19 81 A8
High La
Bickerstaffe L39 22 C8
Ormskirk L39, L40 14 A8
Highlands Rd WA7 84 F1
Highmarsh Cres WA12 46 B4
Highmeadow WN8 25 A6
High Moss L39 13 E3
High Mount CH60 85 F8
Highoaks Rd L25 70 B1
HIGH PARK 5 A8
High Park Pl PR9 5 A8
Highpark Rd CH42 66 C3
High Park Rd PR9 5 A8
High Park St L8 68 A5
High St
Bebington CH62 79 E1
Golborne WA3 47 A8
Hale L24 83 D1
Liverpool L2 90 A4
Liverpool, Wavertree L15 68 F8
Liverpool, Woolton L25 70 A2
Newton-le-W WA12 46 D4
Prescot L34 56 D6
4 Runcorn WA7 84 F2
Skelmersdale WN8 15 E1
Highsted Gr L33 29 F5
Hightor Rd L25 69 F3
HIGHTOWN 18 A3
Hightown Sta L38 18 A4
Highville Rd L16 69 D6
Highwood Ct L33 29 F4
Highwoods Cl WN4 35 B5
Hignett Ave WA9 45 B2
Higson Ct L8 68 A3
Hilary Ave
Golborne WA3 36 D1
Huyton-w-R L14 54 F2
Hilary Cl
Liverpool L4 53 C8
Prescot L34 56 E7
Warrington WA5 74 D6
Widnes WA8 73 E3
Hilary Dr CH49 65 A6
Hilary Mans 1 CH44 51 A4
Hilary Rd L4 53 C8
Hilberry Ave L13 53 E5
Hilbre Ave
Heswall CH60 85 E6
6 Wallasey CH44 51 A4
Hilbre Cl PR9 1 F1
Hilbre Ct CH48 63 A1
Hilbre Dr PR9 1 F1
Hilbre High Sch CH48 63 D3
Hilbre Island Nature Reserve★ CH47 62 B4
Hilbre Point CH47 62 F5
Hilbre Rd CH48 63 B1
Hilbre St
Birkenhead CH41 66 D8
Liverpool L3 90 C3
Hilbre View CH48 63 C2
Hilda Rd L12 54 E5
Hildebrand Cl L4 53 C8
Hildebrand Rd L4 53 C8
Hilden Rd WA2 61 E1
Hillaby Cl L8 68 A6
Hillam Rd CH45 50 D6
Hillary Cres L31 20 D1
Hillary Ct L37 9 E2
Hillary Dr L23 27 A4
Hillary Rd CH62 88 E5
Hillary Wlk L23 27 A4
Hillbark Rd CH48, CH49 64 B1
Hillbeck Cres WN4 34 D4
Hillbrae Ave WA11 33 A1
Hillbrook Dr L9 39 D3
Hillburn Dr CH41 50 E1
Hillcrest
Maghull L31 20 F1
Skelmersdale WN8 24 B8
Hill Crest L20 38 E2
Hillcrest Ave L36 56 A2
Hillcrest Ct 4 CH44 51 A3
Hillcrest Dr CH49 64 C3
Hillcrest Par L36 56 A2
Hillcrest Rd
Crosby L23 27 A4
Liverpool L4 39 D1
Ormskirk L39 13 E6
Hillcroft Rd
Liverpool L25 69 F4
Hillcroft Rd *continued*
Wallasey CH44 51 C2
Hilldean WN8 25 C8
Hillerton Cl L12 40 B2
Hillfield Dr CH61 76 F3
Hillfoot Ave L25 82 C8
Hillfoot Cl CH43 65 C8
Hillfoot Gn L25 82 A8
Hillfoot Rd L25 82 A9
Hill Gr CH46 64 E7
Hillhead Rd L20 38 E2
Hillingden Ave
Halewood L26 83 A7
Liverpool L26 82 F8
Hillingdon Ave CH61 76 F2
Hillingdon Rd L15 69 B6
Hillock La WN8 16 D7
Hill Rd CH43 65 E6
Hill Ridge CH43 65 D5
Hill Rise View L39 13 A1
Hill School Rd WA10 57 A8
HILLSIDE 3 F1
Hillside Ave
Ashton-in-M WN4 34 F8
Huyton-w-R L36 55 D6
Newton-le-W WA12 45 F2
Ormskirk L39 13 D3
St Helens WA10 43 E6
Hillside Cl
Billinge WN5 33 D5
Birkenhead CH41 66 E4
Bootle L20 38 E2
Hillside Com Prim Sch WN8 24 D8
Hillside Court Flats L25 70 B3
Hillside Cres L36 55 D6
Hillside Ct
Birkenhead CH41 66 E4
Liverpool L25 70 B3
Ormskirk L39 13 D3
Hillside Dr L25 70 B3
Hillside Gr WA5 74 F4
Hillside High Sch L20 38 E3
Hillside Prim Sch CH43 65 D5
Hillside Rd
Birkenhead CH43 65 D8
Birkenhead, Tranmere CH41 66 E4
Heswall CH60 86 A7
Huyton-w-R L36 55 E5
Liverpool L18 69 B5
Southport PR8 3 E1
Wallasey CH44 50 F4
West Kirby CH48 63 D2
Hillside St L6 52 F3
Hillside Sta PR8 3 E1
Hillside View CH43 66 A3
Hills Moss Rd WA9 58 F7
Hills Pl L15 69 A7
Hill St
Crosby L23 26 F3
Liverpool L8 67 E6
7 Prescot L34 56 D6
Southport PR9 4 B7
St Helens WA10 44 A5
Hillsview Rd PR8 7 C4
Hill Top La CH60 86 B8
Hilltop Rd L16 69 D7
Hill Top Rd WA11 32 B2
Hilltop Wlk L39 13 C3
Hillview L17 68 E2
Hill View WA8 72 F5
Hillview Ave CH48 63 B3
Hillview Ct 1 CH43 65 C8
Hill View Dr CH49 65 A6
Hillview Gdns L25 69 F3
Hillview Mans CH48 63 B3
Hillview Rd CH61 76 C7
Hillwood Cl CH63 79 A1
Hilton Cl CH41 66 D6
Hilton Ct L30 27 D4
Hilton Gr CH48 63 A3
Hilton St WN4 35 C3
Hinchley Gn L31 20 B1
Hinckley Rd WA11 44 C6
Hindburn Ave L31 20 F2
Hinderton Cl CH41 66 E4
Hinderton Dr
Heswall CH60 85 F6
West Kirby CH48 63 E1
Hinderton La CH64 87 A1
Hinderton Rd
Birkenhead CH41 66 E5
Neston CH64 87 A1
Hindle Ave WA5 60 F1
Hindley Beech 1 L31 20 C2
Hindley Wlk L24 82 D3
Hindlip St 4 L8 68 A3
Hind St CH41 66 E5
Hinson St 6 CH41 66 E6
Hinton St
Bootle L21 38 B6
Liverpool L6 53 C3
Historic Warship Mus★ CH44 51 D1
HM Customs & Exise National Mus★ L3 90 A2
Hobart Dr L33 29 E6
Hobart St WA9 57 E8
Hobberley Dr WN8 24 E8
Hoblyn Rd CH43 65 E8
Hockenhall Alley L2 90 A4
Hockenhull Cl CH63 79 A2
Hodder Ave L31 20 F2
Hodder Cl WA11 44 B7
Hodder Rd L5 52 F6
Hodder St L5 52 F6
Hodge St PR8 4 B7
Hodgkinson Ave WA5 60 F1
Hodnet Dr WN4 35 C3
Hodson Pl L6 53 A4
Hodson St PR8 4 C6
Hogarth Dr CH43 65 D3
Hogarth St 3 L21 38 A6
Hogarth Wlk L4 52 D8
Hoggs Hill La L37 9 F1
Hoghton Cl WA9 58 F8
Hoghton Gr PR9 4 C8
Hoghton Pl 3 PR9 4 B7
Hoghton Rd
Hale L24 83 E2
St Helens WA9 58 F7
Hoghton St PR9 4 C7
Holbeck St L4 53 C7
Holborn Ct WA8 72 F3
Holborn Dr L39 13 C3
Holborn Hill
Birkenhead CH41 66 E4
Ormskirk L39 13 C4
Holborn Sq CH41 66 E4
Holborn St L7 53 A2
Holbrook Cl
St Helens WA9 58 C6
Warrington WA5 74 E5
Holcombe Ave WA3 47 C8
Holcombe Cl CH49 64 D4
Holden Gr 7 L22 26 C2
Holden Rd
Crosby L22 26 C2
Prescot L35 56 C4
Holden Rd E 2 L22 26 C2
Holden St L8 68 A8
Holden Terr 3 L22 26 C2
Holdsworth St L7 53 B2
Holford Way WA12 46 F3
Holgate L23, L29 27 B7
Holgate Dr WN5 25 E6
Holgate Pk L23 27 B7
Holin Ct CH43 66 A7
Holkham Cl WA8 72 F1
Holkham Gdns WA9 57 D6
Holland Bsns Pk L40 15 C4
Holland Ct
Litherland L30 27 D4
Skelmersdale WN8 24 D2
Holland Gr CH60 76 F1
Holland Ho WN8 25 C6
HOLLAND MOOR 24 F7
Holland Moor Prim Sch WN8 24 E7
Holland Moss WN8 24 A5
Holland Pl 4 L7 53 B1
Holland Rd
Halewood L26 82 E7
Speke L24 82 E3
Wallasey CH45 51 C7
Holland's La WN8 15 A1
Holland St L7 53 D3
Holland Way L26 82 E7
Holley Ct L35 57 C3
Holliers Cl L31 20 E1
Hollies Rd L26 82 F9
Hollies The
Liverpool L25 69 E3
Ormskirk L39 13 A4
Southport PR8 3 F6
Hollingbourne Pl L11 40 A3
Hollingbourne Rd L11 40 A3
Hollinghurst Rd L33 29 F5
Hollingwood Cl WN4 35 A3
Hollingworth Cl L9 39 B3
Hollinhey Cl L30 28 A5
Hollin Hey Cl WN5 33 D3
Hollins Cl
Garswood WN4 34 D4
Liverpool L15 69 A8
Hollins Dr WA2 61 A6
Hollinside L36 55 F2
Hollins La WA2 60 E6
Hollins Park Hospl WA2 60 F6
Hollins Way WA8 84 B5
Hollocombe Rd L12 40 B2
Holloway WA7 84 F1
Hollow Croft L28 41 B1
Holly Ave
Bebington CH63 78 F3
Newton-le-W WA12 46 D3
Hollybank Ct
5 Birkenhead CH41 66 D5
Widnes WA8 72 F1
Holly Bank Ct L18 69 C5
Holly Bank Gr WA9 44 C4
Hollybank Grange L26 82 F9
Hollybank Rd
Birkenhead CH41 66 D5
Liverpool L18 68 E5
Holly Bank St WA9 44 C4
Hollybrook Rd PR8 4 A5
Hollybush Sq WA3 36 E1
Holly Cl
Hale L24 83 D2
Skelmersdale WN8 15 E1
St Helens WA10 43 B4
Westhead L40 14 E4
Holly Cres WA11 32 A5
Holly Ct
Bootle L20 38 B5
14 Wallasey CH45 51 B7
Hollydale Rd L18 69 A5
Holly Dene L32 40 F7
Holly Farm Ct WA8 72 E4
Holly Farm Rd L19 81 D6
Hollyfield Rd L9 38 F5
Holly Fold La L39, WA11 23 E3
Holly Gr
Birkenhead CH42 66 E4
Huyton-w-R L36 55 B2
Seaforth L21 37 F6
Holly Hey L35 56 D1
Holly Ho L23 26 F5
Hollyhurst Cl L8 68 A5
Holly La
Ormskirk L39 13 B4
Skelmersdale L39, WA11 23 E4
Holly Lodge Girls' Coll L13 54 A6
Hollymead Cl L25 70 B4
Holly Mews L23 26 F5
Holly Mount
Liverpool L12 54 A6
St Helens WA10 43 D2
Holly Pl CH46 64 F7
Holly Rd
Golborne WA3 47 C8
Haydock WA11 45 A6
Liverpool L7 53 D2
Warrington WA5 74 E5
Hollyrood L34 56 A5
Holly St L20 38 C4
Holly Terr WA5 74 F5
Hollytree Rd L25 70 B3
Hollywood Rd L17 68 E3
Holman Rd L19 81 D6
Holm Cotts CH43 65 F2
Holmdale Ave PR9 2 C4
Holme Cl L34 57 A7
Holmefield Ave L19 69 A1
Holmefield Gr L31 20 C1
Holmefield Rd L19 69 A1
Holme Rd WA10 43 C3
Holmes Ct 4 CH42 66 C3
Holmes La L21 38 A7
Holmes St L8 68 C7
Holme St L5 52 C6
Holmesway CH61 76 F4
Holmfield CH43 65 F2
Holmfield Gr L36 70 F8
Holmfield Pk L37 9 D4
Holm Hey Rd CH43 65 F1
Holm Hill CH48 63 C1
Holm La CH43 65 F2
Holmlands Cres CH43 65 E2
Holmlands Dr CH43 65 E2
Holmlands Way CH43 65 E2
Holmleigh Rd L25 70 A6
Holmrook Rd L11 40 A3
Holmside Cl CH46 64 F8
Holmside La CH43 65 F2
Holm View Cl CH43 66 A3
Holmville Rd CH63 78 E5
Holmway CH63 78 F5
Holmwood L14 55 A3
Holmwood Ave CH61 77 C5
Holmwood Cl
Ashton-in-M WN4 35 A5
Formby L37 9 D3
Holmwood Dr
Formby L37 9 D4
Heswall CH61 77 C5
Holmwood Gdns L37 9 D4
Holt Ave
Billinge WN5 33 D4
Birkenhead CH46 64 E8
Holt Coppice L39 21 A7
Holt Cres WN5 33 D4
HOLT GREEN 21 A6
Holt Hill CH41 66 E4
Holt Hill Terr CH41, CH42 66 E5
Holt La
Huyton-w-R L27 70 E7
Liverpool L27 70 E6
Rainhill L35 57 A5
Holt Rd
Birkenhead CH41 66 E4
Liverpool L7 53 C2
Holt St WN5 25 D5
Holtswell Cl WA3 36 E1
Holt Way L32 29 D2
Holy Angel's RC Prim Schs L32 29 C2
Holy Cross Cl 5 L3 52 D3
Holy Cross RC Prim Sch
Liverpool L3 52 D3
St Helens WA10 44 B4
Wallasey CH41 50 E1
Holy Family High Sch L23 27 A6
Holy Family RC Prim Sch
Cronton WA8 72 D5
Liverpool L25 70 D1
Southport PR9 4 E7
Holyhead Cl WA5 60 D3
Holy Name RC Prim Sch L10 39 E7
Holyrood L23 26 A4
Holyrood Ave WA8 73 A4
Holy Rosary RC Jun Sch L10 28 D3
Holy Rosary RC Prim Sch L10 28 C3
Holy Spirit RC Prim Sch
Litherland L30 27 D3
St Helens WA9 45 A3
Holy Trinity CE Prim Sch PR9 4 C8

Holy Trinity RC Prim Sch
  L19 . . . . 81 D5
Holywell Cl
  Neston CH64 . . . . 86 B1
  St Helens WA9 . . . . 58 D6
Homebank Ho **1** CH43 . . 66 A4
Homechase Ho **3** PR8 . . . . . 3 F4
Homedove Ho **1** L23 . . . . 26 C4
Home Farm Cl CH49 . . . . . 65 C2
Home Farm Rd
  Birkenhead CH49 . . . . 65 C2
  Knowsley L34 . . . . 41 D2
HOMER GREEN 19 C1
Homer Rd L34 . . . . 41 C3
Homerton Rd L6 . . . . 53 D3
Homesands Ho PR9 . . . . 4 D8
Homestall Rd L11 . . . . 40 A2
Homestead Ave
  Haydock WA11 . . . . 45 E6
  Litherland L30 . . . . 28 B3
Homestead Cl L36 . . . . 56 A3
Homestead Mews
  CH48 . . . . 63 B2
Homewood **2** L23 . . . . . . 26 C3
Honeybourne Dr L35 . . . . . 57 A6
Honey Hall Rd L26 . . . . 82 E7
Honeys Green Cl L12 . . . . . 54 D5
Honey's Green La L12 . . . . . 54 D5
Honey's Green Prec
  L12 . . . . 54 D5
Honey St L35 . . . . 57 C7
Honeysuckle Cl
  Liverpool L26 . . . . 70 D2
  Widnes WA8 . . . . 73 B4
Honeysuckle Dr L9 . . . . . . 39 B3
Honister Ave
  St Helens WA11 . . . . 44 C8
  Warrington WA2 . . . . 61 C2
Honister Wlk L27 . . . . 71 A3
Honiston Ave L35 . . . . 57 B4
Honiton Rd L17 . . . . 68 E1
Honiton Way WA5 . . . . . . 74 E4
Hood Rd WA8 . . . . 72 F1
Hood St
  Bootle L20 . . . . 38 A5
  Liverpool L1 . . . . 90 B4
  Wallasey CH44 . . . . 51 D3
Hoole Rd CH49 . . . . 65 B3
Hoose Ct CH47 . . . . 63 C7
HOOTON 89 A1
Hooton Gn CH66 . . . . 89 B1
Hooton La CH66 . . . . 89 B1
Hooton Rd
  Hooton CH64, CH66 . . . . . 88 D1
  Liverpool L9 . . . . 39 B7
Hooton Sta CH66 . . . . 88 D1
Hooton Way CH66 . . . . . . 89 A2
Hooton Works CH66 . . . . . 88 E1
Hope Pk L16 . . . . 69 D6
Hope Pl L1 . . . . 90 C2
Hope Sch L27 . . . . 70 D7
Hope Sq PR9 . . . . 4 D7
Hope St
  Ashton-in-M WN4 . . . . . . 35 D5
  Birkenhead CH41 . . . . 66 D7
  Liverpool L1, L8 . . . . 67 F6
  Newton-le-W WA12 . . . . . 46 B3
  Prescot L34 . . . . 56 D6
  Southport PR9 . . . . 4 C7
  Wallasey CH45 . . . . 51 B8
Hope Valley Com Prim
  Sch L5 . . . . 52 F7
Hope Way **8** L8 . . . . 67 F6
Hopfield Rd CH46 . . . . 64 F8
Hopkins Cl WA10 . . . . 43 D4
Hopwood Cl **5** WA3 . . . . 47 F8
Hopwood Cres WA11 . . . . . 32 A5
Hopwood St L5 . . . . 52 D5
Horace St WA10 . . . . 43 E4
Horatio St **5** CH41 . . . . . 66 D6
Hornbeam Cl
  6 Birkenhead CH46 . . . . 64 B8
  St Helens WA11 . . . . 44 F5
Hornbeam Cres WN4 . . . . . 35 B3
Hornbeam Rd
  Halewood L26 . . . . 83 A7
  Liverpool, Walton L9 . . . . . 39 C3
Hornby Ave
  Bebington CH62 . . . . 79 D1
  Bootle L20 . . . . 38 B5
Hornby Bvd L21 . . . . 38 B6
Hornby Chase L31 . . . . 28 D7
Hornby Cl **1** L9 . . . . 38 F4
Hornby Cres WA9 . . . . 58 C6
Hornby Ct CH64 . . . . 79 D1
Hornby Flats L21 . . . . 38 B6
Hornby La
  Liverpool L18 . . . . 69 D5
  Winwick WA2 . . . . 61 A6
Hornby Pk L18 . . . . 69 D5
Hornby Pl L9 . . . . 39 A5
Hornby Rd
  Bebington CH62 . . . . 79 C1
  Bootle L20 . . . . 38 B5
  Liverpool L9 . . . . 38 F5
  Southport PR9 . . . . 2 A4
Hornby St
  Birkenhead CH41 . . . . 66 F6
  Bootle L20 . . . . 38 A6
  Crosby L23 . . . . 26 E4
Hornby Wlk L5 . . . . 52 C4
Horncastle Cl **4** WA3 . . . 47 F8
Horne St L6 . . . . 53 B4
Hornet Cl L6 . . . . 53 A5
Hornhouse La L33 . . . . 41 C7

Hornsey Rd L4 . . . . 53 B7
HORN SMITHIES 55 B5
Hornspit La L11, L12 . . . . . 54 A8
Horridge Ave WA12 . . . . . 46 C5
Horringford Rd L19 . . . . . . 80 F8
Horrocks Ave L19 . . . . 81 D6
Horrocks Cl L36 . . . . 55 D4
Horrocks Rd L36 . . . . 55 D3
Horseman Pl CH44 . . . . . . 51 E2
Horseshoe Cres WA2 . . . . . 61 E3
Horseshoe Dr L10 . . . . 40 B7
Horsey Mere Gdns
  WA9 . . . . 57 E6
Horsfall Gr L8 . . . . 67 E4
Horsfall St L8 . . . . 67 E4
Horton Cl **1** L33 . . . . . . 29 E6
Horwood Ave L35 . . . . 57 B4
Horwood Cl **1** L12 . . . . 40 C2
Hoscar Ct WA8 . . . . 84 D7
Hoscote Pk CH48 . . . . 63 A2
Hose Side Rd CH45 . . . . . . 51 A7
Hosta Cl **5** L33 . . . . . . 29 D5
Hostock Cl L35 . . . . 56 D2
Hotel St WA12 . . . . 46 B3
Hotham St L3 . . . . 90 C4
Hothfield Rd CH44 . . . . . . 51 D3
Hotspur St L20 . . . . 52 C8
HOUGH GREEN 72 B2
Hough Green Rd WA8 . . . . 72 B3
Hough Green Sta WA8 . . . . 72 B2
Houghton Cl
  Newton-le-W WA12 . . . . . 46 B3
  Widnes WA8 . . . . 73 D2
Houghton Croft WA8 . . . . . 72 C5
HOUGHTON GREEN 61 E4
Houghton La **4** L1 . . . . . 90 B3
Houghton Rd CH49 . . . . . . 65 B3
Houghton's La
  Skelmersdale WN8 . . . . . . 16 C1
  St Helens WA10 . . . . 42 F6
Houghtons Rd WN8 . . . . . . 16 B3
Houghton St
  Liverpool L1 . . . . 90 B3
  Newton-le-W WA12 . . . . . 46 B3
  Prescot L34 . . . . 56 D6
  Rainhill L35 . . . . 57 C3
  Widnes WA8 . . . . 73 D2
Houghton Way **7** L1 . . . 90 B3
Houghwood Grange
  WN4 . . . . 34 F3
Hougoumont Ave L22 . . . . 26 E1
Hougoumont Gr L22 . . . . . 26 E1
Houlding St **7** L4 . . . . . 53 A6
Houlgrave Rd L3, L5 . . . . . 52 C5
Houlston Rd L32 . . . . 29 B2
Houlston Wlk L32 . . . . . . 29 B2
Houlton St **1** L7 . . . . . . 53 C2
Hoveton Gdns WA9 . . . . . 57 E6
Howard Ave CH62 . . . . . . 88 D8
Howard Cl
  Litherland L21 . . . . 27 C2
  Maghull L31 . . . . 20 F1
Howard Ct
  Neston CH64 . . . . 86 F1
  Southport PR9 . . . . 1 D1
Howard Dr L19 . . . . 81 A7
Howard Florey Ave
  L30 . . . . 27 F4
Howards La WN5 . . . . 25 F7
Howard's La WA10 . . . . . . 42 F4
Howards Rd CH61 . . . . 77 B6
Howard St WA10 . . . . 57 D8
Howbeck Cl CH43 . . . . 65 F6
Howbeck Dr CH43 . . . . . . 65 F5
Howbeck Rd CH43 . . . . . . 65 F5
Howden Dr L36 . . . . 55 A3
Howell Dr CH49 . . . . 64 D2
Howell Rd CH62 . . . . 79 A7
Howells Cl L31 . . . . 20 D2
Howe St L20 . . . . 38 B1
Howson Rd WA2 . . . . 61 C3
Howson St CH42 . . . . 66 F2
HOYLAKE 63 B5
Hoylake Cottage Hospl
  CH47 . . . . 63 C8
Hoylake Gr WA9 . . . . 58 C4
Hoylake Holy Trinity CE
  Prim Sch CH47 . . . . 63 C7
Hoylake Rd
  Birkenhead CH46 . . . . 64 D8
  Wallasey, Bidston CH41,
   CH43 . . . . 50 D1
  Wallasey, Leasowe CH46 . . 49 F1
Hoylake Sta CH47 . . . . 63 B6
Hoyle Ct CH47 . . . . 63 B8
Hoyle Rd CH47 . . . . 63 C8
Huddleston Rd CH49 . . . . . 65 C3
Hudleston Rd L15 . . . . 54 B1
Hudson Gr **9** WA11 . . . . 47 E8
Hudson Prim Sch L31 . . . . 28 D6
Hudson Rd
  Maghull L31 . . . . 28 D7
  Wallasey CH46 . . . . 50 A4
  Warrington WA2 . . . . 61 E2
Hudswell Cl L30 . . . . 28 B1
Hugh Baird Coll L20 . . . . . 38 C2
Hughenden Rd L13 . . . . . . 53 F5
Hughes Ave
  Prescot L35 . . . . 56 D4
  Warrington WA2 . . . . 61 D2
Hughes Cl L7 . . . . 53 C1
Hughes Dr L20 . . . . 38 E6
Hughes La CH43 . . . . 66 B3
Hughes Pl WA2 . . . . 61 D2
Hughes St
  Liverpool, Garston L19 . . . . 81 C5
  Liverpool L6 . . . . 53 A4

Hughes St continued
  St Helens WA9 . . . . 58 D8
Hughestead Gr L19 . . . . . . 81 B6
Hughson St L8 . . . . 67 E5
HULME 61 B3
Hulme St PR8 . . . . 4 A7
Hulmewood CH63 . . . . 79 A4
Hulton Ave L35 . . . . 56 F4
Humber Cl
  Liverpool L4 . . . . 52 E8
  Widnes WA8 . . . . 73 F3
Humber Cres WA9 . . . . 58 C6
Humber Rd WA2 . . . . 61 E2
Hume Ct CH47 . . . . 63 C8
Humphreys Hey L23 . . . . . 27 B5
Humphrey St L20 . . . . 38 D6
Huncote Ave WA11 . . . . . 44 D6
Hunslett Rd L9 . . . . 39 B6
Hunstanton Cl CH49 . . . . . 65 A7
Hunter Ave WA2 . . . . 61 B3
Hunter Ct **4** L34 . . . . . . 56 E6
Hunters Chase WN5 . . . . . 25 E1
Hunter's La L15 . . . . 69 A7
Hunter St
  Liverpool L3 . . . . 90 B4
  St Helens WA9 . . . . 44 C2
Huntingdon Cl **4** CH46 . . 64 B8
Huntingdon Gr L31 . . . . . . 20 C4
Huntley Ave WA9 . . . . 58 C7
Huntley Gr WA9 . . . . 58 C7
Huntly Rd L6 . . . . 53 C3
Hunt Rd
  Haydock WA11 . . . . 45 E6
  Maghull L31 . . . . 20 D1
Hunt's Cotts PR9 . . . . 2 A1
HUNT'S CROSS 82 C7
Hunts Cross Ave
  Liverpool L25 . . . . 70 B3
  Liverpool L25 . . . . 70 C2
Hunts Cross Prim Sch
  L25 . . . . 82 C7
Hunt's Cross Sta L25 . . . . . 82 C8
Hunt's Cross Sh Pk The
  L24 . . . . 82 A7
Huntsman Cl L25 . . . . 70 D1
Huntsman Wood L12 . . . . . 54 E8
Hurlingham Rd L4 . . . . . . 39 C2
Hurlston Ave WN8 . . . . . . 24 C8
Hurlston Dr L39 . . . . 13 E7
Hurrell Rd CH41 . . . . 50 D1
Hursley Rd L9 . . . . 39 E4
Hurst Bank CH42 . . . . 78 F8
Hurstlyn Rd L18 . . . . 69 C1
Hurst Park Cl L36 . . . . 56 A4
Hurst Park Dr L36 . . . . 56 A4
Hurst Rd L31 . . . . 28 E7
Hurst's La L39 . . . . 22 B2
Hurst St L1 . . . . 90 B2
Hurstwood L37 . . . . 9 E5
Huskisson St L8 . . . . 67 F7
Huskisson Way WA12 . . . . 46 B4
Hutchinson St
  Liverpool L6 . . . . 53 A3
  Widnes WA8 . . . . 84 F6
Hutchinson Wlk L6 . . . . . . 53 A3
Huttfield Rd L24 . . . . 83 A4
Hutton Ct WN8 . . . . 15 D1
Hutton Rd WN8 . . . . 15 D1
Hutton Way L39 . . . . 13 E5
Huxley Cl **5** CH46 . . . . . 64 B8
Huxley St L13 . . . . 53 D7
HUYTON 55 F3
Huyton Ave WA10 . . . . . . 43 E6
Huyton Brook L36 . . . . . . 70 F8
Huyton Bsns Pk
  Huyton-w-R, Huyton Quarry
   L36 . . . . 56 A1
  Huyton-w-R, Huyton
   L36 . . . . 55 F1
  Huyton-w-R, Windy Arbor
   L36 . . . . 71 B8
Huyton Church Rd L36 . . . . 55 F2
HUYTON FARM 55 C4
Huyton Hall Cres L36 . . . . . 55 E2
Huyton Hey Rd L36 . . . . . . 55 F2
Huyton House Cl L36 . . . . . 55 B4
Huyton House Rd L36 . . . . 55 B4
Huyton La L34, L36 . . . . . . 56 A5
HUYTON PARK 55 E1
HUYTON QUARRY 56 B1
Huyton Sta L36 . . . . 55 E2
Huyton Way L36 . . . . 55 E2
HUYTON-WITH-ROBY
  . . . . 55 C3
Huyton with Roby CE Prim
  Sch L36 . . . . 55 D3
Hyacinth Ave L33 . . . . 29 D5
Hyacinth Cl WA11 . . . . . . 45 F6
Hyacinth Gr CH46 . . . . . . 50 A2
Hyde Rd L22 . . . . 26 D1
Hyde's Brow WA11 . . . . . 32 A8
Hydrangea Way WA9 . . . . 59 A7
Hydro Ave CH48 . . . . 63 B1
Hydro The CH48 . . . . 63 A1
Hygeia St L6 . . . . 53 B4
Hylton Ave **3** CH44 . . . . 51 A4
Hylton Ct L36 . . . . 81 D8
Hyslop St L8 . . . . 67 E6
Hythe Ave L21 . . . . 38 C8
Hythe Cl PR8 . . . . 4 E3
Hythedale Cl **8** L17 . . . . 68 C2

I

Ibbotson's La L17, L18 . . . . 68 E4
Iberis Gdns WA9 . . . . 59 A7
Ibstock Rd L20 . . . . 38 B5
Iffley Cl CH49 . . . . 64 D5
Ikin Cl CH43 . . . . 50 C1
Ilchester Rd
  Birkenhead CH41 . . . . 50 F1
  Liverpool L16 . . . . 54 E1
  Wallasey CH44 . . . . 51 D3
Ilex Ave WA2 . . . . 61 B7
Ilford Ave
  Crosby L23 . . . . 26 C5
  Wallasey CH44 . . . . 51 B3
Ilford St L3 . . . . 52 F7
Ilfracombe Rd WA9 . . . . . . 58 C5
Iliad St L5 . . . . 52 E4
Ilkley Ave PR9 . . . . 2 C6
Ilkley Wlk L24 . . . . 82 D5
Ilsley Cl CH49 . . . . 64 F4
Imber Rd L32 . . . . 40 F8
Imison St L4 . . . . 38 F3
Imison Way L4 . . . . 38 E3
Imperial Ave CH45 . . . . . . 51 C6
Imperial Chambers **13**
  L3 . . . . 90 A4
Imrie St L4 . . . . 38 F2
Ince Ave
  Bebington CH62 . . . . 88 C3
  Bootle L21 . . . . 38 B7
  Crosby L23 . . . . 26 C5
  Liverpool L4 . . . . 53 B8
INCE BLUNDELL 18 E4
Ince Cl CH43 . . . . 65 F4
Ince Cres L37 . . . . 9 D3
Ince Gr CH43 . . . . 65 F4
Ince La L23, L38 . . . . 27 A8
Incemore Rd L18 . . . . 69 B1
Ince Rd L23 . . . . 27 A7
Inchcape Rd
  Liverpool L16 . . . . 54 E1
  Wallasey CH45 . . . . 50 D5
Inchfield WN8 . . . . 16 B2
Index St L4 . . . . 38 F1
India Bldg L2 . . . . 90 A3
Ingestre Ct CH43 . . . . 66 A3
Ingestre Rd CH43 . . . . 66 A3
Ingham Ave WA12 . . . . . . 46 C1
Ingham Rd WA8 . . . . 72 F4
Ingleborough Rd CH42 . . . 66 D2
Ingleby Rd
  Bebington CH62 . . . . 79 B8
  Wallasey CH44 . . . . 51 A3
Ingledene Rd L18 . . . . 69 D5
Ingle Gn L23 . . . . 26 A5
Inglegreen CH60 . . . . 86 B8
Ingleholme Gdns L34 . . . . . 57 A7
Ingleholme Rd L19 . . . . . . 69 A1
Inglemere Rd CH42 . . . . . . 66 E2
Inglemoss Dr WA11 . . . . . 32 C1
Inglenook Rd WA5 . . . . . . 74 F4
Ingleside Ct **1** L23 . . . . . 26 C3
Ingleton Cl
  Birkenhead CH49 . . . . 64 D4
  Newton-le-W WA12 . . . . . 46 B4
Ingleton Dr WA11 . . . . . . 33 B1
Ingleton Gn L32 . . . . 40 F8
Ingleton Rd
  Kirkby L32 . . . . 40 F8
  3 Liverpool L18 . . . . . . 68 F5
  Southport PR8 . . . . 4 E3
Inglewhite WN8 . . . . 16 A2
Inglewood L12 . . . . 41 A2
Inglewood Ave CH46 . . . . . 64 D7
Inglewood Rd WA11 . . . . . 43 C8
Inglis Rd L9 . . . . 39 B7
Ingoe Cl L32 . . . . 29 B1
Ingoe La L32 . . . . 40 B8
Ingram WN8 . . . . 16 B2
Ingrave Rd L4 . . . . 39 C2
Ingrow Rd **9** L6 . . . . . . 53 B3
Inigo Rd L13 . . . . 54 B4
Inley Cl CH63 . . . . 79 A4
Inley Rd CH63 . . . . 79 A4
Inman Ave WA9 . . . . 45 B2
Inman Rd
  Birkenhead CH49 . . . . 64 E6
  Bootle L21 . . . . 38 B7
Inner Forum L11 . . . . 39 E2
Insall Rd
  Liverpool L13 . . . . 54 B1
  Warrington WA2 . . . . 61 F2
Inskip WN8 . . . . 16 A2
Inskip Ct WN8 . . . . 16 B2
Inskip Rd PR9 . . . . 2 A4
Intake La
  Maghull L39 . . . . 19 E8
  Skelmersdale L39 . . . . 23 B2
Interchange Motorway Ind
  Est L36 . . . . 56 A1
Inverclyde Ct **7** L23 . . . . 26 B3
Inveresk Ct CH43 . . . . 65 E6
Invergarry Ct CH47 . . . . . . 62 F6
Invergarry Rd L11 . . . . 40 B4
Invincible Cl L30 . . . . 38 E8
Invincible Way L11 . . . . . . 40 C6
Inwood Rd L19 . . . . 81 D7
Iona Cl L12 . . . . 41 A3
Iona Gdns WA9 . . . . 58 D7
Ionic Rd L13 . . . . 54 A4
Ionic St
  Birkenhead CH42 . . . . 66 F2
  Seaforth L21 . . . . 37 F7
IRBY 76 D6
Irby Ave **7** CH44 . . . . . . 51 A4
Irby Farm CH61 . . . . 76 D5

IRBY HILL 76 C8
Irby Prim Sch CH61 . . . . . 76 E7
Irby Rd
  Heswall CH61 . . . . 76 E3
  Liverpool L4 . . . . 53 C8
Irbyside Rd CH48 . . . . 64 B1
Ireland Rd
  Hale L24 . . . . 83 E1
  Haydock WA11 . . . . 45 C6
Ireland St WA8 . . . . 73 D2
Irene Ave WA11 . . . . 44 C7
Irene Rd L16 . . . . 69 D6
Ireton St L4 . . . . 38 F2
Iris Ave CH41 . . . . 65 F7
Iris Cl WA8 . . . . 72 C2
Iris Gr **7** L33 . . . . 29 D5
Iris Park Wlk **3** L31 . . . . 29 A3
Irlam Dr L32 . . . . 29 E2
Irlam Ho **3** L20 . . . . 38 B3
Irlam Pl L20 . . . . 38 B4
Irlam Rd L20 . . . . 38 B4
Ironbridge View **7** L8 . . . 67 F4
Ironside Rd L36 . . . . 55 D3
Irton Rd PR9 . . . . 4 E8
Irvin Ave PR9 . . . . 2 C5
Irvine Rd CH42 . . . . 66 D2
Irvine St L7 . . . . 53 C1
Irvine Terr CH62 . . . . 79 C8
Irving Cl L9 . . . . 39 C8
Irving St PR9 . . . . 1 D1
Irwell L16 . . . . 38 A3
Irwell Chambers L3 . . . . . . 52 B2
Irwell Cl L17 . . . . 68 E3
Irwell Ho L17 . . . . 68 E3
Irwell La L17 . . . . 68 E3
Irwell Rd WN5 . . . . 25 F7
Irwell St L3 . . . . 90 A3
Irwin Rd WA9 . . . . 58 C7
Isaac St L8 . . . . 67 F4
Isabel Gr L13 . . . . 53 E7
Isherwood Cl WA2 . . . . . . 61 E3
Island Pl L19 . . . . 81 C6
Island Rd L19 . . . . 81 C6
Island Rd S L19 . . . . 81 D6
Islands Brow WA11 . . . . . 44 C6
Isleham Cl L19 . . . . 81 D8
Islington
  Crosby L23 . . . . 26 D4
  Liverpool L3 . . . . 90 C4
Islington Gn WA8 . . . . 73 D4
Islington Sq L3 . . . . 52 F2
Islip Cl CH61 . . . . 76 D7
Ismay Dr CH44 . . . . 51 D5
Ismay Rd L21 . . . . 38 B7
Ismay St L4 . . . . 38 F1
Ivanhoe Ave WA3 . . . . . . 36 D1
Ivanhoe Rd
  Crosby L23 . . . . 26 C4
  Liverpool L17 . . . . 68 C4
Ivatt Way L7 . . . . 53 C1
Iver Cl WA8 . . . . 72 C6
Ivernia Rd L4 . . . . 39 B2
Ivor Rd CH44 . . . . 51 C5
Ivory Dr L33 . . . . 29 E5
Ivy Ave
  Bebington CH63 . . . . 78 C5
  Liverpool L19 . . . . 81 B7
  Newton-le-W WA12 . . . . . 46 C2
  Rainhill L35 . . . . 57 A4
Ivybridge WN8 . . . . 16 B2
Ivy Ct WA9 . . . . 44 C3
Ivydale WN8 . . . . 16 B2
Ivydale Rd
  Birkenhead CH42 . . . . 66 E3
  Liverpool, Hartley's Village
   L9 . . . . 39 B4
  Liverpool, Mossley Hill
   L18 . . . . 69 A4
Ivy Farm Ct L24 . . . . 83 D1
Ivy Farm Rd L35 . . . . 57 B4
Ivy House Rd WA3 . . . . . . 36 D1
Ivyhurst Cl L19 . . . . 80 F8
Ivyhurst Manor L19 . . . . . 80 F8
Ivy La CH46 . . . . 49 E1
Ivy Leigh L13 . . . . 53 E5
Ivy Rd WA3 . . . . 47 B8
Ivy St
  Ashton-in-M WN4 . . . . . . 35 B3
  Birkenhead CH41 . . . . 66 F6
  Southport PR8 . . . . 4 D6

J

Jack McBain Ct L3 . . . . . . 52 C4
Jack's Brow L34 . . . . 41 E2
Jacksfield Way L19 . . . . . . 80 F7
Jackson Cl
  Bebington CH63 . . . . 78 F8
  Haskayne L39 . . . . 11 F5
  Rainhill L35 . . . . 57 C1
Jacksons Pond Dr L25 . . . . 69 F7
Jackson St
  Birkenhead CH41 . . . . 66 E5
  Burtonwood WA5 . . . . . . 59 E6
  Haydock WA11 . . . . 45 A4
  Liverpool L19 . . . . 81 C6
  St Helens WA9 . . . . 44 C2
Jacobs Cl L21 . . . . 38 B6
Jacob St L8 . . . . 67 F4
Jacqueline Ct L36 . . . . 55 C2
Jacqueline Dr L36 . . . . 56 A4
Jade Cl L33 . . . . 30 A3
Jade Rd L6 . . . . 53 B4
Jamaica St L1 . . . . 90 B1
Jamesbrook Cl CH41 . . . . . 66 A8
James Clarke St L5 . . . . . . 52 C4

James Court Apartments
L25. . . . . **70** B2
James Ct L25. . . . . **70** B2
James Dunne Ave L3,
L5. . . . . **52** C5
James Gr WA10. . . . . . . **43** E2
James Holt Ave L32. . . . **29** D2
James Hopkins Way 1
L4. . . . . **52** D7
James Larkin Way L4 . . **52** D7
James Rd
Haydock WA11. . . . . . . **45** F7
Liverpool L20. . . . . **70** B2
James Simpson Way
L30. . . . . **27** F4
James St
Ashton-in-M WN2. . . . . **35** E7
Birkenhead CH43. . . . . **66** C4
Liverpool, Garston L19. . **81** C6
Liverpool L2. . . . . **90** A3
St Helens WA9. . . . . . . **58** D3
7 Wallasey CH44. . . . **51** E2
James Street Sta L2 . . . **90** A3
Jamieson Ave L23 . . . . . **27** A4
Jamieson Rd L15. . . . . . **68** E7
Jane's Brook Rd PR8. . . . **4** E4
Jane St WA9. . . . . **58** F7
Janet St L7. . . . . **53** B1
Japonica Gdns WA9 . . . **59** A7
Jarrett Rd L33. . . . . **30** A4
Jarrett Wlk L33. . . . . . . **30** A4
Jarrow CH43. . . . . **66** B4
Jasmine Cl
Birkenhead CH46,
CH49. . . . . **64** D7
Liverpool L5. . . . . **52** F4
Jasmine L36 . . . . **55** F5
Jasmine Gdns WA9 . . . . **59** A7
Jasmine Gr WA8. . . . . . . **84** D8
Jasmine Mews L17 . . . . **68** A3
Jason St L5. . . . . **52** E6
Jason Wlk L5. . . . . **52** E6
Java Rd L4. . . . . **39** D1
Jean Wlk L10. . . . . **40** B6
Jedburgh Dr L33. . . . . . **29** D6
Jeffereys Cres L36. . . . . **55** B2
Jeffereys Dr L36. . . . . . . **55** A2
Jefferson Gdns WA8. . . . **72** F3
Jeffreys Dr CH49. . . . . . **64** D5
Jellicoe Cl CH48. . . . . . **75** D6
Jenkinson St L3 . . . . . . **52** E3
Jenner Dr CH46. . . . . . . **50** A2
Jennet Hey WN4. . . . . . **34** F6
Jennings Park Ave
WN2. . . . . **36** C7
Jericho Cl L17. . . . . **68** D2
Jericho Farm Cl L17. . . . **68** D1
Jericho Farm Wlk L17. . . **68** D1
Jericho La L17. . . . . **68** D1
Jermyn St L8. . . . . **68** B6
Jerningham Rd L11. . . . . **39** D3
Jersey Ave L21 . . . . **27** B1
Jersey Cl L20. . . . . **38** C3
Jersey St
Bootle L20. . . . . **38** C3
St Helens WA9. . . . . . . **58** C3
Jesmond St L15. . . . . . . **68** D8
Jessamine Rd CH42. . . . **66** E3
Jessop Ho WA7. . . . . . . **84** E3
Jet Cl L6. . . . . **53** B4
Jeudwine Cl L25. . . . . . . **70** B1
Joan Ave
Birkenhead, Greasby
CH49. . . . . **64** E4
Birkenhead, Moreton
CH46. . . . . **64** D8
Jocelyn Cl CH63. . . . . . . **79** A3
John Bagot Cl L5 . . . . . **52** E5
John Hunter Way L30. . . **27** F4
John Lennon Dr L6 . . . . **53** B3
John Middleton Cl L24. . **83** E2
John Moores Cl L7 . . . . **68** A8
John Moores Uni L3 . . . **52** F1
John Moores Univ
Liverpool, Edge Hill L7. . . . **67** F8
Liverpool L1. . . . . **90** C2
Liverpool L3. . . . . **90** B4
Liverpool L3. . . . . **90** C3
Liverpool, Vauxhall L3. . **52** F1
John Moores Univ Avril
Roberts Ctr L3 . . . . . . **90** A4
John Moores Univ IM
Marsh Campus L17. . . . **68** F1
Johns Ave WA11. . . . . . **45** E7
John Smith Ho L20 . . . . **38** B5
Johnson Ave
Newton-le-W WA12. . . . . **46** B5
Prescot L35. . . . . **56** D4
Johnson Gr L14. . . . . . . **54** E5
Johnson Rd CH43. . . . . . **65** F1
Johnson's La WA8. . . . . **73** E1
Johnson St
Liverpool L1, L2, L3. . . . **90** B4
Southport PR9. . . . . **4** B8
St Helens WA9. . . . . . . **44** C4
Johnson Wlk 10 L7. . . . **53** C1
John St
Ashton-in-M WN4 . . . . . **35** D5
Birkenhead CH41. . . . . . **66** F7
Golborne WA3. . . . . . . **47** A8
Liverpool L3. . . . . **52** F3
Johnston Ave L20. . . . . . **38** E6
Jones Farm Rd L25. . . . **70** C4
Jones St L3 . . . . **90** C3
Jonson Rd CH64. . . . . . **86** E1
Jonville Rd L9. . . . . **39** C7
Jordan St L1. . . . . **90** B1

Joseph Gardner Way
L20. . . . . **38** B5
Joseph Lister Cl L30. . . . **27** F3
Joseph St
St Helens WA9. . . . . . . **58** E7
Widnes WA8. . . . . **73** C2
Joshua Cl L5. . . . . **52** E6
Joyce Wlk L10. . . . . **40** C7
Joy La
Burtonwood WA5. . . . . . **59** E4
St Helens WA8, WA9. . . . **58** E2
Joy Wlk WA9. . . . . **58** E3
Jubilee Ave
Liverpool L14. . . . . **54** D1
Ormskirk L39. . . . . **13** F6
Orrell WN5. . . . . **25** D4
Warrington WA5 . . . . . . **74** E4
Jubilee Cres
Bebington CH62. . . . . . **79** B5
Haydock WA11. . . . . . . **45** F7
Jubilee Ct
Birkenhead CH43. . . . . **66** A5
Golborne WA3. . . . . . . **36** A1
Jubilee Dr
Litherland L30. . . . . . . **28** A1
Liverpool L7. . . . . **53** B2
Prescot L35. . . . . **56** D2
Skelmersdale WN8. . . . **23** E8
West Kirby CH48. . . . . . **63** B3
Jubilee Rd
Bootle L21. . . . . **38** B7
Crosby L23. . . . . **26** C3
Formby L37. . . . . **9** D1
Jubilee Way WA8. . . . . . **72** E1
Jubits La
St Helens WA8, WA9. . . . **58** B2
Widnes WA8. . . . . **73** A8
Juddfield St WA11. . . . . **45** A7
Judges Dr L6. . . . . **53** C4
Judges Way L6. . . . . **53** C4
Julian Way WA8. . . . . . . **72** F4
Julie Gr L12. . . . . **54** F5
Juliet Ave CH63. . . . . . . **78** E7
Juliet Gdns CH63. . . . . . **78** E7
July Rd L6. . . . . **53** D5
July St L20. . . . . **38** C5
Junction La
Newton-le-W WA12. . . . . **46** B3
St Helens WA9. . . . . . . **58** F7
Junction One Ret Pk
CH44. . . . . **50** D3
Junction Rd WA11. . . . . **31** E8
June Ave CH62. . . . . **88** E8
June Rd L6. . . . . **53** D5
June St L20 . . . . **38** C4
Juniper Cl
Birkenhead CH49. . . . . **64** C2
Huyton-w-R L28. . . . . . **55** B8
St Helens WA10. . . . . . **43** D4
Juniper Gdns L23. . . . . . **27** B6
Juniper St L20. . . . . **52** C8
Jurby Cl WA2. . . . . **61** F1
Justene Cl WA3. . . . . . . **36** A2
Justin Way L35. . . . . . . **57** B5
Juvenal Pl L3. . . . . **52** E4
Juvenal St L3. . . . . **52** D4

K

Kaigh Ave L23. . . . . **26** D5
Kale Cl CH48. . . . . **63** B1
Kale Gr L33. . . . . **30** A5
Kara Cl L20. . . . . **38** C3
Karan Way L31. . . . . **29** B3
Karen Cl WA5. . . . . **60** A6
Karonga Rd L10. . . . . . . **39** F7
Karonga Way L10. . . . . . **39** F7
Karslake Rd
Liverpool L18. . . . . **68** F5
Wallasey CH44. . . . . . . **51** D3
Katherine Wlk L10. . . . . **40** C7
Kearsley Cl L4. . . . . **52** E7
Kearsley St L4. . . . . **52** E7
Keates St WA9. . . . . **58** F8
Keats Ave
Longshaw WN5 . . . . . . **25** D1
Prescot L35. . . . . **56** F3
Keats Cl WA8. . . . . **84** F8
Keats Gn L36. . . . . **56** A1
Keats Gr WA2 . . . . **61** C2
Keats St L20. . . . . **38** B5
Keats Terr PR8. . . . . **4** F6
Keble Dr
Aintree L10. . . . . **28** C3
Wallasey CH45. . . . . . . **50** D6
Keble Rd L20. . . . . **38** C2
Keble St L6, L7. . . . . **53** A3
Kedleston St L8. . . . . . . **68** A4
Keegan Dr CH44. . . . . . . **51** E2
Keele Cl CH43. . . . . **50** C2
Keel Hey CH64. . . . . **88** B1
Keel Wharf
Liverpool L3. . . . . **90** A1
Liverpool L3. . . . . **90** A2
Keenan Dr L20. . . . . **38** E5
Keene Ct L30. . . . . **27** D4
Keepers La CH63. . . . . . **78** B5
Keighley Ave CH45. . . . . **50** E5
Keightley St 8 CH41. . . . **66** D7
Keir Hardie Ave L20. . . . **38** C5
Keith Ave
5 Liverpool L4. . . . . . **39** A1
Warrington WA5 . . . . . . **74** E6
Keith Ct 4 L4. . . . . **38** F1
Keith Dr CH63. . . . . **88** D5
Keithley Wlk L24. . . . . . **82** E5
Kelbey Cl 18 L8. . . . . . . **68** A4

Kelbrook Cl WA9. . . . . . **58** D6
Kelburn Gr L12. . . . . **54** D8
Kelda Ct L25. . . . . **70** A6
Kelday St L33. . . . . **29** E2
Kelk Beck Cl L31. . . . . . . **20** F2
Kellet's Pl CH42. . . . . . . **66** F3
Kellett Rd CH46. . . . . . . **50** B3
Kellitt Rd L15. . . . . **68** E7
Kelly Dr L20. . . . . **38** E5
Kelly St L34. . . . . **56** E6
Kelmscott Dr CH44. . . . . **50** E4
Kelsall Ave
Bebington CH62. . . . . . **88** F3
St Helens WA9. . . . . . . **58** B4
Kelsall Cl
Bebington CH62. . . . . . **88** E3
Birkenhead CH43. . . . . **65** F3
Widnes WA8 . . . . **72** D1
Kelsey Cl WA10. . . . . . . **43** D4
Kelso Cl L33. . . . . **29** D6
Kelso Rd L6. . . . . **53** C3
Kelton Gr L17. . . . . **68** E2
Kelvin Gr WN4. . . . . **34** D4
Kelvin Ct CH44. . . . . **51** E1
Kelvin Gr L8. . . . . **68** A6
Kelvin Pk CH44. . . . . . . **51** E1
Kelvin Rd
Birkenhead CH41. . . . . **66** E4
Wallasey CH41, CH44 . . **51** E1
Kelvinside
Crosby L23. . . . . **26** F3
Wallasey CH44. . . . . . . **51** E1
Kemberton Dr WA8. . . . . **73** A5
Kemble St
Liverpool L7. . . . . **53** B2
Prescot L34. . . . . **56** D6
Kemlyn Rd L4. . . . . **53** A7
Kempsell Way L26. . . . . **83** A7
Kempsell Wlk L26. . . . . . **83** A7
Kempsey Gr WA9. . . . . . **57** E7
Kempson Terr CH63. . . . **78** F4
Kempston St L3 . . . . . . **52** F2
Kempton Cl
Huyton-w-R L36. . . . . . . **55** D1
Newton-le-W WA12. . . . . **46** D5
Kempton Park Fold PR8. . . **4** A7
Kempton Park Rd L10. . . **28** E2
Kempton Rd
Bebington CH62. . . . . . **79** B8
Liverpool L15. . . . . **68** D8
Kemsley Rd L14 . . . . **54** F4
Kenbury Cl L33. . . . . **30** A4
Kenbury Rd L33. . . . . . . **30** A4
Kendal Ave WA2 . . . . . . **61** C2
Kendal Cl
Bebington CH63. . . . . . **78** F6
Rainford WA11. . . . . . . **23** F2
Kendal Dr
Maghull L31. . . . . **20** E2
Rainford WA11. . . . . . . **23** F2
Rainhill L35. . . . . **57** A4
St Helens WA11. . . . . . **44** B8
Kendal Gr WN4 . . . . **35** B4
Kendal Pk L12. . . . . **54** D6
Kendal Rd
Kirkby L33. . . . . **29** D4
Liverpool L16. . . . . **69** E7
Wallasey CH44. . . . . . . **51** A2
Widnes WA8. . . . . **72** C1
Kendal St 15 CH41. . . . . **66** E6
Kendal Way PR8. . . . . **7** B3
Kendrick's Cross L35. . . . **57** F4
Kendricks Fold L35 . . . . **57** B3
Kenham Ct 9 CH45. . . . . **51** A8
Kenilworth Cl L25. . . . . . **69** E3
Kenilworth Dr CH61. . . . **76** F5
Kenilworth Gdns
Birkenhead CH49. . . . . **64** E6
Newton-le-W WA12. . . . . **46** C1
Kenilworth Rd
Crosby L23. . . . . **26** C3
Golborne WA3. . . . . . . **47** E7
Liverpool L16. . . . . **69** D7
Southport PR8. . . . . **7** A4
Wallasey CH44. . . . . . . **51** E3
Kenilworth St 2 L20. . . . **38** B3
Kenilworth Way L25 . . . . **69** E3
Kenley Ave WA8. . . . . . . **72** D5
Kenmare Rd L15. . . . . . . **68** E6
Kenmay Way L33. . . . . . **30** A3
Kenmore Gr 7 L26. . . . . **26** E1
Kenmore Gr WN4. . . . . . **34** D4
Kenmore Rd CH43. . . . . **65** E1
Kennelwood Ave L33. . . . **29** F3
Kennessee Cl L31. . . . . . **28** E8
Kenneth Cl L30. . . . . **27** E3
Kenneth Rd WA8. . . . . . . **84** C8
Kennet Rd
Bebington CH63. . . . . . **78** D5
Haydock WA11. . . . . . . **45** C6
Kennford Rd L11. . . . . . . **40** C5
Kennington Pk WA8. . . . **72** E4
KENSINGTON **53** B2
Kensington L6, L7. . . . . . **53** B2
Kensington Ave WA8. . . . **58** C7
Kensington Cl WA8. . . . . **73** D4
Kensington Com Prim Jun
Sch L7. . . . . **53** B2
Kensington Ct 1 L10 . . . **43** A3
Kensington Dr L34. . . . . **56** A5
Kensington Gdns CH46. . . **64** E8
Kensington Ind Pk PR9. . . . **4** C6
Kensington Rd
Formby L37. . . . . **9** E1
Southport PR9. . . . . **4** C6
Kensington St L6, L7. . . . **53** A2
Kent Ave
Formby L37. . . . . **10** A1

Kent Ave continued
Litherland L21. . . . . . . **38** C8
Kent Cl
Bebington CH63. . . . . . **88** B8
Bootle L20. . . . . **38** D4
Kentmere Ave WA11. . . . **33** C1
Kentmere Dr CH61. . . . . **76** F4
Kentmere Pl WA2. . . . . . **61** A3
Kenton Cl
Formby L37. . . . . **9** F6
Liverpool L25. . . . . **70** B7
Kenton Rd L26. . . . . **83** A7
Kent Rd
Formby L37. . . . . **10** A1
Southport PR8. . . . . **4** A4
St Helens WA9. . . . . . . **58** D7
Wallasey CH44. . . . . . . **51** A3
Kents Bank L11. . . . . . . **40** C1
Kent St
Birkenhead CH43. . . . . **66** B4
Liverpool L1. . . . . **90** B2
Widnes WA8. . . . . **73** B1
Kent Way WA12. . . . . . . **46** C1
Kentwell Gr L12. . . . . . . **54** D7
Kenview Cl WA8. . . . . . . **84** A4
Kenway WA11. . . . . **32** A6
Kenwood Cl L27. . . . . . . **70** F5
Kenworthys Flats PR9. . . . **4** B8
Kenwright Cres WA9. . . . **58** D8
Kenwyn Rd CH45. . . . . . **51** B5
KENYON **47** F3
Kenyon Ave WA5. . . . . . **74** E5
Kenyon Cl L33. . . . . **29** F6
Kenyon Ct 4 L8. . . . . . . **67** F6
Kenyon La
Golborne, Kenyon WA3 . . **47** F3
Golborne WA3. . . . . . . **47** F5
Kenyon Rd L15. . . . . **69** A5
Kenyon's La WN8. . . . . . **23** C8
Kenyon's La N WA11. . . . **45** F8
Kenyon's La S WA11. . . . **45** F7
Kenyons Lo L31. . . . . . . **20** E3
Kepler St L21. . . . . **38** A6
Keppel St L20. . . . . **38** B1
Kerfoot's La WN8. . . . . . **23** C8
Kerman Cl L12. . . . . **40** B1
Kerr Cl 2 L33. . . . . **29** E6
Kerr Gr WA9. . . . . **44** E3
Kerris Cl L17. . . . . **68** C2
Kerrysdale Cl 4 WA9 . . . **58** D7
Kersey Rd L32. . . . . **40** F8
Kersey Wlk L32. . . . . **40** F8
Kershaw Ave L23. . . . . . **26** F3
Kershaw St WA8. . . . . . . **72** D1
Kershaw Way WA12. . . . **46** C1
Kerslake Way L38. . . . . . **18** A4
Kerswell Cl WA9. . . . . . . **58** D6
Kerton Row PR8. . . . . **3** F4
Keston Ho L36. . . . . **82** F7
Kestral Dene L10. . . . . . **40** A6
Kestral Ave CH49. . . . . . **64** D6
Kestrel Cl
Birkenhead CH49. . . . . **64** D6
St Helens WA11. . . . . . **44** B6
Kestrel Ct PR9. . . . . **4** D7
Kestrel Dr WN4. . . . . **35** C6
Kestrel Gr L26. . . . . **70** D1
Kestrel Mews WN8. . . . . **16** C4
Kestrel Pk WN8. . . . . . . **16** C4
Kestrel Rd
Birkenhead CH46. . . . . **64** C8
Heswall CH60. . . . . **86** C7
Keswick Ave
Bebington CH63. . . . . . **88** C4
Warrington WA2 . . . . . . **61** C2
Keswick Cl
Maghull L31. . . . . **20** E2
Southport PR8. . . . . **7** C3
Widnes WA8. . . . . **72** C1
Keswick Cres WA2. . . . . **61** C2
Keswick Dr L33. . . . . **38** E8
Keswick Gdns CH63. . . . **88** C5
Keswick Pl CH43. . . . . . . **50** D1
Keswick Rd
Liverpool L18. . . . . **69** D2
St Helens WA10. . . . . . **43** E6
Wallasey CH45. . . . . . . **50** D1
Keswick Villas L16. . . . . **70** A8
Keswick Way
Huyton-w-R L16. . . . . . **70** A8
Rainford WA11. . . . . . . **23** F2
Ketterer Ct WA9. . . . . . . **44** C2
Kettering Rd PR8. . . . . . . **7** B5
Kevelioc Cl CH63. . . . . . **78** F3
Kew Gardens WA8. . . . . **73** D4
Kew House Dr PR8. . . . . . **5** A2
Kew Rd
Formby L37. . . . . **9** D1
Southport PR8. . . . . **4** B3
Kew Ret Pk PR8. . . . . **5** A4
Kew St L5. . . . . **52** D5
Kew Woods Prim Sch
PR8. . . . . **4** F3
Keybank Rd L12. . . . . . . **54** A8
Kiddman St L4. . . . . **38** F3
Kid Glove Rd WA3. . . . . . **36** B1
Kidstone Cl 6 WA9. . . . . **58** D7
Kielder Cl WN4. . . . . **34** F7
Kilbuck La WA11. . . . . . . **46** A8
Kilburn Ave
Ashton-in-M WN4 . . . . . **35** D4
Bebington CH62. . . . . . **88** E6
Kilburn Gr WA9. . . . . **57** E7
Kilburn Rd WN5. . . . . . . **25** C5
Kilburn St L21. . . . . **38** B6
Kildale Cl L31. . . . . **20** C2
Kildare Cl L24. . . . . **83** D2

Kildonan Rd L17. . . . . . . **68** E2
Kilford Cl WA5. . . . . **60** E2
Kilgarth Sch CH41. . . . . **66** B8
Kilgraston Gdns L17. . . . **68** F1
Killarney Gr 3 CH44. . . . **51** A3
Killarney Rd L13. . . . . . . **54** B3
Killester Rd L25. . . . . . . **70** B4
Killington Way L4. . . . . . **52** E8
Kilmalcolm Cl CH43. . . . **65** F4
Kilmore Cl L9. . . . . **39** C8
Kilmory Ave L25. . . . . . . **70** C2
Kiln Cl WA10. . . . . **43** C5
Kiln Hey L12. . . . . **54** C5
Kiln La
Skelmersdale WN8. . . . **15** E1
St Helens WA10. . . . . . **43** C5
Kiln Rd CH49. . . . . **65** A3
Kilnyard Rd L23. . . . . . . **26** D4
Kilrea Cl L11. . . . . **53** F8
Kilrea Lo L11. . . . . **53** F8
Kilrea Rd L11. . . . . **53** E8
Kilsail Rd 3 L32. . . . . . . **41** A7
Kilsby Dr WA8. . . . . **73** E2
Kilshaw Rd WA5. . . . . . . **59** F6
Kilshaw St L6. . . . . **53** A4
Kilsyth Cl WA2. . . . . **61** F4
Kimberley Ave
Crosby L23. . . . . **26** D3
St Helens WA9. . . . . . . **57** F7
Kimberley Cl L8. . . . . . . **68** A4
Kimberley Dr L23. . . . . . **26** D3
Kimberley Pl WN4. . . . . . **35** C3
Kimberley Rd CH45. . . . . **51** B6
Kindale Rd CH43. . . . . . . **65** E1
Kinder Gr WN4. . . . . **34** F6
Kinder St L6. . . . . **52** F3
Kine Ave L20. . . . . **38** E5
King David High Sch
. . . . **69** C7
King David Prim Sch
. . . . **69** C7
King Edward Cl L35. . . . . **57** B4
King Edward Ind Est
. . . . **52** B2
King Edward Rd
Rainhill L35. . . . . **57** B4
St Helens WA10. . . . . . **43** E6
King Edward's Dr CH62. . . **79** B6
King Edward St L3. . . . . **52** B2
Kingfield Rd L9. . . . . **38** F5
Kingfisher Bsns Pk
L20. . . . . **38** C7
Kingfisher Cl
Kirkby L33. . . . . **29** E6
Liverpool L27. . . . . **70** F5
Kingfisher Ct
Ashton-in-M WN4 . . . . . **35** B6
Maghull L31. . . . . **20** B4
Southport PR9. . . . . **4** D8
Kingfisher Dr WA11. . . . . **44** B6
Kingfisher Gr L12. . . . . . **40** F1
Kingfisher Ho
Birkenhead CH41. . . . . **67** A6
Liverpool CH13. . . . . . . **54** A1
Kingfisher Pk WN8. . . . . **16** C4
Kingfisher Way CH49. . . . **64** D6
King George Cl WN4 . . . . **35** B3
King George Dr CH44,
CH45. . . . . **51** D6
King George Rd WA11. . . **46** A7
King George's Dr CH62. . . **79** B6
King George V Coll PR8. . . **4** E5
Kingham Cl
Liverpool L25. . . . . **70** C2
3 Widnes WA8. . . . . . **73** D1
Kingham Mews L25. . . . **70** C2
Kinglake Rd CH45. . . . . . **51** D5
Kinglake St L7. . . . . **53** B1
Kinglass Rd CH63. . . . . . **79** B3
King's Ave
Golborne WA3. . . . . . . **47** F7
Hoylake CH47. . . . . **63** D8
Kingsbrook Way CH63. . . **78** D8
King's Brow CH63. . . . . . **78** D6
King's Bsns Pk L34. . . . . **56** A5
Kingsbury Cl PR8. . . . . . . **7** B4
Kingsbury Ct WN8. . . . . **16** C4
Kingsbury Prim Spec Sch
WN8. . . . . **15** D1
Kingsbury Rd WA8. . . . . **73** D4
Kings Cl
Bebington CH63. . . . . . **78** D7
Formby L37. . . . . **9** E2
2 Liverpool L17. . . . . **68** C2
Kingscourt Rd L12. . . . . **54** C5
Kings Ct CH47. . . . . **63** A7
King's Ct
Bebington CH63. . . . . . **78** D6
Birkenhead CH43. . . . . **66** B4
Kingsdale Ave
Birkenhead CH42. . . . . **66** D2
Rainhill L35. . . . . **57** D3
Kingsdale Rd
Liverpool L18. . . . . **69** A5
Warrington WA5 . . . . . . **74** F7
Kings Dock St L1. . . . . . **90** B1
Kingsdown Rd
Abram Brow WN2. . . . . **36** B7
Liverpool L11. . . . . **40** B1
Kingsdown St CH41. . . . . **66** E4
Kings Dr
Huyton-w-R L34. . . . . . **56** A5
Liverpool, Netherley L27. . **70** D5
Liverpool, Woolton L25. . **70** B2

King's Dr
Heswall CH61 .... 76 F6
West Kirby CH48 ..... 75 D8
Kingsfield Rd L31 ...... 28 C7
King's Gap The CH47 ..... 63 A6
Kingsheath Ave L14 ..... 54 F5
Kings Hey Dr PR9 ....1 F1
King's La CH63 .... 78 E8
Kingsland Bldgs CH42 .. 66 C4
Kingsland Cres L11 ... 39 E3
Kingsland Rd
Birkenhead CH42 ..... 66 C4
Liverpool L11 .... 39 E3
Kingsley Ave CH62 ..... 88 E3
Kingsley Cl
Heswall CH61 .... 77 A3
Maghull L31 .... 20 C5
Kingsley Com Sch L8 .. 68 B7
Kingsley Rd
Liverpool L8 .... 68 A5
St Helens WA10 ...... 43 D6
Wallasey CH44 .... 51 B3
Kingsley St CH41 ...... 66 A8
Kings Mdw PR8 .... 7 D3
Kingsmead Dr L25 .... 82 B8
Kingsmead Gr CH43 .... 65 F5
Kings Meadow Prim Sch
PR8 .... 7 D3
Kingsmead Rd
Birkenhead CH43 ..... 65 F5
Wallasey CH46 .... 49 F2
Kingsmead Rd N CH43 .. 65 F5
Kingsmead Rd S CH43 .. 65 F5
Kingsmead Sch CH47 ... 63 C8
KINGS MOSS 32 E7
King's Moss La WA11 .. 32 F7
Kings Mount CH43 ..... 66 C4
Kingsnorth L35 .... 56 F2
Kings Par L3 .... 90 A1
King's Par
Wallasey CH45 .... 37 A1
Wallasey CH45 .... 50 E8
Kings Pk L21 .... 37 F7
Kings Rd
Crosby L23 .... 26 D4
Formby L37 .... 9 E2
Golborne WA3 .... 47 A7
St Helens WA10 ...... 43 D2
King's Rd
Ashton-in-M WN4 ..... 35 A5
Bebington CH63 ...... 78 D7
Bootle L20 .... 38 C1
King's Sq CH41 .... 66 F6
King St
Birkenhead CH42 ..... 67 A1
Crosby L22 .... 26 D1
Liverpool L19 .... 81 C4
Newton-le-W WA12 .... 46 B3
Southport PR8 .... 4 A4
St Helens WA10 ...... 43 F4
Wallasey CH44 .... 51 D4
Kings Terr L20 .... 38 C1
Kingsthorne Pk L25 ... 82 C7
Kingsthorne Rd L25 ... 82 C7
Kingston Ave WA5 ..... 74 E6
Kingston Cl
Birkenhead CH46 ..... 64 E8
Liverpool L12 .... 54 E5
Kingston Cres PR9 .... 2 C5
Kingston Lo 2 CH43 ... 66 C5
King's View CH47 ..... 62 F6
Kingsville Rd CH63 ... 78 E5
Kingsway
Bebington CH63 ...... 78 D7
Crosby L22, L23 ..... 26 E2
Heswall CH60 .... 86 C6
Huyton-w-R L36 ...... 55 D4
Newton-le-W WA12 .... 46 C2
Prescot L34, L35 .... 56 E5
Southport PR8 .... 4 A7
St Helens WA11 ...... 44 A8
Wallasey CH45 .... 51 A6
Widnes WA8 .... 73 A1
Kingsway Ct 4 L3 ..... 52 D4
Kingsway Ind Pk L3, L5.. 52 D4
Kingsway Par L36 ..... 55 C4
Kingsway Prim Sch
CH44 .... 51 D2
Kingsway (Tunnel) L3,
CH44 .... 52 B3
Kingswell Cl L7 ...... 68 B8
Kings Wharf CH44 ..... 51 F1
Kings Wlk
Birkenhead CH42 ..... 67 A1
West Kirby CH48 ..... 63 C2
KINGSWOOD 60 B2
Kingswood
Huyton-w-R L36 ...... 55 D3
Warrington WA5 ...... 60 B2
Kingswood Ave
Crosby L22 .... 26 F2
Liverpool L9 .... 39 B2
Kingswood Bvd CH63 ... 78 E8
Kingswood Ct 3 L33 .. 29 F4
Kingswood Dr L23 .... 26 D3
Kingswood Ho PR8 .... 3 F5
Kingswood Pk PR8 .... 3 F5
Kingswood Rd
4 Wallasey CH44.... 51 C5
Warrington WA5 ...... 60 A2
Kington Rd CH48 ...... 63 A3
Kinley Gdns L20 ...... 38 E5
Kinloch Cl L33 .... 83 A7
Kinloch Way L39 ...... 13 D6
Kinloss Rd CH49 ...... 64 C3

Kinmel Cl
Birkenhead CH41 ..... 66 D7
Liverpool L4 .... 53 D8
Kinmel St
Liverpool L8 .... 68 A5
St Helens WA9 .... 58 C8
Kinnaird Rd CH45 ..... 51 A6
Kinnaird St L8 .... 68 A3
Kinnerton CH46 .... 64 B8
Kinnock Pk WA5 .... 59 E6
Kinross Ave WN4 ...... 34 C4
Kinross Cl WA2 .... 61 F4
Kinross Rd
Liverpool L10 .... 39 F7
Seaforth L22 .... 37 E8
Wallasey CH45 .... 50 D6
Kinsman Ho L19 .... 80 F7
Kintbury Cl WN2 ...... 35 F7
Kintore Cl CH63 ...... 88 C4
Kintore Dr WA5 .... 74 D6
Kintore Rd L19 .... 81 B7
Kipling Ave
2 Birkenhead CH42 .. 66 F1
Huyton-w-R L36 ...... 71 A8
Warrington WA2 ...... 61 C1
Kipling Cres WA8 ..... 84 F8
Kipling Gr WA9 .... 58 A3
Kipling St L20 .... 38 A5
Kirby Cl CH48 .... 63 C1
Kirby Mount CH48 ..... 75 C8
Kirby Park Mans 2
CH48 .... 63 B1
Kirby Pk CH48 .... 63 C1
Kirby Rd L20 .... 38 D6
Kirby's Cotts L31 .... 21 B3
Kirkacre Ave WA12 .... 60 C8
Kirkbride Cl L27 ..... 71 A4
Kirkbride Lawn L27 ... 71 A4
Kirkbride Wlk L27 .... 71 A4
Kirkburn Cl 13 L8 .... 67 F4
KIRKBY 29 E1
Kirkby Bank Rd L33 ... 30 C2
Kirkby CE Prim Sch
L33 .... 29 E2
KIRKBY PARK 29 C3
Kirkby Row L32 .... 29 D3
Kirkby Row Cotts 3
L32 .... 29 C3
Kirkcaldy Ave WA5 .... 74 D6
KIRKDALE 52 E8
Kirkdale Gdns WN8 .... 25 A7
Kirkdale Rd L5 .... 52 E6
Kirkdale St Lawrence CE
Prim Sch L4 .... 52 D8
Kirkdale Sta L20 ..... 38 D1
Kirkdale Vale L4, L5 . 52 E7
Kirket Cl CH63 .... 79 A4
Kirket La CH63 .... 79 A4
Kirkfield Gr CH42 .... 67 A1
Kirkham Ave WA3 ...... 47 E6
Kirkham Rd
Southport PR9 .... 2 A4
Widnes WA8 .... 73 C2
Kirkham St WN2 .... 36 B8
Kirklake Bank L37 .... 9 C2
Kirklake Rd L37 ...... 9 D2
Kirkland Ave CH42 .... 66 D2
Kirkland Cl L9 .... 38 F7
Kirkland Rd CH45 ..... 51 C8
Kirkland St WA10 ..... 43 F4
Kirklands The CH48 ... 63 C2
Kirklees Rd PR8 ...... 3 F1
Kirkmaiden Rd L19 .... 81 B8
Kirkman Fold L35 ..... 57 B3
Kirkmore Rd L18 ...... 69 A2
Kirkmount CH49 .... 65 A5
Kirk Rd L20 .... 38 C6
Kirkside Cl L12 ...... 40 D3
Kirk St L5 .... 52 E6
Kirkstall Dr L37 ..... 10 B2
Kirkstall Rd PR8 ..... 3 F2
Kirkstead Way WA3 .... 47 A8
Kirkstead Wlk L31 .... 29 B3
Kirkstone Ave
St Helens WA11 ...... 44 C8
Warrington WA2 ...... 61 C2
Kirkstone Rd N L21 ... 27 C1
Kirkstone Rd S L21, L30,
L20 .... 38 D8
Kirkstone Rd W L21 ... 27 B2
Kirkway
Bebington CH63 ...... 78 D7
Birkenhead, Greasby
CH49 .... 64 E4
Birkenhead, Upton CH49.. 64 F5
Wallasey CH45 .... 51 B7
Kitchener Dr L37 ..... 38 F6
Kitchener St WA10 .... 43 E4
Kitchen St L1 .... 90 B1
Kitling La L34 .... 41 B5
Kitling Rd L34 .... 41 C5
Kiverley Cl L18 ...... 69 E3
Kiveton Dr WN4 .... 35 C4
Knap The CH60 .... 86 A6
Knaresborough Rd
CH44 .... 50 F4
Knighton Rd L4 .... 39 D1
Knight Rd L34 .... 59 F6
Knightsbridge Cl WA8.. 73 D4
Knightsbridge Ct CH43.. 65 D3
Knightsbridge Wlk
L33 .... 29 D6
Knights Grange WA9 ... 44 C4
Knight St L1 .... 90 C1
Knightsway L22 .... 26 F2
Knightswood Ct L18 ... 81 C8
Knob Hall Gdns PR9 ....1 F1

Knob Hall La PR9 ....1 F3
Knoclaid Rd L13 ...... 53 E7
Knolle Park Mews L25 . 69 F3
Knoll The CH43 .... 66 A3
KNOTTY ASH 54 C3
Knotty Ash Prim Sch
L14 .... 54 D4
Knotty Cross L25 ..... 70 C3
Knotty Mews L25 ...... 70 C3
Knowle Ave PR8 .... 7 C6
Knowle Cl L12 .... 40 C2
Knowles House Ave
WA10 .... 42 F3
Knowles St
Birkenhead CH41 ..... 66 C7
2 Widnes WA8 ...... 73 C2
Knowle The 5 L23 .... 26 B3
Knowl Hey Rd L26 .... 83 A6
KNOWSLEY 41 C4
Knowsley Ave WA3 .... 36 B1
Knowsley Bsns Pk L34. 41 B6
Knowsley Cl CH42 .... 67 A1
Knowsley Com Coll
(Kirkby Campus) L32 . 29 D2
Knowsley Comm Coll
L36 .... 55 D3
Knowsley Ct CH42 .... 67 A1
Knowsley Expressway
Halewood L35, WA8 .. 83 F8
Tarbock Green L35 ... 71 D4
Whiston L35 .... 71 D4
Knowsley Hey Sch L36 . 55 F2
Knowsley Hts L36 .... 55 E5
Knowsley Ind Pk
Kirkby L33 .... 30 C2
Knowsley L33 .... 41 B7
Knowsley La
Huyton-w-R L34, L36 . 55 D6
Knowsley L34 .... 41 C4
Knowsley Park La L34. 56 C7
Knowsley Rd
Birkenhead CH42 ..... 67 A1
Bootle L20 .... 38 B5
Liverpool L19 .... 81 A6
Ormskirk L39 .... 13 F5
Rainhill L35 .... 57 D2
Southport PR9 .... 1 C1
St Helens WA10 ...... 43 D3
Wallasey CH45 .... 51 A6
Knowsley Safari Pk*
L34 .... 42 C2
Knowsley St 1 L4 ... 38 F2
Knowsley View WA11 .. 31 E8
Knowsley Village Sch
L34 .... 41 C3
Knox Cl CH62 .... 79 B6
Knox St CH41 .... 66 F6
Knutsford Cl WA10 ... 43 B2
Knutsford Gn CH46 ... 49 E1
Knutsford Rd CH46 ... 49 E1
Knutsford Wlk L31 ... 20 C4
Kramar Wlk 1 L33 ... 29 F2
Kremlin Dr L13 .... 54 A5
Kylemore Ave L18 .... 69 A2
Kylemore Cl CH61 .... 76 E3
Kylemore Ct L26 ..... 82 E8
Kylemore Dr CH61 .... 76 F3
Kylemore Rd CH43 .... 66 A4
Kylemore Way
Heswall CH61 .... 76 E3
Liverpool L26 .... 82 E8
Kynance Rd L11 ...... 40 D5

L

Laburnum Ave
Huyton-w-R L36 ...... 70 E8
St Helens WA11 ...... 44 D7
Laburnum Cres L32 ... 29 D3
Laburnum Ct 14 L8 ... 68 A4
Laburnum Dr WN8 ..... 15 D1
Laburnum Gr
Irby CH61 .... 76 D6
Liverpool L15 .... 69 A8
Maghull L31 .... 20 E1
Southport PR8 .... 4 F7
Laburnum La WA5 ..... 74 C5
Laburnum Pl L20 ..... 38 D3
Laburnum Rd
Birkenhead CH43 ..... 66 C4
Golborne WA3 .... 47 F7
Liverpool L7 .... 53 D3
Wallasey CH45 .... 51 B7
Laburnum St WN4 ..... 35 B2
Lace St L3 .... 90 B4
Lacey Rd L34 .... 56 E5
Lacey St WA10 .... 57 D8
Laddock Cl L4 .... 53 C7
Lady Alice's Dr L40 . 14 E8
Ladybarn Ave WA3 ... 46 F7
Ladybower Cl
Birkenhead CH49 ..... 64 E6
Liverpool L7 .... 68 B8
Lady Chapel Cl L1 ... 90 C1
Ladyewood Rd CH44 ... 51 C3
Ladyfield CH43 .... 65 C7
Ladyfields L12 .... 54 B5
LADY GREEN 18 D4
Lady Green Cl L38 ... 18 E3
Lady Green La L38 ... 18 D4
Lady Lever Art Gall The*
CH62 .... 79 B6
Ladymount RC Prim Sch
CH61 .... 76 E1
Ladypool L24 .... 83 C2
Ladysmith Ave WN4 ... 35 C3
Ladysmith Rd L10 .... 39 F6
Lady's Wlk L40 ...... 14 C6

Ladywood Rd WA5 ..... 60 D1
LAFFAK 44 D7
Laffak Rd WA11 ...... 44 D7
Lafford La WN8 ...... 25 C8
Lagan Ho CH46 .... 49 E4
Laggan St L7 .... 53 B2
Lagrange Arc 9 WA10 . 44 A3
Laird Cl CH41 .... 65 F8
Lairds Pl L3 .... 52 D4
Laird St CH41 .... 66 A8
Laithwaite Cl WA8 ... 58 B3
Lakeland Ave WN4 ... 35 C4
Lakeland Cl L1 ...... 90 B2
Lakemoor Cl WA9 .... 58 D7
Lakenheath Rd L26 .. 82 E7
Lake Pl CH47 .... 63 B7
Lake Rd
Hoylake CH47 .... 63 B7
Liverpool L15 .... 69 A7
Lakes Dr WN5 .... 25 E6
Lakeside Ave WN5 ... 25 E3
Lakeside Cl WA8 ..... 84 A8
Lakeside Ct
Rainford WA11 .... 32 A6
Wallasey CH45 .... 51 C6
Lakeside Gdns WA11 .. 32 A6
Lakeside Lawn L27 ... 71 A3
Lakeside View L22 ... 37 D8
Lakes Rd L9 .... 39 D7
Lake St 5 L4 .... 53 A7
Lake View L15 .... 71 E8
Lake View Ct L4 .... 39 A2
Laleston Cl WA8 ..... 84 E8
Lambert St 1 L3 ... 90 C4
Lambert Way L3 ...... 90 C4
Lambeth Cl CH47 ..... 63 A7
Lambeth Rd L4, L5 ... 52 D7
Lambeth Wlk L4 ..... 52 D7
Lambourn Ave WA8 ... 72 C5
Lambourne WN8 ...... 16 B4
Lambourne Gr WA9 ... 45 A4
Lambourne Rd L4 .... 39 D1
Lambrigg Row 18 L4 . 52 F7
Lambshear La L31 ... 20 C4
Lambton Rd L17 ..... 68 B3
Lamerton Cl WA5 .... 74 D4
Lammermoor Rd L18 . 69 A2
Lampeter Cl WA5 .... 60 E2
Lampeter Rd L6 ..... 53 C6
Lamport Cl WA8 ..... 73 E3
Lamport St 2 L8 ... 67 E5
Lanark Cl WA10 ..... 43 F2
Lanark Gdns WA8 .... 72 A3
Lancashire Gdns WA10. 43 F2
Lancaster Ave
Crosby L23 .... 26 D3
Golborne WA3 .... 47 C8
Liverpool L17 .... 68 D6
Prescot L35 .... 56 D3
Wallasey CH45 .... 51 C5
Widnes WA8 .... 72 A2
Lancaster Cl
Bebington CH62 ...... 79 B6
Liverpool L5 .... 52 A6
Maghull L31 .... 20 F1
Newton-le-W WA12 .... 45 F4
Southport PR8 .... 3 E4
Lancaster Cres WN8 . 15 C1
Lancaster Dr PR9 ... 2 F5
Lancaster Gate PR9 . 2 F5
Lancaster Gdns PR8 . 3 E4
Lancaster Ho PR8 ... 3 E4
Lancaster Rd
Formby L37 .... 9 E1
Huyton-w-R L36 ...... 56 A4
Southport PR8 .... 3 E4
Widnes WA8 .... 73 B3
Lancaster St
Liverpool L5 .... 52 D6
Liverpool, Walton L9 . 38 F3
Lancaster Wlk L36 .. 56 A4
Lance Cl L5 .... 52 F5
Lancefield Rd L9 ... 38 F5
Lance Gr L15 .... 69 A7
Lance La L15 .... 69 A7
Lancelyn Ct CH63 ... 79 A3
Lancelyn Terr CH63 . 78 F4
Lancing Ave WA2 .... 61 A4
Lancing Cl L25 ..... 70 C1
Lancing Dr L10 ..... 28 D2
Lancing Rd L25 ..... 70 C1
Lancing Way L25 .... 70 C1
Lancots La WA9 ..... 58 D8
Land End L31 .... 21 C1
Lander Rd L21 ...... 38 C6
Lander Road Prim Sch
L21 .... 38 C6
Landford Ave L9 .... 39 E4
Landford Pl L9 ..... 39 E4
LAND GATE 35 A8
Landgate Ind Est WN4. 35 A8
Landgate La WN4 .... 35 B8
Landgate Sch WN4 .. 35 A8
LANDICAN 77 C8
Landican La CH43, CH49,
CH63 .... 77 E7
Landican Rd CH49,
CH61 .... 77 B7
Landican La PR9 .... 2 D4
Landor Cl
Golborne WA3 .... 47 E8
Liverpool L3 .... 52 C5
Landseer Rd L5 ..... 52 F5
Lane Ends WA8 ...... 83 D5
LANE HEAD 47 E6
Lane Head Ave WA3 . 47 F8

Lanfranc Cl L16 ..... 69 E8
Lanfranc Way L16 ... 69 E8
Langbar L35 .... 56 E2
Langdale Ave
Formby L37 .... 9 D2
Golborne WA3 .... 36 C1
Heswall CH61 .... 76 F4
Langdale Cl
Formby L37 .... 9 D2
Kirkby L32 .... 29 F1
Warrington WA2 ...... 61 E2
Widnes WA8 .... 84 C8
Langdale Cres WN2 .. 36 B8
Langdale Dr L31 .... 20 E2
Langdale Gdns PR8 .. 3 E1
Langdale Gr WA11 ... 44 B7
Langdale Rd
Bebington CH63 ...... 78 F4
Liverpool L15 .... 68 E6
Wallasey CH45 .... 51 A7
Langdale St L20 .... 38 D3
Langfield CH43 ...... 47 E7
Langfield Gr CH62 .. 88 D5
Langford L24 .... 83 C2
Langford Rd L19 .... 80 F8
Langham Ave L17 ... 68 C3
Langham Ct L4 ..... 52 F8
Langham St Ind Est L4. 52 F8
Langham St L4 ..... 52 F8
Langholme Hts L11 . 39 F4
Langholm Rd WN4 ... 34 C4
Lang La CH48 .... 63 B3
Langland Cl
Liverpool L4 .... 53 D8
Warrington WA5 ...... 60 E2
Lang Lane S CH48 .. 63 C2
Langley Ave WA12 ... 46 C1
Langley Cl
Bebington CH63 ...... 79 A2
Golborne WA3 .... 36 C1
Hightown L38 .... 17 F2
Liverpool L12 .... 40 F3
Langley Rd CH63 ... 79 A2
Langley St 2 L8 ... 67 E6
Langrove St L5 .... 52 E5
Langsdale St
Liverpool L3 .... 52 E3
Liverpool L3, L6 .... 52 F3
Langshaw Lea L27 .. 70 F4
Langstone Ave CH49 . 64 C3
Langton Cl
Newton-le-W WA12 .... 46 A4
Widnes WA8 .... 72 B3
Langton Rd
Kirkby L33 .... 29 F5
Liverpool L15 .... 68 D7
Langtree WN8 .... 16 B3
Langtree St WA9 .... 44 C3
Langtry Cl L4 ..... 52 D8
Langtry Rd L4 ..... 52 D8
Lansbury Ave WA9 .. 44 E3
Lansbury Bridge Sch
WA9 .... 44 E3
Lansbury Rd L36 ... 56 A2
Lansdown L12 ...... 54 A6
Lansdowne Cl CH41 . 66 A8
Lansdowne Ct 6 CH43. 65 F8
Lansdowne Ho CH41 . 66 F6
Lansdowne Pl
5 Birkenhead CH43 . 65 F8
Liverpool L5 .... 52 F6
Lansdowne Rd
Birkenhead CH41,
CH43 .... 65 F8
Southport PR8 .... 4 E6
Wallasey CH45 .... 50 F7
Lansdowne Way L36 . 55 E2
Lanville Rd L9 .... 39 B1
Lanyork Rd L3 ..... 52 B3
Lapford Cres L33 .. 30 A4
Lapford Wlk L33 ... 30 A4
Lapwing Cl
Golborne WA3 .... 47 D8
Liverpool L12 .... 40 F1
Newton-le-W WA12 .... 46 C3
Lapwing Ct L26 .... 70 E1
Lapwing Rise CH60 . 85 F6
Lapworth Cl 3 CH46. 64 B8
Lapworth St L5 .... 52 D6
Larch Ave
Newton-le-W WA12 .... 46 C2
Warrington WA5 ...... 74 C5
Widnes WA8 .... 73 B2
Larch Cl
Billinge WN5 .... 33 D5
Golborne WA3 .... 47 F6
Liverpool L19 .... 80 F7
Skelmersdale WN8 .... 15 E1
Larch Ct 13 L8 .... 68 A4
Larchdale Gr L9 ... 39 B4
Larchfield Rd L23 . 27 B5
Larch Gr
Birkenhead CH43 ..... 65 E8
Liverpool L15 .... 54 A1
Larch Lea 2 L6 .... 53 B5
Larch Rd
Birkenhead CH41 ..... 66 D5
Haydock WA11 .... 45 F4
Huyton-w-R L36 ...... 55 D3
Larch St PR8 .... 4 E6
Larchtree Mews L12 . 54 E8
Larch Way L37 ...... 9 D4
Larchwood Ave L31 .. 28 C7
Larchwood Cl
Heswall CH61 .... 76 F3
Liverpool L25 .... 70 B5
Larchwood Dr CH63 . 78 F7
Larcombe Ave CH49 . 64 C6

Larkfield Cl L17 . . . . **68** C2
Larkfield Ct PR9 . . . . **2** A3
Larkfield Gr L17 . . . . **68** C2
Larkfield La PR9 . . . . **2** A3
Larkfield Prim Sch PR9 . . . **2** A3
Larkfield Rd L17 . . . . **68** C2
Larkfield View L15 . . . . **68** E8
Larkhill WN8 . . . . **16** B4
Larkhill Ave CH49 . . . . **65** A7
Larkhill Cl L13 . . . . **53** E7
Larkhill Gr L38 . . . . **17** F3
Larkhill La
Formby L37 . . . . **9** C4
Liverpool L13 . . . . **53** E7
Larkhill Pl L13 . . . . **53** F7
Larkhill View L13 . . . . **53** F7
Larkhill Way CH49 . . . . **65** A7
Larkin Cl CH62 . . . . **79** A7
Lark La L17 . . . . **68** C4
Larkspur Cl 3 PR8 . . . . **4** D6
Larkspur Ct 5 L31 . . . . **29** A3
Larksway CH60 . . . . **86** B8
Lark Way L17 . . . . **68** C3
Larne Ct WA8 . . . . **72** E2
Larton Farm Cl CH48 . . . . . **63** E3
Larton Rd CH48 . . . . **63** E3
Lartonwood CH48 . . . . **63** E3
Lascelles Rd L19 . . . . **81** D7
Lascelles St WA9 . . . . **44** C3
Latchford Rd CH60 . . . . **86** B6
Late Moffatt Rd W L9 . . . . **39** B7
Latham Ave
Newton-le-W WA12 . . . . **46** C4
Ormskirk L39 . . . . **14** A5
Latham Ct L7 . . . . **53** D2
Latham Ho WA12 . . . . **46** B4
Latham St L5 . . . . **52** D6
Latham Way CH63 . . . . **79** B2
Lathbury La L17 . . . . **68** E5
Lathom Ave
2 Seaforth L21 . . . . **37** F6
Wallasey CH44 . . . . **51** B4
Lathom Cl
Huyton-w-R L36 . . . . **56** A6
1 Seaforth L21 . . . . **37** F6
Lathom Dr
Maghull L31 . . . . **20** E3
Rainford WA11 . . . . **31** F7
Lathom High Sch WN8 . . . **15** F3
Lathom Ho L40 . . . . **15** B7
Lathom La L40 . . . . **14** C7
LATHOM PARK **15** C7
Lathom Rd
Bickerstaffe L39 . . . . **22** F8
Bootle L20 . . . . **38** C5
Huyton-w-R L36 . . . . **55** E2
Southport PR9 . . . . **1** C1
Lathum Cl L35 . . . . **56** E5
Latimer Cl 2 WN5 . . . . **25** F7
Latimer St L5 . . . . **52** D5
Latrigg Rd L17 . . . . **68** E2
Lauder Cl L33 . . . . **29** D6
Launceston Dr WA5 . . . . . **74** E3
Laund The CH45 . . . . **50** F5
Laurel Ave
Bebington CH63 . . . . **78** E4
Heswall CH60 . . . . **76** F1
Newton-le-W WA12 . . . . **46** D3
Laurel Bank WA8 . . . . **73** A3
Laurelbanks CH60 . . . . **76** E1
Laurel Ct WA11 . . . . **44** B7
Laurel Dr
Skelmersdale WN8 . . . . **15** E2
St Helens WA10 . . . . **42** F4
Willaston CH64 . . . . **88** B1
Laurel Gr
Ashton-in-M WN4 . . . . **35** B4
Crosby L22 . . . . **26** D2
Golborne WA3 . . . . **47** D8
Huyton-w-R L36 . . . . **70** E8
Liverpool L8 . . . . **68** C6
Southport PR8 . . . . **4** E7
Laurelhurst Ave CH61 . . . . **77** A4
Laurel Rd
Birkenhead CH42 . . . . **66** D4
Liverpool L7 . . . . **53** D2
Prescot L34 . . . . **56** E6
St Helens, Blackbrook
WA11 . . . . **44** F5
St Helens, West Park
WA10 . . . . **43** D2
Laurels The CH46 . . . . **49** E3
Laurence Deacon Ct 1
CH41 . . . . **66** D7
Lauren Cl L36 . . . . **56** B2
Lauren Ho L35 . . . . **56** F5
Lauriston Rd L4 . . . . **39** C1
Laurus Cl L27 . . . . **70** F5
Lavan Cl L6 . . . . **53** A3
Lavan St 3 L6 . . . . **53** A3
Lavender Cres 7 L34 . . . . . **56** E6
Lavender Gdns
Crosby L23 . . . . **27** B5
St Helens WA9 . . . . **59** A7
Lavender Way L9 . . . . **39** B4
Lavender Wlk WN4 . . . . . . **34** D5
Lavrock Bank L8 . . . . **67** E4
Lawford Dr CH60 . . . . **86** C8
Lawler Gr L34 . . . . **56** E7
Lawler St L21 . . . . **38** B6
Lawnhurst Gr L17 . . . . **80** E8
Lawns Ave
Bebington CH63 . . . . **88** B6
Orrell WN5 . . . . **25** C5
Lawnside Cl CH42 . . . . **66** F1
Lawns The
Birkenhead CH43 . . . . **65** D7
6 Crosby L23 . . . . **26** B3
Lawns The *continued*
Southport PR9 . . . . **1** F2
Lawrence Cl L19 . . . . **81** A7
Lawrence Com Prim Sch
L15 . . . . **68** D7
Lawrence Ct WN2 . . . . **36** B8
Lawrence Gr L15 . . . . **68** E7
Lawrence Rd
Liverpool L15 . . . . **68** E7
St Helens WA10 . . . . **43** C6
Lawrenson St WA10 . . . . . . **43** E3
Lawson St PR9 . . . . **5** A7
Lawson Wlk L12 . . . . **40** D3
Lawswood L37 . . . . **9** E5
Lawton Ave L20 . . . . **38** E5
Lawton Rd
Crosby L22, L23 . . . . **26** D2
Huyton-w-R L36 . . . . **55** C1
Rainhill L35 . . . . **57** D2
Lawton St L1 . . . . **90** C3
Laxey St L8 . . . . **67** E6
Laxton Rd L25 . . . . **82** C8
Layford Cl L36 . . . . **55** D6
Layford Rd L36 . . . . **55** D5
Layton Ave CH43 . . . . **65** F1
Layton Cl L25 . . . . **70** C2
Layton Rd L25 . . . . **70** C2
Lazenby Cres WN4 . . . . **34** F3
Lazonby Cl 4 CH43 . . . . . . **65** C8
Leach Croft L28 . . . . **55** A7
Leach La
St Helens, Sutton Leach
WA9 . . . . **58** D5
St Helens WA9 . . . . **58** D6
Leach St 4 WA10 . . . . **43** F4
Leach Way CH61 . . . . **76** C6
Lea Cl CH43 . . . . **65** E4
Lea Cres L39 . . . . **13** F7
Leacroft WN4 . . . . **34** F6
Lea Cross Gr WA8 . . . . **72** C3
Lea Ct L39 . . . . **13** E7
Leadenhall Cl L5 . . . . **52** F6
Leafield Cl CH61 . . . . **76** F6
Leafield Rd L25 . . . . **82** B7
Leagate L10 . . . . **39** F8
LEA GREEN **57** F5
Lea Green Bsns Pk
WA9 . . . . **57** F4
Lea Green Ind Est
WA9 . . . . **58** A3
Lea Green Rd WA9 . . . . **58** A4
Lea Green Sta WA9 . . . . . . **58** B5
Leamington Ave
Newton-le-W WA12 . . . . **46** C1
Southport PR8 . . . . **7** D5
Leamington Com Prim Sch
L11 . . . . **39** D2
Leamington Rd
Liverpool L11 . . . . **39** D2
Southport PR8 . . . . **7** D5
Leander Rd CH45 . . . . **51** A5
Lea Rd CH44 . . . . **51** D5
LEASOWE **50** A4
Leasowe Ave CH45 . . . . **50** E6
Leasowe Gdns CH46 . . . . . **49** E4
Leasowe Prim Sch
CH46 . . . . **50** B3
Leasowe Rd
Liverpool L9 . . . . **39** B7
Wallasey CH45, CH46 . . . . . **50** C5
Leasoweside CH46 . . . . **50** A4
Leasowe Sta CH46 . . . . **50** A2
Leas Pk CH47 . . . . **63** A4
Leas The
Heswall CH61 . . . . **77** B6
Wallasey CH45 . . . . **50** E7
Leatherbarrows La
Kirkby L31 . . . . **29** A6
Maghull L31 . . . . **28** F7
Leather La L2 . . . . **90** A4
Leather's La L26 . . . . **82** F8
Leathwood L31 . . . . **28** E8
Leaway CH49 . . . . **64** D4
Leawood Gr CH46 . . . . **64** F8
Leckwith Rd L30 . . . . **28** B2
Leda Gr 3 L17 . . . . **68** C4
Ledburn WN8 . . . . **16** B3
Ledbury Cl
Birkenhead CH43 . . . . **65** E2
Liverpool L12 . . . . **40** F4
St Helens WA10 . . . . **43** B3
Ledger Rd WA11 . . . . **45** A5
Ledmore Gr WN4 . . . . **34** D3
Ledsham Cl CH43 . . . . **65** E4
Ledsham Rd L32 . . . . **29** C2
Ledsham Wlk 7 L32 . . . . . **29** C2
Ledson Gr L39 . . . . **21** B7
Ledson Pk L33 . . . . **29** F6
Ledsons Gr L31 . . . . **29** A3
Leece St L1 . . . . **90** C2
Lee Cl L35 . . . . **57** D1
Leecourt Cl L12 . . . . **54** D5
Lee Ct WA2 . . . . **61** C2
Leeds St L3 . . . . **52** C3
Lee Hall Rd L25 . . . . **70** C5
Lee La WN2 . . . . **36** B8
Leeming Cl L19 . . . . **81** C5
Lee Park Ave L25 . . . . **70** C5
Lee Rd CH47 . . . . **63** C7
Lees Ave CH42 . . . . **66** F2
Leeside Ave L32 . . . . **29** F1
Leeside Cl L32 . . . . **29** F1
Lees La
Liverpool L12 . . . . **54** D7
Skelmersdale WN8 . . . . **16** E7
Lees Rd L33 . . . . **30** B2
Lee St WA9 . . . . **58** E8
Leeswood
6 Crosby L22 . . . . **26** E1
Skelmersdale WN8 . . . . **16** B3
Leeswood Rd CH49 . . . . . . **65** A4
Lee Vale Rd L25 . . . . **70** C4
Leeward Dr L24 . . . . **82** A5
Legh Ct WA3 . . . . **47** A8
Legh Rd
Bebington CH62 . . . . **79** B7
Haydock WA11 . . . . **45** B6
Legh St
Ashton-in-M WN4 . . . . **35** B2
Golborne WA3 . . . . **47** A8
Newton-le-W WA12 . . . . **46** A3
Legh Vale Prim Sch
WA11 . . . . **45** B6
Legion La CH62 . . . . **79** D1
Legion Rd WA10 . . . . **57** D8
Leicester Ave L22 . . . . **26** D2
Leicester Rd L20 . . . . **38** D4
Leicester St
Southport PR9 . . . . **4** B8
St Helens WA9 . . . . **57** D8
Leigh Ave WA8 . . . . **73** A1
Leigh Bridge Way L5 . . . . . **52** C5
Leigh Green Cl 4
WA8 . . . . **84** C8
Leigh Pl L1 . . . . **90** B3
Leigh Rd CH48 . . . . **63** B3
Leighs Hey Cres L32 . . . . . **29** F2
Leigh St L1 . . . . **90** B3
Leighton Ave
Hoylake CH47 . . . . **63** E8
Maghull L31 . . . . **20** D2
Leighton Chase CH64 . . . . **86** D1
Leighton Cotts CH64 . . . . . **86** D5
Leighton Rd
Birkenhead CH41 . . . . **66** E4
Neston CH64 . . . . **86** D2
Leighton St L4 . . . . **38** E1
Leinster Gdns WA7 . . . . . . **84** F3
Leinster Rd L13 . . . . **54** B3
Leinster St WA7 . . . . **84** F3
Leison St L4 . . . . **52** D7
Leiston Cl CH61 . . . . **76** E7
Lemon Cl L7 . . . . **53** C1
Lemon Gr L8 . . . . **68** C6
Lemon St L5 . . . . **52** D6
Lemon Tree Wlk WA10 . . . **43** D1
Lendel Cl L37 . . . . **9** E3
Lenfield Dr WA11 . . . . **44** F6
Lenham Way L24 . . . . **82** B5
Lennox Ave CH45 . . . . **51** B7
Lennox La CH43 . . . . **50** C1
Lenthall St L4 . . . . **38** F2
Lenton Ave L37 . . . . **9** D4
Lenton Rd L25 . . . . **70** C5
Lentworth Ct L17 . . . . **80** F7
Leo Cl L14 . . . . **54** F4
Leominster Rd CH44 . . . . . **51** B4
Leonard Cheshire Dr
L30 . . . . **27** F3
Leonards Cl L36 . . . . **55** D6
Leonard St WA9 . . . . **58** F7
Leon Cl WA5 . . . . **74** D7
Leopold Gr WA9 . . . . **58** C5
Leopold Rd
Crosby L22 . . . . **26** C2
Liverpool L7 . . . . **53** B2
Leopold St CH44 . . . . **51** E3
Lesley Rd PR8 . . . . **4** E7
Leslie Ave CH49 . . . . **64** D3
Leslie Rd WA10 . . . . **57** C8
Lesseps Rd L8 . . . . **68** C7
Lessingham Rd WA8 . . . . . **72** F3
Lester Cl L4 . . . . **52** E7
Lester Dr
Irby CH61 . . . . **76** C7
St Helens WA10 . . . . **43** A5
Lester Gr L36 . . . . **55** F4
Lestock St L8 . . . . **90** C1
Leta St
Liverpool L4 . . . . **38** F1
Liverpool L4 . . . . **39** A1
Letchworth St L6 . . . . **53** C5
Lethbridge Cl L5 . . . . **52** D6
Lethbridge Rd PR8 . . . . **4** D5
Letitia St L8 . . . . **67** F5
Levens Hey CH46 . . . . **64** D8
Leven St L4 . . . . **52** E8
Levens Way 1 WA8 . . . . . . **84** C8
Lever Ave 11 CH44 . . . . . . **51** E2
Lever Cswy CH63 . . . . **78** B7
Leveret Rd L24 . . . . **83** A3
Leverhulme Ct CH63 . . . . . **79** A4
Lever St WA9 . . . . **58** D3
Lever Terr CH42 . . . . **66** E3
Leveson Rd L13 . . . . **54** B1
Lewis Ave WA5 . . . . **60** F2
Lewis Ct PR9 . . . . **4** D8
Lewis Gr WA8 . . . . **72** D1
Lewisham Rd
Bebington CH62 . . . . **79** C6
Liverpool L11 . . . . **40** A1
Lewis St WA10 . . . . **43** E3
Lewis Wlk 4 L33 . . . . **29** E6
Lexham Rd L14 . . . . **54** C3
Lexington Way L33 . . . . . . **29** D6
Lexton Dr PR9 . . . . **2** B3
Leybourne Ave PR8 . . . . **7** F7
Leybourne Cl L25 . . . . **70** A6
Leybourne Gn L25 . . . . **70** A6
Leybourne Gr L25 . . . . **70** A5
Leybourne Rd L25 . . . . **70** A6
Leyburn Cl L32 . . . . **40** E7
Leyburn Rd CH45 . . . . **50** F6
Ley Cl WA9 . . . . **58** C4
Leyfield Cl L12 . . . . **54** D6
Leyfield Ct L12 . . . . **54** D6
Leyfield Rd L12 . . . . **54** D6
Leyfield Wlk L12 . . . . **54** D6
Leyland Cl PR9 . . . . **2** E5
Leyland Gr WA11 . . . . **45** B6
Leyland Green Rd
WN4 . . . . **34** C5
Leyland Rd
Rainford WA11 . . . . **31** F6
Southport PR9 . . . . **1** C1
Leyland St 8 L34 . . . . **56** D6
Leyland Way L39 . . . . **13** F5
Liberton Ct 10 L5 . . . . **53** A6
Liberty St L15 . . . . **68** E7
Libra Cl L14 . . . . **55** A5
Library St 3 WA10 . . . . **44** A3
Lichfield Ave
Crosby L22 . . . . **26** D3
Golborne WA3 . . . . **47** D8
Lichfield Cl L30 . . . . **28** A1
Lichfield Gr WN4 . . . . **35** C2
Lichfield Rd
Halewood L26 . . . . **82** E7
Liverpool, Wavertree Green
L15 . . . . **69** A6
Lichfield St CH45 . . . . **51** C7
Lickers La L35 . . . . **56** E2
Liddell Ave L31 . . . . **29** B4
Liddell Ct CH45 . . . . **50** D5
Liddell Rd L12 . . . . **53** F7
Lidderdale Ct L15 . . . . **68** E6
Lidderdale Rd L15 . . . . **68** E6
Lidgate Cl L33 . . . . **29** F5
Liege Ho CH49 . . . . **64** F6
Lifeboat Rd L37 . . . . **9** B1
Liffey St L8 . . . . **68** B7
Lifton Rd L33 . . . . **30** A2
Lightbody St L5 . . . . **52** C5
Lightburn St 6 WA7 . . . . . **84** F1
Lightfoot Cl CH60 . . . . **86** B7
Lightfoot La CH60 . . . . **86** B7
Lighthorne Dr PR8 . . . . **7** A4
Lighthouse La L37 . . . . **10** A1
Lighthouse Rd CH47 . . . . . **63** B6
Lightoaks Dr L26 . . . . **71** B1
Lightshaw La WA3 . . . . **36** B4
Lightwood Dr 3 L7 . . . . . . **68** C8
Lightwood St 5 L7 . . . . . . **68** C8
Lilac Ave
Downall Green WN4 . . . . . . **34** D5
Southport PR8 . . . . **7** D2
Widnes WA8 . . . . **73** B2
Lilac Gr
Billinge WN5 . . . . **33** D4
Huyton-w-R L36 . . . . **70** D8
Skelmersdale WN8 . . . . **15** E1
St Helens WA11 . . . . **44** F5
Lilac Rd WA3 . . . . **36** A1
Lilford Ave L9 . . . . **38** F6
Lilford Dr WA5 . . . . **74** F6
Lilley Ct L7 . . . . **53** D3
Lilley Rd L7 . . . . **53** D2
Lillian Rd L4 . . . . **53** B6
Lillie Cl 3 CH43 . . . . **65** C8
Lillyfield CH60 . . . . **85** F6
Lilly Gn L4 . . . . **39** B1
Lilly Gr L4 . . . . **39** B1
Lilly Vale L7 . . . . **53** D3
Lily Ave WA12 . . . . **46** D2
Lily La WN2 . . . . **35** F7
Lily Pl WN4 . . . . **35** C2
Lily Rd L21 . . . . **38** B6
Lily St WN4 . . . . **35** E5
Limbo La CH49 . . . . **76** D8
Lime Ave
Bebington CH63 . . . . **78** D4
3 Widnes WA8 . . . . **73** B2
Lime Cl
Abram Brow WN2 . . . . **36** C7
Liverpool L13 . . . . **54** A4
Lime Ct
Liverpool L1 . . . . **90** C3
Skelmersdale WN8 . . . . **15** E1
Limedale Rd L18 . . . . **69** B5
Limefield Dr WN8 . . . . **24** E7
Lime Gr
Bootle L21 . . . . **38** A6
Golborne WA3 . . . . **47** E6
Liverpool L8 . . . . **68** C6
Rainford WA11 . . . . **31** F6
Skelmersdale WN8 . . . . **15** E1
Limehurst Gr CH62 . . . . **88** D6
Limekiln La
Burtonwood WA5 . . . . **59** E3
1 Liverpool L3 . . . . **52** D3
Liverpool L3, L5 . . . . **52** D4
Wallasey CH41, CH44 . . . . . **51** A2
Limerick Cl WA8 . . . . **72** E3
Lime St
Liverpool L1 . . . . **90** B4
Southport PR8 . . . . **4** E6
Limes The
Birkenhead CH49 . . . . **64** F5
Golborne WA3 . . . . **47** D6
Lime Street Sta L3, L1 . . . . **90** C4
Lime Tree Cl L9 . . . . **39** B4
Lime Tree Gr CH60 . . . . **86** C8
Lime Tree Way L37 . . . . **9** C2
Lime Vale Rd WN5 . . . . **33** C3
Limont Rd PR8 . . . . **7** D5
Linacre La
Bootle L20 . . . . **38** D5
Maghull L37 . . . . **19** B7
Widnes WA8 . . . . **72** E5
Linacre Prim Sch L20 . . . . **38** C5
Linacre Rd L20, L21 . . . . . . **38** B6
Linaker Dr L39 . . . . **12** B8
Linaker Prim Sch PR8 . . . . . . **4** B5
Linaker St PR8 . . . . **4** B5
Linbeck Gr WA3 . . . . **36** E1
Lincoln Ave WA3 . . . . **36** D1
Lincoln Cl
Huyton-w-R L36 . . . . **56** B3
Liverpool L6 . . . . **53** B4
Lincoln Cres WA11 . . . . **44** B6
Lincoln Ct L20 . . . . **38** C2
Lincoln Dr
Aintree L10 . . . . **28** D3
Ashton-in-M WN4 . . . . **35** D2
Wallasey CH45 . . . . **51** C6
Lincoln Gn L31 . . . . **28** B8
Lincoln Rd
Southport PR8 . . . . **4** A1
St Helens WA10 . . . . **43** D2
Lincoln Sq WA8 . . . . **73** B2
Lincoln St
Birkenhead CH41 . . . . **51** A1
Liverpool L19 . . . . **81** D4
Lincoln Way
Huyton-w-R L36 . . . . **56** B3
Rainhill L35 . . . . **57** D1
Lincombe Rd L36 . . . . **55** C4
Lindale Cl CH46 . . . . **50** A1
Lindale Dr 11 WA9 . . . . **58** C4
Lindale Rd L7 . . . . **53** E3
Lindby Cl L32 . . . . **41** A8
Lindby Rd L32 . . . . **41** A8
Linden Ave
Ashton-in-M WN4 . . . . **34** F5
Crosby L23 . . . . **26** C4
Litherland L30 . . . . **27** F2
Orrell WN5 . . . . **25** E6
Linden Ct
1 Crosby L23 . . . . **26** B3
Orrell WN5 . . . . **25** E6
Widnes WA8 . . . . **72** F4
Linden Dr
Birkenhead CH43 . . . . **65** E1
Huyton-w-R L36 . . . . **70** E8
Linden Gr
Billinge WN5 . . . . **33** C3
Orrell WN5 . . . . **25** E6
Wallasey CH45 . . . . **51** B7
Linden Rd L27 . . . . **70** E5
Lindens WN8 . . . . **16** B4
Lindens The
3 Birkenhead CH43 . . . . . . **66** C5
Maghull L31 . . . . **28** C7
Linden Way
St Helens WA10 . . . . **43** B4
Widnes WA8 . . . . **72** F4
Linden Wlk WN5 . . . . **25** E6
Lindenwood 6 L32 . . . . **40** F8
Lindeth Ave CH44 . . . . **51** B3
Lindfield Cl 4 L8 . . . . **67** F4
Lindholme WN8 . . . . **16** C3
Lindisfarne Ct WA8 . . . . . . **72** F6
Lindisfarne Dr L12 . . . . **41** A3
Lindley Ave WN5 . . . . **25** C5
Lindley Cl 6 L7 . . . . **68** C8
Lindley St L7 . . . . **68** C8
Lindrick Cl L35 . . . . **57** A4
Lindsay Rd L4 . . . . **53** D8
Lindsay St WA9 . . . . **58** E3
Lind St L4 . . . . **38** F1
Lindwall Cl CH43 . . . . **50** C1
Linear Pk CH46 . . . . **49** C1
Linear View WA12 . . . . **46** C1
Lineside Cl L25 . . . . **70** B5
Linford Gr WA11 . . . . **44** C5
Lingdale Ave CH43 . . . . **65** F6
Lingdale Ct
Birkenhead CH43 . . . . **65** F7
Hoylake CH48 . . . . **62** F3
Lingdale Rd
Birkenhead CH41,
CH43 . . . . **65** F7
West Kirby CH48 . . . . **63** A3
Lingdale Rd N CH41 . . . . . . **65** F7
Lingdales L37 . . . . **10** B5
Lingfield Cl
Huyton-w-R L36 . . . . **55** D1
Litherland L30 . . . . **28** A1
Lingfield Gr L14 . . . . **54** D2
Lingfield Rd
Liverpool L14 . . . . **54** D2
Runcorn WA7 . . . . **84** E1
Lingford Cl L27 . . . . **70** F4
Lingham Cl CH46 . . . . **49** D2
Lingham La
Wallasey CH46 . . . . **49** C3
Wallasey, Moreton CH46 . . . **49** D1
Lingham Prim Sch
CH46 . . . . **49** D1
Lingholme Rd WA10 . . . . . . **43** E4
LINGLEY GREEN **74** C7
Lingley Green Ave
WA5 . . . . **74** D8
Lingley Mere Bsns Pk
WA5 . . . . **74** D8
Lingley Rd WA5 . . . . **74** D6
Lingmell Ave WA11 . . . . . . **33** C1
Lingmell Rd L11, L12 . . . . . **54** B8
Ling St L7 . . . . **53** B2
Lingtree Rd L32 . . . . **29** B3
Lingwell Ave WA8 . . . . **72** D2
Lingwell Pk WA8 . . . . **72** E2
Lingwood Rd WA5 . . . . **74** F6
Linhope Way L17 . . . . **68** C3
Link 25 Bsns Pk WN4 . . . . . **34** F8
Link Ave
Crosby L23 . . . . **27** A5
St Helens WA11 . . . . **44** E5

Linkfield Cl L27 . . . 70 D6
Link Rd L36 . . . 56 B1
Links Ave PR9 . . . 1 F3
Links Cl
Bebington CH63 . . . 88 B6
Wallasey CH45 . . . 50 F7
Links Hey Rd CH48 . . . 75 E6
Linkside CH63 . . . 78 D7
Linkside Ave WA2 . . . 61 B6
Linkside Ct L23 . . . 26 A5
Linkside Rd L25 . . . 70 C1
Links Rd L32 . . . 30 A1
Links The CH43 . . . 65 F5
Linkstor Rd L25 . . . 69 F3
Links View
Birkenhead CH43 . . . 65 E5
Wallasey CH45 . . . 50 F8
Linksway CH45 . . . 50 F7
Linkway WA10 . . . 43 B6
Linkway Ave WN4 . . . 35 E5
Linkway E WA10, WA9 . . . 44 B2
Linkway W WA10 . . . 44 A2
Linner Rd L24 . . . 82 D4
Linnet Cl
Liverpool L17 . . . 68 C5
Newton-le-W WA12 . . . 46 C3
Warrington WA2 . . . 61 D3
Linnet Ct L17 . . . 68 C4
Linnet Ho L8 . . . 68 B5
Linnet La L17 . . . 68 C4
Linnets Way CH60 . . . 85 E8
Linnet Way L33 . . . 29 E7
Linslade Cl L33 . . . 29 F4
Linslade Cres 2 L33 . . . 29 F4
Linton Ave WA3 . . . 35 F2
Linton Pl L32 . . . 29 C3
Linton St 1 L4 . . . 38 F1
Linum Gdns WA9 . . . 59 B7
Linville Ave L23 . . . 26 B4
Linwood Gr L35 . . . 56 E2
Linwood Rd CH42 . . . 66 E3
Lionel St WA9 . . . 58 F7
Lions Cl 2 CH43 . . . 65 F6
Lipton Cl L20 . . . 38 C2
Lisburn La L13 . . . 53 E7
Lisburn Rd L17 . . . 68 E2
LISCARD . . . 51 B6
Liscard Cres CH44, CH45 . . . 51 B4
Liscard Gr CH44, CH45 . . . 51 A4
Liscard Ho 4 CH44 . . . 51 B4
Liscard Prim Sch CH44, CH45 . . . 51 C5
Liscard Rd
Liverpool L15 . . . 68 D7
Wallasey, Liscard CH44 . . . 51 C4
Wallasey, Seacombe CH44 . . . 51 D3
Liscard Village CH45 . . . 51 B5
Liscard Way CH44 . . . 51 B4
Lisleholme Cl L12 . . . 54 C6
Lisleholme Cres L12 . . . 54 C6
Lisleholme Rd L12 . . . 54 C6
Lismore Ct L23 . . . 26 C4
Lismore Pk PR8 . . . 3 E4
Lismore Rd L18 . . . 69 A2
Lister Cres L7 . . . 53 C2
Lister Dr L13, L6 . . . 53 E4
Lister Jun & Inf Schs L13 . . . 53 E5
Lister Rd L7 . . . 53 C2
Liston St L4 . . . 38 F2
Litcham Cl CH49 . . . 65 A7
Litchborough Gr L35 . . . 57 A6
LITHERLAND . . . 27 D1
Litherland Ave CH46 . . . 49 D1
Litherland Cres WA11 . . . 44 C7
Litherland High Sch L21 . . . 27 D2
Litherland Moss Prim Sch L21 . . . 27 D1
Litherland Pk L21 . . . 38 B8
Litherland Rd
Bootle L20 . . . 38 C4
Bootle L20 . . . 38 C5
Lithou Cl L5 . . . 52 D5
Little Acre L31 . . . 28 E8
LITTLE ALTCAR . . . 10 A1
Little Barn Hey L30 . . . 27 D5
Little Bongs L12 . . . 54 D4
Little Brewery La L37 . . . 9 F6
Little Brook La L32 . . . 40 D8
Little Canning St 5 L8 . . . 67 F7
Little Catharine St L8 . . . 67 F7
Littlecote Cl 16 WA9 . . . 58 C4
Little Croft L35 . . . 56 D3
LITTLE CROSBY . . . 26 D8
Little Crosby Mus* L23 . . . 26 D7
Little Crosby Rd L23 . . . 26 E6
Little Ct L3 . . . 52 C4
Littledale L14 . . . 54 D3
Littledale Rd
Wallasey CH44 . . . 51 D3
Warrington WA5 . . . 74 F7
Little Delph WA11 . . . 45 C7
Little Digmoor Prim Sch WN8 . . . 24 B6
Little Hardman St 2 L1 . . . 90 C2
Little Heath Rd L24 . . . 82 E4
Little Heyes St L5 . . . 53 A6
Little Hey La L37 . . . 10 B4
Little Howard St L3 . . . 52 B4
Little Huskisson St L8 . . . 67 F7
Little La
Neston CH64 . . . 86 C1
Southport PR9 . . . 2 B1
Littlemore Cl CH49 . . . 64 D5
Little Moss Hey L28 . . . 55 C7
Little Parkfield Rd L17 . . . 68 B4
Littler Rd WA11 . . . 45 A5
Little St Bride St 12 L7, L8 . . . 67 F8
Little St WA9 . . . 44 E1
Littlestone Cl WA8 . . . 73 A4
LITTLE STORETON . . . 78 A6
Little Storeton La CH63 . . . 78 A6
Littleton Cl CH43 . . . 65 E4
Littlewood Cl L35 . . . 56 E2
Little Woolton St L69 . . . 53 A1
Littondale Ave L35 . . . 57 D2
Liver Ind Est L9 . . . 39 C4
Livermore Ct L8 . . . 68 C6
LIVERPOOL . . . 90 A1
Liverpool Ave PR8 . . . 7 D5
Liverpool Coll L18 . . . 68 F4
Liverpool Com Coll
Liverpool L1 . . . 90 C2
Liverpool L3 . . . 52 C3
Liverpool L3 . . . 90 C3
Liverpool Com Coll (Bankfield) L13 . . . 53 F5
Liverpool Com Coll (Old Swan Ctr) L13 . . . 54 A3
Liverpool Com Coll The Arts Ctr L7 . . . 67 F8
Liverpool Film Acad L4 . . . 38 E1
Liverpool Hope Univ L16 . . . 69 D6
Liverpool Hope Univ Coll L3 . . . 52 F3
Liverpool Inst (Blackburne House) L8 . . . 67 F8
Liverpool Inst for the Performing Arts L1 . . . 90 C2
Liverpool Int Bsns Pk L24 . . . 81 E3
Liverpool John Lennon Airport L24 . . . 82 C2
Liverpool Mus & Planetarium* L3 . . . 90 B4
Liverpool One L2 . . . 90 A3
Liverpool Pl WA8 . . . 72 C1
Liverpool Rd
Ashton-in-M WN4 . . . 35 A3
Bickerstaffe L39 . . . 22 C5
Birkdale Hills PR8 . . . 7 E6
Crosby L22, L23 . . . 26 E3
Formby L37 . . . 10 A1
Garswood WA11, WN4 . . . 34 D2
Haydock, Stanley Bank WA11 . . . 45 A7
Hightown L37 . . . 18 A8
Huyton-w-R L36 . . . 55 D4
Maghull L31 . . . 20 D4
Neston CH64 . . . 86 F1
Ormskirk L39 . . . 13 B2
Royal Oak L39 . . . 21 F4
Skelmersdale WN8 . . . 23 C8
Southport PR8 . . . 4 A3
St Helens WA10 . . . 43 F3
Warrington WA5 . . . 74 E6
Widnes WA8 . . . 72 C1
Liverpool Rd N L31 . . . 20 C2
Liverpool Rd S
Maghull L31 . . . 20 C1
Maghull L31 . . . 28 C7
Liverpool Row WA12 . . . 60 D8
Liverpool South Parkway Sta L19 . . . 81 D6
Liverpool St WA10 . . . 43 F3
Liverpool Womens Hospl L8 . . . 68 A8
Liversidge Rd CH42 . . . 66 D4
Liver St L1 . . . 90 A2
Livesley's La
Great Altcar L37 . . . 10 F2
Haskayne L37 . . . 11 A2
Livingston Ave L17 . . . 68 C4
Livingston Ct L17 . . . 68 C3
Livingston Dr L17 . . . 68 C3
Livingston Dr N L17 . . . 68 C3
Livingston Dr S L17 . . . 68 C3
Livingstone Gdns CH41 . . . 66 C7
Livingstone Rd CH46 . . . 50 B4
Livingstone St
2 Ashton-in-M WN4 . . . 35 A5
Birkenhead CH41 . . . 66 C7
Llanrwst Cl L8 . . . 67 E5
Lloyd Ave CH41 . . . 66 B7
Lloyd Cl L6 . . . 52 F4
Lloyd Cres WA12 . . . 45 F3
Lloyd Dr CH49 . . . 64 D3
Lloyd Rd L34 . . . 56 E7
Lloyd St WA11 . . . 44 F6
Lobelia Ave L9 . . . 39 B4
Lochinvar St L9 . . . 38 F3
Lochmore Rd L18 . . . 69 B1
Lochryan Rd L19 . . . 81 B8
Locker Ave WA2 . . . 61 B2
Lockerbie Cl WA2 . . . 61 E3
Lockerby Rd L7 . . . 53 D2
Locker La WN4 . . . 35 F4
Locker Pk CH49 . . . 64 C4
Locke St L19 . . . 81 C4
Lockett Bsns Pk WN4 . . . 35 C5
Lockett Rd
Ashton-in-M WN4 . . . 35 C6
Widnes WA8 . . . 73 B3
Lockfields View L3, L5 . . . 52 C5
Lockington Cl 22 L8 . . . 68 A4
Lock Rd CH62 . . . 89 A8
Lock St WA9 . . . 44 C5
Lockton Rd L34 . . . 41 B5
Loddon Cl CH49 . . . 65 B7
Lodge La
Bebington CH62 . . . 79 B6
Haydock WA11, WA12, WN4 . . . 46 B8
Liverpool L8 . . . 68 B7
Rainford L39, WA11 . . . 23 D1
Widnes WA8 . . . 72 B4
Lodge Rd
Orrell WN5 . . . 25 E4
Widnes WA8 . . . 84 B8
Lodge The CH43 . . . 65 D6
Lodwick St L20 . . . 38 B1
Lofthouse Gate WA8 . . . 72 F4
Logan Rd CH41 . . . 51 B1
Logfield Dr L19 . . . 81 D4
Lognor Rd L32 . . . 29 C2
Lognor Wlk L32 . . . 29 C2
Logwood Rd L36 . . . 71 A8
Lois Ct CH45 . . . 51 C6
Lombard Rd CH46 . . . 49 F2
Lombardy Ave CH49 . . . 64 B2
Lomond Gr CH46 . . . 64 F8
Lomond Rd L7 . . . 53 E2
Londonderry Rd L13 . . . 53 E7
London Fields WN5 . . . 33 E5
London La PR8 . . . 8 D8
London Rd
Liverpool L3 . . . 52 F2
Liverpool L3 . . . 90 C4
London Row WA12 . . . 60 D8
London Sq 2 PR8 . . . 4 B7
London St PR8, PR9 . . . 4 B7
Longacre PR9 . . . 1 F3
Longacre Cl CH45 . . . 50 D5
Longacres CH46 . . . 64 D5
Long Acres Rd CH64 . . . 86 E2
Long Ave L9 . . . 39 B6
Longborough Rd L34 . . . 41 C2
Longcliffe Dr PR8 . . . 7 C4
Longcroft Ave L19 . . . 81 E7
Longcroft Sq L19 . . . 81 E7
Longdale La L29 . . . 27 D8
Longden Rd WN4 . . . 35 A3
Longdown Rd L10 . . . 40 B6
Longfellow Cl L32 . . . 40 D8
Longfellow Dr CH62 . . . 79 A7
Longfellow St
Bootle L20 . . . 38 A5
Liverpool L8 . . . 68 C7
Longfield L37 . . . 10 B5
Longfield Ave L23 . . . 26 E6
Longfield Cl CH49 . . . 64 D4
Longfield Pk WA9 . . . 58 D4
Longfield Rd
Bootle L21 . . . 38 B6
Warrington WA2 . . . 61 C1
Longfield Wlk L23 . . . 26 E6
Longfold L31 . . . 20 E1
LONGFORD . . . 61 B1
Longford Dr WA8 . . . 72 E2
Longford Rd PR8 . . . 4 A2
Longford St L8 . . . 68 A3
Longhey WN8 . . . 16 C4
Long Hey L35 . . . 56 D2
Long Hey Rd CH48 . . . 75 E7
Long Heys or Back La WN8 . . . 16 F5
Long La
Bickerstaffe L39 . . . 22 B7
Crosby L23, L29 . . . 27 A8
Formby L37 . . . 9 E4
Liverpool, Garston L19 . . . 81 C7
Liverpool, Hartley's Village L9 . . . 39 C5
Liverpool, Norris Green L9 . . . 39 E4
Liverpool, Wavertree L15 . . . 68 F8
Maghull L29 . . . 19 B1
Ormskirk L39 . . . 21 F8
Skelmersdale WN8 . . . 24 E3
Warrington WA2 . . . 61 B1
Longland Rd CH45 . . . 51 B6
Long Mdw
Heswall CH60 . . . 85 F6
St Helens WA10 . . . 43 B4
Longmead Ave WN4 . . . 35 C4
Longmeadow Rd L34 . . . 41 D4
Long Meanygate PR9 . . . 5 F8
Longmoor Cl L10 . . . 39 E7
Longmoor Com Prim Sch L9 . . . 39 B6
Longmoor Gr L9 . . . 39 B6
Longmoor La L10, L9 . . . 39 D7
Long Moss L30 . . . 27 C2
Longreach Rd L14 . . . 54 F3
Longridge Ave
Birkenhead CH49 . . . 64 E6
St Helens WA11 . . . 44 D5
Longridge Wlk 10 L4 . . . 52 E8
LONGSHAW . . . 25 E1
Longshaw Ave WN5 . . . 25 E1
Longshaw Cl WN5 . . . 25 E1
Longshaw Comm
Billinge WN5 . . . 33 E8
Longshaw WN5 . . . 25 E1
Longshaw Old Rd WN5 . . . 25 E1
Longshaw St WA5 . . . 60 F1
Longstone Wlk L7 . . . 68 B8
Longton Ave WA3 . . . 47 C7
Longton Ct PR8 . . . 7 C5
Longton Dr L37 . . . 10 A6
Longton La L35 . . . 57 B4
Longton Lane Com Prim Sch L35 . . . 57 B5
LONGVIEW . . . 55 F4
Longview Ave
Rainhill L35 . . . 57 A4
Wallasey CH45 . . . 51 B5
Longview Com Sch L36 . . . 55 E6
Longview Cres L36 . . . 55 F3
Longview Dr L36 . . . 56 A3
Longview La L36 . . . 55 F4
Longview Rd
Huyton-w-R L36 . . . 55 F3
Rainhill L35 . . . 57 A4
Longville St L8 . . . 67 E5
Longwood Cl WA11 . . . 32 C1
Longworth Way L25 . . . 70 A3
Lonie Gr WA10 . . . 57 C8
Lonsboro Rd CH44 . . . 51 C3
Lonsdale Ave
Ormskirk L39 . . . 13 F7
St Helens WA10 . . . 57 B7
Wallasey CH45 . . . 51 A6
Lonsdale Cl
Litherland L21 . . . 27 B2
Warrington WA5 . . . 74 F8
3 Widnes WA8 . . . 84 C8
Lonsdale Mews L21 . . . 27 B2
Lonsdale Rd
Formby L37 . . . 9 F3
Litherland L21 . . . 27 B2
Liverpool L26 . . . 82 E7
Southport PR8 . . . 4 D4
Lonsdale Villas CH45 . . . 51 A6
Looe Cl WA8 . . . 72 E2
Looe Rd L11 . . . 40 D5
Looms The CH64 . . . 86 B2
Loomsway CH61 . . . 76 D6
Loraine St L5 . . . 52 F5
Lordens Cl L14 . . . 55 A5
Lordens Rd L14 . . . 55 A5
Lord Nelson St L1, L3 . . . 90 C4
Lord St W PR8 . . . 4 A6
Lords Ave CH43 . . . 65 C8
Lord Sefton Way L37 . . . 10 E2
Lords Fold WA11 . . . 31 E7
Lord St
Ashton-in-M WN4 . . . 35 D4
Birkenhead CH41 . . . 66 E7
Liverpool, Garston L19 . . . 81 D4
Liverpool L2 . . . 90 A3
Newton-le-W WA12 . . . 46 A3
Runcorn WA7 . . . 84 F3
Southport PR8, PR9 . . . 4 B7
St Helens WA10 . . . 44 A5
Loreburn Rd L15 . . . 69 B6
Lorenzo Dr L11 . . . 53 F8
Loretto Dr CH49 . . . 65 A6
Loretto Rd CH44 . . . 50 F4
Lorn Ct 17 CH41 . . . 66 E6
Lorne Ct CH43 . . . 66 B4
Lorne Rd
Birkenhead CH43 . . . 66 A5
Crosby L22 . . . 26 D1
Lorne St L7 . . . 53 E3
Lorn St CH41 . . . 66 E6
Lorton Ave WA11 . . . 44 A8
Lorton St L8 . . . 68 B7
Lostock Cl WN5 . . . 33 E5
Lothair Rd L4 . . . 53 A7
Lothian St L8 . . . 68 A5
Lotus Gdns WA9 . . . 59 A7
Loudon Gr L8 . . . 68 A6
Lough Gn CH63 . . . 79 A2
Loughlin Dr L33 . . . 30 A5
Loughrigg Ave WA11 . . . 33 B1
Louis Braille Cl L30 . . . 27 F4
Louis Pasteur Ave L30 . . . 27 F4
Lourdes Hospl L18 . . . 68 F5
Love La
Liverpool L3 . . . 52 B4
Wallasey CH44 . . . 51 B3
Lovelace Rd L19 . . . 81 B7
Lovel Rd L24 . . . 82 D4
Lovel Terr WA8 . . . 84 B5
Lovel Way L24 . . . 82 D4
Lovett Dr L35 . . . 56 E5
Low Bank Rd WN4 . . . 34 F4
Lowbridge Ct L19 . . . 81 D6
Lowcroft WN8 . . . 16 C3
Lowden Ave L21 . . . 27 B1
Lowell St L4 . . . 38 F1
Lower Alt Rd L38 . . . 17 F4
Lower Appleton Rd WA8 . . . 73 B1
Lower Bank View L20 . . . 38 B1
LOWER BEBINGTON . . . 79 A5
Lower Breck Rd L6 . . . 53 C5
Lower Carr La L37 . . . 19 B7
Lower Castle St L2 . . . 90 A3
Lower Cl L26 . . . 83 A8
Lower Farm Rd L25 . . . 70 A7
Lower Flaybrick Rd CH43 . . . 65 E8
Lower Gill St L3 . . . 52 F2
Lower Gn CH49 . . . 65 A3
Lower Hey L23 . . . 27 B5
LOWER HOUSE . . . 84 E8
Lower House La
Liverpool L11 . . . 40 A3
Widnes WA8 . . . 84 F8
Lower La L10, L9 . . . 39 F6
Lower Lee Sch L25 . . . 69 E4
Lower Mersey View L20 . . . 38 B1
Lower Prom
Southport PR8 . . . 4 A7
Southport PR9 . . . 4 B8
Lower Rd
Bebington CH62 . . . 79 B6
Halewood L26, WA8 . . . 83 C7
Lower Sandfield L25 . . . 70 B4
Lowerson Cres L11 . . . 53 E8
Lowerson Rd L11 . . . 53 E8
Lower Thingwall La CH61 . . . 77 C5
Lowe St S WA10 . . . 43 F3
Lowes Gn L37 . . . 10 B3
Lowe's La WN8 . . . 15 F8
Lowe St
Golborne WA3 . . . 47 A8
St Helens WA10 . . . 43 F4
Lowestoft Dr L19 . . . 81 B6
Loweswater Cl WA2 . . . 61 B3
Loweswater Cres WA11 . . . 45 A6
Loweswater Way L33 . . . 29 D4
Lowfield Ind Est WA9 . . . 57 F5
Lowfield La WA9 . . . 57 F5
Lowfield Rd L14 . . . 54 C3
Lowfields Ave CH62 . . . 88 E3
Lowfields Cl CH62 . . . 88 E3
Low Hill L6 . . . 53 A3
Lowlands Rd 6 WA7 . . . 84 F2
Lowndes Rd L6 . . . 53 D6
Lowry Bank CH44 . . . 51 E3
Lowry Cl L33 . . . 29 E6
Lowther Ave
Aintree L10 . . . 28 D2
Maghull L31 . . . 20 F2
Lowther Cres WA10 . . . 57 B8
Lowther Dr L35 . . . 57 C3
Lowther St L8 . . . 68 A7
LOWTON . . . 47 E8
Lowton Gdns WA3 . . . 47 B5
LOWTON HEATH . . . 47 C6
Lowton Rd WA3 . . . 36 C1
LOWTON ST MARY'S . . . 47 F8
Lowton West Prim Sch WA3 . . . 47 D8
Lowwood Gr CH41 . . . 66 D5
Low Wood Gr CH61 . . . 77 C4
Lowwood Rd CH41 . . . 66 D5
Low Wood St 10 L6 . . . 53 A2
Loxdale Cl 23 L8 . . . 68 A4
Loxley Rd PR8 . . . 4 D4
Loxwood Cl L25 . . . 70 B7
Loyola Hey L35 . . . 72 E8
Lucania St L19 . . . 81 C4
Lucan Rd L17 . . . 68 E2
Lucerne Rd CH44 . . . 51 D2
Lucerne St L17 . . . 68 C3
Lucius Cl L9 . . . 38 F7
Lucknow St 4 L17 . . . 68 C4
Ludlow WN8 . . . 16 C4
Ludlow Ct 1 CH48 . . . 63 B1
Ludlow Dr
Ormskirk L39 . . . 13 D7
West Kirby CH48 . . . 63 B1
Ludlow Gr CH62 . . . 79 D1
Ludlow St L4 . . . 38 F1
Ludwig Rd 7 L4 . . . 53 B6
Lugard Rd L17 . . . 68 E2
Lugsmore La WA10 . . . 43 D1
Luke St
Ashton-in-M WN4 . . . 35 D5
Liverpool L8 . . . 67 F6
Wallasey CH44 . . . 51 E2
Lulworth WN8 . . . 16 C4
Lulworth Ave L22 . . . 26 C1
Lulworth Lo PR8 . . . 3 F5
Lulworth Rd
Liverpool L25 . . . 70 C5
Southport PR8 . . . 3 F5
Lumber La WA5 . . . 59 F8
Lumina CH62 . . . 79 E1
Lumley Rd CH44 . . . 51 D3
Lumley St L19 . . . 81 B7
Lumley Wlk L24 . . . 83 E1
Lunar Dr L30 . . . 27 F4
Lunar Rd L9 . . . 39 B6
Lunds Cl L40 . . . 14 E4
Lune Ave L31 . . . 20 E2
Lunehurst 12 WA3 . . . 47 E8
Lunesdale Ave 3 L9 . . . 39 B7
Lune St L23 . . . 26 E4
Lune Way WA8 . . . 72 C1
Lunsford Rd L14 . . . 54 F4
LUNT . . . 27 D8
Lunt Ave
Litherland L30 . . . 28 A2
Prescot L35 . . . 56 E3
Lunt La L29 . . . 27 D8
Lunt Rd
Bootle L20 . . . 38 C5
Lunt L29 . . . 27 D8
Maghull L29 . . . 19 C1
LUNTS HEATH . . . 73 A5
Lunts Heath Prim Sch WA8 . . . 73 B5
Lunt's Heath Rd WA8 . . . 73 B5
Luntswood Gr WA12 . . . 46 A4
Lupin Dr WA11 . . . 45 F6
Lupton Dr L23 . . . 27 A4
Luscombe Cl L26 . . . 83 A8
Lusitania Rd L4 . . . 39 B2
Luther Gr WA9 . . . 45 B2
Luton Gr L4 . . . 52 F8
Luton St L5 . . . 52 C6
Lutyens Cl 2 L4 . . . 52 F7
Luxmore Rd L4 . . . 39 A1
Lycett Rd
Liverpool L4 . . . 53 C7
Wallasey CH44 . . . 50 E5
Lyceum Pl 15 L1 . . . 90 B3
Lydbrook Cl 6 CH42 . . . 66 F3

Lydbury Cl WA5 60 D2
Lydbury Cres L32 40 F8
Lydford Rd L12 54 B8
Lydia Ann St L1 90 B2
LYDIATE 20 D4
Lydiate La
Crosby L23, L29, L30 27 C6
Liverpool L25, L26 70 D2
Willaston CH64 87 E1
Lydiate Pk L23 27 B6
Lydiate Prim Sch L31 20 C4
Lydiate Rd L20 38 C5
Lydiate Station Rd L31 19 E5
Lydiate The
Heswall CH60 85 F7
Willaston CH64 87 D1
Lydia Wlk L10 40 B7
Lydieth Lea L27 70 E6
Lydney Rd L36 55 B4
Lydstep Ct WA5 60 E2
Lyelake Cl L32 29 F1
Lyelake Gdns L32 29 F1
Lyelake La L40 14 F2
Lyelake Rd L32 29 F1
Lyle St L5 52 D5
Lyme Cl L36 56 A6
Lyme Com Prim Sch WA12 45 F4
Lymecroft L25 69 F2
Lyme Cross Rd L36 55 F6
Lyme Gr L36 55 F5
LYME GROVE 56 A6
Lyme St
Haydock WA11 45 E6
Newton-le-W WA12 45 F4
Lymington Gr L30 27 F3
Lymington Rd CH44 50 F4
Lymm Rd CH43 65 C7
Lynas Gdns L19 81 B8
Lynas St CH41 66 D8
Lynbridge Cl WN5 25 E5
Lyncot Rd L9 39 B8
Lyncroft Rd CH44 51 C2
Lyndale WN8 16 B4
Lyndale Ave
Bebington CH62 88 E4
Warrington WA2 61 F2
Lyndale Sch The CH62 88 F5
Lyndene Rd L25 70 A7
Lyndhurst
Maghull L31 20 D1
Skelmersdale WN8 16 B4
Lyndhurst Ave
Heswall CH61 77 A3
Liverpool L18 69 A3
Lyndhurst Cl CH61 77 A5
Lyndhurst Rd
Crosby L23 27 A4
Hoylake CH47 48 E1
Irby CH61 76 C6
Liverpool L18 68 F3
Southport PR8 4 B2
Wallasey CH45 50 F6
Lyndon Dr L18 69 B4
Lyndor Cl L25 70 B1
Lyndor Rd L25 70 B1
Lyneham L35 56 F2
Lynholme Rd L4 53 B7
Lynmouth Rd L17 80 E8
Lynnbank CH43 66 B4
Lynnbank Rd L18 69 D5
Lynn Cl WA10 43 C4
Lynscott Pl L16 69 D8
Lynsted Rd L14 54 F3
Lynton Cl
Heswall CH60 86 B6
Liverpool L19 81 B8
Warrington WA5 74 E4
Lynton Cres WA8 72 E2
Lynton Ct
Crosby L23 26 B4
Hoylake CH47 63 A6
Lynton Dr
Bebington CH63 79 A3
Southport PR8 3 E1
Lynton Gn L25 69 F4
Lynton Gr WA9 58 C5
Lynton Rd
Huyton-w-R L36 56 B3
Southport PR8 3 E1
Wallasey CH45 50 E6
Lynton Way WA10 43 B6
Lynwood Ave
Golborne WA3 47 E6
Ormskirk L39 13 C3
Wallasey CH44 51 A3
Lynwood Cl WN8 24 D7
Lynwood Dr CH61 76 E6
Lynwood End L39 13 C3
Lynwood Gdns L9 38 F5
Lynwood Rd L9 39 A5
Lynxway The L12 54 D4
Lyon Cl WA10 43 F3
Lyon Rd L4 53 B6
Lyons Cl CH46 49 E1
Lyons Pl L25 82 D9
Lyons Rd
Southport PR8 4 A5
Wallasey CH46 49 E1
Lyon St
Ashton-in-M WN4 34 F7
Liverpool L19 81 D4
St Helens WA10 43 F3
Lyra Rd L22 26 D1
Lysander Dr WA2 61 E2
Lyster Rd L20 38 A3
Lytham Cl L10 28 F1
Lytham Ct L32 29 C3
Lytham Rd
Ashton-in-M WN4 34 F5
Southport PR9 2 A4
Widnes WA8 73 C2
Lytham Way L12 54 E6
Lytles Cl L37 10 A2
Lyttelton Rd L17 68 E2
Lytton Ave CH42 66 F1
Lytton Gr L21 38 A6
Lytton St L6 52 F3

M

Mab La L12, L14 54 F7
Mab Lane JMI Sch L12 54 F7
McAllester Ct CH43 65 F4
Macalpine Cl CH49 65 A6
Macbeth St L20 38 C1
McBride St L19 81 C6
Mc Clellan Pl WA8 73 B1
McCormack Ave WA9 44 E3
McCulloch St WA9 44 C3
Macdermott Rd WA8 84 F5
Macdona Dr CH48 75 B8
Macdonald Ave WA11 44 E5
Macdonald Dr CH49 64 D3
Macdonald Rd CH46 64 C8
Macdonald St L15 68 E8
McElloen Rd WN2 36 C7
Mace Rd L11 40 C3
McFarlane Ave WA10 43 C4
MacFarren St 2 L13 54 A3
McGill Ct 9 CH41 66 D7
McGough Cl WA9 58 A3
McKeagney Gdns WA8 84 C7
McKee Ave WA2 61 B2
Mackenzie Rd CH46 50 B3
McKeown Cl 2 L5 52 D5
Mackets Cl L25 70 C1
Macket's La L25 82 C8
Mack Gr L30 27 D2
Mckinley Way WA8 72 F3
McMinnis Ave WA9 45 B2
MacQueen St 2 L13 54 A2
McVinnie Rd L35 56 F6
Maddock Rd CH44 51 D5
Maddocks St 1 L13 54 A2
Maddock St CH41 66 C8
Maddrell St L3 52 B4
Madeira Dr L25 70 B7
Madelaine St L8 68 A6
Madeley Cl CH48 63 B1
Madeley Dr CH48 63 B1
Madeley St L6 53 C3
Madeline McKenna Ct WA8 72 C3
Madison Sq L1 90 C2
Madryn Ave L33 30 A2
Madryn St L8 68 A5
Maelor Cl CH63 88 C6
Mafeking Cl 1 L15 68 F8
Mafeking Pl WN4 35 C3
Magazine Ave CH45 51 B7
Magazine Brow CH45 51 C7
Magazine La CH45 51 C7
Magazine Rd CH62 79 D3
Magazines Prom CH45 51 C7
Magazine Wlk CH62 79 D3
Magdala St L7, L8 68 C7
Magdalen Dr WN4 34 F4
Magdalene Sq L30 27 F4
Maggots Nook Rd WA11 24 A1
MAGHULL 20 B1
Maghull Com Prim Sch L31 28 C7
Maghull High Sch L31 28 C8
Maghull La L31 21 B1
Maghull Smallholdings Est L31 20 F3
Maghull Sta L31 28 E7
Magnolia Cl
Liverpool L26 70 D2
St Helens WA11 44 F5
Magnolia Wlk CH49 64 C2
Magnus Cl L13 53 F5
Maguire Ave L20 38 E4
Maharishi School of the Age of Enlightenment L40 16 A5
Mahon Ave L20 38 D6
Mahon Ct 4 L8 67 F7
Maiden Cl WN8 15 C2
Maiden La L13 53 D7
Maidford Rd L14 54 F4
Maidstone Cl L25 82 C8
Maidstone Dr L14 54 F5
Main Ave WA10 57 C7
Main Cl WA11 45 A6
Main Dr L35 56 E1
Main Front L35 71 E8
Main La WA3 47 F3
Main Rd CH62, CH63 79 B4
Mains Ave WN2 35 F7
Mainside Rd L32 29 F1
Main St WN5 33 E5
Maintree Cres L24 83 A4
Mainwaring Rd
Bebington CH62 88 D8
Wallasey CH44 51 D3
Mairscough La L39 12 B1
Maitland Cl L8 68 B7
Maitland Rd CH45 51 C8
Maitland St 4 L8 68 B7
Majestic Mews WN5 25 D5
Major St L5 52 D6
Makepeace Wlk 2 L8 67 F6
Makerfield Dr WA12 46 A5
Makin St L4 38 F2
Malahide Ct WA8 72 E2
Malcolm Ave WA2 61 D1
Malcolm Cres CH63 88 C6
Malcolm Gr L20 38 D1
Malcolm Pl L15 53 F1
Malden Rd L6 53 C3
Maldon Cl L26 82 F7
Maldwyn Rd CH44 51 B5
Maley Cl L8 68 A4
Malham Cl
Southport PR8 4 E3
Warrington WA5 74 E8
Malhamdale Ave L35 57 D2
Malika Pl WN4 34 E6
Malin Cl L24 83 D2
Mallaby St CH41 66 A8
Mallard Cl
Halewood L26 70 E1
Liverpool L12 40 F3
Ormskirk L39 13 C2
Warrington WA2 61 D3
Mallard Gdns WA9 57 E6
Mallard Ho L31 20 B4
Mallards The PR9 2 C3
Mallard Way
St Helens WA11 44 B6
Wallasey CH46 49 C1
Mallee Ave PR9 2 A3
Mallee Cres PR9 2 A3
Malleson Rd L13 53 E7
Mallins Cl L8 68 A4
Mallory Ave L31 20 B4
Mallory Gr WA11 44 D6
Mallory Rd CH42 66 D2
Mallowdale Cl CH62 88 F5
Mallow Rd L6 53 C3
Mallow Way L36 70 F8
Mall The L5 53 A5
Malmesbury Cl 2 CH49 64 C4
Malmesbury Rd L11 39 E2
Malpas Ave CH43 66 A2
Malpas Dr CH63 78 E7
Malpas Gr CH45 51 A6
Malpas Rd
Liverpool L11 40 D5
Wallasey CH45 51 A6
Malta Cl L36 55 D3
Malta St L8 67 F5
Malta Wlk 5 L8 67 F5
Malthouse Bsns Pk The L39 13 E6
Malthouse Ct L39 13 E6
Malt House Ct WA10 43 C6
Maltkiln La L39 21 E8
Malton Ave WA3 47 E7
Malton Cl WA8 72 C5
Malton Rd L25 70 C2
Malt St L7 68 B8
Malvern Ave L14 54 F2
Malvern Cl
Ashton-in-M WN4 35 B4
Kirkby L32 29 C4
Malvern Cres L14 54 F2
Malvern Gr
Aintree L10 28 C2
Birkenhead CH42 66 D2
Malvern Prim Sch L14 54 F2
Malvern Rd
Bootle L20 38 C5
Haydock WA9 45 A4
Liverpool L6 53 C3
Wallasey CH45 50 D5
Malverns The CH43 66 A3
Malwood St L8 67 F4
Manchester Rd
Prescot L34 56 C5
Southport PR9 4 C7
Manchester Row WA12 60 D8
Mandela Ct L8 68 B5
Mandela Ho L15 68 E7
Manderston Dr L12 54 D7
Mandeville Rd PR8 7 B5
Mandeville St L4 38 F2
Manfield WN8 16 A3
Manfred St 1 L6 53 A2
Manica Cres L10 39 F6
Manion Ave L31 20 B5
Manion Cl L31 20 B5
Manley Ave WA3 35 F2
Manley Cl CH43 65 F3
Manley Pl WA9 57 E7
Manley Rd
Crosby L22 26 D2
Huyton-w-R L36 71 A8
Mannering Ct 11 L17 68 C4
Mannering Rd L17 68 C4
Manners La CH60 85 E6
Manningham Rd L4, L6 53 C6
Manning Rd PR8 4 E6
Manning St WA10 43 F3
Mannington Cl CH47 63 E8
Mann Island L3 52 B1
Mann St L8 67 E6
Manor Ave
Crosby L23 26 D5
Golborne WA3 47 C8
Newton-le-W WA12 45 F4
Rainhill L35 57 C2
Manorbier Cres L9 39 A3
Manor Cl
Bootle L20 38 E2
Garswood WN4 34 C3
Manor Complex L33 30 B2
Manor Cres L25 70 B1
Manor Ct
Birkenhead CH49 64 C3
Golborne WA3 47 C8
Irby CH61 76 D6
Liverpool L17 68 B3
7 Liverpool, Sefton Park L17 68 C4
St Helens WA9 58 D4
West Kirby CH48 63 A3
Manor Dr
Birkenhead CH49 65 A6
Crosby L23 26 D5
Litherland L30 28 B3
Manor Farm Rd L36 55 F1
Manor Gr
Kirkby L32 29 B2
Skelmersdale WN8 15 F1
Manor Hill CH43 66 A6
Manor Ho CH62 88 D8
Manor House Cl
Billinge WA11 33 B1
Maghull L31 20 C1
Manor House Dr WN8 24 E3
Manor La
Birkenhead CH42 67 A2
Wallasey CH44, CH45 51 C5
Manor Lo
5 Bebington CH62 79 B6
Formby L37 9 E4
Manor Mans 3 CH44 51 C5
Manor Mews CH44 51 C5
Manor Park Cl CH61 77 A6
Manor Pl
Bebington CH62 79 D5
Widnes WA8 72 B1
Manor Prim Sch CH43 65 C7
Manor Rd
Bebington CH62 88 E6
Crosby L23 26 C5
Haydock WA11 45 F7
Hoylake CH47 63 C7
Irby CH61 76 D6
Liverpool L25 70 B1
Southport PR9 2 A2
Thornton Hough CH63 87 A7
Wallasey CH44, CH45 51 C5
Widnes WA8 72 B1
Manor Rd Sta CH47 63 C7
Manorside Cl CH49 64 F6
Manor St
Golborne WA3 36 B1
St Helens WA9 44 C2
Manor The WA11 32 C4
Manor View L12 40 F1
Manor Way L25 70 B1
Manorwood Dr L35 56 F2
Mansart Cl WN4 35 D3
Manse Gdns WA12 46 D4
Mansell Cl WA8 73 C5
Mansell Dr L26 82 E7
Mansell Rd L6 53 B3
Mansfield St
Golborne WA3 35 F1
Liverpool L3 52 E3
Mansion Dr L11 40 B4
Manston Rd WA5 74 F3
Manton Ct 6 CH42 66 C3
Manton Rd L6 53 C3
Manvers Rd L16 54 E1
Manville Rd CH45 51 B7
Manville St WA9 44 C1
Manx Jane's La PR9 2 A4
Maple Ave
Golborne WA3 47 F7
Haydock WA11 45 B7
Newton-le-W WA12 46 D2
5 Widnes WA8 73 B2
Maple Cl
Billinge WN5 33 D5
Bootle L21 38 A6
Formby L37 9 C1
Liverpool L12 40 D3
Prescot L35 56 E3
Maple Cres
Huyton-w-R L36 55 D2
Warrington WA5 74 F3
Maple Ct L34 41 C4
Mapledale Rd L18 69 B5
Maple Dr WN2 36 B7
Maple Gr
Bebington CH62 88 C8
Liverpool L8 68 C6
Prescot L35 56 E5
St Helens WA10 43 C3
Maple Rd WA2 61 B6
Maples Ct CH43 66 A3
Maple St
Ashton-in-M WN4 35 A6
Birkenhead CH41 66 D5
Southport PR8 4 E6
Mapleton Cl CH43 65 E1
Maple Tree Gr CH60 77 C1
Maple View WN8 23 F6
Maplewood
9 Kirkby L32 40 F8
Skelmersdale WN8 16 A4
Southport PR9 1 F2
Maplewood Cl
Liverpool L27 70 E5
Widnes WA8 84 A7
Maplewood Gr CH43 65 E8
Maranatha Bglws CH60 77 A1
Marathon Cl L6 52 F4
Marble Cl L20 38 C2
Marble Place Sh Ctr PR8 4 B7
Marbury Rd L32 29 C2
Marc Ave L31 29 B4
Marcham Way 2 L11 40 B1
Marchant Cl L30 39 B8
Marchbank Rd WN8 15 D1
Marchfield Rd L9 38 F5
March Rd L6 53 D5
Marchwood Way L25 70 A7
Marcien Way WA8 72 F3
Marcot Rd L6 53 D4
Marcross Cl WA5 60 E1
Marcus St CH41 66 D7
Marcus Street Workshops CH41 66 D7
Mardale Ave
St Helens WA11 44 B8
Warrington WA2 61 C3
Mardale Cl
Liverpool L27 71 A3
Southport PR8 7 B4
Mardale Lawn L27 71 A3
Mardale Rd L36 55 C5
Mardale Wlk
Huyton-w-R L36 55 C5
Liverpool L27 71 A3
Mareth Cl L18 69 A2
Marford Rd L12 54 B7
Marfords Ave CH63 88 C7
Margaret Ave
Bootle L20 38 C6
St Helens WA9 58 C8
Margaret Ct WA10 43 D1
Margaret Rd
Crosby L23 26 A5
Liverpool L4 38 E2
Margaret St
Liverpool L6 53 A4
St Helens WA9 58 E3
Margery Rd WA10 43 C1
Marian Ave WA12 45 F3
Marian Cl L35 57 C2
Marian Cl The L30 27 E4
Marian Dr
Birkenhead CH46 64 E8
Rainhill L35 57 B2
Marian Rd WA11 45 E7
Marians Dr L39 13 E7
Marian Sq L30 27 E4
Marian Way The L30 27 E3
Maria Rd L9 38 F3
Maricourt RC High Sch L31 28 E8
Marie Curie Ave L30 27 F3
Marigold Way WA9 59 A7
Marina Ave
Litherland L21 38 B8
St Helens WA9 58 C7
Marina Cres
Huyton-w-R L36 55 D1
Litherland L30 28 A1
Marina Ct CH47 63 A2
Marina Dr WA2 61 C1
Marina Rd L37 9 F1
Marine Cres L22 37 D8
Marine Dr
Heswall CH60 85 D6
Southport, Birkdale PR8 3 E7
Southport, Marshside PR8, PR9 1 D4
Marine Gate Mans PR9 4 B8
Marine Par PR8 4 A8
Marine Park Mans CH45 37 B1
Marine Pk CH48 63 B3
Marine Prom CH45 37 B1
Marine Rd CH47 63 A7
Mariners Ho L1 90 B1
Mariners Rd
Crosby L23 26 B3
Wallasey CH45 51 C7
Mariners Way 3 L20 38 C3
Mariners Wharf L3 67 D6
Marine Terr
Seaforth L22 37 D8
Wallasey CH45 51 C7
Marion Gr L18 69 B2
Marion Pl WN2 35 F8
Marion Rd L20 38 D6
Marion St CH41 66 E6
Maritime Cl WA12 46 C5
Maritime Ct
Birkenhead CH49 65 B1
Litherland L30 27 F5
12 Liverpool L6 53 B3
Liverpool, Sandfield Park L12 54 A8
Southport PR9 4 B8
Maritime Ent Pk L20 38 B4
Maritime Grange 15 CH44 51 E2
Maritime Lo L5 52 F6
Maritime Pk 19 CH41 66 C5
Maritime Pl L3 52 E3
Maritime View CH42 66 D3
Maritime Way L1 90 B2
Marius Cl L4 52 F8
Market App 3 WN4 35 B3
Market Cross 5 L39 13 E5
Market Pl
Birkenhead CH41 66 F6
Prescot L34 56 D6
Market Sq 9 L1 90 B3
Market St
Birkenhead CH41 66 E6
Hoylake CH47 63 B7
Newton-le-W WA12 46 A3

Market St *continued*
Southport PR8 . . . 4 B7
11 St Helens WA10 . . . 44 A3
Market Way
8 Liverpool L1 . . . 90 B3
6 Ormskirk L39 . . . 13 E5
Markfield Cres
Liverpool L25 . . . 70 C1
St Helens WA11 . . . 44 C5
Markfield Rd L20 . . . 38 C5
Markham Dr PR8 . . . 4 E2
Markham Gr CH43 . . . 65 F8
Mark Rake CH62 . . . 79 D1
Mark Rd L38 . . . 17 F4
Mark St L5 . . . 52 E7
Marksway CH61 . . . 77 A4
Marland WN8 . . . 16 A4
Marlborough WN8 . . . 16 A4
Marlborough Ave
Litherland L30 . . . 28 A2
Maghull L31 . . . 20 D3
Marlborough Cres
WA8 . . . 73 A5
Marlborough Ct 1
WN8 . . . 16 B4
Marlborough Gdns 5
PR9 . . . 4 C8
Marlborough Gr CH43 . . . 66 C4
Marlborough Pl 5 L3 . . . 52 C3
Marlborough Rd
Crosby L23 . . . 26 D3
Liverpool L13 . . . 53 E6
Prescot L34 . . . 56 E7
Seaforth L22 . . . 37 E8
Southport PR9 . . . 4 C7
Wallasey CH45 . . . 51 C7
Marlborough St 4 L3 . . . 52 C3
Marlborough Way
WA11 . . . 45 E8
Marlbrook Rd L25 . . . 70 B6
Marlcroft Dr L17 . . . 80 E7
Marldon Ave L23 . . . 26 E2
Marldon Rd L11, L12 . . . 54 B8
Marled Hey L28 . . . 55 A8
Marley Cl L35 . . . 57 E1
Marlfield La CH61 . . . 77 A4
Marlfield Rd L12 . . . 54 B6
Marl Gr WN5 . . . 25 D4
Marline Ave CH63 . . . 88 C6
Marling Pk WA8 . . . 72 B1
Marlowe Cl
Liverpool L19 . . . 81 C5
Widnes WA8 . . . 72 F1
Marlowe Dr L12 . . . 54 A6
Marlowe Rd CH44 . . . 51 A4
Marl Rd
Kirkby L33 . . . 30 C3
Litherland L30 . . . 28 B3
Marlsford St L6 . . . 53 C3
Marlston Ave CH61 . . . 76 F6
Marlwood Ave CH45 . . . 50 E5
Marmaduke St L7 . . . 53 B1
Marmion Ave L20 . . . 38 E7
Marmion Cl WA3 . . . 36 E1
Marmion Rd
Hoylake CH47 . . . 63 B7
Liverpool L17 . . . 68 C4
Marmonde St L4 . . . 52 E8
Marnock Cl WN2 . . . 36 F8
Marnwood Rd L32 . . . 29 D1
Marnwood Wlk 6 L32 . . . 29 C1
Marple Cl CH43 . . . 65 E3
Marquis St
Bebington CH62 . . . 79 B7
Birkenhead CH41 . . . 66 E4
Liverpool L3 . . . 90 C4
Marram Cl CH46 . . . 50 A1
Marron Ave WA2 . . . 61 B2
Marryat Cl WA2 . . . 61 A6
Marsden Ave WA10 . . . 43 D4
Marsden Cl CH44 . . . 51 D5
Marsden Ct
13 Wallasey CH45 . . . 51 B7
Widnes WA8 . . . 72 E4
Marsden Rd
Liverpool L26 . . . 82 F7
Southport PR9 . . . 4 E7
Marsden St 12 L6 . . . 53 A3
Marsden Way 13 L6 . . . 53 A3
Marshall Ave
5 St Helens WA9 . . . 58 C8
Warrington WA5 . . . 60 F2
Marshall Cl L33 . . . 29 F5
Marshall Pl L3 . . . 52 C4
Marshallsay L37 . . . 10 A2
Marshall's Cl L31 . . . 20 C4
MARSHALL'S CROSS . . . 58 B5
Marshalls Cross Rd
WA9 . . . 58 B7
Marshall St CH41 . . . 66 C8
Marsham Cl CH49 . . . 65 A7
Marsham Rd L25 . . . 70 C5
Marsh Ave L20 . . . 38 E6
Marsh Brows L37 . . . 9 E2
Marshfield Cl L36 . . . 55 F3
Marshfield Ct CH46 . . . 49 E3
Marshfield Rd L11 . . . 40 B1
Marshgate WA8 . . . 84 B6
Marshgate Rd L12 . . . 40 C2
Marsh Hall Pad WA8 . . . 73 B4
Marsh La
Bebington CH63 . . . 78 C7
Bootle L20 . . . 38 C4
Hightown L37, L38 . . . 18 E6
Marsh La *continued*
Warrington, Penketh
WA5 . . . 74 C2
Marshlands Rd 1
CH45 . . . 50 E6
MARSHSIDE . . . 1 E4
Marshside Cl L8 . . . 67 F5
Marshside Nature
Reserve* PR9 . . . 1 E5
Marshside Prim Sch
PR9 . . . 2 A5
Marshside Rd PR9 . . . 1 F4
Marsh St
Liverpool L20 . . . 38 D1
St Helens WA9 . . . 44 C3
Marshway Dr WA12 . . . 46 B5
Marsland Gr WA9 . . . 58 E8
Marston Cl
Bebington CH62 . . . 88 E3
Birkenhead CH43 . . . 65 F3
Marston Cres L38 . . . 18 A2
Marsworth Dr 7 L5 . . . 52 F4
Marten Ave CH63 . . . 88 C7
Martensen St L7 . . . 53 B1
Martham Gdns WA9 . . . 57 E6
Martin Ave
Newton-le-W WA12 . . . 46 C5
St Helens WA10 . . . 43 F6
Warrington WA2 . . . 61 E1
Martin Cl
Irby CH61 . . . 76 C6
Liverpool L18 . . . 69 A1
Rainhill L35 . . . 57 A4
Martindale Rd
Bebington CH62 . . . 79 E1
Billinge WA11 . . . 33 C2
Liverpool L18 . . . 69 D5
Martine Cl L31 . . . 29 B4
Martin Gr L35 . . . 56 E5
Martinhall Rd L9 . . . 39 F4
Martin Rd L18 . . . 69 A1
Martins La WN8 . . . 24 D7
Martin's La CH44 . . . 51 C4
Martland Ave
Aintree L10 . . . 28 E2
Golborne WA3 . . . 47 E7
Martland Rd L25 . . . 70 C4
Martlesham Cres CH49 . . . 64 B3
Martlett Rd L12 . . . 54 D5
Martock L35 . . . 56 F2
Marton Cl L24 . . . 82 D4
Marton Gn L24 . . . 82 D3
Marton Rd L36 . . . 55 E6
Marvin St L6 . . . 53 A3
Marwood Twrs L5 . . . 52 E6
Mary Ave PR8 . . . 7 E6
Marybone L3 . . . 52 D3
Maryfield L23 . . . 26 E3
Maryfield Cl WA3 . . . 47 A7
Maryland Ho 8 L20 . . . 38 C3
Maryland La CH46 . . . 49 D1
Maryland St L1 . . . 90 C2
Marylebone Ave WA9 . . . 57 F6
Maryport Cl L5 . . . 52 F6
Mary Rd L20 . . . 38 D6
Mary St WA9 . . . 58 E3
Mary Stockton Ct 5
L21 . . . 38 A6
Maryton Grange L18 . . . 69 D2
Maryville Rd L34 . . . 56 E6
Marywell Cl WA9 . . . 58 D7
Masefield Ave WA8 . . . 84 F8
Masefield Cl CH62 . . . 79 A7
Masefield Cres L30 . . . 38 D8
Masefield Dr WA2 . . . 61 A5
Masefield Gr
Liverpool L16 . . . 69 F8
St Helens WA10 . . . 43 D5
Masefield Pl L30 . . . 38 E8
Masefield Rd L23 . . . 27 C6
Maskell Rd L13 . . . 53 F3
Mason Ave WA8 . . . 73 B4
Mason Cl WN4 . . . 35 D4
Mason St
Abram WN2 . . . 36 B8
Crosby L22 . . . 26 D1
Liverpool L7 . . . 53 A1
Liverpool, Woolton L25 . . . 70 A2
Wallasey CH45 . . . 51 B8
Massam Cl WA11 . . . 32 A6
Massam's La L37 . . . 9 F6
Massey Ave WA5 . . . 60 F2
Massey Pk CH45 . . . 51 A5
Massey St
Birkenhead CH41 . . . 66 D8
St Helens WA9 . . . 58 C8
Masters Way L19 . . . 81 D4
Matchwood Cl L19 . . . 81 D5
Matchworks The L19 . . . 81 E5
Mather Ave
Golborne WA3 . . . 47 E6
Liverpool L18, L19 . . . 69 C2
St Helens WA9 . . . 44 E3
Mather Ct 3 CH43 . . . 66 B5
Mather Rd CH43 . . . 66 B5
Mathew St L2 . . . 90 A3
Mathieson Rd WA8 . . . 84 E5
Matlock Ave
7 Liverpool L9 . . . 39 A6
Southport PR8 . . . 4 B4
Matlock Cl
Southport PR8 . . . 4 B4
Warrington WA5 . . . 60 A1
Matlock Cres PR8 . . . 4 B4
Matlock Rd PR8 . . . 4 B4
Matthew Arnold Prim Sch
L8 . . . 68 A3
Matthew Cl 16 CH44 . . . 51 E2
Matthew St CH44 . . . 51 E2
Maud Roberts Ct L21 . . . 38 A8
Maud St L8 . . . 68 A6
Maunders Ct L23 . . . 27 A5
Maureen Wlk L10 . . . 40 B7
Mauretania Rd L4 . . . 39 A2
Maurice Jones Ct
CH46 . . . 49 E1
Mavis Dr CH49 . . . 65 A3
Mawdsley Cl L37 . . . 10 B3
Mawdsley Terr L39 . . . 13 F7
Max Rd L14 . . . 54 F6
Maxton Rd L6 . . . 53 C3
Maxwell Cl CH49 . . . 65 A6
Maxwell Ct 5 CH42 . . . 66 C3
Maxwell Pl L13 . . . 53 F6
Maxwell Rd L13 . . . 53 F6
Maxwell St WA10 . . . 43 E3
May Ave
Abram Brow WN2 . . . 36 C7
Wallasey CH44 . . . 51 D2
Maybank Cl PR9 . . . 2 A1
Maybank Gr L17 . . . 68 F1
Maybank Rd CH42 . . . 66 D4
Maybury Way L17 . . . 68 C2
May Cl L21 . . . 38 B6
Mayer Ave CH63 . . . 78 F4
Mayew Rd CH61 . . . 76 F6
Mayfair Ave
Crosby L23 . . . 26 E5
Huyton-w-R L14 . . . 54 F3
Mayfair Cl
Hightown L38 . . . 17 F2
1 Liverpool L6 . . . 53 B4
Warrington WA5 . . . 74 D7
Mayfair Ct 1 CH43 . . . 66 C3
Mayfair Gr WA8 . . . 72 D1
Mayfayre Ave L31 . . . 20 B5
Mayfield L4 . . . 52 E8
Mayfield Ave
Formby L37 . . . 9 C1
St Helens WA9 . . . 57 E8
Widnes WA8 . . . 72 B1
Mayfield Cl L12 . . . 54 C6
Mayfield Ct
Formby L37 . . . 9 F5
Widnes WA8 . . . 73 A2
Mayfield Dr CH62 . . . 89 B6
Mayfield Gdns
Liverpool L19 . . . 81 A7
Neston CH64 . . . 86 E1
Mayfield Rd
Bebington CH63 . . . 79 A3
Liverpool L19 . . . 81 A7
Up Holland WN8 . . . 25 B7
Wallasey CH45 . . . 50 F5
Mayfields Ho CH62 . . . 79 B7
Mayfields N CH62 . . . 79 B7
Mayfields S CH62 . . . 79 B7
Mayfield St WN4 . . . 35 A3
Mayflower Ave L24 . . . 82 A7
Mayflower Ind Est L37 . . . 10 A1
Mayford Cl L25 . . . 70 B6
Mayhall Ct L31 . . . 20 D2
May Pl L13 . . . 54 A2
Maypole Ct
Knowsley L34 . . . 41 C5
Litherland L30 . . . 27 D5
May Rd CH60 . . . 86 A8
May St
Bootle L20 . . . 38 C5
Golborne WA3 . . . 36 B2
Liverpool L3 . . . 90 C3
Maytree Cl L27 . . . 70 C6
Maytree Wlk WN8 . . . 16 B4
Mayville Rd L18 . . . 69 B5
Mazzini Cl L5 . . . 52 E4
Mead Ave L21 . . . 38 C8
Meade Cl L35 . . . 57 D1
Meade Rd L13 . . . 53 E6
Meadfoot Rd CH46 . . . 49 D1
Meadow Ave
Southport PR8 . . . 4 C4
St Helens WA9 . . . 58 D3
Meadow Bank
Maghull L31 . . . 20 B2
6 Ormskirk L39 . . . 13 F5
Meadowbank Cl L12 . . . 54 E5
Meadowbarn Cl 3 L32 . . . 29 E1
Meadowbridge Cl L40 . . . 14 E4
Meadow Brook Cl L10 . . . 40 B7
Meadowbrook Rd
CH46 . . . 64 D7
Meadow Brow PR9 . . . 2 D5
Meadow Cl
Newton-le-W WA12 . . . 45 F3
Skelmersdale WN8 . . . 24 D7
Westhead L40 . . . 14 E4
Widnes WA8 . . . 72 D3
Meadow Clough WN8 . . . 16 B4
Meadow Cres CH49 . . . 65 B2
Meadowcroft
Ashton-in-M WN4 . . . 34 F6
Formby L37 . . . 9 F2
Heswall CH60 . . . 77 C1
Skelmersdale WN8 . . . 16 B4
St Helens WA9 . . . 58 C6
Meadowcroft Pk L12 . . . 54 D4
Meadowcroft Rd CH47 . . . 48 E1
Meadow Ct
Liverpool, Croxteth L11 . . . 40 B4
Liverpool, Woolton L25 . . . 70 B3
Meadow Dr
Huyton-w-R L36 . . . 70 F8
Ormskirk L39 . . . 13 C2
Meadowfield 3 WN8 . . . 25 A7
Meadowfield Cl
3 Birkenhead CH42 . . . 66 F2
Meadowfield Cl *continued*
Liverpool L9 . . . 39 A7
Meadow Hey L20 . . . 38 A6
Meadow Hey Cl L25 . . . 70 B3
Meadow La
Birkenhead CH42 . . . 66 F2
Liverpool L11, L12 . . . 54 B8
Maghull L31 . . . 20 F1
Southport PR8 . . . 7 D3
St Helens WA9 . . . 44 F2
Willaston CH64 . . . 87 E1
Meadow Oak Dr L25 . . . 70 A4
Meadow Pk 2 CH42 . . . 66 F2
Meadow Rd CH48 . . . 63 F3
Meadowside CH46 . . . 50 B4
Meadowside Ave WN4 . . . 35 A8
Meadowside Com Prim
Sch WA2 . . . 61 B1
Meadowside Dr L33 . . . 29 F6
Meadowside Rd CH62 . . . 88 D8
Meadowside Sch CH49 . . . 65 B2
Meadow St CH45 . . . 51 A8
Meadows The
Bebington CH62 . . . 88 D7
Maghull L31 . . . 20 D1
Rainhill L35 . . . 57 C3
Meadow The CH49 . . . 65 B3
Meadow View
Litherland L21 . . . 27 B3
Southport PR8 . . . 4 D4
Meadow Way L12 . . . 40 B1
Meadow Wlk CH61 . . . 76 E3
Meads The L34 . . . 57 A7
Meadway
Bebington CH62 . . . 79 C2
Birkenhead CH49 . . . 65 B6
Golborne WA3 . . . 47 D8
Heswall CH60 . . . 85 F6
Litherland L30 . . . 28 A2
Liverpool L15 . . . 69 C8
Maghull L31 . . . 28 B7
Prescot L35 . . . 56 F4
Skelmersdale WN8 . . . 16 A4
Wallasey CH45 . . . 51 A5
Widnes WA8 . . . 72 A1
Mealors Weint CH64 . . . 86 B1
Meander The L12 . . . 40 E1
Measham Cl WA11 . . . 44 C5
Measham Way L12 . . . 40 E3
Medbourne Cres L32 . . . 40 F8
Medbourne Ct 12 L32 . . . 40 F8
Meddowcroft Rd 5
CH45 . . . 51 A6
Medea Cl L5 . . . 52 E6
Medlar Way WN4 . . . 34 F5
Medlock Ct CH43 . . . 66 A5
Medlock St L4 . . . 52 E7
Medway 2 L20 . . . 38 C3
Medway Cl
Ashton-in-M WN4 . . . 34 F6
Warrington WA2 . . . 61 E2
Medway Ct WA9 . . . 44 F3
Medway Rd CH42 . . . 67 A2
Meeting La WA5 . . . 74 E5
Melbourne Cl L24 . . . 82 B5
Melbourne St
St Helens WA9 . . . 57 E7
Wallasey CH45 . . . 51 A8
Melbreck WN8 . . . 16 A4
Melbreck Rd L18 . . . 69 B1
Melbury Rd L14 . . . 55 C6
Melda Cl 3 L6 . . . 52 F3
Meldon Cl L12 . . . 40 C2
Meldreth Cl L37 . . . 9 C1
Meldrum Rd L15 . . . 69 B6
Melford Dr
Ashton-in-M WN4 . . . 35 A4
Birkenhead CH43 . . . 65 E1
Orrell WN5 . . . 25 D3
Melford Gr L6 . . . 53 D6
Meliden Gdns WA9 . . . 58 F7
Melksham Dr CH61 . . . 76 D7
MELLING . . . 28 F5
Melling Ave L9 . . . 39 B7
Melling Ct CH45 . . . 51 C7
Melling Dr L32 . . . 29 E3
Melling La L31 . . . 28 F7
MELLING MOUNT . . . 29 C7
Melling Prim Sch L31 . . . 29 B4
Melling Rd
Bootle L20 . . . 38 C5
Liverpool L9 . . . 39 C8
Southport PR9 . . . 4 E7
Wallasey CH45 . . . 51 C7
Mellings Ave WN5 . . . 25 E1
Melling Way L32 . . . 29 E3
Melloncroft Dr CH48 . . . 75 C7
Melloncroft Dr W
CH48 . . . 75 C7
Mellor Cl L35 . . . 71 A7
Mellor Rd CH42 . . . 66 C2
Mellors Cl PR8 . . . 4 F5
Melly Rd 5 L17 . . . 68 B3
Melmerby Cl WN4 . . . 34 F3
Melrose CH46 . . . 65 A8
Melrose Ave
Burtonwood WA5 . . . 59 F7
Crosby L23 . . . 26 E3
Hoylake CH47 . . . 63 B7
Southport PR9 . . . 2 B5
St Helens WA10 . . . 43 B5
Melrose Cres WN4 . . . 34 C3
Melrose Gdns 5 CH43 . . . 65 F1
Melrose Pk 3 L22 . . . 37 E8
Melrose Rd
Kirkby L33 . . . 29 D6
Liverpool L4, L5 . . . 52 D8
Seaforth L22 . . . 37 E8
Melton Cl CH49 . . . 64 E5
Melverley Rd L32 . . . 29 B2
Melville CH42 . . . 67 B1
Melville Ave CH42 . . . 67 A1
Melville Cl
St Helens WA10 . . . 43 D4
2 Widnes WA8 . . . 73 D1
Melville Gr L8 . . . 68 A8
Melville Pl L7 . . . 68 A8
Melville Rd
Bebington CH63 . . . 78 E5
Bootle L20 . . . 38 C7
Melville St L8 . . . 68 A5
Melwood Dr L12 . . . 54 C7
Menai Mews 5 L34 . . . 56 E6
Menai Rd L20 . . . 38 D6
Menai St CH41 . . . 66 C6
Mendell Cl CH62 . . . 88 E8
Mendell Prim Sch
CH62 . . . 88 E8
Mendip Ave WA2 . . . 61 B3
Mendip Cl
Birkenhead CH42 . . . 66 C1
Liverpool L26 . . . 82 E8
Mendip Gr WA9 . . . 44 F3
Mendip Rd
Birkenhead CH42 . . . 66 C1
Liverpool L15 . . . 69 A6
Menivale Cl PR9 . . . 2 B5
Menlo Ave CH61 . . . 76 F6
Menlo Cl CH43 . . . 65 F4
Menlove Ave L18, L25 . . . 69 D4
Menlove Ct L18 . . . 69 C5
Menlove Gdns N L18 . . . 69 C5
Menlove Gdns S L18 . . . 69 B5
Menlove Gdns W L16,
L18 . . . 69 B5
Menlove Mans L18 . . . 69 C6
Menstone Rd L13 . . . 53 F4
Mentmore Cres L11 . . . 40 B1
Mentmore Rd L18 . . . 69 A2
MEOLS . . . 63 D8
Meols Cl
Formby L37 . . . 9 E2
Hale L24 . . . 83 E2
Meols Cop High Sch
PR8 . . . 4 F5
Meols Cop Rd PR8, PR9 . . . 4 F4
Meols Cop Retail Pk
PR9 . . . 5 A4
Meols Cop Sta PR9 . . . 4 F7
Meols Ct CH47 . . . 63 A6
Meols Dr CH47, CH48 . . . 63 A4
Meols Par CH47 . . . 48 D1
Meols Sta CH47 . . . 63 E8
Meols View Cl PR8 . . . 5 A3
Mercer Ave L32 . . . 29 C1
Mercer Ct
10 Bootle L20 . . . 38 C3
Liverpool L12 . . . 54 E5
Maghull L31 . . . 20 A3
Mercer Dr L4 . . . 52 E8
Mercer Rd
Birkenhead CH43 . . . 65 E8
Haydock WA11 . . . 45 D6
Mercer's La L39 . . . 22 B4
Mercer St
Burtonwood WA5 . . . 59 E6
Liverpool L19 . . . 81 C5
Newton-le-W WA12 . . . 46 D4
Merchants Cres WA3 . . . 36 E1
Merchants Ct L1 . . . 90 A3
Merchant Taylors' Boys'
Sch L23 . . . 26 E3
Merchant Taylors' Sch for
Girls L23 . . . 26 E4
Mercury Way WN8 . . . 24 E8
Mere Ave CH63 . . . 88 B6
Merebank CH43 . . . 65 E4
Mere Bank L17 . . . 68 E4
Merebrook Gr L33 . . . 29 F5
Mere Cl WN8 . . . 15 F2
Merecliff L28 . . . 55 B8
Merecroft Ave CH44 . . . 51 C2
Meredale Rd L18 . . . 69 A4
Meredith St L19 . . . 81 E5
Mere Farm Gr CH43 . . . 65 F4
Mere Farm Rd CH43 . . . 65 F4
Merefield Sch PR8 . . . 7 B4
Mere Gn L4 . . . 39 A1
Mere Gr WA11 . . . 33 B1
Mere Hall CH43 . . . 65 E4
Mereheath CH46 . . . 49 E3
Mereheath Gdns CH46 . . . 49 E3
Mere Hey WA10 . . . 43 A3
Mere La
Heswall CH60 . . . 76 E2
Liverpool L5 . . . 52 F6
Wallasey CH45 . . . 50 E7
Mereland Cl WN5 . . . 25 E6
Mereland Way WA9 . . . 44 F2
Merepark Dr PR9 . . . 2 B4
Mere Park Rd CH49 . . . 64 C3
Mere Pk L23 . . . 26 D4
Mere Rd
Ashton-in-M WN4 . . . 35 C4
Formby L37 . . . 9 D2
Newton-le-W WA12 . . . 46 F4
Meres Rd L9, L10 . . . 39 E7
Meres Way PR8 . . . 4 B2
Mereview Cres L12 . . . 40 D3
Merewood
8 Kirkby L32 . . . 40 F8
Skelmersdale WN8 . . . 16 A4
Merewood Cl WA2 . . . 61 D3
Mereworth CH48 . . . 75 D6
Meribel Cl L23 . . . 27 A5
Meriden Ave CH63 . . . 79 A1

Meriden Cl
Southport PR8 . . . . 7 B5
St Helens WA11 . . . . 44 D6
Meriden Rd L25 . . . . 70 B6
Merlewood Ave PR9 . . . . . . .2 B3
Merlin Ave CH49 . . . . 64 D6
Merlin Cl
Birkenhead CH49 . . . . . . 64 D6
St Helens WA11 . . . . 44 B6
Merlin Ct L26 . . . . 70 D1
Merlin Rd **3** CH42 . . . . . 66 C3
Merlin St L8 . . . . 67 F6
Merrick Cl WA2 . . . . 61 E3
Merrills La CH49 . . . . 65 A5
Merrilocks Gn L23 . . . . . . 26 A5
Merrilocks Rd L23 . . . . . . 26 B5
Merrilox Ave L31 . . . . 20 D3
Merrion Cl L25 . . . . 69 F3
Merritt Ave CH41 . . . . 66 B8
Merrivale Rd L25 . . . . 70 C2
Merrydale Dr L11 . . . . 40 C3
Mersey Ave
Formby L37 . . . . 9 E6
Liverpool L19 . . . . 80 F8
Maghull L31 . . . . 20 F2
Merseybank Ho CH62 . . . . . 79 B7
Mersey Bank Rd CH62 . . . . 79 B7
Mersey Cotts L19 . . . . 81 D5
Mersey Ct
Crosby L23 . . . . 26 C3
14 Wallasey CH44 . . . . . 51 E2
Mersey Ho **3** L20 . . . . . 38 B4
Mersey La S CH42 . . . . . . 67 A2
Mersey Park Prim Sch
CH42 . . . . 66 D3
Mersey Rd
Birkenhead CH42 . . . . . . 67 A2
Crosby L23 . . . . 26 C3
Liverpool L17 . . . . 80 E8
Orrell WN5 . . . . 25 F7
Runcorn WA7 . . . . 84 F3
Merseyside Maritime
Mus★ L3 . . . . 90 A2
Merseyside Mounted
Police HQ L18 . . . . 69 C1
Merseyside Police
Training Coll L18 . . . . . . 69 C1
Mersey St
St Helens WA9 . . . . 45 A3
2 Wallasey CH44 . . . . . 51 E2
Mersey View
Bebington CH63 . . . . 78 D6
Crosby L23 . . . . 26 C2
Liverpool L19 . . . . 81 C6
Mersey View Rd WA8 . . . . 84 B4
Mersham Ct WA8 . . . . 72 F4
Merstone Cl L26 . . . . 82 F8
Merthyr Gr L16 . . . . 54 E1
Merton Bank Prim Sch
WA9 . . . . 44 C4
Merton Bank Rd WA11,
WA9 . . . . 44 C5
Merton Cl L36 . . . . 55 B2
Merton Cres L36 . . . . 55 B2
Merton Dr
Birkenhead CH49 . . . . . . 65 A3
Huyton-w-R L36 . . . . 55 A2
Merton Gr
Bootle L20 . . . . 38 C3
Crosby L23 . . . . 26 C3
Merton Pl CH43 . . . . 66 C6
Merton Rd
Bebington CH65 . . . . 89 B3
Bootle L20 . . . . 38 C3
Wallasey CH45 . . . . 51 B5
Merton St WA9 . . . . 44 C5
Merton Twrs L20 . . . . 38 D3
Mesham Ct CH49 . . . . 64 E5
Metcalf Cl L33 . . . . 29 D6
Meteor Cres WA2 . . . . 61 D2
Methuen St
Birkenhead CH41 . . . . . . 66 A8
Liverpool L15 . . . . 68 E8
Metquarter ★ L1 . . . . 90 B3
Metropolitan Cath of
Christ The King★ L3 . . . . 52 F1
Mews The
Burtonwood WA5 . . . . . . 59 E6
1 Crosby L23 . . . . 26 E3
Huyton-w-R L28 . . . . 55 C7
Liverpool L11 . . . . 68 F1
Southport PR8 . . . . 4 A5
St Helens WA9 . . . . 58 D4
Meyrick Cl WA12 . . . . 46 A3
Meyrick Rd L11 . . . . 39 E2
Micawber Cl L8 . . . . 67 F5
Michael Dragonette Ct
L3 . . . . 52 C4
Michaels Cl L37 . . . . .9 E3
Michael's La L39 . . . . 8 C3
Michigan Cl L27 . . . . 70 E5
Mickering La L39 . . . . 21 C5
Micklefield Rd L15 . . . . . . 68 F6
Mickleton Dr PR8 . . . . .7 A5
Middlecot Cl **2** WN5 . . . . 25 E5
Middlefield Com Prim Sch
L24 . . . . 82 F4
Middlefield Rd L18 . . . . . . 69 E3
Middleham Cl L32 . . . . 29 C1
Middlehey Rd L34 . . . . 41 D4
Middlehurst Ave WA10 . . . . 43 F4
Middlehurst Cl L34 . . . . . . 57 A7
Middlemass Hey L27 . . . . . 70 E5
Middle Moss La
Great Altcar L37 . . . . 10 F3
Haskayne L37 . . . . 11 A2
Middlesex Rd L20 . . . . 38 D4
Middleton Ct L24 . . . . 82 F4

Middleton Rd
Crosby L22 . . . . 26 F2
Liverpool L7 . . . . 53 E3
Middle War L1 . . . . 40 D5
Middle Withins La L37,
L38 . . . . 19 A7
Middlewood
Golborne WA3 . . . . 47 E8
7 Kirkby L32 . . . . 40 F8
Skelmersdale WN8 . . . . . 16 A4
Middlewood Cl L39 . . . . . . 21 C7
Middlewood Dr L39 . . . . . . 21 C7
Middlewood Rd L39 . . . . . . 21 C7
Midghall St L3 . . . . 52 C3
Midhurst Dr PR8 . . . . .7 B4
Midhurst Rd L12 . . . . 41 A3
Midland St
17 Birkenhead CH41 . . . . 66 C5
Widnes WA8 . . . . 73 B1
Midland Terr L22 . . . . 26 D1
Midlothian Dr L23 . . . . . . 26 C3
Midway Rd L36 . . . . 55 F4
Milbrook Cres L32 . . . . . . 29 E3
Milbrook Dr L32 . . . . 29 E3
Milbrook Wlk L32 . . . . 29 E3
Mildenhall Rd L25 . . . . . . 70 B7
Mildenhall Way L25 . . . . . 70 B7
Mildmay Rd
Bootle L20 . . . . 38 B5
Liverpool L11 . . . . 39 E2
Mile End L5 . . . . 52 D4
Miles Cl CH49 . . . . 64 C2
Miles La CH49 . . . . 64 C2
Miles St L8 . . . . 68 A4
Milestone Hey L28 . . . . . . 55 B8
Milford Cl L37 . . . . .9 C1
Milford Dr L12 . . . . 40 E3
Milford St L5 . . . . 52 C6
Milk St **7** WA10 . . . . . . 44 A3
Millachip Ct L6 . . . . 53 B4
Milland Cl L11 . . . . 40 C3
Millar's Pace PR9 . . . . .2 B5
Mill Ave WA5 . . . . 74 E7
Mill Bank L13 . . . . 53 F6
Millbank Ct L9 . . . . 39 D8
Millbank La L13 . . . . 20 F3
Mill Bank Rd CH44 . . . . . . 51 A4
Millbeck Cl **6** L32 . . . . . 29 E4
Millbeck Gr WA11 . . . . . . 33 B2
Millbridge Gdns WA12 . . . . 46 E3
Millbrook Bsns Pk
WA11 . . . . 32 C3
Millbrook Cl **3** L33 . . . . 15 E2
Millbrook Com Prim Sch
L32 . . . . 29 D3
Millbrook Ct
Knowsley L34 . . . . 41 C5
Warrington WA2 . . . . 61 B2
Millbrook La WA10 . . . . . . 43 B4
Millbrook Rd CH44 . . . . . . 51 B1
Mill Brow
Bebington CH63 . . . . 78 D6
Haskayne L39 . . . . 12 A7
St Helens, Eccleston
WA10 . . . . 43 B4
St Helens WA9 . . . . 58 D5
Widnes WA8 . . . . 73 C1
Mill Brow Cl WA9 . . . . 58 D5
Millbutt Cl CH63 . . . . 78 D6
Mill Cl
Birkenhead CH42 . . . . . . 66 D4
Crosby L23 . . . . 26 E6
Warrington WA2 . . . . 61 E4
Mill Cotts CH64 . . . . 87 F1
Millcroft
Crosby L23 . . . . 27 A5
Neston CH64 . . . . 86 E1
Millcroft Ave WN5 . . . . . . 25 D5
Millcroft Pk CH49 . . . . . . 64 B3
Millcroft Rd L25 . . . . 70 C1
Mill Ct L30 . . . . 27 D5
Mill Dam La L40 . . . . 14 D8
Millennium Ct
Crosby L22 . . . . 26 E2
Neston CH64 . . . . 86 E2
Millennium Rd L8 . . . . 68 A4
Miller Ave L23 . . . . 26 D5
Miller's Bridge L20 . . . . . . 38 B2
Millers Cl **7** CH46 . . . . . 64 B8
Millerscroft L32 . . . . 29 C4
Millers Ct L39 . . . . 13 F5
Millersdale **13** WA9 . . . . 58 C4
Millersdale Ave **5** L9 . . . 39 B7
Millersdale Cl CH62 . . . . . 88 F5
Millersdale Rd L18 . . . . . . 69 A4
Millers Fold WA10 . . . . . . 43 B4
Millersmede **6** L5 . . . . . 52 D5
Millers Nook WN8 . . . . . . 25 B7
Millers Way CH46 . . . . . . 64 C8
Mill Farm Cl WA2 . . . . . . 61 E3
Millfield CH64 . . . . 86 E1
Millfield Bsns Ctr
WA11 . . . . 45 E8
Millfield Cl
Bebington CH63 . . . . 78 D5
Liverpool L13 . . . . 54 A6
Millfield La WN4, WA11 . . . 34 E1
Millfield Rd WA8 . . . . 73 C2
Millfields WA10 . . . . 43 B3
Millfields Prim Sch
CH62 . . . . 88 E4
Millgreen Cl
Liverpool L12 . . . . 40 E3
Up Holland WN8 . . . . . . 25 A7
Mill Green La WA8 . . . . . . 73 E5
Mill Green Sch WA12 . . . . . 46 E3
Mill Hey L35 . . . . 57 E1
Mill Hey Rd CH48 . . . . . . 75 D6

Mill Hill CH43 . . . . 66 A3
Mill Hill Rd CH61 . . . . 76 C7
Millhouse Cl CH46 . . . . . . 49 B1
Millhouse Ct L12 . . . . 54 A6
Millhouse La CH46 . . . . . . 49 B1
Millhouse St **7** PR8 . . . . . 7 D5
Mill House View WN8 . . . . 25 C7
Millingford Ave WA3 . . . . . 35 F2
Millingford Gr WN4 . . . . . . 35 B3
Millingford Ind Est
WA3 . . . . 47 A8
Millington Cl
Birkenhead CH43 . . . . . . 65 E1
Widnes WA8 . . . . 84 F8
Mill La
Birkenhead CH49 . . . . . . 64 C2
Bold Heath WA8 . . . . . . 73 D6
Bootle L20 . . . . 38 D3
Cronton WA8 . . . . 72 D6
Haskayne L39 . . . . 12 F1
Heswall CH60 . . . . 86 B8
Kirkby L32 . . . . 29 D4
Knowsley L34 . . . . 41 D5
Liverpool L13 . . . . 90 B4
Liverpool, Olive Mount L13,
L15 . . . . 54 A1
Liverpool, Sandfield Park
L12 . . . . 54 A6
Newton-le-W WA12 . . . . . 46 E3
Rainford WA11 . . . . 32 C4
Rainhill L35 . . . . 57 C1
Skelmersdale, Elmers Green
WN8 . . . . 16 F1
Skelmersdale, Pennylands
WN8 . . . . 15 F2
Skelmersdale, Tawd Valley
Park WN8 . . . . 16 A3
Southport PR9 . . . . 2 A1
St Helens WA9 . . . . 58 D5
Up Holland WN8 . . . . . . 25 A8
Wallasey CH44 . . . . 51 A3
Warrington, Houghton Green
WA2 . . . . 61 E4
Warrington WA2 . . . . 60 F4
Willaston CH64 . . . . 87 F1
Mill Lane Cres PR9 . . . . . . .2 A1
Mill Mdw WA12 . . . . 46 E3
Millom Ave L35 . . . . 57 F4
Millom Gr
Liverpool L12 . . . . 40 C1
St Helens WA10 . . . . 57 C8
Mill Park Dr CH62 . . . . . . 88 E3
Mill Rd
Bebington CH62 . . . . 79 D3
Bebington, Higher Bebington
CH63 . . . . 78 D6
Heswall CH61 . . . . 77 A6
Liverpool L6 . . . . 52 F4
Liverpool L6 . . . . 53 A4
Orrell WN5 . . . . 25 D5
Southport PR8 . . . . 7 D5
Millrose Cl WN8 . . . . 15 F2
Mill Spring Ct L20 . . . . . . 38 D3
Mill Sq L11 . . . . 28 E2
Mill St
Ashton-in-M WN4 . . . . . . 35 C2
Birkenhead CH42 . . . . . . 66 D4
Golborne WA3 . . . . 47 A8
Liverpool, Toxteth L8 . . . . 67 E5
Liverpool, Woolton L25 . . 70 A2
Ormskirk L39 . . . . 13 F5
Prescot L34 . . . . 56 D6
St Helens WA10 . . . . 43 F4
Millstead Rd L15 . . . . 69 B8
Millstead Sch L15 . . . . . . 69 B8
Millstead Wlk L15 . . . . . . 69 A8
Millthwaite Ct **4** CH44 . . 50 F4
Millthwaite Rd CH44 . . . . . 50 F4
Millvale St L6 . . . . 53 C3
Mill View **4** L8 . . . . 67 E5
Mill View Ct L9 . . . . 39 E1
Mill View Dr CH63 . . . . . . 78 C6
Millway Rd L24 . . . . 83 A4
Millwood CH63 . . . . 78 D6
Mill Wood Ave WA10 . . . . . 42 F3
Millwood Cl WN4 . . . . 35 A5
Millwood Ct L24 . . . . 83 A4
Millwood Gdns L35 . . . . . . 56 F2
Millwood Rd L24 . . . . 82 F4
MILL YARD 54 E4
Mill Yd CH61 . . . . 77 B6
Milman Cl
Birkenhead CH49 . . . . . . 64 F4
Ormskirk L39 . . . . 13 D3
Milman Ct L25 . . . . 69 E3
Milman Rd L4 . . . . 39 A1
Milner Cop CH60 . . . . 86 A8
Milne Rd **5** L13 . . . . 53 E8
Milner Rd
Heswall CH60 . . . . 86 A8
Liverpool L17 . . . . 68 E1
Milner St CH41 . . . . 66 A8
Milnthorpe Rd **11** L4 . . . 52 E8
Milnthorpe Rd WA5 . . . . . 59 E6
Milnthorpe St L19 . . . . . . 81 C6
Milroy St **7** L7 . . . . 53 B1
Milton Ave
Huyton-w-R L14 . . . . 54 F2
Newton-le-W WA12 . . . . . 46 B3
Prescot L35 . . . . 56 F3
Widnes WA8 . . . . 84 B4
Milton Cl L35 . . . . 56 E3
Milton Cres CH60 . . . . 77 A1
Milton Dr L39 . . . . 14 A4
Milton Gn CH61 . . . . 77 B6
Milton Gr
Longshaw WN5 . . . . 25 D1

Milton Gr continued
Orrell WN5 . . . . 25 F6
Milton Pavement **7**
CH41 . . . . 66 D6
Milton Rd
Birkenhead CH42 . . . . . . 66 C4
Crosby L22 . . . . 26 E2
Golborne WA3 . . . . 47 D7
Liverpool L7 . . . . 53 E2
Liverpool, Walton on the Hill
L4 . . . . 38 E2
Wallasey CH44 . . . . 51 D2
West Kirby CH48 . . . . . . 63 A3
Widnes WA8 . . . . 84 F8
Milton Rd E CH42 . . . . . . 66 D4
Milton St
Bootle L20 . . . . 38 B4
Southport PR9 . . . . 5 A7
St Helens WA9 . . . . 58 B2
Milton Way L31 . . . . 20 B1
Milvain Dr WA2 . . . . 61 C1
Milverny Way WA9 . . . . . . 44 A2
Milverton St L6 . . . . 53 C4
Mimosa Rd L15 . . . . 69 B7
Mindale Rd L15 . . . . 68 F8
Minehead Gr WA9 . . . . . . 58 D5
Minehead Rd L17 . . . . 80 E8
Miners Way L24 . . . . 83 A3
Mines Ave L17 . . . . 80 F8
Mine's Ave L34 . . . . 56 E6
Mine Way WA11 . . . . 45 F7
Minshull St L7 . . . . 53 A1
Minstead Ave L33 . . . . . . 30 A2
Minster Ct L7 . . . . 68 A8
Minstrel Cl WN2 . . . . 36 B7
Minto Cl L7 . . . . 53 C2
Minto Ho CH47 . . . . 63 C8
Minton Cl L12 . . . . 40 F3
Minton Way WA8 . . . . 73 B5
Mintor Rd L33 . . . . 30 A2
Minto St L7 . . . . 53 B2
Minver Rd L12 . . . . 54 D7
Miranda Ave CH63 . . . . . . 78 E7
Miranda Pl L20 . . . . 38 D1
Miranda Rd L20 . . . . 38 D1
Miranda Rd S **4** L20 . . . . 38 D1
Mirfield Cl
Golborne WA3 . . . . 47 D7
Liverpool L26 . . . . 82 F7
Mirfield St L6 . . . . 53 C3
Miriam Pl **2** CH41 . . . . . 65 F8
Miriam Rd L4 . . . . 53 A6
Miskelly St L20 . . . . 38 C8
Missouri Rd L13 . . . . 53 D7
Mistle Thrush Way **2**
L12 . . . . 40 F3
Miston St L20 . . . . 38 C8
Misty Cl WA8 . . . . 72 C2
Mitchell Ave WA5 . . . . 59 E5
Mitchell Cres L21 . . . . 38 B8
Mitchell Pl L1 . . . . 90 C3
Mitchell Rd
Billinge WN5 . . . . 33 E5
Prescot L34 . . . . 56 C6
St Helens WA10 . . . . 43 C1
Mitchell St
Ashton-in-M WN4 . . . . . . 35 C2
Golborne WA3 . . . . 47 A8
Mithril Cl WA8 . . . . 73 C2
Mitre Cl L35 . . . . 56 D1
Mitten's La L37 . . . . 10 A4
Mitten's La L37 . . . . 10 B3
Mitylene St L5 . . . . 52 E6
Mobberley Way CH63 . . . . 79 A3
Mockbeggar Dr CH45 . . . . 50 D8
Mockbeggar Wharf
CH45 . . . . 50 E7
Modred St L8 . . . . 67 F5
Moel Famau View L17 . . . . 68 B2
Moffatdale Rd L4 . . . . 53 C8
Moffat Rd L9 . . . . 39 C7
Moira Sephton Ct
CH43 . . . . 65 D4
Molesworth Gr L16 . . . . . . 54 F1
Molineux Ave L14 . . . . 54 D1
Molland Cl L12 . . . . 54 D8
Mollington Ave L11 . . . . . . 39 F2
Mollington Link CH41 . . . . 66 F5
Mollington Rd
Kirkby L32 . . . . 29 C2
Wallasey CH44 . . . . 51 C3
Mollington St CH41 . . . . . 66 E5
Molly's La L31 . . . . 41 D7
Molton Rd L15, L16 . . . . . 69 C8
Molyneux Cl
Birkenhead CH49 . . . . . . 64 F5
Huyton-w-R L36 . . . . 55 F2
Prescot L35 . . . . 56 D4
Molyneux Ct
Liverpool, Broad Green
L14 . . . . 54 D1
Liverpool, Dog & Gun
L11 . . . . 40 B3
Molyneux Dr
Prescot L35 . . . . 56 D4
Wallasey CH45 . . . . 51 C8
Molyneux Rd
Crosby L22 . . . . 26 E2
Liverpool L6 . . . . 53 B3
Liverpool, Mossley Hill
L18 . . . . 68 F4
Maghull L31 . . . . 28 F7
Ormskirk L39 . . . . 21 C7
Molyneux Way L10 . . . . . . 28 C3
Monaghan Cl L9 . . . . 39 A7
Monarchs Quay L3 . . . . . . 90 A1
Monash Cl L33 . . . . 29 E6
Monash Rd L11 . . . . 53 F8

Mona St
Birkenhead CH41 . . . . . . 65 F7
Bootle L20 . . . . 38 C6
St Helens WA10 . . . . 43 D3
Monastery La WA9 . . . . . . 58 E7
Monastery Rd
4 Liverpool L6 . . . . . . 53 C6
St Helens WA9 . . . . 58 E7
Mond Rd
Liverpool L10 . . . . 40 A7
5 Widnes WA8 . . . . . . 73 A1
Monfa Rd
Bootle L20 . . . . 38 C6
Bootle L20 . . . . 38 D6
Monica Dr WA8 . . . . 73 A5
Monica Rd L25 . . . . 70 B1
Monica Terr WA5 . . . . 35 B2
Monkfield Way L19 . . . . . . 81 D4
Monk Rd CH44, CH45 . . . . 51 B4
Monks Carr La L37, L38 . . . 19 A6
Monks Cl L37 . . . . 10 A1
Monksdown Prim Sch
L11 . . . . 40 A1
Monksdown Rd L11 . . . . . . 40 A1
Monks Dr L37 . . . . 10 A1
Monks Ferry CH41 . . . . . . 66 F6
Monksferry Wlk L19 . . . . . 80 F7
Monk St
Birkenhead CH41 . . . . . . 66 F6
Liverpool L5 . . . . 52 F6
Monks Way
Bebington CH63 . . . . 78 F4
Liverpool L25 . . . . 70 B2
Monk's Way L48 . . . . 63 C2
Monkswell Dr L15 . . . . . . 69 A8
Monkswell St L8 . . . . 68 A3
Monkswood Cl WA5 . . . . . 60 E2
Monmouth Cres WN4 . . . . 35 D2
Monmouth Dr L10 . . . . . . 28 F1
Monmouth Gr WA9 . . . . . . 44 D2
Monmouth Rd CH44 . . . . . 50 F4
Monro Cl L8 . . . . 67 F4
Monro St L8 . . . . 67 F4
Mons Sq **5** L20 . . . . 38 C3
Montague Rd
Liverpool L13 . . . . 54 A2
Widnes WA8 . . . . 84 A6
Montague Mews L37 . . . . . .9 E5
Montagu Rd L37 . . . . .9 E5
Montclair Dr L18 . . . . 69 B6
Monterey Rd L13 . . . . 54 B2
Montfort Dr L19 . . . . 81 A7
Montgomery Ave PR9 . . . . .5 B6
Montgomery Cl L35 . . . . . 56 D2
Montgomery Hill
Birkenhead CH48 . . . . . . 64 A1
Irby CH48 . . . . 76 A8
Montgomery Ho **8**
L21 . . . . 37 F7
Montgomery Rd
Huyton-w-R L36 . . . . 55 E4
Liverpool L9 . . . . 39 A7
Widnes WA8 . . . . 84 D8
Montgomery Way **3**
L6 . . . . 53 B4
Montpelier Dr **8** L8 . . . . 67 F4
Montpellier Cres CH45 . . . 51 A8
Montpellier Ct **7**
CH45 . . . . 51 A8
Montpellier Ho **5**
CH45 . . . . 51 A8
Montreal Cl L27 . . . . 70 E5
Montreal St WN7 . . . . 36 E4
Montrey Cres WN4 . . . . . . 34 C3
Montrose Ave L21 . . . . 51 E1
Montrose Cl WA2 . . . . 61 F4
Montrose Ct
Hoylake CH47 . . . . 63 B6
Liverpool L12 . . . . 54 F7
Montrose Dr PR9 . . . . .1 F1
Montrose Pl L25 . . . . 82 F7
Montrose Rd L13 . . . . 53 E6
Montrose Way L13 . . . . . . 53 F2
Montrovia Cres L10 . . . . . 39 F6
Monville Rd L9 . . . . 39 C7
Moorbridge Cl L30 . . . . . . 28 A5
Moor Cl
Crosby L23 . . . . 26 F5
Southport PR8 . . . . 7 D2
Moor Coppice L23 . . . . . . 26 F5
Moorcroft Rd
Huyton-w-R L36 . . . . 55 E5
Liverpool L18 . . . . 69 D1
Wallasey CH45 . . . . 50 D5
Moor Ct L10 . . . . 40 A7
Moor Dr
Crosby L23 . . . . 26 F4
Skelmersdale WN8 . . . . . 24 D7
Moore Ave
Birkenhead CH42 . . . . . . 66 E2
St Helens WA9 . . . . 45 B3
Moore Cl WA8 . . . . 73 A1
Moore Dr WA11 . . . . 45 F6
Moore's Ho **11** L4 . . . . . 38 F2
Moore St L20 . . . . 38 B5
Mooreway L35 . . . . 57 F1
Moorfield L33 . . . . 29 F5
Moorfield Ctr The L33 . . . . 29 F6
Moorfield Dr CH64 . . . . . . 86 C1
Moorfield Prim Sch
WA8 . . . . 73 D3
Moorfield Rd
Crosby L23 . . . . 27 A5
St Helens WA10 . . . . 43 D5
Widnes WA8 . . . . 73 D3

Moorfields L2 90 A4
Moorfields Ave CH43 65 D4
Moorfields Sta L2 90 A4
Moorfoot Rd WA9 44 F3
Moorfoot Road Ind Est
WA9 44 F4
Moorfoot Way L33 29 D6
Moorgate L39 13 E4
Moorgate Ave L23 26 F4
Moorgate La 8 L32 41 A8
Moorgate Rd L32 41 A7
Moorgate St 8 L7 53 B1
Moorhead Cl L21 38 A7
Moorhey Rd L31 28 D6
Moor Ho 4 L23 26 E5
Moorhouses L38 17 F3
Moorings Cl CH64 86 B1
Moorings The
6 Birkenhead CH41 66 D5
Heswall CH60 85 C8
Maghull L31 20 B4
West Kirby CH48 63 A2
Moor La
Crosby L23 26 F5
Heswall CH60 85 F8
Ince Blundell L38, L23 18 E2
Liverpool L10 40 A7
Liverpool L32 40 B8
Liverpool, Walton L4 39 A2
Maghull L29 19 D1
Southport PR8 7 C2
Widnes WA8 84 F7
Moorland Ave L23 26 E5
Moorland Cl CH60 86 A7
Moorland Pk CH60 86 A7
Moorland Rd
Ashton-in-M WN4 35 E5
Birkenhead CH42 66 E3
Maghull L31 28 D6
Moorlands Rd L23 27 B6
Moor La S WA8 84 F7
MOOR PARK 26 F6
Moor Pl L3 90 C4
Moor Rd WN5 25 E6
Moorside Cl L23 26 F4
Moorside Com Prim Sch
WN8 24 E7
Moorside Ct WA8 84 F7
Moorside Rd L23 26 F4
Moor St
Liverpool L2 90 A3
Ormskirk L39 13 F5
Moorway CH60 86 B8
Moorwood Cres WA9 58 C4
Moray Cl WA10 43 E5
Morcott La L24 83 D2
Morden Ave WN4 35 B3
Morden St L6 53 C3
Morecambe St L6 53 C5
Morecroft Rd CH42 67 A1
Morella Rd L4 53 C8
Morello Cl WA10 43 F5
Morello Dr CH63 79 B2
Moret Cl L23 27 A5
MORETON 49 D1
Moreton Ave 1 WA9 58 C4
Moreton Cl WA3 35 F1
Moreton Gr CH45 50 E6
Moreton Rd CH49 64 F6
Moreton Sta CH46 49 E2
Morgan Ave WA2 61 C2
Morgan Mews L30 27 D3
Morgan St WA9 44 D3
Morland Ave CH62 88 D6
Morley Ave CH41 66 B8
Morley Ct L14 54 E4
Morley Rd
Southport PR9 4 E8
Wallasey CH41, CH44 51 A3
Morley St
Liverpool L4 52 E7
St Helens WA10 43 F5
Morley Way 1 WA10 43 F4
Morningside L23 26 F3
Morningside Pl L11 39 F1
Morningside Rd L11 53 F8
Morningside View L11 53 F8
Morningside Way L11 53 F8
Mornington Ave L23 26 E2
Mornington Rd
Southport PR9 4 C7
Wallasey CH45 51 B6
Mornington St L8 67 E5
Morpeth Cl CH46 64 B8
Morpeth Rd CH47 63 A5
Morpeth St L8 67 F7
Morpeth Wharf CH41 66 F8
Morris Cl WA11 45 A5
Morris Ct CH43 65 F5
Morris Rd WN8 25 A7
Morrissey Cl WA10 43 D4
Morris St WA9 44 E1
Morston Ave L32 40 E8
Morston Cres L32 40 E8
Morston Wlk L32 40 E8
Mortar Mill Quay CH44 51 E1
Mortimer St CH41 66 F6
Mortlake Cl WA8 72 C3
Morton St L8 67 F5
Morvah Cl 2 L12 40 C2
Morval Cres L4 38 E2
Morven Cl WA2 61 E3
Morven Gr PR8 4 E7
Moscow Dr
Liverpool L13 53 F5
Moscow Dr *continued*
Liverpool L13 54 A5
Mosedale Ave WA11 33 B1
Mosedale Rd
Bebington CH62 79 E2
Liverpool L9 39 A5
Moseley Ave CH44,
CH45 51 A4
Moseley Rd CH63 79 A1
Moses St L8 67 F4
Mosley St PR8 4 B4
Moss Ave WN5 25 D3
MOSS BANK 33 A1
Moss Bank L39 13 D2
Moss Bank Ct L39 13 D2
Moss Bank Pk L21 38 A8
Moss Bank Rd WA11 33 B2
Mossborough Hall La
WA11 31 C2
Mossborough Rd
WA11 31 E4
Moss Brow WA11 31 E7
Mossbrow Rd L36 55 E4
Moss Cotts L40 15 A3
Mosscraig L28 55 C7
Mosscroft Cl L36 56 A4
Mosscroft Prim Sch
L36 56 A3
Mossdale Dr L35 57 D3
Mossdale Rd
Ashton-in-M WN4 35 A8
Kirkby L33 29 F5
Moss Delph La L39 13 C1
Mossdene Rd CH44 50 F4
Moss End Way L33 30 D3
Mossfield Rd L9 38 F6
Moss Gate Gr L14 55 A3
Moss Gate Rd L14 55 A3
Moss Gdns PR8 4 C2
Mossgiel Ave PR8 7 B5
Moss Gn L37 10 B4
Moss Gr
Birkenhead CH42 66 C2
Liverpool L8 68 C6
Moss Green Way WA9 45 A1
Mosshill Cl L31 20 C3
Moss La
Bickerstaffe L39 22 F2
Birkenhead CH42 66 B2
Crank WA11 32 E5
Formby L37, L39 10 E5
Golborne WA3 47 B5
Hightown L38, L23 18 C2
Kirkby L33 29 F7
Kirkby, Northwood L33 30 B3
Litherland L21 27 D1
Liverpool L9, L20 38 F6
Maghull L31 20 E2
Maghull, Lydiate L31 20 D5
Skelmersdale WN8 23 F6
Southport PR9 5 B8
St Helens, Moss Nook
WA9 45 A1
St Helens WA11 43 B7
Mosslands WA10 43 A4
Mosslands Dr CH44,
CH45 50 E4
Mosslands Sch The
CH45 50 E4
Moss Lane View WN8 23 F6
Mosslawn Rd L32 30 A1
Mosslea Pk L18 68 F4
Mossley Ave
Bebington CH62 88 D8
Liverpool L18 68 F5
Mossley Ct L18 69 A3
MOSSLEY HILL 69 A3
Mossley Hill Dr L17 68 E4
Mossley Hill Hospl L18 68 E3
Mossley Hill Rd L18,
L19 68 F2
Mossley Hill Sta L18 69 A3
Mossley Rd CH42 66 E3
MOSS NOOK 44 F1
Moss Nook L39 13 C2
Moss Nook La
Kirkby L31 29 B7
Rainford WA11 31 E6
Rainford WA11 31 F5
Moss Pits Cl L10 39 F7
Mosspits Jun & Inf Schs
L15 69 B6
Moss Pits La
Liverpool, Fazakerley
L10 39 E7
Liverpool, Wavertree Green
L15 69 B7
Moss Rd
Orrell WN5 25 D3
Southport PR8 4 C2
MOSS SIDE 21 A1
Moss Side
Formby L37 10 B4
Huyton-w-R L14 55 A3
Moss St
Liverpool, Garston L19 81 C6
Liverpool L3, L6, L7 52 F2
Prescot L34 56 D7
Moss View
Litherland L21 38 C8
Maghull L31 20 F1
Ormskirk L39 13 E4
Mossville Cl L18 69 A2
Mossville Rd L18 69 B2
Moss Way L11 40 C4
Mossy Bank Rd CH44 51 D4
Mostyn Ave
Aintree L10 28 C2
Mostyn Ave *continued*
Heswall CH60 85 C8
Liverpool L19 81 D8
West Kirby CH48 63 B1
Mostyn Cl L4 52 E7
Mostyn Gdns CH64 86 B1
Mostyn Hall L15 68 E7
Mostyn House Sch
CH64 86 C1
Mostyn Sq CH64 86 B1
Mostyn St CH44 51 B2
Motherwell Cl WA8 72 E3
Motherwell Cres PR8 4 F3
Mottershead Rd WA8 73 A1
Mottram Cl L33 29 F2
Moughland La WA7 84 F1
Mould St L5 52 D5
Mounsey Rd CH42 66 D5
Mount Ave
Bebington CH63 78 D7
Bootle L20 38 D7
Heswall CH60 85 F8
Mount Carmel Sch
L39 13 D2
Mount Cl L32 29 C4
Mount Cres
Kirkby L32 29 C4
Orrell WN5 25 F6
Mount Ct
3 Heswall CH60 85 F8
8 Wallasey CH45 51 A8
Mount Dr CH63 78 D7
Mountfield Ct WN5 25 F7
Mount Gr CH41 66 C5
Mount Grove Pl 5
CH41 66 C5
Mount Haven Cl CH49 65 A5
Mount House Cl L37 10 B5
Mount House Rd L37 10 B5
Mount Mews CH60 85 F8
Mount Olive CH43 66 A3
Mount Park Ct L25 70 A3
Mount Pk
Bebington CH63 78 D7
Liverpool L25 70 A3
Mount Pleasant
Birkenhead CH43 66 B3
Crosby L22 26 D1
Liverpool L1, L3, L7 90 C3
Liverpool L3, L7 52 F1
Widnes WA8 73 B2
Mount Pleasant Ave
WA9 45 B3
Mount Pleasant Cl
CH45 51 B7
Mount Pleasant Flats 6
L22 26 D1
Mount Pleasant Rd
CH45 51 B7
Mount Prim Sch CH45 51 A7
Mount Rd
Bebington CH63 78 D5
Birkenhead, Egerton Park
CH42 66 D1
Birkenhead, Upton CH49 65 A5
Kirkby L32 29 B3
Wallasey CH45 51 A7
West Kirby CH48 63 C1
Mount St
Crosby L22 26 D1
Liverpool L1 90 C2
Liverpool, Woolton L25 70 A2
Southport PR9 4 D7
Widnes WA8 73 B1
Mount The
Heswall CH60 85 F8
Skelmersdale WN8 24 B8
Wallasey CH44 51 C4
Mount Vernon L7 53 A1
Mount Vernon Gn 9
L7 53 A2
Mount Vernon Rd L7 53 A1
Mount Vernon St 6
L7 53 A2
Mount Vernon View 7
L7 53 A2
Mountview Cl 5 L8 68 A5
Mountway CH63 78 D7
Mountwood WN8 16 A4
Mountwood Lo PR8 7 C5
Mount Wood Rd CH42 78 C8
Mowbray Ave WA11 44 C5
Mowbray Ct 1 L20 38 C1
Mowbray Gr
Liverpool L13 54 A1
Liverpool L13 54 A1
Mowcroft La WA5 74 B3
Moxon St WA10 43 D2
Moxon Way WN4 35 D4
Moyles Cl WA8 72 D2
Mozart Cl L8 68 B6
Much Woolton RC Prim
Sch L25 70 B2
Muirfield Cl L12 54 E6
Muirfield Dr PR8 7 C4
Muirfield Rd L36 55 C1
Muirhead Ave L13 53 F7
Muirhead Ave E L11,
L12 40 B1
Mulberry Ave
Golborne WA3 47 F7
St Helens WA10 43 C3
Mulberry Cl L33 29 F6
Mulberry Gr CH44 51 D3
Mulberry Lo L36 55 E3
Mulberry Pl L7 67 F8
Mulberry Rd CH42 66 F2
Mulberry St L7 67 F8
Mulcrow Cl WA9 44 D4
Mulgrave St L8 68 A7
Mullberry St L7 52 F1
Mullein Cl WA3 47 D8
Mullen Cl WA5 60 F1
Mulliner St L7 68 C7
Mullins Ave WA12 46 C5
Mullion Cl
Liverpool L26 82 E9
Southport PR9 2 B5
Mullion Rd L11 40 C5
Mullion Wlk L11 40 C5
Mullrea Cl L27 70 C6
Mullwood Cl L12 40 F3
Mulrankin Ct 4 L13 54 B2
Mulveton Rd CH63 78 F3
Mumfords Gr CH47 48 E1
Mumfords La CH47 48 E1
Muncaster Cl CH62 79 D1
Muncaster Dr WA11 32 B6
Munro Ave WN5 25 E6
Munster Rd L13 54 B3
Murat Gr L22 26 D1
Murat St L22 26 D1
Murcote Rd L14 54 F5
Muriel Cl WA5 74 D6
Muriel St L4 53 A8
Murphy Gr WA9 44 E4
Murrayfield Dr CH46 49 F4
Murrayfield Hospl
CH61 77 D5
Murrayfield Rd L25 70 B6
Murrayfield Wlk L25 70 B6
Murray Gr CH48 63 A3
Musker Ct L23 26 F3
Musker Dr L30 27 C3
Musker Gdns L23 26 F3
Musker St L23 26 F3
Muspratt Rd L21 38 A6
Muttocks Rake L30 27 D5
Myddleton La WA2 61 C6
Myers Ave L35 57 A5
Myerscough Ave L20 38 E5
Myers Ct L23 26 F2
Myers Rd E L23 26 E3
Myers Rd W L23 26 D3
Mynsule Rd CH63 78 F3
Myrtle Ave
Ashton-in-M WN4 34 F6
Haydock WA11 45 B7
Newton-le-W WA12 46 C2
Myrtle Gr
Billinge WN5 33 D4
Crosby L22 26 D2
Southport PR9 4 E7
Wallasey CH44 51 E3
Widnes WA8 84 D8
Myrtle Par L7 67 F8
Myrtle St L7, L8 68 A8
Myrtle Way CH49 65 B4
Mystic Mews 9 L39 13 E5

N

Naburn Dr WN5 25 E5
Naburn Gr CH46 64 F7
Nairn Ave WN8 16 B5
Nairn Cl CH63 88 D4
Nansen Gr 4 L4 39 A1
Nant Park Ct CH45 51 C8
Nantwich Cl CH49 65 A2
Napier Cl WA10 43 E3
Napier Dr CH46 64 F8
Napier Rd CH62 79 B8
Napier St
Bootle L20 38 B1
St Helens WA10 43 E3
Napier Terr PR8 4 A5
Naples Rd CH44 51 D3
Napps Cl L25 69 F7
Napps Way
Heswall CH61 77 A2
Liverpool L25 69 F8
Napps Wlk L25 69 F7
Nares Cl WA5 60 C1
Narrow Croft Rd L39 13 B1
Narrow La L39 13 B1
Narrow Lane (Clieves
Hills) L39 12 E6
Narrow Moss La L39,
L40 13 E8
Naseby Cl CH43 65 C4
Naseby St L4 38 F2
Natal Rd L9 39 B6
Nathan Dr WA11 45 E6
Nathan Gr L33 29 F4
National Wildflower Ctr
The* L16 54 F1
Naughton Lea WA8 72 D3
Navigation Cl L30 28 A4
Navigation Wharf L3 67 D5
Naylor Ave WA3 47 B8
Naylor Rd
Birkenhead CH43 65 E8
Widnes WA8 73 D1
Naylorsfield Dr L27 70 C6
Naylor's Rd
Liverpool L25 70 D5
Liverpool L27 70 D7
Naylor St L3 52 D3
Nazareth House La
WA8 84 C7
Nazeby Ave L23 27 A3
N Brooke Way CH49 65 A3
Neale Dr CH49 64 E3
Neales Fold PR9 2 D5
Neasham Cl L26 82 F9
Nedens Gr L31 20 C3
Nedens La L31 20 C3
Needham Cres CH43 65 D4
Needham Rd L7 53 C2
Needham Way WN8 16 B5
Needwood Dr CH63 78 F3
Neills Rd WA5 59 B6
Neilson Rd L17 68 C3
Neilson St L17 68 B3
Neil St WA8 73 C2
Nell's La L39 20 F5
Nelson Ave L35 56 E2
Nelson Ct
Birkenhead CH42 67 A1
Southport PR8 3 F4
Wallasey CH45 37 B1
Nelson Dr CH61 76 E3
Nelson Ho CH42 67 A1
Nelson Pl L35 56 E2
Nelson Rd
Birkenhead CH42 67 A1
Bootle L21 38 B7
Liverpool L7 53 B1
Nelson's Croft CH63 79 A3
Nelson St
Bootle L20 38 B2
Liverpool L1 90 B1
Liverpool L1 90 C2
Liverpool, Wavertree
L15 68 E8
Newton-le-W WA12 46 A3
Southport PR8 4 A6
Wallasey CH45 51 C7
Nelville Rd L9 39 C7
Neptune Ent Ctr CH41 66 D8
Neptune St CH41 66 D8
Ness Gr L32 29 C2
NESTON 86 D2
Neston Ave WA9 58 B4
Neston Gdns CH41 66 B8
Neston High Sch CH64 86 F1
Neston Rd CH63, CH64 86 F5
Neston Road Cotts
CH63 87 A6
Neston St L4 38 F1
Netherby St L8 67 F4
Netherfield WA8 84 E8
Netherfield Cl CH43 65 C4
Netherfield Rd N L5 52 E6
Netherfield Rd S L5, L6 52 F4
NETHERLEY 70 D5
Netherley Rd L35, L27 71 C3
NETHERTON 28 A5
Netherton Gn L30 27 F5
Netherton Grange L30 28 B3
Netherton Ind Est L30 38 F8
Netherton La L30 27 E5
Netherton Moss Prim Sch
L30 27 E3
Netherton Park Rd
L21 38 D8
Netherton Rd
Birkenhead CH46 64 E8
Bootle L20 38 D6
Liverpool L18, L19 69 A1
Netherton Way L20, L21,
L30 38 E8
Netherwood Rd L11 39 E2
Netley St L4 52 E8
Nettle Hill CH48 63 B3
Nettlestead Rd L11 40 A1
Neva Ave CH46 64 D8
Neverstitch Cl WN8 15 F2
Neverstitch Rd WN8 15 D2
Neville Ave
St Helens WA9 45 B2
Warrington WA2 61 D1
Neville Cl CH43 65 C4
Neville Rd
Bebington CH62 88 E8
Crosby L22 26 E1
Wallasey CH44 51 A4
Neville St WA12 46 A3
Nevill St PR8 4 B7
Nevin St 10 L6 53 A3
Nevison St 12 L7 53 B1
Nevitte Cl L28 55 A8
New Acres Cl CH43 65 C8
Newark Cl
Birkenhead CH43 65 C4
Huyton-w-R L36 55 D6
Litherland L30 28 B5
Newark St L4 38 F1
New Bank Pl WA8 72 B1
New Bank Rd WA8 72 B1
New Barn Ave WN4 35 C3
New Barnet WA8 72 F4
New Bartram Ct 9
L17 68 C4
New Bird St L1 90 B1
Newbold Cres CH48 63 E3
New Bold Ct WA9 59 A7
Newbold Gr L12 40 F2
Newborough Ave
Crosby L23 27 A4
9 Liverpool L18 68 F5
Newborough Cl WA5 60 E2
Newborough Sch L25 69 F3
NEW BOSTON 45 E7
Newbridge Cl
Birkenhead CH49 65 B3
Garswood WN4 34 D3
Warrington WA5 60 D2
NEW BRIGHTON 51 B8
New Brighton Prim Sch
CH45 51 C8
New Brighton Sta
CH45 51 A8

Newburn CH43 66 B5
Newburn Cl WN8 16 B5
Newburns La CH43 66 B3
Newburn St 7 L4 39 A2
Newbury Cl
Huyton-w-R L36 55 D1
Widnes WA8 73 A3
Newbury Rd WN8 16 B5
Newbury Way
Liverpool L12 54 E5
Wallasey CH46 49 F3
Newby Ave L35 57 A4
Newby Cl PR8 7 B3
Newby Ct L37 9 F3
Newby Dr
Huyton-w-R L36 55 C3
Skelmersdale WN8 16 B5
Newby Gr L12 40 C2
Newby Pl WA11 44 A8
Newby St L4 52 F8
New Carr La L31 19 E7
Newcastle Rd L15 69 A6
New Century Bldg 14 L3 90 A4
New Chester Rd
Bebington CH42, CH62 79 C5
Bebington, Eastham CH62 88 E7
Birkenhead CH41, CH42 66 F4
Newchurch Cl L27 70 F4
Newcombe St L6 53 B5
New Cotts L12 54 E8
New Court Way L39 13 F5
Newcroft Rd L25 69 F4
New Cross St
Prescot L34 56 D7
6 St Helens, Cowley Hill WA10 43 F4
1 St Helens WA10 43 F3
New Cswy L37, L38 18 B8
New Cut Cl PR8 8 A8
New Cut La
Knowsley L34 42 A8
Rainford L33, WA11 31 B1
Shirdley Hill L39, PR8 8 D6
Newdales Cl CH43 65 C8
Newdown Rd L11 40 D5
Newdown Wlk L11 40 D5
Newell Rd CH44, CH45 51 B5
Newenham Cres L14 54 E3
NEW FERRY 79 B7
New Ferry By-Pass CH62 79 B7
New Ferry Rd CH62 79 B8
Newfield Cl L23 27 C6
Newfields WA10 43 D4
Newfield Sch L23 27 B5
New Fold WN5 25 C4
New Fort Way L20 38 A6
New Foul La PR8 5 A4
NEWGATE 25 A6
Newgate Rd WN8 24 F7
New Glade Hill WA11 44 E6
New Grey Rock Cl 4 L6 53 B4
New Hall L10 39 F8
New Hall Dr PR8 5 C1
Newhall La CH47 63 B6
New Hall La L11 39 E1
New Hall Manor CH64 86 E6
Newhall St L1 90 C1
Newhaven Rd
Wallasey CH45 51 C7
Warrington WA2 61 B4
New Hedley Gr L5 52 C5
New Henderson St L8 67 E5
New Hey L12 54 B5
New Heyes CH64 86 E1
New Hey Rd CH49 65 C3
NEW HEYS 69 D1
New Heys Comp Sch L19 69 D1
New Heys Dr L18 69 D1
Newholme Cl L12 40 E3
Newhope Rd CH41 66 C7
Newhouse Rd L15 68 D7
New Hutte La L26 82 F7
Newick Pk 8 L32 29 C1
Newick Rd L32 29 C1
Newington L1 90 C3
New Islington L3 90 C4
New La
Haskayne L39 11 E3
Ormskirk L39 13 E2
Southport PR9 2 E3
Newland Cl WA8 72 C3
Newland Ct L17 68 C3
Newland Dr CH44, CH45 51 A4
Newlands Ct CH44 51 D4
Newlands Dr WA3 47 D8
Newlands Rd
Bebington CH63 79 B4
St Helens WA11 44 C7
Newling St CH41 66 C7
Newlyn Ave
Litherland L21 27 B1
Maghull L31 20 E1
Newlyn Cl CH47 48 E2
Newlyn Dr
Ashton-in-M WN4 35 B1
Skelmersdale WN8 24 D7
Newlyn Gdns WA5 74 D3
Newlyn Gr WA11 44 D7
Newlyn Rd
Hoylake CH47 48 E2
Liverpool L11 40 D5
Newlyn Wlk L11 40 D5
New Manesty's La L1 90 B3
Newman St L4 52 D7
Newmarket Gdns WA9 57 C6
New Market Rd L21 38 B7
New Meadow La L37 18 F8
New Mersey Ret Pk L24 81 F5
New Mill Stile L25 70 A3
Newmorn Ct L17 68 C2
New Park Prim Sch L6 53 B3
Newport Ave CH45 50 D7
Newport Cl CH43 65 C4
Newport Ct L5 52 C5
New Quay L3 52 B2
New Rd
Formby L37 10 A5
Liverpool L13 53 E5
Prescot L34 56 E7
New Red Rock View L6 53 B4
New Road Ct L13 53 E5
New School La CH66 89 B1
Newsham Cl WA8 72 B4
Newsham Dr L6 53 D5
Newsham Rd L36 71 A8
Newsham St L5 52 D5
News La WA11 23 F2
Newspaper Ho WA5 74 D3
New St
Ashton-in-M WN4 35 C4
Haskayne L39 12 B8
St Helens WA9 58 C7
Wallasey CH44 51 E2
Newstead Ave L23 26 B3
Newstead Dr WN8 16 B5
Newstead Rd
Hale WA8 83 F6
Liverpool L8 68 C7
Newstet Rd L33 30 C2
NEWTON 63 E2
Newton Bank Sch WA12 46 E4
Newton Cl L12 54 B8
Newton Com Hospl WA12 46 B2
Newton Cross La CH48 63 E2
Newton Ct L13 53 E1
Newton Dr
Skelmersdale WN8 16 B5
West Kirby CH48 63 E2
Newton Gr WA2 61 F3
Newton La WA12 46 E6
NEWTON-LE-WILLOWS 45 E3
Newton-le-Willows Com High Sch WA12 46 D5
Newton-le-Willows Prim Sch WA12 46 C3
Newton-le-Willows Sta WA12 46 E3
Newton Park Dr WA12 46 F3
Newton Park Rd CH48 63 E2
Newton Rd
Billinge WN5 33 F6
Golborne, Town of Lowton WA12, WA3 47 D5
Hoylake CH47 63 C7
Liverpool L13 53 E3
St Helens WA9 45 A3
Wallasey CH44 51 A4
Winwick WA2 61 A5
Newton St
Birkenhead CH41 66 C7
Southport PR9 5 A7
Newton Way
Birkenhead CH49 64 F5
Liverpool L3 52 F1
Newton Wlk 4 L20 38 B4
New Tower Ct CH45 51 C8
NEWTOWN 43 D4
Newtown Gdns L32 29 E2
Newway L14 55 A5
New Way L39 22 C2
New Way Bsns Ctr CH44 51 D2
Nicander Rd L18 68 F5
Nicholas Ct 8 L23 26 B3
Nicholas Rd
Crosby L23 26 B3
Widnes WA8 84 C8
Nicholas St 3 L3 52 D3
Nicholl Rd WA10 43 A5
Nicholls Dr CH61 76 F4
Nicholson St WA9 44 E4
Nickleby Cl L8 67 F5
Nickleford Hall Dr WA8 72 F6
Nicola Ct CH45 51 C6
Nicol Mere Dr WN4 35 A5
Nicol Mere Sch WN4 35 A5
Nicol Rd WN4 35 B5
Nidderdale Ave L35 57 D3
Nigel Rd CH60 86 C8
Nightingale Cl
Kirkby L32 29 B3
Liverpool L27 70 F5
Nightingale Rd L12 40 F3
Nimrod St L4 38 F1
Nine Tree Prim Sch L28 41 A1
Ninth Ave L9 39 D7
Nipe La WN8 24 B5
Nithsdale Rd L15 68 E6
Nixons La WN8 24 D7
Nixon's La PR8 7 E7
Nixon St L4 38 F2
NOCTORUM 65 E5
Noctorum Ave CH43 65 C4
Noctorum Dell CH43 65 D4
Noctorum La CH43 65 E5
Noctorum Rd CH43 65 E5
Noctorum Way CH43 65 D3
Noel Gate L39 13 B1
Noel St L8 68 C7
Nolan St PR8 4 C5
Nook La
Golborne WA3 47 B8
St Helens WA9 44 F1
Nook Rise L15 69 B8
Nook The
Birkenhead CH43 66 B5
Birkenhead, Frankby CH48 64 B2
Liverpool L25 70 C3
St Helens WA10 43 B6
Noonan Cl L9 38 F4
Noon Ct WA12 46 B1
Norbeck Ave L14 54 F2
Norbreck Ave L14 54 F2
Norburn Cres L37 9 F2
Norbury Ave
Bebington CH63 78 E5
Billinge WN5 33 D6
8 Liverpool L18 68 F5
Norbury Cl
Bebington CH63 78 F5
Kirkby L32 29 D2
Southport PR9 2 C5
Widnes WA8 73 E1
Norbury Fold L35 57 E1
Norbury Rd L32 29 D2
Norbury Wlk L32 29 D2
Norcliffe Rd L35 57 B4
Norcote Lo L37 9 E4
Norcott Dr WA5 59 F6
Norfield L39 13 F5
Norfolk Cl
Birkenhead CH43 65 C4
Bootle L20 38 D4
Norfolk Dr
Warrington WA5 74 E6
West Kirby CH48 63 C1
Norfolk Gr PR8 3 F1
Norfolk Pl
Bootle L21 38 A7
Widnes WA8 84 C8
Norfolk Rd
Longshaw WN5 25 E1
Maghull L31 28 C7
Southport PR8 3 F1
St Helens WA10 43 D1
Norfolk St L1 90 B1
Norgate St 16 L4 52 F7
Norlands Ct CH42 66 E1
Norland's La L35, WA8 72 F7
Norlands Pk WA8 72 F6
Norland St WA8 73 D1
Norley Ave CH62 88 E3
Norley Dr WA10 43 B3
Norley Pl L26 82 E7
Norman Ave
Haydock WA11 46 A7
Newton-le-W WA12 46 E3
Normandale Rd L4 39 D1
Normandy Rd L36 55 D3
Normanhurst L39 14 A4
Norman Pannell Sch L27 70 E5
Norman Rd
Bootle L20 38 C7
Crosby L23 26 D3
Wallasey CH44 51 E2
Norman Salisbury Ct 1 WA10 44 A4
Normans Rd WA9 58 F7
Norman St CH41 65 F8
Normanston Cl CH43 66 B4
Normanston Rd CH43 66 B4
Normanton Ave L17 68 C3
Norma Rd L22 26 E1
Normington Cl L31 20 C4
Norris Cl CH43 65 C4
NORRIS GREEN 39 F2
Norris Green Cres L11 39 F1
Norris Green Rd L12 54 B6
Norris Green Way 6 L11 40 A1
Norris House Dr L39 21 C8
Norris Rd L34 56 C6
Norris Way L37 10 B3
Norseman Cl L12 54 B8
Northam Cl PR9 2 A5
NORTH ASHTON 34 E6
North Atlantic Cl L36 55 E4
North Ave
Aintree L10 28 E2
Golborne WN7 36 F4
Liverpool L24 82 A7
North Barcombe Rd L16 69 D7
North Breeze Hill 8 L4, L9 38 F2
Northbrook Cl L8 68 A7
North Brooke Way CH49 65 A3
Northbrook Rd CH44 51 D3
Northbrook St L8 68 A7
North Cantril Ave L12 54 F8
North Cheshire Trad Est CH43 77 E8
North Cl CH62 79 C2
Northcote Cl 1 L5, L6 52 F4
Northcote Prim Sch L9 39 A3
Northcote Rd
Liverpool L9 38 F3
Northcote Rd *continued*
Wallasey CH45 50 D5
Northdale Rd L15 68 F8
North Dingle
Liverpool L4 52 D8
Liverpool L4 52 E7
North Dr
Heswall CH60 86 A7
Liverpool, Sandfield Park L12 54 B6
Liverpool, Victoria Park L15 69 A8
Wallasey CH45 50 F8
North Dunes L38 17 F4
NORTH END 18 B6
North End La
Hightown L38 18 A6
Liverpool L26 70 E3
Northern La WA8 72 A3
Northern Perimeter Rd L30 28 B5
Northern Rd L24 82 E5
Northern Rd The L23 26 F4
Northfield WN8 16 B4
Northfield Cl
Kirkby L33 30 A4
St Helens WA9 58 D3
Northfield Ct WN3 36 C1
Northfield Rd L20 38 E6
NORTH FLORIDA 45 D8
North Florida Rd WA11 45 D8
North Front L35 56 E1
Northgate Rd L13 54 A5
North Gr L18 69 C1
North Hill St L8 68 A6
North John St
Liverpool L2 90 A3
St Helens WA10 43 F3
3 St Helens WA10 44 A4
North Leach Dr PR8 7 A5
North Linkside Rd L25 70 C1
North Liverpool Acad L4 53 B7
North Manor Way L25 70 C2
North Meade L31 20 C2
Northmead Rd L19 81 E7
North Mersey Bsns Ctr L33 30 D4
North Moor La L39 12 F8
North Moss La L37 10 D7
North Mossley Hill Rd L17, L18 68 F3
North Mount Rd L32 29 C4
Northolt Ct WA2 61 E1
Northop Rd 8 CH45 51 A6
North Par
Hoylake CH47 63 B7
Kirkby L32 29 E2
Liverpool L24 82 E4
Neston CH64 86 B2
North Park Brook Rd WA5 60 E1
Northpark Ct CH44 51 E3
North Park Rd L32 29 C4
North Parkside Wlk L12 54 A8
North Perimeter Rd L33 30 D4
North Rd
Bebington CH65 89 E3
Birkenhead CH42 66 D3
Halewood L26 82 E6
Liverpool, Broad Green L13, L14 54 C2
Liverpool, Cressington Park L19 81 A6
Southport PR9 2 C4
St Helens WA10 43 F5
West Kirby CH48 63 A2
Northridge Rd CH61 77 A5
North St
Ashton-in-M WN4 35 D5
Haydock WA11 45 E6
Liverpool L1, L2, L3 90 B4
Newton-le-W WA12 45 F4
Southport PR9 4 C8
North Sudley Rd L17 68 E2
Northumberland Gr L8 67 D5
Northumberland St L8 67 E5
Northumberland Terr L5 52 E6
Northumberland Way L30 27 C3
North View
Huyton-w-R L36 56 A2
Liverpool L7 53 A1
Warrington WA5 74 E7
Northway
Heswall CH60 77 D1
Liverpool L15 54 B1
Maghull L31, L39 20 E4
Ormskirk L39 13 A1
Skelmersdale WN8 16 B2
Warrington WA2 61 B2
Widnes WA8 72 D1
Northway Prim Sch
Liverpool L15 54 B1
Maghull L31 20 E3
Northways CH62 79 D3
Northwich Cl L23 27 B6
North William St 5 CH44 51 E2
North Wirral Coastal Pk* CH46 49 E4
NORTHWOOD 30 A3
Northwood Ave WA12 46 F3
Northwood Rd
Birkenhead CH43 65 F1
Huyton-w-R L36 55 F4
Norton Ave WA5 74 E5
Norton Dr CH61 76 C7
Norton Gr
Maghull L31 28 D6
St Helens WA9 57 D7
Norton Rd CH48 63 A3
Norton St
Bootle L20 38 B5
Liverpool L3 90 C4
Norton Terr L20 38 B5
Norville Rd L14 54 C2
Norwich Ave
Ashton-in-M WN4 35 D3
Golborne WA3 47 D8
Norwich Dr CH49 65 A7
Norwich Rd L15 69 A6
Norwich Way L32 29 E2
Norwood Ave
Ashton-in-M WN4 34 F6
Golborne WA3 47 F7
Litherland L21 27 B1
Southport PR9 4 E7
Norwood Cres PR9 4 E7
Norwood Ct CH49 64 D3
Norwood Gdns PR9 4 F7
Norwood Gr
2 Liverpool L6 53 B4
Rainford WA11 32 A6
Norwood Prim Sch PR9 4 E7
Norwood Rd
Birkenhead CH49 64 D4
Southport PR8, PR9 4 F6
Wallasey CH44 51 B2
Norwyn Rd L11 39 E2
Nostell Rd WN4 35 A5
Notre Dame RC Coll L5 52 F7
Nottingham Cl L35 57 C5
Nottingham Rd L36 55 C1
Nowshera Ave CH61 76 F5
Nuffield Cl CH49 64 F4
Nugent House Sch WN5 33 D4
Nun Cl CH43 66 B3
Nunn St WA9 44 D3
Nunsford Cl L21 27 D2
Nunthorpe Rd L34 41 B5
Nurse Rd CH61 77 B6
Nurseries The L37 10 A2
Nursery Ave L39 14 A6
Nursery Cl
Birkenhead CH43 66 C3
Liverpool L25 82 C9
Widnes WA8 73 D3
Nursery Dr L37 9 F2
Nursery La L19 81 C7
Nursery Rd
Maghull L31 20 C4
St Helens WA9 57 D7
NUTGROVE 57 D6
Nutgrove Ave WA9 57 D7
Nutgrove Hall WA9 57 D6
Nutgrove Hall Dr WA9 57 D6
Nutgrove Methodist Prim Sch WA9 57 D7
Nutgrove Rd WA9 57 D7
Nuthall Rd PR8 4 F3
Nut St WA9 57 D7
Nuttall St L7 53 C1
Nyland Rd L36 55 E5

O

Oak Ave
Abram Brow WN2 36 C7
Birkenhead CH49 64 D6
Golborne WA3 47 B8
Haydock WA11 45 E7
Liverpool L9 39 B6
Newton-le-W WA12 46 D3
Ormskirk L39 13 D4
Oak Bank CH41 66 C5
Oakbank Rd L18 68 E5
Oakbank St CH44 51 C3
Oakbourne Cl 5 L17 68 C2
Oak Cl
Birkenhead CH46 64 D7
Liverpool L12 40 F1
Prescot L35 56 E3
Oak Cres WN8 15 D1
Oakcross Gdns L25 70 C2
Oak Ct 15 L8 68 A4
Oakdale Ave CH44 51 D2
Oakdale Cl 7 L32 29 C1
Oakdale Dr CH49 64 C2
Oakdale Rd
Crosby L22 26 D2
Liverpool L18 69 A5
Wallasey CH41, CH44 51 D2
Oakdene Cl CH62 88 D5
Oakdene Ct L35 57 D2
Oakdene Prim Sch L35 57 D2
Oakdene Rd
Birkenhead CH42 66 C3
Liverpool L4 53 B7
Oakenden Cl WN4 35 A6
Oakenholt Rd
Birkenhead CH46 64 E8
2 Wallasey CH46 49 E1
Oakes St L3 52 F2

Oak Farm L25 82 A8
Oakfield L4 53 B6
Oakfield Ave
Golborne WA3 35 F1
Liverpool L25 70 A4
Oakfield Cl WA9 57 D7
Oakfield Com Prim Sch WA8 84 B8
Oakfield Dr
Formby L37 9 D4
Huyton-w-R L36 70 F8
Widnes WA8 84 A8
Oakfield Gr L36 70 F8
Oakfield Rd
Bebington CH62 88 C8
Hightown L38 17 F2
Liverpool L4 53 A6
Oakfields L39 14 A5
Oakgate Cl L11 40 B3
Oak Gn L39 13 F5
Oak Grange L26 82 F9
Oakham Ct PR9 4 C8
Oakham Dr
Aintree L10 28 F1
Wallasey CH46 49 B1
Oakham St L8 67 E6
Oakhill Cl
Liverpool L12 40 D3
Maghull L31 20 D2
Oakhill Cottage La L31 20 D4
Oakhill Dr L31 20 D4
OAKHILL PARK 54 B2
Oakhill Pk L13 54 B2
Oakhill Rd
Liverpool L13 54 B3
Maghull L31 20 D3
Oakhurst Cl L25 70 B5
Oak La L12 40 C2
Oak La N L11, L12 40 D2
Oakland Cl L21 38 C6
Oakland Ct CH43 66 A5
Oakland Dr CH49 65 A6
Oakland Rd L19 80 F8
Oaklands
Bebington CH62 88 D6
Rainhill L35 57 C3
Oaklands Ave L23 26 E5
Oaklands Ct WA9 58 C4
Oaklands Dr
Bebington CH63 79 A6
Heswall CH61 77 A1
Oaklands Rd WA3 47 F7
Oaklands Terr CH61 77 A2
Oakland Vale CH45 51 C8
Oakleaf Mews CH43 65 D5
Oaklea Rd CH61 76 F6
Oaklee Gr L33 30 A4
Oakleigh WN8 24 D2
Oak Leigh L13 53 E5
Oakleigh Gr CH63 78 F6
Oakley Ave WN5 33 E6
Oakley Cl L12 40 E3
Oak Meadows Ct L35 57 E1
Oakmere Cl
Liverpool L9 39 A7
Wallasey CH46 49 E4
Oakmere Dr
Birkenhead CH49 64 C4
Warrington WA5 74 F3
Oak Rd
Bebington CH63 78 F7
Hooton CH66 88 E1
Huyton-w-R L36 70 D8
Prescot L35 56 E3
Warrington WA5 74 F3
Oakridge Cl CH62 79 C2
Oakridge Rd CH62 79 C2
Oaks Cl WA9 58 D3
Oaks Gdns WA5 74 E4
Oaks La CH61 77 A4
Oaksmeade Cl L12 40 F2
Oak St
Bootle L20 38 C4
Southport PR8 4 E6
St Helens WA9 58 E8
Oaks The
Bebington CH62 88 C8
Liverpool L12 40 F3
Southport PR8 3 F6
St Helens WA9 58 D4
Widnes WA8 73 D4
Oakston Ave L35 57 D2
Oaksway CH60 86 C6
Oak Terr L7 53 C2
Oakthorn Gr WA11 45 C6
Oak Tree Ct WN8 16 D3
Oaktree Pl CH42 66 F3
Oaktree Rd WA10 43 A5
Oak Vale L13 54 B2
OAK VALE PARK 54 B2
Oak View L24 83 A3
Oakwood WN8 16 D3
Oakwood Ave
Ashton-in-M WN4 35 A2
Southport PR8 7 D6
Oakwood Cl L25 70 B5
Oakwood Dr
Birkenhead CH43 65 E8
Huyton-w-R L36 55 F1
Southport PR8 7 E5
Oakwood Pk CH62 88 D5
Oakwood Rd L26 82 F8
Oakworth Cl L33 29 E4
Oakworth Dr
Bebington CH62 79 C7
Oakworth Dr *continued*
Huyton-w-R L36 71 A7
Oarside Dr CH45 51 A6
Oatfield La L21 27 B2
Oatlands Rd L32 29 C2
Oatlands The CH48 63 C1
Oban Dr
Garswood WN4 34 C4
Heswall CH60 86 A8
Oban Rd L4 53 B6
Oberon St L20 38 C1
O'Brien Gr WA9 44 E4
Observatory Rd CH43 65 E8
Oceanic Rd L13 53 F2
Ocean Pk CH44 51 D1
Ocean Plaza PR8 4 A8
Ocean Rd L21 38 B7
Ocean View 10 CH45 51 A8
O'Connell Cl WA11 45 C6
O'Connell Rd L3 52 D4
O'Connor Gr L33 29 E6
Octavia Ct L36 55 F1
Octavia Hill Rd L21 27 C1
October Dr L6 53 D6
Odsey St L7 53 C2
Odyssey Ctr CH41 66 C8
Off Botanic Rd PR9 2 A1
Ogden Cl L11 54 A8
Ogle Cl L35 56 E5
OGLET 82 E1
Oglet La L24 82 E1
Ogle Way L36 55 E5
Oil St L3 52 B4
O'Keeffe Rd WA9 44 C4
Okehampton Rd L16 69 D8
Okell Dr L26 70 D1
Old Acre L38 17 F3
Old Alder La WA2, WA5 60 D5
Old Barn Rd
6 Liverpool L4 53 B6
Wallasey CH44 51 A3
Old Bidston Rd CH41 66 B8
OLD BOSTON 46 A8
Old Boston WA11 46 A7
Old Boston Trad Est WA11 46 B8
Old Boundary Way L39 13 F6
Oldbridge Rd L24 82 F4
Old Chester Rd
Bebington CH42, CH63 78 F8
Birkenhead CH41, CH42 66 F2
Old Church Cl L9 39 B7
Old Church Yd
1 Liverpool L2 90 A3
Liverpool L3 52 B1
Old Clatterbridge Rd CH63 78 F2
Old Coach Rd WA7 84 F3
Old College Pl L7 53 C1
Old Colliery Rd L35 56 D3
Old Colliery Yd WN4 34 C3
Old Court House Rd CH62 79 D5
Old Dover Rd L36 70 C8
Old Eccleston La WA10 43 C3
Old Engine La WN8 15 C2
Oldershaw Sch The CH45 51 A5
Old Farm Rd
Crosby L23 26 F4
Kirkby L32 40 F6
Oldfield L35 56 F4
Oldfield Cl CH60 76 E2
Oldfield Cotts CH60 76 C2
Oldfield Dr CH60 76 D2
Oldfield Gdns CH60 76 D1
Oldfield La CH48 64 A5
Oldfield Rd
Heswall CH60 76 D1
Liverpool L19 81 A8
Wallasey CH45 50 F6
Oldfield St WA10 43 F5
Oldfield Way CH60 76 E1
Old Fire Station The 12 L17 68 C4
Oldgate WA8 84 C7
Old Gorsey La CH41, CH44 51 C1
Old Greasby Rd CH49 64 F5
Old Hall L35 71 E8
Old Hall Cl L31 28 D7
Old Hall Dr WN4 35 A2
Old Hall Farm Bsns Pk PR9 5 A5
Old Hall Gdns WA11 32 A7
Old Hall La L32 29 D2
Old Hall Rd
Bebington CH62 79 F1
Maghull L31 28 D7
Old Hall St L2, L3 90 A4
Oldham Pl L1 90 C3
Oldham St L1 90 C2
Old Haymarket L1 90 B4
Old Hey Wlk WA12 46 C1
Old Higher Rd WA8 83 D5
Old Hutte La L26 83 A6
Old Kennel Cl L12, L14 54 F8
Old La
Formby L37 9 F6
Haskayne L39 11 E3
Heswall CH60 86 D8
Maghull L31 20 E4
Prescot L34, L35 56 F6
Rainford WA11 31 F7
Rainhill L35 57 B3
Old Leeds St L3 52 B2
Old Links Cl PR9 5 B8
Old Lodge Cl L12 54 B8
Old Maryland La CH46 49 E1
Old Mdw L34 41 C4
Old Meadow Rd CH61 76 E4
Old Mill Ave WA9 58 D5
Old Mill Cl
Heswall CH60 86 B7
Liverpool L15 69 A8
Old Mill Hill L39 13 D3
Old Mill La
Formby L37 9 F4
Knowsley L34 41 E4
Liverpool L15 69 A8
Old Mill Lane Cotts L34 41 E4
Old Moss La L39 11 C5
Old Nook La WA11 44 E6
Old Orch L35 56 E1
Old Park La PR9 5 A8
Old Penny La WA11 46 B8
Old Post Office Pl 1 L1 90 B3
Old Prescot Cl L31 21 C2
Old Pump La CH49 64 C3
Old Quarry The L25 70 A2
Old Racecourse Rd L31 28 B8
Old Rd WN4 35 A4
Old Rectory Gn
Aughton L39 21 A7
Sefton L29 27 F7
Old Riding L14 54 F5
Old Roan Sta L30 28 B3
Old Ropery 6 L2 90 A3
Old Rough La L33 29 F2
Old Sch L31 29 A5
Old School House La WA2 61 A7
Old School Pl WN4 35 A3
Old School The L29 27 E6
Old School Way CH41 65 E7
OLD SWAN 54 A3
Old Thomas La L14 54 D1
Old Town Cl WN8 23 D8
Old Town Ct L37 9 E4
Old Town La L37 9 E4
Old Town Way WN8 23 D8
Old Upton La WA8 72 E4
Old Wargrave Rd WA12 46 C3
Old Whint Rd WA11 45 A6
Old Wood Rd CH61 76 F3
Oleander Dr WA10 43 C4
Olga Rd WA9 58 C7
OLGET 82 E1
Olinda St CH62 79 B7
Olive Cl L31 29 A2
Olive Cres CH41 66 E4
Olivedale Rd L18 68 F5
Olive Gr
Huyton-w-R L36 55 D2
Litherland L30 28 A1
Liverpool L15 54 A1
Skelmersdale WN8 15 E1
Southport PR8 4 E7
Olive La L15 69 A8
OLIVE MOUNT 54 A1
Olive Mount
Birkenhead CH41 66 E4
St Helens WA10 43 D2
Olive Mount Hts L15 69 A8
Olive Mount Rd L15 69 A8
Olive Mount Wlk L15 69 B8
Olive Rd L22 37 E8
Oliver La CH41 66 E6
Oliver Lyme Ho 6 L34 56 E6
Oliver Lyme Rd L34 56 E6
Oliver Rd WA10 57 C8
Oliver St E CH41 66 E6
Oliver St CH41 66 D6
Olivetree Rd L15 54 B1
Olive Vale L15 68 F8
Olivia Cl CH43 65 C4
Olivia Mans 4 L36 56 A2
Olivia Mews CH43 65 C4
Olivia St L20 38 D1
Olivia Way L36 56 B2
Ollerton Cl CH43 65 C4
Ollerton Pk WA5 59 E7
Ollery Gn L30 28 B4
Olney St L4 38 F2
Olton St L15 68 E8
Olympia St L6 53 A3
Olympic Way L30 39 B8
Omega Bvd WA5 59 D1
O'Neill St L20 38 B4
Onslow Cres PR8 4 A2
Onslow Rd
Bebington CH62 79 B8
Liverpool L6 53 C3
11 Wallasey CH45 51 B8
Ontario Cl L27 70 E5
Opal Cl
Litherland L21 38 C8
Liverpool L6 53 B3
Opco Complex L24 82 B6
Openfields Cl L26 70 E2
Oppenheim Ave WA10 57 C8
Orange Gr
Liverpool L8 68 C6
Warrington WA2 61 E2
Orange Tree Cl L28 55 B8
Oran Way L36 55 D3
Orb Cl L11 40 C3
Orb Wlk 3 L11 40 C4
Orchard Ave L14, L16 54 D1
Orchard Cl
Eccleston Park L34 57 A7
Orchard Cl *continued*
Prescot L35 56 E1
St Helens WA11 44 D7
Orchard Ct
Birkenhead CH41 66 F3
Maghull L31 20 F1
Orrell WN5 25 D3
Orchard Dale L23 26 F4
Orchard Dene L35 57 C3
Orchard Gdns L35 71 E8
Orchard Grange CH46 64 C7
Orchard Hey
Litherland L30 28 B4
Maghull L31 28 E8
St Helens WA10 43 A3
Orchard La PR8 7 D4
Orchard Lo 1 L39 13 F6
Orchard Rd CH46 49 E1
Orchard St WN4 35 C3
Orchards The
3 Orrell WN5 25 E5
Southport PR8 7 D4
Orchard The
Huyton-w-R L36 55 E2
Liverpool L17 68 F1
Ormskirk L39 13 D5
Wallasey CH45 51 A7
Orchard View L39 13 D1
Orchard Way
Bebington CH63 78 D6
Widnes WA8 72 A3
Orchid Cl WN8 25 B6
Orchid Gr L17 67 F3
Orchid Way WA9 59 B7
O'Reilly Ct L3 52 C4
ORFORD 61 D2
Orford Cl
Golborne WA3 47 A7
Hale L24 83 E2
Orford Gn WA2 61 D1
Orford St L15 68 F8
Oriel Cl
Aintree L10 28 D3
2 Liverpool L2 90 A3
Oriel Cres L20 38 C1
Oriel Dr L10 28 D3
Oriel Lo L20 38 C2
Oriel Rd
Ashton-in-M WN4 34 F4
Birkenhead CH42 66 E3
Bootle L20 38 C2
Liverpool L20 38 C1
Oriel St L3 52 C3
Orient Dr L25 70 B3
Origen Rd L16 54 D1
Oriole Cl WA10 57 B7
Orion Bvd WA5 59 E1
Orith Ave WA10 42 F3
Orkney Cl
St Helens WA11 44 D7
Widnes WA8 73 E3
Orlando Cl CH43 65 C4
Orlando St L20 38 C1
Orleans Rd L13 54 A3
Ormande St WA9 44 B1
Orme Ho L39 14 A5
Ormerod Ct CH63 79 A5
Ormesby Gdns WA9 57 E6
Ormesby Gr CH63 88 B6
Ormiston Rd CH45 51 B7
Ormond Ave L40 14 E4
Ormond Cl WA8 72 C2
Ormonde Ave L31 28 C7
Ormonde Cres L33 30 A2
Ormonde Dr L31 28 C8
Ormond Mews CH43 65 C4
Ormond St
Liverpool L3 90 A4
Wallasey CH45 51 B5
Ormond Way CH43 65 C4
Ormsby St L15 68 E7
Ormside Gr 7 WA9 58 D7
ORMSKIRK 13 C6
Ormskirk Bsns Pk 2 L39 13 F6
Ormskirk CE Prim Sch L39 14 A6
Ormskirk Coll L39 13 E5
Ormskirk & District General Hospl L39 14 A4
Ormskirk Ind Pk L39 14 A6
Ormskirk Lathom Park CE Prim Sch L40 15 A8
Ormskirk Old Rd L39 22 F7
Ormskirk Rd
Aintree L10, L30, L9 28 B2
Bickerstaffe L39 22 E7
Knowsley L34 41 D4
Rainford WA11 23 D1
Rainford WA11 31 E7
Skelmersdale, Tanhouse WN8 24 D7
Skelmersdale WN8 15 C1
Up Holland WN8 25 A7
Ormskirk Sch L39 14 B5
Ormskirk St WA10 44 A3
Ormskirk Sta L39 13 F5
Orms Way L37 9 E3
Orphan Dr
Liverpool L6, L3 53 D4
Liverpool L7 53 D3
Orphan St L7 68 A8
ORRELL
Bootle 38 D6
Wigan 25 D6
Orrell Gdns WN5 25 F6
Orrell Hey L20 38 D7
Orrell Hill La L38 18 C4
Orrell Holgate Prim Sch WN5 25 E5
Orrell La L20, L9 38 F7
Orrell Lo L20 38 E6
Orrell Mount L20 38 C7
Orrell Newfold Com Prim Sch WN5 25 D4
ORRELL PARK 38 F5
Orrell Park Sta L9 39 A6
ORRELL POST 25 E7
Orrell Rd
Bootle L20, L21 38 C7
Orrell WN5 25 E7
Wallasey CH45 51 C7
Orrell St WA9 44 C3
Orrell Sta WN5 25 E4
Orrell Water Pk* WN5 25 E4
Orret's Meadow Rd CH49 65 B3
Orrets Meadow Sch CH46 64 F8
Orrysdale Rd CH48 63 A3
Orry St L5 52 D5
Orsett Rd L32 40 F8
Orston Cres CH63 79 B2
Ortega Cl CH62 79 C7
Orthes St L3 52 F1
Orton Rd L16 69 C8
Orton Way WN4 34 F3
Orville St WA9 58 F7
Orwell Cl
Formby L37 9 D1
St Helens WA9 58 A3
Orwell Rd L4 52 D8
Osbert Rd L23 26 B4
Osborne Ave
Wallasey CH45 51 B7
Warrington WA2 61 D1
Osborne Ct
Bebington CH62 79 B6
St Helens WA10 57 C8
Osborne Gr
Huyton-w-R L34 56 A5
Wallasey CH45 51 B6
Osborne Ho L15 69 A8
Osborne Rd
Ashton-in-M WN4 35 A4
Birkenhead CH43 66 B5
Formby L37 9 E1
Golborne WA3 47 E7
Litherland L21 27 C1
Liverpool L13 53 E6
Southport PR8 7 B6
St Helens WA10 43 A5
Wallasey CH45 51 C7
Osborne Vale 8 CH45 51 B7
Osborne Wood L17 68 D1
Osbourne Cl CH62 88 E7
Osmaston Rd CH42 66 A1
Osprey Cl
Liverpool L27 70 F5
Warrington WA2 61 E3
Ossett Cl CH43 65 C4
Osterley Gdns L9 38 F6
O'Sullivan Cres WA11 44 E5
Oteley Ave CH62 88 D8
Othello Cl L20 38 C1
Otterburn Cl CH46 64 B8
OTTERSPOOL 68 D1
Otterspool Dr L17 80 D8
Otterspool Rd L17 68 D1
Otterton Rd L11 40 C5
Ottery Cl PR9 2 A5
Ottley St L6 53 C3
Oulton Cl
Birkenhead CH43 65 E2
Maghull L31 20 B4
Oulton Gdns WA9 57 E6
Oulton La L36 70 D8
Oulton Rd L16 69 D6
Oulton Way CH43 65 E3
Oundle Dr L10 28 C3
Oundle Pl L25 82 B8
Oundle Rd CH46 49 E1
Our Lady Immaculate RC Prim Sch
Downall Green WN4 34 E6
Liverpool L5 52 E6
Our Lady of Compassion RC Prim Sch L37 10 A3
Our Lady of Good Help RC Prim Sch L15 69 A8
Our Lady of Lourdes RC Prim Sch PR8 4 A1
Our Lady of Lourdes RC Sch CH46 50 B4
Our Lady of Mount Carmel RC Prim Sch L8 67 F5
Our Lady of Perpetual Succour RC Prim Sch WA8 84 A8
Our Lady of Pity RC Prim Sch CH49 64 D2
Our Lady of the Assumption RC Prim Sch L25 70 B6
Our Lady of Walsingham RC Prim Sch L30 27 F2
Our Lady Queen of Peace RC High Sch WN8 15 F4
Our Lady Queen of Peace RC Prim Sch L21 27 B2
Our Lady & St Edward's RC Prim Sch CH41 66 B8
Our Lady & St Philomena's RC Prim Sch L9 39 F4
Our Lady & St Swithin's RC Prim Sch L11 40 C5

Our Lady's Bishop Eton RC Prim Sch L18 ... 69 C5
Our Lady's RC Prim Sch L34 ... 56 D7
Our Lady Star of the Sea RC Prim Sch L21 ... 38 A6
Outer Forum L11 ... 39 E2
Out La L25 ... 70 B3
Outlet La L31, L39 ... 21 F1
Outlook The L38 ... 17 F4
Oval Sports Ctr The CH63 ... 78 F7
Oval The CH45 ... 50 F6
Overbrook La L34 ... 41 C5
Overbury St L7 ... 68 B8
Overchurch Inf Sch CH49 ... 64 F6
Overchurch Jun Sch CH49 ... 64 F6
Overchurch Rd CH46, CH49 ... 64 E6
Overdale Ave CH61 ... 77 D5
Overdale Prim Sch L33 ... 29 F4
Overdale Rd CH64 ... 88 A1
Overdene Wlk L32 ... 29 F1
Overgreen Gr CH46 ... 49 D1
Overstrand CH48 ... 63 A2
Overton Ave L21 ... 27 B1
Overton Cl
- Birkenhead CH43 ... 65 F3
- Kirkby L32 ... 29 D1
Overton Rd CH44 ... 51 B4
Overton St L7 ... 53 B1
Overton Way CH43 ... 65 F3
Ovington Dr PR8 ... 4 E3
Ovolo Rd L13 ... 54 A4
Owen Ave L39 ... 13 F6
Owen Cl WA10 ... 43 D1
Owen Dr L24 ... 82 B4
Owen Rd
- Knowsley L33 ... 41 C7
- Liverpool L4 ... 52 D8
- Rainhill L35 ... 57 C2
Owen's La L39 ... 11 E2
Owen St WA10 ... 43 D1
Owlsfield WA12 ... 46 E3
Oxborough Cl WA8 ... 72 F4
Oxbow Rd L12 ... 54 E8
Oxendale Cl L8 ... 68 B7
Oxenham Rd WA2 ... 61 A3
Oxenholme Cres L11 ... 40 A1
Oxford Ave
- Bootle L20 ... 38 E3
- Litherland L21 ... 38 B8
Oxford Cl L17 ... 68 C2
Oxford Ct
- Crosby L22 ... 26 C2
- [6] Southport PR8 ... 3 F4
Oxford Dr
- Crosby L22 ... 26 C2
- Halewood L26 ... 83 A8
- Heswall CH63 ... 86 F6
Oxford Gdns PR8 ... 3 E4
Oxford Ho L20 ... 38 E3
Oxford Rd
- Bootle L20 ... 38 D3
- Crosby L22 ... 26 C1
- Huyton-w-R L36 ... 56 A3
- Liverpool L9 ... 39 B8
- Orrell WN5 ... 25 F8
- Skelmersdale WN8 ... 15 E1
- Southport PR8 ... 3 E4
- Wallasey CH44 ... 51 C4
Oxford St E L7 ... 53 A1
Oxford St
- Liverpool L7 ... 52 F1
- Newton-le-W WA12 ... 46 B3
- St Helens, Cowley Hill WA10 ... 43 F5
- [2] St Helens WA10 ... 43 F4
Oxhouse Rd WN5 ... 25 D4
Ox La L35 ... 71 C6
Oxley Ave CH46 ... 50 B3
Oxley St WA9 ... 58 D7
Oxrton Lawn Apartments [2] CH43 ... 66 A4
OXTON ... 66 A4
Oxton Cl
- Kirkby L32 ... 40 B8
- Liverpool, Aigburth L17 ... 68 C2
- Widnes WA8 ... 72 C4
Oxton Ct CH43 ... 66 B4
Oxton Rd
- Birkenhead CH41 ... 66 C5
- Wallasey CH44 ... 51 B3
Oxton St Saviour's CE Prim Sch CH43 ... 66 A3
Oxton St L4 ... 52 F8

P

Pacific Chambers L2 ... 90 A3
Pacific Rd
- Birkenhead CH41 ... 66 F7
- Bootle L20 ... 38 B4
Packenham Rd L13 ... 53 F6
Padbury St L8 ... 68 A5
Paddington L7 ... 53 A1
Paddock Cl L23 ... 26 B6
Paddock Dr CH64 ... 86 D2
Paddock Gr WA9 ... 58 D3
Paddock Hey L27 ... 70 D6
Paddock Rd WN8 ... 24 C5
Paddock The
- Ashton-in-M WN4 ... 34 F6
- Birkenhead, Saughall Massie CH46 ... 64 C7

Paddock The *continued*
- Birkenhead, Upton CH49 ... 65 B5
- Formby L37 ... 10 A5
- Heswall CH60 ... 86 C8
- Kirkby L32 ... 40 D7
- Liverpool L25 ... 70 B4
- Ormskirk L39 ... 13 C3
- Prescot L34 ... 56 F7
- Southport PR8 ... 7 C4
Padeswood Cl WA9 ... 58 C6
PADGATE ... 61 F1
Padgate Com High Sch WA2 ... 61 F2
Padstow Cl
- Liverpool L26 ... 70 E1
- Southport PR9 ... 2 A5
- Warrington WA5 ... 74 E3
Padstow Dr WA10 ... 43 B6
Padstow Rd
- Birkenhead CH49 ... 64 C2
- Liverpool L16 ... 69 D8
Pagebank Rd L14 ... 55 A3
Page Ct L37 ... 9 F3
Pagefield Rd [1] L15 ... 69 A6
Page Gn L36 ... 55 C3
Page La WA8 ... 73 C1
PAGE MOSS ... 55 B3
Page Moss Ave L36 ... 55 B4
Page Moss La L14, L36 ... 55 A3
Page Moss Par L36 ... 55 B4
Page Wlk L3 ... 52 E3
Pagewood Cl CH43 ... 65 D4
Paignton Cl
- Billinge WN5 ... 33 E8
- Huyton-w-R L36 ... 56 B3
- Warrington WA5 ... 74 E4
Paignton Rd
- Liverpool L16 ... 69 D8
- Wallasey CH45 ... 50 F6
Paisley Ave
- Bebington CH62 ... 88 E4
- St Helens WA11 ... 44 E7
Paisley St L3 ... 52 B3
Palace Arc [1] WN4 ... 35 B3
Palace Rd
- Liverpool L9 ... 39 A6
- Southport PR8 ... 3 E5
Palatine Arc [10] WA10 ... 44 A3
Palatine Rd
- Bebington CH62 ... 79 C1
- Southport PR8 ... 3 F5
- Wallasey CH44 ... 51 D2
Palatine The [6] L20 ... 38 C3
Palermo Cl CH44 ... 51 D2
Paley Cl L4 ... 52 F7
Palin Dr WA5 ... 74 F6
Palladio Rd L13 ... 54 B4
Pall Mall L2, L3 ... 52 C3
Palm Ave WN4 ... 34 D5
Palm Cl L9 ... 39 C3
Palm Ct
- [10] Liverpool L8 ... 68 A4
- Skelmersdale WN8 ... 15 E2
Palmer Cl
- Birkenhead CH43 ... 65 D3
- [7] St Helens WA10 ... 43 F4
Palmerston Ave L21 ... 38 A7
Palmerston Cl L18 ... 68 F3
Palmerston Cres L19 ... 81 C6
Palmerston Ct L18 ... 69 A3
Palmerston Dr
- Bootle L21 ... 38 B7
- Liverpool L25 ... 82 D9
Palmerston Rd
- Liverpool, Garston L19 ... 81 C6
- Liverpool L18 ... 68 F3
- Southport PR9 ... 4 F6
- Wallasey CH44 ... 50 F4
Palmerston Sch L25 ... 69 E3
Palmerston St CH42 ... 66 F2
Palm Gr
- Birkenhead CH43 ... 66 B5
- Liverpool L25 ... 70 B1
- Southport PR8 ... 4 E6
Palm Hill CH43 ... 66 B4
Palmwood Ave L35 ... 57 D2
Palmwood Cl CH43 ... 65 E1
Paltridge Way CH61 ... 76 F4
Pamela Cl L10 ... 40 B6
Pampas Gr L9 ... 39 B4
Pankhurst Rd L21 ... 27 C2
Pansy St L5 ... 52 D7
Papillon Dr L9 ... 39 D8
Parade L3 ... 67 B8
Parade Cres L24 ... 82 E3
Parade St WA10 ... 44 A4
Parade The
- Liverpool L15 ... 54 B1
- Neston CH64 ... 86 B1
Paradise Gdns L15 ... 68 F7
Paradise La
- Formby L37 ... 10 A6
- Prescot L35 ... 56 D2
Paradise St
- Liverpool L1 ... 90 B2
- Liverpool L1 ... 90 B3
Paragon Cl WA8 ... 73 B5
Parbold Ave WA11 ... 44 D6
Parbold Ct WA8 ... 84 D8
Parbrook Cl L36 ... 55 D6
Parbrook Rd L36 ... 55 D5
Parchments The WA12 ... 46 D4
Parish CE Prim Sch WA10 ... 44 B4
Parish Mews [1] L14 ... 54 E4
Park Ave
- Crosby L23 ... 26 E5
- Eccleston Park L34 ... 57 A7

Park Ave *continued*
- Formby L37 ... 9 F1
- Golborne WA3 ... 35 F2
- Haydock WA11 ... 45 A6
- Liverpool, Fazakerley L9 ... 39 D7
- Liverpool L18 ... 68 E3
- Longshaw WN5 ... 25 E1
- Maghull L31 ... 20 D3
- Ormskirk L39 ... 13 E5
- Rainhill L35 ... 57 C4
- Southport PR9 ... 4 E8
- Wallasey CH44 ... 51 D3
- Widnes WA8 ... 73 B1
Park Ave N WA12 ... 46 C2
Park Ave S WA12 ... 46 C2
Parkbourn L31 ... 21 A2
Parkbourn Dr L31 ... 21 A2
Parkbourn N L31 ... 21 A2
Parkbourn Sq L31 ... 21 A2
Parkbridge Rd CH42 ... 66 C3
Park Brow Com Prim Sch L32 ... 41 A8
Park Brow Dr L32 ... 29 F1
Parkbury Ct CH43 ... 66 A3
Park Cl
- Birkenhead CH41 ... 66 C6
- Hightown L37 ... 17 E8
- Kirkby L32 ... 29 B3
Park Cres
- Haskayne L39 ... 11 F4
- Southport PR9 ... 1 D1
Park Ct
- [5] Crosby L22 ... 26 E1
- [2] Kirkby L32 ... 29 C3
- Liverpool L17 ... 68 B4
- West Kirby CH48 ... 63 A2
Parkdale CH48 ... 75 D6
Parkdale Ave L9 ... 39 A7
Park Dr
- Birkenhead CH41, CH43 ... 66 A7
- Birkenhead, Claughton CH41, CH43 ... 66 C6
- Crosby, Blundellsands L23 ... 26 A4
- Crosby, Thornton L23 ... 27 A7
Parkend Rd CH42 ... 66 C3
Parker Ave L21 ... 37 F7
Parker Cl L30 ... 28 B1
Parker Cres L39 ... 13 F7
Parker St L1 ... 90 B3
Parkfield Ave
- Birkenhead CH41 ... 66 D6
- Litherland L30 ... 28 A1
Parkfield Cl L39 ... 13 C4
Parkfield Dr CH44 ... 51 B4
Parkfield Gr L31 ... 20 C1
Parkfield Mews [8] L17 ... 68 C4
Parkfield Pl CH41 ... 66 D6
Parkfield Rd
- Bebington CH63 ... 79 A3
- Crosby L22 ... 26 F2
- Liverpool L17 ... 68 B4
Parkfields WN2 ... 36 B6
Parkfields La WA2 ... 61 F2
PARKGATE ... 86 C1
Parkgate Cl L17 ... 68 E1
Parkgate Ho
- Neston CH64 ... 86 B1
- Neston CH64 ... 86 B2
Parkgate La CH64 ... 86 F5
Parkgate Prim Sch CH64 ... 86 C1
Park Gr CH41 ... 66 D5
Park High Sch
- Birkenhead CH41 ... 66 A7
- Birkenhead, Claughton CH43 ... 66 B6
PARK HILL ... 23 D2
Park Hill Ct [12] L8 ... 67 F4
Parkhill Rd CH42 ... 66 C3
Park Hill Rd L8 ... 67 F4
Parkholme [4] L22 ... 26 E1
Parkhurst Rd
- Birkenhead CH42 ... 66 C2
- Liverpool L11 ... 39 F1
Park Ind Est WN4 ... 34 E3
Parkinson Rd L9 ... 39 A4
Park La
- Aintree L30 ... 39 A8
- Bootle L20 ... 38 E7
- Golborne WN2, WN7 ... 36 D6
- Litherland L30 ... 28 A1
- Liverpool L1 ... 90 B2
- Maghull L31 ... 20 F3
- Wallasey CH47 ... 49 A2
Parkland Cl [6] L8 ... 68 A5
Parkland Ct
- Birkenhead, Bidston CH43 ... 65 C8
- [6] Birkenhead, Woodchurch CH49 ... 65 A2
Parklands
- Knowsley L34 ... 41 E3
- Liverpool L17 ... 68 D2
- Rainford WA11 ... 31 F7
- Skelmersdale WN8 ... 16 D2
- Southport PR9 ... 4 E8
- Widnes WA8 ... 72 C3
Parklands Dr CH60 ... 86 C6
Parklands High Sch L24 ... 82 E4
Parklands Way L22 ... 26 E1
Park Lane Dr L31 ... 21 B2
Park Lane W L30 ... 27 F2
Park Link L39 ... 13 B1
Park Lodge Day Hospl L6 ... 53 D5

Park Pl
- Bootle L20 ... 38 C3
- Liverpool L8 ... 67 E6
Park Prim Sch CH44 ... 51 B3
Park Rd
- Bebington, Eastham CH62 ... 88 F6
- Bebington, Port Sunlight CH62 ... 79 B5
- Birkenhead CH42 ... 66 E3
- Crosby L22 ... 26 E1
- Formby L37 ... 9 E1
- Golborne WA3 ... 47 A7
- Heswall CH60 ... 86 B8
- Hoylake CH47 ... 48 F1
- Kirkby L32 ... 29 B3
- Liverpool L8 ... 67 F5
- Longshaw WN5 ... 25 F1
- Ormskirk L39 ... 13 E5
- Prescot L34 ... 56 C7
- Southport PR9 ... 1 D1
- Southport PR9 ... 4 D8
- St Helens WA9 ... 44 D4
- Wallasey CH44 ... 51 C3
- Warrington, Orford WA2 ... 61 D1
- Warrington WA5 ... 74 E6
- West Kirby CH48 ... 63 A2
- Widnes WA8 ... 73 B1
Park Rd E CH41 ... 66 C6
Park Rd N
- Birkenhead CH41 ... 66 B7
- Newton-le-W WA12 ... 46 E4
Park Rd S
- Birkenhead CH43 ... 66 B6
- Newton-le-W WA12 ... 46 D2
Park Rd W
- Birkenhead CH43 ... 66 A7
- Southport PR9 ... 1 C1
Park Road Com Prim Sch WA5 ... 74 E6
Parkside
- [1] Bootle L20 ... 38 C4
- Liverpool L17 ... 68 C3
- Wallasey CH44 ... 51 D3
Parkside Ave
- Ashton-in-M WN4 ... 34 F8
- Skelmersdale WN8 ... 23 D8
- St Helens WA9 ... 58 B3
Parkside Bsns Pk WA3 ... 47 A8
Parkside Cl
- Bebington CH63 ... 79 A5
- Liverpool L27 ... 70 E4
Parkside Cres WN5 ... 25 F6
Parkside Ct
- Southport PR9 ... 1 D1
- Widnes WA8 ... 73 A2
Parkside Dr L11, L12 ... 54 B8
Parkside Rd
- Bebington CH63 ... 79 A6
- Birkenhead CH42 ... 66 E3
- Golborne WA12, WA2 ... 47 B2
Parkside St L6 ... 52 F3
Park St
- Birkenhead CH41 ... 66 D6
- Birkenhead CH41 ... 66 E7
- Bootle L20 ... 38 D3
- Haydock WA11 ... 45 A6
- Liverpool L8 ... 67 E5
- St Helens WA9 ... 44 C4
- Wallasey CH44 ... 51 C4
Parks The WA12 ... 35 B1
Parkstile La L11 ... 40 C4
Parkstone Rd CH42 ... 66 C3
Park Terr L22 ... 37 E8
Park The
- Huyton-w-R L36 ... 55 E1
- Warrington WA5 ... 74 D3
Parkvale Ave CH43 ... 77 E8
Park Vale Rd L9 ... 39 A6
Parkview CH49 ... 65 A1
Park View
- Abram WN2 ... 36 B8
- Ashton-in-M WN4 ... 35 B2
- Bebington CH62 ... 88 C8
- Crosby, Thornton L23 ... 27 B7
- Crosby, Waterloo L22, L23 ... 26 D2
- Huyton-w-R L36 ... 55 C4
- Liverpool, Hartley's Village L9 ... 39 A4
- Liverpool L6 ... 53 D5
- Newton-le-W WA12 ... 46 E3
- Warrington WA2 ... 61 E3
Parkview Cl CH41 ... 66 C7
Parkview Ct CH60 ... 85 F8
Park View Ct L17 ... 68 E5
Parkview Dr L27 ... 70 E4
Park View Flats L21 ... 38 A8
Park View Prim Sch L36 ... 55 C4
Parkview Rd L11 ... 40 E5
Park W CH60 ... 85 E7
Park Wall Rd L29, L38 ... 19 B2
Parkway
- Crosby L23 ... 26 F2
- Heswall CH61 ... 76 F7
- Litherland L30 ... 27 F5
- Wallasey CH45 ... 50 E7
Park Way
- Formby L37 ... 9 F1
- Hoylake CH47 ... 48 E1
- Huyton-w-R L36 ... 55 D7
- Liverpool L8 ... 67 F7
Parkway Cl CH61 ... 76 F7
Park Way E L32 ... 29 B3
Park Way W L32 ... 29 B3
Parkwood Cl CH62 ... 88 E8

Parkwood Rd
- Liverpool L25 ... 70 A4
- Prescot L35 ... 56 E2
Parlane St WA9 ... 44 C4
Parle Ct [7] L6 ... 53 B5
Parliament Cl L1 ... 90 C1
Parliament Pl L8 ... 67 F7
Parliament St
- Liverpool L1, L8 ... 90 B1
- St Helens WA9 ... 57 D7
- Up Holland WN8 ... 25 C7
Parlington Cl WA8 ... 84 C7
Parlow Rd [4] L11 ... 53 E8
Parnell Rd CH63 ... 79 A2
PARR ... 44 F2
Parren Ave L35 ... 56 C1
Parr Gr
- Birkenhead CH49 ... 64 C4
- Haydock WA11 ... 45 A6
Parr Ind Est WA9 ... 44 E2
Parrmount Ct WA9 ... 44 C3
Parr Mount St WA9 ... 44 C3
Parrs Corner Trad Est L20 ... 38 C4
Parr's La L39 ... 13 D1
Parrs Rd CH43 ... 66 B3
Parr St
- Liverpool L1 ... 90 B2
- St Helens WA9 ... 44 B3
- [1] Widnes WA8 ... 73 C1
PARR STOCKS ... 44 D3
Parr Stocks Rd WA9 ... 44 D3
Parry St CH44 ... 51 D2
Parsonage Brow WN8 ... 25 A8
Parsonage Cl WN8 ... 25 A7
Parsonage Gn L24 ... 83 E1
Parsonage Rd WN8 ... 25 A7
Parson's Brow WA11 ... 31 E6
Parthenon Dr L11 ... 39 E2
Partington Ave L20 ... 38 E4
Parton St L6 ... 53 C3
Partridge Cl L12 ... 40 F3
Partridge Rd
- Crosby L23 ... 26 B4
- Kirkby L32 ... 29 B3
Part St PR8 ... 4 B6
Pass Way WA11 ... 44 C8
Pasture Ave CH46 ... 49 E2
Pasture Cl
- Ashton-in-M WN4 ... 34 E6
- Liverpool L25 ... 70 B1
- St Helens WA9 ... 58 C4
Pasture Cres CH46 ... 49 E2
Pasture La WA11 ... 32 A4
Pasture Lane Bsns Ctr WA11 ... 32 A4
Pasture Rd CH46 ... 49 D2
Pastures The
- Southport PR9 ... 2 D5
- St Helens WA9 ... 59 A7
- West Kirby CH48 ... 63 F2
Pateley Cl [2] L32 ... 29 C1
Pately Wlk L24 ... 82 F5
Paterson St CH41 ... 66 C6
Patmos Cl L5 ... 52 E6
Paton Cl CH48 ... 63 D3
Patricia Ave CH41 ... 50 F1
Patricia Ct [9] WA10 ... 43 F4
Patricia Gr L20 ... 38 D6
Patrick Ave L20 ... 38 E7
Patten's Cl L30 ... 27 D4
Patten St CH41 ... 66 B8
Patten's Wlk L34 ... 41 E5
Patterdale Ave WA2 ... 61 C2
Patterdale Cl PR8 ... 7 B3
Patterdale Cres L31 ... 20 E2
Patterdale Dr WA10 ... 57 B8
Patterdale Rd
- Ashton-in-M WN4 ... 35 A8
- Bebington CH63 ... 78 F3
- Liverpool L15 ... 68 F6
Patterson St WA12 ... 46 B3
Paul Cl WA5 ... 74 D6
Pauline Wlk L10 ... 40 B7
Paul McCartney Way [2] L6 ... 53 B3
Paul Orr Ct L3 ... 52 C4
Paulsfield Dr CH46, CH49 ... 64 E7
Paul's La PR9 ... 1 F3
Paul St L3 ... 52 D3
Paulton Cl [6] L8 ... 67 F4
Paveley Bank L27 ... 70 D6
Pavilion Cl L8 ... 68 B7
Pavilion Ct WA12 ... 46 A3
Paxton Pl WN8 ... 24 C4
Paxton Rd L36 ... 55 E4
Peacehaven WN8 ... 15 E1
Peacehaven Cl L16 ... 69 F8
Peach Gr
- Haydock WA11 ... 45 E7
- Kirkby L31 ... 29 B4
Peach St L3, L7 ... 52 F1
Peach Tree Cl L24 ... 83 E2
Pearce Cl L25 ... 69 F6
Pear Gr L6 ... 53 B3
Pearl Way L6 ... 53 B4
Pearson Dr L20 ... 38 E7
Pearson Rd CH41, CH42 ... 66 E5
Pearson St L15 ... 68 F8
Peartree Ave L12 ... 40 F1
Pear Tree Cl
- Hale L24 ... 83 E1
- Heswall CH60 ... 77 C1
Pear Tree Rd L36 ... 70 E8

Peasefield Rd L14 55 A4
PEASLEY CROSS 44 C1
Peasley Cross La WA9 44 C2
Peatwood Ave L32 40 F7
Peckers Hill Rd WA9 58 E7
Peckforton Cl L13 53 E6
Peckmill Gn L27 70 F4
Pecksniff Cl 4 L8 67 F5
Peebles Ave WA11 44 E6
Peebles Cl
Garswood WN4 34 C4
Kirkby L33 29 D6
Peel Ave CH42 66 F3
Peel Cl L35 56 E3
Peel Ho L15 68 E7
Peel House La WA8 73 B2
Peel Pl
Liverpool L8 67 F7
St Helens WA10 44 A5
Peel Rd
Bootle L20 38 A5
Skelmersdale WN8 24 E5
Peel St
Liverpool L8 68 A4
Newton-le-W WA12 46 A3
Runcorn WA7 84 F3
Southport PR8 4 F6
Peel Wlk L31 20 B2
Peet Ave
Ormskirk L39 13 D4
St Helens WA10 43 C3
Peet's La PR9 2 A1
Peet St L7 53 B1
Pelham Gr L17 68 C4
Pelham Rd CH44 51 A3
Pemberton Rd
Birkenhead CH49 65 B2
Liverpool L13 54 A3
Windy Arbour WN5 34 A8
Pembertons Ct 9 L34 56 E6
Pemberton St WA10 43 E3
Pembrey Way L25 82 D9
Pembroke Ave CH46 64 E7
Pembroke Cl WA10 43 E2
Pembroke Ct CH41 66 E4
Pembroke Gdns L3 52 F2
Pembroke Ho L6 53 C4
Pembroke Pl L3 52 F2
Pembroke Rd L20 38 C2
Pembroke St L3 52 F2
Pembury Cl L12 40 E3
Penarth Cl L7 68 B8
Pencombe Rd L36 55 C4
Penda Dr L33 29 E6
Pendennis Rd CH44 51 C3
Pendennis St L6 53 B5
Pendine Cl
Liverpool L6 53 C4
Warrington WA5 60 C2
Pendle Ave WA11 44 D5
Pendlebury St WA9 58 C3
Pendle Cl CH49 64 E6
Pendle Ct WN8 24 D3
Pendle Dr
Litherland L21 27 C4
Ormskirk L39 14 A6
Pendle Pl WN8 24 D4
Pendle Rd WA3 36 C1
Pendleton Gn L26 82 E8
Pendleton Rd 8 L4 39 A2
Pendle View L21 27 C4
Pendle Villas L21 27 C3
Penfold L31 20 E1
Penfold Cl L18 69 D5
Pengwern Gr L15 68 D8
Pengwern St 3 L8 68 A5
Pengwern Terr CH45 51 C7
Penhale Cl L17 68 B2
Peninsula Cl CH45 50 E8
PENKETH 74 D4
Penketh Com Prim Sch WA5 74 D4
Penketh Ct WA5 74 D4
Penketh Gn L24 82 E5
Penketh High Sch WA5 74 F5
Penketh Pl WN8 24 C5
Penketh South Com Prim Sch WA5 74 E3
Penkett Ct CH45 51 C6
Penkett Gdns CH45 51 C6
Penkett Gr CH45 51 C6
Penkett Rd CH45 51 C6
Penkford La WA5 45 D2
Penkford Sch WA12 45 E2
Penkford St WA12 45 E3
Penlake Ind Est WA9 58 E6
Penlake La WA9 58 F7
Penley Cres L32 29 B2
Penlinken Dr L6 53 C4
Penmann Cl L26 82 F8
Penmann Cres
Halewood L26 83 A7
Liverpool L26 82 F8
Penmark Cl WA5 60 C2
Penmon Dr CH61 76 F3
Pennant Ave L12 40 C1
Pennard Ave L36 55 D5
Pennine Cl WA9 44 E3
Pennine Dr WA9 44 F3
Pennine La WA3 36 C1
Pennine Pl WN8 24 B6
Pennine Rd
Bebington CH42 78 C8
Wallasey CH44 50 F4
Pennine Rd *continued*
Warrington WA2 61 E2
Pennine Way L32 29 C4
Pennington Ave
Bootle L20 38 E6
Ormskirk L39 13 E6
Pennington Ct 4 L39 13 F6
Pennington Dr WA12 46 E3
Pennington Flash Ctry Pk* WN7 36 F4
Pennington La WA5, WA9 45 D2
Pennington Rd L21 38 C6
Pennington St 2 L4 38 F2
Penn La WA7 84 F1
Pennsylvania Rd L13 53 D7
Pennyford Dr L18 68 E3
Penny La
Collins Green WA5 45 D1
Cronton L35, WA8 72 B6
Haydock WA11 46 B7
Liverpool L18 68 F5
PENNYLANDS 15 E1
Penny Lane Neighbourhood Ctr L15 69 A6
Pennystone Cl CH49 64 D6
Pennywood Dr L35 56 E2
Penpoll Ind Est L20 38 C6
Penrhos Rd CH47 63 A6
Penrhyd Rd CH61 76 D5
Penrhyn Ave
Bootle L21 38 B7
Heswall CH61 77 A6
Penrhyn Rd L34 41 B6
Penrhyn St L5 52 D5
Penrith Ave
Southport PR8 7 C3
Warrington WA2 61 C2
Penrith Cres
Ashton-in-M WN4 35 B4
Maghull L31 20 E2
Penrith Rd WA10 57 B7
Penrith St CH41 66 C5
Penrose Ave E L14 54 F2
Penrose Ave W L14 54 E2
Penrose Gdns WA5 74 D3
Penrose Pl WN8 24 E4
Penrose St L5 52 F6
Penryn Ave WA11 44 D7
Penryn Cl WA5 74 E3
Pensall Dr CH61 76 F2
Pensarn Gdns WA5 60 D2
Pensarn Rd L13 53 F2
PENSBY 76 F4
Pensby Cl CH61 77 A5
Pensby Hall La CH61 76 F2
Pensby High Sch for Boys CH61 76 D4
Pensby High Sch for Girls CH61 76 E3
Pensby Inf Sch CH61 76 F3
Pensby Jun Sch CH61 76 F3
Pensby Park Prim Sch CH61 76 E4
Pensby Rd CH61 77 A4
Penshaw Cl L14 55 A6
Pentire Ave WA10 43 B6
Pentire Cl L10 40 B6
Pentland Ave
6 Liverpool L4 39 A1
St Helens WA9 44 F3
Warrington WA2 61 B3
Pentland Pl WA2 61 B3
Pentland Rd L33 30 A4
Penuel Rd 10 L4 38 F2
Penvalley Cres L6 53 C4
Penwell Fold WN8 24 E8
Peony Gdns WA9 59 B7
Peover St L3 52 D3
Peploe Rd L4 39 D2
Peplow Rd L32 29 B2
Pepper St L24 83 D1
Pera Cl 16 L6 53 A3
Perch Pool La PR9 5 F4
Perch Rock* CH45 37 B2
Percival Ct 2 PR8 4 A6
Percival La WA7 84 E2
Percival Way WA10 43 D4
Percy Rd CH44 51 E2
Percy St
Bootle L20 38 B5
Liverpool L8 67 F7
St Helens WA9 58 F7
Percy Villas L9 39 A4
Perimeter Rd L33 30 E2
Perriam Rd L19 81 D8
Perrin Rd CH45 50 E5
Perrins Rd WA5 59 F6
Perrybrook Wlk WN4 35 D4
Perrygate Cl L7 68 B8
Perry St L8 67 D6
Pershore Gr PR8 7 A4
Pershore Ho CH42 66 B1
Pershore Rd L32 40 E8
Perth Ave WA9 57 E7
Perth Cl
Kirkby L33 29 D6
Warrington WA2 61 F3
Perth St L6 53 A3
Peterborough Dr L30 27 F4
Peterborough Rd L15 69 A6
Peterhouse Sch PR9 2 B3
Peterhouse Wlk WN4 34 F4
Peterlee Cl WA9 57 F7
Peterlee Way L30 28 A1
Peter Mahon Way L20 38 B4
Peter Price's La CH63 78 E4
Peter Rd
Liverpool L4 38 E1
Liverpool L4 38 F2
Petersfield Cl L30 28 A1
Peter's La L1 90 B3
Peter St
Ashton-in-M WN4 35 C3
Golborne WA3 47 A8
Liverpool L1 90 B4
St Helens WA10 43 F4
8 Wallasey CH44 51 E2
Peterstone Cl WA5 60 D2
Peterwood CH42 67 A1
Petham Ct WA8 72 E4
Petherick Rd L11 40 C5
Petre Ct L4 53 C7
Petunia Cl
Huyton-w-R L14 55 A4
St Helens WA9 59 A7
Petworth Ave WA2 61 B3
Petworth Cl L24 82 B5
Petworth Rd PR8 7 B6
Peveril St L9 38 F3
PEWFALL 34 C1
Pex Hill Ct WA8 72 E5
Pex Hill Visitor Ctr* WA8 72 E6
Pharmacy Rd L24 82 C6
Pheasant Field L24 83 C2
Pheasant Gr L26 70 E1
Philbeach Rd L11, L4 39 D2
Philharmonic Ct 5 L8 67 F8
Philip Dr PR8 7 F6
Philip Gr WA9 58 C7
Philip Leverhulme Lo 4 CH62 79 B6
Philip Rd WA8 84 B8
Philips Dr WA5 74 E7
Phillimore Rd L6 53 C3
Phillip Gr L12 54 F5
Phillips Cl L23 27 B6
Phillip's Cl L37 9 F2
Phillip's La L37 9 F2
Phillips St L3 52 C3
Phillips Way CH60 85 E8
Phipps' La WA5 59 E7
Phoenix Ave WA5 60 F2
Phoenix Brow WA9 44 B3
Phoenix Dr L14 55 B5
Phoenix Prim Sch L7 53 E2
Physics Rd L24 82 C6
Phythian Cl L6 53 B3
Phythian Cres WA5 74 F4
Phythian St
Liverpool L6 53 A3
St Helens WA11 44 F6
Picadilly WN5 33 E5
Pickerill Rd CH49 64 D3
Pickering Rake L30 27 D5
Pickering Rd CH45 51 B8
Pickering's Pasture (Nature Reserve)* WA8 84 B3
Pickerings Rd WA8 84 B5
Pickering St L6 53 A5
Pickmere Dr
Bebington CH62 88 F3
Bebington CH62 88 F4
Pickop St 6 L3 52 C3
Pickwick St L8 67 F6
Pickworth Way L31 29 B3
Picow Farm Rd WA7 84 E1
Picow St 2 WA7 84 F1
Picton Cl
Bebington CH62 88 E3
Birkenhead CH43 65 F4
Picton Cres L15 68 E8
Picton Gr L15 68 D8
Picton Rd
Crosby L22 26 D1
Liverpool L15 68 E8
Piele Rd WA11 45 E8
Piercefield Ct L37 10 A5
Piercefield Rd L37 9 F5
Pighue La
Liverpool L13 54 A1
Liverpool L13, L7 53 F1
Pigot St WA10 43 E3
Pigotts Rake L30 27 D5
Pike House Rd WA10 43 A5
Pikelaw Pl WN8 24 C5
Pike Pl WA10 43 B4
Pikes Bridge Fold WA10 43 A4
Pikes Hey Rd CH48 75 F7
Pilch Bank Rd L14 54 E4
Pilch La L14, L36 54 F3
Pilch La E L36 55 A2
Pilgrim Cl WA2 61 A6
Pilgrim St
Birkenhead CH41 66 F6
Liverpool L1 90 C2
Pilkington Rd PR8 4 D5
Pilkington St WA11 31 F6
Pilkington Tech Ctr L40 15 C6
Pilling Cl PR9 1 F5
Pilling La L31 20 A5
Pilling Pl WN8 24 C5
Pilot Gr L15 68 D8
Pimblett Rd WA11 45 E7
Pimblett St WA3 47 A7
Pimbley Gr E L31 28 C6
Pimbley Gr W L31 28 C6
Pimbo La WN8 24 F3
Pimbo Rd
Crank WA11, WN8 32 E7
Skelmersdale WN8 24 C5
Pimhill Cl L8 68 A6
Pimlico Rd WA7 84 E2
Pincroft Way 3 L4 52 D7
Pine Ave
Bebington CH63 78 F3
Newton-le-W WA12 46 D2
Ormskirk L39 13 F7
St Helens WA10 43 F6
4 Widnes WA8 73 B2
Pine Cl
Haydock WA11 45 C6
Huyton-w-R L36 55 D4
Kirkby L32 29 C3
Prescot L35 56 E3
Skelmersdale WN8 15 F1
Pine Crest L39 13 B2
Pine Ct
Birkenhead CH41 66 D6
11 Liverpool L8 68 A4
Pine Dale WA11 31 E7
Pinedale Cl CH43 65 D4
Pine Dr L39 13 F6
Pine Gr
Bootle L20 38 D4
Crosby L22 26 D2
Golborne WA3 47 C8
Ormskirk L39 13 F7
Southport PR9 4 D7
Pinehey CH64 86 D1
Pinehurst Ave
Crosby L22 26 C2
Liverpool L4 53 C7
Pinehurst Prim Sch L4 53 C7
Pinehurst Rd L4 53 C7
Pine Lo L4 53 B8
Pine Mews L1 90 C1
Pinemore Rd L18 69 A2
Pine Rd CH60 86 C8
Pineridge Cl CH62 79 C2
Pines The
Bebington CH63 79 B3
Liverpool L12 40 F4
Southport PR8 3 F6
Widnes WA8 73 D4
Pinetop Cl L6 53 C4
Pine Tree Ave CH43 65 C4
Pinetree Cl
Birkenhead CH46 64 F8
Litherland L30 27 F3
Pinetree Ct CH45 50 F5
Pinetree Dr CH48 63 D1
Pinetree Gr CH46 64 F8
Pine Tree Rd L36 70 D8
Pine View Dr CH61 77 A3
Pine Walks
Bebington CH42 78 B8
Birkenhead CH42 66 B1
Pinewalks Ridge CH63 78 C8
Pine Way CH60 76 E2
Pine Wlks CH48 63 D1
Pinewood
Ashton-in-M WN4 35 A2
Skelmersdale WN8 16 D3
Pinewood Ave
Formby L37 9 D1
Liverpool L12 40 D3
Pinewood Cl
Abram Brow WN2 36 C7
Formby L37 9 D2
Liverpool L27 70 E6
Southport PR8 5 C1
Pinewood Cres WN5 25 E6
Pinewood Dr CH60 86 B8
Pinewood Gdns L33 29 E5
Pinewood Rd WA5 59 F7
Pinfold CH47 63 A4
Pinfold Cl
Litherland L30 27 E5
Southport PR8 7 B3
Pinfold Cres L32 41 A8
Pinfold Ct
3 Crosby L23 26 D5
Prescot L35 56 E3
Pinfold Dr WA10 43 A3
Pinfold La
Knowsley L34 41 C3
Southport PR8 7 B3
West Kirby CH48 63 A4
Pinfold Pl WN8 24 D4
Pinfold Rd L25 82 C8
Pingot Rd WN5 33 E5
Pingwood La L33 30 A5
Pinnington Pl L36 55 E2
Pinnington Rd L35 56 E3
Pintail Cl WA11 44 B6
Piper's Cl CH60 85 D8
Piper's End CH60 85 D8
Piper's La CH60 76 C1
Pipers The
Golborne WA3 47 F8
Heswall CH60 76 D1
Pipistrelle Rise CH43 65 E4
Pipit Ave WA12 46 C3
Pipit Cl L26 70 E2
Pirrie Rd L9 39 D3
Pitch Cl CH49 64 D4
Pit Hey Pl WN8 24 C5
Pit La WA8 73 A4
Pit Pl L25 70 A2
Pitsmead Rd L32 29 E1
Pitts House La PR9 5 B8
Pitt St
Liverpool L1 90 B2
Southport PR9 4 F6
St Helens WA9 44 C3
St Helens WA9 44 C4
Pitville Ave L18 69 A3
Pitville Cl L18 69 A2
Pitville Gr L18 69 A3
Pitville Rd L18 69 A3
Pitville Terr WA8 84 C7
Plane Cl L9 39 C3
Plane Tree Gr WA11 46 A7
Planetree Rd L12 54 F8
Plane Tree Rd CH63 78 E5
Plantation Bsns Pk CH62 79 F2
Plantation Prim Sch L26 82 F9
Plantation Rd CH62 79 F2
Planters The
Birkenhead CH49 64 C4
Litherland L30 28 A4
Platt Gr CH42 79 A8
Platts St WA11 45 A6
Plattsville Rd L18 69 A5
Playfield Rd L12 54 F7
Playfield Wlk L12 54 F7
Pleasance Way WA12 46 D4
Pleasant Hill St L8 67 D6
Pleasant St
Bootle L20 38 B2
Liverpool L3 90 C3
Wallasey CH45 51 B7
Pleasant Street Prim Sch L3 90 C3
Pleasant View L20 38 B2
Pleasington Cl CH43 65 E4
Pleasington Dr CH43 65 E4
Plemont Rd L13 54 A5
Plex La L39 12 C5
Plex Moss La
Haskayne L39 11 D8
Southport PR8, L39, L37 7 E1
Plimsoll St 6 L7 53 B1
Plough La L40 15 A4
Plover Cl WA12 46 C3
Plover Way WA3 47 E8
Pluckington Rd L36 56 B3
Plumbers Way L36 55 F2
Plumer St
Birkenhead CH41 66 A8
Liverpool L15 68 E8
Plumley Gdns WA8 72 A1
Plumpton Cross 6 WA8 73 B2
Plumpton La L39 8 E2
Plumpton St L6 52 F4
Plum Tree Cl
Eccleston Park L35 57 A6
Huyton-w-R L28 55 B8
Plymyard Ave CH62 88 D5
Plymyard Cl CH62 88 D5
Plymyard Ct CH62 88 C6
POCKET NOOK 44 C4
Pocket Nook St WA9, WA10 44 C4
Pocklington Ct WA2 61 F1
Podium Rd L13 54 A4
Poets Cnr CH62 79 B5
Poets Gn L35 56 F3
Poleacre Dr WA8 72 D2
Polinda Gdns WA10 57 C8
Pollard Rd L15 54 A1
POLL HILL 76 F1
Poll Hill Rd CH60 76 F1
Pollitt Cres WA9 58 C3
Pollitt Sq CH62 79 C8
Polperro Cl
Liverpool L11 40 D5
Warrington WA5 74 E3
Pomfret St L8 68 A6
Pomona St L3 90 C3
Pond Cl L6 53 C4
Pond Green Way WA9 44 F1
Pond View Cl CH60 86 C8
Pondwater Cl 2 L32 29 E1
Pond Wlk WA9 45 A1
Ponsonby Rd CH45 50 E5
Ponsonby St L8 68 A6
Pontville Sch L39 13 D3
Pool Bank CH62 79 B6
Poolbank Rd CH62 79 B7
Poole Ave WA2 61 B2
Poole Cres WA2 61 B2
Pool End WA9 44 F2
Poole Rd CH44 51 D5
POOL HEY 5 B3
Pool Hey L28 55 B8
Pool Hey La PR8, PR9 5 B3
Pool La
Bebington CH62 79 D5
Birkenhead, Woodchurch CH49 65 A2
Poolside Wlk PR9 2 C4
Pool St
Birkenhead CH41 66 D7
Southport PR9 2 D5
Poolwood Rd CH49 65 B3
Pope St L20 38 B5
Poplar Ave
Birkenhead CH49 64 F5
Crosby L23 26 F5
Downall Green WN4 34 D5
Newton-le-W WA12 46 D3
St Helens WA10 43 A4
Warrington WA5 74 E3
Poplar Bank
Huyton-w-R L36 55 E2
Southport PR9 1 D1
Poplar Cl L26 71 A1
Poplar Ct 7 L8 68 A4
Poplar Dr
Bebington CH63 79 A4
Kirkby L32 29 D3
Liverpool L5 53 A5

Poplar Dr *continued*
Skelmersdale WN8 15 F1
Poplar Farm Cl CH46 64 C6
Poplar Gr
Haydock WA11 45 C6
Prescot L35 56 E5
Seaforth L21 37 F6
St Helens WA10 43 C3
Poplar Rd
Birkenhead CH43 66 B4
Haydock WA11 45 C6
Liverpool L25 70 A3
Poplars Ave
Warrington, Hulme WA2 61 C3
Warrington, Winwick Quay WA2 61 A4
Poplars Pl WA2 61 D2
Poplar St
Golborne WA3 36 B1
Southport PR8 4 E6
Poplars The WA3 36 B1
Poplar Terr 5 CH45 51 B7
Poplar Way
3 Huyton-w-R L36 56 A2
Liverpool L4 52 D8
Poppleford Cl L25 70 D5
Poppy Cl
Southport PR8 4 B2
Wallasey CH46 50 A2
Poppy La L39 14 B1
Poppy Rd L23 27 B5
Porchester Rd L11 39 F1
Porchfield Cl L11 40 B3
Porlock Ave
Liverpool L16 69 E5
St Helens WA9 58 C5
Porlock Cl
Heswall CH60 86 B6
Warrington WA5 74 E4
Portal Mews CH61 76 F3
Portal Rd CH61 76 F3
Portal Way L10, L11 40 C6
Portbury Cl CH62 79 C6
Portbury Way CH62 79 C6
Portbury Wlk CH62 79 C6
Port Cswy CH62 79 D4
Portelet Rd L13 53 F4
Porter Ave WA12 46 C5
Porter Cl L35 57 E1
Porter St L3 52 B4
Portgate Cl L12 40 C2
Porthcawl Cl WA8 72 C3
Portia Ave CH63 78 E7
Portia Gdns CH63 78 E7
Portia St 2 L20 38 C1
PORTICO 57 A8
Portico Ave L35 57 A6
Portico Ct L35 57 A6
Portico La L35 57 A6
Portland Ave L22 26 C2
Portland Cl WN2 36 A8
Portland Ct CH45 37 A1
Portland Ctr WA9 44 D1
Portland Gdns L3 52 C4
Portland Ho L17 68 B5
Portland Pl L5 52 E4
Portland Prim Sch CH41 66 A8
Portland St
Birkenhead CH41 66 A8
Liverpool L5 52 C4
Newton-le-W WA12 45 F4
Runcorn WA7 84 F3
Southport PR8 4 B5
Wallasey CH45 37 A1
Portland Way WA9 44 F1
Portlemouth Rd L11 40 C5
Portloe Ave L26 70 F1
Portman Rd L15 68 D7
Port of Liverpool Euro Rail Terminal L21 37 E7
Porto Hey Rd CH61 76 D5
Porton Rd L32 29 C1
Portreath Way WA10 43 B6
Portree Ave CH63 88 D5
Portree Cl L9 39 A5
Portrush Cl WA8 72 E3
Portrush St L13 53 E6
PORT SUNLIGHT 79 B5
Port Sunlight Sta CH62 79 B5
Portway L25 82 C8
Portwood Cl L7 68 B8
Post Office Ave 1 PR9 4 B7
Potter Pl WN8 24 D5
Potters La
Hale WA8 83 F5
Liverpool L18 69 C5
Pottery Cl L35 56 C3
Pottery Fields 1 L34 56 E6
Pottery La L35, L36 56 C3
Poulevara Ho L13 54 B2
Poulsom Dr L30 27 D3
Poulter Rd L9 39 B7
POULTON
Bebington 79 B2
Wallasey 51 B2
Poulton Bridge Rd CH41, CH44 51 A3
Poulton Cl L26 82 E7
Poulton Ct PR9 4 F7
Poulton Dr
7 Ashton-in-M WN4 34 F5
Widnes WA8 84 D8
Poulton Green Cl CH63 78 F1
Poulton Hall Rd
Bebington CH63 88 A7
5 Wallasey CH44 51 A3
Poulton Lancelyn Prim Sch CH63 79 A2
Poulton Prim Sch CH44 51 B3
Poulton Rd
Bebington CH63 79 A2
Southport PR9 4 F7
Wallasey CH44 51 C3
Poulton Royd Dr CH63 78 F2
Poulton Vale CH44 51 A2
Poverty La L31 28 F8
Povey Rd WA2 61 D1
Powderworks La L31 21 C3
Powell Dr WN5 33 D3
Powell St WA9 58 E7
Power Rd
Bebington CH62 79 F1
Bebington, Rock Ferry CH42 79 A8
Powis St L8 68 A5
Pownall Sq 7 L3 90 A4
Pownall St L1 90 B2
Poynter St WA9 57 E7
Pratt Rd L34 56 C6
Precinct CH63 79 A3
Precincts The 4 L23 26 E4
Precinct The CH62 79 D1
Preece Cl WA8 72 D4
Preesall Cl PR9 1 F4
Preesall Way L11 40 C5
Premier St
Liverpool L5 52 F5
2 Liverpool L5 53 A5
Prentice Rd CH42 66 E1
PRENTON 66 A1
Prenton Ave WA9 58 C4
Prenton Dell Ave CH43 78 A8
Prenton Dell Rd CH43 77 F8
Prenton Farm Rd CH43 78 A8
Prenton Gn L24 82 E4
Prenton Hall Rd CH43 65 F1
Prenton High Sch for Girls CH42 66 D1
Prenton La CH42 66 B1
Prenton Park Rd CH42 66 C2
Prenton Park (Tranmere Rovers FC) CH42 66 C2
Prenton Prep Sch CH43 66 B3
Prenton Prim Sch CH43 66 A1
Prenton Rd E CH42 66 D3
Prenton Rd W CH42 66 C2
Prenton Village Rd
Bebington CH43 78 A8
Birkenhead CH43 65 F1
Prenton Way CH43 65 D1
Prentonwood Ct CH42 66 C1
PRESCOT 56 C5
Prescot Dr L6 53 E3
Prescot Gn L39 13 D3
Prescot Mus★ L34 56 D6
Prescot Prim Sch L34 56 E6
Prescot Rd
Kirkby L31, L32 29 C6
Liverpool L6, L7, L13 53 E3
Ormskirk L31, L39 21 D6
St Helens WA10 43 D2
Tarbock Green WA8 71 F5
Widnes WA8 72 D2
Prescot Sch L34 56 C7
Prescot Sh Ctr 14 L34 56 D6
Prescot St
Liverpool L3, L7 52 F2
Wallasey CH45 51 A8
Prescot Sta L35 56 E5
Prescott Ave WA3 35 F2
Prescott Rd WN8 24 F4
Prescott St WA3 36 A1
Preseland Rd L23 26 E3
Presfield Sch PR9 2 A3
Prestbury Ave
Birkenhead CH43 65 E2
Southport PR8 7 B5
Prestbury Cl
Birkenhead CH43 65 E2
Widnes WA8 84 E8
Prestbury Dr WA10 43 B3
Prestbury Rd L11 39 F4
Preston Ave L34 56 C5
Preston Gr L6 53 C5
Preston New Rd PR9 2 B4
Preston Rd PR9 4 E8
Preston St
Liverpool L1 90 B4
St Helens WA9 58 A2
Preston Way L23 27 A4
Prestwick Cl WA8 72 F3
Prestwick Dr L23 26 C6
Prestwood Cres L14 54 F4
Prestwood Pl WN8 24 F4
Prestwood Rd L14 54 F4
Pretoria Rd
Ashton-in-M WN4 35 B4
Liverpool L9 39 B6
Price Gr WA9 45 A2
Price's La CH43 66 B4
Price St
Birkenhead CH41 66 D7
Liverpool L1 90 B2
Price Street Bsns Ctr CH41 66 C8
Pride Cl WA12 46 E2
Priesthouse Cl L37 10 A3
Priesthouse La L37 10 A3
Primary Ave L30 28 B4
Primrose Cl
Formby L37 10 B5
Primrose Cl *continued*
Southport PR9 2 C6
Warrington WA2 61 D2
Widnes WA8 72 E1
Primrose Ct
Huyton-w-R L36 55 E6
15 Wallasey CH45 51 B8
Primrose Dr L36 55 E5
Primrose Gr
Haydock WA11 45 E7
6 Wallasey CH44 51 E2
PRIMROSE HILL 12 F8
Primrose Hill
Bebington CH62 79 B6
Liverpool L3 90 B4
Primrose Rd
Birkenhead CH41 65 F7
Liverpool L18 69 C5
Primrose St L4, L5 52 D7
Primrose View WN4 35 C2
Primula Cl WA9 59 A7
Primula Dr
Golborne WA3 47 D8
Liverpool L9 39 B4
Prince Albert Ct 1 WA9 58 F8
Prince Albert Mews L1 90 C1
Prince Alfred Rd L15 69 A6
Prince Andrew's Gr WA10 43 C6
Prince Charles Gdns PR8 3 F4
Prince Edward St CH41 66 C7
Prince Edwin St L5 52 E4
Princes Ave
Bebington CH62 88 E6
Crosby L23 26 D4
Liverpool L8 68 A6
West Kirby CH48 63 B2
Princes Bvd CH63 78 E8
Princes Ct L8 68 B6
Princes Gate E 1 L8 68 B6
Princes Gate Ho 3 L8 68 B6
Princes Gate W 2 L8 68 B6
Princes Gdn PR8 4 E6
Princes Gdns L3 52 C3
Princes Par L3 52 B2
PRINCES PARK 68 B6
Princes Park Man L8 68 B5
Princes Pl WA8 72 E1
Princes Rd
Liverpool L8 68 A6
St Helens WA10 43 C1
Princess Ave
Ashton-in-M WN4 35 C3
Haydock WA11 46 A7
St Helens WA10 43 E6
Warrington WA5 74 E7
Princes Sch L8 68 A7
Princess Dr
Huyton-w-R L14, L36, L12 55 A5
Liverpool L14 54 F7
Princess Pavement 14 CH41 66 E6
Princess Rd
Ashton-in-M WN4 35 C3
10 Wallasey CH45 51 B7
Princes St
Bootle L20 38 B1
Liverpool L2 90 A4
Newton-le-W WA12 46 B3
Southport PR8 4 A6
Princess Terr CH43 66 C5
Princess Way L21 38 A7
Prince St
Ashton-in-M WN4 35 A5
Seaforth L22 37 E8
Princes Way
St Helens WA11 44 A8
Wallasey CH45 51 A6
Prince William St L8 67 E6
Prior Farm Cl L19 81 A7
Priors Cl L25 70 B2
Priorsfield CH46 64 E8
Priorsfield Rd L25 70 C2
Prior St L20 38 B6
Priorswood Pl WN8 24 F4
Priory Cl
Bebington CH63 79 A3
Formby L37 10 B2
Liverpool L17 68 B2
Prescot L35 56 C1
Priory Gdns
Southport PR8 3 F4
St Helens WA10 43 F7
Priory Gr L39 13 D4
Priory Grange PR8 4 A4
Priory Mews
Birkenhead CH41 66 F6
Southport PR8 3 F6
Priory Nook WN8 25 C7
Priory Parish CE Prim Sch The CH41 66 C7
Priory Rd
Ashton-in-M WN4 34 F5
Liverpool L4, L6 53 B7
Up Holland WN8 25 C7
Wallasey CH44 51 E3
West Kirby CH48 63 C2
Priory St
Birkenhead CH41 66 F6
Liverpool L19 81 D4
Priory The
Liverpool L15 53 F1
Neston CH64 86 E1
Priory The *continued*
Rainhill L35 57 C3
Winwick WA2 61 A7
Priory Way L25 70 B2
Priory Wharf CH41 66 F6
Pritchard Ave L21 37 F7
Pritt St L3 52 E3
Private Dr CH61 77 D5
Prizett Rd L19 81 B7
Probyn Rd CH45 50 E5
Procter Rd CH42 67 A1
Proctor Ct L30 27 D4
Proctor Rd
Formby L37 9 C4
Hoylake CH47 63 C6
Proctors Cl WA8 73 D2
Progress Pl 3 L2 90 A4
Promenade
Southport, Ainsdale-on-S PR8 6 F6
Southport PR9 1 C1
Southport PR9 4 B8
Promenade Gdns L17 68 A3
Prophet Wlk L8 67 F5
Prospect Ct L6 53 D3
Prospect Pl WN8 24 F5
Prospect Point L6, L7 52 F2
Prospect Rd
Birkenhead CH42 66 B1
St Helens WA9 44 D4
Prospect St 2 L7 53 A2
Prospect Vale
Liverpool L6 53 D3
Wallasey CH45 50 F5
Prospect Way L30 28 B3
Providence Cres L8 67 E6
Providence Ct 5 WA10 44 A4
Provident St WA9 45 A3
Province Rd L20 38 D6
Prussia St L3 90 A4
Pudsey St L3 90 C4
Pugin St L4 52 F7
Pulford Ave CH43 66 A2
Pulford Rd CH63 78 F5
Pulford St 9 L4 52 F7
Pullman Cl CH60 86 D8
Pumpfields Rd L3 52 C3
Pump La CH48, CH49 64 B4
Pump Rd CH41 66 E8
Punnell's La L31 19 F5
Purbeck Dr CH61 76 D7
Purdy Cl WA5 60 D1
Purley Gr L18 69 A2
Purley Rd 1 L22 26 C2
Purser Gr L15 68 D8
Pye Cl WA11 46 B8
Pyecroft Cl WA5 74 D6
Pyecroft Rd WA5 74 D6
Pye Rd CH60 86 A8
Pye's Cotts L39 20 E7
Pyes Gdns WA11 44 B7
Pyes La L36 55 C7
Pye St L15 69 A7
Pygon's Hill La L31 20 D6
Pym St L4 38 F2
Pyramids The CH41 66 D6

Q

Quadrangle The L18 69 B4
Quadrant The CH47 63 B6
Quail Cl WA2 61 D3
Quaker La CH60 76 E1
Quakers Alley L2 90 A4
Quakers Mdw L34 41 D4
Quarry Ave CH63 79 A4
Quarry Bank
Birkenhead CH41 66 D5
Kirkby L33 29 F3
Quarrybank St 20 CH41 66 C5
Quarrybank Workshops CH41 66 C5
Quarry Cl
Heswall CH61 76 F2
Kirkby L33 29 F3
Liverpool L13 54 A5
Quarry Ct
Heswall CH60 76 E1
Widnes WA8 72 C1
Quarry Dale L33 29 F3
Quarry Dr L39 13 C1
Quarry Gn L33 29 F3
Quarry Hey L33 29 F3
Quarry La CH61 77 A6
Quarry Mount L39 14 A6
Quarry Pl L25 69 F2
Quarry Rd
Bootle L20 38 E2
Crosby L23 27 A6
Liverpool L13 54 A5
Neston CH64 87 C1
Quarry Rd E
Bebington CH63 79 A4
Heswall CH60, CH61 76 F2
Quarry Rd W CH60 76 E1
Quarry St S L25 70 A2
Quarryside Dr L33 30 A3
Quarry St L25 69 F3
Quarry Way 6 L36 56 A2
Quartz Way L21 38 C8
Quayle Cl WA11 45 C6
Quebec Quay L3 67 C6
Quebec St WN2, WN7 36 E5
Queen Anne St
Liverpool L3 52 E3
Queen Anne St *continued*
Southport PR8 4 B7
Queen Ave 5 L2 90 A3
Queen Charlotte Villas PR8 7 C5
Queen Elizabeth Ct L21 38 A8
Queen Ind Bldgs L2 90 A3
Queen Mary's Dr CH62 79 B6
Queens Ave L37 9 E5
Queen's Ave
Ashton-in-M WN4 35 B3
Hoylake CH47 63 D8
Widnes WA8 84 B8
Queensberry St L8 67 F5
Queensbury CH48 63 D3
Queensbury Ave CH62 79 E1
Queensbury Way WA8 72 E3
Queen's Cl
Liverpool L19 81 C6
Runcorn WA7 84 F1
Queenscourt Rd L12 54 C5
Queens Croft L37 9 D2
Queens Ct
Hoylake CH47 63 B6
Liverpool, Everton L6 53 A5
2 Liverpool, Wavertree L15 54 C1
Ormskirk L39 13 E4
Queens Ctyd 7 PR9 4 C8
Queensdale Rd L18 69 A5
Queens Dock Commercial Ctr L1 90 B1
Queens Dr
Birkenhead CH43 66 A1
Golborne WA3 47 C8
Heswall CH60 85 E8
Liverpool L13 54 B4
Newton-le-W WA12 46 C5
St Helens WA10 43 C6
Queens Drive Mossley Hill L18 69 B5
Queens Drive Stoneycroft L13, L14 54 B3
Queens Drive Walton L4 39 B1
Queens Drive Wavertree L15 69 C7
Queens Drive West Derby L13 53 F7
Queens Gn L39 11 F5
Queens Hotel Ct PR9 4 B8
Queens Jubilee Nature Trail★ PR8 3 E5
Queensland Ave WA9 57 E7
Queensland Pl WA9 57 E7
Queensland St L7 68 B8
Queens Mews 11 L6 53 A5
Queens Park CE URC Prim Sch WA10 43 D4
Queens Pk CH60 85 D8
Queen Sq L1 90 B4
Queens Rd
Birkenhead CH42 67 A1
Crosby L23 26 E4
Haydock WA11 46 A7
Orrell WN5 25 C5
Prescot L34 56 E6
Southport PR9 4 C8
St Helens WA10 43 C1
Queen's Rd
Ashton-in-M WN4 35 B4
Bootle L20 38 C2
Formby L37 9 D2
Hoylake CH47 63 B7
Liverpool L6 53 A4
Runcorn WA7 84 F1
Wallasey CH44 51 E4
Queen St
Birkenhead CH41 66 E4
Golborne WA3 47 B8
Liverpool L19 81 C5
Newton-le-W WA12 46 B3
Ormskirk L39 13 E4
Seaforth L22 37 D8
St Helens WA10 44 A5
Wallasey CH44, CH45 51 B5
Queensway
Crosby L22, L23 26 F2
Heswall CH60 86 C6
Rainford WA11 32 A5
Runcorn WA7 84 F3
St Helens WA11 44 A8
Wallasey CH45 51 A6
Widnes WA8 84 F6
Queensway Entrance (Mersey Tunnel) L1 90 B4
Queensway (Mersey Tunnel) CH41 66 F7
Queens Wharf L3 90 A1
Queenswood Ave CH63 78 E7
Quernmore Rd L33 30 A3
Quernmore Wlk L33 30 A3
Quickswood Cl L25 69 F5
Quickswood Dr L25 69 F5
Quickswood Gn L25 69 F5
Quickthorn Cres L28 55 B7
Quigley Ave L30 28 A1
Quigley St CH41 66 E4
Quinesway CH49 65 A5
Quintbridge Cl L26 82 E9
Quinton Cl PR8 7 A4
Quorn St L7 53 B2

R

RABY 87 C4
Raby Ave CH63 . . . . 88 B6
Raby Cl
  Bebington CH63 . . . . 88 A7
  Heswall CH60 . . . . 85 F7
  Widnes WA8 . . . . 73 E2
Raby Ct CH60 . . . . 77 A1
Raby Dr
  Bebington CH63 . . . . 88 A6
  Birkenhead CH46 . . . . 64 D7
Raby Gr CH63 . . . . 78 D8
Raby Hall Rd CH63 . . . . . . 88 A6
RABY MERE 88 B7
Raby Mere Rd CH63 . . . . . 87 D5
Raby Park Rd CH64 . . . . . . 86 F1
Raby Rd CH63 . . . . 87 B5
Rachel St L5 . . . . 52 D4
Radburn Cl L23 . . . . 27 B5
Radburn Rd L23 . . . . 27 B5
Radford Ave CH63 . . . . 79 B2
Radford Cl WA8 . . . . 84 C7
Radlett Cl WA5 . . . . 74 E3
Radley Dr
  Aintree L10 . . . . 28 C3
  Heswall CH63 . . . . 86 F6
Radley La WA2 . . . . 61 E4
Radley Rd CH44 . . . . 50 F5
Radley's Ct **3** L8 . . . . 67 F6
Radley Wy 57 E7
Radmore Rd L14 . . . . 54 D3
Radnor Ave CH60 . . . . 76 F1
Radnor Cl L26 . . . . 82 E7
Radnor Dr
  Bootle L20 . . . . 38 E4
  Southport PR9 . . . . 1 F3
  Wallasey CH45 . . . . 51 C6
  Widnes WA8 . . . . 72 D2
Radnor Pl
  Birkenhead CH43 . . . . 66 C6
  Liverpool L6 . . . . 53 D5
Radstock Gr WA9 . . . . 58 D5
Radstock Rd
  Liverpool L6 . . . . 53 C3
  Wallasey CH44 . . . . 50 E5
Radway Rd L36 . . . . 55 F5
Raeburn Ave
  Bebington CH62 . . . . 88 E6
  West Kirby CH48 . . . . 63 C3
Raeburn Prim Sch
  CH62 . . . . 88 D6
Raffles Rd CH42 . . . . 66 D5
Raffles St L1 . . . . 90 C1
Rafter Ave L20 . . . . 38 E6
Raglan St L19 . . . . 81 C5
Railbrook Hey L13 . . . . . . 54 A1
Rail Cl WA11 . . . . 23 F2
Railside Ct L5 . . . . 52 C5
Railton Ave L35 . . . . 57 D2
Railton Cl L35 . . . . 57 D2
Railton Rd L11 . . . . 39 E2
Railway App L39 . . . . 13 F5
Railway Ave PR9 . . . . 2 F5
Railway Bldgs CH47 . . . . . 63 B6
Railway Cotts
  Hooton CH66 . . . . 88 E1
  Liverpool L25 . . . . 82 C8
Railway Path L39 . . . . 13 E4
Railway Rd
  Birkenhead CH42 . . . . 67 A1
  Golborne WA3 . . . . 36 B1
  Ormskirk L39 . . . . 13 F5
  Skelmersdale WN8 . . . . . 23 E8
Railway St
  Liverpool L19 . . . . 81 C5
  Newton-le-W WA12 . . . . . 46 B3
  Southport PR8 . . . . 4 B5
  St Helens WA10 . . . . 44 B4
Railway Terr PR8 . . . . 4 A5
Railway View WA5 . . . . . . 45 D1
Rainbow Cl WA8 . . . . 72 C3
Rainbow Dr
  Kirkby L31 . . . . 29 B4
  Liverpool L26 . . . . 82 E9
Raines Cl CH49 . . . . 64 E4
RAINFORD 32 B6
Rainford Ave L20 . . . . 38 E5
Rainford Brook Lodge
  Com Prim Sch WA11 . . . 32 A7
Rainford By-Pass
  WA11 . . . . 32 B3
Rainford CE Prim Sch
  WA11 . . . . 32 A6
Rainford Gdns **14** L2 . . . . 90 B3
Rainford High Tech Coll
  WA11 . . . . 32 C4
Rainford Ind Est WA11 . . . 32 C4
RAINFORD JUNCTION 23 F2
Rainford Rd
  Billinge WA11, WN5 . . . . . 33 C5
  Skelmersdale L39, WA11 . 23 C4
  St Helens WA10, WA11 . . 43 C6
Rainford Sta WA11 . . . . . . 23 F2
Rainham Cl L19 . . . . 81 C8
RAINHILL 57 D3
Rainhill High Sch L35 . . . . 57 E2
Rainhill Rd L35 . . . . 57 C5
Rainhill Sta L35 . . . . 57 C3
RAINHILL STOOPS 57 E1
Rake Cl CH49 . . . . 65 A4
Rake Hey CH46 . . . . 64 B8
Rake Hey Cl CH46 . . . . . . 64 C8

Rake La
  Birkenhead CH49 . . . . 65 A4
  Wallasey CH45 . . . . 51 B6
Rakersfield Ct CH45 . . . . . 51 C8
Rakersfield Rd CH45 . . . . . 51 C8
Rake The CH62 . . . . 88 C8
Raleigh Ave L35 . . . . 56 D2
Raleigh Cl WA5 . . . . 60 D1
Raleigh Rd
  Neston CH64 . . . . 86 F1
  Wallasey CH46 . . . . 50 B4
Raleigh St L20 . . . . 38 B1
Ralph's Wife's La PR9 . . . . 2 E6
Rame Cl L10 . . . . 40 B6
Ramford St WA9 . . . . 44 D2
Ramilies Rd L18 . . . . 68 F5
Ramleh Pk L23 . . . . 26 B3
Rampit Cl L19 . . . . 45 F7
Ramsbrook Cl L24 . . . . . . 82 C5
Ramsbrook La L24,
  WA8 . . . . 83 C3
Ramsbrook Rd L24 . . . . . . 82 C5
Ramsey Cl
  Ashton-in-M WN4 . . . . . . 35 B2
  Liverpool L21 . . . . 81 D8
  Prescot L35 . . . . 56 E3
  Widnes WA8 . . . . 73 E3
Ramsey Ct CH48 . . . . 63 B1
Ramsey Rd L19 . . . . 81 D8
Ramsfield Rd L24 . . . . 83 A4
Ramsons Cl L26 . . . . 70 E1
Randall Cl WA12 . . . . 46 B4
Randall Dr L30 . . . . 27 C3
Randle Ave WA11 . . . . 31 E8
Randle Brook Ct WA11 . . . 31 E8
Randle Cl CH63 . . . . 79 A2
Randles Rd L34 . . . . 41 A5
Randolph Ho CH41 . . . . . . 66 F6
Randolph St **12** L4 . . . . . 52 F7
Randon Gr **5** WA10 . . . . . 43 F4
Ranelagh Ave L21 . . . . 38 A8
Ranelagh Dr PR8 . . . . 7 F7
Ranelagh Dr N L19 . . . . . . 81 A8
Ranelagh Dr S L19 . . . . . . 81 A8
Ranelagh Pl L1 . . . . 90 C3
Ranelagh St L1 . . . . 90 B3
Ranfurly Rd L19 . . . . 81 B7
Range High Sch L37 . . . . . 17 C8
Rangemore Rd L18 . . . . . . 69 A1
Rankin St CH44 . . . . 51 A4
Rankin Way L21 . . . . 79 E1
Ranleigh Dr WN8 . . . . 16 A8
Ranmore Ave WN4 . . . . . . 34 D4
Ranslett Ct L37 . . . . 10 A3
Ranworth Cl L11 . . . . 39 E3
Ranworth Dr WA3 . . . . 47 E7
Ranworth Gdns WA9 . . . . . 57 D6
Ranworth Pl L11 . . . . 39 F3
Ranworth Rd WA5 . . . . 74 E6
Ranworth Sq L11 . . . . 39 F3
Ranworth Square Prim
  Sch L11 . . . . 39 F3
Ranworth Way L11 . . . . . . 39 F3
Rappart Rd CH44 . . . . 51 C5
Rashid Mufti Ct **6** L8 . . . 68 A6
Ratcliff Pl L35 . . . . 57 B4
Rathbone Rd
  Hightown L38 . . . . 17 F4
  Liverpool L15, L13 . . . . . . 68 F8
Rathlin Cl WA8 . . . . 73 E3
Rathmore Ave L18 . . . . . . 69 A3
Rathmore Cl CH43 . . . . . . 66 A3
Rathmore Cres PR9 . . . . . 2 B3
Rathmore Dr CH43 . . . . . . 66 A4
Rathmore Rd CH43 . . . . . . 66 A4
Raven Cl **15** L6 . . . . 53 A3
Ravendale Cl CH43 . . . . . . 65 D4
Ravenfield Cl L26 . . . . 82 E9
Ravenfield Dr WA8 . . . . . . 72 C3
Ravenglass Ave L31 . . . . . 20 D2
RAVENHEAD 43 E1
Ravenhead Ave L32 . . . . . 40 E7
Ravenhead Dr WN8 . . . . . . 25 A7
Ravenhead Foyer WA9 . . . 44 B1
Ravenhead Rd WA10 . . . . . 43 E1
Ravenhead Ret Pk
  WA9 . . . . 44 A2
Ravenhead Way WN8 . . . . 24 F6
Ravenhill Cres CH46 . . . . . 49 F4
Ravenhurst Way L35 . . . . . 56 D1
Raven Meols Hills Nature
  Reserve★ L37 . . . . 17 B7
Raven Meols Hills La L37 . . 9 F2
Raven Meols Lo L37 . . . . . . 9 E2
Ravenna Rd L19 . . . . 81 D8
Ravenscourt L26 . . . . 82 F8
Ravenscroft L37 . . . . 9 F2
Ravenscroft Ave L39 . . . . . 13 E4
Ravenscroft Com Prim
  Sch L33 . . . . 29 E5
Ravenscroft Rd **1**
  CH43 . . . . 66 C5
Ravensdale Cl WA2 . . . . . . 61 D3
Ravens The L37 . . . . 9 F2
Ravensthorpe Gn L11 . . . . 39 F3
Ravenstone Cl CH49 . . . . . 64 F7
Ravenstone Dr WA9 . . . . . 58 D7
Ravenstone Rd L19 . . . . . . 81 B8
Ravenswood Ave CH42 . . . 78 F8
Ravenswood Rd
  Heswall CH61 . . . . 77 A2
  6 Liverpool L13 . . . . . . 54 A3
Rawcliffe Cl WA8 . . . . 72 F4
Rawcliffe Rd
  3 Birkenhead CH42 . . . 66 D5
  Liverpool L9 . . . . 39 A4
Rawlinson Cres L26 . . . . . . 83 B8
Rawlinson Ct PR9 . . . . 4 D8

Rawlinson Gr PR9 . . . . 1 F1
Rawlinson Rd
  Liverpool L13 . . . . 54 A2
  Southport PR9 . . . . 1 E1
Rawlins St L7 . . . . 53 D3
Rawson Cl L21 . . . . 37 F7
Rawson Rd L21 . . . . 37 F7
Raydale Cl
  Golborne WA3 . . . . 36 E1
  Liverpool L9 . . . . 39 A3
Raymond Ave L30 . . . . 28 A1
Raymond Pl L5 . . . . 52 D4
Raymond Rd CH44 . . . . . . 51 C3
Raynham Rd L13 . . . . 53 F2
Reach The L3 . . . . 52 C3
Reade Cl CH63 . . . . 79 A1
Reading Cl L5 . . . . 52 D7
Reading St L5 . . . . 52 D7
Reads Ct L9 . . . . 38 F6
Reapers Way L30 . . . . 28 A4
Reay Ct CH44 . . . . 51 E3
Reay St WA8 . . . . 73 C2
Rebecca Gdns WA9 . . . . . . 58 C7
Recreation Ave WA9 . . . . . 35 D4
Recreation Dr WN5 . . . . . . 33 E5
Recreation St WA9 . . . . . . 44 D4
Rector Rd L6 . . . . 53 C7
Rectory Ave WA3 . . . . 47 C8
Rectory CE Prim Sch
  WN4 . . . . 34 D5
Rectory Cl
  Birkenhead CH42 . . . . 66 D4
  Heswall CH60 . . . . 85 F7
  Winwick WA2 . . . . 61 A6
Rectory Dr L26 . . . . 71 A1
Rectory Gdns WA9 . . . . . . 58 C6
Rectory La
  Heswall CH60 . . . . 85 E7
  Winwick WA2 . . . . 61 A6
Rectory Rd
  Downall Green WN4 . . . . 34 D5
  Southport PR9 . . . . 2 A1
  West Kirby CH48 . . . . 63 B1
Red Bank Ave WA12 . . . . . 46 F1
Red Barnes L37 . . . . 9 F5
Red Barn Rd WN5 . . . . 33 C6
Redbourne Ave L26 . . . . . . 82 F7
Redbourn Dr WA8 . . . . 72 B4
Redbourn St L6 . . . . 53 C6
Redbridge High Sch
  L10 . . . . 39 F8
Redbrook Cl CH62 . . . . 88 D6
Redbrook St L6 . . . . 53 C6
Redbrow Way **1** L33 . . . . 29 E4
Redburn Cl **2** L8 . . . . 68 A4
Redcap Cl CH45 . . . . 50 E8
Redcar Cl PR8 . . . . 4 F3
Redcar Dr CH62 . . . . 88 D5
Redcar Mews **7** L6 . . . . . 53 C6
Redcar Rd CH45 . . . . 50 D6
Redcar St L6 . . . . 53 C6
Red Cat La WA11 . . . . 32 F5
Redcliffe CH45 . . . . 37 A1
Redcliffe Gdns L39 . . . . . . 13 E3
Redcote Ct CH48 . . . . 63 A1
Redcourt-St Anselm's Sch
  CH43 . . . . 66 A3
Redcroft **2** CH49 . . . . 64 C3
Red Cross St L2, L3 . . . . . . 90 A3
Red Cut La L33 . . . . 41 F8
Red Dale L26 . . . . 70 F1
Red Delph La WA11 . . . . . . 23 E1
Redditch Cl CH49 . . . . 64 C4
Redesdale Cl WA2 . . . . 61 E2
Redfern St L20 . . . . 52 C8
Redfield Cl CH44 . . . . 51 D4
Red Fold L39 . . . . 13 C2
Redford Cl CH49 . . . . 64 C4
Redford St L6 . . . . 53 C6
Redgate
  Formby L37 . . . . 10 A2
  Ormskirk L39 . . . . 13 D5
Redgate Ave L23 . . . . 27 A4
Redgate Dr
  Formby L37 . . . . 10 B2
  St Helens WA9 . . . . 44 D3
Redgate Prim Sch L37 . . . 10 A2
Redgate Rd WN4 . . . . 35 B6
Redgrave St **4** L7 . . . . . . 53 C2
Redhill Ave L32 . . . . 41 A8
Red Hill Rd CH63 . . . . 78 B5
Redhills Dr PR8 . . . . 4 F3
Redhouse Bank CH48 . . . . 63 A3
Redhouse La CH48 . . . . . . 63 A3
Redington Rd L19 . . . . 81 E8
Redland Ct WN2 . . . . 35 E7
Redland Rd L9 . . . . 39 B8
Red Lion Cl L31 . . . . 20 C1
Red Lion Sh Ctr L31 . . . . . 20 C1
Red Lomes L30 . . . . 27 D5
Redmain Gr WA3 . . . . 47 E8
Redmain Way L12 . . . . 40 F2
Redmayne Cl WA12 . . . . . . 46 B4
Redmere Dr CH60 . . . . 86 D8
Redmires Cl L7 . . . . 68 B8
Redmond St CH41 . . . . . . 66 E4
Redmoor Cres **3** L33 . . . . 29 E5
Redpoll Gr L26 . . . . 70 E2
Red Rock St L6 . . . . 53 B4
Red Rum Cl L9 . . . . 39 D8
Redruth Ave WA11 . . . . . . 44 D7
Redruth Rd L11 . . . . 40 D5
Red Sands L39 . . . . 13 D3
Redshank Cl WA12 . . . . . . 46 C4
Redstart Cl **7** WA3 . . . . . 47 E8
Redstone Cl CH47 . . . . 63 D8
Redstone Dr CH60 . . . . . . 76 C1

Redstone Pk **3** CH45 . . . . 51 A8
Redstone Rise CH43 . . . . . 65 D6
Redtail Cl WA7 . . . . 84 F3
Redvers Ave CH66 . . . . 89 A2
Redvers Dr L9 . . . . 38 F6
Redwald Cl L33 . . . . 29 F6
Redwing La L25 . . . . 70 A4
Redwing Way L26 . . . . 70 D2
Redwood Ave L31 . . . . 20 C3
Redwood Cl
  Birkenhead CH43 . . . . 65 F2
  Liverpool L25 . . . . 70 B5
Redwood Ct **8** L8 . . . . . . 68 A4
Redwood Dr
  Ormskirk L39 . . . . 13 D4
  St Helens WA11 . . . . 44 F5
Redwood Gr L20 . . . . 38 C4
Redwood Rd L25 . . . . 70 B5
Redwood Way L33 . . . . . . 29 F6
Reedale Cl L18 . . . . 69 A4
Reedale Rd L18 . . . . 69 A4
Reeds Ave E CH46 . . . . . . 49 F3
Reeds Ave W CH46 . . . . . . 49 F3
Reeds Brow WA11 . . . . 32 B8
Reeds La CH46 . . . . 49 F3
Reed's La WA11 . . . . 32 A3
Reeds Rd L36 . . . . 55 F4
Reeds The L39 . . . . 13 D6
Reedville CH45 . . . . 66 B5
Reedville Gr CH46 . . . . 49 F2
Reedville Rd CH63 . . . . . . 78 F5
Reeve Ct WA9 . . . . 57 C6
Reeves Ave L20 . . . . 38 E5
Reeves St WA9 . . . . 44 E3
Regal Cres WA8 . . . . 84 B8
Regal Dr WA10 . . . . 43 C5
Regal Rd L11 . . . . 40 C3
Regal Wlk L4 . . . . 52 F7
Regency Gdns PR8 . . . . 3 E4
Regent Ave
  Ashton-in-M WN4 . . . . . . 34 F5
  Haydock WA11 . . . . 45 B7
  Huyton-w-R L14 . . . . 54 E2
  Litherland L30 . . . . 27 F3
Regent Cl PR8 . . . . 3 F4
Regent Ct **12** PR9 . . . . 4 C8
Regent Mews PR9 . . . . 3 F4
Regent Pk L36 . . . . 55 E5
Regent Rd
  Bootle L20, L5 . . . . 38 B1
  Crosby L23 . . . . 26 D4
  Liverpool L20, L5 . . . . . . 52 B6
  Southport PR8 . . . . 3 F4
  Wallasey CH45 . . . . 50 D6
  Widnes WA8 . . . . 73 B1
Regents Cl CH61 . . . . 77 B6
Regents Rd WA10 . . . . 43 C1
Regent St
  Liverpool L3 . . . . 52 B4
  Newton-le-W WA12 . . . . . 46 A3
Regents Way CH63 . . . . . . 78 D8
Regina Ave L22 . . . . 26 C2
Reginald Rd WA9 . . . . 58 E6
Reginald Rd Ind Pk
  WA9 . . . . 58 E6
Regina Rd L9 . . . . 39 A6
Reigate Cl L25 . . . . 70 C3
Reins Croft CH64 . . . . 86 E1
Renacres La L39 . . . . 8 F6
Renaissance Way L24 . . . . 82 D6
Rendal Cl L5 . . . . 53 A5
Rendcombe Gn L11 . . . . . . 39 F3
Rendel Cl WA12 . . . . 46 D2
Rendelsham Cl CH49 . . . . . 64 E5
Rendel St CH41 . . . . 66 D7
Renfrew Ave
  Bebington CH62 . . . . 88 E5
  St Helens WA11 . . . . 44 E7
Renfrew St L7 . . . . 53 A2
Renfrey Cl L39 . . . . 13 E8
Rennell Rd L14 . . . . 54 C3
Rennie Ave WA10 . . . . 43 C4
Renown Way L24 . . . . 82 A7
Renshaw St L1 . . . . 90 C3
Renville Rd L14 . . . . 54 C2
Renwick Ave L35 . . . . 57 A4
Renwick Rd L9 . . . . 39 B5
Renwick Sq WA3 . . . . 34 F3
Repton Gr L10 . . . . 28 C2
Repton Rd L16 . . . . 69 D8
Reservoir Rd
  Birkenhead CH42 . . . . 66 B1
  Liverpool L25 . . . . 69 F3
Reservoir Rd N CH42 . . . . 66 B1
Reservoir St
  Liverpool L6 . . . . 53 A4
  St Helens WA9 . . . . 57 C7
Rest Hill Rd CH63 . . . . 78 C5
Retford Rd L33 . . . . 30 A2
Retford Wlk **5** L33 . . . . . . 29 F2
Reva Rd L14 . . . . 54 F3
Revesby Cl WA8 . . . . 72 D2
Rex Cohen Ct L17 . . . . 68 E5
Rexmore Rd L18 . . . . 69 A2
Rexmore Way L15 . . . . 68 E7
Reynolds Ave WA9 . . . . . . 45 B2
Reynolds Cl L6 . . . . 53 A4
Reynolds Way L25 . . . . 70 A3
Rhiwlas St L8 . . . . 68 A5
Rhodesia Rd L9 . . . . 39 C6
Rhodesway CH60 . . . . 86 B7
Rhona Cl CH63 . . . . 88 C4
Rhona Dr WA5 . . . . 74 E6
Rhosesmor Cl L32 . . . . 40 F6
Rhosesmor Rd L32 . . . . . . 40 F6
Rhuddlan Ct L13 . . . . 53 F2

Rhyl St
  Liverpool L8 . . . . 67 F5
  Widnes WA8 . . . . 84 F7
Rialto Cl **11** L8 . . . . 67 F7
Ribble Ave
  Maghull L31 . . . . 20 E2
  Rainhill L35 . . . . 57 C3
  Southport PR9 . . . . 2 C4
Ribble Cl WA8 . . . . 73 E3
Ribble Cres WN5 . . . . 33 C3
Ribbledale Rd L18 . . . . 69 A4
Ribble Ho L25 . . . . 70 C3
Ribble Rd L25 . . . . 70 C3
Ribbler's La
  Kirkby L32 . . . . 40 E7
  Kirkby L34 . . . . 40 F6
Ribblesdale Ave **2** L9 . . . . 39 B7
Ribblesdale Cl CH62 . . . . . 88 F5
Ribble St CH41 . . . . 50 F1
Ribchester Way L35 . . . . . 71 A7
Rice Hey Rd CH44 . . . . . . 51 C4
Rice La
  Liverpool L9 . . . . 39 A4
  Wallasey CH44 . . . . 51 D4
Rice Lane Jun Sch L9 . . . . 39 A5
Rice Lane Sta L9 . . . . 39 A5
Rice St L1 . . . . 90 C2
Richard Allen Way **5**
  L6 . . . . 52 F4
Richard Chubb Dr CH44,
  CH45 . . . . 51 D6
Richard Gr L12 . . . . 54 F5
Richard Hesketh Dr
  L32 . . . . 29 C2
Richard Kelly Cl L4 . . . . . . 53 D8
Richard Kelly Dr L4 . . . . . . 39 D7
Richard Kelly Pl L4 . . . . . . 53 D8
Richard Martin Rd L21 . . . 27 C1
Richard Rd L23 . . . . 26 A5
Richards Gr WA9 . . . . 44 E4
Richardson Rd CH63 . . . . . 78 E4
Richardson St L7 . . . . 68 C2
Richland Rd L13 . . . . 53 F5
Richmond Ave
  Haydock WA11 . . . . 45 B7
  Litherland L21 . . . . 38 A8
Richmond Cl
  Bebington CH63 . . . . 79 A6
  Hightown L38 . . . . 17 F2
  St Helens WA10 . . . . 42 F4
Richmond Cres L30 . . . . . . 27 F3
Richmond Ct
  Bootle L21 . . . . 38 B7
  5 Crosby L23 . . . . 26 E5
  Widnes WA8 . . . . 73 D4
Richmond Gdns WA12 . . . 46 C2
Richmond Gr L31 . . . . 20 E3
Richmond Pk L6 . . . . 53 C5
Richmond Rd
  Ashton-in-M WN4 . . . . . . 34 F5
  Bebington CH63 . . . . 78 F6
  Crosby L23 . . . . 26 E5
  Southport PR8 . . . . 3 F2
Richmond Row L3 . . . . 52 E3
Richmond St
  Liverpool L1 . . . . 90 B3
  Wallasey CH45 . . . . 37 B1
  Widnes WA8 . . . . 73 C1
Richmond Terr L6 . . . . 53 B5
Richmond Way
  Heswall CH61 . . . . 76 F2
  Heswall, Thingwall CH61 . . 77 A6
  Huyton-w-R L35 . . . . 71 A7
Rich View CH43 . . . . 66 B3
Rickaby Cl CH63 . . . . 88 C8
Rickman St L4 . . . . 52 D7
Rickman Way L36 . . . . 70 F8
Riddock Rd L21 . . . . 38 B6
Rides The WA11 . . . . 45 D4
Ridgeborne Cl WA5 . . . . . . 60 D2
Ridge Cl PR9 . . . . 2 C5
Ridgefield Rd CH61 . . . . . . 76 F5
Ridgemere Rd CH61 . . . . . 76 F5
Ridge The CH60 . . . . 76 D2
Ridgetor Rd L25 . . . . 70 A4
Ridgeview Rd CH43 . . . . . . 65 D3
Ridgeway L9 . . . . 47 E7
Ridgeway Dr L31 . . . . 20 D3
Ridgeway High Sch
  CH43 . . . . 65 D4
Ridgeway The
  Bebington CH63 . . . . 78 D8
  Cronton WA8 . . . . 72 C6
  Heswall CH60 . . . . 86 B7
  Hoylake CH47 . . . . 63 E7
  Liverpool L25 . . . . 70 A3
Ridgewell Ave **4** WA3 . . . 47 D8
Ridgewell Cl L21 . . . . 38 A7
Ridgewood Dr
  Heswall CH61 . . . . 76 F5
  St Helens WA9 . . . . 58 D6
Ridgewood Way L9 . . . . . . 39 A7
Ridgmont Ave L11 . . . . 39 F2
Riding Cl
  Haskayne L39 . . . . 11 F4
  St Helens WA9 . . . . 58 C4
Riding Fold L26 . . . . 70 D2
Riding Hill Rd L34 . . . . 41 D2
Riding Hill Wlk L34 . . . . . . 41 D2
Riding La
  Ashton-in-M WN4 . . . . . . 35 F5
  Haskayne L39 . . . . 11 E4
Ridings Hey CH43 . . . . 65 D4
Riding St
  Liverpool L3 . . . . 52 F2
  Southport PR8 . . . . 4 B6
Ridings The
  Birkenhead CH43 . . . . 65 D5

Ridings The *continued*
Southport PR9 2 A3
Ridley Gr CH48 63 A3
Ridley La L31 20 D1
Ridley Rd L6 53 C3
Ridley St CH43 66 C5
Ridsdale 2 WA8 84 C8
Ridsdale Lawn L27 71 A3
Riesling Dr L33 29 E5
Rigby Dr CH49 64 D2
Rigby Rd L31 20 B3
Rigby St
Ashton-in-M WN4 35 A3
Golborne WA3 47 A8
Liverpool L3 90 A4
St Helens WA10 43 F4
Riley Ave L20 38 D5
Rimington Ave WA3 36 C1
Rimmer Ave L16 55 A1
Rimmerbrook Rd L25 70 B7
Rimmer Cl L21 38 B7
Rimmer Gn PR8 5 D1
Rimmer Gr WA9 44 E3
Rimmer's Ave
Formby L37 9 E6
Southport PR8 4 B6
Rimmers Ct CH41 65 F7
Rimmer St L3 90 C4
Rimmington Rd L17 68 E2
Rimrose Bsns Pk L20 38 A4
Rimrose Rd L20 38 A4
Rimrose Valley Country Pk* L23 27 A3
Rimrose Valley Rd L23 27 B4
Rimsdale Cl L17 80 E7
Ringcroft Rd L13 54 B2
Ringley Ave WA3 35 F1
Ringo Starr Dr 4 L6 53 B3
Ringsfield Rd L24 83 A2
Ringway CH64 86 E1
Ringway Rd L25 70 C4
Ringways CH62 79 D3
Ringwood CH43 66 A3
Ringwood Ave L14 54 F2
Ringwood Ct CH43 66 A3
Rio Ct L34 56 D7
Rio Ho 8 L36 56 A2
Ripley Ave L21 27 B1
Ripley Cl L31 20 E1
Ripon Ave WA3 47 D8
Ripon Cl
Huyton-w-R L36 56 B3
Litherland L30 27 F1
Newton-le-W WA12 46 C5
Southport PR8 4 F3
Ripon Dr WN4 35 D2
Ripon Rd CH45 50 F6
Ripon St
Birkenhead CH41 66 E4
Liverpool L4 38 F1
Risbury Cl L11 39 F2
Rishton Cl 10 L5 53 A5
Rishton St 8 L5 53 A5
Ritchie Ave L9 39 C6
Ritherup La L35 57 C4
Ritson St L8 68 B6
Rivacre Rd CH62, CH65, CH66 89 C2
River Avon St
3 Liverpool L8 68 B7
1 Liverpool L8 68 C7
Riverbank Cl CH60 85 F6
Riverbank Rd
Bebington CH62 79 F4
Heswall CH60 85 E6
Liverpool L19 81 A7
River Cl L37 10 B1
River Gr CH62 79 B8
Rivermeade PR8 4 D4
Riverpark Gdns L8 67 E6
Riversdale Cl 8 L33 29 F4
Riversdale Ct
Liverpool L19 80 F8
West Kirby CH47 63 A3
Riversdale Mews
Liverpool L19 80 F8
West Kirby CH48 63 A2
Riversdale Rd
Liverpool L17, L19 80 F7
3 Seaforth L21 37 F7
Wallasey CH44 51 D4
West Kirby CH48 63 A2
Riverside
Bebington CH62 79 B5
Hightown L38 17 F4
Liverpool L12 40 E1
West Kirby CH48 75 B8
Riverside Cl L20 38 A5
Riverside Coll Halton Runcorn Campus WA7 84 E3
Riverside Dr L17 68 B2
Riverside Gr WA9 58 D7
Riverside Prim Sch CH44 51 E3
Riverside Trad Est WA5 74 D1
Riverside View L17 68 C1
Riverslea Rd L23 26 B2
Rivers St WN5 25 E6
River St CH41 66 D6
Riverview CH49 65 A1
River View
Bebington CH62 79 C8
9 Crosby L22 26 C2
Riverview Gdns 8 CH42 66 F2
Riverview Rd CH44 51 E3
Riverview Wlk 9 L8 67 F4
Riverwood Rd CH62 79 F1
Riviera Dr
Birkenhead CH42 66 D1
Liverpool L11 40 C4
Rivington Ave
Birkenhead CH43 65 E4
Golborne WA3 36 C1
St Helens WA10 43 F6
Rivington Cl PR8 4 A3
Rivington Dr
Bickershaw WN2 36 F8
Up Holland WN8 25 C7
Rivington Prim Sch WA10 43 E5
Rivington Rd
St Helens WA10 43 D4
Wallasey CH44 51 D3
Rivington St WA10 43 D3
RL Hughes Prim Sch WN4 35 A3
Roadside Ct WA3 47 C8
Roadwater Cl L25 70 B7
Robarts Rd L4 53 B6
Robbin's Bridge L31 20 E5
Robeck Rd L13 54 B1
Robert Dr CH49 64 E3
Robert Gr L12 54 E5
Roberts Ave WA11 45 A5
Roberts Dr L20 38 E7
Robertson St L8 67 E5
Roberts St L3 52 B3
Robert St
4 Birkenhead CH41 66 D7
Widnes WA8 73 B1
Robina Rd WA9 58 D8
Robins La WA9 58 D8
Robin's La WA11 33 A8
Robins Lane Com Prim Sch WA9 58 C8
Robinson Mews CH41 66 F6
Robinson Pl WA9 44 D3
Robinson Rd L21 27 C1
Robin Way CH49 65 B2
Rob La WA12 46 E5
Robsart St L5 52 E5
Robson Pl WN2 36 B8
Robson St
Liverpool, Everton L5 52 F6
Liverpool, Old Swan L13 54 A1
Robson Way 3 WA3 47 F8
ROBY 55 C2
Roby Cl L35 57 C4
Roby Ct L36 55 D1
Roby Mount Ave L36 55 D2
Roby Park Prim Sch L36 55 A3
Roby Rd
Huyton-w-R, Bowring Park L14, L36 54 F1
Huyton-w-R L36 55 C2
Roby St
Bootle L20 38 C4
Liverpool L15 68 E7
St Helens WA10 43 D1
Roby Sta L36 55 C2
Roby Well Way WN5 33 D5
Rocastle Cl 17 L6 53 A3
Rochester Ave L30 27 F1
Rochester Cl WA3 47 A8
Rochester Gdns WA10 43 D1
Rochester Rd CH42 67 A1
Rock Ave CH60 76 F1
Rock Bank CH49 65 A5
Rockbank Rd L13 53 F5
Rockbourne Ave L25 69 F5
Rockbourne Gn L25 69 F5
Rockbourne Way L25 69 F5
Rock Cl CH42 66 F2
ROCK FERRY 66 F1
Rock Ferry By-Pass CH42 67 A2
Rock Ferry High Sch CH42 78 F8
Rock Ferry Prim Sch CH42 66 F2
Rock Ferry Sta CH42 66 F2
Rockfield Cl WA8 72 D2
Rockfield Gdns 2 L31 20 C2
Rockfield Rd L4 53 A7
Rockford Ave L32 40 E7
Rockford Cl L32 40 E7
Rockford Wlk L32 40 E7
Rock Gr L13 54 A3
Rockhill Rd L25 70 B2
Rockhouse St L6 53 C5
Rockingham Ct 4 L33 29 F4
Rock La
Aintree L31 28 F5
Widnes WA8 72 F4
Rock La E CH42 67 A2
Rockland Rd
Crosby L22 26 E2
Wallasey CH45 50 F7
Rocklands Ave CH63 79 A7
Rocklands La CH63 87 C8
Rock La W CH42 66 F1
Rockley St 8 L4 52 E8
Rock Mount Cl L25 69 F3
Rock Mount Pk L25 69 F3
Rockmount Rd L17 68 F1
ROCK PARK 67 B1
Rock Park Rd CH42 67 B1
Rockpoint Ave CH45 51 C7
Rock Ret Pk CH41 66 F5
Rockside Rd L18 69 A1
Rock St
Golborne WA3 36 A2
Rock St *continued*
Liverpool L13 54 A3
St Helens WA10 57 C8
Rock View
Kirkby L31 29 A4
Liverpool L5 52 E6
Rockville Rd L13, L14 54 C1
Rockville St CH42 66 F2
Rockwell Cl L12 54 D8
Rockwell Rd L12 54 E8
Rocky Bank Rd CH42 66 D3
Rocky La
Heswall CH60 85 F8
Liverpool, Anfield L6 53 C5
Liverpool, Childwall L15, L16 69 D8
Rocky La S CH60 86 A8
Roderick Rd 1 L4 39 A2
Roderick St 3 L3 52 E3
Rodick St L25 69 F2
Rodmell Rd L9 39 B6
Rodney Ct CH45 37 B1
Rodney St
Birkenhead CH41 66 E5
Liverpool L1 90 C2
St Helens WA10 43 E4
Roe Alley L1 90 B3
Roeburn Way WA5 74 D3
Roedean Cl
Liverpool L25 82 B9
Maghull L31 20 D2
Roehampton Dr L23 26 C6
Roe La PR9 4 E8
Roemarsh Cl L11 40 B2
Roe-Park Mews PR9 4 D8
Roe St L1 90 B4
Roften Ind Est CH66 88 D1
Roger Arden Ct L20 38 D4
Rogers Ave L20 38 E5
Rogerson's Gn L26 70 E2
Rokeby Ave WA3 36 D1
Rokeby Cl L3 52 E3
Rokeby St L3 52 E3
Rokeden WA12 46 D4
Roker Ave 6 CH44 51 A3
Rokesmith Ave L7 68 C8
Roklis Ct CH49 65 A4
Roland Ave
Bebington CH63 78 E6
Runcorn WA7 84 F1
St Helens WA11 44 C7
Roleton Cl L30 28 B4
Rollesby Gdns WA9 57 E6
Rolleston Dr
Bebington CH63 79 A4
Wallasey CH45 50 F6
Rolling Mill La WA9 58 F8
Rollo St L4 52 E7
Roman Cl WA12 46 C2
Roman Rd
Ashton-in-M WN4 35 A5
Bebington CH43, CH63 78 A8
Hoylake CH47 48 D1
Rome Cl L36 55 D3
Romer Rd L6 53 C3
Romford Way L26 82 F7
Romiley Dr WN8 15 F2
Romilly St L6 53 B3
Romley St L4 38 F1
Romney Cl WA8 73 E2
Romsey Ave L37 10 B2
Romulus St L7 53 D2
Ronald Cl L22 26 F1
Ronald Rd L22 26 F1
Ronald Ross Ave L30 27 F3
Ronaldshay WA8 73 E2
Ronald St L13 53 F3
Ronaldsway
Birkenhead CH49 64 F6
Crosby L23 27 A6
Halewood L26 83 A8
Heswall CH60 85 F6
Liverpool L10 40 A7
Ronan Cl L20 38 A4
Ronan Rd WA8 84 E5
Rone Cl CH46 64 D8
Roofers Way 1 L36 56 A2
Rookery Ave WN4 35 B2
Rookery Dr
Liverpool L19 80 F8
Rainford WA11 32 A5
Rookery La WA11 32 B5
Rookery Rd PR9 1 F1
Rookery The WA12 46 D4
Rookley Cl L27 70 F4
Rooks Way CH60 85 E8
Rooley The L36 55 D1
Roosevelt Dr L9 39 B8
Ropers Bridge Cl L35 56 D2
Roper St
Liverpool L8 67 F5
St Helens WA9 44 C4
Ropewalks Sq 4 L1 90 C2
Rosalind Ave CH63 78 E7
Rosalind Way L20 38 D1
Rosclare Dr CH45 50 F6
Roscoe Ave WA12 46 E3
Roscoe Cl L35 71 A7
Roscoe Inf Sch L13 53 E7
Roscoe Jun Sch L13 53 E7
Roscoe La L1 90 C2
Roscoe Pl L1 90 C2
Roscoe St
Liverpool L1 90 C2
St Helens WA10 43 D3
Roscommon St L5 52 E4
Roscommon Way WA8 72 E3
Roscote Cl CH60 85 F7
Roscote The CH60 85 F7
Roseacre CH48 63 A3
Roseate Ct CH45 50 E8
Rose Ave
Abram Brow WN2 36 B7
Bootle L20 38 C7
Haydock WA11 45 E6
St Helens WA9 58 C7
Rosebank Rd L36 55 C5
Rose Bank Rd L16 69 D7
Rosebank Way L36 55 C5
Rosebay Cl L37 10 A3
Roseberry Rd WN4 35 A5
Rosebery Ave
Crosby L22 26 C2
Wallasey CH44 51 C4
Rosebery Ct CH44 51 C4
Rosebery Gr CH42 66 B2
Rosebery Rd WA10 43 D5
Rosebery St
Liverpool L8 68 A7
Southport PR9 5 A6
Rosebourne Cl L17 68 C2
Rose Brae L18 69 B4
Rose Brae Ct CH60 77 A1
Rose Brow L25 70 A4
Rose Cl L26 83 A7
Rose Cres
Skelmersdale WN8 15 E1
Southport PR8 7 C2
Widnes WA8 84 F7
Rosecroft CH62 88 C6
Rosecroft Cl L39 13 E6
Rosecroft Ct CH47 63 A6
Rose Ct
9 Birkenhead CH41 66 D6
Liverpool L15 68 E7
Rosedale Ave
Crosby L23 26 F4
Golborne WA3 47 C7
Rosedale Cl L9 39 B4
Rosedale Rd
Birkenhead CH42 66 E3
Liverpool L18 69 B5
Rose Dr WA11 32 A5
Rosefield Ave CH63 78 E7
Rosefield Rd L25 70 C1
Rosegarth Gn L14 54 B4
Roseheath Dr L26 83 A6
ROSE HILL 34 F7
Rose Hill
Liverpool L3 52 D3
Southport PR8, PR9 4 D6
Rosehill Ave WA9 59 B5
Rosehill Bsns Pk 1 PR9 4 D6
Rosehill Ct L25 70 A4
Rosehill Dr L39 13 C2
Rosehill Mans L39 13 C2
Rose Hill View WN4 34 F7
Rose La L18 69 A3
Roseland Cl L31 20 B4
Roselands Ct CH42 66 E1
Rose Lea Cl WA8 73 A4
Roselea Dr PR9 2 C4
Rosemary Cl
Birkenhead CH43 65 E8
Liverpool L7 68 A8
Rosemary Ct L37 9 F3
Rosemary Dr WA12 46 F3
Rosemary La
Formby L37 9 F3
Haskayne L39 12 B4
Rosemead Ave CH61 77 A4
Rosemont Rd L17 68 F2
Rosemoor Dr L23 27 A5
Rosemoor Gdns L11 40 A2
Rose Mount
Birkenhead CH43 66 B4
Crosby L22 26 C1
Rosemount Cl CH43 66 A3
Rosemount Cotts WA2 61 B8
Rose Mount Dr CH45 51 A6
Rosemount Pk CH43 66 A3
Rose Path L37 10 A2
Rose Pl
Birkenhead CH42 66 D4
Liverpool L3 52 D3
Liverpool L3 52 E3
Ormskirk L39 13 D2
Rainford WA11 32 A5
Roseside Dr L27 70 F6
Rose St
Liverpool L1 90 B4
Liverpool, Woolton Hill L25 69 F2
Widnes WA8 84 F7
Rose Terr L18 69 A4
Rose Vale L5 52 E5
Rose View Ave WA8 73 A2
Rose Villas L15 69 A7
Rosewarne Cl L17 68 B2
Rosewell Ct L28 55 B6
Rosewood Cl
Abram Brow WN2 36 B7
Huyton-w-R L28 55 B7
Liverpool L27 70 E5
Rosewood Dr CH46 64 B8
Rosewood Farm Ct WA8 72 E4
Rosewood Gdns 1 L11 40 B1
Rosewood Gr WA8 84 B8
Roseworth Ave L9 39 A7
Rosina Cl WN4 34 F6
Roskell Rd L25 82 C8
Roslin Ct CH43 66 B4
Roslin Rd
Birkenhead CH43 66 B4
Roslin Rd *continued*
Irby CH61 76 D6
Roslyn St CH42 66 F3
Rossall Ave L10 28 D3
Rossall Cl L24 83 E2
Rossall Ct CH46 49 F2
Rossall Rd
Liverpool L13 54 B2
Wallasey CH46 49 F1
Widnes WA8 73 D2
Ross Ave CH46 50 C4
Ross Cl
Billinge WN5 33 E6
Knowsley L34 41 D3
Ross Ct CH62 79 B7
Rossendale Cl CH43 65 D4
Rossett Ave L17 68 E6
Rossett Cl WA5 60 E2
Rossett Rd L23 26 C3
Rossett St L6 53 C5
Rossini St L21 38 A6
Rosslyn Ave L31 28 B8
Rosslyn Cres CH46 64 E8
Rosslyn Dr CH46 64 E8
Rosslyn Pk 1 CH46 64 E7
Rosslyn St L17 68 B3
Rossmore Gdns L4 53 C8
Ross St WA8 73 B1
Ross Tower Ct CH45 51 C8
Rostherne Ave
Golborne WA3 47 D8
Wallasey CH44 51 A3
Rostherne Cres WA8 72 D2
Rosthwaite Gr WA11 33 B1
Rosthwaite Rd L12 54 C6
Rostron Cres L37 9 E1
Rosyth Cl WA2 61 F3
Rothay Dr WA5 74 D3
Rothbury Cl CH46 64 C8
Rothbury Ct WA9 58 B2
Rothbury Rd L14 54 F6
Rotherham Cl L36 55 F4
Rotherwood CH43 65 D5
Rotherwood Cl CH63 78 D6
Rothesay Ct CH63 78 F4
Rothesay Dr
Bebington CH62 88 E4
Crosby L23 26 F3
Rothesay Gdns 3 CH43 65 F1
Rothley Ave PR8 7 A4
Rothsay Cl WA11 44 E6
Rothwell Cl L39 13 D5
Rothwell Dr
Ormskirk L39 13 B2
Southport PR8 7 A4
Rothwell Rd WA3 36 C1
Rothwells La L23 27 B7
Rothwell St 5 L6 53 A4
Rotten Row PR8 3 F6
Rotunda St L5 52 D5
Roughdale Ave
Kirkby L32 40 F7
St Helens WA9 58 B4
Roughdale Cl L32 40 F7
Roughsedge Ho L28 55 B8
Roughwood Dr L33 29 F3
Roundabout The WA8 72 D6
Round Hey L28 55 A8
Round Meade The L31 20 C2
Roundway The L38 17 F3
Roundwood Dr WA9 44 B1
Routledge St WA8 73 B1
Rowan Ave
Golborne WA3 47 F7
Liverpool L12 40 F1
Rowan Cl
St Helens, Blackbrook WA11 44 F5
St Helens, Laffak WA11 44 D7
Warrington WA5 74 F6
Rowan Ct
Bebington CH63 78 D6
Birkenhead CH49 64 C2
Liverpool L17 68 E2
Rowan Dr L32 29 D3
Rowan Gr
Bebington CH63 78 E4
Huyton-w-R L36 70 D8
Rowan La WN8 16 B4
Rowan Park Sch L21 27 D2
Rowans The
Aughton L39 21 A7
Widnes WA8 73 D4
Rowan Tree Cl CH49 64 B3
Rowena Cl L23 26 F4
Rowlings Way 11 L32 40 F8
Rowsley Gr L9 39 B7
Rowson Ct 7 CH45 51 B8
Rowson St
Prescot L34 56 D7
Wallasey CH45 51 B7
Row The CH47 63 B7
Rowthorn Cl WA8 84 E8
Rowton Cl CH43 65 F3
Roxborough Cl WA5 60 A6
Roxborough Wlk L25 70 C3
Roxburgh Ave
Birkenhead CH42 66 D2
Liverpool L17 68 C3
Roxburgh St L20, L4 38 E1
Royal Ave WA8 72 A1
Royal Birkdale Golf Links PR8 3 D3
Royal Cl L37 10 A1

Royal Cres L37 . . . . 10 A1
Royal Croft L12 . . . . 54 B4
Royal Gr WA10 . . . . 43 D1
Royal Liver Building
L3 . . . . 52 B1
Royal Liverpool Univ
Dental Hospl L3 . . . . 52 F2
Royal Liverpool Univ
Hospl L3, L7 . . . . 52 F2
Royal Mail St L3 . . . . 90 C3
ROYAL OAK 21 F4
Royal Pk PR8 . . . . 3 E4
Royal Pl WA8 . . . . 84 B8
Royal Quay L3 . . . . 90 A2
Royal School for the Blind
The L15 . . . . 69 A7
Royal St L4 . . . . 52 E7
Royal Standard Ho **9**
CH42 . . . . 66 F3
Royal Standard Way **8**
CH42 . . . . 66 F3
Royal Terr PR8 . . . . 4 A7
Royal The CH47 . . . . 62 F6
Royden Ave CH44 . . . . 51 D5
Royden Cres WN5 . . . . 33 E5
Royden Ho CH41 . . . . 66 C7
Royden Pk★ CH48 . . . . . . 64 A1
Royden Pk Visitor Ctr★
CH48 . . . . 76 B8
Royden Rd
Billinge WN5 . . . . 33 E5
Birkenhead CH49 . . . . 64 E6
Royden Way L3 . . . . 67 E3
Royhsay Cl L5 . . . . 52 F4
Roysten Gdns WA9 . . . . . . 44 D2
Royston Ave CH44 . . . . 51 D4
Royston Cl **2** WA3 . . . . . . 47 E8
Royston St L7 . . . . 53 B1
Royton Rd L22 . . . . 26 F2
Rubbing Stone CH48 . . . . . 75 D6
Ruby Cl L21 . . . . 38 C8
Ruby St L8 . . . . 68 A3
Rudd Ave WA9 . . . . 45 B2
Ruddington Rd PR8 . . . . 4 E2
Rudd St CH47 . . . . 63 B7
Rudgate L35 . . . . 56 F2
Rudgrave Cl CH44 . . . . 65 D4
Rudgrave Mews CH44 . . . . 51 D5
Rudgrave Pl CH44 . . . . 51 D5
Rudgrave Sq CH44 . . . . . . 51 D5
Rudley Wlk L24 . . . . 82 F3
Rudloe Ct WA2 . . . . 61 F1
Rudston Jun & Inf Schs
L16 . . . . 69 D8
Rudston Rd L16 . . . . 69 D7
Rudyard Cl L14 . . . . 54 C3
Rudyard Rd L14 . . . . 54 D3
Ruff La L39, L40 . . . . 14 B4
Rufford Ave L31 . . . . 20 E3
Rufford Cl
Liverpool L10 . . . . 39 F8
Prescot L35 . . . . 56 F5
Widnes WA8 . . . . 72 C2
Rufford Dr PR9 . . . . 2 F5
Rufford Rd
Bootle L20 . . . . 38 C5
Liverpool L6 . . . . 53 D3
Rainford WA11 . . . . 31 F8
Southport PR9 . . . . 2 C4
Wallasey CH44 . . . . 51 C3
Rufford St **4** WN4 . . . . . . 34 F5
Rufford Wlk WA11 . . . . 44 E6
Ruffwood Sch L33 . . . . 29 F3
Rugby Cl WN5 . . . . 25 E5
Rugby Dr
Aintree L10 . . . . 28 F1
Orrell WN5 . . . . 25 F8
Rugby Rd
Liverpool L9 . . . . 39 B8
Wallasey CH44 . . . . 50 F4
Ruislip Cl L25 . . . . 70 C2
Ruislip Ct WA2 . . . . 61 F1
Rullerton Rd CH44,
CH45 . . . . 51 A4
Rumford Pl L2, L3 . . . . 90 A4
Rumford St L2 . . . . 90 A3
Rumney Pl L4 . . . . 52 E8
Rumney Rd L4 . . . . 52 E8
Rumney Rd W L4 . . . . 52 D8
RUNCORN 84 D2
Runcorn Docks Rd
WA7 . . . . 84 E2
Runcorn Sta WA7 . . . . 84 F2
Rundle Rd L17 . . . . 68 E1
Rundle St CH41 . . . . 66 A8
Runic St L13 . . . . 53 F2
Runnell's La L23 . . . . 27 C5
Runnell The CH64 . . . . 86 D4
Runnymede L36 . . . . 55 D4
Runnymede Cl L25 . . . . 70 A4
Runnymede Ct **2** WA8 . . 73 C1
Runnymede Dr WA11 . . . . . 45 A6
Runnymede Gdns **5**
WA8 . . . . 73 C1
Runnymede Wlk **3**
WA8 . . . . 73 C2
Runton Rd L25 . . . . 70 C5
Rupert Dr L6 . . . . 53 A3
Rupert Rd L36 . . . . 55 D3
Ruscar Cl L26 . . . . 70 E2
Ruscolm Cl WA5 . . . . 74 D7
Ruscombe Rd L14 . . . . 55 A5
Rushden Rd L32 . . . . 30 A1
Rushey Hey Rd L32 . . . . . . 29 F1
Rushgreen Cl CH43 . . . . . . 65 C7

Rushlake Dr L27 . . . . 70 D5
Rushmere Rd L11 . . . . 39 F2
Rushmoor Ave WN4 . . . . . . 35 E4
Rusholme Cl L26 . . . . 83 A6
Rushton Ave WA12 . . . . . . 46 B4
Rushton Cl
Burtonwood WA5 . . . . . . 59 F7
Widnes WA8 . . . . 72 F3
Rushton Pl L25 . . . . 70 A2
Rushton's Wlk L30 . . . . 27 D4
Rushy View WA12 . . . . 46 A4
Ruskin Ave
Birkenhead CH42 . . . . . . 66 F1
Newton-le-W WA12 . . . . . 46 C4
Wallasey CH44 . . . . 51 A3
Warrington WA2 . . . . 61 C2
Ruskin Cl L20 . . . . 38 C3
Ruskin Dr WA10 . . . . 43 D5
Ruskin St L4 . . . . 38 E1
Ruskin Way
Birkenhead CH43 . . . . . . 65 E3
Huyton-w-R L36 . . . . 55 D1
Rusland Ave CH61 . . . . 76 F4
Rusland Rd L32 . . . . 40 F8
Russel Ct WA8 . . . . 73 B4
Russell Ave PR9 . . . . 5 A7
Russell Ct PR9 . . . . 2 B4
Russell Pl L3 . . . . 90 C3
Russell Rd
Birkenhead CH42 . . . . . . 67 A2
Huyton-w-R L36 . . . . 56 B2
Liverpool, Garston L19 . . . 81 C6
Liverpool L18 . . . . 68 F5
Runcorn WA7 . . . . 84 E1
Southport PR9 . . . . 5 A6
Wallasey CH44 . . . . 50 E5
Russell St
Birkenhead CH41 . . . . . . 66 C1
Liverpool L3 . . . . 90 C3
Russet Cl
Liverpool, Netherley
L27 . . . . 70 E5
St Helens WA10 . . . . 43 F5
Russian Ave L13 . . . . 53 F5
Russian Dr L13 . . . . 53 F5
Rutherford Cl L13 . . . . 53 E1
Rutherford Rd
Liverpool L18 . . . . 69 B6
Maghull L31 . . . . 28 E2
St Helens WA10 . . . . 43 C6
Rutherglen Ave L23 . . . . . . 26 F2
Ruth Evans Ct L35 . . . . 57 A4
Ruthin Cl WA5 . . . . 60 E3
Ruthven Ct L21 . . . . 38 A7
Ruthven Rd
Litherland L21 . . . . 38 A7
Liverpool L13 . . . . 54 B1
Rutland Ave
Golborne WA3 . . . . 47 D7
Halewood L26 . . . . 83 A8
Liverpool L17 . . . . 68 D6
Rutland Cl **4** L5 . . . . 53 A5
Rutland Cres L39 . . . . 13 E7
Rutland Dr WN4 . . . . 35 C4
Rutland Ho
Crosby L23 . . . . 26 B3
Liverpool L17 . . . . 68 D5
Rutland Rd PR8 . . . . 4 D5
Rutland St
Bootle L20 . . . . 38 D4
 1 Runcorn WA7 . . . . . . 84 F2
St Helens WA10 . . . . 43 F5
Rutland Way L36 . . . . 56 B3
Rutter Ave WA5 . . . . 60 F2
Rutter St L8 . . . . 67 E5
Rycot Rd L24 . . . . 82 C5
Rycroft Rd
Hoylake CH47 . . . . 63 E8
Liverpool L10 . . . . 39 E7
Wallasey CH44 . . . . 51 C2
Rydal Ave
Birkenhead CH43 . . . . . . 65 C5
Crosby L23 . . . . 26 F2
Formby L37 . . . . 9 D3
Orrell WN5 . . . . 25 F7
Prescot L34 . . . . 56 F6
Rydal Bank
Bebington CH63 . . . . 79 A7
Wallasey CH44 . . . . 51 C4
Rydal Cl
Aintree L10 . . . . 28 F2
Ashton-in-M WN4 . . . . . . 35 C4
Heswall CH61 . . . . 76 F4
Kirkby L33 . . . . 29 D4
Rydal Gr WA11 . . . . 44 A7
Rydal Pl WN2 . . . . 36 B8
Rydal Rd L36 . . . . 55 E1
Rydal St
Liverpool L5 . . . . 53 A5
Newton-le-W WA12 . . . . . 46 C3
Rydal Way WA8 . . . . 72 C1
Rydecroft L25 . . . . 69 F2
Ryder Cl
Ormskirk L39 . . . . 13 C1
Rainhill L35 . . . . 57 A4
Ryder Cres
Ormskirk L39 . . . . 13 C1
Southport PR8 . . . . 7 E7
Ryder Rd WA8 . . . . 73 B4
Rydinge The L37 . . . . 10 A6
Rye Cl WA9 . . . . 58 D4
Ryecote L32 . . . . 40 E7
Ryecroft L21 . . . . 27 B3
Ryecroft Ave WA3 . . . . 61 F5
Ryecroft Rd CH60 . . . . 86 C7
Ryedale Cl L8 . . . . 68 B7
Ryefield La L21 . . . . 27 B3

Ryegate Rd L19 . . . . 81 B8
Rye Gr L12 . . . . 54 E6
Ryeground La L37 . . . . 10 A5
Rye Hey Rd L32 . . . . 29 F2
Rye Moss La L37 . . . . 19 B8
Ryland Pk CH61 . . . . 77 A5
Rylands Hey CH49 . . . . 64 D4
Ryleys Gdns L2 . . . . 90 A4
Rymer Gr **2** L4 . . . . 39 A1
Rymers Gn L37 . . . . 9 E4

S

Sables Ct **4** CH45 . . . . . . 51 A8
Sackville Rd WA10 . . . . . . 43 C6
Sacred Heart RC Coll
L23 . . . . 26 E3
Sacred Heart RC Prim Sch
Liverpool L7 . . . . 53 A2
Wallasey CH46 . . . . 49 F1
Saddle Cl L9 . . . . 39 D8
Saddlestone Gr **5** L8 . . . 67 E5
Sadler's La WA11 . . . . 42 E7
Sadler St WA8 . . . . 73 C1
Saffron Cl WA3 . . . . 47 E8
Saffron Gdns WA9 . . . . 44 D2
Saffron Mews L23 . . . . 27 B6
Sagar Fold L39 . . . . 21 D8
St Aelred's RC Tech Coll
WA12 . . . . 46 D4
St Agnes RC Prim Sch
L36 . . . . 55 F1
St Agnes Rd
Huyton-w-R L36 . . . . 55 F1
Liverpool L4 . . . . 52 D8
St Aidan's CE Com Prim
Sch WN5 . . . . 33 E5
St Aidan's Cl WN5 . . . . 33 E6
St Aidans Ct WA9 . . . . 58 E3
St Aidan's Ct CH43 . . . . . . 65 F6
St Aidan's Dr WA8 . . . . 72 F6
St Aidan's Gr L36 . . . . 55 C7
St Aidan's RC Prim Sch
L36 . . . . 55 F1
St Aidan's Terr **1**
CH43 . . . . 65 F6
St Aidan's Way L30 . . . . . . 27 E3
St Alban Rd WA5 . . . . 74 E5
St Albans L5 . . . . 53 B5
St Albans Cl WA11 . . . . 46 A7
St Albans Ct L5 . . . . 52 C5
St Alban's RC Prim Sch
CH44 . . . . 51 B4
St Alban's Rd
Birkenhead CH43 . . . . . . 66 A6
Bootle L20 . . . . 38 C3
Wallasey CH44 . . . . 51 B4
St Alban's Sq L20 . . . . 38 C2
St Albert's RC Prim Sch
L28 . . . . 55 A8
St Alexander Cl **3** L20 . . 38 D1
St Aloysius RC Prim Sch
L24 . . . . 83 A2
St Ambrose Barlow RC
Coll L25 . . . . 28 A5
St Ambrose Croft L30 . . . . 27 E4
St Ambrose Gr L4 . . . . 53 B6
St Ambrose RC Prim Sch
L24 . . . . 83 A2
St Ambrose Rd WA8 . . . . . 73 C1
St Ambrose Way **6** L5 . . 52 F4
St Andrew Gdns L3 . . . . . . 90 C4
St Andrew Rd L4 . . . . 53 B6
St Andrews Ave L12 . . . . . . 54 E6
St Andrew's CE Prim Sch
Bebington CH63 . . . . 78 F6
Warrington WA2 . . . . 61 C3
St Andrews Ct
Birkenhead CH43 . . . . . . 65 D6
Seaforth L22 . . . . 37 E8
Southport PR8 . . . . 4 B6
St Andrew's Dr L23 . . . . . . 26 C6
St Andrew's Dr L36 . . . . . . 55 C7
St Andrews Gr WA11 . . . . . 44 B6
St Andrew's Gr L30 . . . . . . 27 C3
St Andrew's Maghull CE
Prim Sch L31 . . . . 20 D1
St Andrews Pl L17 . . . . 68 C3
St Andrew's Pl PR8 . . . . 4 B6
St Andrews Rd
Bebington CH63 . . . . 79 A4
Bootle L20 . . . . 38 C6
St Andrew's Rd
Birkenhead CH43 . . . . . . 66 B6
Crosby L23 . . . . 26 B6
St Andrew St L3 . . . . 52 F1
St Andrew's View **8**
L33 . . . . 29 E5
St Andrews Villas L36 . . . . 55 B3
St Andrew The Apostle RC
Prim Sch L26 . . . . 82 D8
St Anne Gr CH41 . . . . 66 C8
St Anne's Cl
 6 Birkenhead CH41 . . . 66 D7
Formby L37 . . . . 9 F6
St Anne's Cotts L14 . . . . . . 54 C3
St Annes Ct
Liverpool, Aigburth L17 . . 68 E1
Liverpool L3 . . . . 52 E1
St Anne's Ct L13 . . . . 53 F3
St Annes Gdns L17 . . . . . . 68 E1
St Annes Gr L17 . . . . 68 E1
St Anne's Path L37 . . . . 9 F6
St Anne's Pl CH41 . . . . 66 C8
St Anne's RC Prim Sch
Bebington CH42 . . . . 78 F3
Huyton-w-R L36 . . . . 55 D1

St Anne's RC Prim Sch
continued
Liverpool L7 . . . . 68 B8
Ormskirk L39 . . . . 13 E4
St Helens WA9 . . . . 58 E7
St Annes Rd PR9 . . . . 1 F4
St Anne's Rd
Formby L37 . . . . 9 F6
Huyton-w-R L36 . . . . 55 F1
Liverpool L17 . . . . 68 F1
Ormskirk L39 . . . . 13 D4
Widnes WA8 . . . . 73 B2
St Anne's (Stanley) JMI
Sch L13 . . . . 54 A3
St Anne St
Birkenhead CH41 . . . . . . 66 C8
 5 Birkenhead CH41 . . . 66 D7
Birkenhead CH41 . . . . . . 66 D7
Liverpool L3 . . . . 52 E3
St Annes Way CH41 . . . . . . 66 D7
St Anne Terr CH41 . . . . 66 C7
St Ann Pl L35 . . . . 57 C4
St Ann's CE Prim Sch
L35 . . . . 57 C3
St Anns Rd WA10 . . . . 43 C3
St Anselm's Coll CH43 . . . . 66 A6
St Anthony of Padua RC
Prim Sch L18 . . . . 68 F4
St Anthony Pl WA2 . . . . . . 61 B6
St Anthony's Cl L36 . . . . . . 55 C7
St Anthony's Gr L30 . . . . . . 27 D3
St Anthony's Rd L23 . . . . . 26 B4
St Anthony's Sh Ctr **5**
L5 . . . . 52 D5
St Asaph Dr WA5 . . . . 60 E3
St Asaph Gr L30 . . . . 27 F1
St Augustine of
Canterbury RC High Sch
WA11 . . . . 44 E5
St Augustine St **1** L5 . . . 52 D5
St Augustine's Way
L30 . . . . 27 E4
St Austel Cl WA5 . . . . 74 E3
St Austell Cl CH46 . . . . 49 B1
St Austells Rd L4 . . . . 38 E2
St Austin's RC Prim Sch
Liverpool L19 . . . . 81 A7
St Helens WA9 . . . . 57 D7
St Bartholomew's RC Prim
Sch L13 . . . . 57 E1
St Basil's RC Prim Sch
WA8 . . . . 72 A2
St Bedes Cl L39 . . . . 13 D3
St Bede's RC High Sch
L39 . . . . 13 D3
St Bede's RC Inf Sch
WA8 . . . . 73 A1
St Bede's RC Jun Sch
WA8 . . . . 73 A1
St Benedicts Coll L19 . . . . 81 D6
St Benet's RC Prim Sch
L30 . . . . 27 F4
St Benet's Way L30 . . . . . . 27 E3
St Bernard's Cl
Litherland L30 . . . . 27 D3
 7 Liverpool L8 . . . . . . 68 D7
St Bernard's Dr L30 . . . . . . 27 D3
St Brendan's Cl L36 . . . . . . 55 C7
St Brides Cl WA5 . . . . 74 E3
St Bride's Rd CH44 . . . . . . 51 D5
St Bride St **10** L8 . . . . . . 67 F8
St Bridget's CE Prim Sch
CH48 . . . . 63 B1
St Bridgets Cl WA2 . . . . . . 61 F3
St Bridget's Gr L30 . . . . . . 27 D3
St Bridget's La CH48 . . . . . 63 B1
St Bridget's RC Prim Sch
WA2 . . . . 61 E3
St Brigid's Cres L5 . . . . . . 52 C5
St Brigid's RC Prim Sch
L28 . . . . 55 A7
St Catherines Cl L36 . . . . . 55 E1
St Catherines Gdns
CH42 . . . . 66 D4
St Catherine's Hospl
CH42 . . . . 66 D3
St Catherine's RC Prim
Sch WA3 . . . . 47 C2
St Catherine's Rd L20 . . . . 38 C3
St Cecilia's RC Inf Sch
L13 . . . . 53 E5
St Cecilia's RC Jun Sch
L13 . . . . 53 E5
St Chad's Dr L32 . . . . 29 E2
St Chad's Par L32 . . . . 29 E2
St Charles RC Prim Sch
L17 . . . . 68 C2
St Christopher's Ave
L30 . . . . 27 D4
St Christopher's Dr
L36 . . . . 55 C7
St Christopher's RC Prim
Sch L24 . . . . 82 D5
St Clair Dr PR9 . . . . 2 A1
St Clares RC Prim Sch
L15 . . . . 68 C6
St Cleopas' CE Jun Mix &
Inf Sch L8 . . . . 67 F4
St Columba's Cl L41 . . . . . 51 D5
St Columba's RC Prim Sch
L36 . . . . 55 E5
St Cuthbert's Cl
 3 Liverpool L12 . . . . . 40 E3
Southport PR9 . . . . 2 A2
St Cuthbert's RC Com Coll
WA9 . . . . 44 C4
St Cuthbert's RC Prim Sch
L13 . . . . 53 F3

St Cuthbert's Rd PR9 . . . . . . 2 A2
St Cyrils Cl L27 . . . . 70 C6
St Cyrils Ct L27 . . . . 70 C6
St Damian's Croft L30 . . . . 27 E3
St David Rd
Bebington CH62 . . . . 89 A6
Birkenhead CH43 . . . . . . 66 A6
St Davids Cl L35 . . . . 57 C4
St Davids Dr WA5 . . . . 60 E2
St Davids Gr L30 . . . . 27 D2
St Davids La CH43 . . . . 65 D3
St Davids Rd L14 . . . . 55 B5
St David's Rd **5** L4 . . . . . 53 B6
St Domingo Gr L5 . . . . 53 A6
St Domingo Rd L5 . . . . 52 E6
St Domingo Vale L5 . . . . . . 53 A6
St Dominic's RC Jun & Inf
Sch L14 . . . . 55 B6
St Dunstan's Gr L30 . . . . . 27 D3
St Edmond's Rd L20 . . . . . 38 C2
St Edmund Arrowsmith RC
High Sch
Ashton-in-M WN4 . . . . . . 35 B2
Prescot L35 . . . . 56 F5
St Edmund of Canterbury
RC High Sch L14 . . . . . . 55 B6
St Edmund's RC Prim Sch
WN8 . . . . 15 F1
St Edmunds Rd CH63 . . . . 78 F5
St Edmund's & St Thomas'
RC Prim Sch L22 . . . . . . 26 D1
St Edwards Cl CH41 . . . . . 66 B8
St Edward's Coll L12 . . . . . 54 B5
St Edwards Mews
CH41 . . . . 66 B8
St Elizabeth's RC Prim Sch
L21 . . . . 38 C6
St Elmo Rd CH44 . . . . 51 B5
SS Peter & Paul RC High
Sch WA8 . . . . 72 F2
SS Peter & Paul's RC Prim
Sch L33 . . . . 29 F5
St Finbar's RC Prim Sch
L14 . . . . 68 A3
St Francis de Sales RC Inf
Sch L4 . . . . 38 E2
St Francis de Sales RC
Jun Sch L4 . . . . 38 E1
St Francis of Assisi RC
Prim Sch WN8 . . . . 24 D7
St Francis of Assisi RC
Prim Sch, Garston
L19 . . . . 81 C6
St Francis Xavier's Coll
L25 . . . . 69 F4
St Gabriel's Ave L36 . . . . . 56 A2
St Gabriel's CE Prim Sch
L36 . . . . 56 A2
St George of England
Specialist Engineering
Coll L20 . . . . 38 D6
St Georges Ave CH42 . . . . 66 D2
St Georges Ave WA10 . . . . 43 C5
St Georges Ct L31 . . . . 28 D8
St George's Ct WA8 . . . . . . 84 D8
St Georges Gr
Birkenhead CH46 . . . . . . 64 D8
Litherland L30 . . . . 27 D2
St George's Hill L5 . . . . . . 52 F5
St George's Mount
CH45 . . . . 51 B8
St George's Pk CH45 . . . . . 51 B8
St George's Pl
Liverpool L1 . . . . 90 B4
Southport PR9 . . . . 4 B7
St George's Prim Sch
CH45 . . . . 51 B8
St George's Prim Sch
(Annexe) CH45 . . . . 50 F6
St George's RC Prim Sch
L31 . . . . 28 D7
St Georges Rd WA10 . . . . . 43 D2
St George's Rd
Formby L37 . . . . 9 E4
Hightown L38 . . . . 17 F5
Huyton-w-R L36 . . . . 55 F5
Wallasey CH45 . . . . 50 F6
St George's Way
 11 Liverpool L1 . . . . . 90 B3
Thornton Hough CH63 . . . 87 A7
St Gerard's Cl L5 . . . . 52 D6
St Gregory's Croft L30 . . . . 27 E4
St Gregory's RC Prim Sch
Liverpool L27 . . . . 70 C5
Maghull L31 . . . . 20 C4
ST HELENS 44 B5
St Helens Central Sta
WA10 . . . . 44 B3
St Helen's Cl CH43 . . . . . . 66 B6
St Helens Coll WA10 . . . . . 43 F3
St Helens Coll Newton
Campus WA12 . . . . 46 B4
St Helens Coll (Tech
Campus) WA9 . . . . 44 B4
St Helens Hospl WA9 . . . . . 44 C1
St Helens Junction Sta
WA9 . . . . 58 F2
St Helens Linkway L35,
WA9 . . . . 57 F4
St Helens Rd
Ormskirk L39 . . . . 14 A2
Prescot L34, WA10 . . . . . 56 E7
Rainford WA11 . . . . 32 B1
St Helens Ret Pk WA9 . . . . 44 B3
St Helens RLFC WA10 . . . . 43 C3
St Hilary Brow CH44 . . . . . 50 F4
St Hilary Dr CH45 . . . . 50 F5

St Hilda's CE High Sch
  L17 . . . . **68** D5
St Hildas Ct L17 . . . . **68** D6
St Hilda St **9** L4 . . . . **52** E8
St Hugh's Cl CH43 . . . . . . **66** B6
St Hugh's RC Prim Sch
  L7 . . . . **68** D7
St Ives Cl CH43 . . . . **66** A7
St Ives Gr L13 . . . . **53** F3
St Ives Rd CH43 . . . . **66** A6
St Ives Way L26 . . . . **70** F1
St James' CE Prim Sch
  WA11 . . . . **45** E6
St James Cl
  Birkenhead CH49 . . . . . . **64** D4
  Ormskirk L40 . . . . **14** C3
St James' Cl L12 . . . . **54** A6
St James Cres WN2 . . . . . . **36** F8
St James Ct **4** CH45 . . . . **51** B8
St James Dr L20 . . . . **38** B4
St James Mews L20 . . . . . . **38** B4
St James Mount L35 . . . . . **57** C2
St James Pl
  Liverpool L8 . . . . **67** E6
  Southport PR8 . . . . **4** B5
St James' RC Prim Sch
  WN5 . . . . **25** D4
St James' RC Sch WN8 . . . **16** B4
St James Rd
  Birkenhead CH41,
    CH43 . . . . **65** F8
  Liverpool L1 . . . . **90** C1
  Rainhill L35 . . . . **57** C2
  Wallasey CH45 . . . . **51** B8
St James' Rd
  Huyton-w-R L36 . . . . . . **55** E1
  Orrell WN5 . . . . **25** D4
  Prescot L34 . . . . **56** E6
St James St
  Liverpool L1 . . . . **90** B1
  Southport PR8 . . . . **4** B6
St James Way L30 . . . . **27** C4
St Jerome's RC Prim Sch
  L37 . . . . **9** C3
St Jerome's Way L30 . . . . . **27** E4
St John Bosco Arts Coll
  L11 . . . . **40** B3
St John Bosco RC Prim
  Sch L31 . . . . **20** B2
St John Fisher RC Prim
  Sch
  Knowsley L34 . . . . **41** D4
  Widnes WA8 . . . . **73** D1
St John Plessington RC
  Coll CH63 . . . . **79** A4
St John's Ave L9 . . . . **39** A5
St John's CE Prim Sch
  Crosby L22 . . . . **26** D1
  Southport PR9 . . . . **2** C5
St John's Cl CH47 . . . . **63** D8
St Johns Ct PR8 . . . . **7** D4
St John's Ct L22 . . . . **26** D1
St John's La L1 . . . . **90** B4
St John's Pavement **6**
  CH41 . . . . **66** D6
St John's Pl L22 . . . . **26** D1
St John's RC Inf Sch
  CH63 . . . . **78** F7
St John's RC Jun Sch
  CH63 . . . . **78** F7
St John's RC Prim Sch
  Liverpool L14 . . . . **54** F2
  Skelmersdale WN8 . . . . . **16** C1
St John's Rd
  Bebington CH62 . . . . . . **89** A5
  Crosby L22 . . . . **26** D1
  Huyton-w-R L36 . . . . . . **55** F1
  Liverpool L20 . . . . **38** C1
  Southport PR8 . . . . **3** F1
  Wallasey CH45 . . . . **50** E5
St John's Sq
  Birkenhead CH41 . . . . . . **66** D6
  10 Liverpool L1 . . . . . . **90** B3
St John's St WN2 . . . . **36** B8
St John St
  Birkenhead CH41 . . . . . . **66** D6
  Newton-le-W WA12 . . . . . **46** A3
  St Helens WA10 . . . . **43** D1
St John's Terr L20 . . . . **38** B1
St John Stone RC Prim
  Sch PR8 . . . . **7** D2
St John's Way **5** L1 . . . . . **90** B3
St John Vianney RC Prim
  Sch WA9 . . . . **57** E6
St Josephs Cl WA9 . . . . . . **44** C1
St Joseph's Cl L36 . . . . **55** C7
St Josephs Cl WA5 . . . . . . **74** E5
St Josephs Cres L3 . . . . . . **52** E3
St Joseph's RC Prim Sch
  CH43 . . . . **66** B3
St Joseph's RC Prim Sch
  Birkenhead, Upton
    CH49 . . . . **65** A5
  Huyton-w-R L36 . . . . . . **55** F3
  Wallasey CH44 . . . . **51** D2
  Warrington WA5 . . . . . . **74** E5
St Joseph's The Worker
  RC Prim Sch L32 . . . . . . **29** E1
St Jude's Cl L36 . . . . **55** C7
St Julie's RC High Sch
  L25 . . . . **70** A1
St Julie's RC Prim Sch
  WA10 . . . . **43** A4
St Kevin's Dr L32 . . . . **29** E4
St Kilda's Rd CH46 . . . . . . **64** D7
St Laurence Cl **10**
  CH41 . . . . **66** D7

St Laurence Dr **11**
  CH41 . . . . **66** D7
St Laurence Gr L32 . . . . . . **40** F8
St Laurence's RC Prim Sch
  Birkenhead CH41 . . . . . . **66** D7
  Kirkby L32 . . . . **29** F1
St Lawrence Cl **1** L8 . . . . **68** A4
St Leonard's Ct L30 . . . . . . **27** D4
St Leo's & Southmead RC
  Prim Sch L35 . . . . **56** E2
St Lucia Rd L14 . . . . **51** D5
St Luke's Ave WA3 . . . . . . **47** D8
St Luke's Bldg **2** PR8 . . . . **4** D6
St Luke's CE Prim Sch
  Formby L37 . . . . **9** D1
  Golborne WA3 . . . . **47** E7
St Luke's Church Rd L37,
  L38 . . . . **17** C8
St Lukes Cl L14 . . . . **54** F6
St Luke's Cres WA8 . . . . . . **73** B4
St Luke's Ct L4 . . . . **39** A2
St Luke's Dr
  Formby L37 . . . . **9** C2
  Orrell WN5 . . . . **25** E4
St Luke's Gr
  Litherland L30 . . . . **27** D4
  Southport PR9 . . . . **4** E7
St Luke's Halsall CE Prim
  Sch L23 . . . . **26** D5
St Lukes Ho WN4 . . . . **35** D4
St Luke's Pl **3** L1 . . . . . . **90** C2
St Luke's RC Prim Sch
  L35 . . . . **56** F4
St Luke's Rd
  Crosby L23 . . . . **26** E4
  Southport PR9 . . . . **4** D7
  St Helens WA10 . . . . **43** D4
St Luke's Way L36 . . . . . . **55** C7
St Malachy's RC Prim Sch
  L8 . . . . **67** E5
St Margaret Mary's RC Inf
  Sch L14 . . . . **54** F4
St Margaret Mary's RC Jun
  Sch L14 . . . . **54** F4
St Margaret of Antioch CE
  Prim Sch L8 . . . . **67** F7
St Margaret's Anfield CE
  Prim Sch L6 . . . . **53** C5
St Margaret's Ave
  WA2 . . . . **61** D1
St Margarets CE High Sch
  L17 . . . . **68** E1
St Margaret's CE Prim Sch
  WA2 . . . . **61** D1
St Margaret's Gr L33 . . . . . **27** C3
St Margaret's Rd CH47 . . . . **63** A6
St Marie's RC Prim Sch
  L33 . . . . **30** A3
St Marks Ct **2** CH43 . . . . **66** B5
St Mark's Gr L30 . . . . **27** C4
St Mark's RC Prim Sch
  L26 . . . . **83** A8
St Mark's Rd L36 . . . . **55** F1
St Mark's St WA11 . . . . . . **45** A6
St Martins Gr L32 . . . . **40** F7
St Martin's Mews **1**
  L5 . . . . **52** E4
St Mary & St Paul's CE
  Prim Sch L35 . . . . **56** D4
St Mary's Arc **13** WA10 . . . **44** A3
St Mary's Ave
  Billinge WN5 . . . . **33** C4
  4 Liverpool L4 . . . . **39** A2
  Wallasey CH44 . . . . **51** B4
St Mary's CE Prim Sch
  CH62 . . . . **89** A5
St Mary's CE Prim Sch,
  West Derby L12 . . . . **54** B7
St Mary's Cl **1** L20 . . . . . **38** B3
St Mary's Cl
  Hale L24 . . . . **83** E2
  Liverpool L13 . . . . **53** F1
St Mary's Coll L23 . . . . . . **26** E4
St Marys Ct L25 . . . . **70** A2
St Mary's Ct CH49 . . . . . . **65** A4
St Mary's Gate CH41 . . . . . **66** F6
St Mary's Gdns PR8 . . . . . . **7** F7
St Mary's Gr
  Litherland L30 . . . . **27** C2
  5 Liverpool L4 . . . . **39** A2
St Mary's Hospl The
  Phineas Gage Ctr
  WA2 . . . . **61** B1
St Mary's La L4 . . . . **39** A2
St Mary's Mkt WA10 . . . . . **44** A3
St Mary's Pl **6** L4 . . . . . . **39** A2
St Mary's RC Coll CH45 . . . **50** E6
St Mary's RC Inf Sch
  WA12 . . . . **46** C4
St Mary's RC Jun Sch
  WA12 . . . . **46** B3
St Mary's RC Prim Sch
  L23 . . . . **26** D8
St Mary's Rd
  Crosby L23 . . . . **26** F1
  Huyton-w-R L36 . . . . . . **55** F2
  Liverpool L19 . . . . **81** B7
  Warrington WA5 . . . . . . **74** F5
St Mary's & St Thomas' CE
  Prim Sch WA10 . . . . . . **43** F4
St Mary's St
  Liverpool, Woolton L25 . . **70** A2
  Wallasey CH44 . . . . **51** B4
St Mathews Cl L4 . . . . **39** D2
St Mathew's Cl L36 . . . . . . **55** F3
St Matthews Ave L21 . . . . . **38** D8
St Matthews Gr WA10 . . . . . **57** C8

St Matthew's RC Prim Sch
  L4 . . . . **53** E8
St Mawes Cl WA8 . . . . **72** E2
St Mawes Way WA10 . . . . . **43** B6
St Mawgan Ct WA2 . . . . . . **61** F2
St Michael & All Angels
  RC Prim Sch CH41 . . . . . **65** D2
St Michael in the Hamlet
  Com Prim Sch L17 . . . . . **68** B3
St Michael Rd L39 . . . . **20** F7
St Michael's CE High Sch
  L23 . . . . **26** C6
St Michael's Church Rd
  L17 . . . . **68** C2
St Michael's Cl
  Liverpool L17 . . . . **68** C2
  Southport PR9 . . . .**1** F3
  Widnes WA8 . . . . **84** C7
St Michaels Ct L36 . . . . . . **55** E3
St Michaels Dr CH46 . . . . . **64** D8
St Michael's Gr
  Litherland L30 . . . . **27** C3
  Liverpool L6 . . . . **53** B4
St Michael's Gr
  L23 . . . . **68** B2
St Michael's Ind Est
  WA8 . . . . **84** C7
St Michaels Mews
  CH42 . . . . **66** C4
St Michaels Pk L39 . . . . . . **21** A7
St Michael's Pk **3**
  CH62 . . . . **79** B6
St Michael's RC Prim Sch
  Liverpool L6 . . . . **53** B4
  Widnes WA8 . . . . **84** C7
St Michaels Rd WA9 . . . . . . **58** A3
St Michael's Rd
  Crosby L23 . . . . **26** C6
  Liverpool L17 . . . . **68** B3
  Widnes WA8 . . . . **84** C7
St Michael's Sta L17 . . . . . **68** B2
St Monica's Dr L10 . . . . . . **27** D4
St Monica's RC Prim Sch
  L20 . . . . **38** E5
St Nicholas CE Prim Sch
  L23 . . . . **26** B3
St Nicholas' Dr L30 . . . . . . **27** D4
St Nicholas Gr **1** WA9 . . . **58** D7
St Nicholas Pl L3 . . . . **52** B1
St Nicholas Rd L35 . . . . . . **56** D1
St Nicholas' Rd CH45 . . . . . **50** D5
St Nicholas RC Inf Sch
  L3 . . . . **52** F1
St Oswald's Ave CH43 . . . . **50** C1
St Oswald's CE Prim Sch
  L30 . . . . **27** F3
St Oswalds Cl WA2 . . . . . . **61** B6
St Oswalds Cl L30 . . . . **27** F3
St Oswald's La L30 . . . . . . **27** F3
St Oswald's Mews
  CH43 . . . . **50** C1
St Oswald's RC Inf & Jun
  Schs L13 . . . . **54** A2
St Oswalds Rd WN4 . . . . . . **35** A3
St Oswalds St L13 . . . . **54** A2
St Paschal Baylon Bvd
  L16 . . . . **70** A8
St Paschal Baylon's RC
  Prim Sch L16 . . . . **69** F8
St Patrick's Cl **1** L33 . . . . **29** E5
St Patrick's Dr L30 . . . . . . **27** D4
St Patrick's RC Prim Sch
  Liverpool L8 . . . . **67** F6
  Southport PR9 . . . . **2** A2
St Paul of the Cross RC
  Prim Sch WA5 . . . . **59** E6
St Paul's Ave **10** CH44 . . . **51** E2
St Pauls Cl L33 . . . . **29** D5
St Paul's Cl CH42 . . . . **66** E2
St Pauls Cl WA8 . . . . **56** D4
St Pauls Mans **4** PR8 . . . . **4** A6
St Paul's Pas PR8 . . . . **4** A6
St Paul's Pl L20 . . . . **38** D2
St Paul's RC Jun Sch
  L12 . . . . **54** C6
St Paul's RC Prim Sch
  CH43 . . . . **65** C4
St Paul's Rd
  Birkenhead CH42 . . . . . . **66** F3
  Wallasey CH44 . . . . **51** E2
St Paul's & St Timothy's
  RC Inf Sch L12 . . . . **54** C6
St Paul's Sq
  Liverpool L3 . . . . **90** A4
  Southport PR8 . . . . **4** A6
St Paul St WA10 . . . . **43** E3
St Paul's Villas **1**
  CH42 . . . . **66** F2
St Peter & St Paul RC
  Prim Sch WA11 . . . . **44** B7
St Peter & St Paul's RC
  Prim Sch CH45 . . . . **51** B8
St Peter's Ave L37 . . . . **9** D4
St Peter's CE Prim Sch
  WA12 . . . . **46** E4
St Peters Cl **4** L33 . . . . . . **29** D5
St Peter's Cl
  Formby L37 . . . . **9** D4
  Heswall CH60 . . . . **85** F7
St Peters Ct L7 . . . . **68** B4
St Peter's Ct CH42 . . . . . . **67** A1
St Peter's Mews CH42 . . . . **67** B1
St Peter's RC High Sch
  Visual Arts Coll WN5 . . . . **25** F7

St Peter's RC Prim Sch
  CH45 . . . . **65** C4
St Peter's Rd
  Birkenhead CH42 . . . . . . **67** A1
  Liverpool L9 . . . . **39** C1
  Southport PR8 . . . . **4** A3
St Peter's Row L31 . . . . . . **28** D6
St Peter's Sq L1 . . . . **90** C2
St Peter's Way CH43 . . . . . **65** C4
St Philip's Ave L21 . . . . . . **38** C7
St Philip's CE Prim Sch
  Bootle L21 . . . . **38** C8
  Southport PR8 . . . . **4** C5
St Philip (Westbrook) CE
  Prim Sch WA5 . . . . **60** B1
St Richards Cl **2** L20 . . . . **38** D1
St Richard's Cl
  WN8 . . . . **15** D1
St Robert Bellarmine RC
  Prim Sch L36 . . . . **28** D7
St Sebastian's RC Prim
  Sch L7 . . . . **53** D2
St Seiriol Gr CH43 . . . . **66** A6
St Silas CE Prim Sch
  L8 . . . . **68** A5
St Stephen Rd WA5 . . . . . . **74** F5
St Stephen's Ave WA2 . . . . **61** B3
St Stephens Cl
  Heswall CH60 . . . . **86** C6
  Liverpool L25 . . . . **70** C5
St Stephens Ct CH42 . . . . . **66** B1
St Stephen's Ct L25 . . . . . . **70** B4
St Stephen's Gr L30 . . . . . . **27** D3
St Stephen's Pl **4** L3 . . . . **52** D3
St Stephen's RC Prim Sch
  WA2 . . . . **61** B2
St Stephen's Rd
  Birkenhead CH42 . . . . . . **66** B1
  Hightown L38 . . . . **17** F4
St Teresa of Liseaux RC
  Inf Sch L11 . . . . **39** F2
St Teresa's RC Inf Sch
  PR8 . . . . **4** A4
St Teresa's RC Jun Sch
  L11 . . . . **39** F2
St Teresa's Rd WA10 . . . . . **43** D4
St Theresa's RC Prim Sch
  WA9 . . . . **58** C3
St Thomas CE Jun & Inf
  Sch WA3 . . . . **36** B1
St Thomas Ct
  Ashton-in-M WN4 . . . . . **35** C3
  Maghull L31 . . . . **20** D4
St Thomas Ct WA8 . . . . . . **72** E1
St Thomas's Ct WN8 . . . . . **25** C7
St Thomas of Canterbury
  RC Prim Sch WA10 . . . . **43** D6
St Thomas's Ct WN8 . . . . . **25** C7
St Thomas's Dr L30 . . . . . . **27** D3
St Thomas Terr WA8 . . . . . **72** E1
St Thomas the Martyr CE
  Prim Sch WN8 . . . . **25** B7
St Vincent de Paul RC
  Prim Sch L1 . . . . **90** B2
St Vincent Rd
  Birkenhead CH43 . . . . . . **66** A6
  Wallasey CH44 . . . . **51** D5
  Warrington WA5 . . . . . . **74** F5
St Vincent's Cl L12 . . . . . . **54** E6
St Vincent's RC Prim Sch
  WA5 . . . . **74** F3
St Vincent St L3 . . . . **90** C4
St Vincent's Way L4 . . . . . . **4** A4
St Werburgh's RC Prim
  Sch CH42 . . . . **66** D5
St Werburgh's Sq **13**
  CH41 . . . . **66** E6
St Wilfrid's RC High Sch
  L21 . . . . **38** C7
St Wilfrids RC Prim Sch
  WN4 . . . . **35** D4
St William of York RC
  Prim Sch L23 . . . . **27** B5
St William Rd L23 . . . . **27** B5
St William Way L23 . . . . . . **27** B5
St Winifred Rd
  Rainhill L35 . . . . **57** B5
  15 Wallasey CH45 . . . . . **51** B7
St Wyburn Ct PR8 . . . .**3** F5
Saker St **17** L4 . . . . **52** F7
Salacre Cl CH49 . . . . **65** A4
Salacre Cres CH49 . . . . . . **65** A4
Salacre La CH49 . . . . **65** A4
Salacre Terr CH49 . . . . **65** A5
Salcombe Dr
  Liverpool L25 . . . . **82** B8
  Southport PR9 . . . . **2** C5
Salem View CH43 . . . . **66** B3
Salerno Dr L36 . . . . **55** D3
Saleswood Ave WA10 . . . . . **43** A3
Salford Ct PR8 . . . . **7** C5
Salford Rd PR8 . . . . **7** C5
Salhouse Gdns WA9 . . . . . . **57** E6
Saline Cl L14 . . . . **55** A6
Salisbury Ave
  Litherland L30 . . . . **28** A1
  West Kirby CH48 . . . . . . **63** A2
Salisbury Ct CH42 . . . . **66** E1
Salisbury Dr CH62 . . . . **79** B7
Salisbury Ho **2** L20 . . . . . **38** B4
Salisbury Pk L16 . . . . **69** D5
Salisbury Rd
  1 Ashton-in-M WN4 . . . **35** A5
  Bootle L20 . . . . **38** B5
  Haydock WA11 . . . . **45** E8
  Liverpool, Anfield L5 . . . . **53** A6

Salisbury Rd continued
  Liverpool, Cressington Park
    L19 . . . . **81** A6
  Liverpool, Wavertree
    L15 . . . . **68** D8
  Wallasey CH45 . . . . **51** A8
Salisbury St
  Birkenhead CH41 . . . . . . **66** D5
  Golborne WA3 . . . . **47** A8
  Liverpool L3 . . . . **52** F3
  3 Prescot L34 . . . . **56** D6
  Southport PR9 . . . . **5** A6
Salisbury Terr L15 . . . . **68** F8
Salkeld Ave L34 . . . . **34** F3
Sallowfields WN5 . . . . **25** D5
Sally's La PR9 . . . . **2** A2
Salop St L4 . . . . **52** F8
Saltash Cl L26 . . . . **82** E9
Saltburn Rd CH45 . . . . **50** D5
Saltergate Rd **19** L8 . . . . . **68** A4
Salthouse Quay L3 . . . . **90** A2
Saltney St L3 . . . . **52** B4
Saltpit La L31 . . . . **20** E1
Salvia Way **8** L33 . . . . . . **29** D5
Salvin St WN4 . . . . **35** D3
Salwick Cl PR9 . . . .**1** F5
Samaria Ave CH62 . . . . **79** C7
Samaria Ho L41 . . . . **66** A4
Sambourn Fold PR8 . . . . . . **7** A5
Samphire Gdns WA9 . . . . . **59** B7
Samuel St WA9 . . . . **57** D7
Samwoods Ho WN4 . . . . . . **35** A5
Sanbec Gdns WA8 . . . . **72** A5
Sandalwood L23 . . . . **26** D4
Sandalwood Cl
  Liverpool L6 . . . . **53** B5
  Warrington WA2 . . . . . . **61** D2
Sandalwood Dr CH43 . . . . . **65** D4
Sandalwood Gdns
  WA9 . . . . **58** C7
Sandbeck St **67** F3
Sandbourne CH46 . . . . **65** A8
Sandbrook Ct CH46 . . . . . . **64** E8
Sandbrook Gdns WN5 . . . . **25** D5
Sandbrook La CH46 . . . . . . **64** F8
Sandbrook Prim Sch
  CH46 . . . . **65** A8
Sandbrook Rd
  Liverpool L25 . . . . **70** A7
  Orrell WN5 . . . . **25** C5
  Southport PR8 . . . . **7** C3
Sandbrook Way PR8 . . . . . . **7** C3
Sandeman Rd L4 . . . . **53** D8
Sanderling Rd
  Kirkby L33 . . . . **30** A3
  Newton-le-W WA12 . . . . . **46** C4
Sanderson Cl WA5 . . . . **74** D6
Sandfield L36 . . . . **55** D2
Sandfield Ave CH47 . . . . . . **48** D1
Sandfield Cl
  Bebington CH63 . . . . . . **78** D6
  3 Golborne WA3 . . . . . **47** E8
  Liverpool L12 . . . . **54** C5
Sandfield Cotts L13 . . . . . . **12** C2
Sandfield Cres WA10 . . . . . **43** F3
Sandfield Hall WA3 . . . . . . **47** A4
Sandfield Hey L12 . . . . **54** C6
SANDFIELD PARK **54** B5
Sandfield Park Sch
  L12 . . . . **54** B5
Sandfield Pk
  Heswall CH60 . . . . **85** D8
  Ormskirk L39 . . . . **13** D2
Sandfield Pk E L12 . . . . . . **54** C6
Sandfield Pl L20 . . . . **38** B4
Sandfield Rd
  Bebington CH63 . . . . . . **78** D6
  Birkenhead CH49 . . . . . . **65** B2
  Bootle L20 . . . . **38** D3
  Liverpool L25 . . . . **70** B4
  St Helens WA10 . . . . **43** A5
  Wallasey CH45 . . . . **51** B7
Sandfield Terr **4** CH45 . . . **51** B7
Sandfield Wlk L13 . . . . **54** B4
Sandford Dr L31 . . . . **20** D2
Sandford Rd WN5 . . . . **25** C5
Sandforth Cl L12 . . . . **54** A6
Sandforth Ct L12 . . . . **54** A5
Sandforth Rd L12 . . . . **54** B6
Sandgate Cl L24 . . . . **82** B5
Sandham Gr CH60 . . . . **86** D7
Sandham Rd L24 . . . . **83** A4
Sandhead St L7 . . . . **68** D8
Sandhey Rd CH47 . . . . **63** C8
Sandheys CH64 . . . . **86** C1
Sandheys Ave L22 . . . . **26** C1
Sandheys Cl L4 . . . . **52** F2
Sandheys Dr PR9 . . . .**1** F1
Sandheys Gr L22 . . . . **26** C2
Sandheys Rd **9** CH45 . . . . **51** B7
Sandheys Terr L22 . . . . **26** C1
SANDHILLS **52** B7
Sandhills L38 . . . . **17** F3
Sandhills Bsns Pk L5 . . . . . **52** C6
Sandhills Ind Ctr L5 . . . . . . **52** C7
Sandhills La L20 . . . . **52** C7
Sandhills Sta L20 . . . . **52** C7
Sandhills The CH45 . . . . . . **49** E3
Sandhills View CH45 . . . . . **50** D5
Sandhurst **2** L23 . . . . **26** C4
Sandhurst Cl
  Formby L37 . . . . **9** C1
  Seaforth L21 . . . . **37** F7

Sandhurst Dr L10 . . . . **28** E2
Sandhurst Rd
 Halewood L26 . . . . **83** A6
 Rainhill L35 . . . . **57** B4
Sandhurst St L17 . . . . **68** B3
Sandhurst Way L31 . . . . . . **20** B5
Sandicroft Rd L12 . . . . **40** F2
Sandilands Gr L38 . . . . **17** F3
Sandino St L8 . . . . **67** E6
Sandiway
 Bebington CH63 . . . . **88** C6
 Hoylake CH47 . . . . **48** D1
 Huyton-w-R L36 . . . . **55** F1
 Prescot L35 . . . . **56** D2
Sandiway Ave WA8 . . . . . . **72** A1
Sandiway Ct PR9 . . . . **4** E8
Sandiways L31 . . . . **20** E1
Sandiways Ave L30 . . . . . . **28** A2
Sandiways Rd CH45 . . . . . . **50** E6
Sandlea Ho CH48 . . . . **63** A2
Sandlea Pk CH48 . . . . **63** A2
Sandlewood Gr **1** L33 . . . . **29** F4
Sandling Dr WA3 . . . . **36** A2
Sandon Cl L35 . . . . **57** B4
Sandon Ct **7** L22 . . . . **26** D1
Sandon Gr WA11 . . . . **32** A6
Sandon Ind Est L5 . . . . **52** B6
Sandon Lo **8** L21 . . . . **38** A6
Sandon Pl WA8 . . . . **73** D1
Sandon Prom CH44 . . . . . . **51** E4
Sandon Rd
 Southport PR8 . . . . **3** F1
 Wallasey CH44 . . . . **51** E4
Sandon St
 Crosby L22 . . . . **26** D1
 15 Liverpool L8 . . . . **67** F8
Sandon Way L5 . . . . **52** B6
Sandown Ct
 3 Liverpool L15 . . . . **68** F8
 10 Southport PR9 . . . . **4** C8
Sandown La L15 . . . . **68** F8
Sandown Park Rd L10 . . . . **28** E3
Sandown Rd
 Liverpool L15 . . . . **53** F1
 Seaforth L21 . . . . **37** F7
Sandpiper Cl
 Birkenhead CH49 . . . . **64** D6
 Newton-le-W WA12 . . . . . **46** C4
Sandpiper Gr L26 . . . . **70** C1
Sandpipers CH47 . . . . **63** B7
Sandpipers Ct **3** L23 . . . . **26** C2
Sandra Dr WA12 . . . . **46** E3
Sandridge Rd
 Heswall CH61 . . . . **76** F5
 Wallasey CH45 . . . . **51** B7
Sandringham Ave
 Hoylake CH47 . . . . **63** C7
 2 Seaforth L22 . . . . **37** E8
Sandringham Cl
 Bebington CH62 . . . . **79** A7
 Hoylake CH47 . . . . **63** C7
 4 Kirkby L33 . . . . **29** E5
Sandringham Ct
 Golborne WA3 . . . . **47** E7
 Southport PR9 . . . . **4** B8
Sandringham Dr
 Liverpool L17 . . . . **68** B4
 St Helens WA9 . . . . **58** C7
 Wallasey CH45 . . . . **51** A8
Sandringham Mews
 CH47 . . . . **63** C7
Sandringham Rd
 Formby L37 . . . . **9** E1
 Liverpool L13 . . . . **53** E6
 Maghull L31 . . . . **28** C8
 Seaforth L22 . . . . **26** C1
 Southport, Ainsdale PR8 . . . . **7** C5
 Southport PR8 . . . . **3** E3
 Widnes WA8 . . . . **73** A4
Sandrock Mews CH45 . . . . **51** B8
Sandrock CH45 . . . . **51** B7
Sandrock Rd CH45 . . . . **51** B7
Sands Rd L18 . . . . **68** F4
Sandstone Cl L35 . . . . **57** C1
Sandstone Dr
 Rainhill L35 . . . . **57** A5
 West Kirby CH48 . . . . **63** E2
Sandstone Mews WA8 . . . **72** E4
Sandstone Rd E L13 . . . . . . **54** A4
Sandstone Rd W L13 . . . . . **53** F4
Sandstone Wlk CH60 . . . . . **86** A7
Sandwash Cl WA11 . . . . . . **32** B4
Sandway Cres L11 . . . . **40** A2
Sandy Brow La
 Golborne WA3 . . . . **47** E2
 Kirkby L33 . . . . **41** E8
Sandy Gn L9 . . . . **39** C6
Sandy Gr L13 . . . . **53** F6
Sandy Ho **5** L21 . . . . **37** F7
Sandy Knowe L15 . . . . **69** A8
Sandy La
 Bold Heath WA8 . . . . **74** B6
 Cronton WA8 . . . . **72** D5
 Golborne WA3 . . . . **46** F8
 Heswall CH60 . . . . **77** A1
 Hightown L38 . . . . **18** A3
 Irby CH61 . . . . **76** C7
 Kirkby L33 . . . . **29** A6
 Liverpool, Hartley's Village
 L9 . . . . **39** C6
 Liverpool, Tuebrook L13 . . . **53** F6
 Maghull, Holt Green L39 . . . **21** B6
 Maghull, Lydiate L31 . . . . . **20** C5
 Ormskirk L40 . . . . **14** D7
 Orrell WN5 . . . . **25** D4
Sandy La continued
 Seaforth L21 . . . . **38** A7
 Skelmersdale WN8 . . . . . . **15** D1
 St Helens WA11 . . . . **43** F8
 Wallasey CH45 . . . . **50** E6
 Warrington, Longford
 WA2 . . . . **61** C2
 West Kirby CH48 . . . . **63** B1
Sandy La Ctr WN8 . . . . **15** D1
Sandy La N CH61 . . . . **76** C8
Sandy La W WA2 . . . . **61** B3
Sandymount Dr
 Bebington CH63 . . . . **78** F4
 Wallasey CH45 . . . . **51** A7
Sandy Rd
 Seaforth L21 . . . . **37** F7
 Seaforth L21 . . . . **38** A7
Sandyville Gr **2** L4 . . . . . . **53** E8
Sandyville Rd L4 . . . . **53** E8
Sandy Way CH43 . . . . **66** A5
Sanfield Cl L39 . . . . **13** E6
Sangness Dr PR8 . . . . **4** E3
Sankey for Penketh Sta
 WA5 . . . . **74** F6
Sankey Rd
 Maghull L31 . . . . **28** D7
 St Helens WA11 . . . . **44** F5
Sankey St
 Golborne WA3 . . . . **47** A8
 Liverpool L1 . . . . **90** C2
 Newton-le-W WA12 . . . . . **46** A3
 St Helens WA9 . . . . **44** D2
Sankey Valley Ind Est
 WA12 . . . . **46** A2
Sankey Valley Pk★
 Newton-le-W WA12 . . . . . **45** D3
 St Helens WA11 . . . . **44** E2
Santon Ave L13 . . . . **53** E5
Santon Dr WA3 . . . . **47** E8
Sanvino Ave PR8 . . . . **7** D5
Sapphire Dr L33 . . . . **29** E5
Sapphire St L13 . . . . **53** F1
Sarah's Croft L30 . . . . **27** E3
Sark Rd L13 . . . . **53** F4
Sarsfield Ave **1** WA3 . . . . **47** D8
Sartfield Cl L16 . . . . **69** E8
Sarum Rd L25 . . . . **70** B7
Satinwood Cl WA3 . . . . **34** F2
Satinwood Cres L31 . . . . . . **29** A2
SAUGHALL MASSIE **64** C6
Saughall Massie La
 CH49 . . . . **64** F5
Saughall Massie Rd
 Birkenhead CH46,
 CH49 . . . . **64** D6
 West Kirby CH48 . . . . **63** E4
Saughall Rd CH46 . . . . **64** C6
Saunby St L19 . . . . **81** C4
Saunders Ave L35 . . . . **56** D4
Saundersfoot Cl WA5 . . . . . **60** E2
Saunders St PR9 . . . . **1** C1
Saunderton Cl WA11 . . . . . **45** C7
Saville Rd
 Liverpool L13 . . . . **54** B2
 Maghull L31 . . . . **20** C3
Savio High Sch L30 . . . . . . **38** E8
Savon Hook L37 . . . . **10** B1
Savoylands **6** L17 . . . . **68** C2
Sawdon Ave PR8 . . . . **4** A8
Sawley Ave WA3 . . . . **36** D1
Sawpit La L36 . . . . **55** F2
Sawyer Dr WN4 . . . . **35** D3
Saxby Rd L14 . . . . **55** A6
Saxenholme PR8 . . . . **3** F5
Saxon Cl L6 . . . . **53** B5
Saxon Ct WA10 . . . . **43** E4
Saxonia Rd L4 . . . . **39** B2
Saxon Lo
 Southport PR8 . . . . **3** F5
 Southport PR8 . . . . **4** A5
Saxon Rd
 Crosby L23 . . . . **26** D3
 Hoylake CH47 . . . . **63** C8
 Southport PR8 . . . . **3** F5
 Wallasey CH46 . . . . **49** F1
Saxon Terr **4** WA8 . . . . . . **73** B1
Saxon Way L33 . . . . **29** E6
Saxony Rd L7 . . . . **53** A2
Sayce St WA8 . . . . **73** B1
Scafell Ave WA2 . . . . **61** C3
Scafell Cl CH62 . . . . **88** D3
Scafell Lawn L27 . . . . **71** A3
Scafell Rd WA11 . . . . **44** A7
Scafell Wlk L27 . . . . **71** A4
Scaffold La L38 . . . . **18** D4
Scape La L23 . . . . **26** E5
Scargreen Ave L11 . . . . **39** F3
Scarisbrick Ave
 Bootle L21 . . . . **38** B7
 Southport PR8 . . . . **4** A7
Scarisbrick Cl L31 . . . . **20** E3
Scarisbrick Cres L11 . . . . . **39** D3
Scarisbrick Ct PR8 . . . . **4** C6
Scarisbrick Dr L11 . . . . **39** D2
Scarisbrick Ho **3** L39 . . . . **13** F5
Scarisbrick New Rd
 PR8 . . . . **4** D5
Scarisbrick Pl L11 . . . . **39** D2
Scarisbrick Rd
 Liverpool L11 . . . . **39** D2
 Rainford WA11 . . . . **31** F7
Scarisbrick St
 Ormskirk L39 . . . . **13** E6
 Southport PR9 . . . . **4** B7
Scarsdale Rd L11 . . . . **39** F1
SCARTH HILL **14** B1
Scarth Hill La
 Ormskirk L39 . . . . **14** A2
Scarth Hill La continued
 Ormskirk L40 . . . . **14** B2
Scarth Hill Mans L39 . . . . . **13** E2
Scarth Pk WN8 . . . . **24** C7
Sceptre Cl WA12 . . . . **46** A3
Sceptre Rd L11 . . . . **40** C3
Sceptre Wlk L11 . . . . **40** C3
Scholar St L7 . . . . **68** C7
Scholes La WA10, WA9 . . . . **57** C7
Scholes Pk WA10 . . . . **57** B7
Scholes The WA10 . . . . **57** B7
Schomberg St L6 . . . . **53** B3
School Ave L37 . . . . **9** F3
School Brow WN5 . . . . **33** E5
School Cl
 Liverpool L27 . . . . **70** C7
 Ormskirk L39 . . . . **13** C1
 Southport PR8 . . . . **4** B2
 Wallasey CH46 . . . . **49** F1
School Dr WN5 . . . . **33** E5
Schoolfield Cl CH49 . . . . . . **65** B2
Schoolfield Rd CH49 . . . . . . **65** B2
School Hill CH60 . . . . **85** F7
School House Cotts
 CH47 . . . . **63** C7
School House Ct WA11 . . . . **31** F6
School House Gn L39 . . . . . **13** F5
School La
 Aintree L10 . . . . **28** E1
 Bebington, Higher Bebington
 CH63 . . . . **78** D5
 Bebington, New Ferry
 CH62 . . . . **79** B7
 Bold Heath WA8 . . . . **73** E7
 Bootle L21 . . . . **38** A7
 Formby L37 . . . . **9** F3
 Garswood WN4 . . . . **34** C3
 Haskayne L39 . . . . **11** F4
 Hooton CH66 . . . . **88** F1
 Hoylake CH47 . . . . **63** B7
 Hoylake, Meols CH47 . . . . **48** D1
 Huyton-w-R L36 . . . . **56** A2
 Irby CH61 . . . . **76** B6
 Kirkby L31 . . . . **29** A5
 Knowsley L34 . . . . **41** B5
 Litherland L21 . . . . **38** B8
 Liverpool, Hunt's Cross
 L25 . . . . **82** B9
 Liverpool L1 . . . . **90** B3
 Maghull L31 . . . . **21** A1
 Neston CH64 . . . . **87** B2
 Neston, Parkgate CH64 . . . . **86** B1
 Skelmersdale WN8 . . . . . . **15** E1
 St Helens L35 . . . . **57** F1
 Up Holland WN5, WN8 . . . . **25** C7
 Wallasey, Bidston CH43 . . . **50** C1
 Wallasey CH44 . . . . **50** E5
 Westhead L40 . . . . **14** E3
School Rd
 Hightown L38 . . . . **17** F4
 Warrington WA2 . . . . **61** C1
School St
 Ashton-in-M WN4 . . . . . . **35** D5
 Golborne WA3 . . . . **47** A8
 Newton-le-W WA12 . . . . . **46** B3
 St Helens WA11 . . . . **44** F6
School Terr WA3 . . . . **47** A8
School Way
 Liverpool L24 . . . . **82** B5
 Widnes WA8 . . . . **73** D3
Science Rd L24 . . . . **82** C5
Scone Cl L11 . . . . **40** C3
Scorecross WA9 . . . . **58** B8
Score La L16 . . . . **69** D8
Scoresby Rd CH46 . . . . **50** B3
Score The WA9 . . . . **58** A7
Scorpio Cl L14 . . . . **55** A5
Scorton St L6 . . . . **53** C5
Scotchbarn La L34, L35 . . . . **56** F6
Scoter Rd L33 . . . . **29** F2
Scotia Ave CH62 . . . . **79** C7
Scotia Rd L13 . . . . **53** A4
Scotia Wlk **1** WA3 . . . . . . **47** F8
Scotland Rd L3, L5 . . . . **52** D4
Scott Ave
 Huyton-w-R L36 . . . . **71** A8
 Prescot L35 . . . . **56** F3
 Widnes WA8 . . . . **84** F8
Scott Cl
 Liverpool L4 . . . . **52** F7
 Maghull L31 . . . . **20** D1
Scott Dr L39 . . . . **13** F7
Scott Rd WA3 . . . . **36** D2
Scotts Ave WA3 . . . . **58** A3
Scotts Pl CH41 . . . . **65** F7
Scotts Quays CH44 . . . . . . **51** F1
Scott St
 Bootle L20 . . . . **38** B5
 Southport PR9 . . . . **5** A7
 Wallasey CH45 . . . . **51** B5
Scott Wlk WA12 . . . . **46** C1
Scythes The
 Birkenhead CH49 . . . . **64** D4
 Litherland L30 . . . . **28** A4
Scythia Cl CH62 . . . . **79** C7
Seabank Ave CH44 . . . . **51** C5
Seabank Cott CH47 . . . . . . **48** E2
Seabank Ct CH48 . . . . **63** A1
Seabank Rd
 Heswall CH60 . . . . **85** E6
 Southport PR9 . . . . **4** B8
 Wallasey CH44, CH45 . . . . **51** C5
Seacole Cl L8 . . . . **68** B6
SEACOMBE **51** D1
Seacombe Aquarium★
 CH44 . . . . **51** F2
Seacombe Prom CH44 . . . . **51** E3
Seacombe View CH44 . . . . . **51** E2
Seacroft Cl L14 . . . . **55** A6
Seacroft Cres PR9 . . . . **2** B5
Seacroft Rd L14 . . . . **55** A6
Sea Ct CH45 . . . . **50** F7
Seafield L37 . . . . **10** A2
Seafield Ave
 Crosby L23 . . . . **26** F4
 Heswall CH60 . . . . **85** E6
Seafield Dr CH45 . . . . **51** A7
Seafield Rd
 Bebington CH62 . . . . **79** B8
 6 Bootle L20 . . . . **38** B4
 Liverpool L9 . . . . **38** F5
 Southport PR8 . . . . **7** C6
Seaford Pl WA2 . . . . **61** A4
Seafore Cl L31 . . . . **20** B4
SEAFORTH **37** E7
Seaforth Dr CH46 . . . . **64** E7
Seaforth & Litherland Sta
 L21 . . . . **38** A7
Seaforth Rd L21 . . . . **38** A6
Seaforth Vale N L21 . . . . . . **38** A6
Seaforth Vale W L21 . . . . . . **38** A6
Seagram Cl L9 . . . . **39** C8
Sealand Ave L37 . . . . **9** E2
Sealand Cl
 Formby L37 . . . . **9** D2
 Warrington WA2 . . . . **61** C1
Sealy Cl CH63 . . . . **79** A1
Seaman Rd L15 . . . . **68** E7
Seaport St L8 . . . . **68** B6
Sea Rd CH45 . . . . **50** F7
Seascale Ave WA10 . . . . . . **57** B8
Seath Ave WA9 . . . . **44** E4
Seathwaite Cl L23 . . . . **26** B3
Seathwaite Cres L33 . . . . . . **29** D4
Seaton Cl L12 . . . . **41** A3
Seaton Gr WA9 . . . . **57** D6
Seaton Pl WN8 . . . . **15** E3
Seaton Rd
 Birkenhead CH42 . . . . **66** C4
 1 Wallasey CH45 . . . . . . **51** A6
Seaton Way PR9 . . . . **2** A5
Seaview CH47 . . . . **63** B7
Seaview Ave
 Bebington CH62 . . . . **89** B6
 Irby CH61 . . . . **76** D6
 Wallasey CH45 . . . . **51** B5
Seaview La CH61 . . . . **76** D6
Seaview Rd CH44, CH45 . . . . **51** A5
Sea View Rd L20 . . . . **38** B4
Seaview Terr L22 . . . . **26** C1
Seawood Gr CH46 . . . . **64** D7
Second Ave
 Aintree L9 . . . . **39** D7
 Birkenhead CH43 . . . . **65** C6
 Crosby L23 . . . . **26** D4
 Liverpool, Fazakerley L9 . . . **39** E6
 Rainhill L35 . . . . **57** B4
Sedbergh Ave L10 . . . . **28** C3
Sedbergh Rd CH44 . . . . **50** F5
Sedburgh Gr L36 . . . . **55** C3
Sedburn Rd L32 . . . . **41** A4
Seddon Cl WA10 . . . . **42** F3
Seddon Pl WN8 . . . . **15** E3
Seddon Rd
 Liverpool L19 . . . . **81** C6
 St Helens WA10 . . . . **57** B8
Seddons Ct **1** L34 . . . . **56** D6
Seddon St
 Liverpool L1 . . . . **90** B2
 St Helens WA10 . . . . **43** F7
Sedgefield Cl CH46 . . . . . . **65** A8
Sedgefield Rd CH46 . . . . . . **65** A8
Sedgemoor Rd L11 . . . . **39** F3
Sedgewick Cres WA5 . . . . . **59** E6
Sedgley Wlk L36 . . . . **55** F5
Sedley St L6 . . . . **53** B5
Sedum Gr L33 . . . . **29** D5
Seeds La L9 . . . . **39** C8
Seeley Ave CH41 . . . . **66** A4
Seel Rd L36 . . . . **56** A2
Seel St L1 . . . . **90** B2
SEFTON **27** F7
Sefton Ave
 Bootle L21 . . . . **38** B7
 Orrell WN5 . . . . **25** D5
 Widnes WA8 . . . . **73** A3
Sefton Bsns Pk L30 . . . . . . **39** A8
Sefton Cl
 Kirkby L32 . . . . **29** C3
 Orrell WN5 . . . . **25** D5
Sefton Dr
 Aintree L10 . . . . **28** E2
 Crosby L23 . . . . **27** A4
 Kirkby L32 . . . . **29** C3
 Liverpool L8 . . . . **68** C5
 Maghull L31 . . . . **28** B8
Sefton Fold Dr WN5 . . . . . . **33** D5
Sefton Fold Gdns WN5 . . . . **33** D5
Sefton Gdns L39 . . . . **21** D7
Sefton Gr L17 . . . . **68** C4
Sefton Ho L9 . . . . **39** B7
Sefton Lane Ind Est
 L31 . . . . **28** A8
Sefton Mill Ct L29 . . . . **27** F7
Sefton Mill La L29 . . . . **27** F7
Sefton Moss La L30 . . . . . . **27** D2
Sefton Moss Villas L21 . . . . **38** B8
SEFTON PARK **68** D4
Sefton Park Palm Ho★
 L17 . . . . **68** D4
Sefton Park Rd L8 . . . . **68** B5
Sefton Rd
 Ashton-in-M WN4 . . . . . . **34** F6
 Bebington CH62 . . . . **79** A8
Sefton Rd continued
 Birkenhead CH42 . . . . **67** A1
 Bootle L20 . . . . **38** D5
 Formby L37 . . . . **9** E2
 Litherland L21 . . . . **38** B8
 Liverpool, Fazakerley L9 . . . **39** E7
 Liverpool, Norris Green
 L9 . . . . **39** A4
 Orrell WN5 . . . . **25** D5
 Wallasey CH45 . . . . **51** B7
Sefton St
 Litherland L21 . . . . **38** B7
 Liverpool L3, L8 . . . . **67** D5
 Newton-le-W WA12 . . . . . **45** F3
 Southport PR8 . . . . **4** C5
Sefton View
 Crosby L23 . . . . **27** A4
 Litherland L21 . . . . **38** B7
 Orrell WN5 . . . . **25** D5
Sefton Villas L20 . . . . **38** B8
Segar's La PR8, L39 . . . . **8** B4
Seiont Ho **3** L8 . . . . **67** F5
Selborne L35 . . . . **56** F2
Selborne Cl **1** L8 . . . . **68** A7
Selborne St L8 . . . . **68** A7
Selbourne Cl CH49 . . . . **65** C3
Selby Cl WA10 . . . . **43** D2
Selby Dr L37 . . . . **10** B2
Selby Gr L36 . . . . **56** B3
Selby Pl WN8 . . . . **15** D2
Selby Rd L9 . . . . **39** A6
Selby St CH45 . . . . **51** B5
Seldon St L7 . . . . **53** B2
Selina Rd L4 . . . . **38** F2
Selkirk Ave
 Bebington CH62 . . . . **88** E4
 Garswood WN4 . . . . **34** D4
Selkirk Dr WA10 . . . . **43** B5
Selkirk Rd L13 . . . . **53** F2
Sellar St L4 . . . . **52** E7
Selsdon Rd L22 . . . . **26** C2
Selsey Cl L7 . . . . **68** B8
Selside Lawn L27 . . . . **71** A4
Selside Wlk L27 . . . . **70** F4
Selston Cl CH63 . . . . **79** A2
Selworthy Gn L16 . . . . **69** D6
Selworthy Rd
 Southport PR8 . . . . **3** D3
 Southport PR8 . . . . **3** D3
Selwyn Cl
 Newton-le-W WA12 . . . . . **46** B3
 Widnes WA8 . . . . **73** E3
Selwyn St L4 . . . . **38** E1
Senate Bsns Pk L30 . . . . . . **38** E7
Senator Rd WA9 . . . . **57** D7
Sennen Rd L32 . . . . **40** F8
Sentinel Way L30 . . . . **39** A8
Sephton Dr L35 . . . . **13** F7
September Rd L6 . . . . **53** D6
Serenade Rd L33 . . . . **29** F6
Sergeant Rd L12 . . . . **54** E7
Sergrim Rd L36 . . . . **55** D3
Serin Cl WA12 . . . . **46** C3
Serpentine N The L23 . . . . . **26** A5
Serpentine Rd CH44 . . . . . . **51** C4
Serpentine S The L23 . . . . . **26** B4
Serpentine The
 Crosby L23 . . . . **26** A4
 Liverpool L19 . . . . **81** A8
 Ormskirk L39 . . . . **21** D8
Servia Rd L21 . . . . **38** B7
Servite Cl L22 . . . . **26** C2
Servite Ct L25 . . . . **70** C1
Servite Ho
 Liverpool L16 . . . . **68** B4
 Wallasey CH45 . . . . **51** B7
Sessions Rd L4 . . . . **52** E7
Seth Powell Way L36 . . . . . **55** D5
Settrington Rd L11 . . . . **39** F1
Seven Acre Rd L23 . . . . **27** B5
Seven Acres La CH61 . . . . . **77** A5
Sevenoak Gr L36 . . . . **71** B7
Sevenoaks Ave PR8 . . . . **7** B5
Sevenoaks Cl L5 . . . . **52** E5
Seventh Ave L9 . . . . **39** D7
Seventh Vale L25 . . . . **70** C6
Severn Cl
 Billinge WN5 . . . . **33** D3
 St Helens WA9 . . . . **58** C6
 Warrington WA2 . . . . **61** C2
 Widnes WA8 . . . . **73** F3
Severn Rd
 Ashton-in-M WN4 . . . . . . **35** E5
 Kirkby L33 . . . . **29** F6
 Rainhill L35 . . . . **57** B3
Severn St
 Birkenhead CH41 . . . . **51** A1
 Liverpool L5 . . . . **52** F6
Severs St L6 . . . . **53** B4
Sewell St L34 . . . . **56** D6
Sexton Ave WA9 . . . . **45** B2
Sexton Way L14 . . . . **54** E2
Seymour Ct
 Birkenhead CH42 . . . . **66** E4
 Liverpool L14 . . . . **54** D1
Seymour Dr L31 . . . . **20** E3
Seymour Pl W **16** CH45 . . . . **51** B8
Seymour Rd
 Bootle L21 . . . . **38** B7
 Liverpool L14 . . . . **54** D2
Seymour St
 Birkenhead CH42 . . . . **66** E4
 Bootle L20 . . . . **38** B7
 Liverpool L3 . . . . **90** C4
 Wallasey CH45 . . . . **51** B8
Seymour Terr L3 . . . . **90** C4
Shacklady Rd L33 . . . . **30** A4
Shackleton Rd CH46 . . . . . . **50** B4

Shadowbrook Dr L24 82 B7
Shadwell St L5 52 B5
Shaftesbury Ave
Southport PR8 8 A8
Warrington WA5 74 E2
Shaftesbury Gr PR8 4 A1
Shaftesbury Rd
Crosby L23 26 D4
Southport PR8 4 A1
Shaftesbury St L8 67 E6
Shaftesbury Terr L13 54 A3
Shaftesbury Way WA5 59 F7
Shaftsbury Ave L33 29 E5
Shaftway Cl WA11 45 F7
Shakespeare Ave
Birkenhead CH42 66 F1
Kirkby L32 29 D1
Shakespeare Cl L6 53 A4
Shakespeare Gr WA2 61 C2
Shakespeare Rd
Neston CH64 86 E1
St Helens WA9 58 A3
Wallasey CH44 51 D2
Widnes WA8 73 A1
Shakespeare St
Bootle L20 38 A5
Liverpool L19 81 C4
Liverpool L19 81 C5
Southport PR8 4 B5
Shalcombe Cl L26 83 A7
Shaldon Cl 3 L32 41 A8
Shaldon Gr 2 L32 41 A8
Shaldon Rd L32 41 A8
Shaldon Wlk 5 L32 41 A8
Shalem Ct CH63 78 D6
Shalford Gr CH48 63 D2
Shallcross Ct L6 53 A4
Shallcross Pl 1 L6 53 A4
Shallmarsh Cl CH63 78 D5
Shallmarsh Rd CH63 78 D5
Shalom Ct L17, L18 68 E5
Shamrock Rd CH41 65 F7
Shand St L19 81 C4
Shanklin Cl WA5 74 C6
Shanklin Rd L15 53 F1
Shankly Ct L4 53 A7
Shannon Gr WA8 72 E2
Shannon Ho CH46 49 E4
Shannons La L34 41 C1
Shannon St CH41 50 F1
Shard Cl L11 40 B5
Shard St WA9 58 E7
Sharon Sq WN2 35 F8
Sharpeville Cl 9 L4 52 D7
Sharples Cres L23 27 A3
Sharrock St 7 PR8 4 B7
Sharwood Rd L27 70 F4
Shavington Ave CH43 65 F3
Shawbury Ave CH63 78 D7
Shaw Cl L39 8 F6
Shaw Cres L37 10 B3
Shawell Ct WA8 73 E2
Shaw Entry L35, WA8 72 A7
Shaw Hill St L1 90 B4
Shaw La
Birkenhead CH49 64 C2
Haskayne L39 11 E6
Prescot L35 56 E4
Shaw Rd L24 82 D6
Shaws Alley L1 90 B2
Shaw's Ave PR8 4 A1
Shaws Dr CH47 63 D8
Shaws Garth L39 8 F6
Shaw's Rd PR8 4 A1
Shaw St
Ashton-in-M WN4 35 B5
Birkenhead CH41 66 D5
Haydock WA11 45 E6
Hoylake CH47 63 B7
Liverpool L3, L6 52 F3
Runcorn WA7 84 F2
St Helens WA10, WA9 44 B4
Shawton Rd L16 69 D8
Shearman Cl CH61 77 A4
Shearman Rd CH61 77 A4
Shearwater Cl L27 70 F4
Sheen Rd CH45 51 C7
Sheffield Row WA12 60 D8
Sheila Wlk L10 40 B6
Sheilings The WA3 47 F8
Sheil Pl L6 53 C3
Sheil Rd L6 53 C3
Shelagh Ave WA8 73 A1
Sheldon Cl CH63 79 A1
Sheldon Rd L12 54 D8
Shelley Cl L36 56 A1
Shelley Ct L32 40 D8
Shelley Dr L39 13 D6
Shelley Gr
Liverpool L19 81 C5
Southport PR8 4 F6
Shelley Pl L35 56 F3
Shelley Rd WA8 73 A1
Shelley St
Bootle L20 38 B4
St Helens WA9 58 B2
Shelley Way CH48 75 B8
Shellfield Rd PR9 2 A4
SHELL GREEN 73 E1
Shellingford Rd L14 55 A4
Shelmore Dr 5 L8 67 F4
Shelton Cl
Liverpool L13 54 A2
Widnes WA8 73 F3
Shelton Dr PR8 7 A4
Shelton Rd CH45 51 A6
Shenley Cl CH63 78 F6
Shenley Rd L15 69 C8
Shenley Way PR9 2 D5
Shenstone St L7 53 B1
Shenton Ave WA11 44 D6
Shepherd Cl CH49 64 C4
Shepherds Fold Cl 4 L8 68 A6
Shepherd's La L39 12 E5
Shepherd St L6, L7 52 F2
Sheppard Ave L16 70 A8
Shepston Ave 7 L4 39 A1
Shepton Rd L36 55 D6
Sherborne Ave
Litherland L30 27 E4
Liverpool L25 82 D9
Sherborne Rd CH44 50 F5
Sherborne Sq L36 55 E2
Sherbourne Way WA5 59 F6
Sherbrooke Cl L14 54 E4
Sherburn Cl L9 39 D8
Sherdley Bsns Pk WA9 58 B8
Sherdley Park Dr WA9 58 B7
Sherdley Prim Sch WA9 58 C6
Sherdley Rd
St Helens, Peasley Cross WA9 44 B1
St Helens, Sutton Heath WA9 57 F7
St Helens WA9 58 A8
Sherford Cl L27 70 F4
Sheridan Ave WA3 47 D7
Sheridan Pl WA2 61 A5
Sheri Dr WA12 46 E2
Sheriff Cl 3 L5 52 E4
Sheringham Cl
Birkenhead CH49 65 A7
St Helens WA9 44 D3
Sheringham Rd WA5 74 E6
Sherlock Ave WA11 45 E7
Sherlock La CH44 51 A2
Sherman Dr L35 57 D1
Sherrat St WN8 15 D1
Sherringham Rd PR8 3 E2
Sherry Ct L17 68 E5
Sherry La CH49 65 A2
Sherwell Cl L15 54 A1
Sherwood Ave
Ashton-in-M WN4 35 C4
Crosby L23 26 D5
Irby CH61 76 C7
Ormskirk L39 13 C2
Sherwood Cl
Rainhill L35 57 C5
Widnes WA8 72 C1
Sherwood Cres WA5 59 E6
Sherwood Ct
Huyton-w-R L36 55 F2
Liverpool L12 40 F3
Sherwood Dr
Bebington CH63 78 E7
Prescot L35 56 F2
Skelmersdale WN8 16 D3
Sherwood Gr CH47 63 F7
Sherwood Ho PR8 7 C5
Sherwood Lo PR8 3 F5
Sherwood Rd
Crosby L23 26 C5
Hoylake CH47 63 F8
Wallasey CH44 51 C3
Sherwood Row L26 82 E7
Sherwood's La L10 39 F8
Sherwood St L3 52 B4
Sherwyn Rd L4 53 C8
Shetland Cl
Warrington WA2 61 E4
Widnes WA8 73 E3
Shetland Dr CH62 88 E8
Shevington Cl
St Helens WA9 58 C7
Widnes WA8 73 E3
Shevington's La L33 29 E6
Shevington Wlk WA8 73 E3
Shewell Cl CH42 66 D4
Shiel Rd CH45 51 B7
Shimmin St L7 53 A1
Shipley Wlk L24 82 D5
Shipton Cl
Birkenhead CH43 65 E1
Liverpool L19 81 B8
Widnes WA8 72 D3
Shirdley Ave L32 40 F7
Shirdley Cres PR8 7 C3
SHIRDLEY HILL 8 F6
Shirdley Wlk L32 40 F7
Shirebourne Ave WA11 44 B7
Shireburn Rd L37 9 D5
Shiregreen 6 WA9 58 C6
Shires The WA10 43 F2
Shirewell Rd WN5 25 E5
Shirley Rd L19 81 C8
Shirley St CH44 51 E3
Shirwell Gr WA9 58 C4
Shobdon Cl L12 40 F4
Shop La L31 20 C1
Shop Rd L34 41 C4
Shore Bank CH62 79 C8
Shore Dr CH62 79 C6
Shorefields CH62 79 C7
Shorefields Ho CH62 79 C7
Shorefields Sch L8 68 A3
Shorefields Village L8 67 F3
Shore Rd
Birkenhead CH41 66 E7
Birkenhead CH41 66 F7
Seaforth L21 37 F5
Southport PR8 7 B6
West Kirby CH48 75 C7
Shore Road Pumping Sta Mus* CH41 66 F7
Shoreside Prim Sch PR8 7 B4
Short Cl WA12 45 E3
Shortfield Rd CH49 65 A4
Shortfield Way CH49 65 A4
Short St
Golborne WA3 36 B1
Haydock WA11 45 E6
Newton-le-W WA12 45 E3
Shortwood Rd L14 54 F3
Shorwell Cl WA5 74 C7
Shottesbrook Gn L11 39 F3
Shrewsbury Ave
Aintree L10 28 D2
Crosby L22 26 D3
Shrewsbury Cl 3 CH43 65 F6
Shrewsbury Dr CH49 65 A6
Shrewsbury Mews L25 82 D9
Shrewsbury Pl L19 81 C6
Shrewsbury Rd
Birkenhead CH43, CH41 66 A5
Heswall CH60 77 A1
Liverpool L19 81 C6
Wallasey CH44 50 F5
West Kirby CH48 63 A1
Shrewton Rd L25 70 B7
Shropshire Cl L30 28 A4
Shropshire Gdns WA10 43 F2
Shuttle Hillock Rd WN2 36 F7
Sibford Rd L12 54 D5
Sibley Ave WN4 35 D4
Siddall St WA10 43 F7
Siddeley Dr WA12 45 F4
Siddeley St L17 68 C3
Sidgreave St WA10 43 E3
Siding La
Kirkby L33 30 C7
Rainford WA11 23 C1
Sidings The CH42 66 F2
Sidlaw Ave WA9 44 F3
Sidmouth Cl
St Helens WA10 43 C6
Warrington WA5 74 E4
Sidney Ave CH45 51 A8
Sidney Cl CH64 86 F1
Sidney Ct CH42 66 E4
Sidney Pl L7 68 A8
Sidney Powell Ave L32 29 C2
Sidney Rd
Birkenhead CH42 66 E4
Bootle L20 38 D2
Neston CH64 86 F1
Southport PR9 4 F8
Sidney St
Birkenhead CH41 66 E7
St Helens WA10 43 D4
Sidwell St L19 81 C5
Sienna Cl L27 70 C6
Signal Works Rd L9, L10 39 E8
Silcock St WA3 36 A1
Silcroft Rd L32 40 E8
Silkstone Cl
Liverpool L7 68 B8
St Helens WA10 43 D3
Silkstone St WA10 43 D3
Silver Ave WA11 45 A5
Silverbeech Ave L18 69 B4
Silverbeech Rd CH44 51 C3
Silverbirch Gdns CH44 50 E5
Silver Birch Gr WN4 35 A5
Silver Birch Way L31 20 B5
Silverbrook Rd L27 70 D7
Silverburn Ave CH46 49 E1
Silverdale PR8 3 E4
Silverdale Ave L13 53 E5
Silverdale Cl L36 70 E8
Silverdale Ct PR8 4 E4
Silverdale Dr L21 38 D8
Silverdale Gr WA11 44 A8
Silverdale Rd
Bebington CH63 78 F7
Birkenhead CH43 66 A4
Newton-le-W WA12 46 B4
Silverlake Cl L9 39 A3
Silverlea Ave CH45 51 B5
Silver Leigh L17 68 D1
Silverlime Gdns L35 57 C7
Silverstone Dr L36 70 D8
Silverstone Gr L31 20 B4
Silverthorne Dr PR9 1 F1
Silverton Rd L17 80 E8
Silverwell Rd L11 40 D5
Silverwell Wlk L11 40 D5
Silvester St L5 52 D5
Simms Ave WA9 44 E3
SIMM'S LANE END 34 B5
Simm's Rd L6 53 D6
Simnel Cl L25 70 B6
Simon Ct CH48 63 A2
Simonsbridge CH48 75 D6
Simons Cl L35 71 D8
Simon's Croft L30 27 C3
Simonside WA8 72 C2
Simonstone Gr 5 WA9 58 D7
Simonswood Ind Pk L33 30 B6
Simonswood La
Kirkby L33 30 A2
Royal Oak L39 21 F3
Simonswood Prim Sch L33 29 F2
Simonswood Wlk L33 30 A2
Simpkin St WN2 36 C8
Simpson St
Birkenhead CH41 66 D6
Liverpool L1 90 B1
Sim St L3 52 E3
Sinclair Ave
Prescot L35 56 F5
Warrington WA2 61 B2
Widnes WA8 84 F8
Sinclair Cl L35 56 F6
Sinclair Dr L18 69 B6
Sinclair St L19 81 C4
Sineacre La L33, L39 30 E8
Singleton Ave
Birkenhead CH42 66 C3
St Helens WA11 44 D5
Singleton Dr L34 41 D3
Sir Alfred Jones Meml Hospl L19 81 C6
Sirdar Cl L7 68 B8
Sir Howard St 13 L8 67 F8
Sir Howard Way 14 L8 67 F8
Sir Thomas St L1 90 B4
Siskin Cl WA12 46 C3
Siskin Gn L25 70 A4
Sisters Way CH41 66 D6
Sixpenny La L37 7 D1
Sixth Ave
Aintree L9 39 D7
Liverpool, Fazakerley L9 39 D7
Skeffington L35 56 E2
Skelhorne St L1, L3 90 C3
SKELMERSDALE 16 A1
Skelmersdale Coll (Westbank Campus)
Skelmersdale WN8 16 B1
Skelmersdale WN8 24 B8
Skelmersdale Rd L39, WN8 23 B7
Skelmersdale Sports Ctr WN8 24 C7
Skelton Cl WA11 44 A7
Skelton St WN4 34 F6
Skerries Rd L4 53 A7
Skiddaw Rd CH62 79 E2
Skipton Ave PR9 2 C6
Skipton Rd
Huyton-w-R L36 56 B3
Liverpool L4 53 B7
Skirving Pl L5 52 D6
Skirving St L5 52 E6
Skye Cl WA8 73 E3
Sky Lark Rise WA9 45 A3
Slackey La PR9 2 C4
Slag La
Golborne WA3 36 F2
Haydock WA11 45 B7
Slaidburn Cres
Golborne WA3 35 F2
Southport PR9 2 B5
Slaidburn Ind Est PR9 2 B5
Slate La WN8 15 C2
Slater Pl L1 90 B2
Slater St L1 90 B2
Slatey Rd CH43 66 B5
Sleaford Rd L14 55 B6
Sleepers Hill L4 52 F7
Slessor Ave CH48 63 D3
Slim Rd L36 55 E3
Slingsby Dr CH49 65 A4
Small Ave WA2 61 C2
Small Cres WA2 61 C2
Small La
Ormskirk, Clieves Hills L39 13 A3
Ormskirk L39 13 F4
Small La S L39 12 D6
Smallridge Cl CH61 76 E4
Smallshaw Cl WN4 35 A2
Smallwoods Mews CH60 76 E1
Smeaton St L4 38 E1
Smethurst Hall Pk WN5 25 C2
Smethurst Rd WN5 25 C2
Smilie Ave CH46 49 C1
Smith Ave CH41 66 B8
Smithdown Gr L7 68 B8
Smithdown La L7 53 A1
Smithdown Pl 5 L15 69 A5
Smithdown Prim Sch L7 68 B8
Smithdown Rd L15, L7 68 D7
Smith Dr L20 38 E5
Smithfield St
Liverpool L2, L3 90 A4
St Helens WA9 44 D2
Smithford Wlk L36 71 B7
Smith Pl L5 52 D6
Smith Rd WA8 84 F7
Smith St
Liverpool L5 52 E6
2 Prescot L34 56 E6
Skelmersdale WN8 15 D1
St Helens WA9 58 E7
Smithy Brow WA3 61 F7
Smithy Cl
Cronton WA8 72 C5
Formby L37 10 B4
Smithy Glen Dr WN5 25 E4
Smithy Gn L37 10 B4
Smithy Hey CH48 63 C2
Smithy Hill CH63 87 A6
Smithy La
Aughton L39 21 A6
Cronton WA8 72 C5
Haskayne L39 12 A6
Smithystone Cl L15 69 A7
Smock La WN4 34 C4
Smollett St
Bootle L20 38 B6
Liverpool L7 53 B2
Smugglers Way CH45 50 E8
Smythe Croft PR9 2 A2
Smyth Rd WA8 73 D2
Snaefell Ave L13 53 E5
Snaefell Gr L13 53 E5
Snape Gn PR8 5 E1
SNAPE GREEN 5 E1
Snave Cl L21 38 B5
Snowberry Cl WA8 73 E4
Snowberry Rd L14 55 A7
Snowden Rd CH46 64 C8
Snowdon Cl WA5 74 E6
Snowdon Gr WA9 58 C7
Snowdon La L5 52 C5
Snowdon Rd CH42 66 D2
Snowdrop Ave CH41 65 F7
Snowdrop Mews L21 38 B6
Snowdrop St L5 52 D7
Soane Cl WN4 35 D3
Soho Pl L3 52 E3
Soho St L3 52 E3
Solar Rd L9 39 B6
Solly Ave CH42 66 E2
Solomon St L7 53 B2
Solway Cl
Ashton-in-M WN4 35 A4
Warrington WA2 61 F4
Solway St E L8 68 B7
Solway St W L8 68 B7
Solway St CH41 51 A1
Soma Ave L21 38 C8
Somerford Ho 9 L23 26 B3
Somerford Rd L14 55 A4
Somerford Wlk WA8 73 E3
Somerley Cl L12 54 D8
Somerset Dr PR8 7 C3
Somerset Pl L6 53 D5
Somerset Rd
Bootle L20 38 D4
Crosby L22 26 C2
Heswall CH61 76 E4
Wallasey CH45 50 E5
West Kirby CH48 63 C3
Somerset St WA9 44 D2
Somerton St L15 68 E8
Somerville CH44 51 C3
Somerville Cl CH63 88 B6
Somerville Gr L22 26 D2
Somerville Prim Sch CH44 51 D3
Somerville Rd
Crosby L22 26 D2
Widnes WA8 84 D8
Sommer Ave L12 54 A7
Sonning Ave L21 27 B1
Sonning Rd L4 39 D2
Sorany Cl L23 27 B6
Sorogold St WA9 44 C3
Sorrel Cl CH43 65 D5
Sougher's La WN4 34 F7
Sougher's Lane End WN4 34 E6
South Albert Rd L17 68 C4
South Ave
Golborne WN7 36 F4
Prescot L34 56 C5
South Bank CH43 66 B3
Southbank Rd PR8 4 C5
South Bank Rd
Liverpool, Elm Park L7 53 D2
Liverpool, Grassendale L19 81 B7
South Bank Terr WA7 84 F3
South Barcombe Rd L16 69 E7
South Boundary Rd L33 41 C8
Southbourne Rd CH45 50 D5
Southbrook Rd L27 70 C7
Southbrook Way L27 70 C6
South Cantril Ave L12 54 F7
South Chester St L8 67 F6
Southcroft 7 L33 29 E4
Southcroft Rd CH45 50 D5
South Dale WA5 74 F5
Southdale Rd
Birkenhead CH42 66 E2
Liverpool L15 68 F8
Southdean Rd L14 55 B6
SOUTHDENE 40 E8
South Dr
Birkenhead CH49 65 A6
Heswall CH60 86 A7
Irby CH61 76 C5
Liverpool, Sandfield Park L12 54 B5
Liverpool, Victoria Park L15 69 A8
Southern Cres L8 67 E5
Southern Rd
Liverpool L24 82 E3
Southport PR8 4 A6
Southern's La WA11 32 A6
Southey Cl WA8 84 F8
Southey Gr L31 28 D6
Southey Rd WA10 57 C8
Southey St
Bootle L20 38 B4
Liverpool L15 68 E7
South Ferry Quay L3 67 D5
Southfield Rd L9 38 F6

Southfields Ave WA5 74 F6
South Front L35 71 E8
Southgate Cl L12 40 E3
Southgate Rd L13 54 B3
South Gr
Liverpool, Dingle L8 68 A4
Liverpool, Mossley Hill L18 69 C1
South Hey Rd CH61 76 D5
South Highville Rd L16 69 D6
South-Hill Gr CH43 66 B3
South Hill Gr 25 L8 68 A4
South Hill Rd
Birkenhead CH43 66 C4
Liverpool L8 68 A4
South Hunter St 1 L1 67 F8
South John St
Liverpool L1 90 A3
St Helens WA9 44 C3
South La
Warrington WA5, WA8 74 E5
Widnes WA8 73 F4
South Lancashire Ind Est WN4 35 B6
Southlands Ave WA5 74 F3
Southlands Ct 9 WA7 84 F1
Southlands Mews 8 WA7 84 F1
South Lane Entry WA8 73 F5
South Manor Way L25 70 C1
South Meade L31 20 B1
Southmead Gdns L19 81 E7
Southmead Rd L19 81 E7
South Mossley Hill Rd L19, L18 81 B8
Southney Cl L31 29 B3
South Par
Crosby L23 26 F3
Kirkby L32 29 E2
Liverpool L24 82 E3
West Kirby CH48 63 A1
Southpark Ct CH44 51 E3
South Park Ct L32 29 C3
South Park Rd L32 29 C3
South Parkside Dr L12 54 C6
South Parkside Wlk L12 54 B2
South Park Way L20 38 D2
SOUTHPORT 4 C3
Southport Botanic Gdns* PR9 2 B2
Southport Coll PR9 4 C7
Southport Ent Ctr PR9 5 A6
Southport FC PR8 4 E5
Southport & Formby District General Hospl PR8 4 E4
Southport General Infmy PR8 4 D5
Southport Holiday Ctr PR8 6 F6
Southport New Rd PR9 2 F5
Southport Old Rd L37 10 B7
Southport Rd
Bootle L20 38 E4
Crosby L23 27 A7
Formby L37 10 A5
Haskayne L39 12 A6
Maghull L31, L39 20 B5
Ormskirk L39, L40 13 D8
Southport PR8 5 B2
Southport St WA9 45 A3
Southport Sta PR8 4 B7
South Quay L3 90 A1
South Rd
Birkenhead CH42 66 D3
Crosby L22 26 E1
Liverpool, Broad Green L14 54 D2
Liverpool, Cressington Park L19 80 F6
Liverpool, Fazakerley L9 39 D6
Speke L24 82 F5
West Kirby CH48 63 B1
Southridge Rd CH61 77 A5
South Sefton Bsns Ctr L20 38 B2
South St
Liverpool L8 68 A5
St Helens WA9 57 D7
South Station Rd L25 70 B4
South Sudley Rd L19 81 A8
South Terr L39 13 E4
South View
Bebington CH62 79 D5
Huyton-w-R L36 56 B2
Seaforth L22 37 E8
South View Ct 4 L22 37 E8
South Villas 11 CH45 51 B7
Southward Rd WA11 46 A7
Southwark Gr L30 27 F1
Southway
Skelmersdale WN8 16 B1
Widnes WA8 84 D8
South Way L15 69 B8
Southwell Cl WA3 47 C8
Southwell Pl 3 L8 67 E5
Southwell St L8 67 E5
Southwick Rd CH42 66 E3
South Wirral High Sch CH62 88 D4
South Wirral Ret Pk CH62 79 D3
Southwold Cres WA5 74 E5
Southwood Cl 9 L32 41 A8
Southwood Rd L17 68 B3
Southworth La WA2, WA3 61 E7
Southworth Rd WA12 46 F4
Sovereign Cl WA3 47 E7
Sovereign Hey 1 L11 40 C3
Sovereign Rd L11 40 C3
Sovereign Way
Liverpool L11 40 C3
Wallasey CH41 51 D1
Spa Fold L40 15 A4
Spa La L40, WN8 15 C4
Sparks La CH61 77 B6
Sparling St L1 90 B1
Sparrow Hall Cl L9 39 F4
Sparrow Hall Rd L9 39 F4
Sparrowhawk Cl L26 70 E1
Spawell Cl WA3 47 E8
Speakman Ave WA12 46 C5
Speakman Rd WA10 43 D5
Speakman St WA7 84 F3
Speedwell Cl
11 Golborne WA3 47 E8
Heswall CH60 86 C8
Speedwell Dr CH60 86 C8
Speedwell Rd CH41 65 F7
SPEKE 82 D4
Speke Bvd
Halewood L24, L26, WA8 83 B5
Liverpool L24, WA8 82 D5
Speke Church Rd L24 82 B4
Speke Hall* L24 81 F2
Speke Hall Ave L24 82 B4
Speke Hall Rd L25 82 B7
Speke Ho L24 83 A2
Spekeland Rd L7 68 C8
Speke Rd
Liverpool, Garston L19 81 D5
Liverpool, Walton L25 82 C9
Speke L19, L24 81 E5
Widnes WA8 84 C6
Speke Town La L24 82 C5
Spellow La L4 52 F8
Spence Ave L20 38 D5
Spencer Ave CH46 50 A1
Spencer Cl L36 70 F8
Spencer Gdns WA9 58 D8
Spencer Pl L20 38 D7
Spencers La WN8 24 B7
Spencer's La
Aintree L10, L31 28 F3
Orrell WN5 25 D7
Southport L39 8 B3
Spencer St L6 52 F4
Spenser Ave CH42 66 F1
Spenser Cl WA8 72 F1
Spenser Lo 6 CH42 66 F1
Spenser Rd CH64 86 E1
Spenser St L20 38 B4
Spicer Gr L32 29 E2
Spice St L9 39 B5
Spindle Cl 3 L6 52 F4
Spindle Hillock WN4 34 D4
Spindrift Ct CH48 63 A1
Spindus Rd L24 82 B4
Spinnakers The L19 80 F7
Spinners Dr 3 WA9 58 F8
Spinney Ave WA8 72 A1
Spinney Cl
Kirkby L33 41 C8
Ormskirk L39 13 D3
St Helens WA9 58 C4
Spinney Cres L23 26 B6
Spinney Gn WA10 43 A2
Spinney Rd L33 41 D8
Spinney The
Bebington CH63 79 B3
Formby L37 10 A5
Heswall CH60 86 C5
Huyton-w-R L28 55 A7
Neston CH64 86 D1
Prescot L34 56 C7
Rainford WA11 31 F6
West Kirby CH48 63 E2
Spinney View L33 41 D8
Spinney Way L36 55 C3
Spion Kop WN4 35 A3
Spire Gn L9 39 A6
Spires Gdns WA2 61 A7
Spires The WA10 43 A4
SPITAL 79 C3
Spital Heyes CH63 79 B3
Spital Rd CH62 79 C3
Spital Sta CH63 79 B3
Spitfire Rd L24 81 F6
Spofforth Rd L15, L7 68 D8
Spooner Ave L21 38 C8
Sprainger St L3 52 B4
Sprakeling Pl L20 38 E7
Spray St WA10 43 E4
Spreyton Cl L12 40 C2
Sprig Cl L9 39 D8
Spring Bank Rd 1 L4 53 B5
Springbourne Rd L17 68 B2
Springbrook Cl WA10 43 A4
Spring Cl
Kirkby L33 30 A5
Southport PR8 4 A5
Springcroft CH64 86 C1
Springdale Cl
Liverpool L12 54 D7
Wallasey CH46 50 A1
Springfield L3 52 E3
Spring Field WA11 23 E2
Springfield Ave
Golborne WA3 46 F8
Springfield Ave continued
Litherland L21 38 C8
West Kirby CH48 63 F2
Springfield Cl
Birkenhead CH49 65 C2
Formby L37 9 C2
St Helens WA10 57 C8
Springfield Cotts 2 L23 26 D5
Springfield Ho 2 L37 10 A3
Springfield La WA10 43 A4
Springfield Pk WA11 45 C7
Springfield Rd
Maghull L39 20 F6
St Helens WA10 57 C8
Widnes WA8 84 A8
Springfield Sch L32 40 E7
Springfield Sq L4 52 F8
Springfield Way L12 54 E8
Spring Gdns L31 28 E8
Spring Gr L12 54 C6
Springhill Ave CH62 88 D6
Springhill Ct 3 L15 69 A6
Springmeadow Rd L25 70 A5
Springmount WA3 47 E7
Springpool WA9 58 D7
Spring Rd WN5 25 F8
Springs Cl L20 38 D4
Springside Cl L14 55 C6
Spring St CH41 66 F3
Spring Vale
Rainford WA11 32 A8
Wallasey CH45 50 E7
Springvale Cl L32 29 D1
Springville Rd L9 39 C7
Springwell Ct L20 38 D6
Springwell Rd
Bootle L20 38 D6
Bootle L20 38 D7
Springwood Ave L19, L25 81 E7
Springwood Ct L19 81 D7
Springwood Gr L32 40 F7
Springwood Heath Prim Sch L19 81 D8
Springwood Way CH62 79 A8
Spruce Cl
4 Birkenhead CH42 66 D4
Golborne WA3 47 F7
Spruce Gr L28 55 B7
Spruce Way L37 9 C3
Sprucewood Cl 3 L6 53 B5
Spur Cl L11 40 C3
Spurgeon Cl L5 52 F5
Spurling Rd WA5 59 F6
Spurrier's La L31 29 D8
Spurstow Cl CH43 65 F3
Spur The L23 26 D3
Spymers Croft L37 10 A6
Squibb Dr CH46 50 A2
Squires Cl WA11 45 B6
Squires St L7 68 A8
Squirrel Gn L37 9 C5
Stable Cl CH49 64 D4
Stables Bsns Ctr The L13 53 E7
Stables Ct WA9 44 C2
Stable Yd L12 40 D1
Stackfield The CH48 63 F3
Stadium Ct CH62 79 F2
Stadium Mews L20 38 E4
Stadium Rd CH62 79 E2
Stadt Moers Ctry Pk* L35 56 C2
Stafford Cl L36 56 A4
Stafford Moreton Way L31 20 D1
Stafford Rd
Southport PR8 4 A1
St Helens WA10 43 D1
Staffordshire Cl L5 52 E6
Stafford St
Liverpool L3 90 C4
Skelmersdale WN8 15 D1
Stag Rd L24 81 E6
Stainburn Ave L11 39 F3
Stainer Cl
Liverpool L14 54 F5
Newton-le-W WA12 46 B5
Stainton Cl
Liverpool L26 82 E9
St Helens WA11 44 B8
Stairhaven Rd L19 69 B1
Stakes The CH46 49 E3
Stalbridge Ave L18 68 F5
Staley Ave L23 26 F3
Staley St L20 38 D6
Stalisfield Ave L11 40 A1
Stalisfield Gr L11 40 A2
Stalisfield Pl L11 40 A2
Stalmine Rd L9 39 A4
Stamford Ct L20 38 D3
Stamfordham Dr L19 81 D7
Stamfordham Gr L19 81 D7
Stamfordham Pl L19 81 D7
Stamford Rd
Skelmersdale WN8 15 D2
Southport PR8 4 B2
Stamford St L7 53 C2
Stanbury Ave CH63 79 A6
Standale Rd L15 68 F8
Standard Rd L11 40 C4
Standedge Way L14 55 A6
Standen Cl WA10 43 E4
Stand Farm Rd L12 40 F3
Standhouse La L39 13 C2
Standish Ave WN5 33 E5
Standish Ct WA8 84 D8
Standish Dr WA11 32 A7
Standish St
Liverpool L3 90 B4
St Helens WA10 44 B4
Stand Park Ave L30 27 F2
Stand Park Cl L30 27 F2
Stand Park Rd L16 69 D6
Stand Parkway L30 27 E3
Standring Gdn WA10 57 B8
Standside Pk WN8 23 D8
Stanfield Ave L5 52 F5
Stanfield Dr CH63 78 F3
Stanfield Merchant Taylors' Jun Sch L23 26 E3
Stanford Ave 3 CH45 51 B7
Stanford Cres L25 82 D9
Stangate L31 20 B2
Stanhope Dr
Bebington CH62 79 D1
Huyton-w-R L36 55 C3
Stanhope St
Liverpool L8 67 E6
St Helens WA10 43 F5
Stanier Way L7 53 C1
Staniforth Pl L16 54 D1
Stanlawe Rd L37 9 E6
STANLEY
Liverpool 53 F3
Skelmersdale 15 E3
Stanley Ave
Bebington CH63 78 C8
Rainford WA11 31 F7
Southport PR8 3 F3
Wallasey CH45 50 D6
Warrington WA5 74 D7
STANLEY BANK 45 A7
Stanley Bank Rd WA11 45 A7
Stanley Bank Way
Haydock WA11 45 A7
St Helens WA11 44 F6
Stanley Bglws L34 41 C3
Stanley Cl
Liverpool L4 52 D7
Wallasey CH44 51 E2
Widnes WA8 73 C2
Stanley Cres L34 56 C6
Stanley Ct CH42 66 F3
STANLEY GATE 22 E7
Stanley Gdns L9 38 F5
Stanley High Sch Sports Coll PR9 1 F4
Stanley Ho L20 38 B4
Stanley La CH62 88 F4
STANLEY PARK 27 C1
Stanley Park Ave N L4 39 B2
Stanley Park Ave S L4 53 B8
Stanley Pk L21 27 B1
Stanley Rd
Bebington CH62 79 A8
Bootle L20 38 C3
Formby L37 9 E6
Hoylake CH47 62 F6
Huyton-w-R L36 55 E3
Liverpool L5 52 D5
Maghull L31 28 C6
Seaforth L22 37 E8
Up Holland WN8 25 B7
Wallasey CH41 50 F1
Stanley Sch CH61 77 A6
Stanley St
Liverpool, Fairfield L7 53 E3
Liverpool, Garston L19 81 C4
Liverpool L1, L2 90 A3
Newton-le-W WA12 46 A3
Ormskirk L39 13 F5
Southport PR9 4 B8
Wallasey CH44 51 E2
Stanley Terr
Liverpool L18 69 A3
7 Wallasey CH45 51 B7
Stanley Villas 7 WA7 84 F1
Stanley Way WN8 15 E3
Stanlow View L19 80 F6
Stanmore Pk CH49 64 B3
Stanmore Rd L15 69 B6
Stannanought Rd WN8 16 E2
Stanner Cl WA5 60 D2
Stanney Cl CH62 88 E3
Stannyfield Cl L23 27 B6
Stannyfield Dr L23 27 B6
Stansfield Ave L31 20 F1
Stanstead Ave WA5 74 F3
Stanton Ave L21 27 A1
Stanton Cl
Haydock WA11 45 C6
Litherland L30 27 D5
Stanton Cres L32 29 C2
Stanton Rd
Bebington CH63 78 F3
6 Liverpool L18 68 F5
Stanton Rd Prim Sch CH63 79 A3
Stanwood Cl WA10 42 F3
Stanwood Gdns L35 56 E3
Stapehill Cl L13 54 B2
Stapeley Gdns L26 83 A6
Staplands Rd L14 54 D2
Stapleford Rd L25 70 C6
Staplehurst Cl L12 40 E3
Stapleton Ave
Birkenhead CH49 64 D4
Liverpool L24 82 D4
Rainhill L35 57 C4
Stapleton Cl
Liverpool L25 70 B7
Rainhill L35 57 C4
Stapleton Rd
Formby L37 9 D1
Stapleton Rd continued
Rainhill L35 57 C5
Stapleton Way WA8 84 B5
Stapley Cl WA7 84 F1
Star Inn Cotts WA11 32 A5
Starling Gr L12 40 F1
Star St L8 67 E6
Startham Ave WN5 33 D3
Starworth Dr CH62 79 C7
Statham Ave WA2 61 C2
Statham Rd
Birkenhead CH43 65 C8
Skelmersdale WN8 15 E3
Statham Way L39 13 E4
Station App
Hoylake CH47 63 E8
Ormskirk L39 13 F5
Wallasey CH46 49 E2
Station Ave WN5 25 D5
Station Mews
Garswood WN4 34 D3
Kirkby L32 29 C3
Station Rd
Banks PR9 2 F5
Birkenhead CH41 50 F1
Garswood WN4 34 C3
Haskayne L39 11 E7
Haydock WA11 45 C6
Heswall, Barnston CH61 77 E5
Heswall CH60 85 F6
Hoylake CH47 63 B6
Huyton-w-R L36 55 C2
Kirkby L31 29 B3
Liverpool L25 70 B5
Maghull L31 28 E8
Maghull, Lydiate L31 20 A6
Ormskirk L39 13 F6
Prescot L34 56 D5
Rainhill L35 57 C3
Runcorn WA7 84 F2
Southport PR8 7 C5
St Helens WA9 58 E7
Thurstaston CH61 75 F4
Wallasey CH44 51 A4
Warrington, Penketh WA5 74 E3
Warrington WA5 74 F6
Station St L35 57 C3
Station Way 2 L36 56 A2
Statton Rd L13 54 B1
Staveley Rd
Liverpool L19 81 B8
Skelmersdale WN8 15 E3
Southport PR8 7 D4
Stavert Cl L11 40 B3
Staverton Pk L32 29 C1
Stavordale Rd CH46 65 A8
Steble St L8 67 F5
Steel Ave CH45 51 C6
Steel Ct L5 52 C6
Steeplechase Cl L9 39 C8
Steeple The CH48 75 D6
Steeple View L33 29 E5
Steers Croft L28 55 A8
Stein Ave WA3 47 E8
Steinberg Ct L3 52 C4
Steley Way L34 56 D5
Stella Prec L21 38 A6
Stephens La L2 90 A4
Stephenson Ct 11 L7 53 C1
Stephenson Ho L7 68 A8
Stephenson Rd
4 Liverpool L13 54 A2
Newton-le-W WA12 46 D2
Stephenson St WN2 36 B8
Stephenson Way
Formby L37 10 C3
Liverpool L13, L15 53 E1
Stephen Way L35 57 B5
Stepney Gr 1 L4 39 A1
Sterling Way L5 52 D6
Sterndale Cl L7 68 B8
Sterrix Ave L30 27 C2
Sterrix Gn L21 27 C2
Sterrix La L21, L30 27 C2
Steve Biko Cl 2 L8 68 B7
Stevenage Cl WA9 57 F7
Stevenson Cres WA10 43 D4
Stevenson Dr CH63 78 F3
Stevenson St L15 68 F8
Stevens Rd CH60 86 C7
Stevens St WA9 57 D8
Steward Ct L35 56 F5
Steward's Ave WA8 84 F8
Stewart Ave L20 38 E4
Stewart Cl CH61 76 F3
Stewerton Cl WA3 35 F2
Stile Hey L23 27 B5
Stiles Rd L33 29 F6
Stiles The L39 13 E5
Stillington Rd L8 68 A4
Stirling Ave L23 26 E3
Stirling Cres WA9 58 C6
Stirling Ct PR9 2 A2
Stirling Dr WN4 34 D4
Stirling La L25 82 D9
Stirling Rd L24 82 B4
Stirling St CH44 51 B2
Stockbridge La L36 55 C5
Stockbridge Pl 6 L5 53 A5
Stockbridge St L5 53 A5
STOCKBRIDGE VILLAGE 55 A8
Stockdale Cl 2 L3 52 C3
Stockdale Dr WA5 74 E7
Stockley Cres L39 22 E6
Stockmoor Rd L11 39 F3
Stockpit Rd L33 30 D2

Stocks Ave WA9 44 E3
Stocks Ct The WA3 47 D8
Stocks La WA5 74 D5
Stockswell Rd WA8 71 F4
Stockton Cres L33 29 E6
Stockton Gr WA9 57 D6
Stockton Wood Com Prim Sch L24 82 C4
Stockton Wood Rd L24 82 C4
Stockville Rd L18 69 E4
Stockwell Farm Ct WA8 72 E4
Stoddart Rd 2 L4 39 A2
Stoke Cl CH62 88 E3
Stoker Way L9 39 A5
Stokesay CH43 65 D6
Stokes Cl L26 71 A1
Stokesley Ave L32 29 C2
Stoke St CH41 66 C8
Stonebarn Dr L31 20 C3
Stonebridge La L10, L11 40 B6
Stoneby Dr CH45 51 A7
Stonechat Cl
10 Golborne WA3 47 E8
Liverpool L27 70 E4
Stonecrop L18 69 E5
Stonecross Dr L35 57 D1
Stone Cross Dr WA8 72 E5
Stone Cross La N WA3 47 C7
Stone Cross La S WA3 47 C6
Stone Cross Pk WA3 47 B7
Stonedale Cres L11 40 B4
Stonefield Rd L14 55 A4
Stonefont Cl L9 39 A3
Stonegate Dr L8 67 F4
Stone Hall La WN8 16 F4
Stonehaven Cl L16 69 F8
Stone Hey L35 56 D1
Stonehey Dr CH48 75 C8
Stonehey Rd L32 40 E8
Stonehey Wlk L32 40 E8
Stonehill Ave
Bebington CH63 79 A6
4 Liverpool L4 53 B6
Stonehill St L4 53 B6
Stonehouse Mews L18 69 D3
Stonehouse Rd CH44 50 E5
Stoneleigh Cl PR8 7 C4
Stoneleigh Gr CH42 78 F8
Stonemasons Ct L25 70 A3
Stone Pit Cl WA3 36 F1
Stone Pit La WA3 47 F2
Stoneridge Ct CH43 65 C8
Stone Sq L20 38 E6
Stone St
Liverpool L3 52 B4
6 Prescot L34 56 D6
Stoneville Rd L13 54 A4
Stoneway Ct 1 CH60 85 F8
STONEYCROFT 54 B4
Stoneycroft L13 54 B4
Stoneycroft Cl L13 54 A5
Stoneycroft Cres L13 54 A5
Stoney Hey Rd CH45 51 A7
Stoneyhurst Ave L10 28 C3
Stoney La L35 57 A3
Stoney La Ind Est L35 57 A4
Stoney View L35 57 B3
Stonham Cl CH49 64 E5
Stonyfield L30 27 E5
Stonyhurst Cl WA11 44 B7
Stonyhurst Rd L25 70 B1
Stopford St 11 L8 67 F4
Stopgate La
Kirkby L33 30 C7
Liverpool L11, L9 39 D3
Store St L20 38 D1
STORETON 78 B5
Storeton Cl CH43 66 B3
Storeton La CH61 77 C4
Storeton Rd CH42, CH43 66 B2
Stormont Rd L19 81 B7
Storrington Ave L11 40 B3
Storrsdale Rd L18 69 B3
Storwood Cl WN5 25 E5
Stour Ave L35 57 C3
Stourcliffe Rd CH44 51 A4
Stourport Cl 1 CH49 64 C4
Stourton Rd
Kirkby L32 40 F8
Southport PR8 7 C4
Stourton St CH44 51 C2
Stourvale Rd L26 82 F8
Stowe Ave L10 28 E2
Stowe Cl L25 82 B8
Stowell St L7 67 F8
Stowford Cl L12 40 C2
Strada Way L3 52 F3
Strafford Dr L20 38 E4
Straight Up La PR9 5 D8
Strand Ave WN4 35 B4
Strand Ho 7 L20 38 C3
Strand Rd
Bootle L20 38 B3
Bootle L20 38 C4
Hoylake CH47 63 B7
Strand Sh Ctr L20 38 C3
Strand St L1, L3 90 A3
Strand The
Ashton-in-M WN4 35 B4
Liverpool L2, L3 90 A3
Strand View L20 38 A3
Strange Rd WN4 34 D3
Stratford Cl PR8 7 A6
Stratford Rd L19 80 F8
Strathallan Cl CH60 76 E2
Strathcona Rd
Liverpool L15 68 E8
Wallasey CH45 51 C6
Strathearn Rd CH60 85 F7
Strathlorne Cl 7 CH42 66 F3
Strathmore Ave WN4 35 A5
Strathmore Dr L23 26 E3
Strathmore Gr WA9 58 C6
Strathmore Rd L6 53 C4
Stratton Cl
Liverpool L18 69 E3
Wallasey CH44 51 C5
Stratton Dr WA9 57 D6
Stratton Pk WA8 72 F5
Stratton Rd L32 29 C1
Stratton Wlk 4 L32 29 C1
Strauss Cl L8 68 B6
Strawberry Rd L11 39 E2
Streatham Ave L18 68 F5
Streatham House Sch L23 26 D4
Street Hey La CH64 88 B1
Stretford Cl L33 29 E5
Stretton Ave
Billinge WN5 33 E5
Golborne WA3 47 E7
St Helens WA9 44 F3
4 Wallasey CH44 51 A4
Stretton Cl
Bebington CH62 88 E3
Birkenhead CH43 65 E3
Liverpool L12 41 A3
Stretton Dr PR9 4 F8
Stretton Way L36 71 C8
Strickland St WA10 44 B4
Stringhey Rd CH44, CH45 51 C5
Stroma Rd L18 69 B1
Stroud Cl CH49 64 C3
Stuart Ave
Liverpool L25 82 C8
Wallasey CH46 49 F1
Stuart Cl CH46 65 A8
Stuart Cres WN5 33 E5
Stuart Dr L14 54 E3
Stuart Gr L20 38 D1
Stuart Rd
Birkenhead CH42 66 D3
Bootle L4, L9 38 F2
Crosby L22, L23 26 F2
Kirkby L31 29 B3
St Helens WA10 43 C6
Stuart Rd N L20 38 F4
Stubbs La CH43 65 E3
STUBSHAW CROSS 35 D5
Studholme St L20 52 C7
Studland Rd L9 39 E4
Studley Ct PR9 1 D1
Studley Rd CH45 50 F6
Sturdee Rd L13, L15 54 B1
Sturgess Cl L39 13 F7
Sturgess St WA12 45 F3
Suburban Rd 6 L6 53 C6
Sudbrook Cl WA3 47 E8
Sudbury Cl L25 70 D2
Sudbury Gdns WA9 57 C6
Sudbury Rd L22 26 B2
Sudell Ave L31 20 F2
Sudell La L31, L39 20 E6
Sudley Grange L17 68 F1
Sudley House Mus & Art Gall* L18 68 F2
Sudley Inf Sch L17 68 E2
Sudley Jun Sch L17 68 E1
Sudworth Rd CH45 51 A7
Suez St WA12 46 B3
Suffield Rd L4 52 D8
Suffolk Pl WA8 84 C7
Suffolk Rd PR8 8 A8
Suffolk St
Bootle L20 38 D4
Liverpool L1 90 B2
Runcorn WA7 84 F3
Suffton Pk L32 29 C1
Sugar La L34 41 D3
Sugar St L9 39 B5
Sugnall St 3 L7, L8 67 F8
Sulby Ave L13 53 E5
Sulby Cl PR8 3 F3
Sulgrave Cl L16 54 C1
Sullington Dr L27 70 E6
Sullivan Ave CH49 64 F4
Sullivan's Way WA9 58 B8
Sumley Cl WA11 44 D5
Summercroft Cl WA3 47 A7
Summerfield CH62 79 D2
Summerfield Ave
St Helens WA10 42 F3
Warrington WA5 60 F2
Summerford Cl CH42 66 E3
Summerhill Dr L31 28 F7
Summerhill Prim Sch L31 28 F8
Summers Ave L20 38 E4
Summer Seat
Bootle L20 38 A3
Liverpool L3 52 D4
Summers Rd L3 67 D4
Summer St WN8 16 A4
Summertrees Ave CH49 64 D4
Summertrees Cl CH49 64 D4
Summer Way L20 38 C5
Summerwood CH61 76 D7
Summerwood La L39 12 D8
Summit The CH44 51 C5
Summit Way L25 69 F3
Sumner Ave L39 11 F4
Sumner Cl
Liverpool L5 52 C5
Rainhill L35 57 D1
Sumner Gr L33 29 F5
Sumner Rd
Birkenhead CH41, CH43 65 F8
Formby L37 9 F3
Sumner St WA11 45 A6
Sunbeam Cl WA7 84 F3
Sunbeam Rd L13 54 B3
Sunbeam St WA12 46 C3
Sunbourne Rd L17 68 B2
Sunbury Dr PR8 7 B4
Sunbury Rd
Liverpool L4 53 B7
Wallasey CH44 51 C3
Sunbury St WA10 57 C8
Suncourt PR8 3 F6
Suncroft Rd CH60 86 C7
Sundale Ave L35 56 F6
Sundene Lo L22 37 E7
Sundew Cl L9 38 F7
Sundridge St 24 L8 68 A4
Sunfield Rd CH46 49 F2
Sunflower Cl WA9 59 A7
Sunlight Lo 6 CH62 79 B6
Sunlight St L6 53 C5
Sunloch Cl L9 39 D8
Sunningdale CH46 65 A8
Sunningdale Ave WA8 72 B1
Sunningdale Cl
Burtonwood WA5 59 F6
Huyton-w-R L36 55 C1
Sunningdale Dr
Bebington CH63 88 B6
Crosby L23 26 C6
Heswall CH61 77 A5
Sunningdale Gdns L37 9 E3
Sunningdale Rd
2 Liverpool L15 68 F8
Wallasey CH45 50 F8
Sunny Bank
Bebington CH63 78 D6
Birkenhead CH49 64 F6
Sunnybank Ave CH43 65 D4
Sunnybank Cl WA12 46 C4
Sunny Bank Cotts WA8 74 A4
Sunny Bank Rd L16 69 D7
Sunnydale L35 57 D3
Sunny Dr WN5 25 F6
Sunnyfields L39 14 A5
Sunnygate Rd L19 81 B8
Sunnymede Dr L31 20 D3
Sunnymede Sch PR8 3 F6
Sunny Rd PR9 2 A2
Sunnyside
Liverpool L8 68 B5
Ormskirk L39 21 C7
Southport PR8 3 F3
Wallasey CH46 49 D2
Warrington WA5 74 E6
Sunnyside Ct PR9 1 C1
Sunnyside Rd
Ashton-in-M WN4 34 F7
Crosby L23 26 D3
Sunrise Cl L19 81 B7
Sunsdale Rd 6 L18 69 A5
Sunset Cl L33 30 A5
Sunshine Vision Mus* CH62 79 B6
Superior Cl L27 70 E5
Surby Cl L16 69 E8
Surlingham Gdns WA9 57 E6
Surrey Ave CH49 64 E5
Surrey Cl PR9 2 C5
Surrey Dr CH48 75 C8
Surrey St
Bootle L20 38 D4
Liverpool L1 90 B2
St Helens WA9 44 D3
Wallasey CH44 51 A3
Susan Dr WA5 74 D5
Susan Gr CH46 64 D8
Susan St WA8 73 C2
Sussex Cl
Bootle L20 38 D4
Heswall CH61 76 E4
Sussex Gr WA9 44 C2
Sussex Rd
Maghull L31 28 D7
Southport PR8, PR9 4 D6
West Kirby CH48 63 C3
Sussex St
Bootle L20 38 D4
5 Crosby L22 26 C2
Widnes WA8 73 D1
Sutcliffe St L6 53 B3
Sutherland Dr CH62 88 D4
Sutherland Rd L34 56 E6
SUTTON 58 E8
Sutton Cl CH62 88 E3
Sutton Ct WA9 58 F7
Sutton Fold WA9 58 D8
SUTTON HEATH 57 E6
Sutton Heath Rd WA9 57 F7
Sutton High Sports Coll WA9 58 B6
Sutton L Ctr WA9 58 B6
SUTTON LEACH 58 D5
SUTTON MANOR 58 A2
Sutton Manor Com Prim Sch WA9 58 A2
Sutton Mews L25 82 D9
Sutton Moss Rd WA9 58 F8
Sutton Oak CE Prim Sch WA9 58 E8
Sutton Oak Dr WA9 44 D1
Sutton Park Dr WA9 58 C7
Sutton Rd
Formby L37 9 E1
St Helens WA9 44 D1
Wallasey CH45 51 B7
Sutton's La L37 10 E3
Sutton St L13 53 E5
Sutton Wood Rd L24 82 C4
Suzanne Boardman Ho L6 53 C5
Swainson Rd L10 39 F7
Swale Ave L35 57 C3
Swaledale Ave L35 57 D3
Swaledale Cl
Bebington CH62 88 E5
Warrington WA5 74 F7
Swalegate L31 20 C2
Swallow Cl
Kirkby L33 29 E7
Liverpool L12 40 F3
Liverpool, Netherley L27 70 F5
Swallow Ct WA10 43 D3
Swallow Fields L9 39 F4
Swallowhurst Cres L11 40 A2
Swan Alley 2 L39 13 E5
Swan Ave WA9 45 A2
Swan Cres L15 69 B8
Swan Ct CH43 65 F2
Swan Delph L39 13 C2
Swanfield Wlk WA3 35 F2
Swan Gdns WA9 57 E6
Swan Hey L31 28 E7
Swan La L39 20 F6
Swanpool La L39 13 C2
Swan Rd WA12 45 E4
Swansea Cl L19 81 B6
SWANSIDE 54 F2
Swanside Ave L14 54 E3
Swanside Par L14 54 F3
Swanside Rd L14 54 E3
Swan St L13 53 F3
Swanston Ave 8 L4 39 A1
Swan Wlk L31 28 E7
Sweden Gr L22 26 D1
Sweet Brier Ct WA9 58 D2
Sweeting St L2 90 A3
Swift Cl WA2 61 E3
Swift Gr L12 40 F4
Swift's Cl L30 27 D4
Swift's Fold WN8 23 D8
Swifts La L30 27 E3
Swift's La L30 27 D4
Swift St WA10 44 A5
Swinbrook Gn L11 39 F3
Swinburne Cl L16 69 F8
Swinburne Rd WA10 43 D5
Swinburn Gr WN5 25 D1
Swindale Ave WA2 61 B3
Swindale Cl L8 68 B7
Swinderby Dr L31 29 B3
Swindon Cl
Birkenhead CH49 64 C4
7 Liverpool L5 52 D7
Swindon St L5 52 D7
Swinford Ave WA8 73 E2
Swisspine Gdns L35 57 C7
Swiss Rd L6 53 C3
Switch Island L Pk L30 28 A3
Sword Cl 4 L11 40 C3
Sword Wlk L11 40 C3
Swynnerton Way WA8 73 B5
Sybil Rd L4 53 A7
Sycamore Ave
Birkenhead CH49 64 D6
Crosby L23 26 F6
Golborne WA3 36 A1
Haydock WA11 45 A5
Liverpool L26 82 F7
Newton-le-W WA12 46 C3
Widnes WA8 73 B2
Sycamore Cl
Birkenhead CH49 64 D7
Liverpool L9 39 C3
St Helens WA10 43 B4
Sycamore Ct 9 L8 68 A4
Sycamore Dr 1 WN8 15 E2
Sycamore Gdns WA10 43 E6
Sycamore Gr L37 9 C1
Sycamore Pk L18 69 D2
Sycamore Rd
Birkenhead CH42 66 D4
Crosby L22 26 E2
Huyton-w-R L36 70 E8
Sycamore Rise CH49 64 C2
Sydenham Ave L17 68 C6
Sydenham Ho L17 68 C5
Syders Gr L34 41 C3
Sydney Pl L7 53 A1
Sydney St L9 39 A6
Sylvan Ct L25 70 B1
Sylvandale Gr CH62 79 D2
Sylvania Rd L4 39 A2
Sylvester Prim Sch The L36 55 F1
Sylvia Cl L10 40 B6
Sylvia Cres WA2 61 D1
Syren St L20 52 C8
Syston Ave WA11 44 C6

T

Tabby's Nook WN8 16 A8
Tabley Ave WA8 72 D2
Tabley Cl CH43 65 F2
Tabley Gdns WA9 57 D6
Tabley Rd L15 68 D7
Tabley St L1 90 B2
Tace Cl L8 67 F7
Tadlow Cl L37 9 C1
Taggart Ave L16 69 D6
Tagus Cl L8 68 B6
Tagus St L8 68 B7
Tailor's La L31 28 E8
Talaton Cl PR9 2 A5
Talbot Ave CH63 78 A1
Talbot Cl WA10 43 F4
Talbot Ct
Birkenhead CH43 66 A4
Huyton-w-R L36 55 E1
Talbot Dr PR8 4 B6
Talbot Ho 7 CH43 66 B5
Talbot Rd CH43 66 A4
Talbot St
Golborne WA3 47 A8
Southport PR8 4 A6
Talbotville Rd L13 54 C1
Talgarth Way L25 70 A7
Taliesin St L5 52 D5
Talisman Way L20 38 A4
Talland Cl L26 70 E1
Tallarn Rd L32 29 B2
Tall Trees WA9 58 B8
Talman Gr WN4 35 D3
Talton Rd L15 68 D7
Tamar Cl L6 53 A4
Tamar Gr CH46 64 D8
Tamarisk Gdns L35 57 C7
Tamar Rd WA11 45 C6
Tamerton Cl L18 69 E2
Tamneys The WN8 15 F1
Tam O'Shanter Urban Farm* CH43 65 E7
Tamworth Gr 1 CH46 64 B8
Tamworth St
Liverpool L8 67 E5
Newton-le-W WA12 46 A3
St Helens WA10 43 E4
Tanar Cl CH63 79 B3
Tanat Dr L18 69 B4
Tancaster WN8 15 E1
Tancred Rd
Liverpool L4 53 A7
Wallasey CH45 51 A5
Tanfields WN8 15 F1
TANHOUSE 24 D8
Tan House La WA5 60 A5
Tanhouse Rd
Crosby L23 27 B5
Skelmersdale WN8 24 E7
Tanner's La WA3 47 B8
Tannery La WA5 74 D3
Tansley Cl CH48 63 E2
Tanworth Gr CH46 49 B1
Tapestry Gdns CH41 50 F1
Tapley Pl L13 53 F2
Taplow St 2 L6 53 B6
Tapton Way L13 53 F1
TARBOCK GREEN 71 D4
Tarbock Rd
Huyton-w-R L36 70 F8
Liverpool L24 82 D5
Tarbot Hey CH46 64 C8
Tarbrock Ct L30 27 D5
Target Rd CH60 85 C8
Tariff St L5 52 D5
Tarleton Cl L26 82 E9
Tarleton Rd PR9 5 A8
Tarleton St L1 90 B3
Tarlswood WN8 15 F1
Tarlton Cl L35 57 B5
Tarn Brow L39 13 C3
Tarn Cl WN4 35 B5
Tarncliff L28 55 C8
Tarn Gr WA11 44 B8
Tarn Rd L37 9 D3
Tarnside Rd WN5 25 E6
Tarnway WA3 47 F7
Tarporley Cl CH43 65 F3
Tarragon Cl L23 27 B5
Tarran Dr CH46 49 D2
Tarran Rd CH46 49 D2
Tarran Way E CH46 49 D2
Tarran Way N CH46 49 D3
Tarran Way S CH46 49 D2
Tarran Way W CH46 49 D2
Tarves Wlk 4 L33 29 F2
Tarvin Cl
Golborne WA3 47 E7
Southport PR9 2 D5
St Helens WA9 58 B3
Tarvin Rd CH62 88 F3
Tasker Terr L35 57 C4
Tasman Gr WA9 57 E7
Tate Cl WA8 72 D2
Tate Gallery* L3 67 B8
Tate St L4 52 F8
Tatlock Cl WN5 33 E5
Tatlock St L5 52 C4
Tattersall Rd L21 38 B7
Tattersall Way L7 53 E2
Tatton Dr WN4 34 F4

Tatton Rd
Birkenhead CH42........66 D5
Liverpool L9...........39 A6
Taunton Ave WA9........58 D5
Taunton Dr L10..........28 F2
Taunton Rd
Huyton-w-R L36........56 B2
Wallasey CH45..........50 E6
Taunton St L15..........68 E8
Taurus Pk WA5..........60 D3
Taurus Rd L14..........55 A4
Tavener Cl CH63.........88 C5
Tavington Rd L26.........71 A1
Tavistock Dr PR8.........7 B6
Tavistock Rd
Wallasey CH45..........50 E6
Warrington WA5.........74 E4
Tavlin Ave WA5..........60 F1
Tavy Rd L6.............53 A4
TAWD BRIDGE...........24 B7
Tawd Rd WN8...........24 C8
Tawd St L4.............52 E8
TAWD VALLEY PARK........16 A2
Taylforth Cl L9.........39 A5
Taylor Ave L39.........14 A5
Taylor Cl WA9..........58 E8
Taylor Rd WA11.........45 F7
Taylors Cl L4..........38 E3
Taylors La L9..........38 F3
Taylor's La WA5.........74 A2
Taylor St
Birkenhead CH41........66 E7
Golborne WN3..........36 C1
Liverpool L5...........52 E5
Skelmersdale WN8.......15 C1
St Helens WA9..........58 E8
Widnes WA8............73 C1
Taylor Street Heritage
Ctr★ CH41............66 E7
Taylor Street Ind Est
L5...................52 E5
Teakwood Cl L6.........53 B5
Teal Cl
Ormskirk L39..........13 C2
St Helens WA11.........44 B6
Warrington WA2.........61 E3
Teal Gr L26...........70 E1
Teals Way CH60.........85 E8
Tears La WN8..........15 F8
Teasville Rd L18........69 E4
Tebay Cl L31..........20 F2
Tebay Rd CH62.........88 E8
Teck St L7............53 A2
Tedburn Cl L25.........70 C4
Tedbury Cl L32.........40 E8
Tedbury Wlk L32........40 E8
Tedder Ave PR9.........5 A7
Tedder Sq WA8.........84 D8
Teehey Cl CH63.........78 D6
Teehey Gdns CH63.......78 D6
Teehey La CH63.........78 D6
Tees Cl L4............38 D1
Teesdale Cl WA5.........74 F7
Teesdale Rd
Bebington CH63.........78 E4
Haydock WA11..........45 C7
Tees Pl L4............38 D1
Tees St
Liverpool L4...........38 E1
Liverpool CH41.........50 F1
Teigh Cl L6...........53 A4
Teilo St L8...........68 A5
Telary Cl L5...........52 C5
Telegraph Ho 3 L23.......26 E5
Telegraph Rd
Heswall CH60..........86 A7
Irby CH48, CH60, CH61....76 C4
West Kirby CH48........75 F7
Telegraph Way L32........29 E2
Telford Cl
Birkenhead CH43........66 B4
Widnes WA8............72 D4
Telford Ct L7..........53 B1
Telford Dr WA9.........58 F7
Tempest Hey L2.........90 A4
Temple Ct L2...........90 A3
Temple La L2...........90 A3
Templemartin 2 WN8......15 F2
Templemore Ave L18.......69 A3
Templemore Rd CH43.......66 A4
Temple Rd CH42.........66 C2
Temple Sq 6 L2.........90 A4
Temple St L2...........90 A4
Templeton Cres L12.......40 B1
Tenbury Cl WA5.........60 A1
Tenbury Dr WN4.........35 A4
Tenby 2 WN8..........15 E2
Tenby Ave L21..........27 A1
Tenby Cl WA5..........60 F2
Tenby Dr CH46..........64 F8
Tenby St 5 L5.........53 A6
Tennis St N WA10.......43 E5
Tennis St WA10.........43 E5
Tennyson Ave 3 CH42......66 F1
Tennyson Dr
Longshaw WN5..........25 D1
Ormskirk L39..........13 D6
Warrington WA2.........61 C2
Tennyson Rd
Huyton-w-R L36........71 A1
Widnes WA8............73 A1
Tennyson St
Bootle L20............38 B5
St Helens WA9.........58 B2
Tennyson Way L32........29 D1

Tensing Rd L31.........20 D1
Tenterden St L5.........52 D4
Tenth Ave L9..........39 D7
Terence Rd L16.........69 D6
Terminus Rd
Bebington CH62.........79 D3
Huyton-w-R L36........55 C5
Tern Cl
Kirkby L33............29 E7
Widnes WA8............73 B4
Ternhall Rd L9.........39 F4
Ternhall Way L9........39 F4
Tern Way
St Helens WA10........57 A7
Wallasey CH46.........49 B1
Terret Croft L28........55 B7
Tetbury St CH41........66 C5
Tetlow St L4..........52 F8
Tetlow Way L4.........52 F8
Teulon Cl 1 L4........52 F7
Teversham WN8.........15 F2
Teviot 5 WN8.........15 E2
Tewit Hall Cl L24.......82 C4
Tewit Hall Rd L24.......82 C4
Tewkesbury 4 WN8.......15 E2
Tewkesbury
Liverpool, Croxteth L12....40 F4
Liverpool L25.........70 D2
Tewkesbury Rd WA3.......47 B8
Teynham Ave L34........41 D4
Teynham Cres L11.......39 F2
Thackeray Cl L8........67 F6
Thackeray Cl 7 L8......67 F6
Thackeray Gdns L30......38 D8
Thackeray Sq L8........67 F6
Thackeray St 8 L8......67 F6
Thackray Rd WA10.......57 D8
Thames Ave WA2.........61 D2
Thames Dr WN5.........25 F7
Thames Rd WA9.........58 C6
Thames St L8..........68 B6
Thanet WN8...........15 F2
Thatchers Mount WA5.....45 D1
THATTO HEATH..........57 E8
Thatto Heath Com Prim
Sch WA9.............57 E8
Thatto Heath Rd WA10,
WA9.................57 D8
Thatto Heath Sta WA9.....57 D8
Thealby Cl WN8.........15 E2
Thermal Rd CH62........79 E4
Thetford Rd WA5........74 E6
Thickwood Moss La
WA11................32 A5
THINGWALL............77 B5
Thingwall Ave L14.......54 D3
Thingwall Dr CH61.......77 A6
Thingwall Grange
CH61................77 B6
Thingwall Hall Dr L14....54 D2
Thingwall La L14.......54 E3
Thingwall Prim Sch
CH61................77 B6
Thingwall Rd
Irby CH61............76 E6
Liverpool L15.........69 B8
Thingwall Rd E CH61......77 A7
Third Ave
Aintree L9............39 D7
Birkenhead CH43........65 B6
Crosby L23............26 A4
Liverpool, Fazakerley L9...39 E7
Thirlmere Ave
Abram WN2............36 B8
Ashton-in-M WN4.......35 C4
Birkenhead CH43........65 C5
Bootle L21............38 D8
Formby L37............10 A2
Liverpool 1 WN5.......25 F7
St Helens WA11........44 B8
Up Holland WN8........25 B7
Warrington WA2........61 C3
Thirlmere Cl L31........20 E2
Thirlmere Ct L5.........53 A5
Thirlmere Dr
Bootle L21............38 D8
Southport PR8.........7 B3
Wallasey CH45.........51 B5
Thirlmere Gn L5........53 A5
Thirlmere Rd
Golborne WA3..........36 C1
Hightown L38..........18 A4
Liverpool L5..........53 A5
Thirlmere Way WA8.......84 C8
Thirlmere Wlk L33.......29 C4
Thirlstane St L17.......68 B3
Thirsk WN8...........15 E2
Thistledown Cl 3 L17.....68 A3
Thistleton Ave CH41......65 F8
Thistleton Mews 3 PR9....15 E8
Thistlewood Rd L7.......53 E2
Thistley Hey Rd L32......29 F2
Thomas Cl L19.........81 C5
Thomas Ct L14.........54 D3
Thomas Dr
Liverpool L14.........54 C2
Prescot L35...........56 C4
Thomas Gray Prim Sch
Bootle L20............38 B4
Bootle L20............38 B5
Thomas La
Liverpool, Broad Green
L14................54 D2
Liverpool L1..........90 A3
Thomas St
Birkenhead CH41........66 E5
7 Birkenhead CH41......66 E6
Golborne WA3..........47 A8

Thomaston St L5........52 E6
Thomas Winder Ct L5......52 D6
Thompson Ave L39.......14 B5
Thompson Cl WA12.......46 C1
Thompson St
Ashton-in-M WN4.......35 D4
Birkenhead CH41........66 E4
St Helens WA9.........43 D1
Thomson Rd L21........38 A7
Thomson St L6.........53 B4
Thorburn Cl CH62.......79 B8
Thorburn Cres CH62......79 B8
Thorburn Ct CH62.......67 B1
Thorburn Lo CH62.......67 B1
Thorburn Rd CH62.......79 B8
Thorburn St L7.........53 B1
Thorley Cl L15.........54 A1
Thornaby Gr WA9........57 D6
Thornbeck Ave L38.......17 F3
Thornbeck Cl 3 L12......40 F3
Thornber 1 WN8........15 F2
Thornbridge Ave L21......38 D8
Thornbrook Cl L12.......54 D7
Thornbury WN8.........15 F2
Thornbury Ave WA3.......47 E7
Thornbury Rd L4........53 C7
Thornbush Cl WA3.......36 E1
Thornby 3 WN8........15 F2
Thorn Cl WA5..........74 F3
Thorncliffe Rd CH45......51 A3
Thorncroft Dr CH61......77 B4
Thorndale 4 WN8........15 F2
Thorndale Rd L22.......26 D2
Thorndyke Cl L35.......57 E1
Thornes Rd 11 L6.......53 B3
Thorness Cl CH49.......64 C2
Thorneycroft St CH41.....66 A8
Thornfield WA3.........47 C8
Thornfield Hey CH63......79 A2
Thornfield Rd
Crosby L23............27 A6
Liverpool L9..........38 F5
Thornham Ave WA9.......58 C8
Thornham Cl CH49.......65 A7
Thornhead La L12.......54 D6
Thornhill WN8.........21 B8
Thornhill Cl L39.......21 B8
Thornhill Rd
Garswood WN4.........34 C4
Liverpool L15.........69 A7
Thornhills WA8........72 A3
Thornholme Cres L11......40 A1
Thornhurst L32........40 E7
Thornleigh Ave CH62......88 F3
Thornley Rd CH46.......64 C7
Thorn Rd WA10.........43 C3
Thornridge CH49........65 A8
Thorns Dr CH49........64 C2
Thornside Wlk L25......70 B4
Thorns The L31.........20 B2
THORNTON............27 B6
Thornton
Skelmersdale WN8......15 F2
Widnes WA8............84 E8
Thornton Ave
Bebington CH63........78 D8
Bootle L20............38 D7
Thornton Cl WN4........34 F4
Thornton Common Rd
CH63................87 D7
Thornton Cres CH60......86 B6
Thorntondale Dr WA5......74 F7
Thornton Gr CH63.......78 D8
Thornton Ho CH63.......87 B6
THORNTON HOUGH........87 A7
Thornton Hough Prim Sch
CH63................87 B7
Thornton Prim Sch
L23................27 B6
Thornton Rd
Bebington CH63........78 D8
Bootle L20............38 C5
Liverpool L16.........54 D1
Southport PR9.........4 F7
4 Wallasey CH45......51 A4
Thornton St
Birkenhead CH41........66 A8
Bootle L21............38 B6
Thorntree Cl L17.......68 A3
Thorn Tree Cl L24.......83 E2
Thornvale WN2.........36 C7
Thornwood WN8........15 F2
Thornwood Cl 4 L6......53 B5
Thornycroft Rd L15......68 D7
Thorpe WN8...........15 F2
Thorpe Bank CH42.......78 F8
Thorstone Dr CH61.......76 C7
Thorsway
Birkenhead CH42........66 F2
West Kirby CH48........75 D8
Threadneedle Ct WA9......58 F8
Three Acres Cl L25......69 E3
Three Butt La L12, L13....54 A7
Three Lanes End CH48.....64 B5
Three Pools PR9........2 C3
Three Sisters Rd WN4......35 B7
Three Sisters Recn Area★
WN4................35 C7
Three Tuns La L37.......9 F3
Threlfall's La PR9.......1 F2
Threlfall St L8.........68 A4
Thresher Ave 4 CH49.....64 C4
Threshers The L30.......28 A4
Throne Rd L11.........40 C3
Throne Wlk 2 L11.......40 C4
Thurcroft Dr WN8.......15 E2
Thurlby Cl WN4........35 D4
Thurlow WA3..........47 E7

Thurne Way L25........70 A6
Thurnham St L6.........53 C5
Thursby Cl
2 Liverpool L32.......40 F8
Southport PR8.........7 B3
Thursby Cres 1 L32......40 F8
Thursby Rd CH62........79 E2
Thursby Wlk 3 L32......40 F8
THURSTASTON...........76 A5
Thurstaston Rd
Heswall CH60..........85 F8
Irby CH61............76 C6
Thurston WN8.........15 E2
Thurston Rd L4.........53 B6
Tibbs Cross La WA8.......73 D8
Tichbourne Way 2 L6......52 F3
Tickle Ave WA9.........44 E3
Tideswell Cl L7........68 B8
Tide Way CH45.........50 E8
Tilbrook Dr WA9........58 D6
Tilcroft WN8..........15 E2
Tillotson Cl L8.........67 E5
Tilney St L9..........39 A6
Tilstock Ave CH62.......79 B8
Tilstock Cl L26........71 A2
Tilstock Cres CH43.......65 F2
Tilston Cl L9..........39 D3
Tilston Rd
Kirkby L32............29 C2
Liverpool L9..........39 D4
6 Wallasey CH45......51 A6
Time Pk L35..........56 F5
Timmis Cres WA8........73 A1
Timms Cl L37.........9 F5
Timms La L37.........9 F5
Timon Ave L20.........38 E5
Timor Ave WA9.........57 E8
Timpron St L7.........68 C8
Timway Dr L12.........54 E8
Tinas Way CH49........65 A5
Tinling Cl 3 L34.......56 E6
Tinsley Ave PR8........4 E3
Tinsley Cl L26.........70 E2
Tinsley's La PR8.......5 A1
Tinsley St 4 L4........53 A7
Tintagel WN8..........15 E2
Tintagel Rd L11........40 D5
Tintern Ave WN4........35 D3
Tintern Cl WA5.........60 E2
Tintern Dr
Birkenhead CH46........64 E8
Formby L37............10 B2
Tiptree Cl L12.........40 F4
Titchfield St L3, L5.....52 D4
Tithebarn CH60........85 F7
Tithebarn Dr CH64.......86 B2
Tithebarn Gr L15.......69 A7
Tithebarn La
Kirkby, Melling L31......29 A5
Kirkby, Westvale L32.....29 D1
Tithebarn Rd
Crosby L23............26 F4
Garswood WN4.........34 D2
Knowsley L34..........41 D4
Southport PR8.........4 E6
Tithebarn St
Liverpool L2, L3......90 A4
Up Holland WN8........25 B7
Titherington Way L15......68 D6
Tiverton Ave
Skelmersdale WN8......15 E2
1 Wallasey CH44......51 B4
Tiverton Cl
Huyton-w-R L36........56 B3
Widnes WA8............72 C3
Tiverton Rd L26........82 C7
Tiverton Sq WA5........74 E4
Tiverton St L15........68 E8
Tivoli Villa's CH45......37 C1
Tobermory Cl WA11.......45 A5
Tobin Cl L3...........52 C4
Tobin St CH44.........51 D4
Tobruk Rd L36.........55 D4
Todd Rd WA9..........44 B3
Toft Cl WA8..........72 F1
Toft St L7...........53 C2
Toftwood Ave L35.......57 D1
Toftwood Gdns L35.......57 D1
Tokenspire Pk L33.......41 B8
Toleman Ave CH63.......79 A5
TOLL BAR.............43 C1
Toll Bar Cnr CH62.......79 B7
Toll Bar Pl WA2........61 A4
Toll Bar Rd WA2........61 A3
Tollemache Rd CH41.......65 E7
Tollemache St CH45......37 C1
Tollerton Rd L12.......54 A7
Tolpuddle Rd L25.......69 F2
Tolpuddle Way L4.......52 D8
Tolver Ho 4 WA10.......44 A4
Tolver St WA10.........44 A4
Tom Mann Cl L3........52 D3
Tonbridge Cl L24.......82 B5
Tonbridge Dr L10.......28 D3
Tongbarn WN8.........15 E2
TONTINE.............25 D5
Tontine Cl L25.........70 C4
Tontine Mkt WA10.......44 A3
Tontine Rd WN5, WN8.....25 C6
Toothill Rd WN4........35 B5
Top Acre Rd WN8.......24 C7
Topaz Cl L4..........38 E2
Topcliffe Gr L12.......41 A3
Topgate Cl CH60........86 B8
Topham St L9.........28 B1
Topsham Cl L25........70 C4
Torcross Cl PR9........9 C7

Torcross Way
Halewood L26..........70 F1
Liverpool, Gateacre L25...70 C4
Tordelow Cl L6.........53 A4
Toronto St CH44........51 E3
Torquay Dr WN5........33 E8
Torr Dr CH62..........89 A7
Torrington Dr
Heswall CH61..........77 B6
Liverpool L26.........82 E7
Torrington Gdns CH61.....77 B7
Torrington Rd
Liverpool L19.........81 B7
Wallasey CH44, CH45....51 A4
Torrisholme Rd L9.......39 D3
Torr St L5...........52 E6
Torus Rd L13.........54 A4
Tor View Rd L15.......69 A6
Torwood CH43.........65 D6
Totland Cl
Liverpool L27.........70 F4
Warrington WA5........74 C7
Totnes Ave L26........70 F1
Totnes Dr PR9.........2 A5
Totnes Rd L11.........40 C5
Tourney Gn WA5........60 A2
Towcester St L21.......38 D8
Tower Bldg L3.........52 B1
Tower Bldgs 11 PR9......4 C8
Tower Coll L35.........57 D1
Tower Dene Sch PR9......1 F2
Tower End L37.........9 C5
Tower Gdns L3.........90 A3
TOWER HILL...........29 F5
Tower Hill
Birkenhead CH42........66 D3
Ormskirk L39..........14 A5
Tower Hill Rd WN8.......25 B6
Towerlands St L7........53 B1
Tower Nook WA8........25 A5
Tower Prom CH45.......37 C1
Tower Quays CH41.......66 E8
Tower Rd
Birkenhead CH42........66 E8
Birkenhead, Devonshire Park
CH42................66 D3
Birkenhead, Prenton
CH42................66 B1
Tower Rd N CH60........76 F2
Tower Rd S CH60........76 F1
Towers Ave L31........20 C2
Towers Rd L16.........69 C6
Tower St L3..........67 E4
Towers The CH42........66 D2
Tower Way L25.........70 A3
Tower Wharf CH41.......66 E8
TOWN CENTRE..........16 C1
Towneley Ct WA8........72 C6
TOWN END............13 D4
Town End Cl L39.......13 D4
Townfield Ave WN4.......35 B2
Townfield Cl CH43.......65 E3
Townfield Ct CH43.......66 A4
Townfield Ctr CH43.......65 E3
Townfield Gdns CH63......78 F7
Townfield La
CH43................65 E3
Townfield Prim Sch
CH43................65 E3
Townfield Rd CH48.......63 B2
Townfields WN4........35 A3
Town Fields 2 CH45......50 E6
Towngate Bsns Ctr
WA8................84 B7
TOWN GREEN
Ashton-in-Makerfield.....35 C4
Ormskirk.............21 D7
Town Green Ct L39.......21 C8
Town Green Gdns L39.....21 C8
Town Green La L39.......21 C8
Town Green Sta L39......21 C8
Town La
Bebington CH63........78 E7
Hale L24, WA8.........83 E2
Southport PR8.........4 E3
Town Lane Inf Sch
CH63................78 E6
Town Lane (Kew) PR8......4 E3
Town Meadow La
CH46................49 C1
TOWN OF LOWTON........47 B5
Town Rd CH62..........66 E3
Town Row L12.........54 B6
Townsend Ave L11, L4.....39 E2
Townsend La L13, L6.....53 C6
Townsend St
Liverpool L5..........52 C6
Wallasey CH41.........50 F1
Townsend View
Litherland L21.........27 B2
Liverpool L11.........39 E3
Townsfield La WA2.......61 A5
Townshend Ave CH61......76 D4
Town View 13 CH41,
CH43................66 C5
Town View Mews 14
CH43................66 C5
Towson St L5..........52 F6
TOXTETH.............67 E5
Toxteth Com Coll L7......67 F5
Toxteth Gr L8.........68 A4
Toxteth St L8.........67 F5
Tracks La WN5.........25 D3
Tracy Dr WA12.........46 E3
Tradewind Sq L1........90 B2
Trafalgar Ave CH44......51 D5
Trafalgar Ct PR8.......3 E1

Trafalgar Dr CH63 79 A4
Trafalgar Rd
Southport PR8 3 E3
Wallasey CH44 51 C5
Trafalgar St WA10 43 E4
Trafalgar Way 4 L6 52 F3
Tragan Dr WA5 74 D3
Tramway Rd L17 68 C3
TRANMERE 66 E3
Trap Hill L37 9 C2
Trapwood Cl WA10 43 B3
Travanson Cl L10 40 B6
Travers' Entry WA9 59 A7
Traverse St WA9 44 C3
Travis Dr L33 29 F5
Trawden Way L21 27 C4
Treborth St 4 L8 68 A5
Trecastle Rd L33 30 A4
Treen Cl PR9 2 B6
Treesdale Cl PR8 3 F4
Treetop Ct L6 53 C4
Treetops Dr CH41 50 D1
Treetop Villas PR9 1 F4
Tree View Ct L31 28 E8
Treforris Rd CH45 50 F7
Trefula Pk L12 54 A6
Trelawney Cl L25 70 B6
Tremore Cl L12 40 C1
Trendeal Rd L11 40 D5
Trent Ave
Huyton-w-R L14 54 F2
Maghull L31 20 F2
Trent Cl
Liverpool L12 40 D3
Rainhill L35 57 B3
St Helens WA9 58 C5
Widnes WA8 73 B4
Trentham Ave L18 68 F5
Trentham Cl WA8 73 B4
Trentham Rd
Kirkby L32 29 C1
Wallasey CH44 51 C3
Trentham St WA7 84 F3
Trentham Wlk 1 L32 29 C1
Trent Pl L35 57 B3
Trent Rd
Ashton-in-M WN4 35 E5
Billinge WN5 33 D3
Rainhill L35 57 B3
Trent Way
Heswall CH60 86 C6
Litherland L21 27 A1
Tressel Dr WA9 58 A3
Tressell St L9 38 F3
Trevelyan Dr WN5 25 D1
Trevelyan St L4 38 F3
Treviot Cl L33 29 D6
Trevor Dr L23 26 F4
Trevor Rd
Liverpool L9 39 A6
Southport PR8 7 C4
Trimley Cl CH49 64 E5
Tring Cl CH49 65 A7
Trinity CE Sch WN8 15 F1
Trinity Ct CH47 63 B7
Trinity Gdns
Ashton-in-M WN4 34 F4
Hoylake CH47 63 B7
Southport PR8 4 A6
Trinity Gr L23 26 B2
Trinity La CH41 66 E7
Trinity Mews PR9 4 C7
Trinity Pl L20 38 D3
Trinity RC Prim Sch The
L3 52 C4
Trinity Rd
Bootle L20 38 C2
Hoylake CH47 63 B7
Wallasey CH44 51 C5
Trinity St Peter's CE Prim
Sch L37 10 A5
Trinity St
Birkenhead CH41 66 C7
St Helens WA9 44 C3
Trinity Wlk 4 L3 52 E3
Trispen Cl L26 82 E9
Trispen Rd L11 40 D4
Trispen Wlk L11 40 D4
Tristram's Croft L30 27 D3
Triumph Trad Pk The
L24 81 F6
Triumph Way L24 82 A7
Troon Cl
Bebington CH63 88 C5
Haydock WA11 45 A5
Liverpool L12 54 F6
Trossach Cl WA2 61 E2
Trotwood Cl L9 39 D8
Troutbeck Ave
Maghull L31 20 E2
Newton-le-W WA12 45 E4
Troutbeck Cl 3 CH49 65 A2
Troutbeck Gr WA11 33 B2
Troutbeck Rd
Ashton-in-M WN4 35 C5
Liverpool L18 69 D5
Trouville Rd L4 53 C7
Trowbridge St L3 90 C3
Trueman Cl CH43 65 C8
Trueman St L1, L2, L3 90 B4
Truman Cl WA8 72 F3
Trundle Pie La L39 12 C6
Truro Ave
Litherland L30 27 F4
Southport PR9 2 B5
Truro Cl WA11 44 D7
Truro Rd L15 69 A6
Tudor Ave
Bebington CH63 79 A3
Wallasey CH44 51 E2
Tudor Cl
Liverpool L7 52 F1
Rainford WA11 31 E8
Tudor Ct
Liverpool L19 81 A7
Ormskirk L39 13 F6
Tudor Gdns L38 17 F4
Tudor Grange CH49 64 D3
Tudor Mans PR8 3 F6
Tudor Rd
Birkenhead CH42 66 E3
Crosby L23 26 D3
Liverpool L25 82 C8
Southport PR8 7 B6
Tudor Street N L6 53 B3
Tudor Street S L6 53 B3
Tudor View L33 29 E5
Tudorville Rd CH63 78 F5
Tudorway CH60 86 B8
TUEBROOK 53 E6
Tue La WA8 72 B6
Tuffins Cnr L27 70 D5
Tulip Ave CH41 65 F7
Tulip Rd
Haydock WA11 45 F6
Liverpool L15 69 B7
Tulketh St PR8 4 B7
Tulliallen L22 37 E8
Tullimore Rd L18 69 A1
Tullis St WA10 43 E2
Tulloch St L6 53 B3
Tully Ave WA12 45 F3
Tumilty Ave L20 38 E4
Tunnage Sq L1 90 B2
Tunnel Rd
Birkenhead CH41 66 F5
Liverpool L7 68 B8
Tunstall Cl CH49 64 E5
Tunstall St L7 68 C7
Tunstall's Way WA9 58 D4
Tupelo Cl L12 40 F4
Tupman St 2 L8 67 F5
Turmar Ave CH61 77 B6
Turnacre
Formby L37 10 B6
Huyton-w-R L14 54 E3
Turnall Rd WA8 84 B7
Turnberry WN8 15 D2
Turnberry Cl
Huyton-w-R L36 55 C1
Liverpool L12 54 F6
Wallasey CH46 49 B1
Turnberry Way PR9 2 D5
Turnbridge Rd L31 20 C3
Turner Ave L20 38 E7
Turner Cl
Liverpool L8 68 A3
Widnes WA8 72 D3
Turner Gr L33 29 E6
Turneris View CH64 86 D2
Turners Ct L25 70 C3
Turner St 6 CH41 66 C5
Turney Rd CH44 51 A4
Turnill Dr WN4 35 B2
Turning La PR8 5 A1
Turnpike Rd L39 13 A2
Turnstone Ave WA12 46 C4
Turnstone Cl L12 40 E3
Turnstone Dr L26 70 E1
Turret Hall Dr 1 WA3 47 E8
Turret Rd CH45 51 A6
Turriff Dr CH63 88 C4
Turriff Rd L14 55 A5
Turton Cl L24 83 E1
Turton St
Golborne WA3 47 A8
Liverpool L5 52 D6
Tuscan Cl WA8 73 B5
Tuson Dr WA8 72 F4
Tutor Bank Dr WA12 46 D3
Tweed Cl L6 53 C4
Tweed St CH41 51 A1
Twickenham Dr
Huyton-w-R L36 55 D1
Wallasey CH46 50 A3
Twickenham St 1 L6 53 B6
Twigden Cl L10 39 F8
Twig La
Huyton-w-R L36 55 C4
Maghull L31 20 E1
Twist Ave WA3 47 C8
Twistfield Cl PR8 3 F5
Two Butt La L35 57 A5
Twomey Cl L5 52 C4
Two Saints Pl 8 L39 13 E5
Twyford Ave L21 27 B1
Twyford Cl
Maghull L31 20 E1
Widnes WA8 73 B5
Twyford La WA8 73 D6
Twyford Pl WA9 44 C3
Twyford St L6 53 B6
Tyberton Pl L25 82 C7
Tyburn Cl CH63 78 F2
Tyburn Rd CH63 78 F2
Tyndall Ave L22 37 F8
Tyne Cl
Liverpool L4 52 E8
St Helens WA9 57 D6
Warrington WA2 61 E2
Tynemouth Cl 9 L5 53 A5
Tyne St CH41 50 F1
Tynron Gr CH43 65 D5
Tynville Rd L9 39 C7
Tynwald Cl L13 53 F4
Tynwald Cres WA8 72 F5
Tynwald Hill L13 53 F4
Tynwald Pl L13 53 F4
Tynwald Rd CH48 63 A2
Tyrer Gr L34 56 E7
Tyrer Rd
Newton-le-W WA12 46 C1
Ormskirk L39 13 F7
Tyrer's Ave L31 20 B5
Tyrers Cl L37 9 F2
Tyrer St
3 Liverpool L1 90 B3
Wallasey CH41 50 F1
Tyrer Wlk 2 WA3 47 F8

U

Uldale Cl
Liverpool L11 40 A2
Southport PR8 7 B3
Uldale Way L11 40 A2
Ullet Rd L17, L8 68 C5
Ullet Wlk L17 68 D5
Ullswater Ave
Ashton-in-M WN4 35 B5
Birkenhead CH43 65 D6
Orrell WN5 25 F7
St Helens WA11 44 B8
Warrington WA2 61 D3
Ullswater Cl L33 29 D4
Ullswater Ct WA3 36 C1
Ullswater Ho L17 68 D2
Ullswater Rd WA3 36 C1
Ullswater St L5 53 A5
Ulster Rd L13 54 B3
Ultonia St L19 81 C4
Ulverscroft CH43 65 F4
Ulverston Ave WA2 61 B4
Ulverston Cl
Haydock WA11 45 A6
Maghull L31 20 E2
Ulverston Lawn L27 70 F4
Umbria St L19 81 C4
Undercliffe Rd L13 54 A4
Underhill Rd WA10 43 D2
Underley St L7 68 C7
Underley Terr CH62 79 B7
Unicorn Rd L11 40 C4
Unicorn Way CH41 66 F5
Union Bank La WA8 58 C1
Union Cl WN5 25 E5
Union Ct L2 90 A3
Union St
Birkenhead CH42 66 F3
Liverpool L3 52 B2
Southport PR9 4 C8
St Helens WA10 44 A4
Wallasey CH44 51 D4
Union Terr CH45 37 B1
Unit Rd PR8 7 D5
Unity Gr L34 41 A5
University Rd L20 38 D2
Univ Hospl Aintree L9 39 E6
Univ of Liverpool
Liverpool L3, L7 52 F1
Liverpool L69 67 F8
Univ of Liverpool Art
Gall★ L7 52 F1
Unsworth Ave WA3 36 E1
Unsworth Ct WA2 61 F1
Upavon Ave CH49 64 B3
Upchurch Cl 2 L8 67 F4
UP HOLLAND 25 B6
Up Holland High Sch
WN5 25 C4
Upholland Rd WN5 25 D2
Upholland Sta WN8 24 F4
Upland Dr WN4 35 D4
Upland Rd
Birkenhead CH49 65 A6
St Helens WA10 57 C8
Uplands Cl WA10 57 B8
Uplands Rd CH62 79 C2
Uplands The CH43 65 E4
Upper Aughton Rd PR8 4 B4
Upper Baker St L6 53 A3
Upper Beau St 9 L5 52 E4
Upper Beckwith St
CH41 66 B8
Upper Brassey St
CH41 66 A8
Upper Bute St 5 L5 52 E4
Upper Duke St L1 90 C2
Upper Essex St L8 67 F5
Upper Flaybrick Rd CH41,
CH43 65 E7
Upper Frederick St
Liverpool L1 90 B2
Liverpool L1 90 C1
Upper Hampton St L8 67 F7
Upper Harrington St
L8 67 E6
Upper Hill St 1 L8 67 F6
Upper Hope Pl 4 L8 67 F8
Upper Huskisson St L8 68 A7
Upper Mann St
Liverpool L8 67 E6
Liverpool, Toxteth L8 67 E5
Upper Mason St L7 53 A1
Upper Newington L3 90 C3
Upper Park St L8 67 F5
Upper Parliament St
L8 68 A7
Upper Pitt St L1 90 C1
Upper Pownall St L1 90 B2
Upper Raby Rd CH64 87 A2
Upper Rice La CH44 51 C5
Upper Stanhope St
Liverpool L8 67 F7
Liverpool L8 90 C1
Upper Warwick St L8 67 F6
Upper William St L3 52 B4
Uppingham WN8 15 D1
Uppingham Ave L10 28 E2
Uppingham Rd
Liverpool L13 53 F5
Wallasey CH44 50 F5
UPTON
Birkenhead 64 F6
Widnes 72 C4
Upton Ave PR8 7 B6
Upton Barn L31 20 C2
Upton Bridle Path
WA8 72 F4
Upton By Pass CH49 64 E5
Upton Cl
Birkenhead CH49 64 F5
Golborne WA3 47 D8
Liverpool L24 82 E4
Upton Ct CH49 65 A6
Upton Dr WA5 74 F5
Upton Gn L24 82 E4
Upton Grange WA8 72 D4
Upton Hall Sch CH49 64 F5
Upton La WA8 72 F4
Upton Park Dr CH49 65 A6
Upton Rd
Birkenhead, Noctorum CH41,
CH43 65 D6
Birkenhead, Upton CH46 64 E8
UPTON ROCKS 72 E4
Upton Rocks Ave WA8 72 E4
Upton Rocks Mews
WA8 72 E4
Upton Sta CH43 65 C5
Upwood Rd WA3 47 D7
Urmson Rd CH45 51 B5
Urmston Ave WA12 46 B5
Ursula St L20 38 D1
Ursuline RC Prim Sch
L23 26 B3
Utkinton Cl CH43 65 F3
Utting Ave L4 53 B8
Utting Ave E L11 39 F2
Uveco Bsns Ctr CH41 51 B1
Uxbridge St L7 68 B8

V

Vale Cres PR8 7 C2
Vale Croft WN8 25 A6
Vale Ct 4 L21 38 A6
Vale Dr CH45 51 C7
Vale Gr L32 30 A1
Vale La L40 15 F5
Vale Lo L9 39 A4
Valencia Gr L34 56 F7
Valencia Rd L15 69 A8
Valentia Rd CH47 63 B7
Valentine Gr L10 28 E1
Valentine Rd WA12 45 F3
Valentines Way L9 28 C1
Vale Owen Rd WA2 61 D1
Vale Rd
Crosby L23 26 D4
Liverpool L25 69 F2
Valerian Rd CH41 65 F7
Valerie Cl L10 40 B6
Valescourt Rd L12 54 C5
Valewood Prim Sch
L23 26 D5
Valiant Cl
Liverpool L12 41 A3
Warrington WA2 61 F2
Valiant Ho CH41 66 F6
Valiant Way CH41 66 F4
Valkyrie Rd CH45 51 A5
Vallance Rd L4 53 C7
Valleybrook Gr CH63 79 B2
Valley Cl
Aintree L10 28 F1
Crosby L23 27 B4
Valley Ct WA2 61 F1
Valley Rd
Bebington CH62 88 D8
Kirkby L32 29 D1
Liverpool, Anfield L4 53 B6
Liverpool L10, L32 40 B8
Wallasey CH41 50 E1
Valley View WA12 46 B1
Vanbrugh Cres L4 53 C7
Vanbrugh Rd L4 53 D7
Vancouver Rd L27 70 E5
Vanderbilt Ave L9 39 B8
Vanderbyl Ave CH62 79 C2
Vandries St L3 52 B4
Vandyke St L8 68 C7
Vanguard St L5 52 F6
Vanguard Way CH42 66 F3
Vardon St CH41 66 D8
Varley Rd
Liverpool L19 69 A1
St Helens WA9 44 C4
Varlian Cl L40 14 C3
Varthen St 6 L5 53 A7
Vaughan Cl L37 9 D4
Vaughan Rd
Southport PR8 4 B4
Wallasey CH45 51 C8
Vaughan St CH41 65 F8
Vaux Cres L20 38 D5
VAUXHALL 52 C3
Vauxhall Cl WA5 74 F4
Vauxhall Rd L3, L5 52 C4
Vaux Pl L20 38 D5
Venables Cl CH63 79 B1
Venables Dr CH63 79 A1
Venice St L4, L5 52 F6
Venmore St L5 53 A6
Ventnor Cl WA5 74 D7
Ventnor Rd L15 68 F8
Venture Ct CH41 66 F5
Venture Point W L24 82 B6
Venture Works L33 30 C1
Verdala Pk L18 69 C2
Verda St WN2 36 B8
Verdi Ave L21 38 A6
Verdi St L21 37 F6
Verdi Terr L21 37 F5
Vere St L8 67 E5
Vermont Ave L23 26 D4
Vermont Cl L33 29 D6
Vermont Rd L23 26 D4
Vermont Way L20 38 C4
Verne Wlk WN4 35 D3
Verney Cres L19 81 C8
Verney Cres S L19 81 C8
Vernon Ave
Hooton CH66 89 A2
Wallasey CH44 51 D2
Vernon Ct PR8 4 D5
Vernon Rd PR9 5 A8
Vernon St
Liverpool L1, L2 90 A4
St Helens WA9 44 C4
Verona St L5 52 F6
Veronica Cl L12 40 E3
Veronica Mews WA8 72 D1
Verulam Cl L8 68 A7
Verulam Rd PR9 2 B3
Verwood Cl CH61 76 D7
Verwood Dr L12 41 A3
Veryan Cl L26 70 F1
Vescock St L5 52 D4
Vesta Rd L19 81 D4
Vesuvian Dr L19 81 D4
Vesuvius Pl L5 52 D6
Vesuvius St L5 52 D6
Viaduct St WA12 46 A3
Vicarage Cl
Birkenhead CH42 66 B1
Formby L37 9 D4
Hale L24 83 E1
Liverpool L18 69 B2
Ormskirk L40 14 B3
Vicarage Dr WA11 45 B7
Vicarage Gr CH44 51 C5
Vicarage La
Banks PR9 2 F7
Ormskirk L40 14 C3
Vicarage Lawn L25 70 C5
Vicarage Pl L34 56 C6
Vicarage Rd
Abram WN2 36 B8
Ashton-in-M WN4 35 B2
Formby L37 9 D4
Haydock WA11 45 A7
Orrell WN5 25 D4
Vicarage Row CH62 89 A5
Vicarage Wlk L39 13 E5
Vicar Rd L6 53 C7
Viceroy Ct 3 PR8 4 A6
Viceroy St L5 52 F6
Vickers Dr WN8 24 E8
Vickers Rd WA8 84 F4
Victoria Ave
Crosby L23 26 C4
Heswall CH60 86 A6
Liverpool, Broad Green
L14 54 D2
5 Liverpool L15 68 F8
St Helens WA11 44 A8
Warrington WA5 74 D6
Widnes WA8 73 A3
Victoria Bldgs L37 9 E5
Victoria Bridge Rd PR8 4 C6
Victoria Central Hospl
CH44 51 B4
Victoria Cl L17 68 E3
Victoria Ct
7 Birkenhead CH41 66 D7
Birkenhead, Rock Ferry
CH42 67 A1
Liverpool, Sefton Park
L17 68 B4
Liverpool, Victoria Park
L15 69 A8
Skelmersdale WN8 15 D1
4 Southport PR8 3 F4
Victoria Dr
Birkenhead CH42 67 A1
Liverpool L9 38 F6
West Kirby CH48 63 A2
Victoria Falls Rd L27 70 F4
Victoria Fields CH42 66 D4
Victoria Gdns CH43 66 B4
Victoria Gr WA8 73 A3
Victoria Ho
12 Prescot L34 56 D6
Rainford WA11 31 F7
Victoria La CH43 66 B4
Victoria Mews PR9 4 D7
Victoria Mount CH43 66 B4
Victoria Par CH45 37 C1
VICTORIA PARK
Bootle 38 F7
Liverpool 69 A8
Victoria Park Rd CH42 66 D2
Victoria Pk WN8 15 C1

Victoria Pl
- Rainhill L35 57 C3
- Wallasey CH44 51 F2

Victoria Rd
- Bebington CH63 78 D6
- Birkenhead CH42 66 D4
- Crosby L23 26 D5
- Formby L37 9 D5
- Garswood WN4 34 D4
- Huyton-w-R L36 55 F2
- Ince Blundell L38 18 E3
- Liverpool L17 68 E3
- Liverpool, Tuebrook L13 53 E6
- Newton-le-W WA12 46 C3
- Ormskirk L39 13 C2
- Seaforth L22 37 E8
- Wallasey CH45 51 B8
- Warrington, Penketh WA5 74 D4
- West Kirby CH48 63 B1

Victoria Rd W L23 26 D4
Victoria Sq 2 WA10 44 A3
Victoria St
- Bebington CH62 79 B5
- Liverpool L1, L2 90 B4
- Rainford WA11 31 F7
- Rainhill L35 57 C3
- Southport PR9 4 B8
- St Helens WA10 44 A5

Victoria Terr
- Bickershaw WN2 36 F8
- 4 Liverpool L15 69 A6
- Rainhill L35 57 C3

Victoria Trad Est L35 57 C3
Victoria Way
- Formby L37 9 D5
- Southport PR8 3 F7

Victor St L15 68 D8
Victory Ave PR9 5 A7
Victory Cl L30 38 E8
Vienna St L5 52 F6
Viennese Rd L25 70 B6
Viewpark Cl L25 69 F7
View Rd L35 57 C2
Viking Cl
- Litherland L21 38 A7
- Southport PR8 4 A4

Village Cl
- Skelmersdale WN8 23 D8
- Wallasey CH45 50 E6

Village Courts L30 27 F5
Village Ct
- Birkenhead CH43 66 A4
- Irby CH61 76 D6
- Liverpool L17 68 C2

Village Green Ct CH43 65 C8
Village Mews 4 CH45 50 E6
Village Nook L10 28 E2
Village Rd
- Bebington CH63 78 D6
- Birkenhead CH43 66 A4
- Heswall CH60 85 F7
- West Kirby CH48 63 C1

Village Row PR8 7 C5
Village St L6 52 F4
Village The CH63 79 A5
Village View WN5 33 E5
Village Way
- Hightown L38 17 F4
- Skelmersdale WN8 23 D8
- Wallasey CH45 50 E6

Villa Gloria Cl L19 81 A8
Villas Rd L31 21 B2
Villiers Cres WA10 42 F4
Villiers Ct L34 41 B5
Villiers Rd L34 41 C6
Vincent Ct L1 90 B2
Vincent Naughton Ct CH41 66 F5
Vincent Rd
- Litherland L21 27 C1
- Rainhill L35 57 C4

Vincent St
- 4 Birkenhead CH41 66 D6
- Liverpool L13 54 A1
- St Helens WA10 44 A4

Vine Cres WA5 74 F6
Vine Ho L21 38 A6
Vineries The L25 69 E3
Vineside Rd L12 54 D6
Vine St L7 68 A8
Vine Terr WA8 72 A2
Vineyard St L19 81 E5
Vining Rd L35 56 F6
Vining St L8 67 F6
Viola Cl L33 29 D5
Viola St L20 38 C1
Violet Rd
- Birkenhead CH41 65 F7
- Bootle L21 38 B6

Violet St WN4 35 B2
Virgil St
- Liverpool L5 52 E4
- St Helens WA10 43 E4

Virginia Ave L31 20 D3
Virginia Gr L31 20 C3
Virginia Rd CH45 37 B1
Virginia St PR8 4 C6
Virgin's La L23 27 A6
Viscount Ctr L24 82 D6
Viscount Rd WA2 61 E2
Vista Ave WA12 46 A4
Vista Rd WA11, WA12 46 A6
Vista Way WA12 46 A4
Vitesse Rd L24 81 F6
Vittoria Cl CH41 66 D7
Vittoria St CH41 66 D7
Vivian Ave 12 CH44 51 E2
Vivian Dr PR8 4 A2
Vixen Gr WA8 72 F4
Voelas St L8 68 A6
Vogan Ave L23 27 A3
Volunteer St 3 WA10 43 F4
Vronhill Cl L8 68 A6
Vulcan Cl
- Birkenhead CH41 65 F8
- Newton-le-W WA12 46 C1
- Warrington WA2 61 F2

Vulcan Ind Est WA12 46 D1
Vulcan St
- 3 Birkenhead CH41 65 F8
- Bootle L20 38 B4
- Liverpool, Garston L19 81 C4
- Liverpool, Vauxhall L3 52 B4
- Southport PR9 4 C7

VULCAN VILLAGE 60 C8
Vyner Cl CH43 65 E6
Vyner Ct CH43 65 E6
Vyner Pk CH43 65 E6
Vyner Prim Sch CH43 50 D1
Vyner Rd CH45 50 F5
Vyner Rd N
- Birkenhead CH43 65 D7
- Liverpool L25 70 A5

Vyner Rd S
- Birkenhead CH43 65 D6
- Liverpool L25 70 B5

Vyrnwy St 1 L5 53 A6

W

WADDICAR 29 B4
Waddicar La L31 29 B4
Waddington Cl
- Golborne WA3 47 F8
- Warrington WA2 61 F1

Wadebridge Rd L10 40 B6
Wade Deacon High Sch WA8 73 A2
Wadeson Rd L4 39 D2
Wadham Pk L20 38 C1
Wadham Rd L20 38 C2
Wagon La WA11 45 B6
Waine Gr L35 57 A5
Waine St
- St Helens, Blackbrook WA11 44 F6
- St Helens, Finger Post WA9 44 D4

Wainwright Cl 2 L7 68 C8
Wainwright Gr L19 81 B6
Wakefield Dr CH46 49 F4
Wakefield Ind Est L30 28 B3
Wakefield Rd L30 28 A2
Wakefield St
- Golborne WA3 47 A7
- Liverpool L3 52 E3

Walby Cl CH49 65 C2
Walden Rd L14 54 C3
Waldgrave Pl L15 54 B1
Waldgrave Rd L15 54 B1
Waldron WN8 23 D8
Waldron Cl 3 L3 52 C3
Walford Cl CH63 78 F2
Walford Rd WN4 35 C3
Walkden Cotts L39 30 E8
Walkden Ho 8 WN4 34 F5
Walker Art Gallery* L3 90 B4
Walker Ave WA9 58 B3
Walker Cl L37 9 F2
Walker Dr L20 38 C7
Walker Mews CH42 66 D3
Walker Pl CH42 66 D3
Walker Rd L21 38 A7
Walker's Croft CH45 50 F5
Walkers La
- St Helens WA9 58 A3
- Warrington WA5 74 E3

Walker St
- Bebington CH62 79 B6
- Birkenhead CH42 66 D3
- Hoylake CH47 63 B7
- Liverpool L6 53 A3

Walker Way L9 38 F6
Walk The
- Liverpool L24 82 A3
- Southport PR8 4 A5

Wallace Ave L36 56 A4
Wallace Dr L36 56 A4
Wallace St L9 39 A6
Wallacre Rd CH44 50 F4
WALLASEY 50 D4
Wallasey Bridge Rd CH41 50 F2
Wallasey Grove Road Sta CH45 50 E6
Wallasey Rd CH44, CH45 51 A4
Wallasey Sch CH46 50 A3
Wallasey Village CH44, CH45 50 E6
Wallasey Village Sta CH45 50 E5
Wallbrook Ave WN5 25 D1
Wallcroft St WN8 23 E8
Waller Cl L4 52 E7
Waller St L20 38 B6
Wallgate Rd L25 69 F6
Wallgate Way L25 69 F6
Wallingford Rd CH49 64 F4
Wallrake CH60 85 F7
Wallsend Ct WA8 72 F3
Walmer Ct PR8 3 F4
Walmer Rd
- Seaforth L22 37 E8
- Southport PR8 4 A3

Walmesley Dr WA11 32 A5
Walmesley Rd WA10 43 A5
Walmsley St
- Liverpool L5 52 C5
- Newton-le-W WA12 46 D4
- Wallasey CH44 51 C5

Walney Rd L12 54 A8
Walney Terr L12 54 A8
Walnut Ave L9 39 C3
Walnut Gr
- Kirkby L31 29 A2
- 1 St Helens WA9 58 C8

Walnut St PR8 4 C4
Walpole Ave L35 56 F3
Walpole Gr WA2 61 C2
Walro Mews PR9 2 A3
Walsham Gdns WA9 57 E6
Walsh Cl
- Liverpool L3 52 C4
- Newton-le-W WA12 46 C5

Walsh Rd L14 54 C2
Walsingham Ct CH44 51 D3
Walsingham Rd
- Liverpool L16 69 E8
- Wallasey CH44 51 D3
- Warrington WA5 74 F5

Walter Beilin Ct L17 68 E5
Walter Gr WA9 58 F7
Walters Green Cres WA3 36 A2
Walter St
- Ashton-in-M WN4 35 D4
- Liverpool L5 52 B5
- Widnes WA8 73 D1

Waltham Rd L6 53 C6
Waltho Ave L31 20 E1
WALTON 39 A2
Walton Ave WA5 74 E5
Walton Breck Rd L4, L5 52 F7
Walton Hall Ave L11, L4 39 C2
Walton Hospl L9 38 F3
Walton La L4 52 F8
WALTON ON THE HILL 39 A2
Walton Pk L9 39 A4
Walton Progressive Sch L9 38 F3
Walton Rd
- Liverpool L4, L5 52 E7
- St Helens WA10 43 D6

Walton St Mary CE Prim Sch L4 38 F2
Walton St
- 16 Birkenhead CH41 66 E6
- Southport PR9 4 C8

Walton Sta L9 38 F4
Walton Vale L9 39 A6
Walton Village L4 39 A2
Wambo La L25 70 C5
Wandsworth Rd L11 39 F1
Wandsworth Way WA8 84 F5
Wango La L10 28 F1
Wanishar La L39 12 A5
Wansfell Pl WA2 61 A3
Wantage View L36 70 C8
Wapping L1 90 A2
Wapshare Rd L11 53 E8
Warbler Cl L26 70 D2
Warbreck Ave L9 39 A6
Warbreck Moor L9 39 B7
WARBRECK PARK 39 A6
Warbreck Rd L9 39 A6
Warburton Hey L35 57 C4
Ward Ave L37 9 D2
Ward Cl WA5 60 B1
Warden St 6 L4 52 E8
Wardgate Ave L12 40 E3
Ward Gr CH42 78 F8
Ward rake L30 27 D4
Ward Rd L23 26 A5
Ward St
- Liverpool L3 90 C4
- Prescot L34 56 D7
- St Helens WA10 44 A4

Ware Cl WN4 35 D4
Wareham Cl WA11 45 C7
Wareing Rd L9 39 C6
Waresley Cres L9 39 E4
WARGRAVE 46 D3
Wargrave CE Prim Sch WA12 46 C1
Wargrave House Sch WA12 46 C1
Wargrave Mews WA12 46 C1
Wargrave Rd WA12 46 C2
Warham Rd L4 53 C7
Waring Ave
- Birkenhead CH42 66 D2
- St Helens WA9 45 B2

Warkworth Cl
- Huyton-w-R L36 71 A8
- Widnes WA8 72 C3

Warmington Rd L14 54 C3
Warner Dr L4 53 C8
Warnerville Rd L13 54 B1
Warnley Cl WA8 72 D3
Warren Ct
- 4 Crosby L23 26 C3
- Southport PR8 3 E5

Warrender Dr CH43 65 F8
Warren Dr
- Birkenhead CH43 65 C6

Warren Dr *continued*
- Newton-le-W WA12 46 F4
- Wallasey CH45 50 F8

Warren Gn L37 9 D3
Warren Hey CH63 79 A1
Warrenhouse Rd
- Crosby L22 26 B2
- Kirkby L33 30 B4

Warren Hurst 6 CH45 51 A8
Warrenhurst Ct 2 L23 26 B3
Warren Pk CH45 50 F7
Warren Rd
- Crosby L23 26 B4
- Hoylake CH47 63 A7
- Southport PR9 5 A8
- Warrington, Orford WA2 61 D1

Warren St L3 90 C3
Warren The
- Birkenhead CH49 65 B5
- Newton-le-W WA12 46 A3

Warren Way CH60 76 D1
WARRINGTON 61 D4
Warrington Bsns Pk WA2 61 C1
Warrington Collegiate WA2 61 B1
Warrington New Rd WA9 44 B3
Warrington Old Rd WA9 44 B2
Warrington Rd
- Abram Brow WN2 36 B7
- Ashton-in-M WN4 35 B2
- Bold Heath L35, WA8 73 D7
- Cronton L35 72 F8
- Golborne WA3, WA12 47 A6
- Prescot L34, L35 56 E5
- Rainhill L35 57 A4
- Warrington WA5 74 F4
- Widnes WA8 73 D1

Warrington St CH41 66 E4
Warton Cl L25 70 C2
Warton St L20 38 B6
Warton Terr L21 38 B6
Warwick Ave
- Ashton-in-M WN4 35 D2
- Crosby L23 26 D3
- Newton-le-W WA12 46 E2
- Warrington WA5 74 D7

Warwick Cl
- Birkenhead CH43 66 C5
- Huyton-w-R L36 56 A3
- Southport PR8 4 B4

Warwick Ct 3 L8 68 A6
Warwick Dr
- Wallasey CH45 51 C6
- West Kirby CH48 75 C8

Warwick Rd
- Birkenhead CH49 64 F6
- Bootle L20 38 D4
- Huyton-w-R L36 56 A3

Warwick St
- Liverpool L8 67 E6
- Southport PR8 4 B4
- St Helens WA10 43 D3

Wasdale Ave
- Maghull L31 20 F2
- St Helens WA11 44 B8

Wasdale Rd
- Ashton-in-M WN4 35 A8
- Liverpool L9 39 A5

Washbrook Ave 2 CH43 65 C8
Washbrook Cl WA10 43 B4
Washbrook Way L39 13 E4
Washington Cl WA8 72 F3
Washington Dr L33 29 D6
Washington Par L20 38 C3
Washington Rd L27 70 F4
Washway La WA10, WA11 44 A7
Wasley Cl WA2 61 F3
Wastdale Ct CH46 49 C1
Wastdale Dr CH46 49 C1
Wastdale Mews CH46 49 C1
Wastle Bridge Rd L36 55 E5
Watchyard La L37 10 A4
Waterdale Cres WA9 58 D7
Waterdale Pl WA9 58 D7
Waterfall Dr L9 39 A3
Waterfield Cl CH63 78 D5
Waterfield Way L21 27 A1
Waterfoot Ave PR8 7 B3
Waterford Rd
- Birkenhead CH43 65 F5
- Liverpool L27 70 C6

Waterfront Bsns Area Parliament St N
- Liverpool L1 90 B1
- Liverpool L1 90 C1

Waterfront Bsns Area Parliament St S
- Liverpool L8 67 D6
- Liverpool L8 90 C1

Watergate La L25 70 B2
Watergate Way L25 70 B2
Waterhouse Cl 8 L6 53 B6
Waterhouse St L5 52 F4
Water La
- Southport PR9 2 D5
- Tarbock Green L35, WA8 71 D5

Waterland La WA9 44 F2
WATERLOO 26 D2
Waterloo Cl L22 37 D8
Waterloo Ct CH63 79 A6
Waterloo EMI Day Hospl L22 26 E1
Waterloo Pl CH41 66 E5
Waterloo Prim Sch L22 26 E1
Waterloo Quay L3 52 B3
Waterloo Rd
- Liverpool L3, L5 52 B3
- 3 Runcorn WA7 84 F2
- Runcorn WA7 84 F3
- Seaforth L22 37 E8
- Southport PR8 3 E2
- Wallasey CH45 37 B1

Waterloo St
- Liverpool L15 69 A7
- 5 St Helens WA10 44 A3

Waterloo Sta L22 26 E1
Waterloo Warehouse L3 52 B3
Watermede WN5 25 E3
Waterpark Cl CH43 65 F1
Waterpark Dr L28 55 A7
Waterpark Rd CH42, CH43 66 A2
Waters Edge L23 26 A4
Waters Edge Apartments CH45 37 C1
Waterside
- Litherland L30 27 E5
- St Helens WA9 44 B4

Waterside Ct
- Runcorn WA7 84 E3
- St Helens WA9 44 B4

Waterside La WA8 84 C5
Waterside Pk L36 55 D1
Water St
- Bebington CH62 79 C5
- Birkenhead CH41 66 F6
- Crosby L23 27 B6
- Liverpool L2 90 A3
- Newton-le-W WA12 46 C4
- 1 Seaforth L22 37 E8
- St Helens WA10 43 F3
- Wallasey CH44 51 D4

Waterstone Cl L11 40 B3
Waterway Ave L30 28 B3
Waterworks Cotts L39 21 F4
Waterworks Dr WA12 46 F4
Waterworks La
- Hooton CH66 88 E1
- Winwick WA2 61 B7

Waterworks Rd L39 14 A6
Waterworks St L20 38 D3
Watery La
- St Helens WA9 44 E1
- Winwick WA2 60 E6

Watford Rd L4 53 B7
Watkin Cl L30 28 B1
Watkins Ave WA12 45 F3
Watkinson St L1 90 B1
Watkinson Way WA8 73 C5
Watling Ave L21 27 B1
Watling Way L35 57 A5
Watmough St 6 L5 52 E4
Watson Ave
- Ashton-in-M WN4 35 C3
- Golborne WA3 35 F1

Watson Ct CH41 66 F7
Watson St CH41 66 D7
Watton Beck Cl L31 20 F2
Watton Cl L12 41 A2
Watts Cl L33 30 A4
Watts Clift Way WA9 44 B3
Watts La L20 38 E6
Wauchope St L15 68 E8
Wavell Ave
- Southport PR9 5 B7
- Widnes WA8 84 D8

Wavell Cl PR9 5 B7
Wavell Rd L36 55 E4
Waverley WN8 15 D1
Waverley Ct
- 10 Liverpool L17 68 C4
- St Helens WA9 44 C1

Waverley Dr L34 55 F5
Waverley Gr CH42 66 C2
Waverley Rd
- Crosby L23 26 C3
- Golborne WA3 36 D1
- Hoylake CH47 63 C7
- Liverpool L17 68 C4

Waverley St
- Bootle L20 38 B3
- Southport PR8 4 A7

Waverton Ave CH43 65 E2
WAVERTREE 68 F7
Wavertree Ave
- Liverpool L13, L7 53 F1
- Widnes WA8 84 F8

Wavertree Bvd L7 53 D1
Wavertree Bvd S L7 53 E1
Wavertree CE Prim Sch L15 69 A7
Wavertree Gn L15 69 A7
WAVERTREE GREEN 69 B7
Wavertree Ho L13 54 A1
WAVERTREE NOOK 54 C1
Wavertree Nook Rd L15 69 C8
Wavertree Rd L15, L7 53 B1
Wavertree Ret Pk L7 53 C1
Wavertree Tech Pk L7 53 E1
Wavertree Tech Pk Sta L13 53 F1
Wavertree Trad Est L15 68 E7
Wavertree Vale L15 68 D8
Wayfarers Arc PR8 4 B7
Wayfarers Dr WA12 46 E2
Waylands Dr L25 82 B8
Wayville Cl L18 69 B2

Waywell Cl WA2 . . . . 61 F3
Weardale Rd L15 . . . . 68 E6
Wearhead Cl WA3 . . . . 46 F7
Weasdale Cl WA9 . . . . 58 D7
Weates Cl WA8 . . . . 73 F3
Weatherhead High Sch & Media Arts Coll CH44 . . . 50 F3
Weaver Ave
Kirkby L33 . . . . 29 F6
Rainhill L35 . . . . 57 C3
Weaver Ct L25 . . . . 70 C3
Weaver Gr WA9 . . . . 45 A3
Weaver Ho L25 . . . . 70 C3
Weaver Ind Est L19 . . . . . . 81 C3
Weavers La L31 . . . . 28 F6
Weaver St L4 . . . . 38 F3
Webb Cl 8 L7 . . . . 53 C1
Webb Dr WA5 . . . . 59 F6
Webber Rd L33 . . . . 30 C1
Webb St
Liverpool L7 . . . . 68 C7
St Helens WA9 . . . . 44 D1
Webster Ave
Bootle L20 . . . . 38 E4
Wallasey CH44 . . . . 51 D6
Webster Dr L32 . . . . 29 E2
Webster Rd L15, L7 . . . . 68 D7
Websters Holt CH49 . . . . . . 64 F6
Webster St
Bootle L21 . . . . 38 C6
Liverpool L3 . . . . 90 B4
Wedge Ave WA11 . . . . 45 A5
Wedgewood Gdns
WA9 . . . . 57 C6
Wedgwood St L7 . . . . 53 B2
Wedgwood Dr WA8 . . . . . . 73 B4
Wednesbury Dr WA5 . . . . . 74 F6
Weedon Ave WA12 . . . . 46 B5
Weightman Gr 4 L9 . . . . . 39 A6
Weirside WA9 . . . . 58 D6
Welbeck Ave
Liverpool L18 . . . . 68 F5
Newton-le-W WA12 . . . . 46 D2
Welbeck Ct 3 L22 . . . . 26 D1
Welbeck Rd
Ashton-in-M WN4 . . . . 35 C4
Southport PR8 . . . . 4 A4
Welbeck Terr PR8 . . . . 4 A4
Welbourne WN8 . . . . 15 D1
Welbourne Rd L16 . . . . 54 C1
Welburn Cl WN5 . . . . 25 E5
Weldale Ho 5 PR8 . . . . 3 F4
Weld Blundell Ave L31 . . . 20 B5
Weld Dr L37 . . . . 9 D4
Weldon Dr L39 . . . . 13 F4
Weldon St L4 . . . . 38 F2
Weld Par 2 PR8 . . . . 3 F4
Weld Rd
Crosby L23 . . . . 26 C3
Southport PR8 . . . . 3 F5
Welfield Pl L8 . . . . 68 A4
Welford Ave
Birkenhead CH43 . . . . 65 F2
Golborne WA3 . . . . 47 C7
Welland Cl L26 . . . . 82 E7
Welland Rd
Ashton-in-M WN4 . . . . 35 E5
Bebington CH63 . . . . 78 D5
Wellbank Dr L26 . . . . 71 A1
Wellbrae Cl CH49 . . . . 64 D5
Wellbrook Cl L24 . . . . 82 D5
Wellbrooke Cl WN4 . . . . . . 35 C3
Wellbrook Gn L24 . . . . 82 D4
Well Brow Rd L4 . . . . 39 A2
Wellcroft Rd L36 . . . . 55 F4
Wellcross Rd WN8 . . . . 25 B6
Weller St L8 . . . . 67 F5
Weller Way 6 L8 . . . . 68 A4
Wellesbourne Com Prim Sch L11 . . . . 39 F2
Wellesbourne Pl L11 . . . . . 40 A2
Wellesbourne Rd L11 . . . . 40 A3
Wellesley Cl WA12 . . . . 46 B5
Wellesley Gr CH63 . . . . 79 A6
Wellesley Rd
Liverpool L8 . . . . 68 A4
Wallasey CH44 . . . . 51 B4
Wellfarm Cl L9 . . . . 39 D3
Wellfield
Rainford WA11 . . . . 32 A4
Widnes WA8 . . . . 73 A3
Wellfield Ave L32 . . . . 29 F1
Wellfield La L40 . . . . 14 C3
Wellfield Rd L9 . . . . 39 A4
Wellgreen Rd L25 . . . . 70 A7
Wellgreen Wlk L25 . . . . 70 A7
Wellington Ave L15 . . . . . . 68 E7
Wellington Cl
Aintree L10 . . . . 28 C3
Bebington CH63 . . . . 79 A6
Newton-le-W WA12 . . . . 46 A3
Skelmersdale WN8 . . . . 24 E8
Warrington WA2 . . . . 61 F2
Wellington Ct CH43 . . . . . . 66 A4
Wellington Fields L15 . . . . 68 D6
Wellington Gate L24 . . . . . 83 E2
Wellington Gdns
5 Crosby L22 . . . . 26 D1
Newton-le-W WA12 . . . . 46 A3
Wellington Gr L15 . . . . 68 F8
Wellington Rd
Bebington CH63 . . . . 79 A6
Birkenhead CH43 . . . . 66 A4
Bootle L21 . . . . 38 A7
Liverpool L8 . . . . 67 F4
Liverpool, Wavertree L15 . . . . 68 E7
Wallasey CH45 . . . . 37 A1
Wellington St
Crosby L22 . . . . 26 D1
Liverpool, Garston L19 . . . . 81 C6
2 Liverpool L3 . . . . 52 D3
Newton-le-W WA12 . . . . 46 A3
1 Southport PR8 . . . . 4 A6
Wellington Terr
Birkenhead CH41 . . . . 66 D5
2 Liverpool L8 . . . . 68 A5
St Helens WA10 . . . . 44 A5
Well La
Bebington CH63 . . . . 78 D6
Birkenhead, Greasby CH49 . . . . 64 C3
Birkenhead, Tranmere CH42 . . . . 66 E2
Bootle L20 . . . . 38 D3
Haskayne L39 . . . . 11 E6
Heswall CH60 . . . . 86 B6
Liverpool L16, L25 . . . . 69 F7
Warrington WA5 . . . . 74 F3
Well Lane Gdns L20 . . . . . . 38 D3
Well Lane Prim Sch CH42 . . . . 66 E3
Wells Ave WN5 . . . . 33 D6
Wells St L15 . . . . 68 F8
Wellstead Cl L15 . . . . 69 A8
Wellstead Rd L15 . . . . 69 A8
Wellstead Wlk L15 . . . . 69 A8
Welsby Cl WA2 . . . . 61 F3
Welshpool Cl WA5 . . . . 60 D2
Welsh Rd CH66 . . . . 89 A1
Welton Ave CH49 . . . . 64 F5
Welton Cl L24 . . . . 82 D4
Welton Gn L24 . . . . 82 D4
Welton Rd CH62 . . . . 79 E3
Welwyn Ave PR8 . . . . 7 E6
Welwyn Cl WA9 . . . . 57 F6
Wembley Gdns L9 . . . . 38 F6
Wembley Rd
Crosby L23 . . . . 26 F3
Liverpool L18 . . . . 69 B5
Wendell St L8 . . . . 68 C7
Wendover Ave L17 . . . . 68 C3
Wendover Cl
Birkenhead CH43 . . . . 65 D4
Haydock WA11 . . . . 45 D7
Wendron Rd L11 . . . . 40 D5
Wenger Rd WA8 . . . . 73 B5
Wenlock Ct L26 . . . . 82 E8
Wenlock Dr L26 . . . . 82 E8
Wenlock Rd L4 . . . . 53 B7
Wenning Ave L31 . . . . 20 E2
Wennington Rd PR9 . . . . . . 4 F7
Wensley Ave L26 . . . . 82 F8
Wensleydale L9 . . . . 39 A7
Wensleydale Ave
Bebington CH62 . . . . 88 E5
Rainhill L35 . . . . 57 D3
Wensleydale Cl
Maghull L31 . . . . 20 B2
Warrington WA5 . . . . 74 F8
Wensley Rd
Golborne WA3 . . . . 47 E7
Liverpool L9 . . . . 39 A7
Wentworth Ave CH45 . . . . . 51 B7
Wentworth Cl
Birkenhead CH43 . . . . 65 D4
Southport PR8 . . . . 7 C4
Widnes WA8 . . . . 73 A5
Wentworth Dr
Bebington CH63 . . . . 88 C5
Liverpool L5 . . . . 52 F4
Wentworth Gr L36 . . . . 55 B2
Wentworth Rd WN4 . . . . . . 35 A5
Wernbrook Cl CH43 . . . . . . 65 D4
Wernbrook Rd L4 . . . . 53 C7
Wervin Cl CH43 . . . . 65 E2
Wervin Rd
Birkenhead CH43 . . . . 65 E2
Kirkby L32 . . . . 29 D1
Wescoe Cl WN5 . . . . 25 E5
Wesley Ave
Haydock WA11 . . . . 45 F7
Wallasey CH44 . . . . 51 C5
Wesley Gr CH44 . . . . 51 E3
Wesley Grange CH49 . . . . . 65 B3
Wesley Hall Gdns WA9 . . . 57 D6
Wesley Pl L15 . . . . 68 F8
Wesley St
Seaforth L22 . . . . 37 D8
Southport PR8 . . . . 4 B7
West Albert Rd L17 . . . . . . 68 B4
West Alfred Ct 23 CH43 . . . . 66 C5
West Allerton Sta L18 . . . . . 69 B1
West Ave WA3 . . . . 36 B1
Westbank Ave CH45 . . . . . . 51 C7
West Bank Dock Est WA8 . . . . 84 E5
Westbank Rd CH42 . . . . 66 C3
West Bank Rd L7 . . . . 53 E2
Westbourne Ave
Crosby L23 . . . . 27 B6
West Kirby CH48 . . . . 63 B2
Westbourne Gdns PR8 . . . . 3 D4
Westbourne Gr CH48 . . . . . 63 B2
Westbourne Rd
Birkenhead CH43 . . . . 66 C5
Southport PR8 . . . . 3 D4
Wallasey CH44 . . . . 50 F4
West Kirby CH48 . . . . 63 B2
Westbourne Sch CH45 . . . 51 C6
West Bridge L31 . . . . 20 C1
Westbrook Ave L34 . . . . . . 56 B6
WESTBROOK CENTRE 60 B1
Westbrook Cres WA5 . . . . 60 B2
Westbrook Ctr WA5 . . . . . . 60 C1
Westbrook Rd
Birkenhead CH46 . . . . 64 C7
Liverpool L25 . . . . 70 C5
Westbrook Way WA5 . . . . . 60 B1
West Brow Gdns CH43 . . . 65 C8
Westbury Cl
Liverpool L25 . . . . 82 D9
Liverpool, Otterspool L17 . . . . 68 C1
Westbury St CH41 . . . . 66 E4
West Cl
Birkenhead CH43 . . . . 65 D5
Eccleston Park L34 . . . . 57 A7
Westcliffe Ct
Southport PR8 . . . . 3 F5
Widnes WA8 . . . . 73 B4
Westcliffe Rd
Liverpool L12 . . . . 54 A7
Southport PR8 . . . . 3 F5
Westcombe Rd L4 . . . . 53 C7
Westcott Rd L4 . . . . 53 B6
Westcott Way CH43 . . . . . . 65 D3
Westdale Rd
Birkenhead CH42 . . . . 66 E2
Liverpool L15 . . . . 68 F8
Westdale View L15 . . . . . . 68 F8
Westdene PR9 . . . . 1 D1
WEST DERBY 54 D7
West Derby Rd
Liverpool L6 . . . . 53 B4
Liverpool, Tuebrook L13, L6 . . . . 53 E5
West Derby Sch L13 . . . . . 54 A5
West Derby Sch (Bankfield Wing) L13 . . . 53 F6
West Derby St L7 . . . . 53 A2
West Derby Village L12 . . . . 54 B7
West Dr
Birkenhead CH49 . . . . 65 A5
Heswall CH60 . . . . 86 A7
West End Gr WA11 . . . . 45 A6
West End Prim Sch L39 . . . . 13 E7
West End Rd
Haydock WA11 . . . . 45 A6
St Helens WA11 . . . . 44 F6
West End Terr PR8 . . . . 4 A7
Westerhope Way WA8 . . . 72 F3
Westerings The CH62 . . . . 88 C6
Western Approaches Mus★ L2 . . . . 90 A4
Western Ave
Bebington CH62 . . . . 79 D3
Huyton-w-R L36 . . . . 55 B3
Liverpool L24 . . . . 82 C4
Western Dr L19 . . . . 81 A7
Westerton Rd L12 . . . . 54 E6
Westfield Ave
Ashton-in-M WN4 . . . . 35 A4
Huyton-w-R L14 . . . . 54 E2
Westfield Cres WA7 . . . . . . 84 E1
Westfield Dr L12 . . . . 40 E3
Westfield Mews WA7 . . . . 84 F1
Westfield Prim Sch WA7 . . . . 84 E1
Westfield Rd
Liverpool L9 . . . . 38 E6
Runcorn WA7 . . . . 84 E1
Wallasey CH44 . . . . 51 D1
Westfield St WA10 . . . . 43 F3
Westfield Wlk
Kirkby L32 . . . . 29 B1
Kirkby L32 . . . . 29 B2
Westgate
Skelmersdale WN8 . . . . 23 D8
Widnes WA8 . . . . 84 B7
Westgate Dr WN5 . . . . 25 D5
Westgate Rd
Bebington CH62, CH63 . . . . 79 B4
3 Liverpool L15 . . . . 69 A5
WEST GILLIBRANDS 23 E8
West Gillibrands Ind Est WN8 . . . . 23 E8
West Gr CH60 . . . . 85 F8
Westhaven PR9 . . . . 4 D8
Westhaven Cres L39 . . . . . 13 C1
WESTHEAD 14 D4
Westhead Ave
Golborne WA3 . . . . 36 E1
Kirkby L33 . . . . 29 F2
Westhead Cl L33 . . . . 30 A1
Westhead Lathom St James' CE Prim Sch L40 . . . . 14 E4
Westhead Wlk L33 . . . . 29 F2
Westholme Ct PR9 . . . . 1 C1
Westhouse Cl CH63 . . . . . . 88 C5
WEST KIRBY 63 B2
West Kirby Gram Sch CH47 . . . . 63 A3
West Kirby Prim Sch CH47 . . . . 63 A3
West Kirby Rd CH46, CH48 . . . . 64 C6
West Kirby Residential Sch CH47 . . . . 63 A3
West Kirby Sta CH48 . . . . . 63 A2
West La L37 . . . . 9 F6
Westland Dr WA2 . . . . 61 E2
Westlands Cl CH64 . . . . 86 F1
Westleigh Pl WA9 . . . . 58 C5
West Lodge Dr CH48 . . . . . 63 A3
West Mains L24 . . . . 83 A3
West Meade L31 . . . . 20 B2
Westminster Ave L30 . . . . 27 F4
Westminster Cl
Liverpool L4 . . . . 38 E1
Widnes WA8 . . . . 84 B8
Westminster Ct CH43 . . . . 65 F5
Westminster Dr
Bebington CH62 . . . . 88 D7
Haydock WA11 . . . . 45 F7
Southport PR8 . . . . 7 A4
Westminster Gr L34 . . . . . . 56 A5
Westminster Rd
Liverpool L4 . . . . 52 E8
Wallasey CH44 . . . . 51 B4
Westmoreland Pl 3 L5 . . . . 52 D5
Westmoreland Rd
Southport PR8 . . . . 4 D5
Wallasey CH45 . . . . 51 C7
Westmorland Ave
Litherland L30 . . . . 27 C3
Widnes WA8 . . . . 73 B1
Westmorland Dr L3 . . . . . . 52 C3
Westmorland Rd L36 . . . . . 55 E2
West Mount WN5 . . . . 25 F6
West Oakhill Pk L13 . . . . . 54 A2
Westonby Ct WN4 . . . . 35 D3
Weston Ct L23 . . . . 26 B3
Weston Gr
Halewood L26 . . . . 83 A6
Maghull L31 . . . . 28 D6
Weston Point Expressway WA7 . . . . 84 E2
Weston Rd WA7 . . . . 84 F1
West Orchard La L9 . . . . . . 39 D7
Westover Cl L31 . . . . 20 C1
Westover Rd L31 . . . . 20 C1
WEST PARK 43 D2
West Park Cl WN8 . . . . 23 D8
West Park Gdns CH43 . . . . 65 C8
West Park Rd WA10 . . . . . . 43 D2
WEST PIMBO 24 D4
West Pimbo Ind Est WN8 . . . . 24 D4
West Pk PR9 . . . . 1 D1
Westport Bsns Pk L20 . . . . 52 C7
West Quay Rd WA2 . . . . . . 60 F3
West Rd
Birkenhead CH43 . . . . 65 D5
Liverpool, Broad Green L14 . . . . 54 C2
Liverpool, Walton L9 . . . . . . 38 F3
Westry Cl CH46 . . . . 64 B8
West Side WA9 . . . . 44 C2
West Side Ave WA11 . . . . . 45 A6
Westside Ind Est WA9 . . . . 44 C2
West St
Prescot L34 . . . . 56 C6
Southport PR8 . . . . 4 A7
St Helens WA10 . . . . 43 D1
Wallasey CH45 . . . . 51 B5
WESTVALE 29 C2
Westvale Prim Sch L32 . . . . 29 B2
West View
Birkenhead CH41 . . . . 66 F4
Huyton-w-R L36 . . . . 56 B2
1 Ormskirk L39 . . . . 13 F5
Rainford WA11 . . . . 31 F6
Warrington WA2 . . . . 61 F1
West View Ave L36 . . . . . . 56 B2
Westview Cl CH43 . . . . 65 D4
West View Cl L36 . . . . 56 B2
Westward Ho CH48 . . . . . . 75 D6
Westward View
Crosby L22 . . . . 26 B2
Liverpool L17 . . . . 68 A3
Westway
Birkenhead, Greasby CH49 . . . . 64 E4
Birkenhead, Noctorum CH43 . . . . 65 D4
Heswall CH60 . . . . 85 F6
Hightown L38 . . . . 17 F4
Liverpool L15 . . . . 69 B8
Maghull L31 . . . . 20 C2
West Way CH46 . . . . 49 E1
Westway Sq CH46 . . . . 49 E1
Westwick Pl L36 . . . . 55 B3
Westwood Cl PR8 . . . . 4 E3
Westwood Ct
Birkenhead CH43 . . . . 65 F5
Neston CH64 . . . . 86 E2
Westwood Gr 2 CH44 . . . . 51 A4
Westwood Rd
Birkenhead CH43 . . . . 65 C6
Liverpool L18 . . . . 81 C8
Wetherby Ave CH45 . . . . . . 50 E5
Wetherby Cl WA12 . . . . 46 C5
Wetherby Ct L36 . . . . 55 C5
Wethersfield Rd CH43 . . . . 65 E4
Wetstone La CH48 . . . . 63 C1
Wexford Ave L24 . . . . 83 D2
Wexford Cl
Birkenhead CH43 . . . . 65 E4
Haydock WA11 . . . . 45 D7
Wexford Rd CH43 . . . . 65 F4
Wexford Wlk CH43 . . . . 65 F4
Wexwood Gr L35 . . . . 56 F2
Weybourne Cl CH49 . . . . . . 65 A7
Weyman Ave L35 . . . . 56 E3
Weymoor Cl CH63 . . . . 78 F2
Weymouth Ave WA9 . . . . . 44 F1
Weymouth Cl L16 . . . . 69 F8
Weymouth Rd WA5 . . . . . . 59 F6
Whaley La CH61 . . . . 76 F6
Whalley Ave
Rainford WA11 . . . . 31 F6
St Helens WA10 . . . . 43 E7
Whalley Ct L30 . . . . 27 D4
Whalley Dr
Formby L37 . . . . 10 A2
Ormskirk L39 . . . . 21 D8
Whalley Gr WA8 . . . . 73 D3
Whalley Rd 2 CH42 . . . . . . 66 D5
WHALLEYS 16 A5
Whalleys Rd WN8 . . . . 16 B5
Whalley St L8 . . . . 67 F4
Wharfedale Ave CH42 . . . . 66 B2
Wharfedale Dr
Bebington CH62 . . . . 88 F5
Rainhill L35 . . . . 57 D3
Wharfedale Rd CH45 . . . . . 50 F6
Wharfedale St L19 . . . . 81 E5
Wharf Rd WA12 . . . . 45 E2
Wharf St CH62 . . . . 79 C5
Wharmby Rd WA11 . . . . . . 45 E6
Wharncliffe Rd L13 . . . . . . 54 A3
Wharton Cl CH49 . . . . 64 D6
Wharton St WA9 . . . . 44 B1
Wheatacre WN8 . . . . 23 E8
Wheatcroft Rd L18 . . . . 69 D2
Wheatear Cl L27 . . . . 70 E4
Wheatfield Cl
Birkenhead CH46 . . . . 64 F7
Litherland L30 . . . . 28 B3
Wheatfield Rd WA8 . . . . . . 72 C5
Wheatfield View L21 . . . . . 27 B2
Wheat Hill Rd L27, L36 . . . . 70 E8
Wheathills Ind Est L27 . . . 70 E6
Wheatland Bsns Pk CH44 . . . . 51 D2
Wheatland Cl WA9 . . . . 58 C4
Wheatland La CH44 . . . . . . 51 D2
Wheatland Rd CH60 . . . . . . 86 C7
Wheatley Ave
Bootle L20 . . . . 38 E5
Newton-le-W WA12 . . . . 46 C5
Wheatsheaf Ave WA9 . . . . 58 D6
Wheatsheaf Wlk 4 L39 . . . . 13 E5
Wheeler Dr L31 . . . . 29 B4
Whelan Gdns WA9 . . . . 57 E6
Wheldon Rd WA8 . . . . 83 F7
Whernside WA8 . . . . 72 C3
Whetstone Ct 4 CH41 . . . . 66 D5
Whetstone La CH41, CH42 . . . . 66 D5
Whickham Cl WA8 . . . . 72 F3
Whimbrel Ave WA12 . . . . . 46 C3
Whimbrel Pk L26 . . . . 70 E1
Whinberry Dr L32 . . . . 29 D1
Whinbury Ct 15 WA9 . . . . . 58 C4
Whinchat Ave WA12 . . . . . 46 C4
Whinchat Cl WA3 . . . . 47 E7
Whincraig L28 . . . . 55 C7
Whinfell Rd L12 . . . . 54 C5
Whinfield Rd
Crosby L23 . . . . 27 B6
Liverpool L9 . . . . 38 F6
Whinhowe Rd L11 . . . . 40 B2
Whinmoor Cl CH43 . . . . 65 D6
Whinmoor Rd
Liverpool L10 . . . . 40 A7
Liverpool, Sandfield Park L12 . . . . 54 C5
Whinney Gr E L31 . . . . 28 C6
Whinney Gr W L31 . . . . 28 C6
WHISTON 56 E4
WHISTON CROSS 56 D3
Whiston Hospl L35 . . . . 56 F4
Whiston La L36 . . . . 56 B4
WHISTON LANE ENDS 56 C2
Whiston Sta L35 . . . . 56 E3
Whiston Willis Com Prim Sch L35 . . . . 56 E3
Whitburn WN8 . . . . 15 D1
Whitburn Cl WN4 . . . . 34 D4
Whitburn Rd L33 . . . . 30 A4
Whitby Ave
Southport PR9 . . . . 2 D6
Wallasey CH45 . . . . 50 E5
Warrington WA2 . . . . 61 D2
Whitby St L6 . . . . 53 D6
Whitcroft Rd L6 . . . . 53 D3
Whitebeam Cl L33 . . . . 29 F6
Whitebeam Dr L12 . . . . 40 D3
Whitebeam Gdns WA9 . . . 57 C6
Whitebeam Wlk CH49 . . . . 64 B2
Whitechapel L1 . . . . 90 B3
Whitecroft Ave WA3 . . . . . . 36 E1
Whiteeside Cl CH49 . . . . . . 65 A4
Whitefield Ave
Liverpool L4 . . . . 52 E8
Newton-le-W WA12 . . . . 46 E2
Whitefield Cl
Birkenhead CH49 . . . . 65 B3
Golborne WA3 . . . . 47 A8
Hightown L38 . . . . 17 F2
Whitefield Dr L32 . . . . 29 C1
Whitefield La L35 . . . . 71 A6
WHITEFIELD LANE END 71 B8
Whitefield Prim Sch L6 . . . . 53 A4
Whitefield Rd
Liverpool L6 . . . . 53 B5
St Helens WA10 . . . . 43 D5
Whitefield Way 2 L6 . . . . 53 A4
Whitefriars WA10 . . . . 43 A4
Whitegate Cl L34 . . . . 41 D4
Whitegates Cl CH64 . . . . . . 87 E1
Whitegates Cres CH64 . . . . 87 E1
Whitehall Cl L4 . . . . 38 E1

Whitehart Cl L4 39 B1
Whitehaven Cl PR8 7 B3
Whitehaven Rd L5 52 F6
Whiteheath Way CH46 49 F3
Whitehedge Rd L19 81 B7
Whitehey WN8 23 E8
Whitehey Rd WN8 23 E8
Whitehorn Dr L28 55 B8
Whitehouse Ave L37 10 A3
White House Cl WA11 45 B6
Whitehouse La
Formby L37 10 A3
Heswall CH60, CH63 77 D1
Whitehouse Rd L13 54 B2
Whitelands Mdw CH49 64 E5
Whiteledge Rd WN8 24 B6
Whiteleys La L40 14 D2
White Lodge Ave L36 55 D3
White Lodge Cl CH62 88 D5
White Lodge Dr WN4 35 D4
Whitely Gr L33 30 A6
White Meadow Dr L23 27 A6
WHITE MOSS 23 F7
Whitemoss Bsns Pk WN8 23 F6
White Moss Rd WN8 23 C7
White Moss Rd S WN8 23 D7
White Oak Lo L19 80 F7
Whiterails Dr L39 13 D6
Whiterails Mews L39 13 D6
White Rock St L6 53 B4
Whiteside Ave WA11 44 E5
Whiteside Cl
Birkenhead CH49 65 A4
Liverpool L5 52 D5
Whiteside Rd WA11 45 B6
White St L1 90 B2
Whitestock WN8 23 E8
Whitestone Cl L34 41 C2
Whitethorn Ave WA5 74 F5
White Thorn Sch L9 39 D7
Whitewell Dr CH49 64 F7
Whitewood Cl WN4 35 A6
Whitewood Pk L9 39 D6
Whitfield Ct [1] CH42 66 D4
Whitfield Gr WA11 45 A6
Whitfield La CH60 77 A1
Whitfield Lodge WA9 58 D4
Whitfield Rd L9 39 A5
Whitfield St CH42 66 D4
Whitford Rd CH42 66 D4
Whitham Ave L23 26 F3
Whithorn St L7 68 D8
Whitland Rd L6 53 D3
Whitledge Gn WN4 35 A5
Whitledge Rd WN4 35 A5
Whitley Cres WN2 36 B7
Whitley Dr [1] CH44, CH45 51 C5
Whitley St L3 52 B4
Whitlow Ave WA3 35 F1
Whitman St L15 68 E7
Whitmoor Cl L35 57 E1
Whitney Pl L25 70 C2
Whitney Rd L25 70 C2
Whitstable Pk WA8 72 E4
Whitstone Cl L18 69 E2
Whitstone Dr WN8 24 D7
Whittaker Ave WA2 61 D2
Whittaker Cl L13 53 F1
Whittaker St WA9 44 D1
Whittier St L8 68 C7
Whittle Ave
Haydock WA11 45 A5
Warrington WA5 60 A1
Warrington WA5 74 F8
Whittle Cl L5 52 E6
Whittle Dr L39 13 E7
Whittle Hall La WA5 74 F6
Whittle St
Liverpool L5 52 E6
St Helens WA10 43 D1
Whittlewood Ct L33 29 F4
Whitwell Cl WA5 74 D7
Wicket Cl L11 40 D5
Wickham Cl CH44 51 E2
Wicks Cres L37 9 C4
Wicks Gdns L37 9 D3
Wicks Gn L37 9 C3
Wicks Green Cl L37 9 C3
Wicks La L37 9 D3
Widdale Ave L35 57 D3
Widdale Cl WA5 74 F7
Widgeons Covert CH63 86 F5
Widmore Rd L25 70 C4
WIDNES 72 F2
Widnes Rd
Cuerdley Cross WA5, WA8 73 F2
Warrington WA5 74 C3
Widnes Sta WA8 73 A3
Wiend The
Bebington CH63 79 A5
Birkenhead CH42 66 D1
Wigan Rd
Ashton-in-M WN4 35 A5
Billinge WN5 33 F7
Golborne WA3 36 B3
Ormskirk L39 14 A5
Skelmersdale WN8 23 F8
Westhead L40 14 E4
Wightman Ave WA12 46 C5
Wightman St L6 53 B3
Wight Moss Way PR8 4 D3
Wignall Cl L32 40 E7
Wignalls Mdw L38 17 F3
Wigston Cl PR8 7 B4
Wilberforce Rd L4 39 B2
Wilbraham Pl [4] L5 52 D5
Wilbraham St
[19] Birkenhead CH41 66 E6
Liverpool L5 52 D5
St Helens WA9 58 E3
Wilburn St L4 38 F1
Wilbur St WA9 58 E7
Wilcock Cl L5 52 D5
Wilcock Rd WA11 46 B8
Wilcote Cl WA8 73 C4
Wilcove WN8 15 F1
Wild Arum Cl [8] WA3 47 E8
Wildbrook Dr CH41 50 D1
Wildcherry Gdns L35 57 C7
Wilde St L3 90 C4
Wild Pl L20 38 E7
Wilfer Cl [4] L7 68 C8
Wilfred Owen Dr CH41 65 E7
Wilkes Ave CH46 50 B3
Wilkie St L15 68 E7
Wilkinson Ct L15 68 E8
Wilkinson St [18] CH41 66 C5
Wilkin St L4 52 E7
Willan St CH43 66 B4
Willard Ave WN5 25 D3
Willard St L20 38 D6
WILLASTON 88 A1
Willaston Dr L26 83 A6
Willaston Rd
Liverpool L4 39 B1
Thornton Hough CH63, CH64 87 D4
Wallasey CH46 49 D1
Willedstan Ave L23 26 E3
William Beamont Com High Sch WA2 61 C1
William Brown St L3 90 B4
William Ct CH64 86 F2
William Gladstone CE Sch L21 38 A7
William Harvey Cl L30 27 F3
William Henry St
Bootle L20 38 B2
Liverpool L3, L6 52 E3
William Jessop Way L3 52 B2
William Morris Ave L20 38 E5
William Moult St L5 52 D5
William Penn Cl WA5 74 E5
William Rd WA11 44 F6
William Roberts Ave L32 29 C2
Williams Ave
Bootle L20 38 E5
Newton-le-W WA12 46 C5
Williamson Art Gall & Mus★ CH43 66 B5
Williamson Ct
[4] Liverpool, Halewood Village L26 71 A1
Liverpool, Woolton L25 70 C1
Williamson Sq [13] L1 90 B3
Williamson St
Liverpool L1 90 B3
St Helens WA9 44 C4
Williamson Student Village L7 53 A1
Williamson Tunnels Heritage Ctr★ L7 53 A1
Williams St L34 56 D6
William St
Birkenhead CH41 66 E6
[2] St Helens WA10 44 A4
Wallasey CH44 51 E2
Widnes WA8 73 C1
William Wall Rd L21 27 B2
Willingdon Rd L16 54 E1
Willington Ave CH62 88 E3
Willink Rd WA11 44 C7
Willis Cl L35 56 D2
Willis La L35 56 D2
Williton Rd L16 69 E5
Willmer Rd
Birkenhead CH42 66 D5
Liverpool L4 53 B7
Willoughby Cl WA5 60 C1
Willoughby Dr WA10 57 B8
Willoughby Rd
Crosby L22 26 E1
Huyton-w-R L14 54 F2
Wallasey CH44 51 A4
Willow Ave
Huyton-w-R L36 70 E8
Kirkby L32 29 C3
Newton-le-W WA12 46 E4
Prescot L35 56 E3
[2] Widnes WA8 73 B2
Willowbank Cl L36 55 C5
Willow Bank Est WA12 46 F4
Willowbank Holiday Home & Touring Pk PR8 7 B2
Willowbank Rd
[2] Bebington CH62 79 B6
Birkenhead CH42 66 D3
Willowbrow Rd CH63, CH64 87 D3
Willow Cl L14 54 E2
Willowcroft Rd CH44 51 C2
Willow Ct
Bebington CH63 78 D6
Bootle L20 38 C2
[17] Liverpool L8 68 A4
Newton-le-W WA12 46 D4
St Helens WA9 58 D4
Willow Ct continued
[14] Wallasey CH45 51 B8
Warrington WA2 60 F3
Willowdale WA12 46 E3
Willowdale Rd
Liverpool, Hartley's Village L9 39 A4
Liverpool L18 68 F5
Willowdene Ct L11 40 D5
Willow Dr WN8 15 E1
Willowfield Gr WN4 35 A2
Willow Gn
Liverpool L25 69 F4
[5] Ormskirk L39 13 F5
Willow Gr
Ashton-in-M WN4 35 E5
Birkenhead CH46 64 D7
Formby L37 9 F4
Golborne WA3 36 A1
Liverpool L15 69 A8
Prescot L35 56 E5
Southport PR9 4 E7
Willow Grove Prim Sch WN4 35 E5
Willowherb Cl L26 70 D2
Willowhey PR9 1 F4
Willow Hey
Maghull L31 28 E7
Skelmersdale WN8 15 F1
Willow Ho [7] L21 38 A6
Willow La CH63, CH64 87 D3
Willow Lea CH43 66 A4
Willowmeade L11 40 B3
Willow Moss Cl CH46 50 A2
Willow Pk
Birkenhead CH49 64 C4
Southport PR8 4 A5
Willow Rd
Haydock WA11 45 E7
Liverpool L15 68 E8
Newton-le-W WA12 46 E4
St Helens WA10 43 C3
Willows The
Newton-le-W WA12 46 D4
Southport PR8 3 F6
[3] St Helens WA9 58 C4
Wallasey CH45 50 E7
Warrington WA5 74 F5
Willow Tree Ave WA9 58 D4
Willow Tree Ct WA8 73 D2
Willow Tree Prim Sch WA9 58 D4
Willow Way
Crosby L23 26 E5
Liverpool L11 40 D6
Willow Wlk WN8 16 B4
Wills Ave L31 20 C2
Willsford Ave L31 29 B3
Wilmcote Gr PR8 7 B4
Wilmere La WA8 73 A6
Wilmot Ave WA5 74 F6
Wilmot Dr WA3 46 F7
Wilne Rd [3] CH45 51 A6
Wilsden Rd WA8 72 B1
Wilsford Cl WA3 36 B1
Wilsham Rd WN5 25 E5
Wilshaw Terr CH63 87 B6
Wilson Ave CH44 51 E4
Wilson Cl
St Helens WA10 43 F3
[4] Widnes WA8 73 D1
Wilson Gr L19 81 C6
Wilson Rd
Huyton-w-R L36 56 A1
Prescot L35 56 D4
Wallasey CH44 51 E4
Wilsons La L21 38 B8
Wilstan Ave CH63 78 D5
Wilstone Cl [8] L5 52 F4
Wilton Gr [6] L13 54 A2
Wilton Grange CH47 63 A4
Wilton Rd
Birkenhead CH42 67 A1
Huyton-w-R L36 55 D1
Wiltons Dr L34 41 D3
Wilton St
Liverpool L3 90 C4
[6] Wallasey CH44 51 B4
Wiltshire Dr L30 27 D3
Wiltshire Gdns WA10 43 F2
Wimbald Cl L25 70 C5
Wimbledon St
Liverpool L15 68 E7
Wallasey CH44, CH45 51 B5
Wimborne Cl L14 55 B6
Wimborne Pl L14 55 B5
Wimborne Rd L14 55 B5
Wimborne Way CH61 76 D7
Wimbourne Ave CH61 77 A5
Wimbrick Cl
Birkenhead CH46 64 F8
Ormskirk L39 13 D4
Wimbrick Cres L39 13 D3
Wimbrick Ct CH46 64 F8
Wimbrick Hey CH46 65 A8
Wimpole St L7 53 B2
Winchester Ave
Aintree L10 28 D3
Ashton-in-M WN4 35 A3
[1] Crosby L22 26 D3
Winchester Cl
Liverpool L25 82 B8
[4] Orrell WN5 25 F7
Winchester Dr CH44, CH45 51 A5
Winchester Pl WA8 84 C8
Winchester Rd
Ashton-in-M WA11 34 E1
Winchester Rd continued
Liverpool L6 53 C6
Longshaw WN5 25 D2
Winchfield Rd L15 68 F6
Windbourne Rd L17 68 C2
Windermere Ave
St Helens WA11 44 B8
Warrington WA2 61 D3
Widnes WA8 73 B4
Windermere Cres PR8 7 C3
Windermere Ct [8] CH41 66 C5
Windermere Dr
Kirkby L33 29 D4
Liverpool L12 40 C1
Maghull L31 20 E2
Rainford WA11 23 F2
Windermere Ho L17 68 D2
Windermere Pl WA11 44 A8
Windermere Rd
Abram WN2 36 B8
Birkenhead CH43 65 C5
Haydock WA11 45 B6
Hightown L38 18 A4
Orrell WN5 25 F8
Windermere St
Liverpool L5 53 B5
Widnes WA8 73 B4
Windermere Terr L8 68 B5
Windfield Cl L33 30 A6
Windfield Gn L19 81 D3
Windfield Rd L19 81 D4
Windgate WN8 15 F1
Windle Ash L31 20 C2
Windle Ave L23 27 A3
Windlebrook Cres WA10 43 B6
Windle City WA10 43 F6
Windle Ct CH64 86 E2
Windle Gr WA10 43 C6
Windle Hall Dr WA10 43 E7
WINDLEHURST 43 F6
Windlehurst Ave WA10 43 E6
Windleshaw Rd WA10 43 E5
Windle Smithies WA10 43 C7
Windle St WA10 43 F5
Windle Vale WA10 43 E5
Windmill Ave
Crosby L23 26 F5
Ormskirk L39 13 F5
Windmill Cl [2] L33 29 E5
Windmill Gdns
Birkenhead CH43 65 C8
St Helens WA9 44 D4
Windmill Ho PR9 1 F2
Windmill Hts WN8 25 A8
Windmill La WA5 74 E5
Windmill Rd WN8 24 F7
Window La L19 81 C4
Windrows WN8 15 F1
Windsor Ave
Litherland L21 38 A8
Newton-le-W WA12 46 D2
Windsor Cl
Bebington CH62 79 A7
Birkenhead CH49 64 D3
Litherland L30 27 F5
Windsor Com Prim Sch L8 67 F6
Windsor Ct
[1] Bootle L20 38 E5
[6] Liverpool L8 67 F6
Southport PR8 3 E4
Windsor Day Hospl L8 67 F7
Windsor Dr WA11 46 A7
Windsor Mews CH62 79 A7
Windsor Park Rd L10 28 E3
Windsor Rd
Ashton-in-M WN4 35 C1
Billinge WN5 33 F5
Bootle L20 38 E5
Crosby L23 26 D5
Formby L37 9 F1
Golborne WA3 47 C8
Huyton-w-R L36 55 B3
Liverpool, Tuebrook L13 53 D6
[5] Liverpool, Warbreck Pk L9 39 A6
Maghull L31 28 C8
Prescot L35 56 F4
Southport PR9 4 D7
St Helens WA10 43 D4
Up Holland WN8 25 A8
Widnes WA8 73 A4
Windsor St
Birkenhead CH41 66 C5
Liverpool L8 67 F6
Wallasey CH45 37 B1
Windsor View L8 68 B7
Windus St WA10 43 E3
Windward Dr L24 82 A5
WINDY ARBOR 71 C8
Windy Arbor Brow L35 71 C8
Windy Arbor Cl L35 56 D1
Windy Arbor Rd L35 56 D1
WINDY ARBOUR 34 B8
Windy Bank CH62 79 B6
Windy Bank Ave WA3 47 E8
Windy Harbour Rd PR8 7 E7
Wineva Gdns L23 26 F3
Winford St CH44 51 D3
Winfrith Cl CH63 78 F2
Winfrith Dr CH63 78 F2
Winfrith Rd L25 70 C4
Wingate Ave WA9 57 D6
Wingate Cl CH43 65 E4
Wingate Rd
Bebington CH62 88 E5
Wingate Rd continued
Kirkby L33 29 F3
Liverpool L17 68 E2
Wingate Wlk L33 30 A3
Wingfield Cl L29 27 D8
Wingrave Way L11 40 B1
Winhill L25 70 A4
Winhill Lo L25 70 A4
Winifred La L39 21 B8
Winifred Rd L10 40 B7
Winifred St L7 53 B1
Winkle St [1] L8 67 F5
Winmoss Dr L33 30 A5
Winnard St WA3 36 B2
Winnington Rd CH47 63 A4
Winnipeg Dr L27 70 E5
Winsford Cl WA11 45 F7
Winsford Dr WA5 59 E7
Winsford Rd L13 53 F6
Winsham Cl L32 40 F8
Winsham Rd L32 40 F8
Winskill Rd L11 40 A1
Winslade Ct L4 39 B2
Winslade Rd L4 39 B2
Winslow St L4 52 F8
Winstanley Coll WN5 25 F3
Winstanley Ho
Bebington CH62 79 B7
[1] Crosby L22 26 E1
Winstanley Ind Est WA2 61 B1
Winstanley Rd
Ashton-in-M WN2 35 F8
Bebington CH62 79 B7
Crosby L22 26 E2
Garswood WN4, WN5 34 B6
Orrell WN5 25 F3
Skelmersdale WN8 23 F8
Winster Dr L27 71 A3
Winsters The WN8 15 F1
Winston Ave
Newton-le-W WA12 46 C3
St Helens WA9 45 B2
Winston Cres PR8 4 E2
Winston Dr CH43 65 C5
Winstone Rd L14 55 A4
Winston Gr CH46 64 E8
Winterburn Cres L12 54 D7
Winter Gr WA9 45 B3
Winterhey Ave CH44 51 B3
Winterlea Dr L26 83 A6
Winter St [9] L6 53 A3
Winthrop Pk CH43 65 E5
Winton Cl CH45 51 A8
Winton Rd WA3 47 E6
WINWICK 61 A6
Winwick CE Prim Sch WA2 61 B6
Winwick La WA3 47 E3
Winwick Link Rd WA2, WA3 61 C6
Winwick Park Ave WA2 61 A5
WINWICK QUAY 61 A3
Winwick Rd
Newton-le-W WA12 46 F1
Warrington WA2 61 A2
Winwick View WA5 45 D1
Winwood Hall L25 70 A1
Wirral Bsns Ctr CH41 51 C1
Wirral Bsns Pk The CH49 64 F3
Wirral Cl CH63 78 F3
Wirral Country Pk★ CH48 75 D5
Wirral Ctry Pk★ CH60 76 B2
Wirral Gdns CH63 78 F3
Wirral Gram Sch for Boys CH63 78 F4
Wirral Gram Sch for Girls CH63 78 F4
Wirral International Bsns Pk CH62 79 E3
Wirral L Pk CH62 79 E3
Wirral Metropolitan Coll CH62 89 A7
Wirral Mount
Wallasey CH45 50 F5
West Kirby CH48 63 D3
Wirral Mus★ CH41 66 F6
Wirral View L19 80 F6
Wirral Villas CH45 50 E6
Wirral Way CH43 65 C5
Wisteria Way WA9 59 A7
Witham Cl L30 28 A4
Witham Rd WN8 15 D1
Withburn Cl CH49 64 E5
Withensfield CH45 51 B6
Withen's La CH44, CH45 51 C5
Withens Rd L31 20 D3
Withens The L28 55 B8
Withert Ave CH63 78 D8
Withill Wlk [4] WN4 35 A5
Withington Rd
Liverpool L24 82 F4
Wallasey CH44 51 D3
Withins Field L38 17 F3
Withins La L37 19 A7
Withins Rd WA11 45 F8
Within Way L24 83 E1
Withnell Cl L13 54 B2
Withnell Rd L13 54 B2
Withycombe Rd WA5 74 E4
Witley Ave CH46 49 E1
Witley Cl CH46 49 E1
Witney Cl CH49 64 C3
Wittenham Cl CH49 64 F4
Wittering La CH60 85 D7

Witterings The CH64 86 E1
Witton Rd L13 53 E6
Witton Way WA11 32 A7
Woburn Ave WA12 46 D2
Woburn Cl
Haydock WA11 45 F7
Liverpool L13 53 F4
Woburn Dr WA8 72 D6
Woburn Gn L13 53 F4
Woburn Hill L13 53 F4
Woburn Pl CH42 66 F2
Woburn Rd
Wallasey CH45 51 B6
Warrington WA2 61 A4
Wokefield Way WA10 43 C5
Wokingham Gr L36 70 E8
Wolfenden Ave L20 38 E5
Wolferton Cl CH49 65 B7
Wolfe St 1 L8 67 E5
Wolfrick Dr CH63 79 B1
Wolfson Sq WN4 34 F4
Wollaton Dr PR8 4 F3
Wolmer St WN4 35 A4
Wolseley Rd WA10 43 F4
Wolsey Cl WN4 35 A5
Wolsey St L20 38 C1
Wolstenholme Sq L1 90 B2
Wolverton WN8 23 F8
Wolverton St L6 53 C5
Womack Gdns WA9 57 E6
Woodale Cl WA5 74 E7
Wood Ave L20 38 F5
Woodbank Cl L16 69 F8
Woodbank Pk CH43 65 F4
Woodberry Cl
Birkenhead CH43 65 D4
Kirkby L33 29 F6
Woodbine St L5 52 D7
Woodbourne Rd L12, L14 54 D4
Woodbridge Ave L26 70 D2
Woodbrook Ave L9 38 F7
Woodburn Bvd CH63 78 E8
Woodburn Dr CH60 85 F6
WOODCHURCH 65 B3
Woodchurch CE Prim Sch CH49 65 B2
Woodchurch Ct CH42 66 C3
Woodchurch High Sch Engineering Coll CH49 65 C3
Woodchurch La CH42 66 C2
Woodchurch Rd
Birkenhead CH42, CH43 66 C3
Birkenhead, Woodchurch CH43, CH49 65 D1
Liverpool L13 54 A4
Woodchurch Road Prim Sch CH42 66 C3
Wood Cl
Birkenhead CH41 66 D7
Kirkby L32 29 D2
Woodclose CH66 89 A1
Woodcote Bank CH42 79 A7
Woodcote Cl
Kirkby L33 30 A4
Warrington WA2 61 D1
Woodcotes The CH62 88 D6
Woodcot La CH60 76 E1
Woodcroft WN8 23 F8
Woodcroft Dr CH61 76 F2
Woodcroft La CH63 78 E8
Woodcroft Rd L15 68 D7
Woodcroft Way 4 WA9 58 C4
Woodedge WN4 35 A3
Woodend
Heswall CH61 76 F5
Prescot L35 71 E8
Woodend Ave
Crosby L23 26 E6
Liverpool L24, L25 82 C6
Maghull L31 28 C7
Wood End Ct WA8 73 D2
Woodend La L24 82 C5
Woodene Cl 1 L32 41 A7
Woodfarm Hey L28 55 A8
Woodfield Ave CH63 78 E8
Woodfield Cres WN4 35 A2
Woodfield Rd
Bebington CH63 79 A3
Heswall CH61 76 E4
Huyton-w-R L36 55 C2
Liverpool L9 38 F5
Ormskirk L39 13 D3
Woodford Ave WA3 47 D7
Woodford Rd
Bebington CH62 79 B8
Liverpool L14 54 E4
St Helens WA10 43 C6
Woodgate L27 70 C6
Woodger St L19 81 C5
Wood Gn
Birkenhead CH43 65 C8
Prescot L34 56 C6
Wood Gr L13 53 F2
Woodgreen Rd L13 54 A4
Woodhall Ave CH44 51 D4
Woodhall Rd L13 54 A3
Woodhead Rd CH62 79 C6
Woodhead St CH62 79 B7
Wood Heath Way CH62 89 A7
WOODHEY 78 F7
Woodhey Ct CH63 78 F7
Woodhey Gr CH63 78 F7
Woodhey Rd
Bebington CH63 78 F7
Liverpool L19 81 A8
Woodholme Ct L25 70 B4
Woodhouse Cl L4 52 E7
Woodhurst Cl L14 55 C6
Woodhurst Cres L14 55 A4
Woodin Rd CH42 79 A8
Woodkind Hey CH63 79 A2
Wood La
Birkenhead CH49 64 D4
Haskayne L37, L39 11 D1
Huyton-w-R L36 56 B2
Liverpool L27 70 F4
Neston CH64 86 D2
Prescot L34 56 C6
Wallasey CH45 50 E6
Woodland Ave
Hoylake CH47 48 D1
Newton-le-W WA12 46 F3
Widnes WA8 72 F1
Woodland Dr
Ashton-in-M WN4 35 B5
Birkenhead CH49 65 A3
Wallasey CH45 51 C7
Woodland Gr CH42 78 F8
Woodland Pk★ L30 27 E5
Woodland Rd
Bebington CH42 78 F8
Birkenhead CH49 65 A3
Halewood L26 82 E8
Kirkby L31 29 A4
Liverpool L4 53 D8
Seaforth L21 37 F7
West Kirby CH48 63 E2
WOODLANDS 70 F3
Woodlands Cl
Formby L37 9 D2
Ormskirk L39 14 A4
Southport PR9 4 D8
Woodlands Com Prim Sch WN8 16 C2
Woodlands Dr CH61 77 C4
Woodlands Ind Est WA12 46 C6
Woodlands La CH48 63 D1
Woodlands Pk
Liverpool L12 54 A5
Newton-le-W WA12 46 C6
Woodlands Prim Sch
Birkenhead CH41 66 D5
Formby L37 9 D3
Woodlands Rd
Formby L37 9 D3
Huyton-w-R L36 55 C2
Irby CH61 76 D5
Liverpool, Fazakerley L9 39 D7
Liverpool L17 68 E2
St Helens WA11 44 C7
Woodlands Sq L27 71 A4
Woodlands The
1 Birkenhead CH41 66 D5
Birkenhead, Upton CH49 64 F6
Prescot L34 56 F7
Southport PR8 7 C5
Woodland View L23 27 A7
Woodland Wlk CH62 79 C1
Wood Lea L12 40 E3
Woodlea Cl
Bebington CH62 88 D5
Southport PR9 2 D5
Woodlee Rd L25 70 C4
Woodleigh Cl L31 20 B5
Woodley Fold WA5 74 F4
Woodley Park Rd WN8 16 B4
Woodley Rd L31 28 D6
Woodmoss La PR8, L40 5 E2
Woodpecker Cl
Birkenhead CH49 64 D5
Liverpool L12 40 F1
Woodpecker Dr L26 70 E2
Wood Rd L26 82 F8
Woodrock Rd L25 70 B1
Woodrow WN8 23 E8
Woodruff St L8 67 F4
Woods Cl L39 12 A4
Woods Ct WA12 46 A3
Woodside Ave
Ashton-in-M WN4 35 A8
Birkenhead CH46 64 D7
Southport PR8 7 B3
St Helens WA11 43 F8
Woodside Bsns Pk CH41 66 F7
Woodside Cl
Liverpool L12 54 B8
Up Holland WN8 25 C8
Woodside Rd
Haydock WA11 45 E7
Irby CH61 76 E6
Warrington WA5 74 F6
Woodside St 10 L7 53 B1
Woodside Way L33 29 F5
Wood's La WN4 35 C5
Woods-Lee Cotts CH62 79 D2
Woodslee Prim Sch CH62 79 D2
Woodsome Pk L25 70 C3
Woodsorrel Rd
Birkenhead CH41 65 F7
Liverpool L15 69 B7
Wood Sorrel Way WA3 47 E8
Wood St
Bebington CH62 79 B5
Birkenhead CH41 66 E7
Bootle L21 38 B6
Golborne WA3 47 B8
Wood St *continued*
Hoylake CH47 63 B7
Liverpool, Garston L19 81 C6
Liverpool L1 90 C3
Prescot L34 56 D6
St Helens WA9 44 C4
Widnes WA8 73 C1
Woodstock Ave WA12 46 D2
Woodstock Dr PR8 7 F8
Woodstock Gr WA8 72 D2
Woodstock Rd CH44 51 A3
Woodstock St L5 52 D5
WOODVALE 7 B2
Wood Vale WA9 57 E6
Woodvale Cl
Birkenhead CH43 65 C8
Warrington WA2 61 E1
Woodvale Dr WA3 36 E1
Woodvale Rd
Liverpool, Croxteth L12 40 F3
Liverpool, Woolton L25 70 B2
Southport PR8 7 D2
Woodview L34 41 D3
Woodview Ave CH44 51 E2
Woodview Cres WA8 84 A8
Woodview Rd
Liverpool L25 69 F4
Widnes WA8 84 A8
Woodville Ave L23 26 D3
Woodville Pl WA8 72 D1
Woodville Rd CH42 66 C4
Woodville St WA10 44 B4
Woodville Terr L6 53 B5
Woodward Rd
Bebington CH42 79 A8
Kirkby L33 30 D4
Woodway CH49 64 D4
Woodyear Rd CH62 88 E7
Woolacombe Ave WA9 58 C5
Woolacombe Rd L16 69 E6
Wooler Cl CH46 64 C8
Woolfall Cl L36 55 B4
Woolfall Cres L36 55 B4
WOOLFALL HEATH 55 D5
Woolfall Heath Ave L36 55 D5
Woolfall Terr 2 L21 38 A6
Woolhope Rd L4 39 B2
Woolmoore Rd L24 82 C7
Woolston Rd WA11 45 C7
WOOLTON 70 A2
Woolton Cl WN4 34 F5
Woolton Ct
Liverpool, Woolton L25 70 B2
Liverpool, Woolton Park L25 69 F2
WOOLTON HILL 69 F3
Woolton Hill Rd L18, L25 69 F4
Woolton Jun & Inf Schs L25 70 B3
Woolton Mews L25 70 A2
Woolton Mount L25 70 A3
WOOLTON PARK 70 A3
Woolton Park Cl L25 70 A3
Woolton Pk L25 70 A3
Woolton Rd
Liverpool, Allerton L19, L25 81 E7
Liverpool L15, L16, L18, L25 69 D5
Woolton St L25 70 B2
Woolton Views L25 82 D9
Worcester Ave
Crosby L22 26 D2
Golborne WA3 47 B8
Liverpool L13 53 D7
Worcester Cl WA10 43 F2
Worcester Ct L20 38 D3
Worcester Dr L13 53 D7
Worcester Dr N L13 53 D7
Worcester Rd
Birkenhead CH43 65 D8
Bootle L20 38 D3
Wordsworth Ave
1 Birkenhead CH42 66 F1
Longshaw WN5 25 D1
Orrell WN5 25 F6
St Helens WA9 58 A3
Widnes WA8 84 F8
Wordsworth Cl L39 13 D6
Wordsworth Ct L32 40 D8
Wordsworth St
Bootle L20 38 A5
Liverpool L8 68 C7
Wordsworth Way L36 55 F1
Wordsworth Wlk CH48 75 B8
World of Glass Mus★ WA10 44 A3
Worrow Cl L11 40 B3
Worrow Rd L11 40 B3
Worsley Brow WA9 58 E8
Worsley St
Golborne WA3 47 A8
St Helens WA11 44 F6
Worthing Cl PR8 3 F3
Worthing St 6 L22 26 C2
Worthington St L8 67 D6
Wortley Rd L10 39 E7
Wotton Dr WN4 35 D3
Wray Ave WA9 58 D4
Wrayburn Cl L7 68 C8
Wrekin Cl L25 70 B1
Wrekin Dr L10 28 E2
Wrenbury Cl CH43 65 F2
Wrenbury St 3 L7 53 C2
Wrenfield Gr L17 68 C2
Wren Gr L26 70 E1
Wrexham Cl WA5 60 E1
Wrights La WA5 73 F2
Wright's La WA5 59 F3
Wright St
Abram Brow WN2 36 B7
Ashton-in-M WN4 35 A6
Liverpool L5 52 D5
Southport PR9 4 C7
Wallasey CH44 51 D4
Wrights Terr
Liverpool L15 69 A7
Southport PR8 4 B3
Wrigley Rd WA11 45 E6
Wrigleys Cl L37 9 F5
Wrigleys La L37 9 F5
Wroxham Cl CH49 65 A4
Wroxham Ct CH49 65 A5
Wroxham Dr CH49 65 A4
Wroxham Rd WA5 74 E6
Wroxham Way CH49 65 A5
Wr Twr Rd CH64 86 E1
Wryneck Cl WA10 57 B7
Wrynose Rd CH62 88 E8
Wulstan St 2 L4 52 D7
Wyatt Gr WN4 35 D3
Wycherley Rd CH42 66 D3
Wycherley St 2 L34 56 D6
Wychwood CH49 64 F5
Wycliffe Rd
Haydock WA11 45 E7
Liverpool L4 53 C7
Wycliffe St CH42 66 F2
Wye Cl CH42 66 F3
Wyedale Rd WA11 45 C6
Wye St L5 52 F6
Wyke Cop Rd PR8, PR9 5 D2
Wykeham St L4 52 D7
Wykeham Way L4 52 D7
Wyke La PR8, PR9 5 E6
Wyken Gr WA11 44 C5
Wyke Rd L35 56 E5
Wyke Wood La PR9 5 F7
Wyllin Rd L33 30 A2
Wylva Ave L23 27 A3
Wylva Rd L4 53 A7
Wyncroft Cl WA8 84 C7
Wyncroft Rd WA8 84 C7
Wyncroft St L8 68 A4
Wyndale Cl L18 69 B3
Wyndcote Rd L18 69 B5
Wyndham Ave L14 55 A2
Wyndham Rd CH45 50 D5
Wyndham St 3 L4 38 F2
Wynne Rd WA10 43 E5
Wynnstay Ave L31 20 D3
Wynnstay St L8 68 A6
Wynstay Rd CH47 63 C8
Wynwood Pk L36 55 C1
Wyre Rd 5 L5 52 F7
Wyrescourt Rd L12 54 D5
Wyresdale Ave
Southport PR8 4 D4
St Helens WA10 43 E7
Wyresdale Rd L9 39 B7
Wyrevale Gr WN4 35 C3
Wysall Cl WA11 44 D5
Wyswall Cl L26 70 E2
Wythburn Cres WA11 44 C8
Wyvern Rd CH46 64 E8

X

XL Bsns Pk WN8 15 C3

Y

Yanwath St L8 68 B7
Yarcombe Cl L26 70 F1
Yardley Ctr L33 30 C1
Yardley Dr CH63 79 A1
Yardley Rd L33 30 C1
Yarmouth Rd WA5 74 E6
Yarn Cl WA9 58 F8
Yarrow Ave L31 20 F2
Yates' Ct L34 56 D5
Yates St L8 67 E5
Yeadon WN8 16 B1
Yeadon Wlk L24 82 C4
Yellow House La PR8 4 B6
Yelverton Cl L26 70 F1
Yelverton Rd
Birkenhead CH42 66 E3
Liverpool L4 53 C7
Yeoman Cotts CH47 63 C6
Ye Priory Ct L25 69 E1
Yew Bank Rd L16 69 D7
Yewdale WN8 16 A1
Yewdale Ave WA11 33 B1
Yewdale Pk CH43 66 B4
Yewdale Rd
Ashton-in-M WN4 35 A7
Liverpool L9 39 B4
Yew Tree Ave
Newton-le-W WA12 46 A4
St Helens WA9 58 C6
Yewtree Cl CH49 65 A2
Yew Tree Cl L12 54 F6
Yewtree Ct CH42 79 A8
Yew Tree Ct 6 CH60 86 A8
Yew Tree Farm Trad Est WA11 46 A8
Yew Tree Gn L31 29 B4
Yewtree La CH48 63 B2
Yew Tree La L12, L14 54 E6
Yewtree Rd L18 69 D3
Yew Tree Rd
Bebington CH63 78 E4
Huyton-w-R L36 70 E8
Liverpool, Hartley's Village L9 39 A4
Liverpool, Hunt's Cross L25 82 C9
Ormskirk L39 13 E7
Wallasey CH46 49 F1
Yew Tree Way WA3 47 B7
Yew Way CH46 49 F1
Yorkaster Rd L18 69 C1
York Ave
Crosby L23 26 D4
Liverpool L17 68 D6
Southport PR8 4 A5
Wallasey CH44 51 D3
Warrington WA5 74 E7
West Kirby CH48 75 B8
York Cl
Formby L37 9 F6
Litherland L30 27 F5
St Helens WA10 43 F4
York Cotts
Liverpool L25 70 B4
Wallasey CH44 51 D5
York Gdns PR8 4 A5
York Ho L17 68 D5
York Manor PR8 4 A5
York Rd
Ashton-in-M WN4 35 C3
Crosby L23 26 E4
Formby L37 10 A3
Huyton-w-R L36 56 A3
Maghull L31 28 D7
Southport PR8 3 F4
Wallasey CH44 51 D3
Widnes WA8 84 C8
York Rd S WN4 35 C2
Yorkshire Gdns WA10 43 F2
York St
Bebington CH62 79 D5
Golborne WA3 36 A1
Liverpool, Garston L19 81 C4
Liverpool L1 90 B2
Liverpool, Walton L9 38 F3
Seaforth L22 37 D8
York Terr
Liverpool L5 52 E6
4 Southport PR9 4 C8
York Villas 8 L5 52 F7
York Way
Huyton-w-R L36 56 B3
Liverpool L19 81 D3
Youatt Ave L35 56 E4
Youens Way L14 54 E4
Yoxall Dr L33 29 E6
Yvonne Cl WN4 35 D5

Z

Zander Gr L12 40 F3
Zante Cl L5 52 E6
Zara Ct WA11 45 C7
Zenith Wlk L25 70 A7
Zetland Rd
Birkenhead CH41 66 D5
5 Liverpool L18 68 F5
Wallasey CH45 50 F7
Zetland St PR9 4 D7
Zig Zag Rd
Liverpool L12 54 D5
Wallasey CH45 51 B6
Zircon Cl L21 38 C8

Addresses

Name and Address	Telephone	Page	Grid reference

NG	NH	NJ	NK
NM	NN	NO	NP
NR	NS	NT	NU
NX	NY	NZ	
SC	SD	SE	TA
SH	SJ	SK	TF	TG
SM	SN	SO	SP	TL	TM
SR	SS	ST	SU	TQ	TR
SW	SX	SY	SZ	TV

Any feature in this atlas can be given a unique reference to help you find the same feature on other Ordnance Survey maps of the area, or to help someone else locate you if they do not have a Street Atlas.

The grid squares in this atlas match the Ordnance Survey National Grid and are at 500 metre intervals. The small figures at the bottom and sides of every other grid line are the National Grid kilometre values (**00** to **99** km) and are repeated across the country every 100 km (see left).

To give a unique National Grid reference you need to locate where in the country you are. The country is divided into 100 km squares with each square given a unique two-letter reference. Use the administrative map to determine in which 100 km square a particular page of this atlas falls.

The bold letters and numbers between each grid line (**A** to **F**, **1** to **8**) are for use within a specific Street Atlas only, and when used with the page number, are a convenient way of referencing these grid squares.

Example The railway bridge over DARLEY GREEN RD in grid square B1

Step 1: Identify the two-letter reference, in this example the page is in **SP**

Step 2: Identify the 1 km square in which the railway bridge falls. Use the figures in the southwest corner of this square: Eastings **17**, Northings **74**. This gives a unique reference: **SP 17 74**, accurate to 1 km.

Step 3: To give a more precise reference accurate to 100 m you need to estimate how many tenths along and how many tenths up this 1 km square the feature is (to help with this the 1 km square is divided into four 500 m squares). This makes the bridge about **8** tenths along and about **1** tenth up from the southwest corner.

This gives a unique reference: **SP 178 741**, accurate to 100 m.

Eastings (read from left to right along the bottom) come before Northings (read from bottom to top). If you have trouble remembering say to yourself Along the hall, THEN up the stairs !

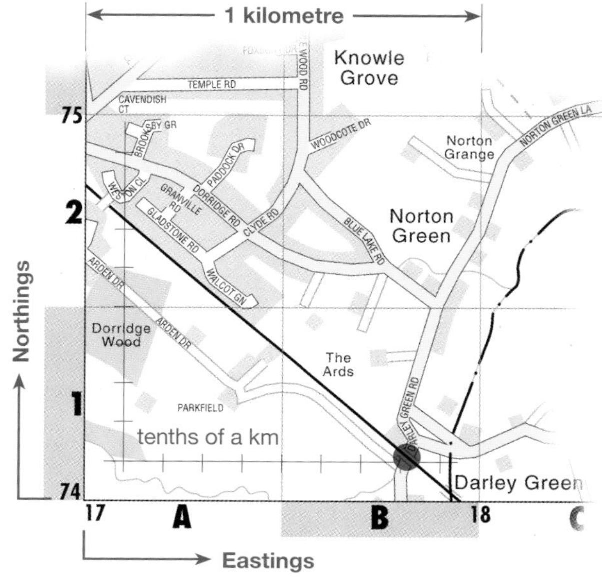

PHILIP'S MAPS

the Gold Standard for drivers

◆ **Philip's street atlases cover every county in England, Wales, Northern Ireland and much of Scotland**

◆ Every named street is shown, including alleys, lanes and walkways

◆ Thousands of additional features marked: stations, public buildings, car parks, places of interest

◆ Route-planning maps to get you close to your destination

◆ Postcodes on the maps and in the index

◆ Widely used by the emergency services, transport companies and local authorities

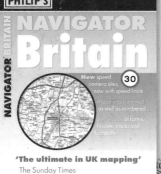

For national mapping, choose **Philip's Navigator Britain** the most detailed road atlas available of England, Wales and Scotland. Hailed by Auto Express as 'the ultimate road atlas', the atlas shows every road and lane in Britain.

'The ultimate in UK mapping'
The Sunday Times

Street atlases currently available

England
Bedfordshire and Luton
Berkshire
Birmingham and West Midlands
Bristol and Bath
Buckinghamshire and Milton Keynes
Cambridgeshire and Peterborough
Cheshire
Cornwall
Cumbria
Derbyshire
Devon
Dorset
County Durham and Teesside
Essex
North Essex
South Essex
Gloucestershire and Bristol
Hampshire
North Hampshire
South Hampshire
Herefordshire Monmouthshire
Hertfordshire
Isle of Wight
Kent
East Kent
West Kent
Lancashire
Leicestershire and Rutland
Lincolnshire
Liverpool and Merseyside
London
Greater Manchester
Norfolk
Northamptonshire
Northumberland
Nottinghamshire
Oxfordshire
Shropshire
Somerset
Staffordshire
Suffolk

Surrey
East Sussex
West Sussex
Tyne and Wear
Warwickshire and Coventry
Wiltshire and Swindon
Worcestershire
East Yorkshire Northern Lincolnshire
North Yorkshire
South Yorkshire
West Yorkshire

Wales
Anglesey, Conwy and Gwynedd
Cardiff, Swansea and The Valleys
Carmarthenshire, Pembrokeshire and Swansea
Ceredigion and South Gwynedd
Denbighshire, Flintshire, Wrexham
Herefordshire Monmouthshire
Powys

Scotland
Aberdeenshire
Ayrshire
Dumfries and Galloway
Edinburgh and East Central Scotland
Fife and Tayside
Glasgow and West Central Scotland
Inverness and Moray
Lanarkshire
Scottish Borders

Northern Ireland
County Antrim and County Londonderry
County Armagh and County Down
Belfast
County Tyrone and County Fermanagh

How to order
Philip's maps and atlases are available from bookshops, motorway services and petrol stations. You can order direct from the publisher by phoning **0207 531 8473** or online at **www.philips-maps.co.uk**
For bulk orders only, e-mail philips@philips-maps.co.uk